Fields in Motion

Fields in Motion
ETHNOGRAPHY IN THE WORLDS OF DANCE

DENA DAVIDA, editor

WILFRID LAURIER UNIVERSITY PRESS

This book has been published with the help of a grant from the Canadian Federation for the Humanities and Social Sciences, through the Aid to Scholarly Publications Programme, using funds provided by the Social Sciences and Humanities Research Council of Canada. Wilfrid Laurier University Press acknowledges the support of the Canada Council for the Arts for our publishing program. We acknowledge the financial support of the Government of Canada through the Canada Book Fund for our publishing activities.

Library and Archives Canada Cataloguing in Publication

Fields in motion : ethnography in the worlds of dance / Dena Davida, editor.

Includes bibliographical references and index.
Issued also in electronic formats.
ISBN 978-1-55458-341-6 (paperback)

1. Dance—Social aspects. I. Davida, Dena

GV1594.D38 2011   306.4'84   C2011-902981-2

Issued also in print format.
ISBN 978-1-55458-377-5 (uPDF)

1. Dance—Social aspects. I. Davida, Dena

GV1594.D38 2011a   306.4'84   C2011-902982-0

Cover photo, by Cylla von Tiedemann, shows Lata Pada dancing in a solo from her choreography *Revealed by Fire*. Cover design by Daiva Villa, Chris Rowat Design. Text design by Catharine Bonas-Taylor.

Page 461 constitutes an extension of this copyright page.

This book is printed on FSC recycled paper and is certified Ecologo. It is made from 100% post-consumer fibre, processed chlorine free, and manufactured using biogas energy.

Printed in Canada

To Joann Kealiinohomoku,
a founding mother of American dance anthropology,
whose crucial proposition that all dances are ethnic was the genesis of this book

In memoriam

Susan McNaughton (1952–2010)

This volume was in production when, on December 4, 2010, author and choreographer Susan McNaughton passed away. Even from her hospital bed she continued revising her chapter in this book and pursuing her doctoral research in anthropology. Her radiant body and mind will be deeply missed in the art worlds of dance.

CONTENTS

FOREWORD

I was introduced to Dena Davida as a young undergraduate student at McGill in Montreal in the 1980s. There was a piece she performed at her alternative performance space Tangente that I still vividly remember. In it she carried individual men from one side of the stage to the other while slides on a screen and a soundtrack recalled her experience on a street corner in Montreal as she asked random men if they would like to be lifted. The piece was mesmerizing. Here was a strong, buff woman in front of my eyes delicately lifting a series of men one by one and lovingly transporting them from one space to another. Simultaneously you heard her recorded voice asking men on the street if they would like to be lifted. Some said no, but those who said yes almost always commented on what a unique and wonderful experience it was—like being cradled by their mother and returning to a place of surprise, calm, and joy in a world that had become frenetic in its intensity.

As I think back on that piece and the journeys Dena and I have taken since that time—me from an aspiring scholar to a tenured professor exploring my place in the dance world at mid-life, and Dena through her roles as dancer, choreographer, and producer to scholar—I am struck by how much she has stayed true to her vision while deepening and expanding its horizons. That early work was an exercise in ethnography "at home" in Montreal where she lived, as she researched the particular movement activity of lifting men; it combined new methods of gathering data with the creation of visceral art dance; it involved collaboration with the men on the street and stage; its aim was to be mutually beneficial (one of the best-known images from the piece is a photographic portrait by Normand Grégoire of Dena holding fellow dancer Daniel Godbout, both with beatific looks on their faces); and it celebrated the power, wisdom, and courage of women to question, experiment, and celebrate new approaches to dance.

Now as I face my own work as a scholar and seek refreshing and creative new ways to challenge the traditional canons of our field, I believe I am in a unique position to value Dena's efforts with this momentous anthology. She has asked that most scary and exciting of questions: What happens when we start with ourselves and our own worlds, draw on our own somatic and intellectual wisdom, and admit the challenges as well as successes of such an approach? So often in the dance world we are working with approaches promoted forty or more years before, holding on to paradigms that were outdated by the time we were born (even the so-called avant-garde of the 1960s is now half a century past us, yet we maintain many of its values in the dance field), often separating theory and practice, privileging the knowledge of the "other" over ourselves, creating linear rather than multi-vocal texts, and honouring male over female approaches.

With *Fields in Motion* Dena Davida has collected a broad range of writings that will greatly enhance the field of dance studies. I am particularly touched by the vulnerability expressed in these pages, as well as the passion for people, who can so easily become objectified in anthropological studies. The autoethnography by Janet Goodridge is for me perhaps the most touching and emblematic article of the anthology. In her piece "The Body as a Living Archive of Dance/Movement: Autobiographical Reflections," this mature dancer/scholar reflects on the layers of somatic, visual, and intellectual memory that exist within herself. Here is someone who has lived through various paradigmatic shifts in the dance world. She is not one of the celebrated greats of dance history; she is someone who loved dance and anthropology, and graces us with her story that is at once typical and unique—embracing generic trends such as Greek dancing and Laban's ideas (among many others), as well as integrating her love for Mandarin Chinese brush-stroke calligraphy, for example.

As she says, it is an "eclectic approach," but isn't that what we all experience as we go through our lives? We are not the pure constructs of a range of discourses, nor are we pillars of independent strength—we are this poetic mixture of visceral, emotional, spiritual, and intellectual elements that creatively blend. And especially as women, we see through these articles the need for sharing and exchanging our experiences in our scholarship as much as in our everyday lives. Since these women are working in their "homes," the importance of self-analysis as well as recognition of others' patterns and individuality are all the more pressing. As in the ethics of care, the authors strive to look out for the needs of their subjects, seeing them as special and deserving of respect. The result is a daring and ground-breaking contribution to dance ethnology, and one which should prove the value of so-called "insider ethnography" in contemporary art dance once and for all.

Naomi Jackson

ACKNOWLEDGEMENTS

There is a vast community of dance scholars, artists, and research participants, whose support—whether through personal conversations and friendships or by way of their writing—was critical to the conception and creation of this book. In particular, numerous members of the Congress on Research in Dance urged me forward on this project year after year, and a fair number of the book's contributors were discovered and recruited during their annual conferences.

The idea of bringing artistic dance into the fold of anthropology was initially proposed by my muse Joann Kealiinohomoku and my dear, departed colleague Cynthia Novack. Rich grounds for this anthology have been previously laid down by first and second generations of the dance anthropology community, notably Gertrude Kurath, Allegra Fuller-Snyder, Anna Peterson Royce, Franziska Boas, Peter Brinson, Judy Alter, Joan Erdman, Sally Ness, Deidre Sklar, Judy Mitoma, and Andriy Nahachewsky. And there have been key conversations along the way about the import of this book with Andrée Grau, Nina de Shane, Georgiana Gore, and Joan Erdmann. And, not to be forgotten, it was ethnomusicologist Nicole Beaudry who spent a decade guiding me through the wilds of the field of arts anthropology in her role as my thesis co-director.

Emerging out of a disciplinary crisis in the wake of post-colonialism, the interdisciplinary crossroads between art and culture at the heart of this book was previously investigated by Clifford Geertz, James Clifford, George Marcus, and Jane Desmond, among others. I am indebted to them for breaking down these barriers.

I am beholden to Lisa Quinn, Leslie Macredie, and Rob Kohlmeier of Wilfrid Laurier University Press for their guidance, and to expert reader number 2, who made me flush with pleasure and relief when pronouncing our anthology an instant classic. My gratitude is also due to the committee of peers at the *Syndicat des Chargé(e)s de Cours* at the *Université du Québec à Montréal* who awarded me a grant to support the last stages of editorial work. And how could I forget Michaël Trahan, poet and formatter par excellence, whose computer savvy was the crucial skill needed to prepare the manuscript for submission and copy editing?

Several of the book's contributors were indispensable to the book-making process. Naomi Jackson contributed hours of insight and her considerable editing skills, functioning as a de facto co-editor, and graciously agreed to pen our Foreword. Monica Dantas assisted me throughout the years in pulling together the community of twenty-eight authors, and Sylvie Fortin stepped in with timely critical advice.

But in the end it is the entire group of dancer-scholars featured in these pages who made this anthology conceivable, feasible, inevitable. Each one gave many hours, and in some cases years, to crafting their narratives so that together we have forged this burgeoning sub-field of artistic dance anthropology. Many are contributing here a first publication of findings from their master's or doctoral work, while others are offering later "secondary" reflections arising from earlier and ongoing research projects.

And as is often the case, the fundamental support that bolstered my patience and confidence throughout the many years of labour came from family members and workplace colleagues: my mother-the-writer Ruth Kanin, new life companion Rainer Waizmann, and the entire staff at Tangente.

Anthropology at Home in the Art Worlds of Dance

DENA DAVIDA

This has been a long and somehow mysterious process of shifting positions, of getting new eyes, new ears, new feelings, new insights and knowledge. (Cazemajou: 25)

I would never have imagined this book without having encountered Keali-inohomoku's essay "An Anthropologist Looks at Ballet as a Form of Ethnic Dance" (1969–70). Nearly forty years after she fleshed out this infamous manifesto, I still witness its ability to exasperate those dance historians, critics, and aesthetic philosophers for whom classical ballet has long held a privileged position. This is an account that has served to widen the horizons of aspiring dance anthropologists and cultural theorists like myself. And it is common sense, as Kealiinohomoku upholds, that all dances were conceived by specific dance-makers at the outset, that they are purposeful products bearing the markings of the society, time, and place that fostered them. *I knew that* The Nutcracker *wasn't just an aesthetic event, but like any tradition, reflected both communal and individual beliefs, as well as culturally revealing attitudes* (Fisher: 47). And so it follows that once classical ballet is seen as a cultural dance form, the same might be said of its modernist and postmodernist progeny. Art is culture (in so many senses).

Assembling this book was a collective effort which I haven chosen to reflect in the structure of this introduction by injecting the contributors' voices directly into the substance of the text rather than describing their chapters second-hand. In the new tradition of global networking, this book was largely consolidated by way of email conversations. The manuscript was conceived, discussed, and edited somewhere out in cyberspace, an electronic domain as mysterious and intangible as dancing itself. (As you might have guessed, I belong to the generation who discovered the potential of word processing and other joys of computing later in life.) This project was also shaped during face-to-face encounters at intercontinental gatherings of dance scholars, such as the Congress on Research in Dance. The journey of generating this anthology was truly a group venture, spanning eight years and five continents, calling on the intellectual labour of three generations of dance researchers. *I did not simply want to present a positivist document of the events as they occurred, but a creative expression of a dynamic interchange* (Thomas: 160). The result is a polyphonic manuscript composed by twenty-eight distinct voices, along with copious contributions from their subjects of study. This venture heralds what I believe to be a novel orientation within the anthropological enterprise at the opening of the twenty-first century: ethnography at home by practitioner-researchers in the art worlds of dance across the globe.

INSIDER MIS/UNDERSTANDINGS

All of the contributors hold the positions of dance world insider and academic researcher. They provide a multitude of responses to Alter's call in the 1990s to move dance scholarship from its habitual use of theoretical models appropriated from other academic fields toward what she termed "dance-based dance theory," grounded in the empirical understandings and kinetic experiences of dancers (Alter 1991*). The revelation that the interpretive writing resembled an act of choreography led me to construct a metaphor and style of writing that felt like "choreographing the data" or "dancing the data"—in other words, examining the BODY of evidence* (Moss: 74). In terms of methodology, these dance ethnographers offer ample information throughout this book about concrete issues involved in doing fieldwork at home in their own dance communities. *Getting to understand what to do—scientifically speaking—with one's own subjective experience seems to me the biggest challenge for the dance insider, and especially for the fieldworker at home* (Cazemajou: 19).

Like the choreographer who simultaneously creates and interprets her own work, these dance researchers found themselves in the predicament of playing the role of protagonist within their own study, their own story. *As an ethnographer writing about her own dancing, I have experimented with multiple writing strategies: starting with the epistemology of dance practice and investigating the epistemological gap between the dance experience and theorizing about it. I have challenged my ethnographer's position, because dance forms my profession. My solution to these predicaments has been partly to encourage myself to create distance from these feelings in order to speak out about them* (Juslin: 185). At some point in their texts each of the authors fleshed out a discussion of the insider/outsider conundrum, or as Dantas put it, "our double subjectivity." *Because I have worked in the dance world for the whole of my professional career, my position as a researcher in the dance institutions that I was studying was a very subtle one.... My background in the dance world meant that I knew, in one way or another, all the participants in my study. Some were even very close friends. This led me to explore the researcher's position as a shifting one between the insider and the outsider in my own home field* (Löytönen: 255–56).

As you will also discover within these pages, in this kind of ethnographic subgenre the fieldworkers were not so much threatened by the dangers of going native, as in the mythology of classic anthropology, but instead faced the quandary of *being* native in their own field. *The boundaries between artist and researcher, normally so blunt and circumscribed in social science research, have here, in this space, become nebulous, soft, and fragmented in the murky overlaps between artist and researcher* (Thomas: 160). They tell us what kinds of strategies they engaged in order to bring their insider presumptions and intuitions to consciousness. They also explained how it was that, over time, they managed to make the familiar strange enough so that they were finally able to take to step backward and gain the necessary perspective to proceed. *Video recording was now a wonderful means of introducing distance, otherness into what was being recorded. It helped in materializing my subject of research. Moreover, I felt that the fact of appearing in front of the group with the camera legitimized my posture as a researcher* (Cazemajou: 24). Some of the research projects, including my own, took place over the span of years. In several cases, however, time spent collecting data in the field was only a week or two, much too short a period to be taken seriously in the tradition of anthropology. But because these authors are native to the culture and community in question, they had actually lived much of their professional lives among their subjects in their field of study. *Although the fieldwork specific to this project took place over a short five-day period, Warwick's long-term experience as a dancer has given him the in-depth knowledge of someone who has inhabited the field over a prolonged period* (Long: 235). Some of the authors chose to write an autoethnography and so became their own object of study. They recount one story (of many that might be told) about their lives as dancers and dance researchers, ranging in scope from the passage of a single day in their life (Barbour) to the epic tale of an entire career in the dance world over decades (Goodridge).

These artist-fieldworkers mostly went to work in their local communities, although in some cases they moved alternately into and away from them, and explained how they gained advantage through their close acquaintance with the field. *My position as a dance teacher at DSW and the assistant for Boyz Ballet allowed me the opportunity to investigate the analogous privileges that male participants in this situation were afforded* (Pike: 295). Among the assets of insider status they noted were: the ease of slipping into the field and gaining participants' trust, the possession of intimate knowledge of the practice being examined, and deep personal comprehension of cultural contexts. But they also made palpable the difficulties and the ways in which they grappled with the politics, assumptions, and logistics of their privileged position. *We had an agreement with Montréal Danse that our participation, apart from the somatic sessions, would be as discreet and passive as possible. However, in doing this, we disempowered ourselves somewhat. Returning home together late each evening exhausted and satiated, we shared our experience, looking for correspondence and corroboration. By the middle of the week, we found ourselves frustrated, longing for a voice in the workshop process* (Newell and Fortin: 199–200). The body-to-body, kinaesthetic empathy that these dance scholars had long cultivated in their lives as dancers provided valuable insights. But at the same time they tell us how this physical sensibility proved difficult to constrain as they sought to gain the requisite scholarly distance from their subjects. In these pages they vividly recount their struggle to align mind with body, the plight of sensuous scholarship. *I became enchanted with watching the way in which the dancers worked out the minute details of a gesture, obsessively repeating a movement sequence in trying to find the precise dynamic required. They were so deeply engaged in embodying the choreographic work. I realized that I also felt frustrated because I was not dancing: the appeal of the movement to my body was so powerful that when I finished my fieldwork with the company, I began a solo choreography* (Dantas: 341–42). In the end, they reveal themselves to be visceral ethnographers with a highly developed kinaesthetic empathy, as much passionate participant as cool-headed observer, a position long championed in the work of dance anthropologist Deidre Sklar (2001).

Not only do these ethnographers expose pertinent details of their personal identities within the first few pages (sometimes at my editorial instance), but their narratives are punctuated by delightful, intimate self-revelations. *As I write this I am confronted once again with the conundrum of writing about bharatanatyam as a Western woman brought up in a primarily Judeo-Christian environment who remembers being unabashedly dazzled by my first viewing of the bejewelled bharatanatyam dancer in her red and gold sari* (McNaughton: 383). Although the measured researcher's voice does in the end predominate these scholarly writings, the first-person "I" is always a strong, if reflexive, presence. As if carrying forward the project of feminist anthropologists to acknowledge the fieldworker's biography at all levels of the ethnographic enterprise, these ethnographers write themselves vividly into the field (for more, see Okeley and Callaway 1992). *When entering the research as a dance-maker, I was confronted by my own enthusiastic relationship to the dance-making process and had to hold in abeyance self-reflexive tendencies to interpret for the choreographer. I wanted to choreograph our encounters, embracing with enthusiasm similarities between their narratives and mine.... By delving into a feast of colours, textures, symbols, and stories that enhanced a "narration of meaning," I was able to piece together a fascinating tapestry of material relationships.... Relevant because of my Latina heritage, I was always/already the subject-for-study, as well as the one who studies* (Suarez: 405–9). Within the conclusion of my own text I describe the moment of revelation, during the research project, in which my point of view as a dance presenter had taken the cultural turn away from the usual utilitarian issues (production budget, audience taste, artistic credibility) toward the wider framework of the dance event (why are we gathering together this evening?). Throughout this book, whether the writing style takes on the tone of a meticulous research report or an imaginative narrative with literary aspirations, each chapter also contains the subtle subplot of its authors' self-transformation by way of the ethnographic process. *All anthropological approaches force the researcher to question the construction of both the research object and field, to ask what motivates her, how she formulates her questions, how she is transformed through contact with the field* (Tardieu and Gore: 313).

Many of the authors remind us that this process of gaining new understandings in the field is a collaborative, dialogic enterprise between researcher and subject. *I had come to understand that the participants needed a clear sense of my honest desire to learn from them, regardless of my professional status as a dance artist-educator pursuing a doctoral degree* (Santos: 151). They approached interviews and fieldwork as mutually beneficial activities for themselves and those they were studying, naming and describing strategies they employed to enhance cooperative collaboration, as they termed it: *"very participative observation"* (Dantas: 341), *"collaborative inquiry"* (Löytönen: 264), *"the process of 'coming together'"* (Thomas: 160), and *"imaginative empathy"* (Wright: 430). *As I conducted interviews with the dancers, I recognized that the information I obtained would benefit from observations of the physical aspects of Boyz Ballet and that in my role as a dancer/ethnographer I could help the informants better articulate their ideas about movement and their experiences in the dance studio* (Pike: 279). The research practices described here are those that generally lie on the softer, qualitative side of

the social science spectrum, seeking at least some of their academic credibility through self-revelation, insider knowledge, and the quality of corroboration with informants. *It was my intention to present the content of my
findings in a way that illuminated the artistic sensibilities of its writer as well
as its subject. In that sense, I didn't see myself as standing on the other side of a
fence from my subject. I am not neutral in my observations. I am subjective, relational, and identified with the subject—and interested in the process of "coming
together" in the trenches of fieldwork* (Thomas: 160).

INTRODUCING ART WORLD DANCES INTO THE ARCHIVE OF DANCE ANTHROPOLOGY

It was in the late 1990s, while searching for theoretical grounds on which
to stage my doctoral study of a contemporary dance event, that I plunged
into the tumultuous debates taking place among anthropologists about the
very survival of the field itself in the wake of post-colonialism. The ethics
of doing fieldwork, a practice at the heart of the matter, was put into question. *Decolonizing entails analyzing and exposing power relationships embedded in the representation of knowledge—who is being studied, by whom and for
what purpose—and measuring those responses against imperialist principles that
have pervaded academic research* (Cauthery: 330). This was a period when
previous frames of reference and methodologies were being reconsidered
in light of the new intellectual order imposed by postmodernism and poststructuralism, and in particular in North America during the 1980s by a
key cohort of male provocateurs, George Marcus being a prominent figure
(see Clifford 1988, Clifford and Marcus 1986, Fisher and Marcus 1985, and
Marcus and Myers 1995). They re-examined the practice of ethnography
through the lens of the politics of power as formulated by cultural studies
theorists, and (among other things) resituated ethnography as a form of
fictional, literary text.

As for the field of dance anthropology, there was understandable enthusiasm among dance researchers for an important philosophical movement
of liberating "body discourses" that examined the human form as a locus
for the study of social repression. *If the reality in which we live is subjectively
inscribed by social and cultural meanings and values, as anthropologists and
cultural critics would have us believe, then our bodies are also a site for the playing out of socially and culturally constructed power relationships* (Long: 251).
At the same time, a decidedly subjective branch of aesthetic philosophy
was being honed within these discourses by American pragmatist Shustermann, arising from the well of his actual bodily experiences, and which he
named somaesthetics. *If dance can propose aesthetic models, it can also polish*

and discipline the body, a body that we use at every instant and which engages us in actions and relationships (Vellet: 221). These new critical anthropologists were bent on shaking the foundations that had historically supported the field of anthropology by questioning the existence of a single coherent field (Amit 2000), the possibility of an objective observer, and especially, the ethical quandry of the outsider-researcher, and more.

No sooner had I discovered the authoritative *Writing Culture* collection of essays from the male cohort mentioned above (Clifford and Marcus 1986) than I came upon its feminist rebuttal, only days later—but written a decade afterwards—in the woman-authored anthology *After Writing Culture*, which reclaimed the value of creative, subjective, and multi-vocal writing (Behar and Gordon 1995). It is interesting to note that I was able to locate only two men to join the twenty-six women contributors for this book. Thus far, like early Euro-American modern dance, our new subfield of artistic dance ethnography appears a woman-centric domain. But in the case of many of the dancer-researchers inscribed in these pages, both female and male, the heart of the matter is the question of how it might even be possible to articulate in written form the somatic phenomena of bodily sensations, intentions, and sensations. *My personal experiences in practice-based artistic research have taught me that philosophical inquiry helps to explain experiential moments. Philosophy assists by narrating the dance movements and the choreographic language, the drafts, methods, and ideas that are used in the process. To my mind, phenomenological narration represents a mode of language that allows my body and its knowledge to speak through speech and writing* (Juslin: 172). And so this book takes its place within an ever-increasing body of writing about dance and demonstrates a multitude of ways in which the immaterial substance, "ineffable nature" (as Moss would have it), of expressive movement can indeed be expressed through words. *Breathing deeply and relaxing my shoulders, I remind myself that just as in dance-making, I can draw together different sources of inspiration for writing—my theoretical readings, creative and poetic writings, and my dancing experiences—and explore how these materials relate through the practice of writing* (Barbour: 112). Dancing has in the past been described in dancers' writing as if it were a literary form or, in a favoured metaphor of postmodern theorists, "a text." The French have adopted the term *écriture chorégraphique*, literally meaning "choreographic writing," as their own. *The dancer possesses an extraordinary ability to generate a poetic universe out of a single movement* (Vellet: 220). During much of the twentieth century, in fact, dance and language have frequently been written about as though they were analogous forms of expression, from expressionist choreographer Wigman's assertion that "dance is a living language which speaks of man" (Wigman 1966: 10) to movement analyst

Hutchison's charting of a "movement family tree" in which the composite elements are subdivided into nouns, verbs, and adverbs (Hutchison 1977: 19). But there does seem to be a consensus around the notion that this "language of dance" is metaphoric. And although it is evident that movement does not make sense in precisely the same way as does a text, it is commonly agreed that the interplay of the worlds of motion and writing is possible and that they work together to produce meaning. *I am deradicalizing the act of dancing by doing it all—dancing the data, deconstructing the practice, documenting the concert, validating in performance and in practice, and articulating and interpreting through a textual dance that will hardly lie flat on the page* (Moss: 80).

Some detractors of this post-colonialist "new ethnography" have expressed fear of an impending end to the tradition of ethnographic fieldwork, a practice that has long been one of the defining characteristics of anthropology. Others have sought to redefine and reorient the field (in both senses of the word). I immersed myself in these discussions, asking: With the weight of a dubious colonialist past, how might anthropologists remain relevant in a globalizing, de-colonizing world in which concepts such as "faraway," "exotic," and "primitive" are now perceived as vestigial remnants of an obsolete and racist Western nostalgia, if not the clichéd fare of the travel industries? The ethnographic texts of the international gathering of dancer-researchers pulled together in this book propose one kind of response to this predicament, one that is reminiscent of one aspect of the Chicago School mandate: send native ethnographers out into their local communities. *As a Taiwanese dancer-researcher-educator, I strive to present my research from an "insider's perspective." Culturally speaking, I am also Han Chinese and my life is also immersed in Chinese elements.... This chapter seeks to establish a new framework for analyzing contemporary Taiwanese performance. I hope that my findings can help lay the foundations for developing new critical theories of performance for critics in Taiwan, a contemporary Asian society with multiple cultural influences* (Huang: 361–62).

Some dance anthropologists have slipped into this new territory with enthusiasm and ease. They are those who embrace the erudite new discourses, often with literary flair, embarking on elegant theoretical narratives in the company of social scientists, literary and feminist theorists, political economists, neurophysicists, philosophers, and other cultural and critical theorists. *Contextualizing Mantsoe's trade in trance requires an understanding of trance both as an artefact and as a commodity. According to James, in his seminal work* On Collecting Art and Culture, *an artefact is something prized for its cultural significance and is very much associated with the imperialist anthropological agenda. An artefact comes to signify something that is*

Other—distanced by time, space, geography, language, and culture, it expands the boundaries of the known world to include that which exists beyond the everyday. It is a reminder of what is achievable and conquerable (Cauthery: 328). These scholars have already produced a substantial body of critical dance ethnographies (Cowan 1990, Desmond 1999, Ness 1996, Novack 1990, Savigliano 1995, and others). And there is ample acknowledgement of these new philosophical frameworks throughout this volume, although the ethnographic texts in this book remain grounded in the empirical evidence gathered in the field and in face-to-face interviews.

Other dance anthropologists have recently turned to their "home fields," one of the binding themes of this book, whether home is located in the place where they currently live or in the land of their forebears (e.g., Giurchescu 1999, Koutsouba 1999, Nahachewsky 1999). This marks a decisive turn away from the exclusive authority of the time-honoured rite of passage of (largely Western) anthropologists in which they must venture out to distant lands for long periods of time (Okeley and Callaway 1992). *If I imagined myself to be an intrepid ethnographer striking out for unknown territory, like a slightly more stylish version of Margaret Mead, it was despite the fact that I was entering a rural Virginia high school auditorium where the local inhabitants put on* The Nutcracker *every year. It was hardly the stuff of perilous journeys* (Fisher: 47). These indigenous dance ethnographers, like the authors in this book, have immersed themselves in the familiar surroundings of their local dance worlds, as had those earlier Eastern European ethno-choreologists who sought to catalogue, notate, and theorize (the now problematized category of) folk dance (see Kealiinohomoku 1972).

ETHNOGRAPHIES OF ART WORLD DANCE

But would dance "art world" ethnography be welcomed in the anthropological archive? The dance research community has traversed a considerable conceptual distance from that day in 1976 when another of Kealiinohomoku's essays, a discussion paper entitled the "Non-art of the Dance," was excluded from the conference proceedings of the Fifth Congress on Research in Dance because the editorial committe had judged it as not credible (Kealiinohomoku: 159). Ironically, it was she who, along with her own muse Gertrude Kurath and elder stateswoman of North American dance ethnology, were among the first to legitimate classical ballet (Kealiinohomoku 1976) and modern dance (Kurath 1965) as topics of interest to anthropologists. In her doctoral study that draws a comparison between differing dance forms (1976), a traditional methodology for dance anthropologists, Kealiinohomoku introduced ballet (and occasionally modern dance) as a foil for Hawaiian and Hopi dances, even as she laid out a first theory and methods for dance anthropology. In this American-grown school, at first called "dance ethnology," the dancing itself is considered as a microcosm of social life and so closely investigated as an embodiment of cultural attributes. *The cultural determinants affect how dancers perform and what their footwear will be.... During a course on material culture, I chose to research the [ballerina's] pointe shoe as an artefact in order to explore in greater depth how a seemingly simple shoe could be so highly charged with meaning for so many people: dancers, audience members, and scholars—male and female alike* (Harris Walsh: 86–87).

On the other hand, dance anthropologists as venerable as Franziska Boas and Theresa Buckland have insisted on the risks of advancing Western art dance as a subject of anthropological study. In her introductory notes to a first seminar on dance and anthropology (1944), Boas faulted modern dancers of the time for directing their work exclusively toward a social and artistic elite, fostering meanings that were not accepted by the entire community. And in a belated response to Kealiinohomoku's essay on ballet (1969–70), Buckland (1999) insisted that because of its powerful cultural capital and the elite status that ballet has maintained in Western society, it is far more important for dance anthropologists to pay attention to the non-Western and non-art dances of the world.

Nevertheless, by the time I stood poised and ready to enter the field during my doctoral study, I was already convinced that the moment was opportune to put forward the notion of art world dance ethnography. *If ethnography as it is rooted in cultural anthropology is to survive its colonialist roots, more methods that move toward collaboration need to emerge. Who better to develop them than scholars who know that the elite form of ballet evolved from folk dance?* (Fisher: 60). In the politically charged climate among researchers on the cusp of the twenty-first century, I hoped that indigenous art world dance ethnography might indeed stand as a challenge to the persistent hierarchy of social values in which Western classical ballet had long claimed the highest position.

Three seminal book-length Western art dance ethnographies were published in the 1990s. The late Cynthia Novack paved the way to an anthropology of Western art world dance by penning *Sharing the Dance* (1990) which she characterized as an ethno-history of the Contact Improvisation dance community, a study in which I played the role of informant as a second-generation Contacter. In Novack's narrative, this postmodern dance "community of experience" and its practices were theorized as emblematic of 1970s American counterculture. Eight years later in 1998, Helena Wulff offered up an ethnographic account of the backstage life of classical ballet dancers in three large-scale dance companies in the United States and Europe, *Ballet across Borders* (1998), a dance culture that she characterized as transnational, with common values and shared dance lore. And in 2003 Jennifer Fisher (with a chapter in this volume) published a book based on her doctoral work, an ethnographic examination of "New World *Nutcracker* ballets." With her experience as a dance critic, she is an engaging writer and so her book proved full of literary delights as well as insights that spring from in-depth research. *Nutcracker Nation* (Fisher 2003) leaves the reader with little doubt of dance anthropology's potential to generate a vibrant analysis of American culture by way of its native artistic dance practices. *Part of my image of myself as a postmodern dance ethnographer seemed to involve ironic nostalgia for iconic explorers. "The natives were friendly and their rituals fascinating," I told friends and colleagues later, knowing that it sounded like a joke about the relative comfort of trekking in the wilds of suburban ballet studios, but also that it was an accurate description of my fieldwork experiences* (Fisher: 47).

These three ethnographies, as well as the book you hold in your hands, bear witness forty years after Kealiinohomoku's seminal text on ballet's cultural origins (1969–70) to the emergence of art world dance ethnography from an ever-expanding group of researchers. I like to think of this collection of case studies as a natural companion to three other anthologies which flesh out the history, theory, methods, and politics of dance ethnography from a post-colonialist perspective (Buckland 1999, Grau and Gore 2005, Kuypers 1988). Furthermore, in 2004, as if to solidify theoretical grounds for this collection, another of the founding mothers of American dance anthropology, Anya Peterson Royce, elaborated a book-length essay for a yet more extensive discipline she termed "an anthropology of the performing arts."

CONSOLIDATING THE FOUR THEMATIC ARENAS

Generally speaking, in terms of form, substance, and style, this is a decidedly eclectic collection of texts drawn from a rich array of scholarly conventions. Taken together, they verify the potential of the "new ethnography" to unearth fresh fields and methods of study, including excavating the body itself as visceral site of knowledge. *[The] impetus for a new study focus came suddenly, early one morning. I had an unusually intense sense of the different dance- and movement-arts styles and techniques experienced throughout my life, prompting an unexpected vision of my body as a living dance museum—an inner archive or repository of dance/movement-arts practice* (Goodridge: 120).

Typical of the current-day academic practice of tightly circumscribed research, each author delved into a narrow area of art world dance practice (choreography, programming, performing, teaching, training, and so on) and posed a precise and clearly bounded set of questions about what was being said and done. Their studies cover a remarkable gamut of concerns: the transmission of "bodily construction" and choreographic movement to dancers by teachers and choreographers; dancers' clothing and costumes as cultural artefact; somatic, health, and ethical issues in dance; the meaning of dancing, choreographing, and presenting dance performances; the incentives, economics, and aesthetics of dancing for a higher power; ethics and power dynamics among dance professionals and academics; new methodologies for artistic dance ethnographers; culture and gender identity in choreography and pedagogy. Some chapters, like my own, outline the results of an entire research project. Others hone in on a single aspect. But Goodridge's text is an exception. She imagined her narrative specifically for this book, and it is the outcome of a lifetime spent as a researcher, an epic ethnographic memoir culled from her "body-as-archive." *Writing this chapter has also brought unexpected understanding, not only of my performance arts experience, but also of my life—not least with discovery of those six key themes. It is a life in which anthropology, as a way of looking at the world, continues to have an influential presence* (Goodridge: 140).

It wasn't until I had discovered as many as ten dance researchers who, like myself, were doing ethnography at home in art world dance that I began to imagine the pertinence of an anthology and began the work of constructing the book. The founding group came together just at the cusp of the millennium: Monica Dantas, Priya Thomas, Susan McNaughton, Sylvie Fortin, Warwick Long, Pamela Newell, Eluza Santos, Janet Goodridge, and Yin-ying Huang. Other authors were uncovered over the years during dance scholars' conferences, through leads provided by other group members, and even by way of listserv postings (on a Scandinavian dance research network website for instance). By the time the number of authors had reached twenty, Naomi Jackson reminded me that it was now time to put some kind of order to the table of contents.

As when crafting the book title, I approached the task of organizing the chapters as a collective project. Two groupings emerged effortlessly from our internet discussions. Section 4 was formed by the six texts that carried the common mandate of revealing choreographies as cultural and spiritual practices. In this long-standing perspective of American dance ethnologists, the attributes of a dance practice are seen as embodied indicators of social and religious practice and belief. *The eventual outcome of this project will be a choreographic reflection of my experiences as a researcher and a performer of "imaginative empathy" in which I demonstrate the potential of dance as a mediator for religious experience between the Christian and secular dance communities* (Wright: 430). Another six chapters were linked together easily in Section 3 as those that examined various aspects of creative processes and pedagogies. They shared a core focus on the process of transmitting dance movement and knowledge from teachers to students, from choreographers to dancers. Dance is not an oral or written tradition for the most part although its transmission does involve speaking and writing. But I suggest that it might be thought of as a "kinaesthetic tradition," one that is principally carried on from body to body. *Poïesis concerns the actions of the choreographer; it tries to grasp the detail and to solve the mystery of the transmission process at the heart of the dialogue between the choreographer and the dancer inside this intimate, secretive dance studio* (Vellet: 223).

Section 2 crystallized suddenly when I realized that five authors had written a first-person tale of their lives in dance: autoethnographic short stories. *I invite you to come on a journey with me as I move through a busy spring day in New Zealand, leaping and stumbling between my shifting responsibilities as dancer, researcher, feminist, and writer* (Barbour: 101). When does autobiography slip into the realm of autoethnography? From evidence in these chapters, it is a matter of self-consciously bringing cultural contexts into play and creating the kind of understandings that come from adopting an anthropological standpoint about the nature and meaning of what one is doing and saying (see Okely and Callaway 1992). *The subjectivity of an ethnographer-artist is essentially bound to the practice itself. The process takes in my life, evoking also cultural and moral values* (Juslin: 185).

But determining the commonality of the texts linked together in Section 1 proved more difficult, the five chapters (including my own) having been literally left over like unclassified residue at the end of a qualitative analysis process. Some time passed before I realized that we were all interested in proposing new strategies for carrying out dance ethnography, hybrid methods that transposed and adapted traditional anthropological practices to the field of art world dance in post-colonial times. *During ... discussions [with informant Kate Cornell], I was able to position myself as an amateur insider in the field, while relying on Cornell's expertise as dancer and dance scholar to link theoretical ideas with her own experiences.... Finally, I have applied a combination of a folklore, dance, and feminist analysis in order to obtain a multi-faceted analysis of footwear in dance. These theoretical approaches complement the ethnographic perspectives formed by my own and Cornell's opinions* (Harris Walsh: 87).

AS WE SAY IN QUÉBEC, *BONNE LECTURE* ...

The field of dance anthropology, as Georgiana Gore reminded me in her comments on this introductory chapter, has always hovered on the margins of either anthropology or dance studies, only recently gaining autonomy as a field of study in its own right. *Fields in Motion* provides a fundamental collection of studies in dance anthropology for its proponents, one that foregrounds the profession of dancing and a companion to the exisiting methodology anthologies. And this may be only a first volume of artistic dance ethnography authored by artist-insiders for, even as I complete this manuscript, I am running into more dance researchers who might have been included.

This anthology is keyworded to lie on the shelf beside ethnographies of traditional social and sport dance studies in the anthropology archive, and not necessarily only in a special section reserved for "art." It is also hoped that it will serve to lessen the perception of elitism that persists in the art world of dance despite the best efforts of current-day artists, policy-makers, and arts presenters to "democratize" the practice. Within these pages, the aesthetic experience of dancing is presumed to be a purposeful *social* activity, emblematic of the culture from which it springs, as Kealiinohomoku insisted so many years ago (1969–70). And now, as you move into these dance writings, prepare both body and mind for luminous insights on the vocation of human dance-making and performance.

[Dancer-choreographer Vincent] Mantsoe is the thing in motion, illuminating the human and social dimensions of his existence and his own agency—the globalizing forces of traditional and contemporary, colonial and post-colonial, a human in touch with the divine, a beautiful and exuberant dancer working with the blessings of the gods at the invitation of the patronizing West. (Cauthery: 333)

Bibliography

Alter, Judy. *Dance-Based Dance Theory: From Borrowed Models to Dance-Based Experience. New Studies in Aesthetics.* Vol. 7. New York and London: Peter Lang, 1991.

Amit, Vered (ed.). *Constructing the Field: Ethnographic Fieldwork in the Contemporary World.* London: Routledge, 2000.

Behar, Ruth, and Deborah A. Gordon. *Women Writing Culture.* Berkeley and Los Angeles: University of California Press, 1995.

Boas, Franziska (ed.). *The Function of Dance in Human Society.* Proceedings from the seminar. New York: Boas School, 1944 (later published in 1972 in New York by Dance Horizons).

Buckland, Theresa (ed.). *Dance in the Field: Theory, Methods and Issues in Dance Ethnography.* New York: St. Martin's Press, 1999.

————. "All Dances Are Ethnic, but Some Are More Ethnic Than Others: Some Observations on Dance Studies and Anthropology." *Dance Research* 17, no. 1 (1999): 3–21.

Clifford, James. *The Predicament of Culture: Twentieth-Century Ethnography, Literature, and Art.* Cambridge, MA, and London: Harvard University Press, 1988.

Clifford, James, and George Marcus (eds.). *Writing Culture: The Poetics and Politics of Ethnography.* Papers from an advanced seminar with ten participants at the School of American Research in Santa Fe, New Mexico. Berkeley, Los Angeles, and London: University of California Press, 1986.

Cowan, Jane K. *Dance and the Body Politic in Northern Greece.* Princeton, NJ: Princeton University Press, 1990.

Desmond, Jane C. *Staging Tourism: Bodies on Display from Waikiki to Seaworld.* Chicago and London: University of Chicago Press, 1999.

Fisher, Michael M.J., and George E. Marcus. *Anthropology as Cutural Critique: An Experimental Moment in the Human Sciences.* Chicago and London: University of Chicago Press, 1986.

Fisher, Jennifer. *Nutcracker Nation: How an Old World Ballet Became a Christmas Tradition in the New World.* New Haven and London: Yale University Press, 2003.

Giurchescu, Anca. "Past and Present in Field Research: A Critical History of Personal Experience." In Theresa Buckland (ed.), *Dance in the Field: Theory, Methods and Issues in Dance Ethnography.* New York: St. Martin's Press, and London: Macmillan, 1999: 41–54.

Grau, Andrée, et Georgiana Wierre-Gore (direction). *Anthroplogie de la danse: Genèse et construction d'une discipline.* Pantin, France: Centre national de la danse, 2005.

Hutchison, Anne. *Labanotation: The System of Analyzing and Recording Movement*, 3rd ed. New York City: Routledge, 1989 (originally published in 1977).

Kealiinohomoku, Joann Wheeler. "Le non-art de la danse: un essai." Trans. Annie Suquet. In Andrée Grau and Georgiana Gore (eds.), *Anthropologie de la danse et construction d'une discipline.* Paris: Centre national de la danse, 2005: 159–66. Originally published as "The Non-Art of the Dance: An Essay," in the *Journal for the Anthropological Study of Human Movement* 1, no. 2 (1980): 38–44.

————. "Theory and Methods for an Anthropological Study of Dance." Unpublished doctoral dissertation, Indiana University, 1976.

————. "Folk Dance." *Folklore and Folklife: An Introduction.* Chicago and London: University of Chicago Press, 1972: 381–404.

————. "An Anthropologist Looks at Ballet as a Form of Ethnic Dance." *Impulse* 20 (1969–70): 24–33.

Koutsouba, Maria. "'Outsider' in an 'Inside' World, or Dance Ethnography at Home." In Theresa Buckland (ed.), *Dance in the Field: Theory, Methods and Issues in Dance Ethnography.* New York: St. Martin's Press, and London: Macmillan, 1999: 185–95.

Kurath, Gertrude Prokosch. "Dance in Modern Culture." In *Half a Century of Dance Research: Essays by Gertrude Prokosch Kurath,* collected by Joann Wheeler Kealiinohomoku. Flagstaff, AZ: Cross-Cultural Dance Resources, 1965: 383–406.

Kuypers, Patricia (ed.). "Nomads de la danse: regards d'anthropologie et d'artistes." *Nouvelles de Danse* 34/35 (printemps/été 1988).

Marcus, George E., and Michael J. Fischer. *Anthropology as Cultural Critique: An Experimental Moment in the Human Sciences*. Chicago and London: University of Chicago Press, 1985.

Marcus, George E., and Fred R. Myers. "The Traffic in Art and Culture, an Introduction." In George E. Marcus and Fred R. Myers (eds.), *The Traffic in Culture: Refiguring Art and Anthropology*. Berkeley, Los Angeles, and London: University of California Press, 1995: 1–51.

Nahachewsky, Andriy. "Searching for Branches, Searching for Roots: Fieldwork in My Grandfather's Village." In Teresa J. Buckland (ed.), *Dance in the Field: Theory, Methods and Issues in Dance Ethnography*. New York: St. Martin's Press, and London: Macmillan, 1999: 175–85.

Ness, Sally Ann. "Dancing in the Field: Notes from Memory." In Susan Foster (ed.), *Corporealities: Dancing Knowledge, Culture and Power*. London and New York: Routlege, 1996.

Novack, Cynthia Jean. *Sharing the Dance: Contact Improvisation and American Culture*. Madison: University of Wisconsin Press, 1990.

Okeley, Judith, and Helen Callaway. *Anthropology and Autobiography*. ASA Monographs 29. London and New York: Routledge, 1992.

Savigliano, Marta E. *Tango and the Political Economy of Passion*. Boulder, San Francisco, and Oxford: Westview Press, 1995.

Shustermann, Richard. "Somaesthetics." *Performing Live: Aesthetic Alternatives for the Ends of Art*. Ithaca, NY: Cornell University Press, 2000: 137–53.

Sklar, Deidre. *Dancing with the Virgin: Body and Faith in the Fiesta of Tortugas, New Mexico*. Berkeley, Los Angeles, London: University of California Press, 2001.

Snyder, Allegra Fuller. "Levels of Event Patterns: A Theoretical Model Applied to the Yaqui Easter Ceremonies." In Lisbet Torp (ed.), *1998 Symposium of the International Council for Traditional Music Study Group on Ethnochoreology "The Dance Event: A Complex Cultural Phenomenon."* Copenhagen: ICTM Study Group on Ethnochoreology, 1989: 1–20.

———. "Past, Present and Future." *UCLA Journal of Dance Ethnology* 16 (1992): 1–28.

Wigman, Mary. *The Language of Dance*. Middletown, CT: Wesleyan University Press, 1966.

Wulff, Helena. *Ballet across Borders: Career and Culture in the World of Dancers*. Oxford and New York: Berg, 1998.

Inventing Strategies, Models, and Methods

CHAPTER ONE

Shifting Positions

FROM THE DANCER'S POSTURE TO THE RESEARCHER'S POSTURE

ANNE CAZEMAJOU

As a dance insider and fieldworker at "home," in France, I set out in this text to produce a reflexive, autobiographical account of how I made my way to a researcher's posture, and of the difficulties encountered in the negotiation of *etic* and *emic* positions.[1] Indeed, as Georgiana Gore puts it, "The use of personal pronoun 'I' is an acknowledgement that the cornerstones of anthropology, fieldwork and ethnographic writing, are reflexive practices and, in some senses, autobiographical."[2] But "in some senses" does not mean just autobiographical. Here lies the difference between what David Pocock calls one's "personal anthropology" as opposed to a recital of "personal, subjective experience."[3] Getting to understand what to do—scientifically speaking—with one's own subjective experience seems to me the biggest challenge for the dance insider, and especially for the fieldworker at home.

So, as my research comes to a close and has to materialize in the writing of a PhD dissertation, I sometimes wonder if I made the right choice concerning my field, which at the time, seemed self-evident. Indeed, while undertaking a degree in drama and performance studies, I first encountered contemporary dance. It was a great shock to me. So, the year after, I undertook a second Diplôme d'Études Approfondies (DEA) specializing in dance.

Following someone's recommendations, I took a contemporary dance class with an American teacher named Toni D'Amelio. Afterwards, I discovered that she had trained in George Balanchine's school in the United States, and, after a career interrupted through injury, was now giving contemporary dance classes in a Paris studio. Toni's classes quickly won me

Figure 1   Summer 2005 intensive course, Peter Goss Studio (Paris). Left to right: Rhizlaine, Emmanuelle, Candy, Emilie, Pauline, Julien, Cécile, Karine, Toni, Anne, and Onyx the dog. Photographer: Audrey Laumonier.

over. She was very concerned with pedagogy, which became part of the topic of the PhD that she had completed in dance at the University of Surrey in the United Kingdom. Toni paid considerable attention to each of her students; she spoke a great deal during the class—satisfying my longing for explanations and indications of all sorts; and seemed to have much knowledge of anatomy as well as of physiology and neurology. Every student thought she was an outstanding teacher.

As Toni had undertaken training to become an Iyengar yoga teacher, and as her pedagogy evolved with the introduction of exercises based on this technique, a group of students, including myself, emerged with whom she started a real process of transmission. We all believed that this process was revealing the functioning of our bodies, and even their reality. It is only quite recently that I have been able to recognize it as one of many possible conceptualizations of the body—Susan Leigh Foster speaks of "a body of ideas"[4]— leading to a specific construction of bodily experience. Indeed, at the beginning of most classes (which took place twice a week except for a special one on Sundays for a few invited students), Toni would announce the theme we were to work on. It might be the psoas; torsionality; the shoulder; the relationship between shoulder blades and sternum, sternum and sacrum, shoulders and shoulder blades, ischia and heels; the pectoral girdle; the pelvis; the internal/external rotation of the hip; the foot; the leg; the arms; the groin; the ilia; the ribs; orientation; and so on.

Thus, the first part of the class, influenced partly by the Feldenkrais Method and partly by Iyengar yoga, was a sort of guided visit of our bodies—mapping them; coordinating, organizing, representing them. It was followed by what Toni called "travelling barres" (*barres ambulantes*), which she used in order to work on specific technical movement sequences that integrated the patterns previously explored. Then, the final dance combination, still exploiting the same patterns, challenged us and our bodies through education. (As Toni would say, "We have a sensation but this sensation is wrong. It is habit. We must educate the body.")

Along the same lines, she organized thematic intensive courses running for one or two weeks during each academic vacation period. Some of the themes tackled between the summer of 2002 and spring of 2005 were the spine; openings (she specified "corporeal and conceptual"); apprehending the body; the arabesque and the arch; preliminary work on the shoulder's movements; choreographic training courses (specifying that "the dance class tries to make the coordination necessary for the production of a danced movement"); contemporary dance through yoga (the morning class, "dedicated to the yoga exercises," was followed in the afternoon by "a contemporary dance class exploiting the anatomic coordination prepared by the work of yoga"); and "yoga and dance: 'tasting,' 'chewing,' 'incorporating.'" As students, we became totally addicted to this learning process, which we viewed, I now realize, as a process of revelation.

After my DEA, I started a job and couldn't attend the dance classes and intensive courses as much as before. I recognized how vital these sessions were to me. As my intention was not to become a professional dancer, I started to ask myself what was really at stake in my intense commitment to these classes. I didn't really set out to formulate a clear answer, but I came to the conclusion that the only way of continuing with this process and of making sense of it was to transform it into a research project. So, after attending this class persistently and being part of the group of students for three years, I decided to investigate the transmission of bodily experience in this specific context. This is how the choice (that I now consider to be double-edged) of a field for my doctoral research was made.

Anthropology, with its fieldwork rite of passage,[5] seemed the ideal approach for my research. Yet, if fieldwork is a wonderful means for the outsider to attain the emic position (the insider point of view), I soon realized that having been in the field for three years as a student of Toni, I was much too inside already, and too involved in a strong emotional tie. That is, I was totally implicated in the situation and did not have the distance I thought was necessary for one to undertake research. As a student told me later during an interview, "I was taking all that Toni said word for word."

Indeed, I found that once you have chosen to trust somebody and to get involved in his or her process of transmission, there is complete faith in what that person proposes. It is a question of belief; and as Michel de Certeau[6] says, belief is not about truth but about "acting" and "the success of an undertaking." Belief is "a disposition to act" and it has to be conceived through the kind of relationship it constructs. It establishes a contract with the other, which is assumed to be "endowed with the power, the will and the knowledge that will make the remuneration effective" (de Certeau, 1981: 372). I completely trusted Toni and the process that she was making us undergo in the belief that the rewards would be forthcoming—those rewards became apparent as I progressively mastered the exercises and increasingly understood what was going on from an insider's perspective.

So, as I first came to this dance class as a student—not as a researcher—and at the time had no intention of researching this context of transmission, I had not been observing the process of acculturation[7] that I underwent and which had gradually made me part of this group. My knowledge and posture were entirely dedicated to action. Therefore, once I wanted to understand this process, to examine it with a critical eye, I was stuck too close to it. I could practise the rule, but I could not theorize about it. I had entered the contract as a dancer and had plunged entirely into the system of belief it entailed.

I remember presenting my work during a seminar at my home university, and the researchers present telling me again and again that my questions and posture were not those of a researcher but of a dancer. They kept asking me, "But what is your question *as a researcher*?" I was desperate: "But what is the difference between a dancer's posture and a researcher's posture?" They were clear: I had to get out of the field and take some distance if I wanted to make sense of it. For a while, I thought that I might succeed in grasping this posture of researcher while staying in the field, by trying to be more alert as to "how" the class developed rather than to "what" we had to do. But gradually, it became obvious that I could not—as I had first thought—hold both postures simultaneously, that of the dancer and that of the apprentice researcher. After conducting my research for one year, I wrote,

The choice is getting crucial. The idea of the research has prevented me in the last few months from doing the same work in dance as I did before. And vice versa, this implication in the field is too deep and prevents me from going on with my research. I can really feel how much I need to stand back. My thinking ability seems to be paralyzed, muddled up, confused.[8]

One thing was clear: I had to get out of the field to carry on with my research.

The main point is this: Quitting the field is not easy, and it has been a long process of going forward and backward, of shifting from outsider to insider and back again. Seven months after I officially started my research, knee injuries suddenly prevented me from taking the class. Not firmly established yet in my posture of researcher, I took this opportunity to sit aside in the studio and try to observe what was going on. But the other students would ask me to watch their movement or give my opinion about an exercise. There is no doubt that I was part of their group, part of this community of believers. And so, one month and a half later, when my knees healed enough to allow me to dance again, I hastened to return to the class.

Six months later, new circumstances prevented me from taking the class for two months; and after that, I decided not to go back. This resolution lasted two months, and in spite of feeling guilty, I couldn't resist jumping into the intensive course offered during winter vacation—even if I did not come back to the class after this lapse.

I then decided to completely assume my posture of researcher, and set out to video record the Easter intensive course. This attempt was a total failure, for I realized afterwards that while video recording, I had been concentrating on the students' movements, dancing somehow with them kinaesthetically. My eye was stuck to the camera in the same way as I was stuck in my dancer's posture. Instead of using the camera as an interface, a chemist's crucible, I was using it as an eye to enlarge my own dancer's desires: sensing, feeling, moving,[9] going further into this experience where a world of its own had started to emerge. Hidden behind the camera, I kept immersing myself in the sensation of movement. But when the music stopped, when the students went to the changing room and I found myself alone in the studio putting away my camera, I was brought back to reality: I was not *inside* any more *and* neither was I a *real* or *true* researcher.

For one year after that incident, I remained totally *out* of the field—except for the summer intensive course that I thought I had well deserved after being outside of the class for five months. But things had now changed. Being inside was not the same. Because of all the literature I had read, all of the arguments I'd had with other researchers, but mainly because of the passage of time, of getting out of the field, my posture had shifted imperceptibly. (I had now been doing my research for two years.) Even if I still felt part of the group, I was relieved of an enormous affective burden that before had acted like blinkers.

Eight months later, after the summer intensive course, I came back with my video again to record the intensive Easter course (one year had passed since my first attempt). And after one hour, I knew something was won: I realized that I had not paid attention to the students themselves, that I had not tried to identify with them, but that I had concentrated somehow on what was in between them,[10] in the way it all was happening. My eye was fresh, I was watching from elsewhere and I got excited about it. Video recording was now a wonderful means of introducing distance, otherness into what was being recorded. It helped in materializing my subject of research. Moreover, I felt that the fact of appearing in front of the group with the camera legitimized my posture as a researcher.

I took advantage of this situation to ask the students for interviews. Indeed, I thought that allowing them to speak would help me to avoid substituting my own experience for theirs and confining my subject of research to pre-established categories. The year before, I had been trained in a specific interview technique, developed by the CNRS[11] researcher Pierre Vermersch. This technique focuses on "explicitation" and allows the subjective bodily experience of the interviewee to be made explicit through its rendering in speech. Indeed, Pierre Vermersch says that "what comes first" in an interview are "generalities, loads of anecdotes larded with my implicit theories."[12] But this "natural posture" (as phenomenologist Husserl calls it) of "grasping" one's experience—an experience that is always already there, already constituted—has to be interrupted if the interviewee wants to reach a deeper experience. Indeed, according to Pierre Vermersch, this kind of generalization, even if interesting in the sense that it gives information about how the interviewee perceives his or her activity, is also "what he or she thinks he or she is doing"—which is not necessarily what the interviewee is "really doing" (Vermersch 1999). In the case of a dance class where the activity recurs regularly, in order for the technique to work, the focus for the duration of the interview has to be on one specific moment of the class that the interviewee wants to talk about.

So that I might grasp the salient elements of this process of transmission, I started with the same open question for each student, according to the structure recommended by the technique. After ascertaining that the student was ready, I asked the following slowly, trying to create the appropriate atmosphere for introspection: "What I suggest, if you agree, is for you to take your time in allowing a moment of the dance class which has interested you, to return." Sometimes I added, "… and which you wish to tell me about" and "Take all the time you need," "It can be any moment," and so on. Sometimes, the student went straight to something that was evident for himself. Sometimes, it was more difficult. He needed more time and I had to help him to get back to the context of the dance class by asking very simple questions such as, "What do you remember of the last class?" "Is there any element that comes back to you?" From what came back, we could start unravelling the narrative thread.

When I was sure that we had found a specific moment and that he or she was reliving it, revealing what Pierre Vermersch calls an "embodied posture of speech"—the main signs being a faraway look, a slowing down of the delivery and the use of the present tense—I started asking questions that brought the student to describe this moment: "What are you doing now?" "What are you are doing when …? "How do you know that …?" and "When you … what happens to you?" Such cues, which got the interview going, allowed us to fragment, that is complexify, the description each time a little more, to reach a sharper level of detail and to go further into the "granularity" of the experience's description.

Through this activity of "reflectiveness" (*réfléchissement*), the technique of accompaniment devised by Vermersch helps the interviewer bring the verbalizations back to the action, and from there, back to the very place of the experience. In this activity of making something conscious—as opposed to the "reflexive activity" which is a conceptual activity—the interviewer and the interviewee subordinate their cognitive activity to a silent open posture, which allows what is not yet conscious, and which exists only in a pre-reflexive, "ante-predicative" manner (before it has been expressed in words), to emerge. This technique creates the conditions to help the interviewee reappropriate his or her experience and to enable sense to be made of what really happened. And what happened during Toni's transmission process, I realized, was an incredible phenomenon of belief, which gathered a strong community of believers. Indeed, most of the time, the students were not doing anything more than what they were asked to do, and they didn't so much as try to feel or wait for a feeling to emerge, trusting that through time and work, feelings would come and bodies would change.

Despite the constraints of this interview technique, the students were eager to talk, and I undertook and transcribed eight interviews. Hearing their voices, their version of events, entering deeply into *their* experience, plunged me into the core of the research, as did the video recording. And now, as I am beginning to analyze this data and to write up the material for my PhD, I know that another process of going forward and backward is waiting for me: from data to theory and back again. But now, as I am entering this process, I am happy to say that I am finally feeling as much satisfaction as a researcher as I did as a dancer. This has been a long and somehow mysterious process of shifting positions, of getting new eyes, new ears, new feelings, new insights and knowledge—which I am sure I would never have achieved if I had stayed in the field, and continued with the classes.

Notes

1 This notional couple was coined by the linguist Kenneth Pike in the 1960s. He writes in *Language in Relation to a Unified Theory of Human Behavior*, 1967 [1st ed. in vol. 3: 1954, 1955, 1960]: 37, "It proves convenient—though partially arbitrary—to describe behavior from two different standpoints, which lead to results which shade into one another. The etic viewpoint studies behavior as from outside of a particular system, and as an essential initial approach to an alien system. The emic viewpoint results from studying behavior as from inside the system. (I coined the words *etic* and *emic* from the words *phonetic* and *phonemic* following the conventional linguistic usage of these latter terms. The short terms are used by dance anthropologists and others in an analogous manner, but for more general purposes.)" Pike's contribution proved of great interest to anthropologists. For example, human-movement anthropologist Adrienne Kaeppler writes in "The Mystique of Fieldwork" (1999: 14), "While observing and participating in activities and events it becomes evident that people of distinctive groups move in distinctive ways and categorize their movements accordingly. Anthropologists try to find the systematic patterns that lead to understanding indigenous categorization—the emic dimension of movement."

2 Georgiana Gore, "Traditional Dance in West Africa," in Janet Adshead-Lansdale and J. Layson (eds.), *Dance History: An Introduction*, 2nd ed. (London: Routledge, 1994), 59.

3 David Pocock, "The Idea of a Personal Anthropology," *Journal of Anthropological Study of Human Movement* 8, no. 1 (1994 [1973]): paragraph 13.4.

4 She writes in "Dancing Bodies" (1997: 235–57), "The daily practical participation of a body in any of these disciplines makes of it a body-of-ideas. Each discipline refers to it using select metaphors and other tropes that make it over. These tropes may be drawn from anatomical discourse or the science of kinesiology; or they may liken the body to a machine, an animal, or any other worldly object or event. They may be articulated as verbal descriptions of the body and its actions, or as physical actions that show it how to behave. Whether worded or enacted, these tropes change its meaning by re-presenting it."

5 Paul Rabinow, in *Reflections on Fieldwork in Morocco* (1977: 4), speaks about "this essential rite of passage, this metaphysical marker which separated anthropologists from the rest." And Sara Delamont, Paul Atkinson and Odette Parry write in *The Doctoral Experience: Success and Failure in Graduate School*, 1999: 73, "Fieldwork is virtually a *sine qua non* of anthropological membership—just as laboratory research is a taken-for-granted facet of the natural scientist's knowledge—and equally distinctive claims to personal competences.... Social anthropology, whether pure or applied, is marked by the strong empirical base of the discipline and a dependence upon fieldwork (Grillo 1985). The symbolic and individual value of anthropological fieldwork goes well beyond the strict requirement of 'research methods' and 'data collection' (Fardon 1990). Generally, fieldwork was described as the essence of anthropological work, distinguishing anthropology from other disciplines in the social sciences." Thus, as Gary P. Ferraro writes in *Cultural Anthropology—An Applied Perspective*, 2006 [2003], p. 94, "Doing firsthand fieldwork has become a necessary rite of passage for becoming a professional anthropologist."

6 Michel de Certeau, "Une pratique sociale de la différence: croire." In *Faire croire: Modalités de la diffusion et de la réception des messages religieux du XIIe au XVe siècles*, 1981: 364–84.
7 Robert Redfield, Ralph Linton, and Melville J. Herskovits write in "Memorandum for the Study of Acculturation," *American Anthropologist* 38 (1936: 149), "Acculturation comprehends those phenomena which result when groups of individuals having different cultures come into continuous first-hand contact, with subsequent changes in the original cultural patterns of either or both groups."
8 Fieldnotes, January 20, 2004.
9 Allusion to Bonnie Brainbridge Cohen's text: *Sensing, Moving and Action: The Experiential Anatomy of Body–Mind Centering* (Northampton: Contact Collaborations, 1993).
10 According to the French philosopher Gilles Deleuze and in his perspective of a renewed empiricism, relations are what happens "between" things, people, animals, and so on—that is, in the middle, and exterior to their terms. See Gilles Deleuze and Claire Parnet, *Dialogues* (Paris: Flammarion, 1996), 68–70.
11 Centre National de la Recherche Scientifique (National Center for Scientific Research), a state structure under the Ministry of Research that employs researchers in all disciplines.
12 Pierre Vermersch, "Pour une psycho-phénoménologie," *Journal du GREX, Expliciter* 13 (février 1996): 1. (My translation.)

Bibliography

de Certeau, Michel. Une pratique sociale de la différence: croire. In *Faire croire: Modalités de la diffusion et de la réception des messages religieux du XIIᵉ au XVᵉ siècles. Actes de la Table ronde organisée par l'Ecole française de Rome*, Rome: Collection de l'Ecole française de Rome, 1981: 363–83.
Delamont, Sara, Paul Atkinson, and Odette Parry. *The Doctoral Experience: Success and Failure in Graduate School*. London: Falmer, 2000.
Deleuze, Gilles, and Claire Parnet. *Dialogues*, Paris: Flammarion, 1996.
Ferraro, Gary P. *Cultural Anthropology: An Applied Perspective*. Belmont, CA: West/Wadsworth. 2006 [2003].
Foster, Susan Leigh. "Dancing Bodies." In Jane C. Desmond (ed.), *Meaning in Motion. New Cultural Studies in Dance*. Durham, NC, and London: Duke University Press, 1997: 235–57.
Gore, Georgiana. "Traditional Dance in West Africa." In J. Adshead-Lansdale and J. Layson (eds.), *Dance History: An Introduction*, 2nd ed. London: Routledge, 1994: 59–80.
Grau, Andrée, and Georgiana Wierre-Gore (eds.). *Anthropologie de la danse. Genèse et construction d'une discipline*. Pantin: Centre National de la Danse, 2005.
Kaeppler, Adrienne L. "The Mystique of Fieldwork." In Theresa Buckland (ed.), *Dance in the Field*. London and New York: Macmillan, 1999: 13–25.
Pike, Kenneth L. *Language in Relation to a Unified Theory of the Structure of Human Behavior*. The Hague-Paris: Mouton [1st ed. in 3 vols.: 1954, 1955, 1960]. (Especially chapter 2: "Etic and Emic Standpoints for the Description of Behaviour," pp. 37–72.)

————. Towards a Theory of the Structure of Human Behavior. In D. Hymes (ed.), *Language in Culture and Society: A Reader in Linguistics and Anthropology.* New York and London: Harper and Row, 1964: 54–62.

Pocock, David. "The Idea of a Personal Anthropology." *JASHM: Journal for the Anthropological Study of Human Movement* 8, no. 1 (1994 [1973]): 11–42.

Rabinow, Paul. *Reflections on Fieldwork in Morocco.* Berkeley and Los Angeles: University of California Press, 1977.

Redfield, Robert, Ralph Linton, and Melville J. Herskovits. "Memorandum for the Study of Acculturation," *American Anthropologist* 38 (1936): 140–52.

Vermersch, Pierre, *L'entretien d'explicitation.* Issy-les-Moulineaux: ESF, 2004 [1994].

————. "Pour une psycho-phénoménologie." *Journal du GREX, Expliciter* 13 (février 1996): 1 (available at www.grex2.com).

————. "Approche du singulier." *Journal du GREX, Expliciter* 30 (mai 1990) (available at www.grex2.com).

Williams, Drid, *Anthropology and the Dance: Ten Lectures.* Chicago: University of Illinois Press, 2004 [1991].

————. "Fieldwork." In Theresa Buckland, *Dance in the Field*: 26–40.

CHAPTER TWO

A Template for Art World Dance Ethnography

THE *LUNA "NOUVELLE DANSE"* EVENT

DENA DAVIDA

Born into an American family of theatre directors, actors, and screenwriters, I inherited the vocation of artist and have always been an insider to the world of the Western performing arts. It was in a contemporary dance studio that I discovered my optimum form of expression and plunged into modern dance technique classes, Laban Movement Analysis (LMA), then later made a postmodern move into the sensuous duet form Contact Improvisation (CI). Along the way, I performed, taught, worked backstage and finally claimed the métier of dance presenter. But, devoted as always to reading and inquisitive by nature, I also deepened my ties with academia throughout the decades. And so one day the life of the mind and the body dovetailed when, enrolled in a master's program, I fell upon Kealiinohomoku's seminal text (1969/1970) on ballet's ethnicity, and began the ethnographic journey to understanding why I dance.

KEALIINOHOMOKU'S ASSIGNMENT

Suddenly, through the common denominator of ethnicity, my small contemporary dance world seemed inevitably linked to a larger world of dancers. (Davida 2006: 12)

My doctoral "research event" begins with a story of its muse, Joann Kealiinohomoku, whose seminal theories about dance anthropology have largely guided my thinking throughout the years. It was by way of a first

29

reading of "An Anthropologist Looks at Ballet as a Form of Ethnic Dance" (1969/1970), a cultural reframing of Western classical ballet, that my dance world was shaken. A powerful sense of dance as a cultural imperative arose from the arguments in her text, suddenly widening my frame of reference.

The concept of doing ethnographic fieldwork among contemporary dancers came to mind one afternoon in 1990. Soon after having been struck by Kealiihonomoku's essay on ballet, I flew south from Montreal to join her summer course at the University of North Carolina at Greensboro. On leaving the classroom one day in her company, I inquired earnestly, "I do understand what you are saying about the ethnicity of ballet, but what about postmodern dance?" With little hesitation, she answered, "That, of course, is *your* project." That project is this book.

Sixteen years later, one by-product of this fateful exchange was an ethnographic doctoral project that I undertook in my adopted home city of Montreal, a case study of *O Vertigo Danse* and choreographer Ginette

Figure 1 Dancer Anne Barry in the moon dress in the *Luna* choreography by Ginette Laurin. Photographer: Georg Anderhub.

Laurin's *Luna* choreographic project. The research spanned eight years from initial proposal to cap-and-gown. By way of a detailed descriptive and interpretive analysis, *Illuminating Luna: An Ethnographic Study of Meaning in a Montréal "Nouvelle Danse" Event* (Davida 2006) advanced a field of thought that I called "contemporary dance ethnography."[1] My methods were largely drawn from time-honoured practices of anthropologists: long-term participant observation in the field; detailed data gathering, including field notes, artefacts, and documents; field photographs; in-depth interviews; focus groups; followed by coding and analysis. The entire process was grounded in general anthropological theories (and especially symbolic interactionism). But theoretical threads were also assembled from an interdisciplinary combination of concepts gleaned from the fields of Western sociology of the arts, cultural and critical studies, and aesthetics.

As have dance ethnographers before me, I addressed questions of nature and function, examined the *who, what, where, when,* and *why* of the dance event. I asked, "Why do we [myself and other contemporary dance event participants] conceive and present these kinds of dance events in the particular way that we do?" But in a break with much of previous practice in dance anthropology, I chose to "make strange the familiar" by doing fieldwork close to home among dancers for whom I was a colleague—acknowledging the tensions in my situation as both a dancer-insider and researcher-outsider. And unlike the time-honoured village dance events that apparently mobilized entire communities and even societies, I wondered at the onset why contemporary artistic dancing persisted among its proponents despite its status as a marginal subculture whose artists laboured under precarious physical and economic conditions (Perreault, 1988).

As an artist and researcher with a progressive frame of mind, I also ventured (if cautiously) into the territory of what was being called in the 1990s the "new ethnography," by way of attending to political dynamics in the field and within the research community. I adopted a self-reflexive attitude and theorized Montreal choreographer Ginette Laurin's dance aesthetic as an intertextual and interdisciplinary constellation of phenomena. Just as I embarked on my research project in 1997, I discovered a field that was immersed in an identity crisis of its own in which the ethics and viability of ethnographic fieldwork were being called into question (Fischer and Marcus 1985). And so I examined the politics of my position as an academic insider ethnographer doing anthropology "at home" (see Jackson 1987 and Messerschmidt 1981) within my own community of Montreal contemporary dancers. An intensive reading period unearthed further subquestions: Why had so few dance anthropologists ventured into the fields of Western art dance? Would contemporary dance ethnography be welcomed in the field of dance anthropology? Judging by recent publications and research, discussed below, I had some reason to think so. And since I had undertaken this project later in life (in my fifties), seeking to refresh my professional practice in the dance world, it came as no surprise that my artistic world view was profoundly reshaped during the process.

MOVING FROM INSIDER TO OUTSIDER AND BACK AGAIN

As an insider working in the same artistic "community of experience" (Novack 1990: 15) as the dance event participants inhabiting my field of my study, I found it often necessary to readjust my physical and philosophical position as fieldworker, vacillating sometimes quite unexpectedly between an insider and outsider frame of mind. It is undeniable that my insider status eased my entry into the public and even very private areas of dance studios and performance venues (such as dressing rooms and board meetings). And my long accumulated knowledge and common sense about this particular contemporary dance world provided the kinds of insights, probably more difficult for an outsider to detect, about phenomena like the somatic life of the dancers, the choreographer's creative intuition, the intricate logistics of organizing dance events and even the technicalities of stagecraft.

But there were times when the differing vantage points of outside fieldworker and dance insider became blurred—suddenly confused or interrupted—as, for instance, when a dancer approached me with a choreographic project in my role as a dance presenter, even as I was taking field notes. Before entering the field, I spent several months charting my own deep-set assumptions about the contemporary dance world, and found it frequently necessary while in the field to re-examine the dynamics of participation and of observation because of a tangle of past relationships linking me to my research subjects.

But it was by finally and fully assuming my role as a university doctoral student over the course of the eight-year study that I managed to achieve the emotional and intellectual shifts in perspective necessary to reflect, interpret, and analyze the goings-on. When in the field, I was best able to do this when in the least familiar, most peripheral positions: e.g., observation from the backstage wings during a performance. I also frequently needed to censor certain of my "insider impulses" such as the desire to massage the tense shoulders of a dancer, or to offer my own interpretations of the *Luna* choreography during audience focus groups. I may not have succeeded completely, for dancer David Rose one day described my anthropologist's field persona as "the fly that occasionally buzzes." And there were times when I felt as if I had slipped inadvertently into the skin of insider participant once again, because of the dancers' eventual perception of me as a kind of *O Vertigo* "company scribe." This realization occurred when a dancer turned toward me unexpectedly one day and called out playfully, "Dena, did you get that?" and at another moment when another exclaimed, "You didn't really write *that* down Dena, did you?!" But it wasn't until over a year after leaving the field that I was able to see myself as really separate from the pile of papers, notebooks, and boxes of data that had accumulated on my office floor, and so able to review the findings in a contemplative frame of mind. I never did lose sight of being a dancer straddling the fence between real world dance pracrice and dance academia, one who was observing close colleagues and who possessed a very personal stake in the outcome of the research.

RECASTING THE TRADITIONAL CONTOURS OF "THE DANCE EVENT" IN THE LIGHT OF *LUNA*

Although I have long been working as a university teacher, my primary art-world vocation for the last three decades has been that of "dance presenter," as English Canadians usually call it (*diffuseur* in Québécois), or as I have inscribed on my calling card, "artistic director." We performing arts event organizers use various titles in view of how we perceive our roles: presenters, producers, programmers, cultural agents, venue directors, curators, and more. Because my work involves the organization of a season of dance performances in Montreal, the anthropologists' notion of the dance event was particularly suited to my "dance presenter's gaze" and perspective. And so I modelled a research design grounded in Kealiinohomoku's theorization of a structure and range of dance event elements (1976: 233–45) and Ronström's discussion of a dance evening as an extraordinary occasion in which the experience of dance and music are the focus (1989: 21–29). But Royce's advocacy of a holistic and contextual "dance event unit," in response to the competing theories in the 1970s about the nature and function of dance (1977: 10–17), was also an early instigation to mount my study, and Snyder's "event levels" diagram pulled my attention to the intricate layers, the macro and micro aspects of dance events in general (1989: 1–20). My first task in conceiving an ethnographic framework for this study was that of remodelling the contours of these concepts to better suit the nature and function of the contemporary dance genre.

A novel paradigm with certain unique features emerged from this transposition. From a dance anthropologist's perspective, of course, answers to questions of function, form, and meaning have traditionally been sought in the words and actions of insider participants and their cultural contexts. The ethnographer observes, analyzes, and writes from an "academic distance," but the ethics of current-day anthropological practice also demand that she seek a balance of power between participant and researcher perspectives. These new ethnography proponents have also sharpened the focus on the literary character of ethnographic writing as well as the political dynamics of dancing and dance "production." But an ethnographic study of this kind of contemporary dance event—with its modernist ethos of artistic and interpretive freedom, of creativity and innovation—required a significant refashioning of who-what-when-where and why components of the dance event framework's habitual contours, as I will elaborate in this section.

Who

A vivid example of how the *Luna* project required a reorganization of the traditional dance event framework can be found in the typology I developed for its dance event participants. Soon after entering *O Vertigo*'s offices and studios, it became apparent that while those engaged in the *Luna* project might fit within the usual categories of dancers and non-dancers,[2] a more useful breakdown might consider a further classification such as dance world professionals and non-professionals, those for whom dancing was a full-time vocation and audience members who devoted only a few hours to attending the dance event, and the dance company and the venue staffs. The *Luna* study included a triad of participant types with their corresponding fields of study, already familiar to dance researchers: spectators (reception theory), creative artists (creativity theory, choreographic composition), and critics (aesthetics). But the *Luna* fieldwork also unearthed numerous but rarely discussed protagonists such as theatre technicians, rehearsal directors, professional visual and sound designers, arts programmers, publicists, production managers and administrators on the staff of the cultural venues and dance companies, "dance *animateurs*," members of boards of directors, summer workshop students, funding agents and cultural policy-makers, tour managers, a community of artistic peers, and more. In the figure with which I concluded the *Luna* study, without a doubt evoked by Howard Becker's model of artworks as the result of the joint cooperation of "an often large number of people" (1982: 1), each of these participant groups is seen as playing a significant role in determining the form and the substance of the dance event. And so, although this kind of dance event is commonly understood by its practitioners as choreographer-centric, for without the dancemaker's creative vision the dance wouldn't materialize, I observed how all participants, by virtue of their roles in the event, contribute in small or significant ways to its form and meaning.

When and Where

The usual temporal and spatial boundaries of the framework also needed reconfiguring in light of the *Luna* study. Where might Day 1 of the dance event be located? At a crucial juncture in my formulation of the research project design, anthropologist Joan Erdman warned me categorically, "There is no beginning and there is no end." This proved true in some small measure. While searching for the elusive Day 1 of "preparation" for the *Luna* event, for instance, I discovered that the beginning of *Luna* might be located in events that happened many months before the first creative session between choreographer and dancer, and much to my dismay, before I had even entered the field! I finally found a plausible point of origin during an interview with company dancer Marie-Claude Rodrigue (2001). She reported her experience of a rehearsal in which the very first images for *Luna* had surfaced in the consciousness of choreographer Laurin, even as she was finishing the creation of the previous choreography. Kealiinohomoku mused about this "origin myth," as she put it, of contemporary dance events during our interview for the *Luna* study:

> Is this the idea [for a contemporary dance event]: that it has to be a clean slate, and you are a creative individual and you are inventing?… At a certain point this mythical person wants to make a work. That's probably day one. (Kealiinohomoku, 1999)

Conversely, I never did discover a moment that might be definitively considered "a final day" of the event. That is to say, in the aftermath, during an indefinite time, there might ensue (and this proved true for *Luna*) more writing and discussion of the choreography, choreographic reconstruction, lingering memories in the minds of participants, and so on. So in the end, I chose the closing performance of *Luna* on tour, in Prague, with which to end the ethnographic narrative, encouraged to do so because of an email from dancer Rodrigue:

> You know that last Saturday we gave the very last performance of *Luna* in Prague and something marvelous happened. There was an eclipse of the moon that evening. I won't tell you how we all felt! We said goodbye to *Luna*, and for many of us, to *O Vertigo*. A new stage begins. (Rodrigue 2003)

But as I suspected might happen, the year after this "last performance" the company decided to remount *Luna* in their home city of Montreal. Without hesitation, I jumped back into the field during the two days of repeat performances.

Is it even possible to speak of a definitive ending for artistic dance events like *Luna*, beyond the requisite final reports to funding agencies, archiving of press books, and storage of costumes and sets? Perhaps closing public performances and their aftermath are more appropriate terms, suggesting the possibility of continuity. And for choreographer Laurin, the seeds for the following creation were apparently embedded in the creative process of the previous work.

But keeping in view Snyder's dance-event levels (1989), the concepts of time and space in *Luna* took other forms as well. In the sense Snyder gives to the "macro level," or the world view, that underlies a contemporary dance event, *Luna* might also be understood as anchored in the time of an artistic era (the local moniker is *nouvelle danse* or *danse contemporaine*) and the space of a geographic location (with Montreal, Quebec, as its home city but restaged in eighty cities while on tour).

On yet another level, what struck me about the element of time in *Luna* as I reviewed the data, was how its regulation was micromanaged in the everyday life of the dance company. There were a multitude of grids, organized by the month, day, hour, minute, and even the second. Every working hour of the project's progress had to be paid and accounted for, and it was the rehearsal director who assumed the role of company timekeeper. In the data pool, I collected documents such as schedules for rehearsal and touring, lists of significant dates in the lives of the dance company and its members, exact timings (to the second) for each section of the choreography in the technical cue sheet. There was not a moment squandered during the creative process, and choreographic timings were controlled precisely by way of "cues" that were "called out" to the technical crew through headphones by the stage manager as the performance took place.

The element of time took on yet another guise, what is often distinguished as "theatrical" vs. "real life" time by performing arts insiders. It's a fluctuating form of consciousness that is experienced vividly by the stage performers and their audiences. Performers spoke about it in terms of "stage presence" or "states," while audience members described it as "being drawn into the performance." I observed and recorded this shifting perception of time most intensely from my backstage vantage point in the offstage wings. In the case of the dancers, it appeared as if some kind of heightened energetic state of consciousness was continuously created and released, one that animated their larger-than-life personas when on stage (theatrical time), only to pull back into a recuperative phase as they exited the stage, letting go of tension and engaging in technical tasks such as changing costumes (real time). As for the spectators, they alternately "suspended their disbelief" as their attention was captivated in the so-called "choreographic universe" of the stage action, and they experienced "real time" when their awareness pulled away from the fictional stage world or if they became distracted during the performance, for instance, and, of course, as the choreography came to an end and it was time to applaud the performers.

As for space, in terms of place, *Luna* was a multi-sited event (Amit 2000). It was created and managed in several venues (dance and recording studios, technical laboratories, offices, etc.), mounted and performed in eighty cities. In order to study the physical organization of the venues at the time of public performance, I charted several distinct areas of simultaneous goings-on. There was (a) an audience waiting area at the entrance with a ticket office and sometimes a café; (b) a seating section of the theatre space reserved for audiences; and (c) a curtained-off stage space reserved exclusively for the performers with its own inner sanctum of dressing rooms, common rooms, and exclusive stage entrances and street exits hidden from public view. But (d) the backstage area, rarely attended to by arts researchers and anthropologists, was called to my attention whenever I observed performances from an off-stage perspective. This area included the so-called wings, "flys," and the technical "box" (usually placed in the back of the audience), where manipulations of the light-and-sound effects by the stage crew accompanied every move of the dancers. The work of the stage technicians was crucial to the outcome of the performance but invisible to audience members. The data recalled yet another sense of space in *Luna*, homologous to the idea of choreographic "timings": the notion of "spacings," i.e., the choreographic use of the stage space.

What

As is true for most dance events in the professional art world in my experience, the performance of *Luna* was the result of many months (more than a year in this case) of planning, fundraising, administrative, promotional, and documentation activities necessary to its favourable outcome. And recalling that traditional non-art dance events usually require the remounting of previously conceived dances, perhaps one of the distinguishing characteristics of *Luna* and similar contemporary dance events is extensive devotion to long creative processes and to the primacy of innovation. For each choreographic project, Laurin and her dance company have been called upon to "make it anew," to reinvent the choreographic material and thematic content. Development of a philosophical basis for this process, in the case of *Luna*, involved ongoing conversations between Laurin, a science-minded company dancer, a visual conceptual artist, and an astrophysicist. A labour-intensive collaborative creative process with dancers; as well as sound and light, visual image, costume, and set designers unfolded in parallel with administrative preparations.

Typical of the contemporary dance genre, the creative processes of *Luna* unfolded in orderly stages, beginning with the development of an initial set of ideas, articulated in the form of a project proposal within a grant application. An inventory of the resources necessary to flesh out Laurin's underlying choreographic vision, along with fundraising and tour-development activities, were set into motion and would determine the scale of the choreographic composition. Creative sessions with Laurin began with the introduction of imaginative movement material through intuitive strategies (in emulation of the Québécois *automatistes*), followed by further movement invention and manipulation with contributions by the dancers, and gradually shaped into a final form. As with her previous choreographies, there was an imperative to seek out a unique way of moving, to crystallize a movement aesthetic to embody the particular concepts announced in the project description. During this same period, *Luna*'s image, sound, and costume collaborators interjected new layers of media into the movement composition, which was finally "mounted" on a theatrical stage by way of a technical residency. Soon after the initial performances in their hometown, the *O Vertigo* dance company began travelling from city to city over three continents, remounting and adapting the *Luna* choreographic event within eighty disparate communities. In each case the performance decorum was the same: spectators and dance specialists sat still and quietly in the dark, bringing the dance into the public sphere and creating the intensive dancer–audience relationship at the core of the dance event. The audience's interpretations and assessments were made manifest in formal and informal post-performance conversations and remained in memory, as well as being recorded in critical writing. Also in the aftermath of the event, there remained final reports to funding agencies, the storage of sets and costumes, and archival activities. And then the cycle of creation would begin again as Laurin began to imagine another new work for the company even as the previous one was touring.

Why

In the *nouvelle danse* world of events like *Luna*, there is little common consensus about either the significance of these dance events in the everyday lives of participants nor a shared understanding of the meaning of the choreography and its performance. In this presentational or "theatrical" dance form in the modernist tradition, itself the historical outcome of an art movement in which the ethos of creative and interpretive freedom have prevailed, meanings are not usually prescribed through a "kinaesthetic tradition." Choreographer Laurin contemplated this ethos of multiple meanings in this way: "There certainly is a sense, but it will be different from one person to another.... For me there are thousands of senses" (Laurin 2002).

Beyond an agreed-upon behaviour at performances (Goffman 1974), the only common consensus among the proponents of the *Luna* event proved to be the general belief that the dance performance was indeed valuable and significant in some way or another. But what function did *Luna* serve for its dancing and non-dancing participants within the ongoing process of their lives? How did the various participants manage to interpret and assess the polysemic choreographic performance?

I am reminded of Geertz's cultural account (1973), resonant with my own understanding of the human compulsion to know and interpret art works, however abstract and ambiguous they may be:

> The perception of something important in either particular works or in the arts generally moves people to talk (and write) about them incessantly. Something that meaningful to us cannot be left just to sit there bathed in pure significance, and so we describe, analyze, compare, judge, classify; we erect theories about creativity, form, perception, social function; we characterize art as a language, a structure, a system, an act, a symbol, a pattern of feeling; we reach for scientific metaphors, spiritual ones, technological ones, political ones; and if all else fails we string dark sayings together and hope someone else will elucidate them for us. (Geertz 1973: 95)

To offer an example from the field of *Luna*, dance spectator Ginette Longueux articulated during an audience focus group how the dynamics of interpretation operated in her own mind as she watched the choreography unfold:

> One makes associations.... I don't force it. I just feel, at certain moments, that was it. But it wasn't important. I don't want to seize [the meaning] at any price.... In any case, one always has a little flash somewhere or other. You're always in the material.... It's also important to feel what the body is expressing. You need to feel something. You can't only be in the abstraction of movement. (Longueux 2001)

If not producing a common understanding of the dance event, analysis of the *Luna* interviews, focus groups, and field notes yielded what I named "sites of consensus." I was able to group together "life meanings" for *Luna*'s artists, personnel, and specialists in ways that referred to general spheres of human activity which I categorized as emotional, spiritual, socio-political, physical, intellectual, and psychological. As for the twenty-two spectators who stayed behind after *Luna* performances, allowing me to put their views on record in the course of three focus groups, I formulated five motive-centred genres of life meaning that I named variously, "I came to feel," "I came to reflect," "I came to admire," "I came to escape," and "I came to explore." During these group discussions, audience members also revealed the attitudes and understandings with which they entered the theatre and also how it was that dance spectating gave meaning to their everyday lives. Referring back to the moment when they sat silently in the dark experiencing the *Luna* performance, I also asked them to describe their individual strategies for interpretation and evaluation of the dancing itself, which I was then able to classify as intellectual, emotional, sensorial and/ or intuitive.

The *Luna* dancers were offered sparse clues to meaning throughout the creative process with the choreographer to elucidate the sense or motivation underlying the gestures they were given to perform. They articulated their sense of the meaing in poetic and metaphoric phrases. For dancer David Rose, the movement must be "made to speak"; Antje Riede spoke about movement energies and human connections; Kha Nguyen looked for a binding thematic thread; Marie-Claude Rodrigue interpreted through a spiritual lens; Donald Weikart constructed the concept of an "imaginary kernel"; and so on. Each one had created a process by which she imbued her performance of the abstract, poetic movements with a personal sense of motive and meaning, or, as dancer Anne Barry expressed it, "[They found] themselves in the universe of *Luna*" (2002).

Also participating in the *Luna* event were a group of dance professionals whose role it was to provids expert interpretations and evaluations of the *Luna* event, including dance critics, consultants, cultural theorists, historians, and aesthetic philosophers. In the narrative ethnography of *Luna*, I

Figure 2 The researcher, Dena Davida, undertaking an audience focus group after a performance, during the pilot project of an earlier work by *O Vertigo Danse* at Jacob's Pillow in New England. Photographer: Robert Duplessis.

positioned these protagonists as both "expressive specialists," employing Ronström's term and concept (1988), and as members of my own dance scholar's community. Each articulated a unique point of view, making aesthetic interpretations and judgments that relied on one or more of the existing contemporary philosophies of art and schools of artmaking. In my own expert account of Laurin's choreography, for instance, I wrote this art historical analysis of *Luna*'s form and function:

> The aesthetics of *Luna* were emblematic of an eclecticism that has been fostered by the tenets of postmodern art. A striking example of this is how Laurin's approach to dance-making integrated elements of previously opposing artistic movements: idea-based Conceptualism, emotionally saturated Expressionism and a belief in the subconscious that belonged to Automatism. (Davida 2006: 454)

While some proceeded as if meaning lay somewhere embedded in the dance work itself and waiting to be "excavated" or uncovered by the shrewd observer, others assumed the viewer-centred position of "constructing" the meaning from the experience of a spectator. Yet other specialists sought to understand the conscious (and perhaps unconscious) intentions of the artistic creator (for more about this, see Bennett 1997 on reception theory and Lavendar 1997 on theories of interpretation). The *Luna* study hints at a possible reconciliation of these divergent viewpoints: that the life meanings and aesthetic interpretations of a dance composition might be seen as a composite of these diverse perspectives. The *Luna* ethnography also expanded this paradigm to include interpretative voices that have been scarcely heard previously in these debates, like those of the dancers, the programmers, the technicians, the funders, and the administrators. And I believe that by meshing together so many vantage and viewpoints from event insiders, this ethnographic approach to telling the story of *Luna*—while it can never claim to be the definitive one—does offer a plausible, dense, and richly situated narrative.

DANCE RESEARCH TRANSFORMING LIFE, TRANSFORMING ART

What might be the effects of this way of envisioning a contemporary dance performance for dance presenters like me? In the field of the professional performing arts, replete with quantitative audience-development strategies aimed at improving box-office revenue and driven by economic models from the cultural industries (large-scale for-profit enterprises), this ethnographic study moves dance presenting in a resolutely subjective and intersubjective direction. In other words, it asks, "What is the qualitative experience of dance audience members?" But within the *Luna* study and its comprehensive event framework, I also ask about the experiences of all kinds of dancing and non-dancing participants, professional and non-professional, and not only those of spectators.

As *Luna*'s "research specialist," I can already confirm that the way in which I go about my work as a dance presenter has been fundamentally changed in the course of forging this particular way of thinking about contemporary dance events. This realization sprang to consciousness one evening while I was attending a dance performance of the Random Dance Company in Roubaix, France, on March 17, 2005. It was there and then that I began to notice a shift in the way my mind was now navigating the occasion of a dance performance. No longer was I initially preoccupied with the usual "presenters' gaze," in which I calculate how many hotel rooms would be needed for the company members on tour, whether the set pieces could be shipped on an airplane, and if this aesthetic would appeal to the audiences and critics in Montreal. This time, the first thought that came to mind as I walked into the lobby and looked around at the goings-on was, "Who are all these people and what are we all doing here together?" This wider frame of reference was now predominated by social and cultural contexts. It was the dynamics of interaction among participants at the centre of my concerns, and the possible range of answers to the question "What do these dance events mean?" that now appeared to be as richly varied as the complex identities and ideologies of its participants. As the *Luna* ethnography concludes,

> In this contemporary dance world it is imperative that each choreographic project be created anew, and that these dance events are occasions for participants to encounter unique, newly imagined visions of the world through the dance. (Davida 2006: 464)

Much had been gained from the long years doing ethnography among my own kind, the Montreal *nouvelle danse* community. But there was also something lost—at last!—and that was the persistent hierarchy of values in which art-world dancing has long claimed the position of highest value. I offer many thanks to my muse Joann Kealiinohomoku for these insights, she who so long ago insisted that all dances are ethnic (1969/1970).

Notes

1 The question of what to call the genre that I had long referred to as postmodern dance has been fraught with difficulty, in the context of both the Montreal dance milieu and among the authors of this book. I settled on *contemporary* for the purposes of my study because it is the most common term among anglophone participants, and *nouvelle danse* for local francophones. In various conversations, Québécois intellectuals rejected the term *postmodern dance* as one that belonged to dance historians of the United States.

2 In her thesis, Kealiinohomoku developed the idea of the "<u>D</u>ancer" effectively distinguishing part-time from the vocational dancers. As she explained it, the <u>D</u>ancer is someone whose "title [of dancer] is not limited in time" and who always remains a dancer even when not dancing (1976: 23).

Bibliography

Amit, Vered (ed.). *Constructing the Field: Ethnographic Fieldwork in the Contemporary World*. London: Routledge, 2000.

Becker, Howard S. *Art Worlds*. Berkeley, Los Angeles, and London: University of California Press, 1982.

Bennett, Susan. *Theatre Audiences: A Theory of Production and Reception*. London and New York: Routledge, 1997.

Boas, Franziska (ed.). *The Function of Dance in Human Society*. Proceedings from the seminar. New York: Boas School, 1944 (later published in 1972 in New York by Dance Horizons).

Buckland, Theresa J. "All Dances Are Ethnic, but Some Are More Ethnic Than Others: Some Observations on Dance Studies and Anthropology." *Dance Research* 17, no. 1 (1999): 3–21.

Clifford, James. *The Predicament of Culture: Twentieth-Century Ethnography, Literature, and Art*. Cambridge, MA, and London: Harvard University Press, 1988.

———, and George Marcus (eds.). *Writing Culture: The Poetics and Politics of Ethnography*. [Papers from an advanced seminar at the School of American Research in Santa Fe, New Mexico.] Berkeley, Los Angeles, and London: University of California Press, 1986.

Davida, Dena. *Illuminating Luna: An Ethnographic Study of Meaning in a Montréal "Nouvelle Danse" Event*. Unpublished doctoral dissertation, University of Quebec in Montreal, 2006.

Desmond, Jane. *Staging Tourism: Bodies on Display from Waikiki to Sea World*. Chicago: University of Chicago Press, 1999.

Fisher, Jennifer. *Nutcracker Nation: How an Old World Ballet Became a Christmas Tradition in the New World*. New Haven, CT, and London: Yale University Press, 2003.

Geertz, Clifford. *The Interpretation of Cultures: Selected Essays*. New York: Basic Books, 1973, 95.

Goffman, Erving. "The Theatrical Frame." *Frame Analysis*. New York: Harper and Row, 1974: 124–55.

Giurchescu, Anca. "Past and Present in Field Research: A Critical History of Personal Experience." In Theresa Buckland (ed.), *Dance in the Field: Theory, Methods and Issues in Dance Ethnography*. New York and London: Macmillan (1999): 41–54.

Jackson, Andrew (ed.). *Anthropology at Home. ASA Monographs, 25*. Selection of Papers from the Association of Social Anthropologists (ASA) 1985 Conference at the University of Keele, UK, 1987.

Kealiinohomoku, Joann Wheeler. "Le non-art de la danse: un essai." Trans. Annie Suquet. In Andreé Grau and Georgina Gore (eds.), *Anthropologie de la danse et construction d'une discipline*. Paris: Centre national de la danse, 2005: 159–66. Originally published as "The Non-Art of Dance: An Essay," in the *Journal for the Anthropological Study of Human Movement* 1, no. 2 (1980): 38–44.

———. "An Anthropologist Looks at Ballet as a Form of Ethnic Dance." *Impulse 20* (1969/1970): 24–33.

———. *Theory and Methods for an Anthropological Study of Dance*. Unpublished doctoral dissertation, Indiana University, 1976.

Koutsouba, Maria. "'Outsider' in an 'Inside' World, or Dance Ethnography at Home." In Theresa Buckland (ed.), *Dance in the Field: Theory, Methods and Issues in Dance Ethnography*. New York and London: Macmillan, 1999: 185–95.

Kurath, Gertrude Prokosch. "Dance in Modern Culture." In Joann Wheeler Kealiinohomoku (ed.), *Half a Century of Dance Research: Essays by Gertrude Prokosch Kurath*. Flagstaff, Arizona: Cross-Cultural Dance Resources, 1965: 383–406.

Lavendar, Larry. "Understanding Interpretation." *Dance Research Journal* 27, no. 2 (Fall 1995): 25–33.

Marcus, George E., and Michael J. Fischer. *Anthropology as Cultural Critique: An Experimental Moment in the Human Sciences*. Chicago and London: University of Chicago Press, 1985.

Marcus, George E., and Fred R. Myers. "The Traffic in Art and Culture: An Introduction." In George E. Marcus and Fred R. Myers (eds.), *The Traffic in Culture: Refiguring Art and Anthropology*. Berkeley, Los Angeles, and London: University of California Press, 1995: 1–51.

Messerschmidt, Donald A. (ed.). *Anthropologists at Home in North America: Methods and Issues in the Study of One's Own Society*. Cambridge, London, New York, Sydney: Cambridge University Press.

Nahachewsky, Andriy. "Searching for Branches, Searching for Roots: Fieldwork in My Grandfather's Village." In Theresa Buckland (ed.), *Dance in the Field: Theory, Methods and Issues in Dance Ethnography*. New York and London: Macmillan, 1999: 175–85.

Novack, Cynthia Jean. *Sharing the Dance: Contact Improvisation and American Culture*. Madison: University of Wisconsin Press, 1990.

Perreault, Michel. "La passion et le corps comme objets de la sociologie: la danse comme carrière (notes de recherche)." *Sociologie et sociétés* 20, no. 2 (1988): 177–86.

Ronström, Owe. "The Dance Event: A Terminological and Methodological Discussion of the Concept." In Lisbit Torp (ed.), *1988 International Council for Traditional Music Study Group on Ethnochoreology Symposium "The Dance Event: A Complex*

Cultural Phenomenon." Copenhagen: ICTM Study Group on Ethnochoreology, 1989: 21–29.

Royce, Anya Peterson. *The Anthropology of Dance.* Bloomington and London: Indiana University Press, 1997.

Snyder, Allegra Fuller. "Levels of Event Patterns: A Theoretical Model Applied to the Yaqui Easter Ceremonies." In Lisbet Torp (ed.), *1998 Symposium of the International Council for Traditional Music Study Group on Ethnochoreology "The Dance Event: A Complex Cultural Phenomenon."* Copenhagen: ICTM Study Group on Ethnochoreology, 1989: 1–20.

Wulff, Helena. *Ballet across Borders: Career and Culture in the World of Dancers.* Oxford and New York: Berg, 1998.

Interviews, Focus Groups, and Correspondence with Participants

Barry, Anne. Interview with researcher in Montreal, QC, March 4, 2002.

Kealiinohomoku, Joann. Interview with researcher in Albuquerque, NM, June 12, 1999.

Laurin, Ginette. Second interview with researcher in Montreal, QC, March 7, 2002.

Longueux, Ginette. Audience focus group in Chicoutimi, QC, November 3, 2001.

Rodrigue, Marie-Claude. Interview with researcher in Montreal, QC, August 24, 2001.

Rodrigue, Marie-Claude. In an email correspondence to researcher from Prague, November 10, 2003.

CHAPTER THREE

Interview Strategies for Concert Dance World Settings

JENNIFER FISHER

If I imagined myself to be an intrepid ethnographer striking out for unknown territory, like a slightly more stylish version of Margaret Mead, it was despite the fact that I was entering a rural Virginia high school auditorium where the local inhabitants put on *The Nutcracker* every year. It was hardly the stuff of perilous journeys. After all, I had just stopped at a mall for directions and noticed that it was "high cappuccino machine per capita" country, with plenty of amenities and free parking. But part of my image of myself as a postmodern dance ethnographer seemed to involve ironic nostalgia for iconic explorers. "The natives were friendly and their rituals fascinating," I told friends and colleagues later, knowing that it sounded like a joke about the relative comfort of trekking in the wilds of suburban ballet studios, but also that it was an accurate description of my fieldwork experiences. After all, I was encountering people who *were* native to a particular tradition, even though it wasn't always called a ritual by the tribes that put the ballet on. I knew that *The Nutcracker* wasn't just an aesthetic event, but like any tradition, reflected both communal and individual beliefs, as well as culturally revealing attitudes. And, of course, "fieldwork at home" was not exactly new, although ballet ethnography is still relatively rare.[1]

These are some of the thoughts I had in 1996, as I began my study of *The Nutcracker*, the Russian ballet that had evolved into a Christmas tradition in North America. My methods included those of traditional participant observation, but because I was on "home turf," investigating a familiar phenomenon in an unfamiliar way, I developed a particular approach to

Figure 1   The ethnographer backstage with *Nutcracker* artefacts at the Loudoun Ballet Company of Virginia, 1997. Photographer: Sheila Hoffmann Robertson.

interviewing, the topic I will focus on here. I was both an "insider" and an "outsider" to the world of the annual *Nutcracker*, in that I had once danced in the ballet, and I shared the ethnic, economic, and cultural background of most *Nutcracker* participants,[2] but I was also a "foreigner" in that I had drifted away from the dance world as an adult, and then returned as an academic, armed with the tools of observing and recording what I saw. Indian-born anthropologist Jayati Lal, who wrote about her return from the United States to India to do her fieldwork, recognized this duality when she said that she felt like "a 'native' returning to a foreign country," because she did fieldwork in places she hadn't been before (Lal 1996: 191–92).

I also have something in common with the "halfie" or "hyphenated" ethnographers discussed by anthropologists Kamala Visweswaran and Lila

Abu-Lughod, although I am not positioned between two ethnic groups as they are (Visweswaran 1994: 131). What I have in common with hyphenated ethnographers, as well as researchers working in their "own" cultural groups (such as Lal, Kondo, and Limón), is the embodied experience of existing in two different worlds. For me, the two worlds were a ballet dancer's realm and that of the academic observer and analyst. I considered it an advantage to have this double or multiple positioning (ex-dancer, dance scholar advocate, "impartial" critic and ethnographer), because acknowledging different vantage points led me to understand that fieldwork is not "a collection of data by a dehumanized machine" (Okley 1992: 3). These different vantage points surely interacted with each other, and if the way I reacted to ballet and *The Nutcracker* arose from a complex of experiences and attitudes that alternately felt entrenched or shifting, I reasoned that the same thing could be true for my respondents.

Fortunately, the days of believing that only outsiders were clear-headed enough to write ethnographies were over before I entered the field. As James Clifford emphasizes, ethnographers who are closely related to the cultures they investigate are uniquely positioned to do their work, since "it probably requires cultural insiders to recognize adequately the subtle ruses of individuality, where outsiders see only typical behavior" (Clifford 1978: 53). In the case of *The Nutcracker*, it was even more complicated than that. Many dance insiders often saw the ballet as "typical" or, more to the point, as "stereotypical," even though they might realize that many individual approaches are involved. In the professional dance world, *The Nutcracker* has often been considered a lightweight phenomenon, suspect because it is widely embraced by non-specialists, families, and children. In the tradition of Western art after the age of modernism, regular repetition of an aesthetic product is often characterized as a static iteration that becomes stale. But an insider to dance studies could easily see that the annual *Nutcracker* phenomenon is a complex, always changing, powerful ritual of some sort.

The difference in viewpoints—the dance-studies ethnographer versus dance-world insiders—would make my fieldwork interview questions perplexing to some respondents. Dancers, producers, and volunteers around *The Nutcracker* were used to being asked about the particulars of their versions in terms of aesthetic values and production details—who staged it, how many snowflakes, who was dancing the Sugar Plum Fairy, and how much snow fell. But they were less used to being asked questions like, "Does it matter that it's ballet?" and "Is there a message in *The Nutcracker*?" They were completely unfamiliar with the idea of a dance-studies ethnographer spending weeks "hanging around" their rehearsals and performances. So, although the annual *Nutcracker* was a well-known phenomenon—indeed, perhaps the best known ballet in the world, given its multitude of versions in cities and towns of North America, and increasingly elsewhere—my role in exploring it puzzled many participants in *Nutcracker* world. What was there to say? It was just *Nutcracker*. But I knew that people close to the ballet often felt a deep attachment to it, even if they didn't have the language to explain it. I sensed that new methods were needed to discover what their relationship with the ballet was and to give them a voice in my work. I suspected there was a lot to discover about the rhetorical terrain surrounding *The Nutcracker* that went beyond the generalities of it being just "the thing you did" at Christmastime, or the thing that made money because tickets sold well. How to encourage this kind of exploration among my respondents? Having also been versed in improvisational performance techniques and journalism, I thought it was useful to bring strategies I had used in these fields to bear on my current research.

SETTING THE SCENE

The annual *Nutcracker* phenomenon, which developed in North America in the second half of the twentieth century, had materially changed the ballet since its 1892 premiere during the golden age of imperial Russian ballet. That original production underwent many changes in Russia, and then in the Soviet states during the Cold War era, but it was never considered a major success in its homeland, despite respect for the Tchaikovsky score. In North America, however, a yearly *Nutcracker* tradition developed as a result of its appeal as a Christmas story and its ability to suit any number of amateur and professional companies and their disparate audiences. I explored the ballet in terms of its similarity to a ritual, and the way it tended to reflect sociocultural values and beliefs in each community where it was performed, highlighting issues of gender, race, and class along the way.[3] I began with historical research about the original Russian *Nutcracker* and its travels to Europe, the United States, and Canada, then documented the evolution of the ballet as a yearly tradition in North America, deciding on two primary field sites to serve as case histories. Representing many regional ballet productions that rely on a community of amateur dancers and volunteers was the Loudoun Ballet, a semi-professional company with a well-structured ballet school attached to it and a tightly knit *Nutcracker* family in Leesburg, Virginia. Representing the elite ballet tradition, the National Ballet of Canada in Toronto had many aspects in common with other professional versions.

Because of my theoretical emphasis on rhetorical hermeneutics— the way people argue for meanings—my main information-gathering technique in the field was participant observation, with an emphasis on interviewing.[4] This took place in both casual and formal settings and included all kinds of "*Nutcracker* participants," meaning anyone connected to the event, whether onstage, backstage, or in the audience. Although I frequently found myself using the word "interview," I also tried to avoid it, because of its inevitable link in the popular imagination to celebrity interviews or job interviews. I requested "talks" and "conversations," but the procedure often took on the character of an interview anyway, and was often perceived as such. I noticed that the mention of "being interviewed" for non-dancers (parents, backstage volunteers, audience members) often made them nervous, while many seasoned dancers and ballet officials seemed to have routine answers for any questions that sounded familiar to them. Even amateur dancers are used to being asked what their audition process was like, or what it feels like to dance a certain role in *The Nutcracker*. But when I got to less typical questions, things were stickier for both groups. What did the Sugar Plum Fairy's dancing tell you about her? What did they think of the fact that many people were bored by the annual repetition of *The Nutcracker*? Respondents would sometimes glance at the tape recorder and wonder what I meant, and if they dared spoil the happy holiday Christmas mood with a negative comment. They fell silent or returned to generalities. An even more challenging question was, "Why aren't there more people of colour in the ballet?" That was a topic rarely discussed in ballet communities, which, even in an increasingly integrated mainstream society, often are comprised of decidedly pale-faced people.

In the following sections, I describe the two primary interview strategies that worked well when asking such questions in my population of mainly urban, fairly well-educated North American respondents who were participants in the *Nutcracker* world.

CHOREOGRAPHING AND IMPROVISING THE INTERVIEW[5]

My fieldwork in Leesburg, Virginia, with the regional Loudoun Ballet, offered me the most intimate opportunity to follow rehearsals and wander backstage and in the audiences of *Nutcracker* performances. I set up more formal interviews in my Toronto location, because of the more regulated rehearsal times and spaces of a unionized professional company; but in both locations, I had conversations that took place on the spot, finding a place to sit down, often chatting while other things went on backstage. Whether the conversation was formally scheduled or not, I became aware of my "performance" as interviewer, as well as the ways I could "choreograph" or "improvise" during the process to make it seem less intimidating.

Although many residents of the *Nutcracker* world expect to be observed and interviewed, they were surprised that I didn't leave after a few hours, as a reporter or critic would. I started explaining my presence by saying that I was writing a book, when the word *dissertation* either drew a blank stare or made people feel even more intimidated. Usually, I tried to make my interview request sound more like an invitation to tea, saying, "I'd just like to know about your experiences" or "I like to talk to all kinds of people and find out what they think." These approaches were sometimes made by phone but more often they occurred as I wandered around ballet classes, theatre lobbies, rehearsals, or backstage areas. I collected information from people on the periphery of the theatre occasionally, but my emphasis was on insiders to each *Nutcracker* community—that is, people who were involved in performance, production, and viewing to a significant extent.

I did not have a strict interview schedule (questions that most often recurred are listed in an appendix at the end of this chapter). My intention was to guide an interview with my questions and then let the conversation proceed in a respondent-driven fashion. I would ask a "grand tour," somewhat value-free question, such as, "What is your history with *The Nutcracker*?" or "Why do you participate?" or "Why do you come every year?" and then follow their "leads" into whatever areas seemed most rich for them. However, I found that since some of my questions involved thinking about things in ways they had not done before ("Do you relate *The Nutcracker* to the rest of your life?"), it helped if I revealed some of my own thoughts about the ballet and those of others. As I proceeded, my interview questions became increasingly "intertextual"—that is, I brought up ideas that had arisen in conversations with other *Nutcracker* participants, such as, "Some people say the Leesburg production is like a big family. Does it seem like this to you?" Or I might say, "I often want to cry at certain points in the ballet. Has that ever happened to you?" This kind of sharing generally seemed to work well, in that my respondents "got the idea" (saw the range of opinions that could arise), and talk flowed more freely than before, whether or not they agreed with me. A group of researchers who investigated similar topics with teenage ballet students have called this aspect of sharing during an interview "engaging in interested conversation ... in the spirit of participant hermeneutics" (Stinson et al. 1990: 16). Oral historian Kristina Minister calls it "mutual self-disclosure" (Minister: 36); other anthropologists have referred to their way of "sharing" as a reassuring, demystifying part of their interview process (Matsumoto 1996: 162–65; Zavella 1996: 146).

The idea of sharing conversation, yet shaping an interview to foreground themes of my study, eventually made me think of the interview as being "choreographed and improvised." It involved everything from the physical arrangement of the interview, to aspects of my own "performance" of the interviewer. The giving and taking of weight in contact improvisation comes to mind when I think of adjusting my conversational style (pace, timing, and humour) to that of my respondent. I might suggest connections and images from my own and others' experiences with ballet, pull back when I see a confused response, provide encouraging body language and noises, leave long enough silences for respondents to think, but not so long a pause that they become uncomfortable. In general, I tried to sense the pace at which I could proceed and the tone that made the respondent most relaxed and reassured. I'm always aware of trying to maintain a "listening" focus, not only showing interest in my eyes, but repeating phrases such as, "That's interesting" and "I see, yes." Minister has described women interviewers as "midwives for women's words," employing methods drawn from their own "sociocommunication subculture" (Minister 1991: 39).

I see my own development as an interviewer less as a function of having learned "women's ways" of communicating (although this could be part of it) and more a result of having been a dancer and an actor, then a journalist—literally a performer before entering the field of performance studies.[6] The ability to listen, to embody or "act out" interest, calibrate emotional levels, and improvise are all skills learned for the stage. You explore energy levels, pacing, projection, and body language while training for performance, and the interview or casual conversation may be as much a performance as a piece of theatre.[7] While I was interviewing actors and other people in power as a journalist, the skill of appearing to be the respondent's "biggest fan" came in very handy. It's not that researchers without theatrical backgrounds would fail at such a "performance," but actors are trained to be especially aware of how to make curiosity and interest apparent, even if fatigue or a momentary lapse of interest sometimes threatens. With anyone not used to being interviewed, I found it seemed to relax them if I "played with" the seriousness of being an interviewer. One Leesburg volunteer kept shying away from me, ducking comically into an alcove when I walked by with my tape recorder. My first instinct was not to press; then I realized that this might be a self-conscious pantomime on the respondent's part. When one day I said with mock sternness, "You can't escape me now, it's time for your official interview," it was readily agreed to.

In the past, I have considered the advantages and disadvantages of using a tape recorder. It can add an element of formality and possibly of fear for the respondent, sometimes resulting in an artificially formal or stilted quality to conversation. But instead of sacrificing the opportunity for a clear record of what was said, I tried to find ways to make the tape recorder less intimidating. I would place it casually by a chair or on a coffee table not directly in the respondent's line of vision; or, conversely, I would talk *about* the tape recorder, saying, "Oh, I just like to make sure I hear everything," as if the machine were just a more accurate ear than my own. I did not tape every conversation, but perhaps most. For one thing, it allows a closer analysis of the way the interview functions as a "communicative event," a concept anthropologist/sociolinguist Charles Briggs emphasizes (Briggs 1982: 1). Adding dimensions to my own notion of the interview as a performative act, Briggs emphasizes the interviewer's role in creating a certain kind of ethnographic truth. He cautions against accepting interview results as "what is out there," instead of something that has been produced as a joint effort by interviewer and respondent (Briggs 1982: 6).

Although I don't engage in Briggs's detailed sociolinguistic analysis of interview transcripts, I find it instructive to keep in mind my own role as "co-participant in the construction of a discourse" (Briggs 1982: 25). What this means to me generally is that I try to pull back from my "engaged conversation" at times and look for ways of getting new viewpoints. For me, the next step in pulling back from the interview was to consider another method of interviewing in which my presence was at least physically removed; this led me to develop what I first called "introspective interviewing," a method that puts the interview respondent and the tape recorder alone in a room, away from the immediate physical presence of the researcher.

THE TAKE-HOME INTERVIEW

The idea for the take-home interview came from a concept called "introspective ethnography," described by anthropologist John L. Caughey as an aspect of cognitive anthropology that can "deepen our understanding of how culture influences our own forms of consciousness" (Caughey 1982: 116). He set out to explore the ways people think and what they can reveal about attitudes and feelings that might otherwise remain hidden, asking informants to catch themselves "mid-reverie" and then reflect and write down their thoughts. His informants (he often included himself) reported that for a large portion of their days, a state occurred that could be called "stream of consciousness," "daydreaming," or "reverie." This state includes a complex and often fragmented flow of sense memories, anticipations, fantasy, and talking to oneself (127). Countering the objection that introspection is too subjective and possibly irrelevant to ethnographers (among anthropologists, Geertz has called too much of it "diary disease"), Caughey pointed out that in other cultures, ethnographers have regularly asked their informants to be introspective—to reflect upon and articulate various features of their existence in a particular culture.

One college-campus experiment by Caughey centred on greeting behaviours and revealed that decisions about whether and how to say "hello" were made almost subconsciously, depending on current circumstances, appearances, moods, and the perceived status of an acquaintanceship. Participants were asked to recall and describe each encounter. As an early experiment with introspective ethnography, it promised a way of making more explicit the rules and procedures of one's own culture, which are often overlooked as "natural." The promise of Caughey's method to me was that it focused on a way of making available previously inchoate thoughts and feelings, and I wanted to find out about the connections between ballet, *The Nutcracker*, and the attitudes and beliefs of my respondents. Even on *Nutcracker* turf, where people think the ballet is crucial, they aren't used to articulating their thoughts about that in any detail. I sometimes asked a question that stumped my respondent, such as, "Does *The Nutcracker* have anything to do with religion? Or something spiritual?" Silence ensued. Then, that person would see me the next day and start with, "You know, I've been thinking about what you asked and it *is* sort of spiritual ..." Then, they found the words. In response, I started to develop what I now call the take-home interview, sending respondents home with a tape recorder and a set of "guiding questions" they could consider and answer at their own pace, away from the interviewer who waits for an answer in conversation.

My version of this methodology developed from an audiocassette correspondence I had with a friend and colleague over a long period of time when we lived across the continent from each other.[8] Although we rarely saw each other for a many years—back in an age before email and cheap long-distance phone rates made keeping in touch easier—the taped letters made me feel as if I knew a lot about her life, almost as if I had been there at times. I recently listened to one of these tapes from the 1980s and heard my friend reflecting on why that method of communicating felt deeper and more intimate than many others. She had just finished talking through an emotionally charged subject, seeming to discover new aspects of it and how she really felt as she went along. Maybe feeling she was spilling too much, she said at one point, "There's something about the tape recorder, this grey box that you are left alone with, that encourages you to be personal, to ruminate in a way that probes what you're thinking, more than in conversation." I also found that making taped letters was a way of "thinking through" a subject, making discoveries, and articulating them in ways I hadn't thought of before.

Before arriving for *Nutcracker* fieldwork in Leesburg in 1995, I had exchanged taped letters with Sheila Hoffmann-Robertson, artistic director of the Loudoun Ballet Company and the Loudoun School of Ballet. Friends since 1988, we had exchanged tapes a few times before my work on this project began, and afterward her communications about the ballet became more detailed and intense. She regularly sent ninety-minute audiotapes that chronicled *Nutcracker* events and also contained stories and reflections about her own dance background, as well as ballet in general. These became an invaluable resource. Already an articulate and astute observer, she was sparked by the challenge of examining and reporting about *Nutcracker* events in Leesburg. Alone with a tape recorder, at her own pace in her own time, she found more and more levels of reflection. It *was* a ritual, she would say, that's why it seemed so monumental every year, and why it felt like a season she couldn't escape. Possible explanations occurred to her about why there were so many trials and tribulations at *Nutcracker* time—for instance, people thought they *owned* it, she decided, and they chafed at their lack of control when she, as artistic director, made casting decisions or changes in the familiar production. For parents, it often wasn't just about a ballet role, it was about their child's successful survival in the world—even their child's perceived worth. Having such a clear "ladder of success" in terms of coveted roles dancers won from year to year, *The Nutcracker* became the site of their greatest triumphs and most heartbreaking defeats. Every artistic director has war stories of how skirmishes break out about who dances Clara, who gets the red bonbon costume, and why little Eloise isn't quite ready for her snowflake tutu yet.

For Hoffmann-Robertson, the audiotapes became a way of sharing the details and stressors of *Nutcracker* time; for me, they became a way of following her particular role and point of view closely through both public and private rituals of the season. She started to report, for instance, the most frequent ways the ballet's importance came up, noticing a rhetorical preference for utopian phrases like "a gift to the community," "one big happy family," and "the story shows that dreams really come true." The habit of talking into her tape recorder as she went through a day brought elements of the experience to light in ways she might have forgotten to mention in more formal conversations. It was she who coined the word *nutmare* one day, when her language articulation fell victim to fatigue after a night of dreaming about what could go wrong with her production.

In my two *Nutcracker* locations, I asked many respondents to take home the tape recorder and my guiding questions, usually after deciding from a first meeting that they might be good candidates. This decision was an intuitive one, based on conversational flow and their willingness to undertake the project. I knew it would attract only a certain kind of person, someone who enjoyed reflecting and articulating ideas while alone—or at least was willing to try—and someone who had the time and place to make a tape (parents often had a privacy problem). I told various groups of ballet students in Leesburg about the "tape project," and asked for volunteers; in Toronto, Laurel Toto, the National Ballet School teacher who directed the students in *The Nutcracker* picked out some of her students for the project, got some volunteers, and set up times for them to use the school's tape recorder.[9] Also in Toronto, I talked to adult amateur ballet students after their class at the National Ballet School and got a few volunteers, discovering at least one of the respondents I ended up identifying as a balletomane.

Over the two-year period of my major research, I handed out dozens of the lists of my guiding questions, which participants could address or use as a start and detour wherever they wished. I often loaned small tape recorders and provided blank, labelled audiocassettes as encouragement. These tapes and/or the list of questions were taken home by over one hundred people, with the understanding that respondents would make a tape only if it turned out to be something they wanted to do. Although mine was not a quantitative study, I noted that my rate of return was about 20 percent. The tapes I got back varied in length, from about ten to twenty minutes (on average) to ninety-minutes (on a few occasions). Compared to face-to-face interviews, I found that many of my questions about *The Nutcracker* and ballet in general were given longer and more detailed answers on the tapes.

In many of the taped monologues, respondents rambled on in reflective tones of voice, warming to particular topics. Although these answers cannot be considered a transparent route to more "real" responses than I heard in face-to-face interviews, it sounded as if the method created a private space in which they felt they had a bit more time and the luxury of thinking things through. This worked particularly well for questions that had seemed to startle or challenge when I asked them in person. The idea of connecting *The Nutcracker* to a spiritual or religious feeling was new to many people, for instance, but on the tapes, they often started to recognize the fervour they brought to ballet in general, that there was something in their enthusiasm and loyalty that resembled spiritual or religious commitment. Some were able to recreate the moments that touched them most deeply and say why—the beauty of children achieving something, a sparking of a memory of their own youth or idealism. Questions that led to gender distinctions and perceptions also received thoughtful reflection, as someone started to talk about a relationship to Clara or the Sugar Plum Fairy that they might have thought sounded silly at first. "She's a fairy, but she's in charge," one respondent said, and another said, "You know, I never even thought of what her partner is called—he just doesn't seem important."

Perhaps the most sensitive of my questions was the one about why more people of colour weren't involved in the ballet world. (I often used the term "people of colour" advisedly, because it's the darkness of skin tone that becomes controversial in the classical ballet world.) In conversation, I had tried to use phrasing and a tone that somehow rendered the question less incendiary, asking in a pensive way, "There don't seem to be a lot of people of colour onstage in ballet, and I'm always wondering why—is that something you've ever thought about?" But still, I could see a wall go up, as if the respondents—who were nearly all white—worried about being accused of racism. I sometimes got defensive answers, offered quickly: "But there *are* African Americans in ballet—there's the Dance Theatre of Harlem, and there are lots of Asians" or "I don't think there's any prejudice in the ballet world, if that's what you mean." Although race was not a major aspect of my study, I thought *The Nutcracker* was a good place to gather some attitudes and opinions about the topic, especially given the fact that each *Nutcracker* community saw itself as a reflection of many values participants agreed upon, such as the warmth of family, communal celebration, and the importance of children who dream and achieve.

I've noticed that at *Nutcracker* time, in fact, the ballet world has tended to embrace more diversity over the years. It was one of the first places where so-called "colour-blind casting" occurred in classical ballet, with families that didn't all look alike in the first act, for instance. But few would deny that professional ballet companies around the world are most often comprised of dancers with light skin colour.[10] In general, my respondents addressed this fairly obvious fact better in their taped monologues than in face-to-face interviews. After having time to think, and perhaps feeling less pressured while speaking into a tape recorder alone, they offered more thoughts than had occurred to them in conversation—that some cultures perhaps don't privilege dancing that reflects European roots, or that some people haven't been exposed to ballet because it's perceived by them to be foreign, elite, or exclusionary. By themselves, some respondents felt safer, perhaps, in admitting that ballet's "white world" *was* a quandary, that perhaps prejudice *did* exist. To me, the time and space given to respondents in this case took away some of the question's power to intimidate them. They seemed to feel free, for instance, to conclude that they simply didn't know why there weren't more people of colour in ballet and wasn't it a shame.

It was very productive to explore this take-home interview methodology. The richness of the material on the tapes continually impressed me. I have tried the experiment only once more and found another instance when the method was unlikely to work well. While following a boys' ballet class during a summer intensive, I asked several of them to try the take-home interview. My questions at that time were meant to get at the reported isolation of boys in ballet and the prejudices and stereotypes they might have encountered. But the preliminary involvement I had with the class (watching it for only a few weeks), combined with their ages (from 8 to 12), perhaps led to the project's relative failure. Some of the *Nutcracker* participants who had made tapes for me a few years before were the same age, but they were highly motivated dancers who knew a lot about that specific ballet—and they had also had the chance to get to know me for longer. I received some wonderfully articulate and insightful tapes back then from *Nutcracker* dancers who were about 10 or 12, either the few hand-picked students from a pre-professional conservatory, or high achievers in the Leesburg cast. But the boys in the summer intensive, although somewhat motivated, were much less inculcated in the ballet world and had met me just a few times. They seemed to finish the project only under parental duress, even though my directive to parents was *never* to insist. What did their friends think about them taking ballet? I got answers like, "Oh, they think it's okay, I guess"—I could almost hear the screen door slamming behind them once they got my questions answered.

The rapport I had with my *Nutcracker* respondents at a fairly cheerful time of year, as well as their affection and experience with a ballet they thought of as "their own," probably increased the effectiveness of the take-home-interview methodology. Their voices sounded different on the tapes—softer, slower, or more authoritative or excited—and I often got the privileged feeling I had had with friends who made taped letters, that someone was allowing you to hear them reveal more deeply the way they think and reflect. Of course, the presence of the ethnographer is perhaps always there, even in the take-home situation. One can't really forget that "ethnographic texts are mainly orchestrated through the anthropologist's towering voice" (Shokeid 1988: 42), and that "quotations are always staged by the quoter" (Clifford 1983: 139). But perhaps the take-home interview can contribute to what has been called "polyphonic ethnography," which "seeks to share ethnographic authority with the voices of the informants" (Sanjek 1990: 406; Clifford 1986). For me, it goes a long way to allowing respondents to become collaborators, allowing them at least some measure of control over the way their voices are recorded.

While my "choreographing and improvising" approach can easily be applied to any interview situation, I think of the take-home interview as particularly suited to my locations in the world of concert dance—in theatres, urban areas, dance studios, and anywhere people might have preconceptions about what the interview should be. In the ballet world, both cognoscenti and fans often indicated to me that they were choosing words carefully in our interviews, wanting to say something "important" about a revered classical form of dance. The topic of ballet, or any form of "art dance" can be intimidating, and perhaps was especially so in my situation, given the fact that I was so often identified as an "expert" of sorts, as a PhD student, as well as a dance critic.[11] Even trained dancers sometimes hedge when faced with questions about dance they perceive as challenging. As noted by one ex-dancer who did research among ballet dancers,

> It is not unusual for a performer to hesitate when asked how he feels about an event. Some seem to need to sort through the range of emotions tied to that situation and separate out their own feelings from those they expect themselves to experience based on the attitude of their teacher, ballet master or other significant contributor to their well-being. (Earl 1988: 57)

Although many of my respondents were less closely allied with ballet's intimidating training system, a certain amount of insecurity often hampered their openness to interviews. They worried about whether they were "worthy" of being interviewed, or whether they had anything "important" to say about ballet. Speaking into a tape recorder alone, they had a bit more time and agency when it came to contributing to the research process. They had time to reflect and to deepen that level of reflection, to work on what they wanted to say, adding thoughts as they occurred, even going back to add more thoughts or to clarify or rephrase.

This take-home interview method is akin to the process of writing and rewriting, which is, after all, what the ethnographer gets to do after the information-gathering event. As the author of my *Nutcracker* study, I had the ability to consider over time, in private, the task of representing experience, then to make decisions and produce a written document. The take-home interview provides the interviewee with just a bit more of a role in the process. If ethnography as it is rooted in cultural anthropology is to survive its colonialist roots, more methods that move toward collaboration need to emerge. Who better to develop them than scholars who know that the elite form of ballet evolved from folk dance; and who better to call on for collaboration than people who do and watch ballet, because they are the folk who are involved now? Everyone is both "at home" and "in performance" for much of the time; in its own way, the take-home interview tries to account for that.

APPENDIX

Guiding questions used by respondents to make audiotape monologues.

[The following explanation of my project and these "guiding questions" were sent home with respondents who agreed to make "introspective tapes" for me regarding their involvement with ballet and The Nutcracker. *The handout had my name, address, and local and permanent phone numbers on it; it also assured respondents' privacy. My study had approval from the human subjects research review board at my university. Over my research period, a few questions were refined, tailored to location, added, or eliminated; this is a representative selection of questions. Many of these questions also duplicate questions asked in face-to-face interviews.]*

Handout

I'm doing research on *The Nutcracker* and on people's reactions to ballet in general—where they fit into different peoples' lives and how you think about and interpret ballet and *The Nutcracker* in particular. This is a project where I ask people to record a sort of diary of thoughts and reactions to ballet on audiocassette tape. You can record as little or as much as you want. You can turn the tape recorder off and on when you want to think or to say something.

These questions are some of the things you can talk about on the tape, but you're free to go in any direction you want. Tell me what you find interesting or important about *The Nutcracker* and ballet in general. There are no wrong answers or wrong conversation—I'm interested in hearing about your experience, thoughts, and opinions.

If you're answering one of these written questions, you might want to read the question out loud on the tape, so I'll know what you're answering.

Beginning the tape: Test the tape recorder first to make sure you can hear yourself clearly. It helps to talk directly into the microphone. Make sure your name is written on the tape. Thank you so much for your participation.

- Tell me about your *Nutcracker* experience, when and what you've seen, if you've been in it, what role, your reactions.
- What's the best role in *The Nutcracker*?
- Why do you think so many people like to see *The Nutcracker*?
- What would you miss if you didn't see *The Nutcracker* or weren't in it? Anything?
- Does it matter that it's ballet?
- If you had to tell someone who had never seen *The Nutcracker* why they should go see it, what would you say?

- Describe the Sugar Plum Fairy. What can you tell about her from her dancing? What about her partner?
- Describe Clara (or Marie). What kind of character is she?
- Is there any message in *The Nutcracker*? What do you get from watching it?
- Is *The Nutcracker* an important event? Why?
- If you know the National Ballet's new *Nutcracker* (or the Loudoun Ballet's *Nutcracker*), how is it different from the old one? Or from other productions? Talk about what the differences mean to you.
- If you're in the National Ballet (or the Loudoun Ballet), is it like a big family in any way?

Questions about Ballet in General

- What kind of people do ballet? What kind of people watch it?
- What's the best part of the ballet? The worst?
- Talk about pointe shoes. Do you like or dislike them? Why?
- If you like to do ballet, do some of your favourite movements right now, then talk about what you're thinking or feeling as you do them, why you like to do them. Are there some you don't like?
- Think about the kind of person you are when you're doing ballet, then describe yourself—what are you like while dancing?
- Is there anything about watching or dancing ballet that makes you feel emotional? What? Talk about these emotions?
- Do you think of ballet in terms of being feminine or masculine? Why?
- Do you think that your parents or friends think of ballet the same way you do? If not—what's the difference?
- Are you interested in choreographing?
- Is there a difference between boys and girls—or men and women—in ballet? What is/are the difference(s)?
- Imagine yourself watching your favourite dance or dancer. Talk about why you like watching them.
- What kinds of roles do women dance in ballet?
- Have you ever thought about why ballerinas don't play lawyers or housewives or mothers in ballets?
- Do you think ballet has anything in common with religion? (Is there anything sacred, for instance?)
- There aren't a lot of people of darker skin colours in ballet (such as African Americans). Have you ever noticed this and thought about why it is? [The example of African Americans was removed for Canadian respondents; eventually, the phrase "people of colour" was used most often.]

- Suppose someone in your life thought you shouldn't do ballet, or watch it. How would you convince them that you should? What would you say?
- Describe the movements of the man and woman in a pas de deux. What's your impression of each of them?
- How do other people see ballet dancers? Your friends, relatives or on TV? Is it realistic?

Notes

1 The only other book-length study of ballet using ethnographic methods that I know of is *Ballet Across Borders: Career and Culture in the World of Dancers*, by Helena Wulff (Berg Publishers, 1998). Wulff mentions an essay that was also most influential for me (alongside Kealiinohomoku 1970): "Ballet, Gender and Cultural Power," by Cynthia Jean Cohen Bull (formerly Novack), in Helen Thomas (ed.), *Dance, Gender and Culture* (London: Macmillan, 1993), 34–48.

2 I share the general ethnic heritage of ballet, meaning its European roots and its linguistic, genetic, and cultural ties (see Kealiinohomoku 1970). My respondents were largely, although not exclusively, white, middle- to upper-class North Americans of European descent, reflecting the cultural origins of ballet itself. Although the constituency of ballet dancers, as well as audiences, has expanded in immigrant-rich North America and elsewhere (with Asian dancers and African American *Nutcracker* versions having a particularly strong presence in *Nutcracker* land), few would disagree that the ballet world has historically tended to be populated by many white Euro-Americans of some means.

3 More *Nutcracker* history and evolution, as well as explanations of theoretical approaches and other aspects of my research, in abbreviated form here, can be found in Fisher (1998 and 2003). My original *Nutcracker* research took place from 1995 to 1998, and continued in the years preceding the completion of my book *Nutcracker Nation* (2003), which was based on my dissertation.

4 Steven Mailloux defines rhetorical hermeneutics as a focus on "how specific interpretive practices function within sociopolitical contexts of persuasion" (Mailloux 1990: 52). My theoretical approach, which I identify as "participant-oriented," combines rhetorical hermeneutics with other approaches drawn from German reception theory, reader-response criticism, feminist ethnography, and performance studies. For elaboration, see chapter 2 of Fisher (1998).

5 An earlier version of some of this material appeared under the title, "Choreographing and Improvising the Interview" in the *Proceedings of the Society of Dance History Scholars 1994 Conference, Provo, Utah: Retooling the Discipline, Research and Teaching Strategies for the 21st Century* (1994), 341–46.

6 Here, I pay homage to my first, unofficial, doctoral work, when I audited classes for a brief but influential time in the New York University Performance Studies Department in 1992. By the time I officially entered the PhD program in dance history and theory at the University of California, Riverside (UCR), my methodological choices and theoretical directions had already been most influenced and adopted from Performance Studies, as well as the master's in dance program of York University, Toronto, where history and ethnography were a major focus. During the time I attended UCR, it called what it did "critical theory" and

"cultural studies," pointedly *not* "performance studies." Today, the term *dance studies* has become common and encompasses these various labels. Within the "variants" of dance studies Susan Manning has suggested exist (Spring 2006 edition of the *Society of Dance History Scholars Newsletter*), my work falls into the one that "emphasizes the blurring of the previously distinct subfields of dance history and dance ethnography."

7 See, for instance, Erving Goffman's *The Presentation of Self in Everyday Life* (1959).

8 This was dancer/choreographer Lenna DeMarco, who, during our correspondence in the late 1970s to early '80s, started teaching in the dance department of Redlands University, moved to Chapman University, and then to the University of California, Irvine. She later relocated to Arizona, where she was a professor at Glendale Community College. My thanks to her for suggesting the cassette letter format, and for allowing me to quote her in this article.

9 I thank Laurel Toto and Mavis Staines at the National Ballet School of Canada for their co-operation and help during my Toronto research period.

10 The prevalence of "colour-blind" casting in the *Nutcracker* world, as opposed to ballet in general, was seen in the 1996 BBC documentary *The House*, about London's Royal Opera House. In a casting session, then-artistic director Anthony Dowell chastised a ballet mistress for wondering if an Asian Clara might seem odd when her parents were non-Asian dancers. "That kind of thing" wasn't a concern these days, Dowell said. His attitude toward this shift wasn't clear, but he was definitive in stating that things had changed since the days when skin tone and "look" were more uniform in the ballet world. However, a quick look at major ballet companies in North America confirms the fact that ballet is still dominated by white-looking dancers.

11 At the time of my *Nutcracker* research in the 1990s, I was a regular contributor of dance writing to the *Los Angeles Times*. The number of times people said to me, "Well, I don't know, you're the expert" convinced me that this was an aspect of my subject-positioning that I constantly needed to counter. I never knew which of my respondents recognized the difference between my part-time role as a dance critic and my full-time commitment to being a dance ethnographer while I was researching.

Bibliography

Abu-Lughod, Lila. *Writing Women's Worlds: Bedouin Stories*. Berkeley: University of California Press, 1993.

Briggs, Charles L. *Learning How to Ask: A Sociolinguistic Appraisal of the Role of the Interview in Social Science Research*. Cambridge: Cambridge University Press, 1986.

Bull, Cynthia Jean Cohen. "Ballet, Gender and Cultural Power." In Helen Thomas (ed.), *Dance, Gender and Culture*. London: Macmillan, 1993: 34–48.

Caughey, John L. "Ethnography, Introspection, and Reflexive Culture Studies." In J. Saltzman (ed.), *Prospects: the Annual of American Cultural Studies*. New York: Bert Franklin 1982: 115–39.

Clifford, James. "Hanging Up Looking Glasses at Odd Corners." In Daniel Aaron (ed.), *Studies in Biography*. Cambridge, MA, and London: Harvard University Press, 1978: 41–65.

————. "On Ethnographic Authority." *Representations* 1, no. 2 (1983): 118–46.

————. "Introduction: Partial Truths, and On Ethnographic Allegory." In James Clifford and George E. Marcus (eds.), *Writing Culture: the Poetics and Politics of Ethnography*. Berkeley, Los Angeles, and London: University of California Press, 1986: 98–121.

Earl, William L. *The Dancer Takes Flight: Psychological Concerns in the Development of the American Male Dancer*. Lanham, MD, and London: University Press of America, 1988.

Fisher, Jennifer. *The Annual Nutcracker: A Participant-Oriented, Contextualized Study of The Nutcracker Ballet as It Has Evolved into a Christmas Ritual in the United States and Canada*. Dissertation, University of California, Irvine, 1998.

————. *Nutcracker Nation: How an Old World Ballet Became a Christmas Tradition in the New World*. New Haven: Yale University Press, 2003.

————. "Choreographing and Improvising the Interview." *Proceedings, Society of Dance History Scholars*. Provo, Utah, February 1994: 341–46.

Kealiinohomoku, Joann. "An Anthropologist Looks at Ballet as a Form of Ethnic Dance." In Roger Copeland and Marshall Cohen (eds.), *What Is Dance?* Oxford: Oxford University Press, 1983: 533–49 (originally published in 1970).

Kondo, Dorinne K. *Crafting Selves: Power, Gender, and Discourses of Identity in a Japanese Workplace*. Chicago and London: University of Chicago Press, 1990.

Lal, Jayati. "Situating Locations: The Politics of Self, Identity, and 'Other' in Living and Writing the Text." In Diane L. Wolf (ed.), *Feminist Dilemmas in Fieldwork*. Boulder, CO: Westview, 1996: 185–214.

Limon, José. "Notes from a Native Anthropologist." In Richard Fox (ed.), *Recapturing Anthropology: Working in the Present*. Santa Fe, NM: School of American Research Press (Seattle: University of Washington Press), 1991.

Mailloux, Steven. "The Turns of Reader-Response Criticism." In Charles Moran and Elizabeth F. Penfield (eds.), *Conversations: Contemporary Critical Theory and the Teaching of Literature*. Urbana, IL: National Council of Teachers of English, December 1990.

Matsumoto, Valerie. "Reflections on Oral History: Research in a Japanese American Community." In *Feminist Dilemmas in Fieldwork*. Boulder, CO: Westview, 1996: 160–69.

Minister, Kristina. "A Feminist Frame for the Oral History Interview." In Sherna Berger Gluck and Daphne Patai (eds.), *Women's Words: The Feminist Practice of Oral History*. New York and London: Routledge, 1991: 27–42.

Sanjek, Roger. "On Ethnographic Validity." In Roger Sanjek (ed.), *Fieldnotes: The Makings of Anthropology*. Ithaca and London: Cornell University Press 1990: 385–418.

Shokeid, Moshe. "Anthropologists and Their Informants: Marginality Reconsidered." *Archives Européennes de Sociologie* 29 (1988): 31–47.

Stinson, Susan W., Donald Blumenfield-Jones, and Jan Van Dyke. "Voices of Young Woman Dance Students: An Interpretive Study of Meaning in Dance." *Dance Research Journal* (1990): 13–22.

Thomas, Helen, ed. *Dance, Gender and Culture*. London: Macmillan, 1993.

Visweswaran, Kamala. *Fictions of Feminist Ethnography.* Minneapolis and London: University of Minnesota Press, 1994.

Wulff, Helena. *Ballet Across Borders: Career and Culture in the World of Dancers.* Oxford and New York: Berg Publishers, 1998.

Zavella, Patricia. "Feminist Insider Dilemmas: Constructing Ethnic Identity with Chicana Informants." *Feminist Dilemmas in Fieldwork.* Boulder, CO: Westview, 1996: 138–59.

CHAPTER FOUR

The "Why Dance?" Projects

CHOREOGRAPHING THE TEXT AND DANCING THE DATA

MICHÈLE MOSS

I have always been interested in dance. My remembrances are often dance re-lated, my imaginings, my perceptions; most of my thinking is oriented toward the language of movement. This has been my world, the landscape within which I find my lived meaning.

Dancing was central to our family celebrations. My sweet sixteenth birth-day celebration was a basement dance party—my cousins taught me to do the Mashed Potato and the Puppet, dances we had seen on American Bandstand. *An avid social dancer, it is little wonder I came to study dance formally.*

As a youngster taking tap dance classes in Liverpool, England, and as a teenager in Québec, dancing to James Brown and watching the American broadcast of Soul Train, *I knew that this was something I needed to do. I had no idea then that I could actually make a career out of dancing, let alone jazz dancing. I have always sought to feed my kinaesthetic tendencies to move and to breathe life through the body, but didn't yet know which dance forms and/or idioms would suit these tendencies best. I studied ballet, but it didn't move me. My early studies at the Negro Community Centre (NCC) in Montreal were compelling and fundamental to my training, especially my "groove" training. Our teacher, I think I remember her name as Chucky, had hoofed on Broad-way and was the quintessential showgirl gypsy: a long-legged tap dancer, who could sing as well as act. Most enticing was her quality of movement: natural, rhythmic, rounded, and grounded. The funny thing is she's now just a shad-ow, a memory hard to bring into focus. But I do remember Chucky seemed to bring the music to life and was the source of inspiration in my adolescent life. My time at NCC was short-lived, as our suburban home was far from the NCC's downtown Montreal location, and all too soon my parents insisted that I stop taking classes. By this time however, I had already decided that my future must always include dancing. In the end, I made dance my career path and, following graduation with a Bachelor of Education in 1984, I embarked on a dance career. I have been making dances since 1986 and have taught dance since 1981. Together with Vicki Adams Willis and Hannah Stilwell, I founded Decidedly Jazz Danceworks in 1984, a professional dance company dedicated to preserving the rich history of jazz music and dance, and to moving the form forward.*

I have always been the happiest, indeed most comfortable, when inquiring with my arms and legs as they manipulate time and space. When harnessing the dancing body as an advocate for self-inquiry and transforming my community, I wonder how some people can still believe in the superiority of the mind over the body. I want to release the body from any perceived tyranny of the mind and acknowledge it's merging with the body as a vehicle for rich knowing. I have found the body to be epistemological, a source of meaning, and meaningfulness. The interpretations I have made of my dancing body move beyond simply a personal expressivity—they are a thoughtful act of agency in the world. Why can't we use dance as way of inquiring into the world? When at last I took to the road, it was through an embodied prism of movement, of dance, that I proceeded out into the world with passion and intent. In the 1980s, I sought out the rhythms of jazz in New York City, Berlin, Paris, and England. Then I tracked the roots of the form in Sénégal and The Gambia and ultimately landed in Conakry, Guinée. It felt like a homecoming.

THE *WHY DANCE?* MISSION

This paper represents a call and a response to the topic of dancing as a way of knowing. For the past decade, my ethnographic field research has been concentrated in Guinée-Conakry and Cuba, fuelling many embodied research projects in my home city of Calgary. The *Why Dance?* concerts, which culminated in 2011, revealed ever more about the dancing body, the knowing mind–body system and the artists of Calgary, Alberta, Canada. The work also features many unseen collaborators on far-off shores who have enriched my understanding of dance and dancing. The mission of my master's thesis project, *Why Dance? Interpreting Lifeworlds Through Dance*, aimed to break down notions of a dualist epistemology, forging together a text, a dance, and a concert in such a way as to view and analyze the dancing body in a more multi-faceted way. The inaugural concert event was held in 2005 and the second concert in 2009. The concerts were used to create an educational DVD. I came to this research project with a multiple identity: as a fully hyphenated, bi-racial and bilingual art practitioner and

Figure 1   Michèle Moss, photographed for *Swerve* magazine, 2008. Photographer: Trudie Lee.

educator, choreographer, and performer, I am a student of many dance forms and have long been devoted to the embodied practices of dance research as practice. It is this passion, the way of life that I have enjoyed since I was three years old, that brought me to formulate this vital group of subquestions that were central to the *Why Dance?* project:

1. What does it mean to dance, reflecting and influencing culture and society?
2. How does dancing encourage critical thinking?
3. How does dance enhance the quality of life?
4. Can dance be an important representation of history and culture?

By reflecting on my practice, listening to the voices of many collaborators, colleagues, students, and teachers, I have discovered that dance and dancing, at home and abroad, is worthy of serious consideration. It is a process that has proved to offer many rewards. In her text "Spectacle and Dancing Bodies That Matter: Or, If It Don't Fit, Don't Force It," Anna Scott constructs a rich metaphor that resonates and speaks to me, in which she cautions us not to mistake dance for a *toy* when it is a *sacred object* (Scott 1997: 267). I am committed to investigating in fields both abroad and at home, through ethnography and autoethnography. I am drawn to the data and its interpretation, the intellectual knowledge and the physical experience and to sharing the evidence in the dance studio and on the page. I have found the research process to be compelling and ambitious. I don't often know where it is leading, and the tasks of interpretation, analysis, and rethinking have been rich and rewarding. The dissemination processes, performance creation, textual projects, and data collection seem equal in compensation. They have been fabulously recursive, repetitive, unending, and enriching. This ongoing synthesis of words, gestures, ideas, steps, lectures, and conversations is a dialectical process that is challenging and sweet.

My West African research—the dances, the people, the setting, and the cultural meaning of the dances—are a great source of inspiration for me. This textual work manifests that inspiration. The rhythms/dances associated with seduction and courtship are especially apt for my contribution to *Fields in Motion.* A song that accompanies one of the dances translates roughly to "Will she or won't she?" The lyrics reference a courtship between a man and a woman, and as you will see below, I use the lyrics to orient the reader to my research quest as I try to understand my need to dance.

Will I ever fully understand my quest and find my answers? Why do others also feel the call, the push, the pull, and begin the quest? Why dance? The metaphor of this *danse des amoureux* serves me in analyzing and interpreting the act of dancing, my life, my work, and my passion. The ethnographic opportunity to unpack and interpret in faraway places is irresistible. To conduct research in my own dance community is an interpretive process that is very exciting. The process is not undertaken alone, and not without a fair amount of passion and love. I hope that by the end of this process, I will be able to recognize and realize its full possibilities and potential. This research is too seductive to deny.

AN EMBODIED RESEARCH PROCESS: SCHOLARSHIP AS COURTSHIP

Because I believe that the body is a thinking space, I have found that my work, dance and the act of dancing, is interdisciplinary, addressing both performance artists and members of the academy. I draw my collaborators from both of these groups. And so, I conceptualized the *Why Dance?* concert and the interviews as a way to reveal the interconnectedness of theory and art practice.

Perhaps, and not surprisingly, I did not initially believe in the possibility and validity of the concert as a part of a thesis paper, although this is common practice among university dance researchers (I was not studying in a fine arts faculty). It was not an easy act for this dancer to move onto the page. The contact with dancers, and the pleasure of music and ideas coming together in the body was paramount. My supervisor encouraged me to fold all my identities, resources, talents, and modes of research representations into the project. Taking the work to the stage was a natural progression. The construction of what I called "body stories" was alluring. It was only gradually that I became committed to pondering the limitations and possibilities of dance within the context of phenomenology as well as feminist and cultural/social theory. An intellectual lens—the words and cognitive functions of the mind—have in the past seemed to be in opposition to the emotional artist within me. The researcher in me recognized the power of text-based language but wondered how to reveal the "language" of my research through my dancing body. My research is usually a kinaesthetic practice, the creation of dances. The ineffable is at play here: as I surrender to the bodily impulses and intentions, a product of my inner landscape and what I sometimes cannot express in words, I feel my power. The written transmission of ideas—of what I know through my muscles and my left-brain—is challenging. Following my instincts and intuitions, those that I readily access in the moment of dancing, creating a moving interpretation of self and the world, is far easier for me, and yet ... I have become committed to this text-based signifying process.

As they dance the popular rhythm called *Yankadi*, and the accompanying faster rhythm called *Macarou*, young people in Guinée would socialize and mingle. Well, that's what they tell me would happen in the village. I have seen the dance recreated in festival settings on the theatrical stage in Conakry only, but I have danced it in workshops at home and in Guinée. The dance is similar to the kind of courtship dances that are common in many cultures. By this I mean there are young people who come together in gender groups to dance and, in times gone by, look for a partner. The young people move together expressing interest in each other through the sharing of a scarf and then move through formations that have them holding hands and creating couples that travel through an arch of arms or some formations have the girls sit on the knee of a boy. I imagine them wondering if their advances will be positively received, their feelings reciprocated. *Will s/he or won't s/he?* I return to the lyrics of the song, to structure and code evident in the dance. As with these dancers, I wonder will my efforts succeed in seducing the reader into coming with me into the world of dance, into the field or onto the concert stage.

Figure 2 *Why Dance? Two* (2009) finale-dancers (from left to right) Caroline Fraser, Tara Wilson, Amanda Bonnell, Jennifer Mahood, and Deanne Walsh. Photographer: Kristian Jones.

There are so many possible questions; there is so much potential. Seeking evidence, I chose a topic of inquiry, reviewed the literature, considered the theories. I entered the field and danced, interviewed, collected, transcribed, and engaged in an ethics process. I returned to the field, thought some more, gathered more data. Returning home, I interpreted the data, created dances and then ... did it all over again.

BODY [OF] EVIDENCE: DATA COLLECTION AND INTERPRETATION

With the *Why Dance?* study, I set out to probe into the lives of both artistic and recreational dancers, to understand the various meanings they ascribed to their engagement with the act of dancing. I plunged into the research vibrantly, eagerly anticipating interpreting the data gathered in the course of interviews and fieldwork. I have always enjoyed gathering and analyzing the meanings people conferred on their own stories and actions, reading autobiographies, biographies, and listening to friends and family recount stories about their lives. I am also committed to practice-as-research. As did Carl Bagley and Mary Beth Cancienne in *Dancing the Data* (2002), I have long danced the data, interpreting conversations, re-interpreting stories, and living qualitative inquiry as a working artist. And in hindsight, I now find that the writing process itself revealed as many possibilities as had the creative act of dancing and dance creation itself.

I could   endeavour
to organize   the page,
to choreograph   the text
                  What I heard
                        of
                        passion
                        and
                        desire.

Most recently, I learned a village-style *Yankadi* and *Macarou*, in a workshop setting in Victoria, Canada. The formations are such that the genders are called to meet each other and called to the dance—an imperative, a response. But even as I dance this style, I am thinking how it is this dance is not often enjoyed in this manner. The dance is now usually presented by a whole group in unison with genderless choreography, or as individual solos. How is it that traditional practices are in flux? It seems things do change, times change—and that is acceptable in the culture, even if some researchers, such as myself, sometimes wish it was unchanging. I am left wondering, "Why isn't anyone dancing *Yankadi* and *Macarou* like they used to?" When I had the opportunity to dance them myself, the skip through the London Bridge–style arches was really fun and had me giggling like a girl. Was it because of the innocence and simplicity? This brings me to realize that the simplicity of the question, "Why dance?" is an illusion because, as it turns out, it is complex and hard to answer and certainly in flux—dependent on so many things.

I chose to conduct interviews as a way of preserving and honouring the voices of this often-silent arts practice. It seemed to me that the act of recording and videotaping constituted, in itself, an artful task. The revelation that the interpretive writing resembled an act of choreography led me to construct a metaphor and style of writing that felt like "choreographing the data" or "dancing the data"—in other words, examining the *BODY* of evidence. In *Dancing the Data*, editors Cancienne and Bagley seek to open discussion and encourage reflection regarding the ways in which familiar methodologies and pedagogical approaches might benefit from new ways of representing findings and new knowledge, as well as exploring various ways of teaching and learning. For instance, their incorporation of a CD-ROM to support the textual readings in the book provided inspiration for my own thesis and my choice to bring bodily experience forward as evidence through the medium of video recording and live performance.

There is a certain irony in operation as I represent this dance work textually, because one of the themes that arose from the interview data was the dancers' belief in the ineffable nature of dancing. For many of the participants in this study, dancing was an expressive choice precisely because it seemed to be beyond the limits of language. They often remarked that if they could say it in words, they would say it, but they couldn't—and so, they dance. Acknowledging the ineffable proved important in understanding and interpreting some of the interviews, and in recognizing the importance of the body stories both as part of the interview/data collection and the performance creation dissemination act concert. I elaborated on these ideas in my field notes in this way:

Singing ... "This is the Universal Break!" (This melodic phrase is a device we sometimes employ when learning the rhythms and breaks played on djembé to remember and identify the pattern that calls us to attention. This call is important to hear, the call, or break, is an imperative. This is an opportunity to find a way to say what is important, a need to express.)

Singing ... "A boro ma
A'ma boro ma, Eh!..."
(The song goes on ...)

"Will she or won't she ... dance *Yankady* when we get to the celebration?" (This first liminal break will describe the journey through my West African dance studies and many theatrical performances that have served as a vital mode to say what I need to say.... It is an inner voice that speaks, my voice, a voice, a summoning voice—an invocation dance opens *Why Dance?*)

The dance is a short creation improvised with a red scarf.

As I stand ready to dance, I am called to attention. I have a heightened sense of being in my skin. I am open to possibility. I will be improvising and don't know exactly what will happen, but I am well prepared and open to the moment. The dance serves to set the scene, allowing the energy to come in—to come through my body ... embodying an interrogative. Preparing the discursive space, others will follow.

I hold the red scarf ready to sweep and move the energetic forces, to open the path, the audience awaits ... (Field notes, Calgary, September 29, 2005)

Seeking the boundaries of this idea, that the dancing body conveys important information about others, and myself, and can reveal the evanescent processes of the mind, I dance, I write, I listen. I agree with Diaz when he speaks of a "discursive collage of meaning," to describe the way in which I make meaning through my words as dancer/choreographer and ethnographer/interpreter. He further notes, "Meaning is temporally located, and always being contested, negotiated and transformed, while appearing to remain the same. The different discursive fields of art and human science research employ different ways of making meaning of the world, of constructing reality" (Diaz 2002: 148).

THE AFRICANIST CALL AND ANSWER AS A FRAMEWORK FOR ARTISTIC INQUIRY

I wonder how do I make my written work look like a dance, feel like a dance, and perform like a dance ... a textual dance? I would like to propose employing an Africanist characteristic and one essential to jazz, the musical structure of *call and answer*. My "discursive collage" is in fact a kind of folk dance, in the sense that it is an improvised mixture of Africanist traditions and personal movement. The stretching and pushing, pulling and recoiling, circling and reaching are a discursive dance collage. The "call" is the pull my research participants spoke of that drew them to express themselves through movement, through dance. I, too, call upon my creative inclinations to reveal the *why*—a recursive and reflexive answer. In West African dance practice, the musical and corporeal expression is often marked by breaks; these calls/signals move dancer and drummer through the dance. These musical transitions serve as small separations or interludes. These occasions can lift the dancer to step higher and can call the drummer to greater attention—to lead or respond—to what the dancer is doing, the collaboration, the dance. These liminal transitions,[1] or discursive calls, can help transform both musician and dancer to "answer," to reach deeper, dance higher, and connect and communicate at a different level. They serve to reconnect me to the root or core research question, its significance, and to the dance as artistic inquiry.

I imagine that I am dancing any one of the many celebration dances, the "dances performed at popular festivals solely for pleasure, relaxation and fun" (Billmeier and Keita 1999: 109). According to Chernoff (1979), it is at this moment that I would be accessing the social function of Guinean dance. Chernoff describes African music as possessing two essential characteristics: community participation and social function. As he explains, the music (and I extend this definition to include dance) can have a "positive influence at many important events in the life of the individual and society at large" (Chernoff cited in Billmeier and Keita: 27).

The textual dance I performed in my thesis used this call-and-answer structure as a framework. The call was a personal one. The call was also from the social sciences to make sense of the world. My participants were happy and ready to answer my call through an act of reflection, to consider why they dance. They undertook this by responding verbally and corporeally—dancing it in the interview process and, when called upon, they also came to the stage.

Internal call ... to dance, dancing in the skin of my ancestors. Dancing my cultural and spiritual memory, my essence as constructed through practice, heritage, even geography. It is a dance marking the motivating force behind this research. I dance an invocation dance to open the concert. It is a signal, a dance that calls out the data representation—I hope to faithfully represent the phenomenon I witnessed, the voices I documented. These "voices" will take the stage representing their own lived experience, speaking, and dancing their own inquiry. I, too, wish to interpret the text, be the text, and gather meaning from the text—all the while the dance moves me, moves the arms and legs, torso, and head, leaving a trail of ... sympathetic responses and visceral interpretations. I recognize I am limited by my personal or interpretive style and movement experiences/background. The red scarf is used to clear the space, to wipe the slate and prepare the way for new insights and meaning; personal and communal. The struggles and the joy, information and impressions, emotion and knowledge.... I dance steps that feel sweet, that I have learned, that I have invented. I use some traditional vocabulary and I just sway. I continue, I continue to move ...

Lurching, spinning, shuffling ... lurching, spinning, shuffling ... lurching, spinning, shuffling ... lurching, spinning, shuffling ... eyes now open, alert ... (Field notes taken from the first *Why Dance?* concert, my solo "*invocation,*" September 25, 2005)

Is this invocation dance presumptuous? Idealistic? Can a dance, or dances, really be so laden with meaning? In giving the act of creation and performance my attention, both in terms of descriptive and interpretive methodology, I wanted the dancers, the dances, to speak for themselves. I hope everyone will be able to hear them, as they have so much to say.

Figure 3   University of Calgary solo dancer Cara Moeller in the field on travel study program, Conakry, 2006. Photographer: Jenna Moeller.

THE GUINEAN COURTSHIP DANCES AS METAPHORS FOR BRINGING TOGETHER TEXT AND DANCE

This effort to make the text look like a dance is not easy but is important to me, I don't really know how to do it. As the "lived meanings" of my research participants and myself are revealed—that is, our way of being in the world—they involve both the everyday and the performative.[2] Research is listening, watching/observing, inquiring, interpreting, and analyzing. This questioning by way of personal and/or collective perspectives can change the way we see or attend to the world. Sometimes, this means just starting and seeing where we end up—guided by our emotions, our senses; guided by the questions and the data, but not privileging answers.

For me, this process is akin to the two Guinean rhythms/dances, *Yankadi* and *Macarou*. These dances of seduction or courtship have proved to be perfect metaphorically vis-à-vis my passion for this subject and my courtship with the language of the social/human sciences. The dances start very slowly, seductively. The couples dance and interact until a male puts his scarf around the neck of a chosen woman. (I have also learned the dance in a modern variation in which the woman puts the scarf around her male partner's neck.) A whistle heralds a change to the fast, spirited *Macarou* section, an échauffement; the drummers play the rhythm with speed and verve and the dancer must respond. Things are heating up and the courtship begins in earnest.

In this instance, the dance is one of courtship, a means of negotiating the world, the world of both relationships and concepts. *The break marks the beginning of the dance:*

Swaying with ease, I slowly move forward and backwards with the pelvis leading and the arms supporting and initiating the oppositional coordination. The weight changes easily, although changing sides is a little tricky, and the way it spirals up the spine is satisfying, twisting and wringing the torso in the most delicious manner. The sedulous dance comes easily to me. This is *Yankadi* and I release into the sensuous helix. I am not yet dancing per se as the first break is for the drummers. To begin the rhythm in earnest, once dancers and drummer have settled in, is to travel up and down the spine with intermittent whips and punches with a lightness in the feet and a confident weight in the pelvis. The signal comes again and I move to another step, another idea but the movement remains circular, recursive, circuitous and always spiralling.... I have danced this dance in the field, in Guinée. I dance this in a Calgary studio, on the stage, in my living room—teaching and learning through this dance, this state of consciousness. I am fully engaged and aware of the body. I am conscious of the tickle in my belly, is this a bubbling up of the magic or is it the connection to the rhythmic impulse? As I dance I am developing a more intimate relationship with others and myself. I am listening for the whistle that heralds a change, a call, a call to step it up and get moving. I know the dance has a more folkloric feel with formations and patterns but I have not learned it this way very often. When I have it has been fun to skip under and through the London Bridge arches with my *partner*. There is a sweetness that reminds me of English country dances—this suits my bi-cultural roots and moving with the community of dancers in formations and patterns familiar to many folk dances pleases me. The whistle sounds, heralding the change to the more spirited rhythm, requires focus, commitment, sweat and effort—no lurching or shuffling allowed. (Field notes from Conakry, May 2006)

Hermeneutic[3] terms such as "circuitous" and "recursive" appear in my field notes, but they are also played out in the dances presented in my concerts. The theme of recursivity is central to my considerations and to those I interviewed for the *Why Dance?* project. I find myself returning often to a central theme, the performative inquiry model as a form of communication. The language of dance speaks about individuals and community and it speaks to them. It speaks of states of engagement, consciousness, action, and compassion. I returned to the theme for my second concert.[4] While the inaugural concert focused on presenting some of the dances of my research participants/collaborators, whom I had interviewed for my textual process, I also presented my own work and developed the community-based research around my choreographic "voice," all the while bringing home ever more elements of my fieldwork from Sénégal (1987 and 2006), Guinée (1999, 2000, 2003, and 2006) and Cuba (1999, 2004, 2005, and 2007).

RECONCILIATION OF BEING "AT HOME" AND "FAR AWAY"

The other important theme of my research has been what I call *empathetic training*. From the various perspectives of tourist dance classes, to deep prolonged investigation, to artistic creation projects, I have enjoyed this dance of seduction, enticed by the *other* and have come to confound "at home" and "away." I enjoyed making strange the familiar at home and feeling in the right place when away. Under these circumstances I have fallen more deeply under the influence of dance and dancing. I have come to create a holistic sphere, a courtship that has resulted in a marriage of fieldwork and home, theory and practice, methods and performance, writing and dancing. For the concert series, it was important to me that my collaborators all have a tradition of engaging in ethnographic practice, as a form of inquiry into the world, as participant-observers. By mixing inquiry and passion into embodied research as a way of making sense of the world, by asking questions, and by seeking a frame that orients my gaze, I am brought back repeatedly to the data and to the question, "Why dance?" I continue … lurching, spinning, shuffling … lurching, spinning, shuffling …

The lurching, spinning, and shuffling allude to the raw inquiry and raw data. How to finesse this process to find the right questions, never mind the answers? Will I or won't I find the path open and stimulating, will I be able to reconcile home and away? Will home provide as rich and as exciting a locale as far-off shores? This global alliance connects me on so many levels to the questions, to the world. With my scarf in hand, I am endeavouring to draw to me my loving subject, dance. With my scarf, I am trying to clear the space, the *bantaba*, a community dance space that allows for both cognitive and kinaesthetic practices to take shape.[5] I can envision a connection of torso and spirit, of arms and legs and heart weaving together a formation of practice and theory, methodology and performance. Moving under the canopy of arms and hearts, so reminiscent of the London Bridge game of my youth, I feel that the structure supports my lurching, spinning, and shuffling by transforming it into a beautiful, youthful, innocent skip. I am skipping with the help of many partners, my nearby community and one of my faraway collaborators in Conakry.

CODA

The work I have completed thus far in the *Why Dance?* research project elaborates on a conversation between theory and practice, and, hence, it is a dialogic process. I believe that it is important not to alienate ourselves as dancers, performers, artists, teacher-educators, and researchers from either the academy or the community. This occasion to underline or to account for the oftentimes ephemeral quality of performance has been an important moment of self-exploration. I recognize that the mind–body system is designed to be flexible, multilingual, and diverse. I am deradicalizing the act of dancing by doing it all—dancing the data, deconstructing the practice, documenting the concert, validating in performance and in practice, and articulating and interpreting through a textual dance that will hardly lie flat on the page.

Notes

1 "Liminal transitions" refers to the suggestions brought forward by Victor Turner (1997). For me, the concept of liminality involves both separation and threshold. I use the liminal breaks as a device to reference the personal understandings gleaned by the act of dancing and writing, writing and dancing. This state, that Turner says is *betwixt and between*, offers the opportunity to reference past and the future. I do think of this as a *universal break*, one that many of us can connect to being in the body and using movement to create a break with the ordinary, the dominance of mental process, and use our legs, arms, and torso to create and reflect the data of daily life and of dreams and possibilities. This act of critical thinking happens in the body as much as in the mind.

2 By "performative," I mean *performance*—a state or action that can express or transform our understanding of the world. It can happen on the stage and in everyday life.

3 The hermeneutic process is often referred to as a circle—I imagine it requires a recursive and circuitous path, and understand this to mean it requires reflection to reveal meaning. The inquiry—interpreting and reinterpreting, searching and seeking—moves forward but also reconsiders and returns to the data. This weaving or knitting action allows us to return to the subject matter and to reconsider and reinterpret the meaning, the text, the body, the narratives. This process is one of seeking meaning while we take in the world as it is. To report from the heart of the matter and to be embedded and engaged, but always reflexive, is at the core of hermeneutics. This dynamic process of analyzing, comparing, judging, and classifying can then unfold and reveal greater meaning. It requires us to be reflexive. Returning to the material, the data, the details, and interpretive acts gives greater meaning to our lived experience. The act of reflection is rooted in social theory and social change.

4 Following the inaugural 2005 concert, *Why Dance?* I presented a second evening *Why Dance? Two*. It was presented at the University of Calgary, by the Dance Department, in a program called the Professional Dance Series. The full title of the second concert was *Why Dance? Two: The Power of One, Plus one, Plus …* A final entry was presented in April 2011, with the title, *A Riddmic Conclusion to the* Why Dance? *Trilogy in 3D*.

5 The *bantaba*, a dance space, is a sacred ground, an area or arena where community assembles to witness and participate in affirmative acts such as dance. I liken this space to a portal, a passageway to possibility and transformation for both the individual and a community as a whole.

Bibliography

Amit, Vered. "Introduction: Constructing the Field." In Vered Amit (ed.), *Constructing the Field: Ethnographic Fieldwork in the Contemporary World*. London and New York: Routledge, 2000: 1–18.

Bagley, Carl, and Mary Beth Cancienne. "Educational Research and Intertextual Forms of (Re)Presentation: The Case for Dancing the Data." In Bagley and Cancienne (eds.), *Dancing the Data*. New York: Peter Lang, 2002: 3–19.

Buckland, Theresa J. (ed.), *Dance in the Field: Theory, Methods and Issues in Dance Ethnography*. New York: St. Martin's Press, 1999.

Billmeier, Uschi, and Mamady Keita. *A Life for the Djembé: Traditional Rhythms of the Malinke*. Brussels: Arun, 1999.

Cummins, Bryan D., and John L. Steckley. *The Ethnographic Experience*. Toronto: Pearson Education Canada, 2005.

Diaz, Gene. "Artistic Inquiry: On Lighthouse Hill." In Bagley and Cancienne (eds.), *Dancing the Data*. New York: Peter Lang, 2002: 147–61.

Geertz, Clifford. *Local Knowledge: Further Essays in Interpretive Anthropology*. New York: Basic Books, 1983.

Gottschild, Brenda Dixon. "Stripping the Emperor: The Africanist Presence in American Concert Dance." In A. Dils and A. Cooper Albright (eds.), *Moving Histories/Dancing Cultures: A Dance History Reader*. Middletown, CT: Wesleyan University Press, 2001: 332–41.

Greene, Maxine. *Releasing the Imagination: Essays on Education, the Arts, and Social Change*. San Francisco: Jossey Bass, 1995.

Grondin, Joan. *The Philosophy of Gadamer*. (K. Plant trans.) Montreal: McGill-Queen's University Press, 2003.

Hamera, Judith. *Dancing Communities: Performance, Difference and Connection in the Global City*. Hampshire, UK: Palgrave Macmillan, 2007.

Hammersley, Martyn, and Paul Atkinson. *Ethnography: Principles in Practice*, 2nd ed. London and New York: Routledge, 1995.

Husserl, Edmund. "The Phenomenology of Internal Time Consciousness." In T. Mooney and D. Moran (eds.), *The Phenomenology Reader*. London: Routledge, 2002: 109–23.

Keller, Pierre. "Husserl and Heidegger on Human Experience." In Donn Welton (ed.), *The New Husserl: A Critical Reader*. Bloomington: Indiana University Press. 2003.

Lansdale, Janet *The Development of Dance Research*. Guildford, UK: University of Surrey, 2003. Retrieved February 23, 2006, from http://www.surrey.ac.uk/Dance/Research/index.html.

Moss, Michèle. *Why Dance? Interpreting Lifeworlds Through Dance*. Unpublished master's thesis. Graduate Division of Educational Research, University of Calgary, 2007.

Papageorgiou, Dimitris. "Field Research on the Run: One More for the Road." In Athena McLean and Annette Leibing (eds.), *The Shadow Side of Fieldwork: Exploring the Blurred borders between Ethnograhy and Life*. Malden, MA: Blackwell, 2007: 221–38.

McNamara, Joann. "Dance in the Hermeneutic Circle." In Sondra Horton Fraleigh and Penelope Hanstein (eds.), *Researching Dance: Evolving Modes of Inquiry*. Pittsburgh: University of Pittsburgh Press, 1999: 162–87.

Ness, Sally Ann. "Dancing in the Field: Notes from Memory." In Susan Leigh Foster (ed.), *Corporealities: Dancing, Knowledge, Culture and Power*. London and New York: Routledge, 1996: 129–54.

Schechner, Richard. "Magnitudes of Performance." In Richard Schechner and Willa Appel (eds.), *By Means of Performance: Intercultural Studies of Theatre and Ritual*. Cambridge, UK: Cambridge University Press, 1990: 19–49.

Scott, Anna Beatrice. "Spectacle and Dancing Bodies That Matter: Or, If It Don't Fit, Don't Force It." In Jane Desmond (ed.), *Meaning in Motion*. Durham, NC: Duke University Press, 1997: 259–66.

Shapiro, Sherry. "Educational Research and Intertextual Forms of (Re)Presentation: The Case for Dancing the Data." In Sherry Shapiro (ed.), *Dance in a World of Change: Reflections on Globalization and Cultural Difference*. Human Kinetics, 2008: 253–374.

Snowber, Celeste. "Bodydance: Enfleshing Soulful Inquiry through Improvisation." In Bagley and Cancienne (eds.), *Dancing the Data*. New York: Peter Lang, 2002: 20–33.

Turner, Victor. "Are There Universals of Performance in Myth, Ritual, and Drama?" In Schechner and Appel (eds.), *By Means of Performance: Intercultural Studies of Theatre and Ritual*. Cambridge: Cambridge University Press, 1997.

Van Manen, Max. *Researching Lived Experience: Human Science for an Action Sensitive Pedagogy*, 2nd ed. London, ON: Althouse Press, 1990.

CHAPTER FIVE

What Is the Pointe?

THE POINTE SHOE AS SYMBOL IN DANCE ETHNOGRAPHY

KRISTIN HARRIS WALSH

When we think of classical ballet, the mind's eye can easily conjure up images of willowy women in gossamer dresses, perched on their toes as they are supported and lifted by their male partners. Why is this the predominant ideal of ballet? Ideas of gender in dance relate not only to plot, character, and choreography, but also to costume. The footwear used is of especial interest. In much of the ballet world, the pointe shoe is an essential tool in the creation and execution of ballet. Moreover, for many in a typical ballet audience, a ballet would not be complete were the women not shod in pointe shoes. This expectation holds in conventional ballet companies globally. The pointe shoe has been used—initially in Europe in the early nineteenth century and spreading globally after that—and lingers as the ultimate image of the ballerina even today. It would be difficult, perhaps even impossible, to imagine a typical production of *Swan Lake* without the thirty-two fouettés, or *Romeo and Juliet* danced in bare feet. Furthermore, the pointe shoe can be regarded as the harbinger of numerous messages; that is, it can imply strength, delicacy, ethereality, or dependence.

However, not all ballet dancers wear pointe shoes. Male dancers, children, and female dancers offstage almost always wear the soft ballet slippers that are not often found on stage. The commonality of the humble ballet slipper also bears examination. Why is it that men wear only soft shoes? Why do women usually wear the same during classes, yet perform ballets in pointe shoes? Why does aesthetic dictate footwear so strongly? In contrast to the world of ballet, numerous dance forms do not require shoes at all. Modern dance and classical East Indian dance styles, among many

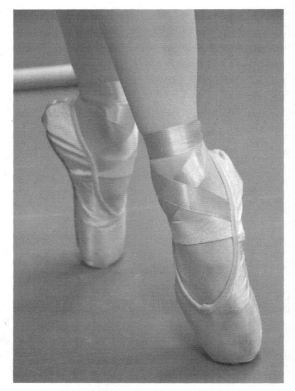

Figure 1 Dancer Sarah Mackey's foot on point. Photographer: Kristin Harris Walsh.

others, require their dancers to dance barefoot, regardless of location or performative situation. Attitudes toward the body, gender, and dance itself all culminate in the uniform that is de rigueur for the dancer of a particular style. The cultural determinants affect how dancers perform and what their footwear will be.[1] All these factors provide a comprehensive indication of some of the differences inherent in these dance forms.

This chapter primarily focuses on ballet, a dance form that contains a class structure, internal hierarchy, and strict gender divisions. During my graduate studies in dance at York University, Toronto, I became especially interested in the role of gender in ballet. I had danced since childhood, and had begun during my university years to seriously question inherent structures and assumed normative behaviours in ballet. Analysis of ballet and gender power relations was a way for me to explore these issues through my love of dance. Once I moved on to doctoral studies in folklore, I became far more intrigued in the role of ethnography as a mode of analysis. During a course on material culture, I chose to research the pointe shoe as an artefact in order to explore in greater depth how a seemingly simple shoe could be so highly charged with meaning for so many people: dancers, audience members, and scholars—male and female alike. It was my first attempt to merge my chosen fields of dance and folklore, something that has been achieved by numerous dance anthropologists and dance ethnologists before me. My work here comes from that initial study.

In order to acquire an emic perspective on this style, I interviewed Kate Cornell, a freelance dance writer, ballet teacher, and dancer in Toronto.[2] I have also drawn on my own experiences in the dance world to augment the information from my interviewee. As a dancer in Toronto and St. John's for more than twenty years, and with nearly ten years of training on pointe, my own experiences complemented my fieldwork with Cornell, adding an autoethnographic layer to my interview findings. During our discussions, I was able to position myself as an amateur insider in the field, while relying on Cornell's expertise as dancer and dance scholar to link theoretical ideas with her own experiences. I will reflect also on how ballet functions in contrast to modern dance in terms of footwear and the affect that it has on various issues. Finally, I have applied a combination of a folklore, dance, and feminist analysis in order to obtain a multi-faceted analysis of footwear in dance. These theoretical approaches complement the ethnographic perspectives formed by my own and Cornell's opinions, and I would venture to assert that our opinions, while merely those of two individuals, are well within the realm of beliefs held by other amateur and professional ballet dancers.

In order to begin looking at ballet, it is perhaps useful to explicitly state that the pointe shoe, as the principal image of ballet, can be regarded as an artefact (Babcock 1992). The shoe's physical components are uniform and have remained largely unchanged for several hundred years. Because pointe shoes are often handmade, each shoe differs slightly in terms of colour, moulding, construction, and surface detail. But the basic shape is uniform. The shoes are made in numerous colours, the most common being pale pink. The outer covering of the shoe is satin. The shoes fit snugly to the foot, but lengthen the look of the foot with the addition of a blocked toe on the end. This stiff cup is called the block or box, and the flat part of the shoe that the dancer stands on is the platform. Other important elements of shoe construction are the vamp, which covers the top of the toes and foot; the shank, the stiff sole that supports the insole; and the quarter, the soft material that covers the heel and sides of the foot. These elements can vary slightly in length or width, yet they all maintain the same function: to aid and support the dancer as she performs on pointe.

It would seem, thus, that the pointe shoe has one function; however, it can be seen to be multi-functional and polysemic. Dancers spend a great deal of time working in their shoes, breaking in or softening the stiff shanks, as well as darning the platform, and sewing on ribbons and elastics.[3] These activities are a ritual for all ballet dancers and, consequently, are an integral aspect of a dancer's life. Furthermore, the shoes function as the demonstration of technical and artistic ability since it is evident on pointe if a dancer is poorly trained or is not a strong performer. Finally, the shoe conveys the entire aesthetic of the ballet world. From her own experiences, Cornell speaks of the physical difference between dancing on pointe and dancing on a soft ballet slipper:

> Someone who hasn't done it would think that you're concentrating on the foot. When I first tried to do it, I was concentrating on the foot, and I think that's why my feet were cramping, I was getting blisters, ingrown toenails, and all that stuff. And then I realized when I had a strong teacher in pointe work, it's really about the pull-up in the butt. It's your legs that are doing the work and I didn't have strong legs when I was fourteen, fifteen, sixteen—and then I started building up strength. And I always have trouble—my feet don't work in the same way. So on demi-pointe, I'm always trying to get my arches over, which, that same thought in pointe work, tends to push you over and you hurt your big toe. So the feeling is completely different—stretch your knees as much as you can and stay on your platform. Because I was one of those people who was back on the platform and I always had to push over.... So I had to learn that where I was trying to sort of force my arches over and get a good platform on demi-pointe, I wasn't supposed to do that as much on pointe and I had to find the real straight column of the strength in my legs as opposed to just depending on my feet. And it took me two, three years to realize the importance of the platform and to get the right shoe to find the platform.... So that was always a big struggle for me to not only understand the difference between standing on demi and standing on pointe, but getting the shoes to help me understand what the difference was.

There are numerous frames of reference that can relate to pointe dancing. Depending on the piece, the dancer, on her pointe shoes, can convey lightness, pain, clumsiness, beauty or effortlessness. This also relates to the shoes' ability to communicate. To a dancer, the right pair of shoes can make her feel powerful and can physically assist her dancing. A poor pair can cause immense pain and, therefore, can affect her ability to perform. Through the shoes themselves, the dancer communicates to the audience. She relays her own feeling about dancing as well as her character's feelings and expression. Thus, the shoe functions simultaneously as both an artist-centred and performance-centred artefact. The ensuing cultural contextual interpretation varies, depending on the interaction. For example, the dancer experiences the shoe in a very different context from the audience member. Moreover, each audience member will understand the shoe in various ways, depending on her own personal history and experience with pointe shoes.[4] Although the image will be the same, the visual message that the artefact sends will be vastly different. On the other hand, the soft shoe conveys very different meanings. It can be made out of leather or canvas, and comes in pink, black, and white. While all three colours are available for women, pink remains the standard. Both white and black are equally acceptable for men. The shoe is essentially the same shape as the pointe shoe, with a few notable exceptions in the construction: the soles are softer, there is no blocked toe, and the shoes are generally more flexible. This leads to a much greater comfort level for dancers wearing these slippers. The technique that the dancers can achieve is less diverse and complex; however, many steps can be fully performed or modified to an acceptable extent.[5]

There is a distinct visual difference between a dancer on demi-pointe in a soft shoe and full pointe in a pointe shoe. Moreover, soft shoes (or the equivalent in boot form, for stage) are the norm for male dancers. With a few rare exceptions, men don't dance on pointe. Cornell mentions two scenarios in which men *do* dance on pointe: some old-school training styles require their male dancers to spend one year dancing on pointe, and companies such as the *Ballets Trockaderos*, an all-male troupe that dances on pointe. Men are given far greater comfort with their shoes and don't have to suffer the physical pain and strain on their bodies in the same way as female ballet dancers. The technique that tends to be preferred in male ballet dancers differs also—it focuses more on high leaps and grand turns rather than the quick footwork and multiple turns that are ideal for the female dancer on pointe. However, Cornell believes that pointe training for men can be extremely helpful in their other dancing:

> I really think that you can see the difference between men who have had to train on pointe, and I think you can see the difference in the articulation of the foot. I'm sure in pas de deux, men who have danced on pointe appreciate how difficult it is to stand in that pirouette position without sinking into your pointe shoe and understand how important it is to support the woman in the right way.

As a means of dress, shoes can imply certain codes, or socially acceptable ways of wearing and using the item.[6] "Fashion has a social significance.… Distinctions among garments imply distinctions among people" (Berger 1995: 91). Berger's thoughts can well be applied to the argument at hand. Footwear in ballet implies the various differentiations that can be made between dancers. The first and most obvious is the gender difference. Women wear pointe shoes and men wear soft shoes. While this is almost always true on stage, the dance class may differ slightly. In this situation, women will often wear soft shoes constructed in the same way as the men's footwear. However, the variation this time will come with the colour of the shoes themselves. Finally, onstage, not all dancers will wear either of these types of shoes. Character roles will usually call for character, or heeled, shoes, which will differ slightly for both men and women. This then creates a hierarchical difference between those dancers who require the more "balletic" shoes to perform as opposed to those who wear the more "theatrical" shoes and, therefore, do more acting than dancing. A class system is quickly put in place.

Pointe work is controversial also in the gender differences it implies. From an aesthetic point of view, the pointe shoe can be considered the primary balletic visual manifestation. In the history of ballet, the Romantic era promulgated the idea of the supernatural being, oftentimes in contrast to a more earthy character. In these ballets, the primary costume and choreographic difference is that while the ethereal character embodies all that is light, gossamer and vertical, her earthy counterpart wears soft slippers or character shoes, and dances in a more grounded, solid way. The pointe shoe, then, easily indicates the desired, unattainable, beautiful themes that run through all Romantic ballets. This is in direct contrast to many twentieth century choreographers, such as George Balanchine, who demanded a long, lean, athletic look in his dancers. There is a split between these two aesthetics. Romantic ballets, particularly in the traditional pas de deux, require that the female dancer be supported and lifted by her male counterpart. She turns, balances, jumps, while he assists her movements and ensures that she remains upright. The gaze is on her, not only from the audience but from her partner as well. It has been seen as a patriarchal constructed frame. Conversely, female solo pointe dancing (found in Balanchine's work) displays the woman as strong and in control. Because pointe work is extremely difficult to perform, particularly without any support, a woman dancing on pointe on her own makes a powerful visual statement. While the gaze is still on her from the audience, this kind of dancing can be seen as counter-hegemonic, as it is clearly the woman who is in control.

From a personal point of view, pointe dancing can be extremely liberating. When I asked Cornell about the emotional feeling she gets from dancing on pointe, her response mirrors how I, and likely many other female ballet dancers, feel about it:

> You would think that it would be, "I hate this. This is so painful. This is so awful." I still have dreams about dancing on pointe. The feeling is like no other in the world. Part of the reason why I wanted to start dancing in the first place was because I love to jump and I love the feeling when you're in the air—that split second—that takes your breath away. And then all of a sudden I got pointe shoes and it's like that but better. It's just standing in that fifth position, completely pulled up, you have a sense of every muscle in your body. It's an incredible feeling, despite all the pain, despite all the frustration. And I still miss it.

Feminist dance criticism has often focused its attention on the ballet genre, and the typical heterosexual and power relations that it often connotes. Ann Daly, Judith Lynne Hanna, Susan Leigh Foster, and Susan Brownmiller have all presented compelling arguments addressing how movement and dance reflect how women are regarded. Further, Laura Mulvey's discussions on issues relating to the gaze are also relevant and applicable.[7] The arguments presented by these women all build upon one another to provide a framework within which to explore how the pointe shoe helps to construct a gender analysis within the ballet genre. The underlying message of all these scholars is similar. "Traditional" ballets are often seen as presenting an old-fashioned, patriarchal hierarchy that has forced women into particular iconographical roles onstage and has suppressed feminine creative and administrative talents offstage. There have been few women ballet choreographers and artistic directors, and female dancers typically portray princesses and wronged lovers, relying (both in plot and choreography) on a man to arrive and support them. While it is true that males dominated the dance world of yore, this should not imply that all women were subservient either as dancers or as characters. It is interesting, therefore, to examine several theories relating to ballet, and ascertain how the pointe shoe, as the primary artefact of the female ballet dancer, fares under this particular microscope. Daly suggests,

> Dance classicism is an ideology devoted to tradition, chivalry, and to hierarchy of all kinds—gender, performer's rank, the distinction between types of roles, spectator's placement, stage organization, the canon. Romanticism's emphasis on personal expression also relies on the theatricalized dichotomy of feminine and masculine temperaments. (Daly 1997: 58)

Indeed, dancing on pointe can be regarded as ascribing to these notions, particularly when examining Classical or Romantic ballets. Certainly, the ability to dance on pointe (and to dance it well) indicates a gender difference—that is, males, in almost all instances, dance only in soft shoes. Cornell asserts that the legacy from the Romantic ballet pervades dance classes today:

> Taglioni is the epitome of ethereal, of unattainable, of hovering, even with the wires [that were supporting her] with the Sylphides [*Les Sylphides*]. And that establishes a classist idea in the dance studio that female dancers who can dance on pointe are somehow better than dancers who can't.... Teaching a couple of years ago, thirteen-, fourteen-, fifteen-year-old girls, the ones who couldn't dance on pointe, when we did that fifteen minutes at the end of class, were the saddest things on the face of the earth. They were so dejected. And somehow, rather ironically, somehow they weren't women because they couldn't dance on pointe but the perfect woman who dances on pointe really looks like a boy anyway, if you think of the Balanchine aesthetic that goes with it. So I think definitely, established from 1830s onwards, there're two types of dancers: ones who can dance on pointe and ones who can't.

This ultimate symbol of femininity in dance, the pointe shoe continues to infiltrate the soul of even the most spirited and feminist-minded young female dancer today. Furthermore, there is a certain class structure present in the professional dance world in that there are solo dancers, corps dancers, and character dancers. Character dancers rarely wear pointe shoes, and may wrongly be seen as less able dancers than those who are on pointe for the entire performance. The shoe is the signifier for the entire ballet canon.

It is also true that there are differences between male and female forms of dance. This is particularly evident when examining which steps are allotted to various dancers in the ballet. The pas de deux receives particular scrutiny. In her article entitled, "Classical Ballet: A Discourse of Difference," Daly discusses Romantic ballet's fondness for the grace and beauty of its dancers, particularly required of female dancers (Daly 1997: 61). Daly argues that stage dynamics in Romantic ballets consist of males denoting power and females denoting fragility. This leads to an asymmetry, the two polarities of which create the balance in the male–female relationship onstage (Daly 1997: 59). Hanna also raises the notion of the pas de deux as the penultimate representation of heterosexuality in dance. Furthermore, it reinforces two ideas: sexual proximity and tension between the two dancers, and (a more contemporary reading) a metaphor for the idea of romantic love (Hanna 1988: 166). The pointe shoe is the indicator of these heteronormative ideals that are inherent in these pieces. Through the shoe, the choreography is structured so that the pas de deux is the central item of a ballet, and gendered ideas are epitomized through the steps. The structure of the choreography of the pas de deux conforms to our prescribed notions of male–female relationships.

In her article "The Ballerina's Phallic Pointe," Susan Foster asserts that all bodies in dance are gendered, through their costuming as well as choreography.[8] She argues that the common dynamic on the stage is for the female to be presented to the audience by her male counterpart. "*He* and *she* do not participate equally in their choreographic coming together. *She* and *he* do not carry equal valence. *She* is persistently put forward, the object of his adoration" (Foster: 1996: 1). While this is the norm in the ballet genre as a whole, contemporary ballets can allow the female dancer to present a very different image on pointe.

Cornell presented these arguments from her own perspective:

> I think it has a lot to do with power relations and, when we're talking classical Petipa ballets, the woman is, with the pointe shoe, put on a pedestal and with the pas de deux, the man stands behind the woman and is always subservient to her dancing and to her style and to her raised position, with the pointe shoe doing that both metaphorically and physically. But then when you get into twentieth-century ballet, the pointe shoe takes on a different meaning for me. With Balanchine, the pointe shoe accentuates how beautiful the woman's leg is, and really adds a sensual line to the end of the foot because with the black bodysuits and the white tights, he just shows off the woman's leg and there's real arrogance in the way I think his women dance a lot of the time.... Then going into William Forsythe who extends the pointe shoe even more and ... again, the woman is really sensual, the woman is not the centre of attention like she is in Petipa, with the pointe shoe and the delicateness and the femininity, but she's strong, she uses the pointe shoe as an exclamation point. And I think the pointe shoe is pivotal to expressing the characters that happen in Forsythe ballets. But then, talking about the relationship between men and women and the shoes they wear, I think an important choreographer is Jyri Kylian, who doesn't put the women in pointe shoes and really, in his pas de deux, men lift men, women lift women, women lift men, and there's a real equality there, and again equality in shoes ... they wear the some shoes. So I think he's a really pivotal choreographer in terms of how gender is perceived through the shoe.

In this passage, Cornell provides an historical and thematic account of how footwear has evolved through several eras in the development of ballet as a dance style. The Romantic style of the 1800s epitomized lightness, grace, and ethereality, and the verticality of the pointe shoe emphasized these ideals. The contrast between the earthy, almost peasant-like, female character and her unattainable, supernatural counterpart evidenced what was considered desirable in terms of femininity. However, more recent and contemporary ballet choreographers have taken a different stance when it comes to representations of the woman through the pointe shoe. Be it the portrayal of women as strong characters, dancing solo on pointe (a difficult feat) or female dancers wearing soft slippers along with the men, equality and/or female dominance can now be found in many instances. The power dynamics are constantly shifting.

The issues of power relate well to Armstrong's assertion that "a very different problem is posed by the man-made thing or event which, while perhaps not having been created primarily for the purpose of being affecting, is nonetheless intentionally concerned with power, as an inevitable condition of being what it is" (Armstrong 1971: 6). These ideas accord well with the thoughts put forward by the feminist dance theorists. The pointe shoe is a symbol of power, regardless of how that power is seen to be wielded. Contemporary readings into the pas de deux do portray it as a stereotypical heterosexual dynamic. The woman leans on the man, who supports her and enables her to perform the steps that the audience sees. The shoes force her to depend on her partner, as she would be able to dance some of these steps on her own if she was wearing soft ballet slippers. With Foster's theory of the pointe shoe as phallus, this further pushes the patriarchal power imbalance. Conversely, some dance scholars believe that the ballerina's prominence, in terms of character importance and choreography, forces the male dancer to seem subservient (Clement and Crisp 1987: 52). Also, as I have argued, women dancing solo on pointe demonstrate their own strength and dominance on stage: the typical dynamic can be averted and a counter-hegemonic ideal can be achieved.

When discussing footwear for an art form that relies so heavily on the foot, body image and physical exertion must also be taken into consideration. Women's feet may he physiologically more suited to pointe shoes than men, but it is for a largely aesthetic reason that women are the ones who don the blocked toe and lace up the pink ribbons. Because of the constant weight and pressure on the foot, women who wear pointe shoes often have bloody feet, ingrown toenails, blisters, bunions, and other unpleasant side effects. Men's feet tend to suffer far less while wearing softer shoes. It is an interesting juxtaposition, then, that the pointe shoe is seen as a thing of beauty, elongating the foot and making it seem elegant:

Kate Cornell: And I think it's interesting that, having taught boys, and just seeing the way that male dancers consider their feet, I think there's this connotation that male feet are ugly. And the pointe shoe just makes the female foot so beautiful.

Kristin Harris Walsh: Especially because professional dancers have terrible feet anyway because of the pointe shoe.

KC: Yes, because of the pointe shoe. But as soon as you cover it up and put the pointe shoe on it, "Oh it's so beautiful, oh, it's so gorgeous, so feminine." But I think that men are really made to be conscious of their feet. Because you know those boots they wear, like in Romeo and Juliet, that almost hide their footwork, whereas the women with the tutus, or whatever dress really, accentuate the foot. And you're really drawn to the foot.

So the pointe shoe is the means by which female dancers can cover up the ugliness of their feet and, at the same time, draw attention to them. Costumes, particularly those that are short, emphasize the leg, which is elongated by the blocked toe of the pointe shoe. By sheathing the foot in delicate pink satin, the ballerina can execute steps, leaps, and turns while projecting the appropriate aesthetic. This is in direct contrast to male footwear, which can be seen to disguise the footwork that men are able to perform. Soft shoes subvert the male foot, allowing the audience's gaze to focus on the grandeur of his leaps and turns.

While ballet footwear contains these apparent gender differences, modern dance eradicates them by eliminating artificial footwear. Instead, it focuses on the foot itself as the shoe, resulting in an equality between men and women that is not found in traditional ballet.

Physically, dancing in bare feet is vastly different from dancing in shoes. Any kind of footwear creates a physical boundary between body and floor, resulting in a less intimate experience. However, technique in different dance styles tends to suit its prescribed shoes. Modern dance tends to be far more grounded and into the floor than the upward verticality of ballet. It is not unheard of, though, for ballet to be performed in bare feet. I asked Cornell about her feelings on this:

Ballet barefoot. Yeah, but not very often…. And I don't think it was until my grade 13 year when I first did modern that I realized the feeling you can't get unless you dance barefoot. But … I really haven't done … any ballet barefoot…. The thing that really bothers me, because I love to turn, is that I have so much trouble turning in a modern class because your feet sweat and then you stick to those plastic floors. It's just so frustrating, when you can do a triple easily in slippers, you can do a double with hardly any push at all in pointe shoes, and then you get in bare feet and it's like, "I can't get around in a single!"

For the exclusively ballet-trained dancer, the shoes can become an essential tool for the performance of particular steps. Cornell's experience seems similar to many others. Ballet dancers are used to ease in terms of friction on the floor, thereby enabling them to perform multiple turns with little effort in terms of push from the legs. Modern dance oftentimes relies on this friction as a part of both its technique and aesthetic. Any kind of crossover (that is, performing ballet in bare feet or performing modern in shoes) can result in emotional or physical discomfort on the part of the dancer.

The choice for modern dancers to perform barefoot is one that was born with the very notion of modern dance. In contrast to ballet's existence as a remnant from the French courts of the seventeenth century, modern dance originated in the United States and grew out of the idea that "it is not so much a system or technique as an attitude toward dance, a point of view that encourages artistic individualism and the development of personal choreographic styles" (Anderson 1992: 165). Early proponents of modern dance revolutionized not only choreography and vision, but also the dance uniform. Perhaps the most notorious of these women was Isadora Duncan, who shocked audiences by wearing loose tunics draped around her, and by dancing barefoot (Thomas 1995: 61). This led the way for numerous other modern artists who also advocated dancing in bare feet as a part of this new aesthetic. Also noteworthy is that most of the modern dance pioneers have been female. This has meant that women have been finally able to attain control of not only dancing but also of choreography and artistic direction. The truly revolutionized modern dance world stands in sharp contrast to the realm of ballet. Additionally, gender roles for men and women seemed more closely entrenched in ballet. As Novack writes of her own experiences with modern dance, "The movement vocabularies for individual women and men and for dancers interacting varied far more in modern dance than in ballet" (Novack 1993: 38). Modern dance, then, provides a far different set of values and expectations from ballet.

While others might place value judgments on one over the other, I hesitate to do so. I have practised both forms of dance and have found joy in both. I spent a short time training in modern dance, and enjoyed the grounded, solid feeling that performing in bare feet gave me. I felt as though it were a "natural" way to dance, feeling every muscle and bone in my foot contact with the floor and engage in a way that I had never felt before. I also love my soft ballet slippers. They are extremely comfortable to wear and provide enough traction so that I can dance without fear of falling, yet are slippery enough so that I can turn effectively and smoothly. These two artefacts symbolize the equality that can be present if only to create an illusion of femininity that is dance, as represented by the primary instrument through which to perform. These two types of footwear differ greatly to my final, and most personally controversial, article of dance shoes—my pointe shoes.

Intellectually, I understand that ballet is fraught with issues that I am used to confronting in daily life. There is a distinct gender inequality present, and men, for the most part still do run ballet companies. While the prima ballerina is often the centre of attention, one must acknowledge theories that show her in subordination to her male partner. And I do think that the way a dancer dances in a pointe shoe can reflect how the dancer feels about her body, her feet, and the choreography she is performing. It can be an extremely uncomfortable tool that functions for a dance performance, only to create an illusion of femininity that is unattainable for most women and is, in fact, essentially non-existent outside of the fantasy world of the stage. I easily relate to Cornell's comments about performing ballet, particularly dancing on pointe. I found it excruciatingly painful and eventually gave it up because of the strain it was putting on my body. There will always be a small part of me, though, that will remember the anticipation of tying the ribbons, of warming up the feet and finally, that perfect moment when every muscle is engaged and the potential is endless. This, to me, is the perfect indication of what footwear can mean to the individual who has donned it and what it can do for a dance performance. The ethnographic and autoethnographic aspects of this discussion show, on a personal level, how the dancer intellectually and emotionally reacts to what may seem to be a purely functional artefact. As illustrated through this discussion, the pointe shoe is indicative of gender and power, and indeed encapsulates the very symbol of ballet.

Notes

1 By "culture," I imply a dual meaning: culture of the dance form, as well as the larger culture in which the particular dance form exists.
2 I conducted a personal interview with Kate Cornell in the winter of 1998.
3 Dancers have developed alternative methods, or shortcuts, to bypass some of the more labour-intensive practices. For example, rather than darning the toe, a dancer may place a piece of moleskin, or a textured stick-on bandage, to provide the necessary friction rather than hem the ends to prevent fraying. Dancers often burn the ends of their ribbons to prevent fraying.

4   That is, a spectator who has danced in pointe shoes will likely better understand the pain and joy inherent in dancing on pointe, whereas someone who has never danced on pointe will tend to appreciate the dancing from a largely visually aesthetic point of view.

5   Most steps performed on full pointe, that is, on the platform of the toe shoe, can be performed on demi-pointe, on the ball of the foot in soft shoes. The effect and feel will be different, but it will usually be adequate for the dancer when rehearsing or marking choreography.

6   In this case, the society to which I am referring is the dance world.

7   Mulvey's writings deal with the visual, and are often used to discuss film and visual arts. In order to fully appreciate her arguments, it is useful to be familiar with Jacques Lacan's theories on the gaze as well.

8   The pointe shoe can be regarded as a part of dance costuming as well as a tool for the achievement of technique.

Bibliography

Anderson, Jack (ed.). *Ballet and Modern Dance: A Concise History*, 2nd ed. Princeton, NJ: Princeton Book Company Publishers, 1992: 165.

Armstrong, Robert Plant. *The Affecting Presence*. Urbana: University of Illinois Press, 1971: 6.

Babcock, Barbara. "Artifact." In Richard Bauman (ed.), *Folklore, Cultural Performances* and *Popular Entertainments*. New York: Oxford University Press, 1992: 204–17.

Berger, Arthur Asa. *Cultural Criticism*. London: Sage, 1995: 91.

Clarke, Mary, and Clement Crisp. *Ballerina: The Art of Women in Classical Ballet*. London: BBC Books, 1987: 52.

Daly, Ann. "Classical Ballet: A Discourse of Difference." In Jane Desmond (ed.), *Meaning in Motion: New Cultural Studies of Dance*. Durham, NC: Duke University Press, 1997: 58.

Foster, Susan Leigh. "The Ballerina's Phallic Pointe." In Susan Leigh Foster (ed.), *Corporealities: Dancing, Knowledge, Culture and Power*. London and New York: Routledge, 1996: 1.

Hanna, Judith Lynne. *Dance, Sex and Gender*. Chicago: University of Chicago Press, 1988: 166.

Mulvey, Laura. *Visual and Other Pleasures*, 2nd ed. London: Palgrave Macmillan, 2009.

Novack, Cynthia. "Ballet, Gender and Cultural Power." In Helen Thomas (ed.), *Dance, Gender and Culture*. New York: St. Martin's Press, 1993: 36.

Thomas, Helen. *Dance, Modernity and Culture*. London: Routledge, 1995: 61.

Embodying Autoethnographies

CHAPTER SIX

Writing, Dancing, Embodied Knowing

AUTOETHNOGRAPHIC RESEARCH

KAREN BARBOUR

INTRODUCTION

I invite you to come on a journey with me as I move through a busy spring day in Aotearoa, New Zealand, leaping and stumbling between my shifting responsibilities as dancer, researcher, feminist, and writer. Negotiating both the university environment and my own movement landscape, I share my experiences in embodied knowing (Barbour 2004, 2006, 2011) through dance-making, and reflect on some of my challenges in writing and dancing.

By way of introduction to my story, I briefly mention here some of my most influential sources of research and methodological inspiration. But this is a brief mention, because rather than outlining the nature of dance as a lived experience (Fraleigh 1987) and the value of feminism and phenomenology for dance research (Barbour 2005, 2011; Fraleigh 1987, 1993, 2000), I seek instead to demonstrate my theorizing in an autoethnographic narrative of the self (Richardson 1998) or personal experience narrative (Barbour 2001b, 2002).

In my narrative, I situate myself as the author and use my first-person experiential dancer's voice and researcher's voice (Denison and Markula 2003; Ellis and Bochner 2000; Fraleigh 2000; Richardson 1998), attempting to shrink the distance between us—myself the writer, and you the reader (Ellis and Flaherty 1992). I share Jim Denison and Pirkko Markula's narrative intention that "the author is alive and well in these [autoethnographic] tales, born to speak, feel, and reflect openly through his or her memories, self-talk, recollections, dreams, and conversations" (2003: 25).

I use literary techniques in my writing to develop coherence, verisimilitude, and interest (Denison and Markula 2003; Richardson 1998), as opposed to being concerned about traditional research expectations of reliability and validity. Through my choice of vivid and visceral words, I aim to stimulate kinaesthetic empathy (Barbour 2011; Foster 1995; Stinson 1995) using thick descriptions, texture, flow, and resonance. As Laurel Richardson commented, "Using dramatic recall, strong metaphors, images, characters, unusual phrasings, puns, subtexts, and allusions, the writer constructs a sequence of events, a 'plot,' holding back on interpretation, asking the reader to 'relive' the events emotionally with the writer" (Richardson 1998: 356). So join with me as I leap and stumble through today.

Bodies still warm from contemporary dance class, Margaret and I relax cross-legged in large chairs outside the campus café. With the spring sun brightening the day, birds chattering, and a stream of oblivious students flowing past, we sip our coffees. We reflect quietly together, Margaret sharing her insights from this morning's breathing exercises. Her gestures and animated expression tell me much about how she values small movement revelations. Our discussion turns to sharing other treasured moments, like when suddenly a previously abstract movement concept becomes meaningful in the repetition of a dance exercise. These moments of insight make the discipline of dance class and attention to small details in movement all worthwhile, we agree. Languidly stretching my legs and sliding into the chair further, I meditate on breathing exercises and the positive effect they can have on my whole day. As a childhood asthmatic, free-flowing breath when I dance is something I value and consciously attend to. Our conversation slows and we slip into companionable silence, enjoying the fresh air and warmth.

Snapping me out of my dreaming, Margaret asks, "So how are you getting on at university, Karen?" in her characteristically direct manner. I sigh. "Well, I'm just trying to get through this semester, and to find some time to write an autoethnographic paper. And I have meetings and dance classes to prepare and ..." Margaret interrupts me before I get too far through my list. "You know, I think you need to take some time to refresh yourself and create some new movement. I worry that choreographically you are not allowing yourself enough time for play and movement exploration, especially as you want to continue developing your solo. I'm the same, too, but I reckon you need to have some fun investigating and searching for those new understandings in your own body, and ..." Perhaps seeing the expression on my face, she lets her sentence tail off. I am both challenged by, and a little despairing, hearing Margaret's perspective. More animatedly, she continues, "Well, you know, what is the point if you are not dancing? It is you who keeps telling me that you're not just being a dance researcher at a desk." "Yeah, I know. You are probably right," I reply with another sigh. I drink my coffee, collecting my thoughts, and am about to respond further ... but suddenly Margaret exclaims, "Sorry—it's five to eleven already! I've got to go catch my bus," and she leans over to hug me. We agree to meet next week after dance class, and then she strides away across campus. I stretch and reluctantly gather together my teaching notes, CDs, and books. Sighing again, I realize there is no point in citing the looming deadlines for my written dance research, meetings and planning to Margaret. She speaks from a position I once occupied, too: that of a full-time dancer. And while still having to balance income with intermittent dance work, Margaret does have the freedom to prioritize improvisation in a way I no longer can. When we were training together as dancers we were taught that we should use focused improvisation in the studio to search the depths of our experience for new motifs. This was the accepted Western dance creative process that we dutifully followed, trawling our emotional depths each time we created a dance. But now as a dance researcher, balancing writing time at my computer, teaching, improvisation, and structured rehearsals is always a challenge. I wonder whether there might be a more sustainable creative process for me to explore now that I have more life experience to directly inform my choreography (Barbour 2006). Nursing the remainder of my coffee, I walk briskly to my office, barely noticing the new blossoms scattering the path with each fresh gust of wind. Lost in memories, I drift into my last solo performance ...

> Lying still ... breath flowing smoothly in and out ... weight and tension releasing as I lie on my side on the wood. The sound of waves rolling against a distant shore fills me, and then warps slowly into a rhythm as my sound score unfolds. Rehearsing my solo dance, each time beginning with this meditation ... but each time it is slowly eroded by a deep base sound. Eventually, the sound warps further, the deep base resounding in my centre and pushing me into movement ... twisting, tying myself in knots and attempting to untangle myself. I'm forced from relaxation into a state of uncomfortable awareness. I roll to crouch, twist up and then turn to collapse. And then twisting to sitting again, faint voices in my memories: "instinct rather than reason came to my rescue." Searching to define my own truth, frustrated by the contradictions. Desiring to share my struggle, I open my awareness to the audience. My arms lock my torso, restricting my breath

and then lift to unwind so I can breathe deeply, and then my struggle continues as I travel across the wooden floor. Staggering as though carrying a heavy burden of care, worry, responsibility, expectation, loss. Contradiction overwhelms me, hindering my movement as I search for a resolution to the tension between the dominant stories I'd been told since childhood about what it was to be a woman, and the flickering instincts I nurture privately. Trying to let my tension go as I cross and uncross my arms. Finding more and more chances to breathe deep. I slowly unload my heavy burden to the floor and step back from it as though to see it for what it is. Feminism has helped me to see this burden and to realize it is time to let it go. Finally succeeding, my lungs expand and I draw a full breath at last. I step back and turn to the audience, vulnerable, but able to breathe.

Leaving behind my burden and walking gently across the stage, my eyes draw me out into the space, desiring to communicate with the watching audience and to explore my differently nuanced world. Fluidly moving, finding joy in unwinding and loosening my limbs and muscles, I explore space. Meditatively, my arms register gravity, swing gently and I turn, as though in slow motion. I thread my arms through each other, reach out, suspend and fall into the floor. A held breath, wood under my shoulders and then hands, before I uncurl and my feet take responsibility again. I respond in movement to gravity and momentum, embodying my intention to explore space, dynamic, freedom and release. Enjoying moving outside my normal movement patterns, I feel empowered. I dance through suspension and release to a state of calm and centeredness. Now I find myself. I open my heart and my lungs to space. I feel. I reach my limbs as though compass points from my centre, extending my imagination out to the audience, beyond the performance venue to my family and friends, deep into the flesh and blood of the land, and across the seas to my ancestors. I heal myself as I dance, allowing my own breath and sense of flow and dynamic to emerge. From where I stand, I send my imagination out. I resolve my embodiment in the here and now of performance, in relation to others and to the world. I stand tall and strong and I dream myself anew. (Barbour 2001b: 5–6)

Abruptly drawn out of my reverie I arrive at the end of the path through the trees. The university buildings loom over me, and I negotiate my way through throngs of students rushing out. Inside, I slip through a gap in a cue of students waiting to collect assignments, flinging greetings as I pass people I know. Making it to the elevator just before the doors close, I gratefully squeeze myself into a cluster of staff returning from their morning tea break. Catching a glimpse of myself in the elevator mirror, I hurriedly adjust my layers of comfortable clothes and retie my hair. Next to these tidily dressed lecturers, my dance clothes and open shoes mark me out-wardly as different from my colleagues.

Recalling Margaret's comments over coffee, I sense that she is right. I spent many hours while first developing my solo dance—exploring and articulating my experiences of knowing in movement. But I haven't had time to work this way recently and I want to extend my solo even more. It is embodied knowing, after all, that I acknowledge as most important for me (Barbour 2004, 2011). As my research continues, I realize again that I actually experience embodied knowing as an epistemological strategy. Embodied knowing allows me to appreciate that knowledge is contextual and experiential, not universal. I experience myself as a creator of, and as embodying, knowledge. This perspective has allowed me to value my own experiential ways of knowing rather than being limited to the narrow, typical Western perspective of knowing as rationalization. Somehow, I've always felt that it was important for me to reconcile accepted academic strategies for knowing with my own embodied strategies (Barbour 2002, 2011). I know that I must critically explore the *knowledges* that I feel are intuitively important with knowledges I have learned from other research-ers and theorists, and be consciously aware as I integrate and embody these knowledges. In this way, I can meaningfully weave different knowledges together with my passions, experiences, and embodied individuality in my life (Barbour 2011).

Escaping the elevator and unlocking my office, I almost stand on my copy of Ann Albright's book (1997), slid under my door by a friend. Albright's discussion on femininity in contemporary dance encouraged me to reflect on how I choreograph myself as a solo dancer. As a competitive sportswoman, I benefit from sporting strength and aerobic fitness, but I never fitted the stereotypical dancer body image. I sometimes struggle to feel confident as a dancer next to some of my thinner, more delicate peers. To help liberate myself from my own judgments, I try to focus on the expe-rience of dancing instead of observing my image in the mirror. Smiling, I remember delving deep into my own movement habits, trying to move away the confines of my previous technique training toward a more per-sonalized movement vocabulary. For me, this process began with recogniz-ing the dominance of Western dance body images and associated training practices, imported from Europe and North America, and the impact of these on my body and creativity. Here in the South Pacific I am surrounded by dancers of amazing expressive capability, substantially different embodi-ments, and who train in community practices that are completely counter to Western stereotypes. Respected feminine, virtuoso performers in Maori dance and Kapa Haka, or in Samoan Siva (as examples), are more likely to be mature, voluptuous Maori or Samoan women than young, petite white women. These women typically dance throughout their lives as part of family and community activities, and their training practices are part of everyday activity rather than learned from a paid, private studio teacher. So I have been influenced by these substantial women and by the perception of dance as integral to family and community life. Nevertheless, as a white feminist choreographing in the broad genre of contemporary dance, I do need to explore Western analyses of dance while retaining an awareness of the need to critique their dominance over me. As a result, I read with relish many sources on women and femininity in dance and attempt to explore an expanded norm of femininity in my dance practice (Albright 1997).

Deep in thought, I recall how Albright discusses dancers she calls "techno bodies" (1997)—highly muscular women whose bodies crossed over gender norms. I was interested in her example of contemporary dancer Louise Lecavalier (from the Canadian company La La La Human Steps), a dancer I had only seen pictures of, but who seemed to have extraordinary musculature and strength. Obviously, Lecavalier was of interest to me because of her embodiment, and I was inspired by successful women dancers whose bodies seemed to challenge feminine norms in shape, size, and muscle mass (Albright 1997). I flick open Albright's book to marked pages and read again how Lecavalier "creates an intense physicality that both literally and figuratively crosses over gender norms, even in the midst of a cultural moment in which both men and women are encouraged to cultivate a muscularly defined look in their bodies" (Albright, 1997: 29). Curiously, though, Albright also writes that she saw a slippage between the actual strength and muscularity of Lecavalier's body and the way in which she continued to perform stereotypical femininity in this particular role with La La La Human Steps (Albright 1997). I feel that Albright's main point is that while contemporary dance training might encourage the development of a fit, muscular body, this sort of body might not actually result in alternative femininity if the dancer continues (or is required by a choreographer) to perform stereotypical feminine behaviour and roles in choreography. I reflect: How might this analysis inform my own choreographic representations?[1]

Considering Albright's analysis further, I recall that she was drawn to Iris Young's phenomenological research on the modalities of feminine movement (1997). Young's work is also one of my favourites for the way in which she validates doing research specifically on women's movement. Young argues that girls and women exhibit typical feminine movement characteristics in activities such as throwing a ball (Young 1980); what she rather abstractly named *ambiguous transcendence, inhibited intentionality*, and *discontinuous unity*. Reading again from Albright, she summarizes Young's research:

> By analysing the ways that young girls and women are trained *not* to take up the space around them, *not* to use the capacity of their whole body in engaging in physical activity, and *not* to fully project their physical intentions onto the world around them, Young describes the tensions inherent in experiencing one's body as a thing and as a capacity for action, both as passive subject and as active subject. (Albright 1997: 47)

So, adding Young's research into her analysis, Albright then argues that, despite Lecavalier's muscular, atypical woman's body, she actually continued to exhibit the existential ambiguity of feminine movement and bodily comportment. I interpret this to mean that in performance, Lecavalier moved her body as a series of disconnected parts, and often without clear spatial intention. Referring again to my well-marked book, I see that Albright says in conclusion, "While her built-up body radically challenges a conventionally feminine body or movement style, Lecavalier's disconnected intentionality reinforces her traditionally gendered role within the spectacle" (Albright 1997: 50). I reflect to myself that Lecavalier is an extraordinary performer, and I wonder what choices she might make in representing herself as a woman, perhaps in her own choreography. Just looking physically different from the stereotypical image of women isn't enough to make a clear statement to challenge this image. So I realize I need to be more choreographically explicit in representing myself and more overt in trying to expand the norm of dancing for women.

Continuing to reread this interesting analysis, I see that Albright then considers the choreographic and performance work of dancer Jennifer Monson in relation to Young's research on the modalities of feminine movement. Monson seems to use physical dance as a basis for her choreographed and improvisational performances, rather than as display of female strength and muscularity. Albright interprets Monson's movement very differently from Lecavalier's movement. Highlighted in my book is Albright's description of Monson's dancing. Perhaps there is something in this description that can help me in my own dancing. I read how Albright describes Monson.

Because her whole body is affected by her movement, she seems to ride the currents of the air around her, emphasising the spatial flow of her dancing rather than directly placing her limbs in a shape. This clarity of weight, spatial intention, and movement flow allow Monson to dance in an explosive, raw manner that is both physically subtle and pleasurably rambunctious. She is strong but contained. (Albright 1997: 50)

Without being able to see Monson perform live, I'm left here imagining what this might actually mean. While Monson is obviously strong and powerful, she doesn't seem to have either a fierce aerobicized physicality or a lithe feminine delicacy. Monson is not deliberately resisting stereotypical femininity, but according to Albright she is dancing an expanding norm of feminine movement through her explorations. For these reasons, Albright writes that Monson's dancing is responsive, enduring, able to accommodate change, and can offer the audience a more profound connection with her dancing experience (Albright 1997). These are characteristics I might use to describe some inspiring women in Maori dance—as dancers, they are responsive to the audience and to other performers around them, enduring in the dance form, able to accommodate changes while maintaining the intent of the performance, and able to offer me a more profound connection with their experiences. In addition, some of the women in New Zealand contemporary dance who I most admire also embody these characteristics—they are mature women in their fifties who integrate improvisation and choreography in real time, engage personally with their audiences through courageously sharing lived experiences, and respond to audiences in the moment of performing solo.[2] Of course, there are also plenty of vacuous, thin, young, dance technicians who leap about on our stages, too. But I'm never much moved by their dancing or convinced that they have something to share with me beyond the act of leaping itself. As always, I remind myself that I need to explore and attempt to embody such ideas as Albright identifies in choreographing and performing myself. I wonder what "sweaty truths" might be revealed to me for my research.

But actually, there are some practical issues in applying Young's work (1980), because she bases her understandings on Merleau-Ponty's account of body comportment, motility, and spatiality—an account he developed from male experiences of movement (of course). And Merleau-Ponty's instrumentalist view of the person, in which he sees the person "as subject is a purposive actor, with specific objectives it moves out into the world to accomplish" (Young 1998: 298), may not actually be applicable to women's experiences of movement in the world. The "instrumentalist-purposive model of action privileges plan, intention, and control. These are attributes of action most typical of masculine-coded comportment and activities" (Young 1998: 288–289). So, in this sense, Young assumes a masculine model of action for women's movement. I know that feminists such as Elizabeth Grosz (1994; Young 1998) have pointed out that the application of masculine models of experience to women's movement experience is inappropriate—a point I acknowledge, too.

However, I still think that there is value for feminists (as Albright demonstrates) in considering Young's (1980, 1998) work as it relates to women's contemporary dance. But a more appropriate understanding of feminine modalities of movement could be developed. In later research, Young (1998) herself asks whether feminine movement might be understood differently by looking for "specifically feminine forms of movement that cannot be brought under the unifying instrumentalist model but are nevertheless about work or accomplishing goals" (Young 1998: 289). Rather than looking for plan, intention, and control in women's movement, Young asked, "What might a phenomenology of action look like which started from the mundane fact that many of us, especially women, often do several things at once?" (Young 1998: 289) A provocative question indeed. It seems to me that dance-making is an ideal context to explore movement that is about work and intention, though not necessarily about identifiable plans, singular intentional activity, or control. Smiling, I remember my colleague Raewyn Thorburn in her solo performance *Sensual Ensemble* (1997), peeling potatoes on stage and talking to the audience while dancing (Barbour 2002; Barbour and Thorburn 2002). She demonstrated in this solo how she tried not to differentiate between dancing and her everyday life. I'm often engaged in several things at once in my everyday life, too—writing, dancing, researching, and teaching. But what might this mean specifically for me when I am creating dance? Can I be choreographing while writing or walking about the campus?

After returning Albright's book to my shelf, I make myself comfortable, drawing my chair away from the desk so I can stretch my legs long. As though readying myself for a ritual, I place fresh notepaper and pens at arm's length to make notes, and close my eyes to focus my thoughts on my recent dancing experiences. Reflecting back on my solo, I recall that my improvisational practices and choreographic strategies had revealed a range of movements for selection. One of the intentions I had in choosing movement was to express and understand my lived experiences. Sometimes, though, I chose movement because I specifically wanted to enhance kinaesthetic empathy with my experiences. Using everyday, pedestrian, and gestural movement I knew that sometimes I was able to evoke a physical response in others, just as yawning (and even reading or writing about yawning) can sometimes evoke a yawn in others. Playing with ways to subvert and resist audience expectations of what I would do as "the dancer" was also fun to try, though I often found it difficult to actually achieve this in performance. And the same movement could also serve to challenge or change stereotypical feminine movement and movement qualities. I make some notes of examples for reference later. I did begin my solo performance by sleeping on stage—hoping to subvert the typical audience–performer relationship and resist their expectations of me as dancer/performer. But sleeping also worked to help me to relax, breathe, and prepare myself for performance. With sleeping and then more specific gestural movement, I was able to expand the possibilities of what might constitute "dance" movement to include pedestrian or everyday movement, potentially enhancing kinaesthetic empathy with my experience. And on another level, I was also inviting the audience to watch me, and yet refusing to acknowledge the audience in the same moment. With these examples in mind, I can see how multiplicity may already be a feature of my solo movement, just like it is in my everyday life.

I value multiplicity in my movement as I also value the way in which my dance-making processes allow me to be both receptive and responsive to my lived experiences. One of my earliest teachers, Alison East, introduced me to environmentally responsive dance by encouraging me to open my awareness and to allow sounds, smells, visual stimuli, and sensations from the natural world to be cues for movement improvisation (East 2001, 2007). When performing in the theatre, I also aim to receive and integrate information from multiple sources, including moment-to-moment changes and understandings developed during performing, audience responses, events in my life, and choreographed and rehearsed movement (Sheets-Johnstone 1999). Responding to these multiple influences in whatever manner I feel appropriate while performing is the fun, and also scary, part. I give myself the opportunity to improvise, adapt, and respond, both thinking *in* and *about* movement as I dance (Sheets-Johnstone 1999). Rather than creating a fixed singular plan, finding control and singular intention, I have moments when I experience multiplicity in intention, and receptivity and responsiveness in dancing my solo. So really, as I dance, I experience modalities of feminine movement alternative to those Young outlined. My movement does not always reflect an instrumentalist (and masculinist) model of action (Young 1998). Instead, my dancing can embody my individual ways of expressing and coming to understand myself. This is a much more empowering, life-giving, and self-sustaining process for me, than just performing choreography repetitively. It also allows me to move outside the constraints and expectations of feminine movement (at least sometimes),

Figure 1   Karen Barbour in *Fluid Echoes Dance*, 2007. Photographer: Cheri Waititi.

and to value intuition and sensation. Instead of merely valuing movement with identifiable plans and structure, then, I can privilege improvisation and play in dance.

Knock knock! "Karen, are you coming to our staff meeting?" Brought immediately back to the reality of administrative responsibilities, I make a mental note to return to my examples, and to these inspirations for further movement investigation. For now, I gather my diary and notes and join my colleague Mere outside the meeting room. "I'll be glad when this semester is over," my peer comments, smoothing her hair and adjusting her shawl before we enter. We congregate with the rest of the staff, grumbling to each other about looming deadlines and delays in textbook orders. I slouch into my chair around the table, and while the meeting is under way I catch myself drifting back into recollections of dancing … air brushing my face, muscles contracting and lengthening with a jump, my heart full of that special sweaty elation …

Suddenly desperate to stretch, I spend a couple minutes trying to unwind my legs and lengthen my back. I get disapproving sidelong looks from a couple of peers, but most are used to my dancerly ways by now. While they debate the merits of various software packages, I whisper quietly to Mere, "I hope you can come to our work-in-progress seminars next month. We have all made real breakthroughs and I want to dance this time, instead of giving a typical seminar." "I doubt I'll make it along, Karen. I've got too much to do myself," Mere whispers back. At the end of the meeting, when I extend the same invitation to the rest my peers, I am met with similar responses.

Later in the day, I sit surrounded by my creative journals containing scrawled reflections on choreography, favourite poems and images, and my blurred attempts to recreate and represent my embodied experiences in words. Piles of texts rise precariously on the floor beside me, threatening to tip as I carefully transfer my body weight to stretch my other hamstring. Surely, there must be a place for these different types of poetic and academic writing in my contribution to *Fields in Motion*. Feeling the pressure to find a place from which to begin writing, as well as mounting heat in my hamstring, I flick through pages of journals. One page falls open to words penned in purple ink: "Each word brighter-bodied for the shadow of the ones we did not say—this is after all the edited life to cut, to prune, select, is my profession ..." (Edmond 1986: 49). Inspired by this fragment from New Zealand poet Lauris Edmond (1986), I had edited and selected experiences in my own life as I began developing my solo dance. As I choreographed my dance, it became apparent to me that I could experiment with dancing an expanded norm of femininity (Albright 1997). It was such an exciting period, and I busied myself in the dance studio for days at a time. I used poems, personal experiences, ongoing reflection, as well as research texts to stimulate my dance-making. It seems to me that the choreographic process of dance-making allowed me to bring personal experiences and research interests together to explore new relationships, juxtapositions, and connections between them. I recall a quote about choreographic process from Australian dance writer Elizabeth Dempster:

The process allows me to bring together in a kind of laboratory, un-alike, incompatible ideas, activities, objects, so that they are held in temporary, sometimes strained relationship. And through this intensification connections which were at first only dimly sensed are revealed. These dances are ... a process of discovery. (Dempster, cited in Gardner and Dempster 1990: 46)

Breathing deeply and relaxing my shoulders, I remind myself that just as in dance-making, I can draw together different sources of inspiration for writing—my theoretical readings, creative and poetic writings, and my dancing experiences—and explore how these materials relate through the practice of writing. Laurel Richardson wrote that writing can be a process of discovery, a process of becoming (1998). I wonder how I can use my dancerly knowing to inform my writing, to help my readers empathize with my research experiences, and to engage them in my lived experiences. Upending the nearest pile of papers, I search for an article I particularly love by dance educator Susan Stinson (1995). She had written somewhere about how choreography informed her writing. Pages worn and covered in notes and underlining, I locate my much-read copy and find the section in which Stinson describes how both choreographers and researchers (and other creative artists, such as poets) select a compelling idea, collect material that seems relevant, focus in detail on all the material to explore relationships, and eventually find ways to make meaning from the process. My eyes are drawn to another underlined block of text, in which Stinson writes that it is the kinaesthetic sense that helps us to understand when we watch movement: "[It helps us] to go inside the dance, to feel ourselves as participants in it, not just as onlookers" (Stinson 1995: 43). Sensing I am on to something interesting, I cross my legs and reach to rummage through my books and papers for writings by Sandra Fraleigh (2000), Jim Denison and Pirkko Markula (2003), and Laurel Richardson (1998). Perhaps I can try writing more kinaesthetically, writing my own autoethnography as a dancer knows the world—full of embodied experience and breath—rather than as a disembodied researcher?

It is not until my muscles scream an hour later that I realize I have reread much of the relevant writing and I need to move on. Stretching slowly, blood recirculating to my toes and into my hip creases, I dig for my office keys, lock the door, and run down the stairs. Puffing, I race past the fifth floor, the third floor, and finally to ground level outside. Now I slow down and inhale the fresh late-afternoon air. Mulling over ideas, I meander across the fields and around the lake, digesting. Just as when I'm improvising in the dance studio to find that satisfying transition between movements, I am walking to search for some flow in my ideas for this autoethnography.

Walking slowly in front of me is the familiar shape of my friend Mere, clad in a flowing green shawl. I hear her humming as I speed up to join her and she smiles in greeting. "Hi, Mere. Nice to catch up with you again today. Are you walking somewhere and can I join you?" "Actually, I'm just taking a break from preparing my research proposal seminar for next week. Let's walk together." Peering closely at me, she remarks with concern, "You look how I feel, Karen. What's up, girl?" I rub my brow and then try to articulate my frustrations, explaining, "Well, you know how I've got this narrative to write? I'm a bit stuck. I think I know what ideas I want to convey, but I can't quite see how to make all the links between the ideas. And I want to write myself into the chapter, as a character in a story, so that readers can relate to my challenges being here at university. I find it hard being a dancer and trying to express in words what I know in moving." "Yeah—I think I know what you mean," replies Mere. "And being a feminist," I continue, "I'm ultimately critical of the ways in which 'knowledge' has been defined in these places. But I also know that universities are

113

supposed to uphold 'knowledge' and tell us the ways in which we should represent our research knowledge. Do you know what I mean?" Mere sighs and replies sympathetically, "Yes, I do understand. In my work, I'm trying to find words to describe ancient songs that just don't 'translate' into English words—they are beautiful, poetic, and meaningful, but so much more has to be understood about why the songs are sung to appreciate the words. My translations just seem to lose the poetics. I feel like I'm ruining these songs I love. It's hard, all right."

Following the stony path, we discuss various options for representing our research, breathing in the cooling air and walking slowly in step together. "For me, I need to be moving to make sense of the theory I've been reading and the research I've done. I guess it is the same with you and singing. And yet when I discover relationships and connections between ideas as I dance, and then figure out how these ideas are relevant in my everyday life, I struggle to articulate my revelations. It's like these sweaty understandings fail to be communicated in words. Writing narratives helps I think, but what my context or scene is for this autoethnography, I'm yet to discover." Swinging my arms loosely at my sides and rolling my shoulders, I reflect and listen for Mere's response. She stops suddenly, lightly touching my shoulder. "But what about writing just what you've told me. You could write about talking as we walk, and being frustrated and all. And, hey, I could even be a character in your story!" Laughing together, we continue walking. Mere sings gently under her breath as we stroll up the rise away from the lake. There is a crisp feel to the afternoon air, and a familiar scent—the blossoms under our feet, I think. Actually, Mere's suggestion is perfect—I could even write about my whole day, about coffee with Margaret and her reminder to keep investigating movement as I continue my research. And meeting Mere and reading in my office ... a day-in-the-life scenario, perhaps. Suddenly, I sense the narrative, like those glimpses of choreography I get sometimes—little visions of what might be expressed. Now I know where to begin.

Mere's singing tails off and she pauses in her step. "Karen, what about if I share that song I was just singing as part of the presentation of my research proposal next week? What do you think?" "Perfect! That will show them! We have to keep our passion for movement and song at the centre of our research. What better way to begin your proposal!" "On that note," Mere grins, "I think I will just run and finish my presentation. I'll see you tomorrow, girl." We hug in parting and I cheerfully retrace my steps back to my office, still strewn with papers and books. I dig out a dance poster, and scrawl on the back in purple ink, noting ideas, adding arrows and links, and

Figure 2 Karen Barbour in *Nightshade,* directed by Sue Cheesman, 2007. Photographer: Cheri Waititi.

thinking about how to bring my world alive on the page. Sighing happily this time, I pin my visual outline of ideas on the wall.

Glancing at the clock, I realize that if I leave right away, I will have a whole hour left to play in the dance studio. And I can just use today's insights as a beginning point for my improvisation. I bet the studio is empty now ...

Notes

1 Sections of this narrative draw from my doctoral thesis (Barbour 2002) and have subsequently been developed into chapters in my book (Barbour 2011).

2 Jan Bolwell (2000a, 2000b), Alison East (1996, 2001), Bronwyn Judge (1998), and Raewyn Thorburn (1997; Barbour and Thorburn: 2002) are mature New Zealand performers whom I would characterize in this way. Each of these women participated in my doctoral research exploring women's solo contemporary dance (Barbour 2002; also see Barbour 2005).

Bibliography

Albright, Ann Cooper. *Choreographing Difference: The Body and Identity in Contemporary Dance*. Hanover, NH: Wesleyan University Press, 1997.

Barbour, Karen. *Dancing across the Page: Narrative and Embodied Ways of Knowing*. Bristol, UK: Intellect Books, 2011.

———. "Embodied Engagement in Arts Research." *International Journal of the Arts in Society* 1, no. 1 (2006): 85–91.

———. "Beyond Somatophobia": Phenomenology and Movement Research. *Junctures. Journal of Thematic Dialogue* 5 (2005): 35–51.

———. "Embodied Ways of Knowing." *Waikato Journal of Education* 10 (2004): 227–38.

———. "Researching Embodied Ways of Knowing in Women's Solo Dance." In Jan Bolwell (ed.), *Tirairaka: Dance in New Zealand*. Wellington, NZ: Wellington College of Education, 2003.

———. "Embodied Ways of Knowing. Women's Solo Contemporary Dance in Aotearoa, New Zealand." Unpublished doctoral thesis, University of Waikato, 2002.

———. *This Is After All the Edited Life*. Hamilton, NZ: WEL Energy Trust Academy of Performing Arts, October 10, 2001a.

———. "Writing about Lived Experiences in Women's Solo Dance Making." In Pirkko Markula (ed.), *Danz Research Forum Proceedings*. Hamilton, NZ: University of Waikato, 2001b: 1–6.

Barbour, Karen, and Charlotte Corner. "Own Path in *This Is After All the Edited Life*." Compact disc. Auckland, NZ: Charlotte 90, 2001.

Barbour, Karen, and Raewyn Thorburn. "Reconstructing Stereotypical Femininity in Women's Solo Dance-Making." *Australia New Zealand Dance Research Society Journal* (2002): 6–13.

Bolwell, Jan. *Off My Chest*. Mary Hopewell Theatre, Dunedin College of Education, Dunedin, NZ: September 15, 2000a.

———. "The Pink Nude." In Margaret Clark (ed.), *Beating Our Breasts: Twenty New Zealand Women Tell Their Breast Cancer Stories*. Auckland, NZ: Cape Catley, 2000b.

Denison, Jim, and Pirkko Markula (eds.). "Introduction: Moving Writing." In *Moving Writing: Crafting Movement in Sport Research*. New York: Peter Lang, 2003.

East, Alison. "Interweaving Philosophies of Dance Teaching and Dance-Making: What Can One Practice Teach the Other?" *Waikato Journal of Education* 13 (2007): 123–38.

————. "Making Dance as if the World Mattered. Eco-choreography: A Model for Dance Making and Dance Teaching in the 21st Century." In Pirkko Markula (ed.), *Danz Research Forum Proceedings, 2001*. Hamilton, NZ: University of Waikato, 2001.

————. "How Being Still Is Still Moving, in *Four Women Dance*." Watershed Theatre, Auckland, NZ: May 29–June 1, 1996.

Edmond, Lauris. "Camellias I: Femme de Letters, in *Seasons and Creatures*." Auckland, NZ: Oxford University Press, 1986.

Ellis, Carolyn, and Michael Flaherty (eds.). *Investigating Subjectivity: Research on Lived Experience*. Newbury Park, CA: Sage, 1992.

Ellis, Carolyn, and Arthur Bochner. "Autoethnography, Personal Narrative, Reflexivity: Researcher as Subject." In Norman Denzin and Yvonne Lincoln (eds.), *Handbook of Qualitative Research*. Thousand Oaks, CA: Sage, 2000: 733–68.

Foster, Susan Leigh. *Choreographing History*. Bloomington: Indiana University Press, 1995.

Fraleigh, Sandra. "Consciousness Matters." *Dance Research Journal* 32, no. 1 (2000): 54–62.

————. "Good Intentions and Dancing Moments: Agency, Freedom, and Self-Knowledge in Dance." In Ulric Neisser (ed.), *The Perceived Self: Ecological and Interpersonal Sources of Self-Knowledge*. Cambridge and New York: Cambridge University Press, 1993: 102–11.

————. *Dance and the Lived Body: A Descriptive Aesthetics*. Pittsburgh, PA: University of Pittsburgh Press, 1987.

Gardner, Sally, and Elizabeth Dempster. "Moving about the World: An Interview with Elizabeth Dempster." *Writings on Dance* 6 (1990): 41–48.

Grosz, Elizabeth. *Volatile Bodies: Toward a Corporeal Feminism*. Sydney, Australia: Allen and Unwin, 1994.

Judge, Bronwyn. *Housework*. Video available from B. Judge, P.O. Box 351, Oamaru, NZ. 1998.

Richardson, Laurel. "Writing: A Method of Inquiry." In Norman Denzin and Yvonne Lincoln, (eds.), *Collecting and Interpreting Qualitative Materials*. Thousand Oaks, CA: Sage, (1998): 345–71.

Sheets-Johnstone, Maxine. *The Primacy of Movement*. Amsterdam and Philadelphia: John Benjamins, 1999.

Stinson, Susan. "Body of Knowledge." *Educational Theory* 45, no. 1 (1995): 34–54.

Thorburn, Raewyn. "Sensual Ensemble." In *Dress Sense: A Night of Contemporary Dance and Sound Performance*. Auckland, NZ: Lopdell House, August 10, 1997.

Young, Iris Marion. "Throwing Like a Girl." In Iris M. Young (ed.), *Throwing Like a Girl*. Bloomington: Indiana University Press, 1980: 141–59.

CHAPTER SEVEN

The Body as a Living Archive of Dance/Movement

AUTOBIOGRAPHICAL REFLECTIONS

JANET GOODRIDGE

But suddenly, as she stood close against a pine tree and breathed in its sharp, bitter scent, a clear space opened to her childhood, as though a wind had sprung from the sea, clearing a mist. It was not a memory from the past, it was the past itself, as alive, as real; and she knew that she and the child of forty years ago were the same person. (Thomas 1999, orig. 1981: 190)

PREFACE: AN ONGOING PROCESS OF DISCOVERY

From the 1970s I was on an extended quest to develop my understanding of anthropology/ethnography in relation to dance/movement arts. I refer to this life process more fully later, but how and why did it begin? After twenty years of training and experience in arts subjects and performance participation, I wanted to expand my knowledge of performance arts world-wide and develop a deeper understanding of their significance in diverse cultural contexts. In 1970s England, dance anthropology did not yet exist as an academic discipline. My way in was through a two-year post-graduate diploma in social anthropology at the London School of Economics (LSE), which offered an appealing anthropology of art option. (Consistent with that training, I frequently use the term *anthropology* to include *ethnography* in this chapter.) I discovered cultural anthropology and ethnomusicology through reading, and then dance anthropology through meetings I sought with various people, especially in the United States. These meetings had a great influence.[1]

My approach always was and remains essentially eclectic. I have never been an anthropologist full-time, nor have I undertaken a prolonged period of fieldwork in an unfamiliar location. However, as a dance/movement-arts practitioner, with interest and experience in a range of contexts and styles, the study of anthropology has been a core influence in my life.

Until recently, my research and writing interests centred primarily on honouring the work of other people. However, for this chapter, I focus on aspects of my own experience, drawing on memories.[2] The original working title for this book was *Interpreting Ourselves*, and thus with that underlying theme still in mind, I am crossing a new threshold.

INTRODUCTION: THE DANCER'S LIVING ARCHIVE

I find that research on one subject often gives rise to research in a different direction. While preparing a paper for a Society of Dance History Scholars conference in 2002, which referred to modern dance in England from the 1930s to the 1950s, I recalled some of my own dance training from those years. At the conference, there were frequent references to many dance styles, several of which I had practised myself. This revived further memories. Perhaps with awareness heightened by the ambient buzz of conference events, impetus for a new study focus came suddenly, early one morning. I had an unusually intense sense of the different dance- and movement-arts styles and techniques experienced throughout my life, prompting an unexpected vision of my body as a living dance museum—an inner archive or repository of dance/movement-arts practice. This was a remarkable realization, and seemed akin to a series of distinctive layers or strata in rock formation, laid down over time. Although this is not entirely satisfactory as a descriptive metaphor for essentially living, vibrant body-movement experience, it relates to Connerton's suggestion about cultural memory that "the past is, as it were, sedimented in the body" (Connerton 1989: 98).

An interest in how memories may contribute to research in dance/performance was fired many years ago, when I first heard recordings of dance artist and choreographer Doris Humphrey speaking of her work.[3] I was instantly struck by the power of her words to transport me into her world and time. More recently, a British Museum exhibition, The Museum of the Mind: Art and Memory in World Cultures, inspired me. Exhibits revealed clusters of meanings associated with memory, and how this is linked with consciousness and a sense of self (Mack 2003). I already discern an influence from anthropology here—that is, knowledge of traditional cultures gleaned by Western anthropologists, notions of respect for elders, honouring ancestors, valuing oral knowledge. The idea of body-memory as a three-dimensional archive, with depth of knowledge retained, is especially relevant to honouring and learning from older dancers, worldwide. But that early-morning realization was in sensing and relating the concept to my own kinaesthetic experience.

KINAESTHETIC MEMORIES

I can stand up right now and do a Mexican folk dance for you! (Lisbeth Bagnold)[4]

Kinaesthetic memories may be of performances, dance/movement techniques, or styles. These may range from snapshot impressions to short or longer sequences of movement. Additionally, as cultural anthropologists, we are also interested in kinaesthetic-memory of movement behaviour learned in social and ritual contexts. All this may be considered as different forms or aspects of knowledge in the body, in tune with Gardner's "bodily kinaesthetic intelligence" (1993: 205–36). Farnell highlights the significance of memory in relation to body knowledge: "Memory [the past] remains with us, not only in words but also in our neuro-muscular patterning and kinaesthetic memories" (1999: 353).

Insights about human movement may be gathered from many sources. With reference to kinaesthetic memory, internationally renowned pianist John Lill has commented, "I've sometimes had the feeling that the fingers themselves are beginning to know what they are supposed to be doing."[5] In his approach to actors' expressive movement, theatre director Roose-Evans advocates "drawing from all the hand movements we have embedded in our memories" (1994: 126). Indeed, the process can be understood through movement patterns learned every day—from threading a needle to using a knife in the kitchen—and includes both expressive and symbolic gestures.

Perhaps dancers retain kinaesthetic memories of performances they have seen, due to a possibly heightened perception of movement. Drawing

Figure 1 Movement behaviour: preparing to participate in a Japanese tea ceremony (in a private home, Shikoku, Japan, 1993). Photographer: Françoise Carter.

on years of experience as both a dancer and a spectator, Steinman states, "Memory is embedded in our very act of seeing" (1986: 71). Furthermore, when watching a performance, it is not uncommon for dancers to respond synaesthetically, finding it "natural" to empathize physically and kinaesthetically with the action. Neuroscientists Daniel Glaser and colleagues have identified how dancers' learned movement is stored in the movement-control area of the brain as a "mirror system." Finely tuned to a dancer's skills, their research reveals that this "system" reacts and is reactivated, particularly when trained dance practitioners are observing dance styles with which they are familiar (Glaser 2004).

Conversations with several dancers have provided me with anecdotal impressions of dance memory. On dancers' observational memory, Mara de Wit commented, "It seems as if the observed movement registers in the body on a cellular level" (April 2005).[6] This perception was echoed in a further comment from Bagnold, who added, "The muscle memory is there; it's like a brain." She also emphasized her memory of dance spaces in the following way: "All kinaesthetically different ... it stays with you."

When focusing on my own kinaesthetic experience, my body-memory was initially of dance techniques, styles, steps, and spaces. Memories from my earliest days include dancing on the dark blue and beige square-patterned sitting-room carpet at home, with my mother at the piano—then class memories of revived Greek dance. These include some details of the syllabus such as the frieze-like arm positions derived from visual arts of ancient Greece, often chanted as we moved: "*straight line ... low V ... high V ... forward ... low oblique ... high oblique ... half-turn and scoop.*"[7] And my first performance (age 4) as a rosebud, at London's Fortune Theatre: "*I vividly recall my starting position, and the sensation of being unable to resist peering out at the auditorium from beneath crossed arms.*"[8]

DISCOVERING MY KEY THEMES

Preparing this chapter led me to take a wider view of my experience. At my desk one day, pencil in hand, I found myself drawing a curving line, which became an autobiographical chronology in the form of a spiral pathway. This traced my training and professional experience of dance/movement, together with evidence of the occurrence and influence of anthropology along the way. To my surprise, a clear pattern emerged. My varied life had always seemed somewhat diffuse, relatively unplanned. Yet six interrelated, recurring features or themes stood out as significant through all the phases of my life, with kinaesthetically sensed memories for each.

Descriptive titles for the themes, my repurposing words familiar from conventional use in other contexts, seemed limiting, and certainly lacking any implication of kinaesthetic experience. This led me in another sudden and surprising direction—related to my Tai Ji practice. In the course of learning this movement-art, I have been introduced to Mandarin Chinese brush-stroke calligraphy: it seemed that the range of meanings or interpretations needed for my titles, might perhaps be more satisfactorily embodied in Chinese characters.[9]

I refer to three of the six themes in this chapter.[10] In the Chinese language, meanings vary according to context, but possible translations are indicated in parentheses in the following pages. As my understanding of the language develops, I anticipate discovery of other characters that may also relate to the themes, so my choice of those selected here is not definitive. Furthermore, these thematic areas are ever expanding and open to creative development and fresh ideas. This is matched by Chinese calligraphy, which I find stimulates comprehension and imagination in new, unexpected ways—through the lines and spaces created from the flowing energy of the brush.[11]

Theme 1

JI (combine, assemble, collect ...)
This theme concerns bringing separate subjects together (or different aspects of a subject), interrelating them, cross-referencing between subjects—a multi-faceted approach.

In this Chinese character, meaning is constructed through the relationship between the upper and lower components. These can be translated as *bird* (x 3) above, and tree below. Hence the theme is represented in terms of diverse birds gathered together from far and near, in a widely spreading tree.

In relation to my central performance arts interest, the process of autobiographical reflection made me realize that I was attracted to this theme in my student days—and during my first teaching experience. Recollections from that period resonate with the growing sense of limitation I felt in the London theatre repertoire and in drama training. This reaction contributed to the introduction of anthropology into my life, bringing its multi-faceted focus and an influence relainge to the theme of JI. These are some of my recent recollections from student days in the early 1950s:

Choice of BA in drama, music, and English literature in 1950 (despite preva-lent view of single-subject degrees as higher status).[12] The interrelated aspects of drama attracted me—e.g., Greek drama with its mix of chorus, individual characters and messengers' reports of events offstage; plays attended by all sections of society; English mediaeval drama's system of guilds and whole community involvement plus varied staging/sites: street, marketplace, church; with use of contrasting spatial levels to represent heaven, earth, and hell. I always loved acting: the rehearsal/performance collaboration process; with continuous series of performances in plays (and choral music) during term, and vacations touring English counties and in continental Europe. Combining academic with practical subjects was unusual then, as when, in 1954, I was the first university graduate to train at Laban's Art of Movement Studio,[13] and next added dance to the mix.... Laban spoke of the universality and variety of dance; at his studio, I was introduced to Yugoslav, Israeli, South American Dance styles, as well as to African drumming technique; some of us visited London's Asian Music Circle for classical Indian music, and danced rock 'n' roll at Cy Laurie's London Jazz Club ...

The numerous postwar London theatre productions I saw as a theatre-loving teenager and onwards lacked influences from continental Europe or beyond, and any real sense of physical theatre. There was fine acting and an increasing number of interesting new plays, but box sets, situated well behind the proscenium arch, predominated. Expressionism and ideas from the early decades of twentieth century theatre (such as those of Mey-erhold, Vakhtangov, Appia, Artaud) were either unknown or ignored, and a whole world away from London. Matters improved through the arrival and influence of Michel Saint-Denis at the Old Vic Theatre (1947) and the work of Theatre Workshop at the Theatre Royal, Stratford East (1953), with Joan Littlewood, and others. Later, Peter Daubeny's World Theatre seasons and rare Japanese Noh and kabuki performances at Sadlers' Wells Theatre enriched London's theatre scene.

By the end of the 1950s, I was in my first job, in St. Gabriel's College, a London teacher-training college. Although I continued to appreciate and enjoy the arts in England, I had become dissatisfied with the bias toward British work in drama (at that time my main teaching responsibility). The general academic assumption seemed to be that the subject began with the Greeks and proceeded linearly through to Marlowe and Shakespeare, with perhaps a later nod to writers from further afield, such as Molière and Ibsen. Interesting as all that was, I began to broaden my teaching syllabus slightly to include some less conventional material from around the world, in courses and in drama productions.

Figure 2 Early student days: in the garden, practising a choreographic sequence from "Annunciation," by tutor Yat Malmgren (Laban Art of Movement Studio, Addlestone, Surrey, 1995). Photographer: S.D. Erridge, the author's father.

When I started teaching, I had adopted and embarked on what I described as "a movement approach to drama" in coursework and productions. My introduction to Laban's work had encouraged this notion, strongly supplemented by Peter Slade's ideas.[14] I recall the lively dancing games of a group of children, gathered from a local school, in one production. This group contributed linking sequences—to a background of traditional American children's songs—in my open-stage adaptation of Carson McCullers's novel *A Member of the Wedding*. Of course, music frequently stimulates movement-memory. Writing this now, I remember my delighted discovery of Peggy Seeger's rendition of the songs, and memories are stirred. As I conjure up an impression of the college hall performance space, and a scene with the central character—twelve-year-old Frankie—I begin to sense some of the movement:

> *first in my feet—step hop, step hop, run, run, run, run, run—"little bird, little bird, go through my window"—we are in Frankie's yard, picking up the steps—body moving, too—side to side—we're smiling—enjoying the pattern—now elbows are lifting a little—and we're linking hands—making a chain—an arch—through we go—into a line: now up the steps and into the house—circling the table—"all around the kitchen cock-a-doodle-doodle-doo"* …

With these kinaesthetic memories, I have a growing impression of being transported to that time and place. I recall the gloomy old wood-panelled hall, and how we managed to transform it; I sense the physical presence of the audience (who shared the floor-level space with us); and even remember surprised looks when they found themselves sitting behind the low picket fence, which surrounded the acting area. Adapting the novel for dramatic presentation is an example of my attraction to JI—an interest in interrelating different forms of expression. Also, the working process brought different groups of people together. In addition to our college students and the children, I was permitted to invite male volunteer students from another London college—St. Mark and St. John—to join the cast: a first in the history of our two colleges.

My interest in interrelating various subjects had also been well met at that time by innovative, integrated project-based schoolwork, to which my colleagues introduced me. Its purpose was to cover a wide range of curriculum subjects, through focus on one topic or piece of literature. Travel books—a frequent choice—were popular with the children, and exposed them to aspects of life in other countries. This experience made a strong impression on me.

JI: Discovering Anthropology

In 1967, I was asked to write a book for teachers on drama and movement, which introduced a wide range of suggested stimuli and diverse sources for dance-drama (Goodridge: 1970). I felt impelled to include a chapter, naively entitled (but seemingly acceptable in the context of that period) *Primitive and Child Drama*. This drew inspiration from myths and themes (such as heroes' journeys) from various sources worldwide. Perhaps it was chiefly my enthusiasm for this subject area, as well as my interest in countries' ways of life, which first drew me to anthropology. But I was only too conscious of my limited background in this field of study. Knowing nothing about anthropology at that stage, my real quest was to find and develop what I had nonetheless begun to think might be an anthropological approach to performance arts. I somehow had the idea that perhaps this could provide a basis for a more satisfyingly inclusive approach, and I took a period away from full-time teaching to pursue the idea.[15]

I discovered the two-year social anthropology course at the LSE in 1972. The course gave me an excellent grounding in the British structural-functionalist tradition of Malinowski, Evans-Pritchard, et al., and I found there that my interest in a multi-faceted focus was met. With obvious thematic connection to JI, we were immediately and primarily encouraged to view all interrelated features of a society. That is, its social, political, legal, economic organization, together with use of symbolism, ritual, and religious or spiritual beliefs—an essentially holistic view.

Thanks to the LSE course, I was already attempting to understand human movement and dance from an anthropological perspective. However, although my chosen anthropology of art option was of great related—and continuing—interest, I had not yet developed a fully fledged anthropological approach to performance arts. More importantly, however, I was developing an awareness of how to avoid ethnocentric, judgmental views and attitudes. Also, I had developed a greater understanding of the nature, purpose, and potential of the arts. Later, as a member of a university dance faculty, I was involved in course design, teaching, and examining on a number of performance arts degree programs that offered "combined" or "integrated" work in dance, drama, and music. My one opportunity and attempt to devise a course based on dance anthropology was established at that time, in 1978, as a year-long option for students in their final year of a Bachelor of Arts in Performance Arts (Dance). Over many years, this enabled me to glimpse the potential of an anthropological perspective and approach to dance and theatre in college education, then rare in England. The students' main focus was contemporary dance performance, but *my* aim for the course was to interest them in cultural diversity, and to ask the *who, where, why, what, with/for whom* questions about all forms of dance and performance-arts events worldwide.

The course included occasional visits off-campus, input from experts in the field and students' individual projects. I encouraged students' interest in community dance, which at that time was not fully developed in England. With one particularly enthusiastic year group, we joined a colleague's music-based folk-arts course. Together, we contributed to an outdoor countryside community event in Wales: memories remain of farandoles and circle dances on rough grass, surrounded by groups of lively musicians, and joined by local people of all ages.

In my other dance teaching, I have found that ideas from anthropology can contribute a useful, wider cross-referencing perspective. This is evident, for example, in discussion of work by contemporary performers who draw on diverse cultures, or with reference to the role of the artist in societies other than one's own, and to indigenous performance aesthetics.

JI: Other Contexts

In the late 1970s, I collaborated with others working in dance/movement arts in London, to form the innovative Many Ways of Moving organization. Our aim was to encourage expansion of the whole notion of dance—beyond the narrow, well-established confines of specific techniques—which we thought was much needed at that time. Many specialists in a single dance style joined the enterprise, along with a wide range of other dance and movement practitioners. We planned a series of participatory workshops through several weeks of a summer vacation. For me, this project had an anthropological aspect, not least since its central concern was to broaden peoples' concept and experience of dance. The objective was not to improve technique, so much as to try something new, dancing and moving together. One of the key founder-members agreed: "Yes, the '-ing' was crucial. It was about the experience of the moment—going out to meet people and bringing other peoples' technique into part of your experience."[16] We all participated, and some of us, with invited collaborators, taught or led sessions. For instance, I joined another participant to devise an outdoor, secular, ritual-like group movement journey, as one session on the opening day, which reflected my background in anthropology and interest in ritual and mythical journey themes.[17]

This background and interest have sometimes been evident in other performance contexts. In 1996, for example, I was employed to provide choreography and actors' movement/dance training for a London and touring production of Shakespeare's *Pericles*. There was calm, sustained ritualistic movement in the play, as well as livelier action. In one scene, King Simonides requests a dance from the six knights who are vying for daughter Thaisa's hand: "Even in your armours, as you are address'd, / Will very well become a soldier's dance" (*Pericles* II.3.103–4). In our production, their "armours" included long, ceremonially borne poles. Incorporating these, we devised a competitive dance. Some background inspiration came not only from experience of using swords in English folk/Morris dance and in a kendo long-sword class in Japan, but also from ethnographic description of expressive, symbolically charged use of sticks in stick-wielding dances elsewhere (for example, see Widness 2000).

Attraction to the interrelating content of key theme JI is again evident in another context: in my interest in changes that occur when an artwork is derived from material that originates elsewhere. Influenced by anthropology, one focus has been on examples that involve transference from one culture to performance in another, where there can be a danger of trivializing the original. An early project was a study of Peter Brook's earth-covered stage production of *The Ik* (Roundhouse Theatre, London: 1976) where I concluded that this trap was avoided.[18]

Figure 3 From research travels: participating in a summer festival dance procession. A moment from my first lesson in classical Japanese dance (Shikoku, Japan, 1993). Photographer: Françoise Carter.

When I travel for research, I am drawn to multi-faceted events. A background in dance with anthropology undoubtedly helps me to learn, observe, and participate in diverse social-cultural contexts. I retain movement memories from very special learning experiences. For instance, again in Japan, I saw ritual behaviour in Matsuyama City temples and during seasonal street processions in Tokyo; I learned the traditional tea ceremony; I took classical Japanese dance classes; and I joined in folk dance at festivals. Closer to home, I have kinaesthetic memories of joining England's possibly oldest surviving traditional dance: Staffordshire's Abbots Bromley Horn Dance, performed once annually. This consists of a day-long, twenty-mile processional tour of the parish, for all to join, with various stops for dancing with music, humour, and refreshment en route. I first met the performers in the early morning, when the weighty reindeer antlers—worn in the dance—are blessed in the church, and where they are held all year for safekeeping.

In Arizona and Mexico, I attended Native American events and ceremonies. With the enormous benefit of anthropologist Dr. Joann Kealiino-homoku's fine guidance, I was able to develop some awareness of preferred, appropriate behaviour—the dance of movement etiquette. The rich experience of attending and participating in those ceremonies—at times of multi-faceted "consecrated community enterprise" (Painter 1971: 8)—made a profound, lasting impression. It gave me an invaluable opportunity to apply any understanding I may have gained from studying anthropology.[19]

Finally, to summarize my dance and work experience in relation to JI, this too has been characterized by diversity: varied movement/dance training, performance and teaching environments combined with academic post-graduate study and independent research.[20]

Theme 2

LÜ (ordered, disciplined, rhythmical ...)
This theme concerns aspects of movement/dance, rhythm, and timing.

The image is assertive, arresting—just as rhythm can be. The brush strokes suggest rhythmic beats, or sharply marked actions, with some variation implied by their differing lengths. A contrasting, curving pattern flows through the spaces between, reminiscent of non-metric rhythm. (In the design of Chinese calligraphy, the spaces are as significant as the lines.) The one sharp-angled change of direction invokes rhythm's potential for surprise. The long emphatic downward thrusting stroke in the component on the right is like a structural lynchpin, holding the rhythm together. Here,

as with the other Chinese characters, one can imagine the visual existing in three-dimensional space, like an artist's mobile, and moving as if in a dance.[21]

Always a subject of paramount concern to anyone involved with dance, the emergence of LÜ as a key theme in my experience is hardly surprising. As well as a lifelong delight, it has been a central interest in my dance-movement practice and research. Indeed, in 1988, my PhD topic—rhythm and timing in human movement with reference to performance events: drama, dance and ceremony—became the focus for my quest to bring theatre arts and anthropology together.[22] I set out to analyze components of movement-rhythm, to consider the role of timing, and to investigate the polyrhythmic nature and structural levels of various kinds of performance events cross-culturally. (This illustrates once again my interest in bringing different aspects of a subject together: a survey of the field included ideas from dance historians, educators, critics, aestheticians, and movement notators, as well as anthropologists.) In relation to dance performance, I observed the role of rhythm in examples of choreographer Twyla Tharp's work, in a solo Kathak recital and in a contemporary version of *Gisèlle*. These observations led to a wider study of rhythm and timing as contributory factors in dance style. For this development, I gratefully acknowledge the invitation to present a keynote paper on that theme for the June 1985 Congress for Research in Dance conference, Performing, Perceiving, Recording Dance: Issues of Style. From a sense of being somewhat isolated in my research area in England, it was my presence at that event, and meeting others there who were interested in the subject, which encouraged me to proceed further with the wider study.

The focus on rhythm and timing certainly helped me in my theatre arts/anthropology quest. I investigated a wide range of ethnographic contextual references and meanings in relation to the presence of rhythm and use of timing. I also began to observe how this presence plays a significant part not only in dance, drama, and ceremony, but also in people's interactions, transactions, and life events in so many different ways around the world. The study includes a detailed categorization of spatio-dynamic characteristics and continuity pattern variables for observation and description of the presence and effect of movement-rhythm in performance events. With examples of kinaesthetic memories, I now refer to selected aspects of three topics: movement-rhythm in the performance environment, timing, and metric patterns.

LÜ: The Performance Environment: Performing in a Landscape
I am invariably intrigued by events that take place over some distance, and
beyond a conventionally sized Western enactment area, whether in or out
of doors. A vivid moment of kinaesthetic-memory recall surprised me and
revealed an early interest in such events:

> *1943–1949: ... in the darkened, dimly lit school hall, music begins as we
> enter ... now we are sitting on the floor, each side of a central gangway ...
> teachers on chairs against the walls ... it's a very special occasion: the annual
> Christmas event in honour of Christ's birth, with the whole school present:
> tableaux by the youngest, readings spoken by the oldest, interspersed with
> carols rehearsed and sung by each class as well as by everyone, a choir of
> about four hundred voices ... simple lighting gradually focuses on the small
> stage, approached by a long central gangway and then a number of steps ...
> a series of tableaux form round the crib ... music sustains the continuous
> flow of the event ... in the near-dark, we see a star, held aloft, suspended on
> a string ... leading the way it's being carefully carried down the hall, slowly,
> slowly ... shepherds follow, on their journey ... then kings, with attendants,
> bearing gifts ...*

This relatively expanded use of performance space was unusual in those days.

In more recent years, I have been interested to observe how elements or
aspects of rhythm attract audience attention and contribute to the sustain-
ment of performance power over distance. Two examples from the 1990s:
first, a Native American traditional event with dances, in celebration of Les
Trois Reyes in Jemez Pueblo, New Mexico. I well recall that chilly morning in January when I witnessed the start of the ceremonies with just a
few other people. As the day dawned, smoke from a ritual fire rose from a
distant high ridge:

> With a growing sense of wonder and excitement, I began to see masked
> figures moving on the skyline.... I could distinguish the outline of a buffalo
> head-dress, later those of deer, ram and antelope.... Sometimes out of sight,
> these figures made their way down the hillside, and eventually arrived
> where we were standing, then continued with drummers into the centre of
> the pueblo. The ceremonies had begun. (From field notes, and reported in
> Goodridge 1999: 73)

When I observe movement rhythm, I include spatial aspects and related
physical factors such as size of movement. This may include use of body
extensions—like the headdresses here, which caught my attention first,

with their irregular pattern of slow/quick, side-to-side changes—in and out of sight. Then, the travelling spatial rhythm dominated, with its directional changes as the procession continued in a roughly zigzag pathway down the hillside: an effect strengthened by the number of participants in the group, and as their step pattern, reinforced by drum beats, became more noticeable.[23]

The second example is from the field of drama: a performance of Shakespeare's *Macbeth* that I attended in Scotland. It again covered a considerable distance, but this time began near the audience—on a boat. We had assembled on the quayside, en route to historic Inchcolm Island in Scotland's Firth of Forth. The first scene of the play was enacted on board, with the three witches emerging among us, from below the shifting deck. Later, across the turbulent water, we saw other characters in preliminary action, fighting on the distant shore. Body extensions once more attracted attention with varied dynamic and spatial rhythms of sword and rapier, thrust and parry, advance and retreat. We disembarked to follow the play, which continued in different locations around the island:

> *I remember stepping over pebbly sand, up a rough path further into the island; sometimes sitting, then walking—timing my own journey from one scene to the next—now in close proximity, sometimes further away from the action as the drama progresses among and through ancient ruins evidence of lives long gone ... there's a wonderful sense of the movement-action of the play developing with us as we travel on ...*[24]

LÜ: Timing
Although frequently considered as part of rhythm and vice versa, I have found it useful to identify timing as a feature in its own right. As generally understood, it has significance in everyday life, just as in sacred or secular performance contexts.

My movement-dance experience from early years was influenced by the time and place of my birth. Now I return to those years. England in the 1930s and '40s was an unsatisfactory era for anyone with modern-dance aspirations: as much a poet's dream as the idea of someone walking on the moon. With just one example from my research, I refer briefly to dancer Leslie Burrowes's experience. In autumn 1931, she returned from Dresden as the first British holder of a Wigman School Diploma with "a somewhat despairing hope to introduce this type of dancing to England."[25] Reviews of Burrowes's solo recitals in London reflect prevalent attitudes, as here: "Her dancing had an overpowering sense of being 'real' almost uncomfortably so.... It is very seldom that we see an emotion permeating every line and every movement of the body."[26]

With American Louise Soelberg as co-director, Burrowes opened her Dance Centre studio on October 3, 1938, as an innovative school with an international program.[27] Perhaps "international" was problematic. In any event, the dance establishment did not give its approval. As Burrowes's daughter recounted, "There was a lack of interest ... it was dismissed ... I think they thought it was a bit of a joke—people dancing around, flapping their arms—bare feet and all that!"[28] The Dance Centre, further imperilled by the war, was forced to close in 1940, and Burrowes left London.[29]

It should be remembered that suspicion of ideas from Germany and general resistance to ideas from "abroad" were not uncommon in the England of those days. As historian Hobsbawm notes, Britain of the 1930s was "extraordinarily blind to the brilliance of the central European Jewish and anti-fascist refugee intellectuals unless they operated in conventionally recognised fields such as classics and physics" (Hobsbawn 2002: 121). Such attitudes were persistent.

However, there was at least one significant gain for me during this period, and to which I referred earlier: the development of revived Greek dance in England. Taken to classes from the age of four by my mother—partly to improve the poor condition of my flat feet and knocked knees—I loved the experience from the start, and did well in spite of physical problems. Recurrent falls were a disturbing factor in everyday life. As I rekindle these memories, I feel the sensation:

> *sharp impact of that rough gravely tarmac on path outside our house ... feeling scared ... being carried into bathroom for slow extraction of loose gravel from knees.... It always seemed to be the knees....*
>
> *Another time at the seaside:*
>
> *falling—splat!—face down in sea-shallows ... I'm sensing the sand in my mouth ...*

Until I was age eight, custom-made, laced-up leather shoes were the order of the day (with arch supports and heavy soles). Feet trapped. No summer sandals allowed. Seemed different from most other people:

> *now I am entering the specialist shoe shop in central London with my mother.... I am asked to climb the steps of a tall box-like X-ray contraption, with binoculars set in the top—I'm peering down at the view inside—a*

strange, green world of my feet in the old shoes—sharp, black nails firmly marked all the way round the feet, grown to their limits ... I am sensing the constriction of those shoes—the sense of feet as alien exhibit—an impediment ...

After about two years of that first special experience of revived Greek dancing, wartime brought other limitations; disturbance, fear, disruption for all—not least for me in my small world:

a shock ... a discovery ... the dance classes have stopped ... an overpowering sense of loss.... I don't know where the wonderful teacher has gone. "She has joined the ambulance service"—what does that mean? I am inconsolable ... is she coming back? Asking, asking through the years ...

London bombing affected us—even in our suburb. We were on the inward-/outward-bound flight path: bombs were sometimes jettisoned to explode locally. I recall ceilings down in our house and glass shattered, despite regulation criss-cross tape. Timing? Planning? Future unknown, unknowable ... *"If wishes were horses, beggars would ride"*—now a vividly recalled, constant refrain from my mother. However, once back from a nine-month evacuation to the distant West country, I settled happily at school. Despite the dangers, bomb damage, and other obvious problems, plus the worries and sadness of wartime, anything was better than being away from home and friends. Youthful high spirits generally prevailed.

Dance at school was limited to a rare folk-dance class in the time-worn, musty gymnasium. But I had always had an unexpressed, unfulfilled longing to dance barefoot in our school hall—a modern, airy, light space— on its beautiful pale-brown parquet wood floor, which we were taught to respect. A recollection: *sitting in school assembly, listening to one of the pieces of classical music we heard each morning ... imagining ... secretly designing dances in my mind ...*

The war compounded the problem of a lack of dance influence from outside England. General ignorance of modern dance work persisted. I had a few treasured books on ballet and the occasional magazine, and I remember gazing endlessly at the photographs. After the war, I attended numerous ballet performances and remained a fan, although my feet, "unsuited to ballet," prevented class participation beyond the beginner level. I had a further year or so of revived Greek dance (with a different teacher), and also had a growing interest in modern ballet style and themes. For instance, I recall being captivated by John Cranko's *Sea Change* (Sadlers' Wells Theatre Ballet, January 1949). But I knew nothing about Mary Wigman, Kurt Jooss, or other modern dance in continental Europe, or anywhere else, until my first unexpected, fortuitous, and ultimately life-changing glimpse of a Laban-trained dancer in 1951.

LÜ: Metric Patterns

I have always attributed the beginning of my enjoyment of rhythm, especially metric patterns, to excellent experience of music at high (or "senior") school—an otherwise unexceptional local school. The key influence was participation in *The Combined Choir* (singing and conducting—our sopranos and altos joined by tenors and basses from a local boys school). Challenging repertoire: unaccompanied early West European polyphonic music, sacred and secular (such as by Byrd, Palestrina), as well as occasional modern pieces (such as by Britten, Vaughan Williams), performed to a high standard. Acquiring a sense of the underlying, shared beat, holding one's vocal line with listening-awareness of others and living the life of changing patterns and dynamics was a wonderful learning experience. Similar repertoire continued for four further years at university, as well as participation in a larger choir for challenging works with orchestra. Obviously, in later years, exposure to music and dance worldwide, and studies from ethnomusicology and dance anthropology contributed even more to my experience of metric patterns and of all aspects of rhythm.

However, in relation to metricity, the process of kinaesthetic memory-access has again brought my early revived Greek dance experience to the fore as an important influence: notably memories of my bare feet in contact with the floor and an emphasis on metric step patterns. These were derived from the rhythmic motifs of ancient Greek poetry and drama.[30]

I now realize how influential this early experience was for me, and it contributes to the question of where in the body kinaesthetic memories begin, since from an almost imperceptible sense of movement in my body centre, mine usually seem to begin in my feet. Toes, heels start to lift—matching a beat or rhythm pattern. Perhaps this is due to later years of "marking" step patterns when learning dance sequences. Or, it may be a further influence from the school choir, where we were told, if need be, to mark the beat silently, invisibly, with our toes inside our shoes. But I am drawn back, yet again, to that early dance-class experience:

I am sensing the effort it is taking to manage the different step patterns ... skips—"simple" and "dotted" ... a mysterious sharp "komat" ... next: one, two, three, hop ... more effort now with "run, run, high leap!" ... finally galloping, galloping around the room ...

Much class time was spent on these patterns, and care was taken to help me overcome the problem with my feet. I learned to enjoy running, even outside, and with fewer tumbles. Years later, I particularly relished covering the ground, striding out, etching pathways, travelling, carving through space. Both acting and dance training taught me to love the floor, as an ally—a partner in the experience of falling, and in making interesting discoveries about shifting weight.

At first, metric rhythm was the basis of my dance experience. Then "free" rhythm and Laban's non-metric, qualitative approach became more important to me. Non-metricity, free rhythm, also featured in my favourite section of the revived Greek dance syllabus, "Nature Rhythms." Here, we were asked to devise a sequence of movements inspired by something in the natural environment. I have recalled a frequent choice:

> *I begin close to the ground ... spiky starting position—"becoming" a pile of twigs, old branches ... into action with sparkings ... flickerings ... flamings ... then gentle, smoky floating, twisting, circling around the room and back to starting place ... subsiding ... dying down ... ashes ...*

A bonfire: I could perform it for you now! Why did I enjoy this classwork feature so much? Enjoyment certainly came from those first experiences of devising and performing movement sequences—simple, yet clearly structured in space and with both metric and non-metric patterning of changing dynamics. Nature rhythms relate to Isadora Duncan's view of dance—and other early modern dance—as "an expression from within," and inspired by nature (see Morrison Brown 1980: 7–11). However, I recall our class experience as being, in general, perhaps more controlled than this view implies, with that emphasis on metricity, as well as with incorporation of the specific arm positions to which I have already referred.[31]

The foregoing allusions to the ground, to free rhythm, nature rhythms— and to Isadora Duncan—lead to my last theme. Recurring through my life, this theme concerns aspects of both nature and spontaneity.[32]

Theme 3

TIAN RAN (natural, unleashed, spontaneous ...)
TIAN (the left character below) can be translated as "heaven or sky." Perhaps the character may be imagined as all of nature spread wide under heaven, yet securely rooted. In RAN (the right-hand character), there are traces of ancient characters for moon, dog/wolf with the four small strokes flaming up at the base representing fire. For me, the image suggests a down surge of

power from above, with the lurking unpredictability of wild nature hinted on the right: a sense of balance, as well as joyous excitement, creative flair.

I recognize that I was drawn to this theme in early childhood, with reinforcement later. Final recollections from those times are followed with some thoughts about spontaneity and nature. I then return to ideas drawn from ethnography and to my dance/movement work.

1930s–1940s: I relished the extremes and surprises of British variable weather conditions (especially heavy rain, mists, even fog; also the less frequent thick snow and clear blue skies); lived near forest—memories of playing among oak, birch, beech, chestnut trees—wading, kicking through leaves; hide and seek around blackberry-bush thickets. Love of the seashore.... To reprise: revived Greek dance class—dancing barefoot; Art of Movement Studio—improvisation, dancing out of doors on the grass—sensing the earth; Peter Slade's movement-drama/improvisatory approach. As a student teacher, though somewhat apprehensive, I sought times when the hall was available for class release from desks for movement ...

Spontaneity and nature are conceptually linked for me. And they are connected in dance/movement-arts work just as they are in human life. An important aspect of this connection has to do with change, impermanence. This is inherent in dance-movement material, just as it prevails in everyday conditions, with varying degrees of unexpectedness and aesthetic interest: clouds, wind in trees—across grasses; shifting weather. We, too, are constantly in physical flux, and must adapt to changing circumstances in daily life.

We experience spontaneity when there is release from thinking in straight, preconceived lines, and when ideas occur on the spur of the moment. There's surely an element of spontaneity in the energy of inspiration, and in the spark of enthusiasm. A key ingredient in the play of imagination, in surprise and humour—spontaneity is present in the response to the unforeseen. It is obviously indispensable in any arts improvisation— which is a vital area of my own movement/dance practice, such as in some drama and contemporary dance, and in Laban-based work. Indeed, spontaneity in movement is related to Laban's concept of *free-flow* (which may be defined as unrestricted fluidity).

Order of some kind may be apparent in performance improvisation, but spontaneity truly occurs when movement or other ideas are allowed to flow unconstrained, whether or not remembered motifs are introduced (as in music or dance). It is inherent in the poetic imagination. To return to anthropology once more, through reading ethnographies, we can expand our horizons here, too. In one fine example, d'Azevedo described variation and expression of individuality in some Gola peoples' solo dance performance, which he observed in Liberia, West Africa, and how this seemed to be considered "a gift of the spirit" (1989: 337).

Turning to aspects of nature, in terms of the natural environment in general, various ethnographic studies of traditional societies have introduced me to specialist knowledge, to lore about trees, plants, and animals—and their symbolic significance for the people concerned. Just as themes from mythology were included in my early teaching days, I now realize that ideas from material such as this have filtered through into my expressive work in later years, consciously or unconsciously. Some knowledge of natural healing ritual processes with plants, for example, was unexpectedly useful as background for a key scene, again in the production of Shakespeare's *Pericles*, when the healer Cerimon brings Marina back to life with the aid of "blest infusions that dwell in vegetives" (*Pericles* III.2.39–40). I attribute my awareness of the life-maintaining importance of nature and of the earth itself, at least partly to an influence from anthropology—from ethnographic studies of peoples who live in intimate contact with the natural world.

Dancers can sometimes develop ideas about using the surrounding space and spatial directions through exploring indigenous ideas that relate to nature. Kurath first alerted me to this possibility, with her clear account of ceremonies performed by the Keresan Pueblo Indians to invoke *Shiwana* (rain gods). In her account, Kurath draws attention to the way in which compass directions, seasons, and colours are linked with specific movements (1960, 312–16).

The world of nature is, of course, a common source of inspiration for dancers, as it is for other artists. This theme of both nature and spontaneity was vitally present in early Western modern dance practice, and is evident in reports of the exuberant and well-grounded dancers of the time.[33] Indeed, a sense of the earth is generally acknowledged as "the founding principle of modern dance" (for example, see Fraleigh 1987).

Awareness of our relationship with the whole natural environment and its energies has undoubtedly developed further for me through my experience of Tai Ji. I find its images and metaphors from nature inspiring: the strong sense of grounding, of the earth deep beneath us, the limitless sky above. "Like the sea, it ebbs and flows.... When I finish a Tai Ji class I feel alive, I feel there's blood flowing in my veins again.... It keeps us in touch with nature."[34] The traditional Chinese concept of the Five Elements (or Five Phases: *wu xing*) is associated with the form of Tai Ji that we practise.[35] This concept relates the Five Elements to dynamic processes in the human body as in the whole of nature represented by earth, fire, water, wood, and metal.

Aspects of all the Chinese Five Elements can be sensed in movement expression, but perhaps water has a particular affinity with dance and the dancer, its fluidity, its life-sustaining presence. Browning, for instance, is one who reveals this link in her study of the Brazilian samba. So, for a final example from one of the many anthropologists who have inspired me, I refer to Browning's evocative description of Yemanja—goddess of salt waters: "[She] who dances with a shimmering, shivering motion of her shoulders which resembles the sea's surface ..."

Figure 4 Practising Tai Ji in Epping Forest, Essex, 2010. Photographer: Janet Bruce.

(Browning 1995: 65). And from Isadora Duncan once more: "My first idea of movement certainly came from the rhythm of the waves" (Morrison Brown 1980: 7–11). Water: "The primary and most essential element for all living processes ... [in] ... close connection with all rhythmical processes in time and space" (Schwenk 1999: 80).[36]

> The great sea
> Has set me adrift
> It moves me
> As the weed in a great river
> Earth and the great weather
> Move me
> Have carried me away
> And move my inward parts with joy
> ("Song of Uvavnuk," Eskimo woman shaman, quoted in Rasmussen 1930: 122)

In concluding my reflections on nature, I return briefly to memory. Some things in the world of nature have memory-like features, such as my initial "repository" image of rock strata through the ages, and the ringed record of past life laid down within the trunk of a tree. And again, water:

artist Paul Schültze intrigued me with an exhibition that demonstrated his exploration of water in connection with memory, change, and consciousness.[37] Surprising experimental scientific work actually demonstrates water's capacity for "memory" storage. There is evidence of this in photographs of 10,000 frozen samples of water from different places (Emoto 1994–99). These reveal information concerning aspects of each sample's history, stored in individual crystals. Such examples may also be thought of as metaphors for a dancer's body—as a repository of dance knowledge through time.

POSTSCRIPT

Writing this chapter has been an ongoing process of discovery. It arose simply from that surprising vision, a sense of my own body as a living archive of dance/movement-arts knowledge. An invitation from our editor to contribute the idea in a chapter for this anthology, and conversation with other dancers, encouraged me to pursue the subject. Writing this chapter has also brought unexpected understanding, not only of my performance-arts experience, but also of my life—not least with discovery of those six key themes. It is a life in which anthropology, as a way of looking at the world, continues to have an influential presence.

Notes

1 Influential meetings, trips undertaken. 1968: first US contemporary-dance-based exploratory trip through friend Jacqueline Davis (post-graduate: Ohio State University, Columbus, later faculty, SUNY Brockport); 1972: Sue Jennings (fellow anthropology student—shared theatre/performance interest); Drid Williams (Oxford PhD student—contacted via Royal Anthropological Institute Library (since I had noted we were the only members borrowing dance books); Professor John Blacking (trip to Queen's University, Belfast); 1980s: in the United States, Dr. Joann Kealiinohomoku—to whom I am most indebted—met at CORD/SDHS events, later with study time at Cross Cultural Dance Resources, Flagstaff; travelled to find other dance-interested anthropologists, notably meetings with Hanna, Royce, Meyerhof, ethnomusicologist Ruth Stone, and Professor Victor Turner (visit with participation in class seminar—including enactment of Ndembu ritual).
2 During the writing process, I was encouraged by discovery of van Manen's positive approach to autobiographically-based research (van Manen 1997).
3 Recordings in the Dance Collection, New York Public Library, Lincoln Center.
4 The former Nikolais Dance Theatre dancer here, in an informal September 2004 conversation with the writer, remembers student days as member of a Mexican Folkloric group.
5 Interview, BBC Radio, March 24, 2004.
6 Mara de Wit, founder Research and Navigation Dance Theatre Company (UK).

7 Revived Greek dance: developed by pioneer of "freer" movement Ruby Ginner (1886–1978); inspired by ancient Greek arts.

8 From memories recalled during chapter writing (as are all subsequent italicized passages).

9 I am indebted to Chungliang Al Huang for teaching (twenty years and ongoing) with inspiring approach to the Chinese ideographic movement-language of calligraphy, also to Gerda Geddes (first Tai Ji teacher). My thanks to Professor George Sang and to artist-calligrapher Yizhou Zhao for tuition and choice of Chinese characters for my themes (School of Oriental and African Studies, University of London). Gratitude also goes to Bob Lambert for his illustrations. (Readers are encouraged to study artist-calligraphers' larger-scale cursive-style renditions for more obvious sense of energy flow, which matches a dancer's kinaesthetic experience.)

10 My three other recurring themes: movement observation (GUAN), groupwork (XIE), and diverse cultures (YI).

11 I later discovered European classical-Renaissance writers' grouped memories in mental pictures of rooms for memory training (Mack 2003: 36–37). Also, sixteenth-century Italian priest Matteo Ricci introduced a memory palace of rooms as memory stimulus to a Jiangxi province governor (Spence 1984). (I myself have found that focus on each of my themes/characters acts mnemonically.)

12 University drama studies in Britain were then offered solely at Bristol (from 1948). Dance was not offered at any British university at that time.

13 In Addlestone: classes with Laban's colleagues, occasionally Laban. I recall performing as Puck in a dance-drama that he directed on themes from *A Midsummer Night's Dream* (1954).

14 See Slade (1954).

15 Initially due to the Social Sciences Research Council's two years of funding.

16 David Henshaw, private conversation with the writer, July 1, 2004.

17 "Ritual" in the sense of marking/sharing a special occasion, in recognition here of our collaborative journey, embarking on a new enterprise. (A modest attempt: I had yet to learn of Anna Halprin's work in this area, and to participate in a session that she led in California.)

18 Source material: *The Mountain People* by anthropologist Colin Turnbull; dramatization by Denis Cannan and Colin Higgins.

19 1990–1994: I am indebted to Dr. Joann Kealiinohomoku for three visits to the four Yaqui Arizona settlement areas, visits to six Yaqui homelands pueblos in northwest Mexico and discussion/archival studies at Cross Cultural Dance Resources; to the library archives staff, University of Arizona, Tucson; to Dr. Françoise Carter for facilitation of my research visit, Shikoku, Japan.

20 Examples—movement/dance work: with actors in Helsinki theatres, in Kubrick's film *Barry Lyndon*; choreography: BBC TV, *Jane Seymour—Wives of Henry VIII*, Double D Company—Yeats's *Plays for Dancers*; Barry Smith's Theatre of Puppets; operas—*HMS Pinafore, La Belle Hélène*; Welsh Youth Theatre, *American Wry*; UK National Youth Theatre, *Salomon Pavey*. Teaching: New England College, UK Campus; Welsh College of Music and Drama, Cardiff; Laban Art of Movement Studio; Bedford College of Physical Education; in the United States: Boston Conservatory of Music; workshops: Ohio University, Athens; University of Maryland; independent research: early modern dance in England; early history of professional dancers touring/teaching in US colleges, with archival work by invitation

on Helen Alkire's dance collection, Ohio State University; dance training: Laban training/influence continued; also, Leeder, Graham, Humphrey-Limon, and Nikolais-based techniques with performance in Patricia Barclay's Dance Theatre Workshop London and classes with Barbara Mettler, Hilde Holger, British "New Dance," Dolmetsch (period style), varied folk dance styles; several vacation dance composition courses with US teachers.

21 In Japanese, this *Kanji* character expresses "the rhythm of life."

22 University College, London University (part-time 1974–88 combined with teaching and performance work)—PhD awarded January 1989.

23 Rhythmic use of "body extensions" in communication over distance: I am reminded of the hand-held, pole-mounted flags of pre-telegraph Morse-coded semaphore, with its dot/dash patterns of small/broad arcs.

24 Production staged by Scottish artist Richard Demarco, whose avant-garde performance-arts promotion has inspired me, together with other experimental work by directors/choreographers/companies such as Mike Alfreds, Pina Bausch, Steven Berkoff, Peter Brook, Nuria Espert (Lorca's *Yerma* staged on a trampoline with varied tension), Lin Hwai-Min (Cloud Gate Dance Theatre), Tadeusz Kantor, Yukio Ninagawa Terayama (*Shintoku-Maru* and Shakespeare plays), James Roose-Evans (Stage Two Company and participation in improvisation workshops), Shared Experience Company, Wlodzmierz Staniewski (Gardzienice Company), Robert Wilson.

25 Dance critic John Martin, "The Dance: British Style," *New York Times*, 21 August 1932.

26 *Daily Express*, July 25, 1932; writer unnamed.

27 "Formed ... as a medium of contemporary thought and feeling ... not as an escape from life but an intensification of it" (Dance Centre manifesto).

28 Jennie Goossens, Burrowes's daughter, private conversation with the writer, spring 2002.

29 Lack of establishment approval for modern dance continued into the 1960s, despite individual initiatives—e.g., John Broome's Dance Theatre Company, 1957–59. After performing with the Sadlers' Wells Ballet, dancer Broome trained with Leeder: "My whole interest was in developing something more expressive and fluent [than ballet]" (in conversation with the writer, 2003). In 1957, I joined Broome's Company and in his *Journey of the Beggars*, my own role was inspired by Breugel's picture of helmeted, breastplated Mad Meg. I recall: *leading the group diagonally across stage from upstage right, gleaming sword in hand, pointing the way....* We aimed to cut through to new forms of dance expression.

30 Motifs based on long/short combinations: e.g., anapaest (- —).

31 See note 7 on revived Greek dance.

32 For further reference to movement-rhythm and timing, see Goodridge, 1999.

33 Demonstrated in photographs of Hertha Feist and Jenny Gert's 1920s Berlin dance groups (Preston-Dunlop and Lahuson: 1990, figures 8–11).

34 Comments from three members of one of my London classes for partially chairbound senior citizens, Kingsgate Community Centre, May 1997.

35 See note 9.

36 See also pioneer-inventor Schauberger's research on the "living intelligence of Nature," including the "vital energies of water" (Cobbald 2006).

37 Alan Cristea Gallery, London, January 2004.

Bibliography

Browning, Barbara. *Samba: Resistance in Motion*. Bloomington: Indiana University Press, 1995.

Cobbald, Jane. *Viktor Schauberger: A Life of Learning from Nature*. Edinburgh: Floris Books, 2006.

Connerton, Paul. *How Societies Remember*. Cambridge: Cambridge University Press, 1989.

d'Azevedo, Warren L. "Sources of Gola artistry." In W.L. d'Azevedo (ed.), *The Traditional Artist in African Societies*. Bloomington: Indiana University Press, 1989: 282–340.

Emoto, Masaru. *Messages from Water*, vols. 1–3. Tokyo: Hado Kyikusha, 1999–2004.

Farnell, Brenda. "Moving Bodies Acting Selves." *Annual Review of Anthropology* 28 (1999): 341–73.

Fraleigh, Sandra Horton. *Dance and the Lived Body: A Descriptive Aesthetics*. Pittsburgh: University of Pittsburgh Press, 1987.

Gardner, Howard. *Frames of Mind: The Theory of Multiple Intelligences*. London: Basic Books (Tenth Anniversary Edition), 1993.

Glaser, Daniel. "Research Report." *Cerebral Cortex Online Journal*, December 22, 2004.

Goodridge, Janet. *Drama in the Primary School*. Oxford: Heinemann Educational Books, 1970. In the United States: *Creative Drama and Improvised Movement for Children*. Boston: Plays Inc., 1971.

———. *Movement Rhythm and Timing in Performance: Drama, Dance and Ceremony*. London: Jessica Kingsley, 1999.

Hobsbawn, Eric. *Interesting Times in Twentieth Century Life*. London: Penguin, 2002.

Huang, C. Al. *Embrace Tiger, Return to Mountain*. Berkeley, CA: Celestial Arts, 1987 (orig. 1973).

Kurath, Gertrude Prokosch. "Research, Methods and Background of Gertrude Kurath." *Congress on Research in Dance. Research Annual* VI (1974): 34–43.

Mack, John. *The Museum of the Mind*. London: British Museum Press, 2003.

Morrison-Brown, Jean. *The Vision of Modern Dance*. London: Dance Books, 1980.

Painter, Muriel Thayer. *A Yaqui Easter*. Tucson: University of Arizona Press, 1971.

Preston-Dunlop, Valerie, and Susanne Lahusen (eds.). *Schrifttanz: A View of German Dance in the Weimar Republic*. London: Dance Books, 1990.

Rasmussen, Knud. *Report of the Fifth Thule Expedition, 1921–1924*, vol. 7, nos. 1–3, Copenhagen, 1930: 122–23.

Roose-Evans, James. *Passages of the Soul: Ritual Today*. Shaftesbury, Dorset: Element Books, 1994.

Schwenk, Theodor. *Sensitive Chaos*. London: Rudolf Steiner Press, 1999.

Slade, Peter. *Child Drama*. London: University of London Press, 1954.

Spence, Jonathan D. *The Memory Palace of Matteo Ricci*. London: Penguin, 1984.

Steinman, Louise. *The Knowing Body*. Boston: Shambhala Publications, 1986.

Thomas, D.M. *The White Hotel*. London: Orion Books, 1999 (orig. 1981).

Widness, Richard. "Musical Structure, Performance and Meaning: The Case of a Stick Dance from Nepal." *Ethnomusicology Forum* 15, no. 2 (November 2006): 179–212.

CHAPTER EIGHT

Self-Portrait of an Insider

RESEARCHING CONTEMPORARY DANCE AND CULTURE IN VITÓRIA, BRAZIL

ELUZA MARIA SANTOS

This narrative has been adapted from the introduction to my dissertation, in which I reflected on my experiences in the world of professional dance performance and research, offering insight into how and why I became interested in researching the cultural significance of Brazilian contemporary dance in my native Vitória. A subtext follows, relating the way in which contemporary dance became implanted and was developed in the environment of this small city, outside, but in proximity to, larger cosmopolitan dance centres. I have purposefully adopted a personal tone here—the better to draw the reader into the predicament of a dancer-researcher whose field was her home city, whose subjects of study were close colleagues. Woven throughout this personal story of fieldwork are discussions of the advantages inherent in, and the challenges posed by, my position as a Brazilian contemporary dance protagonist and insider, and how my vantage point as a doctoral student at Texas Woman's University finally provided the full benefit of an outsider's perspective.

THE STORY BEGINS

It began one day in 1968 during junior high school, as I embarked on my study of modern dance at the Escola de 1 Grau Maria Ortiz in Vitória. Dance instructor Conceição Ferreira Vieira always created a vibrant ambiance in the classroom, playing the piano as we danced and keeping the momentum moving along with her characteristic clarity, fluidity, and boldness. Shortly after starting her classes, I joined the school's dance group, which performed in various dance styles such as modern (Graham), jazz, Afro-Brazilian, and some of the popular dances of Brazil.

It wasn't easy to maintain a fresh, up-to-date outlook during those years in Vitória, because the outside influence of dance performances and workshops by visiting professionals were all too rare. But Vieira's passion and curiosity took her travelling throughout the country and abroad, bringing home to us jazz, Graham, and Limón techniques. She eventually earned a master's degree in dance from the University of Oregon, after which she again returned to Vitória to continue teaching. As it happened, in her absence, she invited me to take over some of her dance classes. And so Vieira became my mentor by offering me opportunities that served to intensify my interest and commitment to the field of dance.

In the 1960s and '70s, the Universidade Federal da Bahia was the only institution to offer a degree program in dance in Brazil. In the end, though, I stayed in Vitória and studied dance in the physical-education department at Universidade Federal do Espírito Santo. With increased professional involvement, I realized that I had begun to follow the pattern of my mentors: taking dance workshops in Rio de Janeiro so that I might bring a wider range of experience to my teaching and creative work.

In 1980, I travelled to the United States to pursue further university studies in dance. I attended Arizona State University, where I spent five years completing a Bachelor of Fine Arts in Dance, and went on to graduate with a master's in the field, too. I finally realized that the scope of my previous academic work with dance in Brazil had been very limited indeed. At ASU, modern dance technique classes seemed to me more challenging, and the varied approaches to choreographic composition brought me deeper familiarity with all aspects of the creative process. Choreographic productions were particularly demanding and rigorous. In addition, the requisite theory classes provided me with completely new historical, aesthetic, and kinesiological perspectives.

It was in this setting that I also began to understand that my way of moving was somehow expressive of my cultural background, a notion which became apparent, for instance, when professors and peers commented on a particular kind of energy in my dancing—a kind of "magnetic" performance, as one of my classmates called it. I began to wonder if this kind of movement quality might be generalized to encompass "a Brazilian way of moving." This led me to delve into creating a choreographic composition for my MFA dance concert in 1985, in which I set out to create an interpretive portrayal of four particular elements of Brazilian culture: *cativeiro*, the slavery period in Brazil; *capoeira*, a form of martial arts; *Candomblé*, one of the Afro-Brazilian religions; and *Carnaval*, the nationwide festival preceding Lent (equivalent to Mardi Gras in the United States). Perhaps because of my long familiarity with the material, the piece seemed to evolve effortlessly. To my immense satisfaction, the choreographic performance was positively assessed by teachers and peers, giving me further confidence in the pertinence of this line of thinking.

Returning to Brazil between 1986 and 1992, I taught first at the Universidade de Uberaba, Minas Gerais, then at Universidade Federal do Espírito Santo. I founded dance companies at these two institutions and continued to choreograph and perform in Brazil. My contact with the United States was maintained through frequent visits with friends living there, and I always took more dance classes, presented workshops at dance-related events, and eventually toured with one of the dance companies I had founded.

It was by way of contrast with my experiences in the United States that I was finally able to isolate and identify three critical aspects of the Brazilian dance context. First, although classical ballet was traditionally considered the main foundation for concert dance, many dancers had all along also been studying elements of Brazilian culture along with their training in Western classical and modern dance styles. In addition, modern dance styles like Graham, imported to Brazil from other countries, had been subjected to various local influences. Finally, it became evident that the theme of cultural identity had long been a major concern for contemporary Brazilian choreographers. And so it followed that when I went to Texas Woman's University to pursue doctoral studies in 1992, my intention was to investigate these, and other, characteristics of Brazilian contemporary dance and their relationship to Brazilian culture.

My home city of Vitória became the site for the study. Even with a limited number of dance companies, it provided me with many case studies and a variety of approaches to dance-making. Surrounded by cultural and artistic centres in the cities of Rio de Janeiro, São Paulo, Minas Gerais, and Bahia, Vitória's geographical location put contemporary choreographers into proximity with artistic trends from this larger region. Another reason for my choosing Vitória was the advantage I had of being an insider: I am deeply familiar with this dance community and have been a protagonist in its development since the beginning. However, although this study was conducted from my insider's perspective, it was also informed by my experiences outside Brazil. Throughout the research process, there was a continual shift between these two perspectives.

RESEARCH METHODOLOGIES AND DESIGN

Novak succinctly described the dance ethnographer's task when she wrote, "What is of interest in the study of structured movement systems is the description and interpretation of the cultures which they stimulate" (1988: 117). In my approach, the goal was also to allow the reader to become fully immersed in my descriptions and not only to know, but to *feel* the interpretations and meanings that were revealed through ethnographic methodologies. Further enhancing the ethnographic mode of inquiry, this study adopted a phenomenological approach. Stemming from my understanding of phenomenology as the study of "lived experiences" (Fraleigh 1987, 1993; Van Manen 1990), I employed my recollection of past events, my activities, and continued involvement in Vitória during the time of this research as phenomenological data. Laban Movement Analysis was also useful in providing a descriptive vocabulary and in identifying movement characteristics and qualities.

The following questions emerged during the research design phase and guided this investigation: How do contemporary dance-makers in Vitória, Brazil, originate and develop their thematic and movement ideas? How do their use of the body and the qualitative characteristics of their movements form an overall impression about the contemporary dance of Vitória? What cultural elements (in the sense of aspects of daily life) are present in their dance-making and in what ways are these elements made manifest, or "voiced" in their dance? What might be the relationship between their dance-making processes and other cultural manifestations in Brazil, such as popular festivals, music, politics, sport, peculiarities found in the natural environment, food, religious rites, etc.? These questions encompassed cultural knowledge, behaviour, and artefacts. They also reflected my understanding and belief that dance is rooted in and manifests its cultural milieu.

Fieldwork was scheduled to take place during the summer of 1995, when I would be returning to Brazil. (It would be winter there.) I left the option open to return in the fall to collect more data. In order to minimize influencing the participants of my study with my own ideas and attitudes about dance and culture, I developed the basic structure for interviews prior to doing my fieldwork. But this structure was also designed to stimulate spontaneous and in-depth conversation, allowing the interviews to range from semi-structured to open-ended.

On my arrival in Vitória, I identified four dance companies that were actively choreographing and performing, to form the core of the study: (1) Advinha quem vem para dançar? (2) Duo Cia. de Dança, (3) Grupo de Dança Afro NegraÔ, and (4) Neo-Iaô Cia. Brasileira de Dança Contemporânea. I also interviewed directors and choreographers from other groups

Figure 1 Neo-Iaô dance company members Marcelo Ferreira (left) and Magno Godoy performing in *The Creation of Man* at the site of the sand dunes, in Espírito Santo. Photo courtesy of the artists.

in Vitória, even though they were less productive during the time of my fieldwork and not all working as professionals: (1) Cia. de Dança Mitzi Martucci, (2) Companhia de Dança Avivar, (3) Grupo de Dança Lenira Borges, (4) Grupo Somas, and (5) Grupo Stein / Arte Maior.

THE INSIDER–OUTSIDER: ISSUES OF CREDIBILITY

Many scholars have discussed intellectual and methodological aspects of fieldwork in terms of being an insider or outsider. For instance, Zinn (1979) proposed that the most frequent objection to insiders acting as researchers is the fact that subjectivity in data gathering and interpretation will bias the investigation without fail. This concern with subjectivity disregards the fact that, like their colleagues in majority groups, minority researchers are trained in the methodological rigours of their disciplines. This is not to say that such training by itself guarantees credibility, but simply that both insiders and outsiders are subject to the standards imposed by the scientific community.

My own position is that a subjective point of view need not disqualify work as scholarship or science as long as data-gathering procedures and values are both made explicit. In a 1996 issue of the *Journal of Contemporary Ethnography*, Bochner and Ellis advocate for liberation from methodological practices that idealize a detached observer who utilizes neutral language to explain raw data:

149

Interactive ethnography *privileges* the way in which investigators are part of the world they investigate and the ways in which they make it and change it, thus breaking away from the epistemology of depiction that *privileges* modes for inscribing a preexisting and stable social world. For writers whose work departs from canonical forms of narrating ethnography, there is a desire to be more author centered and, at the same time, more engaging to readers. (Bochner and Ellis 1996: 4)

In recognizing my own perspective as an insider, I acknowledged myself as a human instrument in the study. More precisely, I could not deny being a Western female dance artist who has long been an insider to the Vitória dance community. I made my values explicit, for example, by revealing my conceptualization of dance as a culturally situated art form.

Particular aspects of the phenomenological approach to research caught my attention. First of all, I found myself resonating with Van Manen's (1990) statement that "[one's] own life experiences are immediately accessible [to oneself] in a way that no one else's are." Nevertheless, this does not end here, he wrote, and concluded that when "drawing up personal descriptions of lived experiences, the phenomenologist knows that one's own experiences are also the possible experiences of others" (1990: 54). Perhaps, then, all ethnographic research might be understood as phenomenological in the sense that it engages the researcher in experiencing and writing personal descriptions of their lived experiences. My own perspective was shaped by my studies in the United States during a period of eighteen years, allowing me to acquire a broader perception of the dance life in Vitória. This intellectual and geographical distance evoked the sensation that I lived a "fresh," to use Fraleigh's description (1987), dance experience every time I returned to my own city, because I engaged in those experiences in a renewed way and perceived things I had not noticed before.

Zinn went further to point out that insider researchers may in fact have some advantages (1979). She advanced the idea that a "unique methodological advantage of insider field research is that it is less apt to encourage distrust and hostility" (1979: 212) from the community being investigated. I also think that insiders may have special insight into matters and nuances of behaviour. It is, of course, true, though, that both insiders and outsiders encounter advantages and limitations while engaged in fieldwork.

I faced many of the problems and experienced the anxieties common to all fieldworkers. After all, even though I was an insider in the dance community of Vitória, I was not an insider to the dance companies that I chose to study. From the start, even though I had a clear idea of what and whom to look for in the field, I had to be careful. For example, since I hadn't been living in Vitória for some time, I realized that the dance companies might also include people I did not know.

My knowledge of that particular dance community also triggered another concern. With so few dance companies in that city, the dance artists knew each other fairly well. And so I needed to reassure them that I was not seeking their assessments of one another but that my intention was to simply inquire about his or her particular process of dance-making and how it embodied culture.

ETHICAL CONCERNS: PROTECTING THE RIGHTS OF INFORMANTS

With these intellectual, methodological, and personal thoughts in mind, I soon became attentive to the ethical issues inherent in my research. Respect and sensitivity toward human subjects have long been widespread ethical concerns, voiced in the writings of many authors (e.g., Erlandson, Harris, Skipper, and Allen 1993; Marshall and Rossman 1989). It is also my belief that the rights of the participants should be considered, first and foremost. Zinn expressed her difficulty with the kind of research on minorities in which "social scientists have systematically (if unintentionally) exploited minority peoples," adding that "researchers who are insiders can also be exploiters ... working toward their own professional advancement" (1979: 211). In other words, even an insider takes something away from the participants of a study—be it their attention, knowledge, energy, or time. In response to these concerns, during my own research process, I cultivated a conscious effort not to deceive, exploit, or harm my subjects.

On the other hand, I realized that the subjects of my study might also be seen to benefit intellectually, artistically, and professionally from their participation. For instance, they might gain an increased understanding about themselves as dance artists within the cultural context of Vitória, and promote their work to the outside world as well. In the spirit of exchanging gifts, I offered to send them, based upon their needs and desires, materials from the United States about dance that couldn't be found in Brazil: books, magazines, musical recordings, and videos.

Partly due to my insider status as "one of them," I experienced immediate and complete receptivity, enthusiasm, and trust. They all signed consent forms without hesitation. In spite of this complete acceptance, I felt humbled by this experience. I had come to understand that the participants needed a clear sense of my honest desire to learn from them, regardless of my professional status as a dance artist-educator pursuing a doctoral degree.

THE FIELDWORK, OR "GOING HOME"

Returning to Brazil on vacation from my doctoral studies, I found myself already informally beginning the study. It was in the course of these visits that my research proposal and the focus of my investigation became gradually defined. But the actual fieldwork took place during the summer, fall, and winter of 1995.

The fieldwork phase of "gaining entree" began on July 11, 1995. My parents' house remained my home as well, and so I stayed there when I came to Brazil. It is indeed helpful to know the community one is studying, and it proved advantageous to be home while conducting fieldwork. I am thinking here about how, soon after arriving in Brazil, I recognized a woman being interviewed on television. She was Carla van den Bergen, producer and lighting designer for one of the newly formed dance companies in Vitória, Duo Cia. de Dança. I suddenly found myself taking field notes about a television interview from the vantage point of my own home.

From my first encounters with dance artists, I sensed a clear, if intuitive, direction opening up for me in my fieldwork. But the process was certainly not free of tensions and uncertainties about becoming overly invasive toward the dancers, and I needed to negotiate a respectful attitude toward my informants from the outset. I soon learned how to react quickly to spontaneous predicaments and seize unforeseen opportunities. Some of my assumptions proved to be erroneous (e.g., about who were the main proponents in that dance community, what currently constituted the "professional" dance milieu, and even where things were happening). I learned to keep asking questions and not to rely on my suppositions only.

Because this was a study of Brazilian dance undertaken in the United States, I often had to address the complexities of translating concepts from the Brazilian culture or the Portuguese language into English. One incident was significant enough to make me pay more attention to the use of language: the moment when dancer Jace Teodoro informed me that the choreographic focus of *Advinha quem vem para dançar?* was *pesquisa gestual.* Translated into English, this means "gestural research." At first, this led me to presume that the choreographic approach of the group was based on the concept of, and in a way limited to, gestures stemming from everyday activities. My assumption was wrong because later in the fieldwork, and aided by more observations, interviews, and many conversations, I realized that he had been implying "a deep exploration of any type of movement." This exploration, or "research," allowed for the surfacing of specific meanings that had become attached to the movements. For example, in the dance *S.Ó.S (By Oneself)* the company explored movement's relationship with water—more specifically, the ocean. By stimulating the creation of choreographic material by way of ideas such as floating and sinking, being agitated and being calm, being on the inside and the outside, and so on, the company created a composition expressing some of the binary dynamics that people might encounter. This type of clarification and deepening of my understanding continued throughout the fieldwork.

As fieldwork progressed, my participation in dance events involving Vitória companies intensified. I even accepted the invitation to travel with Duo and NegraÔ for a joint weekend performance in Guaçuí, a small city in southern Espírito Santo. This proved a fertile period in which I could spend more prolonged time "hanging out" with the dancers and choreographers. I was also able to pay closer attention to the audience's varied reactions to the style of the two groups—one using classical ballet and jazz as its main foundation; the other using Afro-Brazilian themes and movement patterns.

At the beginning of the fall semester, I needed to return to the United States, but I had plans to travel back to Brazil later that semester to conclude my research. During the return visit, I spoke with those additional choreographers, whom I hadn't originally included in my work, by conducting further interviews and then collecting videos of their choreographies to study later. When I left my home in Brazil after this second fieldwork phase, I finally felt a sense of completion.

AWAKENINGS AND DISCOVERIES

The entire research process—data collection, analysis, and interpretation—evoked many awakenings and discoveries for me. In the context of my study, "awakenings" referred to the bringing to consciousness of previous knowledge or understandings, and by "discoveries" I mean the conclusions that arose as a result of the research process.

A first awakening sprang from the process of coming to terms with working definitions of core concepts such as culture, society, ethnicity, and ethnography prior to fieldwork. In addition to this undertaking as a traditional academic practice, I needed to grasp these concepts with clarity so that I might make my intentions transparent to my informants. Once fieldwork began, I realized that it wasn't simple for my subjects to seize the larger sense of these ideas as being part of the broader spectrum of experiences in the course of a person's life. To their minds, only the traditional manifestations of a group were related to those terms. This happened, for example, when I asked members of the *Duo* dance company questions about their dance-making and Brazilian culture. Since their technical and choreographic base was classical ballet and jazz, they hadn't previously perceived any direct relationship between their dance-making and Brazilian cultural elements. I probed further, asking if for instance they used Brazilian music in their choreography. After answering yes, they laughed, having just begun to understand what I was searching for. They finally came to understand that although their artistic foundation was rooted in extracultural (imported) forms of dance—classical ballet and jazz dance—their choreographic style was often honed under the influence of Brazilian cultural elements, especially in their choices of music and literary sources.

Another of my awakenings occurred during my efforts to seize the meaning of the term *contemporary dance* and how it differs from that of *modern dance*. For me, what is called contemporary encompasses the variety of movement aesthetics one sees today, in concert dance form and embedded in its own location and time. This contrasts with the term *modern*, which I believe can be exemplified in a more distilled way, with dances within the Graham, Limon, Cunningham, or Nikolais styles, among others.

I was startled to discover an understanding divergent from my own among most of my informants, some of whom even made a point of strongly and emphatically telling me how they understood these two dance forms. For instance, several dancers informed me that although modern dance was a structured system of dance, it entailed much creative freedom on the part of the artist and so primarily referred to an individual's style. On the other hand, as they explained, the notion of contemporary dance was a question of an individual's message and a contemporary dance artist might employ any number of styles to convey her message. Points of view like this one differed from my own understanding and evoked challenging, unexpected turns of mind for me. In spite of that, dancer Ingrid Mendonça, from Grupo Somas, came closer to my own definitions and offered a vivid metaphor to differentiate the two dance genres. She likened modern dance (and classical ballet) to a turnstile through which only those who "fit" can pass. As for contemporary dance, she envisioned a wide open door through which anyone might enter.

Yet a third moment of awakening was made manifest as I watched van den Bergen's interview on television that first day. It happened when she was expressing her belief that it was necessary for dance "to touch, or do something to the viewer," that the performance quality of dancers' movements needed to go beyond "mere execution." She continued by saying that the audience should leave the theatre with "some kind of sensation." Her implication seemed obvious: she was advocating for the idea that dancing should portray, convey, and generate emotions. She even stated that while she valued technically rigorous training, the ideal dance work was one that blends good dance execution with vivid emotional expression. This focus on the emotional component of dance was one of the factors that I intended to probe more deeply, and to postulate that a local form of expressionism might be a common characteristic of contemporary Brazilian dance artists. The key moment arose during a conversation between seven dancers, as they discussed the merits of two dance festivals, one in Joinville and the other in São Paulo. All seven finally agreed that the latter one was superior because the dances in Joinville didn't, as they put it, "do anything for them." Van den Bergen was among them and reiterated that for her part, dance works must leave her with "some kind of emotion." Then Bianca Corteletti and Patricia Miranda countered that it wasn't precisely a matter of feeling an emotion, but that it was more a matter of feeling "differently." And then, Bianca said something that triggered the third awakening: "I think *enchantment* is the right word." It was then that I began to think about Brazilians in general as being accustomed to having their bodies, and life events, "charged" with emotion but also a certain kind of "energy."

This "charged body" then became a central metaphor, functioning as a thematic thread to link the discoveries arising from the fieldwork and analysis. I was able to isolate a group of key concepts that proved common to all the dancers, in spite of their diverse aesthetic approaches:

- Choreographic diversity and complexity
- Difficulties, oppression, limitations of their social predicament
- Joyful attitude toward life tempered with jeitinho (or cunning approach to life)
- Primacy of emotion
- Intensity, determination, commitment in terms of their dance-making

In other words, on the whole, the discoveries that emerged from this study revealed a group of dance artists who committed to their endeavours with a remarkable intensity, who spoke about the barriers they had to overcome to practise dance, in particular the conditions resulting from the intense poverty and political oppression in their environment. As a result of the struggle to sustain their passion in the face of these difficulties, they viewed their dancing primarily as a form of resistance. And so for these Brazilian dancers it was essential that the dance convey socially charged messages to their audiences.

Figure 2 Eluza Maria Santos in her own choreography, *Folia*. Photographer: Steve Clarke.

LEAVING THE FIELD, BUT "WILL BE BACK HOME SOON"

A recurring theme throughout the accounts of ethnographic researchers about their work has been the conflict between leaving and not leaving the field. Along with many fellow researchers, I also found myself very reluctant to leave the field when the time came. Ties had been forged that I didn't want to bring to an end, having developed friendships that are still present in my life.

Discussing the reasons why researchers remain in, or return to, the field after completing their research, Shaffir and Stebbins elaborated on the "barriers that pull on the researcher to remain in the field, such as the attitude of the group studied toward the withdrawal of members or the intensity of the established relations" (1991: 207). As for my own research project in Vitória, it proved true that "the researcher never leaves completely as a result of secondary involvements that are established during the course of the study" (Shaffir and Stebbins, 1991: 208). Zinn went further, recounting how her subjects had actually become dependent on her (1979). And so, when some of them expressed their disappointment when she had to disengage herself from the field, Zinn had to remove her services and support completely. In my case, this point of extreme interdependence was never reached, but I was aware that my subjects had come to expect my continuing involvement with them. This did happen and would in fact become a core dynamic within my future professional activities, because I was still, in so many ways, an active part of the community that I researched. It was my own desire to keep following the development of contemporary dance in Vitória, hoping to support the work of those artists as well as maintain a link between them and the United States.

I was an associate professor in the Dance Department of the University of North Carolina in Greensboro from 1996 to 2008. The vital connections with my Brazilian roots, the fact that I missed spending time in Brazil, and the deep ties with my family members brought me back to Vitória at least once a year. When I came home, members of the dance community often contacted me and engaged me once again in shared professional activities. After having participated in my research, the contemporary dance artists of Vitória, with little access to dance research, became eager to see the final document and to have it translated into Portuguese. I have done several presentations about my research for these artists.

They know now that they will never lose contact with me, and that I am committed to keeping my promises. Even after everything was finished, my study's participants didn't have to wonder if I would be "one of those researchers who is never seen in the community again once the study is completed" (Zinn, 1979: 217). I always come home. It happened in the past after the conclusion of my MFA. I frequently came home while I was immersed in doctoral studies. And after leaving the University of North Carolina at Greensboro, a major change occurred since I relocated to the greater Vitória area, being active here with a new dance company ElnzaArtes.

However, I continue my professional activities with the Latina Dance Theatre Project, which I co-founded with Licia Perea, Juanita Suarez, and Eva Tessler, artists of Latino origin, in the United States. Even though I like the fact that my work includes connections to another country, my roots are still very deep in Brazil.

Note
This adaptation was completed with assistance from Dena Davida.

Bibliography
Bochner, Arthur, and Carolyn Ellis. "Taking Ethnography into the Twenty-First Century." *Journal of Contemporary Ethnography* 25, no. 1 (1996): 1–5.

Erlandson, David A., Edward L. Harris, Barbara L. Skipper, and Steve D. Allen. *Doing Naturalistic Inquiry: A Guide to Methods*. Newbury Park, CA: Sage, 1993.

Fraleigh, Sondra. *Dance and the Lived Body: A Descriptive Aesthetics*. Pittsburgh: University of Pittsburgh Press, 1987.

———. "Dances I Like: Critical Values and Phenomenology." Paper presentation, SummerDance '93, Texas Woman's University, Summer 1993.

Marshall, Catherine, and Gretchen B. Rossman. *Designing Qualitative Research*. Newbury Park, CA: Sage, 1989.

Novack, Cynthia. "Looking at Movement as Culture: Contact Improvisation to Disco." *Theater Drama Review* 32, no. 4 (1988): 102–19.

Shaffir, William, and Robert Stebbins (eds.). *Experiencing Fieldwork: An Inside View of Qualitative Research*. Newbury Park, CA: Sage, 1991.

Van Manen, Max. *Researching Lived Experience: Human Science for an Action Sensitive Pedagogy*. New York: State University of New York Press, 1990.

Zinn, Maxine B. "Field Research in Minority Communities: Ethical, Methodological and Political Observations by an Insider." *Social Problems* 27, no. 2 (1979): 209–19.

CHAPTER NINE

Reflections on Making the Dance Documentary Regular Events of Beauty

NEGOTIATING CULTURE IN THE WORK OF CHOREOGRAPHER RICHARD TREMBLAY

PRIYA THOMAS

So you think you've finally finished something; in fact, I'm sure it's a familiar feeling to you. You put away a flexed and puckered stack of pages, cross something off a long list of to-do's, and get up from the desk anticipating the false lull of that vague, self-congratulatory feeling. Well, I was in just that state of completion euphoria when an email twinkled from the blue radiation light of my computer screen. It was the *Fields in Motion* editor requesting that I say something about myself to introduce you to this chapter. It was suggested that perhaps I could give you a better view of myself, or present myself formally, before you started to read this ...

So now I am here again feeling daunted, with my toes skimming the surface of those baptismal waters, knowing that I am a different person, with a different sense of identity, than when I first shot and directed the dance documentary video entitled *Regular Events of Beauty*. And then again, perhaps it is this sense of change and transition in the perception of identity that has guided and underpinned my work with Montreal choreographer Richard Tremblay and his culturally hybridized works (Chambers 1994, Young 1995).

In 2002, when I had finished producing my documentary, I would have considered myself a dance writer, enrolled in the graduate program at York University in Toronto. I would perhaps have mentioned that I come from a family of academics; that my father is a Syrian Orthodox minister with a PhD in theology, and that my mother was a physicist before she opted to raise children. I might also have mentioned my ongoing work as a musician.

Today, nine years following the making of the documentary, my context and self-perception has changed; and much of my time is spent producing my own artistic work and writing music. This has necessarily meant that the boundaries between artist and researcher, normally so blunt and circumscribed in social science research, have here, in this space, become nebulous, soft, and fragmented in the murky overlaps between artist and researcher. It was my intention to present the content of my findings in a way that illuminated the artistic sensibilities of its writer as well as its subject. In that sense, I didn't see myself as standing on the other side of a fence from my subject. I am not neutral in my observations. I am subjective, relational, and identified with the subject—and interested in the process of "coming together" in the trenches of fieldwork.

Some of the questions guiding my work were, "Am I neutral in the process of documenting my subject?" "Is it worth pursuing a neutral position?" "Can a neutral position actually exist?" and "Is there a way to document and remain critical and open to questions in a non-neutral relational dynamic?"

As such, I drew from the phenomenological approach (Husserl 1970) that I had encountered as an undergraduate in religious studies, which sought to unify the researcher's act of understanding the subject's experience, with the act of classifying and categorizing the phenomena being studied. I wanted to document the subject's spirit of creativity in artmaking, and also find a way to research the subject creatively. I did not simply want to present a positivist document of the events as they occurred, but a creative expression of a dynamic interchange. So I decided to compile a personal collection of journal entries that rolled childhood memories, journals of field notes, as well as all my formal interviews with the subject, into one multi-dimensional onslaught. It begins:

My first memory of Richard Tremblay is sitting at the kitchen table with my parents over a Sunday afternoon meal. The typical Kerala style chicken in coriander curry sauce and green chillies was ladled over spongy sourdough bread, and onto the casual melamine plates bordered with uneven, imperfect floral patterns. He ate with his hands and spoke attentively, his nacreous hands tracing ideas in the glacial, sunlit air in the idle Montreal afternoon. I must have been at least five, because I sat with my legs dangling off the chair, but not quite touching the carpet, swinging solidly with a to-and-fro kind of restless rocking motion. I eventually crossed my legs up onto the upholstered checkerboard fabric of the dining chair and listened to the proverbially arcane conversations that I came to expect.

Despite what I did not understand as a five-year-old about the content of Richard's conversations with my family, what I did gather was that Richard was unusual. I could understand that he had given something up to pursue his work with dance. I'm not sure I ever figured out the specifics of what he had sacrificed, but that strong sense of sacrifice being central to his work persisted with me.

In other ways, too, Richard became a kind of subtle archetype that crept in and left questions gnawing at me. I became aware in a way that I might not otherwise have noticed, that being an artist was a dignified vocation ... it could be possible to pursue your interests at the cost of so many other creature comforts.

And, finally, Richard was significant to me even as a five-year-old in a way that I could only have intuitively known ... that he was an outsider. I somehow felt he was like me, only on the other side of the cultural fence looking in. If ever I asked myself then,

"What is Richard doing here?" ...

I think I know now. He was throwing a tiny stone into a much larger ocean, and like anyone else, he was making waves. He was closing the cultural gap just by being there on a Sunday afternoon. He was making contact.

Figure 1   Richard Tremblay as costumed dancer. Photo courtesy of Kalashas.

I spent four days at Le Centre Kalashas in Montreal with choreographer Richard Tremblay in December 2002, in order to produce a video of a dance artist working on the margins of Quebec culture. What is extraordinary about Richard Tremblay's work in contemporary choreography is his identification with the margins of Canadian dance culture, and that his choreography draws its movement vocabulary from a dance culture to which he does not belong (Chambers 1994, Ferguson 1990, Fusco 1995).

Richard Tremblay is credited with being the first Canadian to have trained in Kathakali and then choreographed new, cross-cultural works using traditional Kathakali conventions (Tremblay 1982, Zarilli 2000). In 1986, he set up Le Centre Kalashas with musical collaborator Bruno Paquet in order to develop projects and choreographic work. Specifically, Richard Tremblay is a key example of the Canadian experience of global culture, of art in the age of globalization (Fusco 1995, Gilroy 1993, Kitaj 1989). And it was this choreographic process that seems to cross borders, the culturally transgressive dance that I was interested in understanding (Chambers 1994, Chow 1993).

Furthermore, the dance form known as Kathakali in which Tremblay was trained, has suffered from a similarly marginal and underdocumented existence in its native context of South India, in part through the rapid changes brought on by industrialization and the birth of modern city life. In its traditional form, Kathakali is evocative of the sixteenth century highly educated priestly cast traditions, or Kerala Brahminical traditions that have been long discarded with the advent of urban living (Appadurai 1996). As television and the web bring the hegemony of American culture into the homes of Kerala families, traditional dance forms that do not translate well into a television format begin to lose former audiences.

Given the context of Kathakali in Kerala itself, transplantation of the dance form to North America is an ambitious undertaking (Chambers 1994). And in Quebec, the presentation of Kathakali is so rare that one would think it often requires either connoisseurs of the art form in the audience to appreciate its performance or a quick history lesson to understand its value. What is fascinating about Richard Tremblay is that he has found a way to present Kathakali work done on the margins to an audience that is made up of both contemporaries in traditional Kathakali and the completely unschooled. His approach is elastic, negotiable, culturally diverse, and continually in flux. And though in the video he does not elaborate on a method as such for the performance and choreography of hybrid Kathakali works in a new context, it becomes clear that Tremblay does have strong ideas about the choices involved in transplanting or recreating culture (Tremblay 1983).

Richard Tremblay is a French-speaking Quebecer with a background in theatre and linguistics who has studied the highly specialized and rigorous training of Kathakali dance theatre in the exacting methods of training used by the best established and oldest of Kathakali training centres, the Kerala Kalamandalam. Kathakali originated in the sixteenth century in the southwestern state of Kerala and has recently enjoyed a more international appeal, in part fuelled by new academic scholarship and interest in the area of globalization, cross-cultural enterprise, and the Kathakali dance tradition itself (Appadurai 1996). The word *Kathakali* reveals something of its historical background, in that it is a highly Sanskritized Malayalam word that can be split into two just like a dvandva compound in Sanskrit. *Katha* means "story," and *kali* means "play" or "game." Kathakali's peculiar combination of both dance and theatre in equal parts has provided the vocabulary for cross-cultural communication in Tremblay's choreography.

After I had finished my four-day shoot with Tremblay and his musical collaborator Bruno Paquet, I started to think about Tremblay's notion of the myriad choices that affect the choreography of new cross-cultural work. It was in this context that I began to consider the idea of negotiating culture as a theme that could guide the editing process of the video. Specifically, I chose to pay close attention to the negotiations of culture involved in the reworking of Greek epics such as the *Iliad* (which is perhaps Tremblay's best-known work) through the movement vocabulary of Kathakali (Iampolski 1998, Takaki 1995). I started to give some thought to the interview segments with Tremblay in which he spoke about everything from the training process in Kathakali to the politics of arts funding in Canada. Among the many comments that really captured my attention was his idea that the "epic universe" could be transferred from one form to another, in so far as there was responsible accommodation and negotiation with the dance form's native context in borrowing, adapting, and transferring dance forms.

This assumes that all cultural codes and conventions that may be easily read by those within a culture or tradition, can similarly be decoded by strangers to the culture. It occurred to me that this was a tall order. How could this be arranged? Couldn't this be dangerous work in some senses? What if codes are misread and misunderstood and those in the originating culture are left only with a sense of being inappropriately appropriated or misunderstood? And isn't the idea of universals somehow outdated, a fossil of the imperial dream?

I began to really listen to Richard Tremblay. And I noticed that he neither wholly subscribed to the skeptical postmodern relativities of culture, nor did he understand his world in terms of the modernist hope of universals and absolutes. Instead, his is an approach that is aware and sensitive to the post-colonial discourse that surrounds the creation of new artwork in India while being equally sensitive to the context in which he currently works. For example, while listening carefully to Tremblay's words and observing his process, it became apparent to me that the essence of the *Iliad* is not its importance as a towering work of European literature. And neither is the essence of the *BhagavadGita* its stature as a Hindu epic and scripture. Rather, the importance of these works is based in a kind of existential truth, the truth told about the human condition through its characters and through the hybrid and fragmented process itself. The hybrid working process started to make me think that unlike postmodernist choreographers who favour fragmentation over truth, Tremblay's process seems to incorporate the universals and absolutes of a modernist approach along with the fragmentation and multiplicity of the postmodern.

In this sense, Tremblay's work with the *Iliad*, in particular, is reminiscent of the work done by Peter Brook with the theatrical production of the medieval Hindu epic, the *Mahabharata*. Peter Brook's film of the *Mahabharata* was one of the first intercultural productions of the epic. It was originally based on a stage production that involved an international cast. Brook made the choice to use English as the language of the script, however, and insisted that all the actors retain their original accents and not attempt to "correct" or "tidy up" their pronunciation. For anyone who may have seen the piece, this is a noticeable feature of the film and, I think, a statement regarding how Brook would like his *Mahabharata* to be situated both aesthetically and geographically.

The choice to use accents to inform and decorate the English language indicates an interest in language that moves beyond the idea that language must remain pure, untouched, and separate from change and flux. Brook is clear in his statement that fragmented English is still English (Fusco 1995). Brook's English *Mahabharata* is a hybrid production that, like Tremblay's work, tries to throw all of the instabilities of culture, the confusing costumes, the accents, the idiosyncrasies, the politics, and characters all into one colossal production. What results is a production that seems to negotiate with multiple cultures (Lippard 1990). It is a disruptive and destabilizing process that plays with the meanings of all the cultures involved. And if there is finally a universal that can be understood, and can be translated, it is the truth of the non-homogenous human condition. In this sense, the universal truth, the raison d'être, is in the fragmentation and hybridity of the working process (Young 1995).

Another pair of questions that occurred to me in developing my portrait document of Tremblay were, "How does one experience fragmentation enough to then incorporate that into a working process?" and "Is this sense of fragmentation part of Tremblay's self-definition?"

Belonging is an essential part of transmitting culture across generations (Kitaj 1989). And through belonging to a culture, however, we establish ideas of inside and outside. More specifically, the notion of insider and outsider become central to assessments of relevance in any artwork produced in a homogenous environment. Having observed and interviewed Tremblay with regard to his sense of identity in the Montreal dance community, I have noticed an acute sense of interculturality; of finding oneself in the margins rather than in the belonging (Ferguson 1990). Part of my interest in making *Regular Events of Beauty*, then, was to try to understand this experience of self-definition as it emerges through complex negotiations with various communities and cultures.

Particular attention was given editing segments to include the idea of adaptation of a work for a new context. These adaptations provide a very rich source of information on the ways in which choreographers negotiate culture through the borrowing of themes, the transplantation of ideas, and even a reinvention of technique.

Choreographic adaptations also depend on the use of language in transmitting culture. So another emphasis in my video is the use of language as a signifier of culture. I had originally decided that the interview segments would feature Tremblay speaking in French with English subtitles. But during the interviews, I noticed that he would switch languages in mid-sentence quite naturally to find words that would best express his feelings or ideas. So this seemed to me to indicate two important features of Tremblay's new Kathakali: namely, the flexibility involved in the creative process and the multiplicity of languages that characterizes the new context of Kathakali as it specifically operates in Montreal. Furthermore, in trying to capture the hybrid, regular, everyday experience of cultural exchange and negotiation in Tremblay's artistic process in Montreal, I finally decided that I would allow the interview segments to proceed in whatever language was used without the addition of subtitles in order to emphasize exactly this variety of experience.

In an off-camera moment, Tremblay explained to me that he first learned how to speak English in India from people whose first language was Malayalam—and that he had picked up colloquialisms, inflections, and an accent that he would otherwise not have had, had he learned his English in francophone Quebec. He went on to say that his personal experience of the teaching of English in the French school system lacked both context and emotional resonance, so that when he finally learned English in India, it was because the language had found a resonance, a reason to grow, through his study of *Kathakali*. I thought this was yet another complex moment—a remembrance of a cultural negotiation that expressed the layers of cultural dialogue informing Tremblay's work.

In light of the intricacy of Tremblay's creative process, I also decided to document rehearsal footage instead of performance footage. This was a decision made in order to develop an understanding of Kathakali that moves beyond the traditional costume-intensive gaze of cultural otherness; but also a decision to concentrate on the inner world of the work. I chose to emphasize the commonality of *Kathakali* practice by looking at movement as the basic structure behind the work; and to strip away the differences that can sometimes distract a viewer from appreciating the ordinariness, the everyday nature of a Québécois man practising an ancient epic drama in plain rehearsal dress.

Though some of the complexities of Tremblay's decision to navigate between cultures remain unknown (for personal reasons), it is obvious that he identifies with the margins of multiple cultures. It is also clear that in order to function in several communities at once, Tremblay has chosen to form his sense of identity around the idea of not belonging or the "other" rather than through belonging.

I did not ask him whether always identified himself as an outsider; but it occurs to me that Tremblay has made good use of his outsider status, in that this designation has perhaps made him more acutely aware of the negotiations always necessary in producing any new work. These negotiations are an implicit part of the choices any person makes in adapting works to new contexts, reconstructing long lost choreographic works, or even collaborating with other dancers in creating a work. For, in each case, one is ultimately confronted with difference: the difference of a new culture or geography, the difference attributable to a lost or distant history, or the basic difference of another human body.

Since I made *Regular Events of Beauty* in 2002, it has been a project that I have revisited and reconsidered over several years. This is partially because I believe my own personal work with the subject may not be complete; but also because the process of documenting a hybrid dance form that grows out of the margins of a dominant culture demands that all writers and artist-researchers engage continually in a dialogue with this emerging art in order to bring its uncompromising subject matter into wider circles.

The video was my effort as an artist-researcher to document the choreographic process of hybridity as expressed through Tremblay's work. And through making the documentary, I understood what it meant for the artist-researcher to meet the artist-worker in the field, face-to-face, in the trenches in order to express those things that continually escape expression.

I have decided that we are not so different on either side of the fence. The researcher sets up his or her process so as to capture the artist and his/ her work; and the artist designs his or her process to best capture the visions that have yet to manifest. Both are equally engaged in forging work in challenging and disruptive environments. Both sides know what it means to step into another world.

As artist-researchers, we have an intimate relationship to artistic practice; and we use an artistic lens to study art itself. Through a phenomenological approach to research, I like to think we are sensitive enough to skirt objectivity in favour of a more complex, hermeneutic process. The researcher is no longer simply outside the gates of art as an objective observer, but is engaged in the creative process with the camera and the documented artist.

Sympathetic artist-researchers know that the words and tools we employ can describe and accurately detail events—and that we can document dance as if we were dance historians. And yet, like the artist I have chosen to document, I prefer to use a hybrid approach to media to communicate and document (e.g., the use of video still-frames; silences in interviews and essays to evoke and suggest, rather than explain) (Sherman 1998). I like to think that emerging artist-researchers do not deny the chaotic world of inspiration, but exploit the world of half-thoughts and intuition with the same conviction as traditional arguments.

To put it simply, there is an important role that an artist-researcher can play in the continued development of the field; that is, contribute to the discussion the view that art can be discussed in a non-reductionist, complex, confessional, and emotive process that more resembles art than history. In this sense, artist-researchers may be an invaluable resource—a mediating body that can translate between the world of historical research and of art. After all, someone must run interference; someone must navigate in between the nuances of statements such as:

"What you said to me ...," which constitutes the hard facts, the historical accuracy of an event, and,
"How you said it to me ...," which is the arena of nowhereness and multiple meanings—and the ineffable terrain of dance.

Bibliography

Anderson, Benedict. *Imagined Communities*. London: Verso, 1992.

Appadurai, Arjun. *Modernity at Large: Cultural Dimensions of Globalization*. Minneapolis: University of Minnesota Press, 1996.

Bhabha, Homi. *The Location of Culture*. London: Routledge, 1994.

César Augusto Salgado. Hybridity in New World Baroque Theory. *Journal of American Folklore* 445 (Summer 1999): 48–73.

Chambers, Iain. *Migrancy Culture Identity*. London: Routledge, 1994.

Chow, Rey. *Writing Diaspora*, Bloomington: Indiana University Press, 1993.

Clifford, James. *The Predicament of Culture*. Cambridge, MA: Harvard University Press, 1991.

Cubitt, Sean. "Dispersed Visions: About Place." *Third Text* 32 (Autumn 1995): 65–74.

Derrida, Jacques. *Of Grammatology*. Baltimore: Johns Hopkins University Press, 1976.

Ferguson, Russell, et al. (eds.). *Out There: Marginalization and Contemporary Cultures*. Boston: MIT Press, 1990.

Fusco, Coco. *English Is Broken Here: Notes in Cultural Fusion in the Americas*. New York: New Press, 1995.

Gilroy, Paul. *The Black Atlantic: Modernity and Double Consciousness*. Cambridge, MA: Harvard University Press, 1993.

Husserl, Edmund. *The Crisis of European Sciences and Transcendental Phenomenology*. Evanston, IL: Northwestern University Press, 1970.

Iampolski, Mikhail. *The Memory of Tiresias: Intertextuality and Film*. Berkeley, CA: University of California Press, 1998.

Kitaj, R.B. *First Diasporist Manifesto*. London: Thames and Hudson, 1989.

Lippard, Lucy. *Mixed Blessings: New Art in a Multicultural America*. New York: Pantheon, 1990.

Mayne, Judith. *Cinema and Spectatorship*. New York: Routledge, 1993.

Mbembe, Achille. "Figures of the Subject in Times of Crisis." *Public Culture* 7 (1995): 323–52.

Powers, Martin J. "Art and History: Exploring the Counterchange Condition." *Art Bulletin* 77, no. 3 (September 1995): 382–87.

Rogoff, Irit. "Luggage and Borders." In *Terra Infirma: Geography's Visual Culture*. London: Routledge, 2000.

Said, Edward. *Culture and Imperialism*. New York: Alfred Knopf, 1993.

Sherman, Daniel, and Irit Rogoff. *Museum Culture*. Minneapolis: Minnesota University Press, 1994.

Shohat, Ella, and Robert Stam. "Narrativizing Visual Culture: Towards a Polycentric Aesthetics." In Nicholas Mirzoeff (ed.), *The Visual Culture Reader*. London: Routledge, 1998.

Sinha, Ramone. "A Cross-Cultural Trojan Horse." 1997. http://www.silentculture.org/creation/default.asp (accessed January 6, 2002).

Takaki, Ronald. "A Different Mirror." In *Points of Entry: Tracing Cultures: The Friends of Photography*. San Francisco: University of San Francisco Press, 1995.

Thompson, Robert Farris. *Flash of the Spirit: African and Afro American Art and Philosophy*. New York: Random House, 1983.

Tremblay, Richard. "La Danse Ethnique; Inadéquation d'un Concept." *Re-Flex* 21 (Winter 1983): 15–19.

———. "Initiation au travail de la danse de l'Inde." *Les Cahiers de la Danse de l'Inde* 1 (septembre 1982): 3–26.

Young, Robert. *Colonial Desire: Hybridity in Theory, Culture and Race.* London: Routledge, 1995.

Zarilli, Phillip B. *Kathakali Dance-Drama: Where Gods and Demons Come to Play.* New York: Routledge, 2000.

CHAPTER TEN

Angelwindow

"I DANCE MY BODY DOUBLE"

INKA JUSLIN

MY FINNISH ETHNOGRAPHIC BENT WITH PHILOSOPHY

My choreographic career began in the mid-1990s, at a time when the social structure of the Finnish dance field was changing and a young generation of ballet and modern dance theatre artists was beginning to emerge (Sarje 2006: 90–91). Discussing my artistic work has proved more difficult than performing it, yet I believe it is crucial to reflect on the concepts that emerge during creative processes. In terms of ethnography, writing about one's own work proposes narratives, from insider perspectives, on processes and their aftermaths.

A group of artists and arts scholars in Finland begun to enhance creative processes and the knowledge gained from insider perspectives. While focusing on contemporary dance communities in Finnish, European, and North American contexts, they started investigating practice-based modes of gathering information about processes. My impression has been that their artistic research often aligns ethnography with philosophical discussions about the arts and about the body, and that by way of personal approaches they criticize particular Western schemes of aesthetics by building up new philosophical, aesthetic, and artistic ideas about the content of contemporary dance.[1] With this kind of orientation, it has been possible to develop new knowledge about recent dance histories. Finnish contemporary choreographers are well aware of their choreographic roots and the international influences behind their creative ideas.

I attended my first artistic research seminar in early 2000 in Finland. The various research groups that were formed during the seminar focused their attention on artistic processes, bringing together different genres in the art field. I later joined the Art and Narrative Inquiries group during a conference in January 2001 at the Helsinki Theatre Academy. In 2002, I participated in a writing workshop for doctoral students in the arts organized by the Helsinki University of Art and Design; the school had engaged Canadian Rishma Dunlop to teach us expressive writing methods. Dunlop led us to ponder how we might engage with personal narratives in our research by examining the use of life memories and cultural objects, both foreign and familiar, as research data. And in 2003, I took part in yet another workshop at the Zodiak Center for New Dance in Helsinki. The practice-based studio workshop, called Writing from the Body, was led by Diana Theodores of Britain, who focused on both dance and writing. We produced various text fragments, maintaining an awareness while writing of our presence in the moment, constantly using our moving bodies as source material.

I have learned from fellow artists as well as from my own artistic research that the moments of discovering one's own core ideas are those that really count. Bodily experience *can* speak through scholarly and theoretical writing. In her seminal book *A Passage to Anthropology: Between Experience and Theory* (1995), anthropologist Kirsten Hastrup advanced the idea that ethnographic practice is always about something composed from within one's own memory. She further proposed that ethnography was a mixture of experiences, drawn from the life cycle and the full subjectivity of being, thus situating its process as one that lay somewhere between anthropology and autobiography. Without experiences in the field, our artistic practices and our writing about them would lose the essence of speaking out from subjective knowledge (Hastrup 1995: 15).

My personal experiences in practice-based artistic research have taught me that philosophical inquiry helps to explain experiential moments. Philosophy assists by narrating the dance movements and the choreographic language, the drafts, methods, and ideas that are used in the process. To my mind, phenomenological narration represents a mode of language that allows my body and its knowledge to speak through speech and writing.[2] I use phenomenological narrative both as a practical choreographic tool and also when I wish to make sense to myself about my choreographic ideas. In addition, I use it to survey the structures of tacit knowledge in my body, asking what is being revealed during the process. To do this, I often write in a diary while researching the movements. The language I use for this purpose is very metaphorical. I benefit later from the diary descriptions because my writing reveals how I have fulfilled the task: I have been creating work that articulates, in the present moment, the different modes of being. I am aware that through textual descriptions, the artistic information becomes only partially visible, but it surely becomes more comprehensible through the layers of language.

I call the moment that follows my choreographic processes the *aftermath*. It signifies a state to me, one in which I go back to my diary and to the performance, then analyze them in one way or another. If I am able to, I also reflect about them by way of theories of experience, namely those from the anthropological and philosophical literature. To accomplish this kind of aftermath, I need to stay open to my autoethnographic self. I do not let myself doubt its authenticity, but allow the voice of my experience and memory speak. Thus, ethnographic writing about one's own work creates a room in which one moves toward a fuller description of events that have been explored during the choreographic process. But it also touches my life cycle, as I will explain.

Here, I discuss the dance solo *Angelwindow*, which I created during the fall of 2006 and performed for the first time in 2007. Reviewing the choreographic process with phenomenological description suggests that I will follow a mode in which I use my body as "the site of knowledge" (Cancienne and Snowber 2003). Through writing, I further consider how it was that my life as a woman and as a dancer played out during the creative process itself and in its aftermath. This ethnographic account might be considered as a form of arts-based research, one that interfaces anthropological autoethnography with certain philosophies of the body. Various forms of personal narratives—autoethnographic writing, explorations that fall between creative empirical work and various "real-life" aesthetic modes of performative representation—are richly introduced in a book edited by Arthur P. Bochner and Carolyn Ellis, *Ethnographically Speaking: Autoethnography, Literature, and Aesthetics* (2002). Their example has encouraged me to use my voice as a narrator, to describe my first-person experience and to reflect on my artistic intuition.

ABOUT THE PROJECT

Angelwindow is a solo dance project containing both a video and a theatrical component. The video was first presented by itself in an intimate gallery space in April 2007 as part of the Dance Decentralization Zone, a festival of suburban dance and visual arts in Helsinki.[3] In May 2007, I performed the live theatrical version of *Angelwindow* at Dance Theatre Hurjaruuth in the Helsinki Cable Factory. The performance program included three solo choreographies and was called *Diaspora: Traversing the Changing Body*. The two other choreographers who performed their solos alongside my own were Ronja Verkasalo and Otto Akkanen. I also developed *Angelwindow* as a joint video and live performance that was flexible enough to present in smaller spaces, such as galleries. In November 2007, I performed the solo in the Gershwin Living Room in New York City as part of an evening of contemporary Finnish dance called *UNHOLA: The Place Where the Forgotten Memories Live.*[4]

The video of *Angelwindow* became an artistic collaboration with visual artist Outi Länsikunnas, who works with photography, video, graphic arts, and theatrical set designs. Both in our video collaboration and in the live performance, the starting point was that of bodily investigation: the visible and invisible sites of woman's body, its historicity and layers. From the outset, I wanted the project to erase different kinds of questions.

In October 2006, I was ready to show first movement sketches in a workshop in New York City, which was organized by Movement Research and hosted by Korean-born choreographer Sam Kim.[5] Sam's feedback proved essential to my process. She paid attention to my performance rhythm, noticing the particular duration of my movements, and so enhanced the movement logic that was bound to the duration, the slowness and accentuation of the movements. Sam brought me to realize that the duration being produced by my body had created movement syntax of its own. She also noticed the gestures that I was making with my fingertips, as I pointed repeatedly to my face and sacrum. This "keyhole gesture," as she called it, was connected to my vertebrae and to the bottom of my spine and proposed an image of evolution, or of the progression that human beings encompass during their life cycle.[6]

I began shooting the video with Outi Länsikunnas in December 2006. The camera angle was very important to us. One goal of the project was the idea that I would position myself in front of the camera while performing authentic presence with my body. My intention was to look away from the camera and move as if not acknowledging the camera presence, as sometimes occurs in ethnographic video documentation. On the other hand, our recognizing the fact that the video camera is always a powerful tool, even when used as merely an ethnographic device to grasp human presence and the present moment, gave great meaning to our artistic collaboration.

My choreographic goal was to make a solo about the bones and the bony surfaces of my body. The movements were intended to highlight the elbows, knees, and head, with the purpose of revealing the tension and areas of discomfort in my physicality. Sam had commented that the choreographed movements appeared "as if timeless." My choice to shiver my body with minimal gestures created tensions that gave the body a raw and primal appearance, yet not in any way animalistic.[7]

This solo project sprang from my need to address the particularities of a woman dancer's body throughout her life cycle and dance career. I had earlier begun discussions with myself while thinking about my own dance career, and also began sharing information about choreographic processes with colleagues who were similarly preoccupied. Finnish ballet dancer Minna Tervamäki, younger generation choreographers Susanna Leinonen and Ronja Verkasalo, and dancer-scholars Leena Rouhiainen and Susan Kozel were immensely important to my work by sharing and being so open about their own artistry, career, and womanliness.

In *Angelwindow*, I investigated my own corporeal life cycle, accounting that a dancer might live through several phases of relationship to her body throughout her career. I have in fact had many careers as a dancer: first there was my youth, in which I received the requisite corporeal education. My middle career was the phase in which I established contacts, found working partners, and significantly changed habitual behaviours. The next phase is usually radical: the process of aging that dancers experience while still quite young. For me, it was not only the fact that my body was aging, but the process also took place in my mind. It disrupted my performance persona, and it touched the entire domain of my subjectivity. This latter phase was the most influential in my making of *Angelwindow*. As a dancer, I am currently living through new changes to my body and in my career. I have arrived at a phase in which I re-evaluate my body and recontextualize it, pondering how my orientation makes me who I am.

While making the solo, it didn't come as a surprise to me that my adolescence resurfaced. There were even moments when this youthful period predominated in the movement research. Adolescence is a period in a female dancer's life when one usually makes important decisions about the future. And so it is also possible that those years reappear as she starts to ponder aging. My *Angelwindow* narrates an adolescent female body whose experiences were strongly *revisited* in the solo. But, without mediation, they are performed in an adult woman's body. The nature of this double tension is one of the important artistic questions in this solo. I looked back on my adolescence as a nurturing period, the years of my life in which a pathway was opened, leading to the formation of my subjectivity.

SETTINGS FOR THE DANCE VIDEO

Outi Länsikunnas and I decided to use an art school interior for our video shoot. We chose a drawing studio with mismatched tables and white walls to provide a somewhat neutral environment, but also to point to a specific direction with our simple setting. She proposed that I wear white clothes, which proved to loosely resemble the work clothes of artists or painters but which also implied an underlying theme of "cleanliness" and suggested a "clinical attitude" behind the costuming of my video role. My white, long-sleeve shirt and pants suggested the setting of an anatomy class. One could also think about my career as a dancer in this context. I have specifically been interested in my own anatomy, and it is fair to assume that there is no career in dance without attention paid to one's own anatomy and bodily changes. The dancer's body eventually becomes a site for anatomical investigation. Doesn't that also make it clinical? A body of pain, and the feminine body? For, metaphorically speaking, isn't it also the body of menstruation and childbirth?

In the background, we had white wall panels on which there hung a bright yellow painting with the timeline *1950–2000* and the word *Minimalism* written on it. There were also white chairs on the floor that we arranged chaotically. We put a pottery machine (dreija), the potter's wheel, in the background. Part of the pottery machine was painted red.

At the centre, there were two mismatched tables pushed close together. I performed my movements in the middle of the tables so that most of the time my hips were between these two tables. From the camera's point of view, I appeared to be strangely positioned and not at all comfortable, as both of my knees were deeply bent, and one was sometimes in the position of an attitude. My blond hair was pulled back into ponytail, and black ballet shoes and black nail polish contrasted the white clothing.

Figure 1 Triptych of Inka Juslin performing *Angelwindow*. Video-still photographer: Outi Länsikunnas.

During the time that we were making the video, Outi was pregnant—a fact made evident by the way she used the camera. We discussed Outi's situation, wanting to include this ethnographic fact in the shooting. So we let the movements of the camera follow her breathing in such a way that the apparatus would seem as if part of the same flesh as her pregnant body, breathing and moving with the baby. As with her two previous pregnancies, this one changed her breathing patterns and the rhythm of her body. It intensified the circulation of blood and made her whole body more sensitive, its fluids reactive to the life inside her body.

Outi's habitus as an artist, who has often used her experience as a mother in her artworks and in her ways of working with visual devices, became significantly entangled in our video aesthetics. In her 2005 master's thesis, she had investigated the use of the pinhole camera as an environmental device. During her own artistic research process, she came to the conclusion that the camera is not only an instrument, but essentially part of the environment it is coding and, thus, producing.[8] At best, the camera may become one with its user—as if the hand and eye of an artist would make the crucial operational choices, and not visa versa. This makes sense within phenomenological artistic philosophy, in which the camera does not impose such a power on its own, but makes statements through the lens of an artist and through her body. Outi's understanding of the shooting activity of her camera was closely related to Maurice Merleau-Ponty's phenomenology of the body. She has, in fact, found inspiration for her visual art from his phenomenological concepts, as I have for my dance art.

TECHNICALITY OF THE VIDEO MOVEMENTS

I am on one of the two tables posing to the side, keeping quite low at first. My face is turned toward the camera, but my focus is directed inward. My attention is on my body, toward its centre, my bodily gesture is one of pointing toward myself. I shake and shiver my head, which sets my ponytail in motion. My fingers and painted fingernails make the keyhole gesture. As I turn my head slowly to the left, I place my fingers on my forehead as if indicating that I had horns. An animal ready to attack? Then I bring my head up into a pose, reminiscent of a sphinx. I stretch my upper body upward with eyes closed. I bring my head down again, shivering so that my ponytail is once again in motion. I bend down so that my forehead is almost touching the table's surface. I bring my head up once again, even more closely resembling a sphinx. I lean slightly backwards, stretching my left arm, imitating balletic postures with the torso.

Performed in slow motion, the whole image is evocative: I use an outreaching upper-body gesture to express longing, but my movements emphasize the torso only, as my legs are cut off from activity. My sphinx is captured, imprisoned, so that forward and backward movements are prevented. I stretch my legs, which are still but hold no tension. The leg lifted in a bent attitude creates a seemingly uncomfortable posture. There appears to be no use for my legs but to support my torso's outreaching. My buttocks are in extension, as if I was presenting an extended performance of the female body. The posture is in constant, continual tension. It seems as if it took ages of human evolution to develop a body that is this numb.

What follows is a surprise, an unexpected moment. My first finger key-hole gesture hits my forehead, and stays there. Another keyhole gesture is now hitting my lower back, the sacrum. My facial focus introduces tension to the invisible audience behind the camera, although my gaze is inward directed. I open one leg again in an attitude position, turning my torso slightly toward the camera and placing one arm on my waist. I open my body up a bit. I gesture to the side with my arms and drop my upper body downwards. The movement flow is now different, there's more swaying. It is the moment of decision-making.

I drop my head, giving my hands a new supportive role. My elbows are bent; I pull my hips up and let my knees support the drop, using my toes instead. A more released moment of decision-making follows. I drop my head one more time, and then slowly stretch my hips downwards so that they hit the other table. I have moved forward in space, my ankles pointing toward my buttocks: in unison for the first time, both arms and feet create a symmetrical stance.

More tension follows. With my legs pulled closer into my body, my whole body gestures *at me*. I avoid touching one of the tables, which I leave behind. I remain poised on the surface of the other one. I turn my body to face the camera, shiver with my head and bring it even closer to my spine and hips. My head is at the height of the pottery wheel, which evidently creates another tension.

I release the tension a bit, allowing my other leg to stretch so that my pointed foot touches the table behind me. My hand reaches toward that leg, while the other is still bent, and I hold it with my hand. I try bending deeper toward my body's centre, my solar plexus, becoming as small as possible. At the same time, my bodily gesture indicates the table behind me, which remains spatially out of my reach. I appear as if I were a creature without legs.

My next choice is radical. I turn my face toward the camera. My eyes lead the movement, so it is apparent that I am speaking to people behind the camera. My body breathes with the camera lens, the object that has been "looking" at me. In this core moment, the camera also shifts, alters its perspective, and changes its gaze. Now the dialogue begins. I start moving slightly away from the two-table surface. I am hanging partially in the air. My whole body is releasing. Then I communicate with the table behind me by pulling my lower body further up, as if coming closer to a standing position, although I am horizontally positioned. This indicates that there is no longer profiling, setting, and, perhaps, performing?

I move to the centre of the table in front, leaving the other one completely behind me. I place my hand underneath it to get support. For a moment, I look downwards, outside of the table surface, as if asking it to hold my next move. I keep turning in slow motion so that the top of my head is facing the camera and my ponytail hangs loosely outside the table. My left foot has landed on the table and my left hand is around the ankle. Then I set my right foot down slowly, rotating my right arm down with a circular motion, and take hold of my right ankle.

I start turning my head to the left and right, bringing it back to centre while pulling my hips up. I keep pulling, transferring weight from one side to the other. Once I am there, my arms release my ankles, letting them drop partially outside of the table surface to hang in the air. I bring my arms up to point toward the ceiling and make more keyhole gestures with my fingers. Then I bring my arms down, past my head and all the way down. I place my hands on the table for support and to reach out. I bring my hips down. My legs are turned out widely. I stretch my neck backwards so that my face looks at the camera. I pull at my forehead, looking like an alien from the camera's angle. I have wrinkles, my eyes stare, and my mouth is open so that my teeth are partially visible. I stare at the camera in this twisted position. We breathe together.

OUT OF MY CHOREOGRAPHER'S CAVE

I wrote a performance notebook in early 2007, just as we had finished the video, and I was outlining the live theatre performance. My choreographic questions took the form of a puzzle in which I asked myself how I could make my recorded movements, my "restored video body" with the power to communicate in the present moment. The video was technical, autonomous, and worked by itself, but how would the live performance change it? Synchronous video and live movements begged the question of duration. It also obliged me to revisit the concept of adolescence, to think about what it means for a woman to reappear in an adolescent body. I pondered how my present-day woman's body accentuated its historicity and its layers.

How had my dancer's career affected my womanliness? Was I still living some kind of adolescent turbulence in my body because I had chosen to be a dancer? It was partially true, I answered, so going through the process that I called "transgression for the sake of choreography" was not completely false. I felt as if I was "coming out of the cave" with my movements.

As part of my choreographic investigation, I returned to reading philosopher Luce Irigaray's famous work *Speculum* (1985). Here, she undertakes a critical reading of Western psychoanalytical and philosophical texts, unravelling the production of knowledge underlying the concepts. She illustrates Plato's cave metaphor, the core idea of which is metaphysical, but vividly visual. So the cave's imagined interior and spatial climate started nourishing my imagination and became a metaphor that instigated new choreographic visions. This image provided me with a direction, indicated where to go next with my movements and how to encompass my theatrical movements with video technicalities. In *Speculum*, Irigaray writes,

> In Plato's cave, men—sex unspecified—gaze at the shadows projected opposite them on the back of the cave. The fire behind produces nothing but shadows and gazes fascinated by shadows. And whether it be through their own eyes or through the eyes of their companions, the men can see only the projection of the light of the fire striking "objects," "figures," that are always already manufactured. Behind. What else could they see, considering that every one of them is kept in that same position? They are seated, looking fixedly across from them, backs to a supposedly like origin, one and the same, and to the path re-enacted within the cave, to its partition, to the magicians, to the instruments of their prestige, and to their spells. Which are of course always the same. Thus the men can *see* the same images, shadows, fantasies, through the eyes of others. Within this *twisted* cave of Plato's, all are identical to, identified with, prisoners who are the same and other. The community of men is caught in the snare of a symmetrical project that they could only glimpse by turning their heads. But these men are chained above all by the intractability of repetition, by the overdetermination of the one by the other, which both fascinates and escapes them. No sun will ever reduce this overdetermination to an exact truth of perception, to a "nature" clearly seen. (Irigaray 1985: 260)

Shortly after reading this, in February 2007, I began writing in my notebook:

What kinds of movements come out of that cave? Tilt or angle, have to, because otherwise one cannot even start moving. Post-standing, which is kind of a posture after falling? Not the same, but an altered shape of the same. What would happen to me if I were one of the men in Plato's cave? What would the effects be like on my movements? I spiralled, and then made a triangle, a shape never ending and the consecrated one.

I come to sacrum, a full turn; the body swallows itself in a complete turn. Who may complement this, if one is not fully there? The possible alteration begins not in time as we know it, but in an extraction of one's own involvement. It is finally laced into the bony surfaces of the body.

To begin with, Irigaray's Plato-text, here sited as fragment, inspires me. The cave scenery is a completely affective topos. The images and shadows prove there is light, although light is represented here in contradictory terms. And I respect light as a sign of creation, in which poles of representations alter, shift. There is light in two movements, in fascination and in escaping. As a pair, they occupy truthfulness and intensity so that there would be participation in a light. Who would not long for a touch, to parallel touching and to be touched, after—if there is to be an after—being chained forever?

If the cave is the interior, knitted to one's flesh, as the solar plexus, it is inside the body, in my body. That is how I dream it. And here I need to discover what my false images are, and whereupon I mirror my apprehensions. Is it then that I am the one whose image was touched upon in the cave? As an actor, I face my dreams and fears and, in the end, a limited truth. With my movements, I am getting closer to perfection, but not closer to a whole image. Speculum.

My own vulnerability is accentuated by my understanding of my interior. I have knowledge about my impulses, which I want to take deeper and further. I connect this scene of hysteria (the cave, the uterus, the interior) to memories of my adolescent menstruation, for that is the time frame in which I locate myself. Because I am a dancer, I have menstruated less throughout the years. Quite lately, I have returned to re-enter this experience. So have I come to a completely new understanding of feminine creation?

What does it mean to be young and imprisoned by love? In the body, it produces various marks. When my body is changing, I try to inquire where a differentiation commences and how I alter into another shape. I am different from men. I am bleeding; my body is a woman's body. Until now, I have been the same, and now this other *is rapidly weakening. I am bleeding, which makes my body weak. Where is the flow of* flood? *I imagine chains that tie our bodies to their gender. If we are chained in odd positions, our moods are hardly visible. Or perhaps the inner moods of those who are chained cannot be traced?*[9]

ACCOUNTS OF AUTOETHNOGRAPHIC SELF

It has become evident to me that artistic subjectivity is linked to one's working methods and relationships, which are present not only in performance contexts but in one's lifespan and personal history. I argue that art is inevitably intertwined with one's personal growth and evolution. Knowledge produced along with the artistic process recollects and brings together issues that inform us about subjectivities and culture.

In the case of my solo, much of the verbal narration about the process came afterwards. But since *Angelwindow* was an investigation from the very start, posing questions and suggesting new ones, the concepts that came afterwards made an early appearance during the process. The literary expression that was formulated alongside the choreographic process took on the character of what I call a "corporeal language dialect." The concepts I produced with my body in my artistic work were derived from the actual choreographic learning.

My autoethnographic self has passed through various *now-moments*, and is constantly rehearsing how to speak about it, seeking ways in which to communicate its uniqueness. In anthropological terms, I have been investigating how to communicate this particular local dialect of contemporary dance language to audiences. When I pose questions with my movement vocabulary, I am constantly addressing my own dancer's body. This is how I have been able to identify a new language for my body with which to communicate in the now-moment. I admit that this local dance language is full of paradoxes and ruptures, surprises, gaps, and curiosities. In other words, the language is artistic. I use it expressively to carry out creative tasks.

I have posed questions about my artistic work to myself, which in terms of ethnographic methodology might be seen as *the preparation for fieldwork*. I have performed my work for audiences, an activity that corresponds to actual process, to *being in the field*. Coming back from the field would then be *the aftermath*, in which I illuminate the affective aspects of my work. I have already spoken by way of my diary, but the real test of my ethnographic depth is in the questions that I need to further link to my autoethnographic self. To be an ethnographer, I have to give this local child (dance language) continuity, a place where it can live on in future projects.

My own identity is multicultural. To address this is important to me, since without it, this local child has no name. My complex roots are located between east and west. My family histories lie partly hidden; some are rooted back in history, all the way to the Russian Empire and Germany. My roots *now* are contemporary Finnish with an eastern Jewish twist.

Autoethnography and memory must surely touch one's sense of nostalgia, and with it arise sentiments and affects. The recollection of memories is a poetic action, but it doesn't mean that it entirely escapes the reality of real events. To my mind, memory recollection is about identity formation. I allow myself to change during artistic investigation.

My fieldwork has hovered around my subjectivity as a female dancer, taken me into observations in which I have sometimes appeared alien to myself. The video of *Angelwindow* proved to be a personal test because, acting as an artistic narrator for myself, I performed my now-presence in front of the camera in my own vocabulary. How I came to see myself in the video performance has proved to be the most substantial aftermath so far.

What gives me the chance to connect my artistic project and its locality to future dance-making is the notion that there is nothing definite about the process, no closure to obstruct new solutions. Kirsten Hastrup states that to be physically present in the field is to not make something evidentially absolute. The "process of becoming" acts as a metaphor for something yet to be completed (Hastrup 1995: 19). The process of identifying continues after the physical presence is over, and part of that process involves participation.

I have no conclusion to offer about what might come next after this field experience: where my movements will lead me next, where my dancing body will be situated, which movements it will perform.

"I DANCE MYSELF DOUBLE"

Gravity is a force that not only inhabits one's movements while dancing, but it also travels along emotionally with us throughout our lives, with the sensibility that one encounters as a woman and as a dancer. A dancer often becomes connected with a strong mentor, but her self-image also carries divergent thoughts. In practical terms, although one sometimes dances with airborne virtuosity, feelings tend to follow the *earthboundness* of one's own body image. Because I dance, the issue of objectification is also present in my body. The dancer's body is fluid and becoming, and requires rehearsing (Bringinshaw 2001: 78).

Irigaray has compared the perceiving of another's subjectivity to a state of contemplation: if I allow it to, it gives me a sensation of openness as if in a state of meditation. Our subjectivities grow and become energized just by being close to one another (Irigaray 2000: 50–52). This idea can be adapted to the live theatre performance of *Angelwindow*. I am thinking here of an odd moment during the performance where I am performing myself "as double" in which I look at myself in the video, echoing and responding to its technicality, the visual images through movement. On the one hand, my live stage movements correspond to those in the video, but at the same time they create a double movement, perhaps even a double tension: one of myself now looking at the video-image as if it was someone else. And to tell the truth, these are two different things. When I perform truthfully on the stage, my sensing of the video image occurs as if from a state of contemplation. When I am really present on the stage, my body reacts to movements in the video: I remain sensitive to it and capable of showing this doubleness to my theatre audience. Audience members have responded to me in ways, many of those responses indicating that they didn't recognize me in the video. Some people who know me quite well became confused and even asked if I was a teenager when the video was shot. Clearly, many people were unaware that the video was made in conjunction with the theatre performance. The theatre audience easily distinguished the video image and the live dancer from each other, although I at times performed exactly the same movements.

The way I am on the stage has an impact on how my movements progress. I presume that to some extent I also direct the gaze of my audience. This happens in *Angelwindow* through multimodal performance aesthetics. There is a character appearing on video and another one onstage, separately and simultaneously. The multimodality of the work becomes visible and matures during the theatre performance. The way I use my personal space, my bodily space in performance, gives me the status of a strong live performer who overrules the video character, making it appear younger or immature as compared to my womanly stage presence. In the theatre, I intentionally disturb and reshape the video picture by breathing along with mimicking movements—making it more real, making its representation of an adolescent body even more effective.

I believe this kind of multimodality emphasizes artistic processes that foreground the creation of meaning in the minds of audience members. It is not only that videos have become a powerful presence in contemporary dance performances, but video techniques have also had a strong impact on the way we now perceive dance. A multimodal perspective for dance composition provides tools to communicate the visual and gestural modes simultaneously and more effectively than if we used discursive analytical approaches to express meaning (Kress, Leite-García, and van Leeuwen 1997: 257–59).

NEW YORK AFTERMATH

The subjectivity of an ethnographer-artist is essentially bound to the practice itself. The process takes in my life, evoking also cultural and moral values. Hastrup used the metaphor of *horizon* to explain the nature of processing ethnographies. When one moves in space, the horizon shifts (Hastrup 1995: 11). A similar kind of process took place as I choreographed *Angelwindow*. I came to realize that dealing with my life and my artistic career has been a longitudinal process. As an ethnographer writing about her own dancing, I have experimented with multiple writing strategies: starting with the epistemology of dance practice and investigating the epistemological gap between the dance experience and theorizing about it. I have challenged my ethnographer's position, because dance forms my profession. My solution to these predicaments has been partly to encourage myself to create distance from these feelings in order to speak out about them. However, I will admit that my intention has also been to challenge ethnographic writing forms by speaking about these practices in a way that revealed my insider dancer's perspective.

I wrote the following in November 2007, while preparing for my *Angelwindow* performance in New York City. Once again, performance happens in an unknown place. It pushes further backwards in time. And it was exactly the theme of the program, *Unhola: The Place Where the Forgotten Memories Live.*

I come to this performance with a memory. I grew up in a close relationship to architecture, to sketches and models, learning intimately and affectively how to bond with humanity's creations. History always appeared as visual and embodied, closely attached to the bodies of close relatives and family members. I had few words with which to narrate my experience. It is maybe why I chose to dance by enhancing spatiality. My artistry is tied to my body. I am a dancer interested in radical aesthetic experiences, those of a woman, those of an adolescent. Both in one and the same body. I wish to bring forth past experiences and actions, look backwards from now, to give new meaning to them. The performance is memory. Memory is hands. Hands are emotions. The spatiality of past performance experiences appears to me as sensorial and memorable. The feeling of presences, moving bodies sensing one another, alters and shifts the location of my self. Dancing is strongly connected to the self, to the notion of dancing and performing as a site of reworking one's centre. Angelwindow doesn't narrate. But it is the memory of a past performance. I dance east and west encountering each other. If it were a balletic posture, it would be hands of Agrippina Vaganova from the old-time Russian stage. Geographically, high and low culture appears in the same sentence.

Figure 2   Photo of Inka Juslin in her choreography *Angelwindow*. Photographer: Sini Parkkinen.

Notes

1 Among the doctoral theses are my own: Juslin (Välipakka) (2003), as well as Monni (2004), Parviainen (1998), and Rouhiainen (2003). We all handle contemporary dance artistry from philosophical perspectives.
2 Inspired by Merleau-Ponty (1962, 1968), Heinämaa (1996).
3 Festival website: http://www.hajaalue.fi/hajaalue_us.shtml (accessed May 12, 2007).
4 October 29, 2006, at Movement Research. A workshop for choreographers to show works-in-progress and to get feedback.
5 Ibid.
6 Excerpt from my notebook from the MR-workshop, October 29, 2006.
7 Ibid.
8 Outi Länsikunnas, "Harjula, My Favourite Place"—Photography Project, 1–14 September 2005, unpublished MA thesis (University of Lapland, Department of Art Education, 2005). English summary: http://ace.ulapland.fi/Projects/lapland/harjula/harjula.pdf (accessed May 12, 2007).
9 Excerpt from my notebook from February 2007.

Bibliography

Bachelard, Gaston. *The Poetics of Space*. New York: Orion Press, 1964. [*La poétique de l'espace*. Presses universitaires de France, 1958.]

Briginshaw, Valerie A. *Dance, Space and Subjectivity*. Hampshire: Palgrave, 2001.

Bochner, Arthur, and Carolyn Ellis (eds.). *Ethnographically Speaking: Autoethnography, Literature, and Aesthetics*. Walnut Creek, CA: AltaMira Press, 2002.

Cancienne, Mary Beth, and Celeste N. Snowber. "Writing Rhythm: Movement as Method." *Qualitative Inquiry* 9, no. 2 (2003): 237–53.

Hastrup, Kirsten. *A Passage to Anthropology: Between Experience and Theory*. London and New York: Routledge, 1995.

Heinämaa, Sara. *Ele, tyyli ja sukupuoli. Merleau-Pontyn ja de Beauvoirin ruumiinfenomenologia ja sen merkitys sukupuolikysymykselle* [*Gesture, style and gender. Merleau-Ponty's and de Beauvoir's phenomenology of the body and their signification to a question of gender*]. Helsinki: Gaudeamus, 1996.

Irigaray, Luce. *To Be Two*. Translated by Monique M. Rhodes and Morco F. Cocito-Monoc. London: Athlone Press, 2000. [*Essere Due*. Bollati Boringhieri, 1994.]

————. *Speculum of the Other Woman*. Ithaca, NY: Cornell University Press, 1985. [*Speculum de l'autre femme*. Paris: Minuit, 1974.]

(Juslin) Välipakka, Inka. *Tanssien sanat. Representoiva koreografia, eletty keho ja naistanssi* [*Words of the Dances: Representative Choreography, the Lived Body and Women's Dance*]. University of Joensuu Publications in the Humanities 34. University of Joensuu Press, 2003.

Kress, Gunther, Regina Leite-García, and Theo van Leeuwen. "Discourse Semiotics." In Teun A. Van Dijk (ed.), *Discourse as Structure and Process*. London: Sage, 1997: 257–91.

Länsikunnas, Outi. "Harjula, My Favourite Place"—Photography Project, 1–14 September 2005. Unpublished MA thesis. University of Lapland: Department of Art Education, 2005. English summary: http://ace.ulapland.fi/Projects/lapland/harjula/harjula.pdf (accessed May 12, 2007).

Merleau-Ponty, Maurice. *The Phenomenology of Perception*. Translated by Colin Smith. New York: Routledge, 1962. [*Phénoménologie de la perception*. Gallimard, 1945.]

————. *The Visible and the Invisible*. Translated by Alphonso Lingis. Evanston, IL: Northwestern University Press, 1968. [*Le visible et l'invisible*. Gallimard, 1964.]

Monni, Kirsi. *Olemisen poeettinen liike. Tanssin taidefilosofia tulkintoja Martin Heideggerin ajattelun valossa sekä taiteellinen työ vuosina 1999–1996* [*The Poetic Movement of Being: Philosophical Interpretations of the New Paradigm of Dance in the Light of Martin Heidegger's Thinking and the Artistic Work of Years 1999–1996*]. Acta Scenica 15. Helsinki: Theatre Academy, 2004.

Parviainen, Jaana. *Bodies Moving and Moved. A Phenomenological Analysis on the Dancing Subject and the Cognitive and Ethical Values of Dance Art*. Tampere: Tampere University Press, 1998.

Polanyi, Michael. *Personal Knowledge: Towards a Post-Critical Philosophy*. Chicago: University of Chicago Press, 1974 [1958].

Rouhiainen, Leena. *Living Transformative Lives: Finnish Freelance Dance Artists Brought into Dialogue with Merleau-Ponty's Phenomenology*. Helsinki: Theatre Academy, 2003.

Sarje, Aino. "The Change of Power in the Field of Dance Art in Finland." In Päivi K. Pakkanen and Aino Sarje (eds.), *Finnish Dance Research at the Crossroads: Practical and Theoretical Challenges*. Arts Council of Finland. Tampere: Tampere University Press, 2006: 88–95.

Examining Creative Processes and Pedagogies

CHAPTER ELEVEN

The Montréal Danse Choreographic Research and Development Workshop

DANCER-RESEARCHERS EXAMINE CHOREOGRAPHER–DANCER
RELATIONAL DYNAMICS DURING THE CREATIVE PROCESS

PAMELA NEWELL AND SYLVIE FORTIN

THE MAP: TWO DANCER-RESEARCHERS REFLECT ON THEIR COMMUNITIES

Pamela: Throughout the history of concert dance forms, choreographers, dancers, historians and the like have speculated about the dancer's contribution to a choreographer's creative process or, in the words of ballerina Nora Kaye, "where the creator and interpreter take on and leave off" (Newman 1998: 57). Working as a choreographer and dancer in Montreal and Boston, I have been intrigued by the notion of boundaries, in this case, boundaries of artistic practice and geographical boundaries. With my move from Boston to Montreal—two very different cultural communities— I could not resist making spontaneous comparisons that by consequence brought into relief my experience in the creative process. My attitude on the job was often like that of an anthropologist who keenly observes and documents a community or phenomenon. On the one hand, I mentally noted the outward signs in my community of the dancer's evolving status and, on the other, I paid attention to my own experience in the rehearsal studio and creative process. With respect to outward signs, I observed a change in the quantity and quality of descriptive language used to credit dancers in program notes. For example, in some programs, a new collaborative status was being acknowledged. In the studio, I sometimes observed an incongruence between certain collaborative methods, their aesthetic objectives, and my sense of empowerment, health, and well-being.

Sylvie: In my experience as a dance and somatic educator in pre-professional settings, I have often been baffled by the fact that, in some contexts, students are able to manifest signs of empowerment while, in others, these same students adopt a submissive attitude that leads to physical and psychological difficulties. Also puzzling, I have encountered resistance to change and an attachment to habitual practices when trying to implement health promotion guidelines to diminish these difficulties in my working environment. To explain this reluctance, I have heard colleagues say: "That is just the way things are, that is the reality of the milieu." But what exactly is the "reality" of today's contemporary dance scene? What if "the way things are" has changed? And if it has not changed, why are we not trying to change it? Since Lord (1992) demonstrated that students in pre-professional and recreational dance settings tend to replicate the attitudes and behaviours of the professional dance milieu, I was interested to find out if we could challenge this apparent homogeneity of the professional milieu or at least provide an empirical picture of what is actually going on in today's dance studios.

Pamela and Sylvie: Armed with these non-systematic, yet compelling, observations and our "insider" status, we undertook an ethnographic study of the dancer's role in the creative process and the choreographer–dancer relational dynamics that help determine that role. The study was part of Sylvie's larger research project entitled "Healthy Dancing Bodies," which has been examining dancers' constructions of health. Curious to know how choreographer–dancer relationships in the creative process have an impact on dancers' physical, psychological, and even vocational health, we chose to participate in a newly formed workshop (2005) offered by Montréal Danse, a Montreal-based repertory company. The Montréal Danse Choreographic Research and Development Workshop offered four emerging choreographers one week of experimentation with the dancers of Montréal Danse and creative guidance with four experts. The notion of "insiders" doing research at home in their own communities seemed to us to present exciting possibilities for uncovering pertinent and applicable knowledge about the relational component of the dancer's experience in the creative process.

According to Andrews (2004) and Bowring (2004), the status, recognition, and working conditions of dancers in contemporary concert dance forms in Canada are improving through both legislation and grassroots mobilization. But as their status continues to be standardized through efforts such as unionization, it is imperative that their experiences be documented and understood. In Canada, the push to unionize dancers working in contemporary dance forms has been long and arduous. In Montreal at the time of our study, a few collective agreements had been signed with Union des artists—the union that has represented Quebec performing artists from other disciplines since 1937. Certain gains, such as appropriate scheduling of activities and aspects of personal and environmental safety, had, in theory, been achieved. However, other issues that involve questions of intellectual property—such as royalties; copyright; billing in programs, on publicity and in media; rights to dancers' images; and remounting rights—are continually being negotiated. As well, when disputes arise, lack of documentation around the dancer's work puts them at a disadvantage in arbitration. If rights and ownership in dance are to become legal issues, it is important that we, who work in the field, document the nature of the creative process and the dancer's contribution to it.

As far as health is concerned, art that is highly valued in Western society has not typically been associated with healthy practices. On the contrary, pushing the body's limits has often been seen as necessary to innovation; but this excess is not without consequences for dancers' health. Dance researchers (Kelly 2001; Benn and Walters 2001; Long 2002) have documented the underlying utilitarian ethic of dancers when privileging the integrity of the art form over their own safety. But we wonder why one should have to choose between health and art. Our position is that dancers, within the constraints of their artistic environment, are active constructors of their own health.[1]

In the last ten years, dancers have begun to take action in response to the pervasiveness of health problems. Two examples are the process of unionization already mentioned and successful negotiations between dancers and La Commission de la Santé et de la Securité du Travail du Québec (CSST) (Quebec Workers' Compensation Commission), which led to the acceptance of compensation claims from dancers injured during training. These structural efforts reflect an increased interest in health and well-being in the local dance milieu. But, how dancers negotiate health-preserving activities in the creative process, given the aesthetic and socio-economic demands of the art form, is not known.

Motivated by this debate in our community around the recognition of the dancer's role in the making of work and by dancers' vulnerability to career-threatening health risks, we wanted to identify and document the activities and interactions that constitute the choreographic process from the dancer's perspective. Our objective was to define potential roles that dancers assume in the creative process and to examine the socio-political (power) and somatic-health (body) questions that come into play when carrying out those roles. In order to do this, Pamela first devised a conceptual framework of the dancer's role based on her experience as a performer and an analysis of dance literature. We then challenged that framework in the field, the professional contemporary dance creative process. Below, we briefly describe the conceptual framework[2] before reporting in depth the study's fieldwork methods and results.

THE FRAME: FOUR DANCER ROLES

For the purpose of this study, we focus on the way in which dancers' experiences in the creative process are affected by the working relationship established between the choreographer and dancer and on the creative objectives of each individual work. Those experiences and those relationships are as infinite as the variety of potential creative processes, as infinite and varied as dance works themselves. Choreographer–dancer relationships can be seen as falling on a continuum between a traditional model and a decentred model. In a more traditional model, a hierarchy is established; authority and meaning are centred on the choreographer. In a decentred model, the relationships are more horizontal; authority and meaning are shared.

Four dancer roles can be delineated from this hypothetical continuum: *executant, interpreter,*[3] *participant,* or *improviser.* At one extreme, the *executant*, perhaps a classical or modern dancer trained in a specific tradition or technique (Dempster 1993; Foster 1997; Jowitt 1994), maintains a passive role in the creative process. Her[4] primary objective is replication of movement and meaning given by the choreographer. Her body, highly regulated and ordered, is praised for external achievement.

The *interpreter* is characterized by his place as a medium between the choreographer and the audience, a place of "in between" (Huynh-Montassier 1992). He is given more freedom to interpret the meaning behind choreographer-generated movement and, thus, more freedom in its execution. He focuses less on replication and more on appropriation through dialogic exchange (Mappin 2000). Other binaries—such as that between the choreographer's direction, whether physical or verbal, and the dancer's own inner bodily sensation or that between the dancer's body as itself and the dancer's body as artistic material—are often activated (Bossatti 1992; Fraleigh 1987; Lamirande 2003). Somatic awareness and the experiential body are awakened through a diversification of training practices (Schulmann 1997).

The *participant* is appreciated, not only as a bodily filter for ideas, but also as a fully formed human being with a unique biography, morphology, education, and culture. Through improvisation and composed studies, her lived experience, intellectual and perceptual, is solicited in the making of work (Lepecki 1998; Schulmann 1997).

The *improviser* is positioned at the opposite extreme to the executant, in an ostensibly non-hierarchical working relationship with his colleagues (Benoit 1997; Novack 1990). As a creator of spontaneous composition in the moment of performance, the improviser is the embodiment of the choreographer, the performer, and the work itself.

These roles are neither prescriptive nor fixed. Instead, they serve as lenses that bring into focus some of the important issues, such as autonomy, subjectivity, and identity, at stake for the dancer in a creative process. As conceived theoretically, the roles do not stay the same throughout the process; rather, the dancer can move between the diverse demands of each. Figure 1 schematizes this continuum concept of the dancers' roles.[5]

Examining the four roles on the continuum, many somatic-health (body) and socio-political factors (power) associated with each role became apparent. Depending on whether subjectivity is suppressed (executant), negotiated (interpreter), employed (participant), or implicit (improviser), the dancer's body is represented as an object or experienced as a subject. The kinds of experience valued (external, internal) have consequences for an individual's access to and appreciation of her own personal knowledge. Preston-Dunlop and Sanchez-Colberg (2002) explain that dance works make ideas tangible through a body's "corporeality" or its "reification." Corporeality is linked to the concept of embodiment, which involves the "whole person, a person conscious of being a living body, living that experience, giving intention to the movement material" (7). Corporeality emphasizes the human body in all of its complex biological, psychological, and

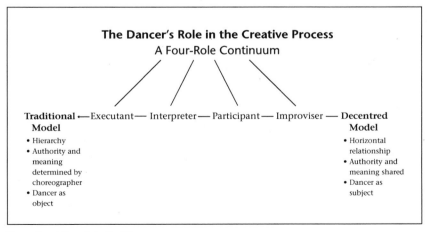

Figure 1   A Four-Role Continuum

cultural processes, whereas reification is achieved through a "negation of all things dialectic concerning the body as socio-political" (10).

An emphasis on the representational or "reified" body, in certain traditional training and choreographic practices, has been associated with a lack of somatic authority, a desensitization of sensory impulses and conformity to dominant systems (Fortin and Girard 2005; Fortin, Long, and Lord 2002; Green 1999, 2001; Salosaari 2002; Smith 1998). For example, dancers who work in this way may not be able to access sensory information that, on the one hand, can be retrieved to develop individual expressive capacities and, on the other, can signal potentially harmful or abusive activities.

THE FIELD: THE MONTRÉAL DANSE CHOREOGRAPHIC RESEARCH AND DEVELOPMENT WORKSHOP

The Montréal Danse Choreographic Research and Development Workshop offered four emerging choreographers one week of experimentation with their company dancers, as well as theoretical presentations on the creative process, direct feedback on their investigations from four facilitators—Kathy Casey, Larry Lavender, Susan Marshall, and Philip Szporer[6]—and in-depth discussions on all aspects of the creative process. Founded in 1986, Montréal Danse is a repertory company that employed seven dancers at the time of the first workshop. Three choreographers or choreographic teams were chosen from Montreal and one from Toronto. The four women and one man ranged in age from mid-twenties to early forties. The choreographers were then matched with two or three dancers. The mean age of the men dancers was 31.5; for the women, it was 37.

While the workshop setting provided an excellent short-term, cross-sectional[7] study sample, questions did arise regarding that event's authenticity as a "naturalistic" professional setting. Our sample—while not a specific creative process culminating in a professional performance—was, however, a creative event in which we participated from beginning to end, engaging in all its components. Furthermore, given that a dance work is made fully manifest only in performance, a mentoring component is an inherent part of dance creation

Figure 2 Montréal Danse Choreographic Research and Development Workshop, 2005. Photographer: Warwick Long.

and professional mentoring opportunities are becoming an increasing part of dance's naturalistic setting (Cools, 2006; Litzenberger, 2005; Szporer, 2003). More importantly, many of the workshop's ostensible limitations— limited time, a lack of pre-existing professional relationships between choreographer and dancers, the absence of a performance platform, and the workshop setting—served, in fact, as valuable parameters for bringing the choreographer–dancer relationship in the creative process into relief.

First, the limited time meant that the focus of the workshop was on the early stages of dance-making, the creation phase of generating, gathering, manipulating, and transforming material, when the choreographer and dancer are in close relationship. This phase can be differentiated from what Leduc (1996) and Lamirande (2003) have called the "appropriation" phase where the dancer takes time to fully embody all aspects of fixed material, and the "performance" phase where the dancer integrates staging components or conditions a touring work (Davida 2006).

Second, because the choreographers and dancers had never worked together before, the dancers' capacity to anticipate choreographers' directions, a skill that comes with familiarity, was at least in part disabled. The freshness of these relationships afforded us the opportunity to witness how the delicate exchange between choreographer and dancer might be initiated.

Third, this study is in no way meant to be directly transferable to a creative process with a professional performance. It is understood that facilitation by experienced, outside observers was meant to provoke unusual risk-taking on the part of the choreographers. Moreover, with the pressure and distractions that go along with making a finished product temporarily suspended, this period of intense exploration was effectively expanded by a concentration of highly focused creative time.

Fourth, the workshop setting allowed us to use a range of data-collection methods, an important contribution of feminist methodologies, which is thought to contribute to the richness of research findings (Maynard and Purvis 1994). Having participated in every aspect of the workshop, we were able to accumulate data from material written by the choreographers before going into the workshop process; notes from the morning creative process seminar; twenty-four hours of afternoon rehearsal observation; presentation observation and videotaping; somatic session observation; evening discussions with facilitators and choreographers; as well as five follow-up interviews with dancers. Table 1 gives an overview of the data-collection methods employed as they relate to the workshop's activities.

Table 1   Data Collection Methods

Time	Activity	Data-Collection Method
9:30 a.m. – 11:00 a.m.	Creative-process seminar	Observation and notation
11:00 a.m. – 12:30 p.m.	Individual meetings: Choreographers and facilitators	Private conferences: no data collected
12:30 p.m. – 4:30 p.m.	Rehearsals	Observations and notation videotape of day 5
4:30 p.m. – 5:30 p.m.	Feldenkrais Awareness through Movement® Session	Observation and notation
6:00 p.m. – 9:00 p.m.	Dinner discussion	Observation, notation, and audiotape
Four months later	Individually scheduled interviews with selected dancers	Semi-structured interviews, taped and transcribed

Since our focus was on the creative process and the data showed the dancer's involvement in the activities as much as the choreographer's, we chose to refer to each workshop process as "Process *n*" in the text, rather than by the choreographer's name alone as is customary when discussing a finished work. As well, some of the participants chose to maintain their anonymity. Therefore, since revealing the identities of some and not others in such a small community would effectively compromise the anonymity of all, we decided to give pseudonyms to all the workshop participants. Table 2 shows the workshop participants by pseudonym and the workshop processes in which they were involved.

Table 2   Research Participants

Workshop Process	Choreographers Observed	Dancers Observed	Dancers Interviewed
1	Laura Michael	Emily Lucie	Lucie
2	Mary	Isabelle Paul	Paul
3	Stephanie	Lise David	Lise
4	Nadine	Daniel Anna Dominique	Daniel

The observational and interview data was analyzed through a series of categorization and constant comparison steps inspired by Paillé's (1994) adaptation of Glaser and Strauss's seminal qualitative methodology grounded theory. Following ethical protocol, each interview participant signed both a consent form before the interview and a corroboration form after reading and verifying the transcript.

METHODOLOGICAL CONSIDERATIONS

According to Sklar (1991), the dance researcher as ethnographer wants to know how a given group makes meaning. An ethnographic perspective offers the researcher a larger view of a particular dance event and goes deeper into its underlying social and cultural significance. Furthermore, it brings into focus the researcher's role in the dance event. Inductive ethnography, with its strong emphasis on data and method, is the most basic form of ethnographic inquiry (Alvesson and Sköldberg 2000). Linking interpretation and theory tightly to data, it falls on the more traditional end of the post-positivist research continuum. At the other end, critical ethnography relies more on theory and emphasizes interpretations that highlight the social and political power issues that emerge from the data.

Because of limited existing documentation of the choreographer–dancer relationship, we took a traditional approach to methodology, aligning the research with inductive ethnography. Nevertheless, the nature of the subject—the dancer's experience of power and body issues—and our sensitivity as researchers added a critical dimension to each stage of our process. For example, although this was not an overtly participatory action-research-oriented study, our feminist commitment sensitized us to the importance of collaborating, giving voice to research participants, appreciating the process as well as the product and developing knowledge that leads to social action or change (Harrison, 2001). It was in this spirit, and as an exchange for access to all activities during the week-long intensive, that we offered to lead a Feldenkrais session as part of the daily activity schedule.

The distinction between participant and non-participant observation in ethnographic research is loosely delineated, and some argue that all social research is participant observation since we cannot separate our study of the social world from our part in it (Atkinson and Hammersley 1994). We had an agreement with Montréal Danse that our participation, apart from the somatic sessions, would be as discreet and passive as possible. However, in doing this, we disempowered ourselves somewhat. Returning home together late each evening exhausted and satiated, we shared our experience, looking for correspondence and corroboration. By the middle of the week, we found ourselves frustrated, longing for a voice in the workshop process. Even the stimulating exchange with research participants that we had hoped for in the somatic sessions was left unrealized. (The sessions had been tacked onto the schedule at the end of the day and, thus, were not well-attended by the dancers.) We had hoped to empower others, but not by disempowering ourselves. We did feel good about the fact that, as the week went on, choreographers and dancers in their respective ways acknowledged our presence more and more. They shared aspects of their process with us, contextualizing what we were observing since we were not able to witness entire rehearsals. Similarly, our presence at the evening discussions was as unobtrusive as possible during sessions at the beginning of the week; but, by the fourth day, we spontaneously began to offer our observations and pose questions.

THE REPORT: CHOREOGRAPHERS AND DANCERS IN CREATIVE PROCESS

Preliminary analysis of the data, which consisted of compiling the observational notation from three principal categories—action, verbatim and the body's perceptual relationship—revealed that the "actional material" (Preston-Dunlop and Sanchez-Colberg, 2002), what we have chosen to call the compositional practices, is the nexus between choreographer and dancer, between power and body. The choreographer and dancer come together in relationship in the creative process through this actional material: the choreographer's direction and dancer's response. We chose, however, the expression "compositional practices" rather than adopt Preston-Dunlop and Sanchez-Colberg's (2002) term "actional material" because we wanted to capture the complexity of the material that the data analysis revealed. For example, we considered that a compositional practice comprised three categories, not only the "activity" but also its goal and the means by which it is carried out. Below, we briefly outline the compositional practices observed, then relate them to each of the four workshop processes and the four dancer roles. Lastly, we discuss the somatic-health and socio-political factors as they relate to two central themes—dancer choice and negotiating an identity—in the section entitled "Dancers' Personal Discernment Processes."

COMPOSITIONAL PRACTICES

Based on our fieldwork data, we broke down the concept of compositional practices into observed rehearsal activities, the goals of those activities, and their component parts. Identifying the overall goal of an activity is important and informative because some of the activities, particularly certain structured improvisations, can resemble each other, but distinguish themselves when the goal is stipulated. Taking inspiration from Lavender's (2005; 2007) concept of four interrelated operational goals—invention, development, evaluation, and assimilation—we formulated appropriate goals that further explicated the activities observed. The goals are to prepare or prime, to generate or instigate, and to evolve through construction/deconstruction. Preparation or "priming" activities set up a foundation for working; they put the body into a kind of creative or specialized state, but are not intended to directly generate or evolve dance material per se. Generation or instigation activities are those that stimulate the production of dance material, gestural and otherwise, in the dancers' bodies. Activities associated with evolution through construction/deconstruction involve existing material—in varying degrees of refinement or specificity—instigated through a generation activity. These activities are intended to alter or transform that material in order to explore or deepen its potential significance. Table 3 provides an overview of the compositional practices observed.

FOUR WORKSHOP PROCESSES OBSERVED AND THE FOUR DANCER ROLES

Our week of observation began by attending Process 1, where Michael and Laura were the choreographers and Emilie and Lucie were the dancers. Each dancer learned a different pre-constructed sequence—movement material that had been fixed on the choreographer's body prior to being presented to the dancers—from one of the choreographers. Michael and Laura worked in a similar fashion, demonstrating short sections of their sequences, while the dancers, copying them from behind, attempted to reproduce the actions. The movement vocabulary was idiosyncratic and seemed to be specialized to the physical and expressive affinities of each choreographer. The movement quality was physically challenging: quick, complex body shifts while maintaining strong muscular tension. Right away, body and power issues became evident. Emilie developed a leg cramp and expressed some frustration at not having the time to prepare her body for the work: "Casey [the artistic director] said to come in the morning [to the theoretical session], but I need to train. I don't want to do that kind

Table 3 Compositional Practices Observed in Study

Main Goal	Rehearsal Activities	Component Parts

1 To prepare or prime	• Structured improvisation
	  – individual focus
	  – relational focus
		• Choreographer verbal direction
		  – Dancer listening
		  – Dancer demonstrating
		  – Specificity/detail level
		  – Proximity

2 To generate or instigate	• Pre-constructed movement sequence
	• Verbal scenario
	• Structured improvisation
	• Dance composition from prompt
		• Choreographer demonstration
		  – Dancer watching
		  – Dancer partnering
		  – Performance level
		  – Rehearsal clothing

3 To evolve through contruction/ deconstruction	• Add, expand, and clarify formal and expressive elements
	• Create and expand relational elements between dancers
	• Sequence construction from dancer improvisations
	• Limited palette improvisations
	• Manipulation of dance material
	• Extraction from dancer composition
	• Kinetic exercise
		• Dancer demonstration/ reproduction
		  – Choreographer observing
		  – Choreographer giving directives
		• Choreographer verbal feedback
		• Dancer verbal feedback
		• Communication between dancers
		• Choreographer–dancer cyclical interchange
		• Dancer's personal discernment process

of work without training in the morning." For Lucie, this way of working raised questions of ownership and demonstrated an imbalance of power. In her interview, she explained her thoughts:

> My sense of them was that they were young choreographers, that their identity as choreographers was found in that they could do something hard, that was hard for their dancers to do, and the whole first day was spent correcting us and teaching us and owning this thing that they could do that we couldn't do…. I felt like I had to prove myself to [Michael] and it created this kind of dynamic where I wasn't an equal.

Through constant repetition, Michael and Laura required a high degree of specificity and detail in the dancers' reproductions. The choreographer's body was treated as the ideal body as Michael and Laura used each other as "outside eyes" to compare the performance of the phrase-creator with that of the phrase-learner.

Figure 3 Montréal Danse Choreographic Research and Development Workshop, 2005. Photographer: Warwick Long.

All of the other choreographers—though Mary in Process 2 only minimally—employed the activity of introducing pre-constructed sequences at some point during the week as a way of generating material; however, we noticed that each seemed to have different expectations for its desired outcomes. Stephanie, the choreographer in Process 3, told the dancers that she was interested in seeing what they "recorded." In our observations, she did not present her pre-constructed material as an ideal rendition, nor did she require precisely accurate replication. The generation activities that centred on reproduction spilled into evolution through construction/deconstruction as she added, expanded, and clarified formal and relational elements through a cyclical interchange with the dancers' own demonstrations. As the week went on, Stephanie's directions became more imagistic and open-ended and the dancers were more active in transformations of the material. By dressing in street clothes and shoes, moreover, she drew attention away from her performing, demonstrative body and seemed to tacitly encourage the dancers to take ownership of the material. Like Stephanie, Nadine's behaviour as the choreographer in Process 4 demonstrated a fairly quick "transfer of authority," to borrow Martin's (1990) term. Nadine's silent, loose demonstrations shifted to fairly open-ended verbal direction as she exchanged with the dancers' broad-stroke reproductions.

The different employment of pre-constructed sequences in the four processes illustrates how the margin of choice offered by a compositional practice can affect the dancer's role. The narrow margin of choice for Emilie and Lucie in Process 1, which centred the authority on the choreographers, tended to put them in the executant's role. Whereas, the emphasis on evolving material through construction/deconstruction and the move away from the choreographer's demonstrative body meant that the dancers in Processes 3 and 4 enjoyed a wider margin of choice and operated as interpreters. Lise explained to us that the dancers' level of interest and engagement increased in Process 3 when the authority shifted to include the dancers' bodies:

> David [the other dancer] responded more, and I think me, too, when [Stephanie] just let us explore something and show it. And her manipulating it a bit, by just visually looking at it, and maybe changing it. But when she was very, very specific about things, it was kind of boring for us. Because we were able to reproduce it, but not exactly like she did it, to our bodies.... So, what I'm thinking is that when she saw us show her things, for her it was way more interesting, the things that we came up with, than the stuff that we reproduced from her body.

In fact, during the course of the week, our observations showed that Stephanie seemed to abandon interest in generating new material and spent most of her rehearsal time expanding existing material through strategies of manipulation, employing the dancers as interpreters. Throughout this construction/deconstruction process, the physical demands and intellectual complexity of movement vocabulary increased. Of the four processes, Stephanie's seemed to us the most overtly challenging to the dancers' physical condition and to their capacity to reorder, record, and reintegrate dance material. While the movement was never without an expressive[8] intent, formal elements were more prominent and perhaps more developed than in the other processes.

It is worth mentioning that by mid-week the workshop facilitators instigated a decisive change in the activities and component parts of Process 1. Instead of focusing on how to more effectively induce the dancers into reproducing Michael and Laura's choreographic style, the facilitators chose to redirect how Michael and Laura were employing the dancers in order to offer the choreographers new possibilities. Michael and Laura moved from pre-constructed sequences and an emphasis on a high degree of specificity to other activities such as verbal scenario, dancer composition from prompt, manipulation of dance material and limited palette improvisation that gave the dancers more choice. Lucie told us that after this shift, the relational dynamic also changed: "There was a lot of dialogue between equals as opposed to us being told what to do and being judged on how well we achieved that."

Mary, the choreographer in Process 2, and Nadine in Process 4 used preparatory activities that seemed to acknowledge the uniqueness of the dancers working with them. Through improvisational games with a relational focus, Mary cultivated a sense of group identity in preparation for other activities, which would harness material specific to those individuals, to that time and place. Nadine started her rehearsal several times employing a particular structured improvisation with an individual focus. Daniel, one of the dancers in Process 4, told us that the improvisation was a time to "be yourself," that the experience brought the group together in a way that other rehearsal activities could not have. Mary and Nadine both participated in these preparatory activities, but not as a demonstrator or an ideal model. Rather, our observations showed that they joined the improvisations as a way of acknowledging, even claiming, their place as an equal member in the group.

These more open-ended preparatory activities that recognized the dancers' individual uniqueness gave them a wide margin of choice and seemed to have significance for the unfolding of other activities. Ostensibly, they seemed to put the dancers in the participant's role. Paul, a dancer in Process 2, explained how these activities helped establish an atmosphere of trust in which the choreographer and dancer could freely exchange as equals:

> The first days were very important for building groundwork, just days of being vulnerable. Doing really not that great stuff, but it being okay and good.... I find it rare that there is that much openness and discussion between choreographer and dancer. I feel like I learned a lot just from watching Isabelle [the other dancer] break down what Mary was asking for, and throw it back at her ... to watch Isabelle disagree.... For me, it was just fantastic. Then I was able to try that myself. And then you can learn to trust your inner creative voice, rather than just be a rule-follower.

Paul adds that when mutual trust is installed, he is not only more engaged, as was Lise when compositional practices afforded her more choice, but he can more easily and deeply access his creativity:

> If you're not trusting your choreographer to work with who you are, then you've already lost something collaborative. It's fake. The mutual respect is gone.... I think you give less; you do less. You're less willing to open up. And as soon as you are unwilling to open up, then you're creating lesser work.... If it's been established that it's a safe environment, I think it's very easy to dive in immediately.

In effect, this deepened access to his creative resources—a consequence of the safe environment—further broadened his margin of choice.

In Process 2, Mary placed the individual experience of the dancers at the centre of the process, giving them a high degree of autonomy and trusting them implicitly. From Mary's initial expressive prompts, they generated and evolved material under varying degrees of supervision. The language of her verbal feedback—which was often prefaced by phases such as "You just gave me an idea"—showed that her inspiration for further development was almost exclusively something she had witnessed in the dancers' demonstrations rather than a preconceived vision she was trying to solicit or impose. Her verbal directions were often intentionally embedded with elements of dancer choice, again prefacing her propositions with "I want to keep the freedom in there to interpret however you want." She acknowledged the internal compositional process at work when dancers demonstrate—either open-ended initial explorations or structured material that has passed a certain level of refinement—by allowing the dancers to explore material uninterrupted.

In Process 4, while the preparatory improvisation had a significant impact on the dancers and seemed to give them choice, other factors seemed to hinder choice. Much of Nadine's research during the week focused on addressing her methods for employing a dancer's knowledge. She clearly stated that she was not as much interested in dance vocabulary itself as in the dancer's state, his "engagement in the process." On several occasions, we observed that she struggled with how much freedom to give the dancers, on the one hand wanting them to stage a "mutiny," as she called it, and on the other wondering if she should give them "more specific prompts." This struggle with creative authority played out at several points during the process, two of which we mention here.

When working with Anna, one of the dancers in Process 4, Nadine's expressed intention was "to take [the movement] from [Anna's] body." But after giving Anna some parameters within which to improvise, Nadine kept interjecting with directives that guided and limited Anna's choices while she demonstrated. To our observations, this method seemed to achieve limited success for Nadine. Furthermore, Anna told us,

> Actually, what bothered me was, while I was doing it, I kept saying to myself that I wasn't giving her what she wanted. Because, as I was doing it, she was guiding me. So, I said to myself, "Okay, that's not it, because now she's saying 'more like this.'"

On Day 3, when Daniel was taking his turn with the preparatory improvisation, Nadine interrupted and redirected his interpretation, provoking some observed discomfort from Daniel and the other dancers. While Daniel had felt the preparatory improvisation was "a space to do whatever you want to do" and that "there were no rules except 'be yourself' there,"

Nadine's choice to intervene when he did not fulfill the spatial instructions of the improvisation was evidence that, at least in this instance, she placed a certain importance on respecting the rules of the compositional practice.

Nadine's de-emphasis on demonstration as a way of generating move-ment, her employment of preparatory activities, and her expressed interest in dancer "rapport" suggest that she wanted the dancers to act as partici-pants—to be the "mutinous" force on which the content was centred or by which it was driven. But our observations suggested that such a shift would have conflicted with her desire for creative control. Consequently, the margin of choice of a compositional practice was not always clear to the dancers, nor was the dancer role always apparent.

To sum up, from the study's data, certain elements of compositional practices could be associated with each of the four roles. High specificity and detail of choreographer demonstration or choreographer verbal instruc-tion tended to put the dancer in the executant's role (Process 1). Activities with a goal to prepare or prime, for example, tended to put dancers in the participant's role (Process 2 and 4). Component parts of the activities, such as the quality of demonstration and verbal direction, that narrowed the dancer's margin of choice and required more conformity to the choreog-rapher's directions, put the dancers in the executant's role (Process 1 and 4). A greater concentration of activities with the goal to evolve existing material tended to put the dancers in the interpreter's role (Process 3). In activities that employed improvisation, formal prompts tended to put the dancers in the interpreter's role (Process 3), while expressive prompts put the dancers in the participant's role (Process 2). Expressed aesthetic objec-tives that emphasized "rapport" tended to put dancers in the interpreter or participant's role (Process 2 and 4), while those that emphasized creating a unique movement vocabulary or "distinct style" tended to put dancers in the executant's role (Process 1).

As suspected when conceiving of the continuum model, the processes could not be identified exclusively with one role. Rather, a complex interre-lation of three roles—whether executant, interpreter, or participant[9]—was active in each process. We discerned, however, a role that was dominant and one that was subordinate in Processes 1, 2, and 3. For Process 4, two dominant roles were given equal value. The dancer's margin of choice helped us determine a dominant dancer role in each process. When com-positional practices offered the dancer more choice and, therefore, more authority, that person seemed to operate at the participant end of the

Table 4   Dominant and Subordinate Roles Observed

Process	Choreographers	Dancers	Dominant Role	Subordinate Role
1	Michael Laura	Emilie Lucie	executant	interpreter
2	Mary	Paul Isabelle	participant	interpreter
3	Stephanie	Lise David	interpreter	participant
4	Nadine	Daniel Anna Dominique	interpreter/ participant	executant

continuum; when they offered less, the dancer was found to be nearer to the executant end. Table 4 shows the dominant and subordinate roles observed in each process.

DANCERS' PERSONAL DISCERNMENT PROCESSES

As illustrated above, margin of choice is an important factor in understanding how a dancer's knowledge and experience will be employed in the creative process. This study suggests that margin of choice widens as the roles on the continuum move from executant to participant and allows opportunities for dancers to engage what we have chosen to call the dancer's personal discernment process. We have chosen the word *discernment* because, in our interpretation, it does not limit the decision-making process to an intellectually oriented or mind-sourced process. Instead, it leaves room for the possibility of bodily or somatic intelligence as a trigger for choice. When responding to direction and engaging their personal discernment processes, dancers seemed to weigh aesthetic, somatic-health, and socio-political factors. Moreover, how dancers balanced those factors echoed an important theme in the documentation of the dancer's experience: negotiating an identity in between the choreographer and the work being created (Huynh-Montassier 1992; Fraleigh 1987; Bossatti 1992).

In spite of the potentially disempowering relational dynamic and the limited choice of compositional practices experienced in the first days of Process 1, Lucie endeavoured to find her place:

I figured out my role within the three other people, was trying to keep it on track. Because Emilie [the other dancer] was really explaining the role of the dancer a lot to [Michael and Laura], and I felt like she was making really valid points. But almost too much, so much so that we were just getting sidetracked all the time and work wasn't getting done. And I wanted them to know that they should respect a dancer's right without having to totally sidetrack their process. And so I felt like I kept trying to keep it going.

Lucie is weighing aesthetic factors ("keep it on track … without having to totally sidetrack their process") against socio-political ones ("respect a dancer's right").

As we mentioned, Process 1 was the only process where overt health issues were observed: a dancer developed a muscle cramp and both dancers expressed some fear around injuring their bodies during certain activities. Lucie expressed a common struggle among the participants when she considered the somatic-health issues against aesthetic ones and asked, "How do you protect yourself and still fulfill someone's vision? And I haven't answered that question, but it's been on my mind."

In Process 3, Lise, like Lucie, struggled to exercise judgment around her somatic-health needs and the aesthetic demands of the work. She asked, "How do I have an 'out' but not compromise the rehearsal? But still take care of myself, and take care of [the choreographer]?" Lise explained in her interview that toward the end of the week when they were getting tired, she and David would decide between themselves to demonstrate sections for Stephanie, emphasizing certain aspects of the choreography rather than performing every aspect at full energy every time.

In Process 2, Paul has also developed tactics for lessening the personal physical risks of the creative process. For example, when asked to compose something on his own—dancer composition from prompt—with a wide margin of dancer choice, he chooses to privilege his somatic-health needs over aesthetic ones. He composes something that he "can repeat a lot and not hurt myself." In so doing, he relies on the choreographer and a dialogic exchange to make the movement aesthetically relevant.

As choreographers, Stephanie in Process 3 and Mary in Process 2, may or may not have noticed the dancers' actions, but for Lise there is always an anxiety and a fear of reprisal around revealing something to the choreographer that might be perceived as weakness. While Emilie in Process 1 and Isabelle in Process 2 felt confident to voice their needs to protect their bodies, our observations showed that dancers also felt some pressure to downplay moments of pain and discomfort in the creative process. "Old-school," as Lise called them, or "survival of the fittest" attitudes sometimes prevailed. She acknowledged that certain attitudes of complete devotion to the choreographer learned through traditional pedagogical practices are hard to change.

Anna also acknowledges the dancers' reluctance to create conflict when discussing the interaction between Nadine and Daniel over the preparatory improvisation in Process 4: "We are trained to listen, to be submissive, to do what the choreographer wants." Anna's comment suggests that the dancers did not necessarily feel in a position to support Daniel's interpretation of the exercise or his decision to follow his inner impulse.

The dancers' personal discernment process was not employed just for protective measures. When compositional practices offered dancers more choice, the data showed that they privileged opportunities for personal and artistic growth. For Daniel in Process 4, striving for innovation, experimentation, and originality governs his decision-making: "When I start a process, it's not to do the same thing.... I want to grow my personality." On a physical level, he is conscious of "not letting my training be an obstacle to the process." In Process 3, Lise also tries to approach creative choice from a fresh place, which stimulates her engagement in a process. She has developed strategies so she doesn't "feel like a robot in the room." By recognizing the less obvious solution when responding to direction, she attends to her growth as an artist and her desire not to be limited by habitual patterns: "Everyone always has the first instinct to push maybe the shoulder or something. So I would say to myself, 'Normally, I would push on the shoulder. But where else would I push someone?' Then I would think, 'Okay, maybe the hip.' So then maybe something else would come from it."

For Paul, however, where there is choice, he privileges the spontaneity of his first impulse when responding to choreographer propositions. Disabling his censoring mechanism in this way, he told us he can go beyond what might be considered acceptable and trust that the editing process will make it appropriate. Moreover, the ideal creative environment is one where he is in a position to access his vulnerability as a potent state for creative transformation. In his interview, he explained,

> What really grabs, in my mind, when I'm doing something, is what Paul does poorly. And not by accident, but what he allows out. Whether it's the faults that he allows out, the fragility that he can let you into. I find that to be the beautiful part of a presentation.

In this case, certain compositional practices (the activities and component parts) allow him to access parts of himself that he might otherwise keep hidden, consciously or unconsciously. His creative ideal is to be able to bring all parts of himself to the negotiation between the creator and the product. Both Paul and Lise felt that a safe and non-judgmental environment—created most often by the choreographers' flexibility toward the outcome of choreographic propositions and their acceptance of a dancer's individuality—gave the dancers a deeper access to their own personal creative process.

DISCUSSION

The study showed us that compositional practices could be associated with different dancer roles that emphasize different degrees of dancer autonomy. The dancers' testimonies reveal that just as the compositional practices in the study have somatic-health and socio-political consequences for the dancers, the somatic-health and socio-political concerns of dancers influence their personal discernment processes, which in turn have consequences for compositional practices. The interview participants are both more willing and better positioned to contribute to the creative process when compositional practices acknowledge their voice and give them access to personal choice; however, they recognize a tendency to censor their own behaviour because of past, repressive training and/or work experience. To offset this predicament, we wonder if dancers' experiences could be enhanced, their situation improved, if at any given moment in the creative process, they knew where they stood on the four-role continuum of knowledge, choice and subjectivity. For example, how much transgression on the dancer's part is sanctioned in a particular compositional practice? For Daniel with Nadine in Process 4, there were apparent limits that were not necessarily made clear to the dancers.

Four out of five of the interviewed dancers saw their role as deferential: they described their job as in some way realizing what the choreographer "wants." Furthermore, most of the interview participants also mentioned that the dancer is always replaceable. Daniel explained to us, "As a dancer, you get comfortable with what you're doing, and you always have an idea of being part of what a person is creating, when actually, you are always an instrument." They also expressed a sense of resignation around their fate. When discussing the complexity of recreating roles on new dancers and the disrespect dancers feel around their contribution, Paul conceded that without the public accountability that money-making ventures demand, people can ultimately do whatever they want: "So you just stand back and shake your head. And the next time they ask you to work, you probably say 'yeah' and do it all over again."

Dancers don't seem to feel they have a foothold to ask for acknowledgement in programs, financial remuneration for increased creative input or "right of first refusal" when a role is remounted. Ginot (2001) sees that in France at the time of her writing the *interprète* is in a particularly advantageous position: the replaceable character of the dancer (a socio-political factor)—and its potentially negative effects—is addressed by accentuating his singularity, the creative authenticity of each dancer (an aesthetic factor). Many choreographers on the French contemporary dance scene place the dancer and his predicament at the centre of their creative inquiries, likely corresponding to the participant's role.

The dancer's balancing act of aesthetic, somatic-health and socio-political factors could also be expressed as one of self and other. When Lucie asks, "How do you protect yourself and still fulfill someone's vision?" she acknowledges that it can no longer be a question of either-or, either the dancer's somatic-health and socio-political needs, or the choreographer's aesthetic ones. Rather, this balancing act of negotiating one's personal and professional needs in a working environment which is affected by outside pressures can perhaps best be expressed as the "simultaneity of human embodiment" that Thomas (2003)—citing Turner who follows up the ideas of philosophers Schilder and Merleau-Ponty—describes as "at once 'personal and impersonal, objective and subjective, social and natural'" (p. 94). In terms of the four-role continuum model, the dancer would ideally be in a position to perform every role, operate at both the subjective and objective ends of the continuum and every place in between, while also being fully aware of where they are operating on the continuum.

As in Martin's (1990) study, the compositional practices present in the four processes show that knowledge and power operate as fluctuations of systems of authority. There are times when the dancer suppresses any desire for a personal authority in order to acquire an unknown movement language. There are others when he is asked to act in total possession of his individual, creative powers and compose. A creative process would perhaps, at its best, epitomize this fluctuation. A detailed account of potential strategies that would make each role and its optimal characteristics a viable, non-threatening working option would be the subject for further study.

THE WRAP: TWO DANCER-RESEARCHERS REFLECT ON THEIR INVESTIGATION

Pamela: The dancers' personal discernment process would ideally also be the topic of further research. Observing these processes has made me want to know more about possible forms of dancer critical thinking and creative problem-solving as they relate to compositional practices. For example, I realized that I had a tendency to think there is less critical thinking activated in the dancer when she is employed as an executant and when compositional practices centre knowledge on the choreographer. The data showed that replication of an external ideal triggers resistance through power issues (Lucie in Process 1) and boredom or apathy (Lise in Process 3). Nevertheless, the critical thinking needed to reproduce an external ideal is not insignificant. Unless the dancer has a high affinity with the choreographer's way of moving or has been trained in a specific technique that serves as the basis for the movement vocabulary, she needs skills that are very different from those employed when carrying out an improvisational or compositional task. Many training methods seem to promote one or the other, but is it possible to promote both?

As I come to the end of this investigation, I find myself in the throes of a creative process for four women where I am the choreographer. Many of my methods are familiar to me as I carry out the process, but many new methods are a direct consequence of this research. While the four-role framework in its theoretical form certainly contributed to my understanding and has influenced how I employ dancers, it is this investigation into the relationship between compositional practices and dancers' roles that has led to concrete changes in my creative process. Primarily, it has helped me to recognize that crafting a rehearsal is as important, or as influential, to its outcome, as creating a piece. In my present process, I find that I get the most out of the process when I intentionally construct activities around a balancing of dancers' roles and of compositional practices—that is, for example, preparation activities that cultivate the dancer as participant; generation activities during which I demonstrate a pre-constructed movement sequence that engages the dancer as executant and during which I can assert control over direction and aesthetic; as well as evolution activities during which the dancers, as interpreters, and I, equally from our respective sides, explore the potential of existing material.

Sylvie: As a restless dance and somatic educator confronted with traditional pedagogical practices in my working environment, I appreciate that this study has allowed me to better understand the resistance I often encounter when attempting to implement health-promotion guidelines. For example, at the time of this study, a colleague, Fernande Girard, and I were developing guidelines for injury management to assist students and teachers throughout the dance curriculum. It took two years to complete this small project, not only because we consulted frequently with the student representatives, part-time teacher representatives and faculty members, but also because addressing somatic-health attitudes and behaviours threatens the department's accepted aesthetic and socio-political norms. When addressing somatic-health issues in dance practices, we cannot help

213

but confront how we mediate socio-political and aesthetic constraints. Change in one realm seems to jeopardize the delicate balance of an already-established complex scaffolding that, as was demonstrated in this study, is not as fixed and homogeneous as people have presumed. The four-role model and the multiple ways in which individuals negotiate within each role force us to question our assumptions and encourage us to appreciate diversity.

Notes

1 We define health in a holistic manner, encompassing social, spiritual, emotional, mental and physical well-being. Our definition goes beyond a mechanistic functioning of the body and conceives health as the way individuals are able to enjoy and adapt to the demands of their environment.
2 The conceptual framework is explained in depth in Newell (2007).
3 The terms *executant* and *interpreter* are borrowed from Igor Stravinsky (1942), who attempted to make distinctions between these two kinds of music performers.
4 We have chosen to alternate the use of the female (she, her) and male (he, his, him) pronouns when the gender is unspecified.
5 Since Pamela first devised this conceptual framework in 2002, we have encountered other attempts to delineate what a dancer does with respect to the demands of a given choreographer or creative process. From a pedagogical perspective, Butterworth (2004) presents a continuum framework of five distinct approaches to the choreographic process. In each process, the choreographer and dancers take specific roles. From a decidedly political point of view, Russell (1993) proposes three heuristic models of the dancer's "work" in a creative process. Martin's (1990) study offers important insights into the fluctuations of systems of authority as they are played out through specific dance material–generating activities undertaken in rehearsal. The transfer of authority from the choreographer to the dancers is made manifest in part in the progressive unfolding of compositional operations.
6 Kathy Casey is artistic director of Montréal Danse; Larry Lavender is a professor at the University of North Carolina at Greensboro; Susan Marshall is artistic director of Susan Marshall and Company; and Philip Szporer is a dance critic, videographer, and arts broadcaster.
7 In social science research, a cross-sectional design is one in which the researcher looks at a sample of individuals or organizations at one particular point in time; it is in contrast with the longitudinal approach where the researcher tracks a sample over an extended period of time (Babbie 2001). The workshop presented us with a limited sample at a precise moment in time.
8 The terms *expressive* and *formal* when referring to images or prompts align most closely with Lavender and Predock-Linnell's (2001) descriptions of "form-based exercises" and "expression-based prompts": "Form-based exercises isolate and focus upon such basic dance elements as space, shape, energy, motif, theme and

variation, to name a few. Expression-based prompts, on the other hand, invite students to delve into their memories, beliefs, hopes, fears, and dreams and then generate simple movement ... that symbolise[s] or represent[s] these facets of the students' unique identities" (196–97).

9 Although all the dancers—and sometimes the choreographers—improvised in the rehearsal activities, none of the four processes engaged the dancers as improvisers per se—that is, as that role was conceived and described in the conceptual framework.

Bibliography

Alvesson, Mats, and Kaj Sköldberg. *Reflexive Methodology*. London: Sage, 2000.

Andrews, P. Megan. "Putting It into Words: An Anecdotal History of the Canadian Alliance of Dance Artists—Ontario Chapter's Professional Standards for Dance." In Naomi Jackson (ed.), *Right to Dance: Dancing for Rights*. Banff, AB: Banff Centre Press, 2004: 173–92.

Atkinson, Paul, and Martyn Hammersley. "Ethnography and Participant Observation." In N. Denzin and S. Lincoln (eds.), *Handbook of Qualitative Research*. London: Sage, 1994: 173–92.

Babbie, Earl. *The Practice of Social Research*, 8th ed. Toronto: Wadsworth, 1998.

Benn, Transin, and Dorcas Walters. "Between Scylla and Charybdis. Nutritional Education versus Bodyculture and the Ballet Aesthetic: The Effects on the Lives of Female Dancers." *Research in Dance Education* 2, no. 2 (2001): 139–54.

Benoit, Agnès (ed.). "On the Edge : Dialogues on Dance Improvisation in Performance" / "Créateurs de l'imprévu: Dialogues autour de la danse et de l'improvisation en spectacle." *Nouvelles de Danse* 32/33 (1997).

Bossatti, P. (ed.). "Interprètes inventeurs." *Cahiers du Renard* 11/12 (1992).

Bowring, Amy. "Sacrifice in the Studio: A History of Working Conditions, Contracts, and Unions for Dance in Canada, 1900–1980." In Naomi Jackson (ed.), *Right to Dance: Dancing for Rights*. Banff, AB: Banff Centre Press, 2004: 135–72.

Butterworth, Jo. "Teaching Choreography in Higher Education: A Process Continuum Model." *Research in Dance Education* 5, no. 1 (2004): 45–67.

Cools, Guy. "De la dramaturgie du corps en danse / On Dance Dramaturgy: A Dramaturgy of the Body." In Brian Webb (ed.), *Encounter/Rencontre: Environmental Encounters*. Ottawa, ON: Canada Dance Festival Society, 2006.

Davida, Dena. "Illuminating *Luna*: An Ethnographic Study of Meaning in a Montréal "Nouvelle Danse" Event." Unpublished doctoral thesis, University of Quebec in Montreal, 2006.

Dempster, Elizabeth. "Women Writing the Body: Let's watch a little how she dances." In S. Sheridan (ed.), *Grafts: Feminist Cultural Criticism*. London: Verso, 1988: 35–54.

Fortin, Sylvie, and Fernande Girard. "Dancers' Application of the Alexander Technique." *Journal of Dance Education* 5, no. 4 (2005): 125–31.

Fortin, Sylvie, Warwick Long, and Madeleine Lord. "Three Voices: Researching How Somatic Education Informs Contemporary Dance Technique Classes." *Research in Dance Education* 3, no. 2 (2002): 155–79.

Foster, Susan Leigh. "Dancing bodies." In Jane C. Desmond (ed.), *Meaning in Motion*, Durham, NC: Duke University Press, 1997: 235–59.

Fraleigh, Sondra. *Dance and the Lived Body*. Pittsburgh, PA: University of Pittsburgh, 1987.

Ginot, Isabelle. "Ceci n'est pas le corps de Chouinard." *Protée* 29, no. 2 (2001): 77–84.

Green, Jill. "Socially Constructed Bodies in American Dance Classrooms." *Research in Dance Education* 2, no. 2 (2001): 155–73.

———. "Somatic authority and the myth of the ideal body in dance education." *Dance Research Journal* 3, no. 2 (1999): 80–100.

Harrison, Deborah. "Can Research, Activism, and Feminism Converge? Some Notes on Collaborative Action-Oriented Inquiry." *An International Feminist Challenge to Theory* 5 (2001): 233–45.

Huynh-Montassier, Emmanuelle. "Passage Secrets." In Marietta Secret and Hervé Robbe (eds.), *Le corps de la danse*. Paris: Ministère de la Culture, 1992: 10–13.

Jowitt, Deborah. "Expression and Expressionism in American Modern Dance." In Janet Adshead-Landsdale and June Layson (eds.), *Dance History: An Introduction*. New York: Routledge, 1994: 169–81.

Kelly, Maree I.E. "Servants to Ballet: The Adolescent Dancer and Injury Management." Unpublished post-graduate diploma thesis. Dunedin, New Zealand: University of Otago, 1999.

Lamirande, Chantal. "Le sentiment d'appropriation d'une oeuvre ouverte: étude d'inspiration phénoménologique du vécu de l'interprétation." Unpublished master's thesis: Université du Québec à Montréal, 2003.

Lavender, Larry. Facilitating Choreographic Process. In Jo Butterworth and Liesbeth Wildschut (eds.), *Contemporary Choreography: A Critical Reader*. London: Routledge, 2009: 71–89.

———. Five Workshops on the Creative Process with Larry Lavender. Workshops presented at the Montréal Danse Choreographic Research and Development Workshop, Montreal, Canada, 2005.

———, and Jennifer Predock-Linnell. "From Improvisation to Choreography: The Critical Bridge." *Research in Dance Education* 2, no. 2 (2001): 195–209.

Leduc, Diane. "Les espaces de l'interprète en danse contemporaine." Unpublished master's thesis, Université du Québec à Montréal, 1996.

Lepecki, André. "Par le biais de la présence: la composition dans l'avant-garde post-bauschienne." *Nouvelles de danse* 36/37 (1998): 183–93.

Litzenberger, Sharon. "Mentorship: Nurturing Creative Potential." *The Dance Current* 7 (2005): 23–25.

Long, Warwick. "Sensing Difference: Student and Teacher Perceptions on the Integration of the Feldenkrais Method of Somatic Education and Contemporary Dance Technique." Unpublished master's thesis, University of Otago, Dunedin, New Zealand, 2002.

Lord, Madeleine. "The Teaching of Dance: A Characterization of Dance Teacher Behaviors in Technique and Choreography Classes at the University level." *Dance Research Journal* 2, no. 1 (1982): 9–19.

Mappin, Jane. "Speaking the Unspeakable in Contemporary Dance: The Dialogue between Choreographer and Interpreter in the Creative Process." Unpublished master's thesis, Université du Québec à Montréal, 2000.

Martin, Randy. *Performance as Political Act: The Embodied Self.* New York: Bergin and Garvey, 1990.

Maynard, Mary, and June Purvis (eds.). *Researching Women's Lives from a Feminist Perspective.* London: Taylor and Francis, 1994.

Newell, Pamela. "Dancers Make Dance: Dancers' Roles in the Creative Process and Their Somatic-Health and Socio-political Implications." Unpublished ·master's thesis, Université du Québec à Montréal, 2007.

Newman, Barbara. "Dancers Talking about Performance." In Alexandra Carter (ed.), *Routledge Dance Studies Reader.* London: Routledge, 1998: 57–65.

Novack, Cynthia. *Sharing the Dance.* Madison: University of Wisconsin, 1990.

Paillé, Pierre. "L'analyse par théorisation ancrée." *Cahiers de Recherche Sociologique,* no. 23 (1994): 147–81.

Preston-Dunlop, Valerie, and Ana Sanchez-Colberg (eds.). *Dance and the Perfomative.* London: Verve, 2002.

Russell, George. "Dancers' Work." In *Proceedings of the Society for Dance History Scholars Conference: Of, for and by the People.* New York, 1993: 193–200.

Salosaari, Paula. "Multiple Embodiment of Ballet and the Dancer's Cultural Agency." In Valerie Preston-Dunlop and Ana Sanchez-Colberg (eds.), *Dance and the Perfomative.* London: Verve, 2002: 219–37.

Schulmann, Natalie. "Paradoxe de l'interprète et de ses interprétations." *Nouvelles de Danse* 31 (1997): 35–43.

Sklar, Deidre. "On Dance Ethnography." *Dance Research Journal* 23, no. 1 (1991): 6–9.

Smith, Clyde. "On Authoritarianism in the Classroom." In Sherry B. Shapiro (ed.), *Dance, Power and Difference,* Champaign, IL: Human Kinetics, 1998.

Stravinsky, Igor. *Poetics of Music.* Cambridge, MA: Harvard University Press, 1942.

Szporer, Philip. "Expanded Creativity." Unpublished manuscript, 2003.

Thomas, Helen. *Body, Dance and Cultural Theory.* New York: Palgrave Macmillan, 2003.

CHAPTER TWELVE

How the Posture of Researcher-Practitioner Serves an Understanding of Choreographic Activity

JOËLLE VELLET

Anthropological tradition, like most anthropological research, forces us to ask whether it is possible and pertinent for a researcher to carry out research on her own social and cultural practice. In this chapter, I put forward some of my thoughts, based on experiences as a practitioner and researcher. I have been studying contemporary choreographic activity and, of course, when studying something that is as close to one's own practice as dance is to me, certain questions necessarily arise.

Is the closeness between one's artistic activity and one's field of research an obstacle to research? Does belonging to the world of dance pose a problem? Alternatively, is it possible that through practice the choreographer's eye is sharper, so that any pertinent problems facing the artist are noticed early and that what the artist is doing to resolve them is readily understood?

On the one hand, I wanted to see the "insider" position as a positive one, and I used it to my advantage. I will explain what I mean by this shortly. On the other hand, I tried to reduce the problems that might arise from being an insider to my own culture and, thus, from possessing a specific, as well as extensive, knowledge of the environment. I think I have been able to overcome these possible complications through my choice of methodologies of observation and analysis.

A CONTEXT AND A LINE OF QUESTIONING

The approach to dance that I have adopted as my own has always influenced my professional commitments as well as my personal experiences. However, when I became a researcher, I discovered the need for distance and objectivity.

My experience of the dance world has been constructed by the various roles I have played in it; for example, that of a dancer, a dance teacher, and a choreographer with a university company and, it goes without saying, a multitude of experiences as a spectator. I currently teach the artistic subject of dance in a French university to student teachers specializing in sports and it was in this capacity that the subject of my PhD dissertation emerged.

My research shows the importance I attach to everything that precedes the production of a work of art and which emerges during the creation of a dance. I am particularly interested in the meaning of the choreographer's activity, and how it brings the dancer to interpret the dance using specific gestural qualities. The viewpoint of the anthropologist allows the researcher to study not only the process begun by those involved in the transmission of the dance (choreographers and dancers) but also the characteristics of the dance and its composition.

My research is about dance transmission by the artists themselves, during creation or teaching. More precisely, I focus on the process of the construction of gesture and on the study of the discourse used during the transmission of the dance—which I call "discourse in situation."

During my PhD project, I engaged in research on contemporary dances in order to understand the choreographer's discourse during the transmission of the dance (during creation and teaching) and how it contributes to the elaboration of the dance gesture and its qualitative nuances. I concentrated on an analysis that focuses on how words and language influence the production and elaboration of movements, and on how they influence perception, imagination, and sensation, in order to allow the specific qualities of a dance to emerge. What follows is a brief explanation of the choices I made when constructing the field and in the constitution of the corpus, and some particularities of this research within the French context.

The dancer possesses an extraordinary ability to generate a poetic universe out of a single movement. How does she inscribe and renew the differences, in terms of subtle nuances, of gestural forms that appear to be the same? The form of the gesture, called here the *figure*, does little to help understand the modalities of what she has done. "The least little variation in the body part that initiates the movement, the flow of intensity that it organizes, the manner in which the dance anticipates and visualizes the movement it will produce, all this results in a figure that doesn't always produce the same meaning" (Godard 1995: 224). In the context of research in France, a certain number of parameters for aesthetics are used to describe the resulting gesture, but they rarely include the internal dynamics of the gesture, such as the processes that brought it to be. The dialogue of "corporeality to corporeality" (*corporéité* in French)[1] that takes place between choreographer and dancer, dancer and choreographer, is associated with an interbody contagion and alteration of shared gestures. But in this oral tradition, there are not only gestures but also words. It is here that my interest is focused: to unveil and understand the processes at work in the construction of the dance gesture. The term *dance* refers to a multiplicity of practices, of thoughts about the body in motion and associated models of dancing bodies. Aesthetics and artistic movements influence the work and also the perception of dancing corporealities. In a certain way, experiences and life histories modulate the body of the choreographer, like that of the dancer. What I have retained throughout this experience is a sensitive approach, a movement language (*écriture du mouvement*)[2] of dance that inscribes its own physical actions as *meaning*, in the sense that Roland Barthes spoke of in *Mythologies* (1957) when he wrote about certain corporeal languages (*écritures*). But if dance can propose aesthetic models, it can also polish and discipline the body, a body that we use at every instant and which engages us in actions and relationships. The body doesn't exist outside of its context; it doesn't exist prior to all that it is based on in everyday life. "Inventing" the body is also the work of a choreographer (Louppe 1997: 246). The creation of a danced gesture falls above and beyond the province of aesthetics, because it is permeated with questions about ethics. If dance can be perceived as a possible site for strong discipline, from which emerges the notion of "the docile body," it is also a place of openness and the construction of an identity, of a certain otherness, to which the choreographer contributes. One part of my research work develops this line of questioning.

The interest that I have developed for certain choreographers over others comes from the fact that they have their own distinct gestural style that they feel compelled to transmit to their dancers. The choreographers I chose to study are also dancers, working on material that has moved through their own corporeality. And though it is not a question of denying a place for the dancer's appropriation (and the transformation that is thus revealed), these choreographers develop material with the dancers and a poetics of dance from these same dancing bodies out of the movement and the gesture that rightly belongs to the dancers. Even the choreographic composition is dependent on a "corporal event."

Choreographer Odile Duboc working with dancer Vincent Druguet. Photographer: Samuel Carnovali.

Odile Duboc is part of a generation of choreographers of the new French dance of the 1980s, an intense period for the recognition of contemporary dance in France and for the emergence of a multi-faceted dance, bearing witness to diverse influences and affinities (Aubry 1991; Ginot and Michel 1995; Izrine 2002). Like her peers, Dominique Bagouet and Daniel Larrieu, Duboc pursued her own personal research about dance movement (*mouvement dansé*). She was also one of the rare choreographers of that period, along with Bagouet, to have contributed to the training of many interpretive dancers. Born in 1941, she danced and created her own school in Aix-en-Provence, where she lived until 1980. In 1983, she founded, along with Françoise Michel, the Compagnie Contre Jour. And in 1991, she was named as the director of one of France's regional choreographic centres, the Centre Chorégraphique National de Franche-Comté à Belfort.

BRIEF ELEMENTS OF A THEORETICAL FRAMEWORK
AND A METHODOLOGY

I adopted an anthropological stance from the start, one that is prominent in traditional ethnography (Copans 1999). Wanting to study transmission situations in their social and cultural human context and to get as close as possible to the ecological situation, I sought to trace the choreographers' and dancers' activity within their professional framework. Thus, my approach favoured the analysis of data collected in the field. This descriptive and ethnographic approach valued the understanding of observations in situ and attempted to understand the activity of these artists at work. Here, the field in which learning about a culture and a mode of thinking takes place, in the sense used by Kilani (1994), was the choreographer's studio.

All anthropological research projects are linked by the method of direct observation of the behaviour of others, beginning with a human relationship and a familiarity with the group that one wants to understand. My anthropological approach, however, is not concerned with a mysterious foreign object or land. Today, the anthropological viewpoint is also validated within a cultural and geographic proximity (Kaeppler 1998: 24–46) based on experiences that have been engendered there (Kealiinohomoku 1998: 47–67). It is not only a matter of letting oneself become permeated by observation: the way in which one observes must be developed (Laplantine 1987). It is not only a matter of describing the transmission channels and the creative channels but of trying to understand them. I have also developed an interest in the active subject and in the relations that tie him to the development of the dance. The study of the processes at work in the creation of the dance is part of *poïesis* as Passeron (1996) defines it. *Poïesis* concerns the actions of the choreographer; it tries to grasp the detail and to solve the mystery of the transmission process at the heart of the dialogue between the choreographer and the dancer inside this intimate, secretive dance studio. The crossing between aesthetics and anthropology in my work leads me to make the claim of being a "*poïetic* anthropologist" (Passeron 1996).

I have chosen to observe dance companies during their creative period in order to understand the choreographer's activity as she tries to bring the dancers to reproduce the specific qualities of the dance she wants. As far as I am concerned, the closeness of one's own artistic and professional practice to the field being studied need not be an obstacle in anthropology. For the researcher, some of the aspects of this situation can be thought of in a positive way.

PROFITING FROM CLOSENESS TO THE FIELD: A FIRST POINT IN FAVOUR OF THIS POSITION

I believe that before embarking on any anthropological research, one must acquire knowledge that can come from the field only. It is this kind of knowledge, coming from the inside, from deeply felt experience, that allows us to build a pertinent, sensitive, and experiential fieldwork question.

I am seeking to know more about the choreographer's activity and to understand why "discourse in situation" is different in dance, in comparison to other kinds of corporal activity, and why it varies with each choreographer. These questions stem from my own experience with different choreographers and from teaching. When I began my research, there were only a few studies on the kinds and functions of discourse in situation. Moreover, these studies focused mainly on teaching classes in North American schools—in other words, not on the context of creation (Vellet 2006: 79–91).

Normally, the researcher is in an etic ("outsider") position, one in which he observes, describes, and interprets the choreographer's actions with few preconceptions. A researcher who is also a dancer, however, can see the problems that arise for the choreographer in the situation of transmission: the difficulty is how to get the dancer to reproduce the specific qualities of the movement or gesture needed by the choreographer. The researcher/ dancer perceives that discourse in situation is one of the tools used by the artist to reduce this difficulty. With a topic such as mine, because of the etic point of view, a researcher can only hope to analyze the discourse, for example, identifying when it appears, its different functions, and so on. But an insider, someone in an emic position, can also analyze a change in the choreographer's strategy, because the insider will also try to understand how the choreographic problem can be resolved. This is because past experience in the dance world allows him to notice it. And so, the analysis of discourse is used to improve understanding, like a tool that serves to gain access to the specific qualities of the gesture.

I will illustrate with a specific situation. I observed that when Odile Duboc wanted to transmit her dance to the dancers, she was confronted with the following problem: seeing only her dancing was not enough for the dancers to grasp it (even if they were professionals). Therefore, she offered them something else, and we can study what she did and said.

First, she explained and described what she did in technical terms. For example she said,

There is a braking motion in the turn and if you don't brake / you are immediately / on top of it / so you must tighten the turn / give it less momentum.... All of you, you went two metres ahead of me at that moment / but I think the turn that you did took you into space immediately / think about braking here and freeze / and try to stop / it is as if there is a precipice in front of you / always think about that idea. (Excerpt from observations, January 2001)

Here, we see that Duboc's precipice metaphor allowed for the understanding of another quality of movement. At first, she tried to make the dancers understand that the turn must be done by braking on arrival. This was not enough, however, so she tried to help them grasp the origin of the movement: braking while integrating the idea of suspension and balance/ unbalance (the precipice). It is obvious that there was depth to the gesture she was trying to transmit. It was the intentionality of the movement that was evoked and constituted one of the elements of its genesis here.

Through discourse in situation, the choreographer helps the dancer to understand what generates the specific qualities of movement: the origins of the movement are revealed. This is why I have called this mode of transmission the "transmission matrix" because it includes factors surrounding the movement such as its origins and intentions.

MOVING AWAY FROM THE PROBLEM OF PROXIMITY

The second point is somewhat unusual in dance research. Being an "insider-dancer" led me to adopt a prudent attitude. I tried to find a methodology that would allow me to keep a necessary distance to preserve as much objectivity as possible. I think I found it in the methodology I chose: the "stimulated recall" interview (*entretien d'autoconfrontation* in French). This methodology ensures sufficient distance during fieldwork, particularly when the researcher knows her subject very well. It was not only a question of letting oneself be impregnated by the observation but of establishing an outlook that comes from the experiences lived in cultural and geographical proximity to the research question.

I placed myself in a theoretical perspective where the activity of transmission took place in a particular context, a kind of "situation ecology," where the actions of the choreographer are evident and meaningful only in contextualized action (Suchman 1987). In my research, the weight I lent to discourse in situation led me to remark that, as in every social or cultural situation, the act of speaking is "indexed" behaviour—that is, it is produced and adapted to the specific context in which it appears (Javeau 1998). I have taken into account the events of a moving, dynamic environment and also the principles and conceptions that form the basis for present thinking about choreography (at this precise moment in the course of its history).

In fact, from an anthropological viewpoint, choreographic activity cannot be understood independently of the significance that it holds for the choreographer. In a transmission situation, the knowledge mobilized by the artist is, in part, implicitly entwined in his know-how. The choreographer might even be unaware of it.

The scientific form of investigation that I have developed focuses on a detailed description of the act of transmission, by which it aims to analyze the knowledge at work driving the artist to act in the way she does. I use the tools of classic ethnography: fieldwork, involving field notes and video recording; informal interviews; and so on. Moreover, it is important for me to compare what I observe in situations of transmission with what the choreographer says about what she intended to do. I do this because it is important for me to listen to what the choreographer has to say, making sure that there is little false interpretation on my part.

To study this further, I looked for investigative tools from other human sciences. These tools aim to give the means of expression back to the choreographer and dancers (analysis of activity in psychology, in ergonomics, in ethno-methodology). So I chose to cross the theoretical and methodological borders between the different social sciences in an interdisciplinary approach. This is why I have adopted my stimulated-recall interviewing approach.

The simple stimulated-recall interviews demonstrate that, as a researcher, I did not want to remain an outsider. I wanted to understand the motivation of the choreographers better from an insider's viewpoint. The proposed methodology corresponds with a desire to know others: an attempt to study the choreographers' particular activities in order to understand humanity more generally.

The stimulated interview is a kind of "autoscopic" method in which the choreographer is shown videos of his own sessions of transmission and is asked to react to his own image. The choreographer then comments on what he did. This is how I obtained new and additional information with which to analyze the significance of the intentions and meanings that lie behind his way of transmitting the dance at that moment. The self-confrontation interview gives me access to part of what the choreographer hopes to do, corresponding to his deep convictions. This also gave me access to the constraints that prevent the practice from living up to one's expectations. What the choreographer does may be considered as the accomplished work but it is only ever "the actualisation of one of the activities possible in a situation where it takes place" (Clot 2001). Therefore, the reality of the activity also includes that which is not carried out; which one tries to do but unsuccessfully; which one would like to do, or could do; which is done unintentionally, and so on. In other words, as Clot would say, going beyond the "realized" to discover "the real of the activity."

Various methods of investigation and of data collection have allowed me to develop an approach that combined three perspectives:

1   I gathered my data using my status as an external researcher with regard to the subject of my work: field observations written into a notebook, audiovisual recordings with a fixed camera and microphone. I tried to capture not only the images in action but also the greatest number of verbal manifestations, constructed discourse, and other vocal forms (onomatopoeia, song). Recording the sound was useful in helping me recount the activity of the choreographer and dancers. During the observation periods, I shared many moments of ordinary life with the dancers outside their work (meals, rests, lodgings). The fact that I am a dancer also allowed me to take part in the company's daily training alongside the dancers. This kind of participatory immersion is an important influence on the way in which the dancers and the choreographer regarded my presence. It may be thought of as an essential gesture toward the choreographer: to be able to taste physically, to share, to immerse in a "doing" of dance that I was then going to observe. My presence was thus accepted at all times, even during those delicate sessions of readjustment and discussion. I had access through my own involvement in dance not only to another form of knowledge but to everything that was said and done outside of the camera's range, just like those things that fall outside the noted, targeted situation of transmission. All these clues picked up in this way make sense of certain elements, which are observed and analyzed. This is also an argument in favour of proximity in the field. My entry into the field and the sharing of work within the dance company are made easier, even when I don't know the choreographer and the dancers personally.

2   I gathered other data from various kinds of documents (e.g., texts written by the choreographers themselves; interviews and articles by art critics or theoreticians on the subject of the choreographic work of the artists involved).

3   I also collected data from a process of dialogue: semi-direct interviews (with the choreographers and dancers of the companies) and stimulated-recall interviews. Thanks to these kinds of interviews, I gained access to the transmitter-choreographer's words—that is, to discourse that is well developed because of the methodology being used. When put into context, the research material stimulates this discourse. The artist was compelled to say more than usual about relations with the dancer or the dance material. The choreographer was not only a subject for study, submitted to observation, but she also participated in the research by dialoguing with the researcher. I regarded the choreographer's own analysis as an element that nourished a theorization of the act of creating a dance, of the act of training the interpretive dancer.

It was this access to intentional and operational elements in the "doing" that allowed me to better understand this weaving together of gesture and discourse. In transmission, things sometimes happen as if only discourse could open the paths to corporeality and to corporal imagination (Vellet 2003, 1999). The earlier precipice metaphor example is testimony to this idea. Here is what the choreographer Duboc said in a stimulated-recall interview:

> In fact I have just spoken about a precipice but it's always this state of emergency / very ad hoc / from all these sensations all that imagining / I don't think that I've got a precipice in front of me, it's not true but / my breath my breathing corresponds to those moments where you're in an emergency, perhaps on a pavement, you're going to fall down and you stay there in the air because you cut your breathing, in fact it's / it's all those sensations / that nourish my dancing. (Excerpt from interview, January 2001)

Through the use that the choreographer made of the metaphorical or imagined proposals, she appealed to the imagination of the dancers and suggested that they find the gestures by way of a search for sensation. As Jullien has proposed, it is in the situation of transmission where a state or a sensation or a quality is being sought; it is the encouragement value of the discourse that is present (Jullien 1995).

In the next example, taken from the teaching of a fragment of choreography, Odile Duboc's discourse in situ described the gesture she was expecting (and she demonstrated it while she was speaking):

From that point you have a circle made by the leg and a circle made by the arm which are the same / and you arrive at the different diagonal with the arm on the shoulder / with the hand on the shoulder / here / behind / the hand on the shoulder / your arm stays hooked here and the other hand comes to rest on the right. (Excerpt from observations, January 2001)

This hand on the shoulder was received like an additional and very descriptive indication of the movement. However, the stimulated-recall interview led the choreographer to reveal deeper meanings of that a movement. Through sensation, she tried to develop a particular relationship with space; it was neither considered as a form nor as an aesthetic of gesture that was being searched for. A state was being sought, one that allowed the relationship to space to be nourished by sensitive listening to one's own body. Understanding this intention is not easy when one looks at the situation of transmission—at no moment were these explanations given to the dancers. On the other hand, during the stimulated-recall interview, the explanations given by Duboc showed that behind this short descriptive commentary, a fundamental aspect of her dance was present:

So the hands it's / it's something, how shall I put it, we'll be a little bit the same there with this left hand which will settle on the right hand / the right hand is there before carrying the arm which / will meet a very slight resistance to this very hand which has settled on top / it's my right arm which will begin the movement and as it's the left hand which is on top, there will be a very light contact / something sensitive which will allow me to develop a relation that I would not otherwise develop if there had not been this hand / but it is what lets me feel sensations / that is why the hand intervenes like that from time to time, one on top of the other / because they're going to let me develop this relation to space. (Excerpt from interview, June 2001)

This cannot be made accessible to dancers without supplementary verbal explanations, or without prior acquisition of know-how, characteristic of the qualitative work of this artist's dancing (acquired by attending daily classes for example).

Finally, in Duboc's words, considered in context, the relationship to gravity is highly valued with all that is meant in terms of weight, of transfer of support. Why approach this dimension rather than another at any given moment? The stimulated-recall interview allowed access to the intentions of these priorities:

So that the dancing can get organised and start to advance / for example the thing about the transfer of support is that it isn't just for me / there will not be the balance necessary there won't be the possibility of braking in what I've just said / and therefore the musicality won't be there / I think the explanations I give justify the necessary musicality I'm speaking about. (Excerpt from interview, June 2001)

In the adjustment to the context, there were choices and priorities that made sense. Duboc gave no explanation of these priority and choices to the dancers. She constructed a contextualized point of view by taking into account the major dimensions of her own dancing at the same time as she took into account a temporal dimension, a relational dimension (professional as well as affective).

Moreover, it is worth noting that dancers seem very interested in this kind of research. The reaction of dancers and choreographers to these studies has been very positive. Interestingly enough, they are as intrigued by the questions as they are by the results. They told me that it enabled them to better understand how they do their daily job; to become conscious of what they are doing and why. For the choreographers, this stimulated recall has held the possibility of producing a new conceptualization of their activity.

Let me conclude by saying that an exclusively etic or emic point of view cannot exist in such studies. For me, it is most interesting to consciously employ both perspectives and so to create a form of research that takes both into account. A kind of permanent dialogue between the researcher and the dancer emerges, producing new, enhanced knowledge.

In the period when this chapter was being written, Odile Duboc passed away, an incalculable loss for dance professionals and dance admirers throughout France.

Notes

1 I have chosen the term "corporeality" (*corporéité*) instead of "body," adhering to the choice proposed by Michel Bernard when he distinguished two conceptions underlying these concepts. In his article, "Les fanstasmagories de la realité spectaculaire" (2001: 85–94), in which he takes up elements already put forward in his 1976 book *Le corps*, Bernard posits that "the body in the Occident is not a universal, permanent or autonomous essence. In spite of the apparent identity of its anatomical structure and its physiological functioning, the body is a sensory-motor network of unstable intensity, submitted to the fluctuations of a double symbolic history: that of the society of the culture in which it appears, and that of the historical and national particularity of its own existence.... Also, to permit a better intelligibility of the creative process and to avoid misunderstandings, illusions, and confusions engendered by the current use of the concept of the

body, I propose that of 'corporeality,' while diverging from the reflexive, idealist and psychological acceptance that has been given to it by phenomenology" (1995: 86). According to this version argued by Bernard, what appears for the observer of the dance "is no longer the anatomical reality of the body as identified in the practice of everyday life but a constellation of mobile and multi-sensorial appearances" (1995: 87).

2 By *écriture du mouvement* ("movement writing"), I mean the construction of the dance gesture of the body in movement, with all of its material and energetic qualities, space and time ... the pathways that are traced by the gesture, by a wilful gesture that is researched and chosen. I distinguish this concept from that of *écriture chorégraphique* ("choreographic writing"), which refers to the ensemble of elements in a performance (relationships between dancers, stage space, artistic proposal, light, music, costumes, and so on).

Bibliography

Aubry, Chantal. "Danse l'invention des langages." *Territoires de la danse*. Paris: Cahiers du Renard, 1991: 11–19.

Bakhtine, Michel. *Esthétique de la création verbale*. Paris: Gallimard, 1984.

Barthes, Roland. *Mythologies*. Paris: Seuil, 1957.

Bernard, Michel. *Le corps*. Paris: Éditions Universitaires, 1976.

———. *De la création chorégraphique*. Paris: Centre National de la Danse, 2001.

Clot, Yves. "Clinique de l'activité et pouvoir d'agir." *Éducation permanente* 146 (2001): 17–34.

Copans, Jean. *Introduction à l'ethnologie et à l'anthropologie*. Paris: Nathan, 1999.

Ginot, Isabelle, and Marcelle Michel. *La danse au XXè siècle*. Paris: Bordas, 1995.

Godard, Hubert. "Le geste et sa perception." In Ginot and Michel (eds.), *La danse au XXème siècle*. Paris: Bordas, 1995: 224–29.

Izrine, Agnès. *La danse dans tous ses états*. Paris: L'Arche, 2002.

Javeau, Claude. *Prendre le futile au sérieux*. Paris: Éditions du Cerf, 1998.

Jullien, François. *Le détour et l'accès, stratégies du sens en Chine*. Paris: Grasset, 1995.

Kaeppler, Adrienne. "La danse selon une perspective anthropologique." *Nouvelles de danse* 34–35 (1998): 24–46.

Keali'inohomoku, Joann. "Une anthropologue regarde le ballet classique comme une forme de danse ethnique." *Nouvelles de danse* 34–35 (1998): 47–67. Originally published in *Impulse* (1969/70). Also in Roger Copeland and Marshall Cohen (eds.), *What Is Dance? Reading in Theory and Criticism*. New York: Oxford University Press, 1983.

Kilani, Monder. *L'invention de l'autre: Essais sur le discours anthropologique*. Lausanne: Payot, 1994.

Korzybski, A. *Le rôle du langage dans les processus perceptuels* (French translation). New York: International Non-Aristotelian Library, 1965, 1951.

Lakoff, George, and Mark Johnson. *Les métaphores dans la vie quotidienne*. Paris: Éditions Minuit, 1980.

Laplantine, François. *Clefs pour l'anthropologie*. Paris: Clefs Seghers, 1987.

Louppe Laurence, *Poétique de la danse contemporaine: La pensée du mouvement*. Bruxelles: Contredanse, 1997.

Mauss, Marcel. *Sociologie et anthropologie*. 7th ed. Paris: Presses Universitaires de France, 1980 [1950].

Passeron, René. *La naissance d'Icare: éléments de poïétique générale*. Valenciennes: Presses Universitaires de Valenciennes and Éditions ae2cg, 1996: 365–86.

Reed, Edward. S. "An Outline of a Theory of Action System." *Journal of Motor Behavior* 14, no. 2 (1982): 98–134.

Straus, Erwin. *Du sens des sens* (French translation, 1989). Grenoble: Million, 1935.

Suchman, Lucy. *Plans and Situated Action*. Cambridge: Cambridge University Press, 1987.

———. "Plans d'action. Problèmes de représentation de la pratique en sciences cognitives." In P. Pharo and L. Quéré (eds.), *Raisons pratiques 1: Les formes de l'action*. Paris: Éditions de l'EHESS, 1990: 149–70.

Vellet, Joëlle. "La transmission matricielle de la danse contemporaine." *Revue STAPS* 72 (2006): 79–91.

———. "Contribution à l'étude des discours en situation dans la transmission de la danse. Discours et gestes dansés dans le travail d'Odile Duboc." Unpublished doctoral dissertation, Université de Paris 8, en Esthétique Sciences et Technologies des Arts, Paris, 2003.

———. "Le chorégraphe passeur d'une musicalité du mouvement." In S. Becuwe et N. Garreau (eds.), *Arts, Sciences et Technologies*. La Rochelle, France: Maison des Sciences de l'homme et de la Société Université de La Rochelle, 2003: 211–24.

———. "Processus de création chorégraphique ... un tissage de gestes et de discours." *La danse une culture en mouvement*. Strasbourg: CREEC, Université Marc Bloch, 1999: 55–64.

CHAPTER THIRTEEN

A Teacher "Self-Research" Project

SENSING DIFFERENCES IN THE TEACHING AND LEARNING OF CONTEMPORARY DANCE TECHNIQUE IN NEW ZEALAND

RALPH BUCK, SYLVIE FORTIN, AND WARWICK LONG

INTRODUCTION

The site of this study was a university dance program in Auckland, New Zealand. There are currently six tertiary dance programs in New Zealand, including polytechnics and universities. These institutions offer graduate and post-graduate diploma and degree courses ranging from; a polytechnic program focused on developing Maori and Pacific Island performing arts, several university programs offering dance majors as part of a Bachelor of Arts degree, to a named bachelor's degree in dance and a dance degree within a Bachelor of Screen and Performing Arts. The context of this research was informed by the particular program offered by the institution participating in the study. In this case, it was a Bachelor of Screen and Performing Arts that was focused on developing practitioners in contemporary dance choreography, as well as technically competent dancers able to contribute to New Zealand's contemporary dance environment. We felt that the strong practical focus of this particular program would be suitable in allowing us to work with a cohort of participants who through the nature of their particular course structure constantly have to reflect on their kinaesthetic sensations and adapt their dance practice to changing demands of different techniques and choreographers. Warwick was an insider, having previously taught at this institution and was therefore familiar with the culture, pedagogical, and administrative structure. This was important, as it facilitated "getting in" to the field, and allowed the research to take place with relative discretion, and without disrupting the curriculum.

CULTURAL CONTEXT

We—Ralph Buck, Sylvie Fortin, and Warwick Long—are experienced teachers with considerable teaching histories honed in New Zealand, Canada, and Australia. We have different fields of expertise and a shared respect for constructivist pedagogy in which knowledge and understanding are made and remade by the participating teachers and students through interaction with each other and their socio-cultural environment. We each have an awareness of the complexities of teaching in tertiary, secondary, and primary school contexts, sharing an interest in the kinds of "holistic" dance educational practices that acknowledge each learner as a unique individual, specific in their movement and their construction of meaning. We all met in 2002 at the University of Otago, School of Physical Education, in New Zealand, and it was here that we discussed the role(s) of dance teachers and dance technique within all levels of dance education. The School of Physical Education at the University of Otago is unique in that it has the oldest university dance program in New Zealand dating back to the 1940s. Its uniqueness is further enhanced by the origins of this program that saw dance an integral part of the education of all students of physical education. Embedded in the values of this program, dance provided ways for students to apply cognitive understandings of the body in a physical, creative, reflective and cooperative environment.

Thus it was under this historical umbrella that we shared our own practices as we taught contemporary dance and Feldenkrais classes (Warwick), dance education pedagogy (Ralph) and dance, health and somatics (Sylvie). While we had all had similar experiences as former dance professionals and educators working in Australia, Europe, New Zealand, and Canada, it is important to note how our distinct cultural backgrounds influenced both our pedagogical approaches and previous experiences in dance. Warwick was born in New Zealand and spent the most part of his professional dance and educational career working in both Australia and New Zealand. Ralph was originally from Australia and had a similar background to Warwick, but also had spent time working in the United Kingdom and Europe. Sylvie was French Canadian and developed her dance and educational career in Montreal. Both Warwick and Sylvie were also Feldenkrais teachers. Our discussions in part reflected the wider pedagogical debate in New Zealand between 1999 and 2004 as the Ministry of Education released the new arts curriculum (inclusive of dance) into all schools. This document proactively supported diverse pedagogies, not least interactive pedagogies that relied on dialogue between teachers and students and curriculum, and recognized that all dance learners have experiences; unique ways of moving and can contribute ideas to share and build upon in pedagogical processes.

Similarly, these views have been championed by Tina Hong (2002), Caroline Plummer and Dr. Ralph Buck (2003), Adrienne Sansom (2001) and Dr. Karen Barbour (2001) across several leading tertiary institutions in New Zealand.

Arguably the emergence of an increasingly interactive pedagogy was (and remains) born from New Zealand educators' increasing awareness of, and respect for, diversity of: dancers' culture, dancers' bodies, dancers' abilities, dancers' values and interests. Within the global postmodern debate about "what is dance" and "who is a dancer," New Zealand dance educators on the whole have firmly embraced a diversity of responses. Stemming from this range of views, these dance educators have worked to develop pedagogies that engendered participation that is inclusive of learners' diversity. It is worthwhile noting that not all tertiary dance programs, educators and dance professionals have shared this pedagogical shift, as some of them, in brief, have maintained that "form" should take precedence over "feeling." As you can see, New Zealand dance educators have been engaged in a process of re-debating through school curriculum, conferences and tertiary degree curriculums, the core values underlying pedagogy philosophy, artistic practices and aesthetic ideals.

AN INSIDER'S PERSPECTIVE

This study is both a "teacher research" into Warwick's own practice and, as will be introduced in the following passages, a constructivist inquiry into student perceptions of the dance technique classes. In terms of situating this study within the parameters of this book, it could be said that although a social-constructivist view guided the course of this project, the methods engaged in doing fieldwork and interpreting the data coincided with those of ethnographic methods.

When completing the write-up in which he described and interpreted experiences of the dance teachers and students, Warwick placed himself as the author in the first person. In doing so, he clearly adopted an emic insider's perspective regarding his own teaching process, discussing the evolution of this process with the other participants, and consequentially synthesizing these experiences in relation to the theoretical frameworks introduced below. It is also of value to note that from an anthropological point of view, although the fieldwork specific to this project took place over a short five-day period, Warwick's long-term experience as a dancer has given him the in-depth knowledge of someone who has inhabited the field over a prolonged period.

To elaborate further on the emic perspective in the data collection, somatic education values the creation of direct knowledge acquired through direct embodied personal experience (Lake 1987–1988). This line of inquiry stems from an emic perspective (Cochran-Smith and Lytle 1993; Eisner 1998; Maykut and Morehouse 1994). In valuing this insider's view, Peshkin (2001) advocates a "quality of attention to lives that otherwise may be demeaned as those of mere actors on the stage of our research settings, simply so sources of data, unclad figures of speech awaiting our—the researchers—interpretation" (Peshkin 2001: 244). And so, by choosing an emic line of inquiry, we are specifically not engaging in an objective analysis of teaching procedure. Our interest is in collecting data from an emic perspective and interpreting and notions of how and why experiences are lived the way they are by their protagonists.

Warwick Long: The Teacher as Researcher

As I shift this narrative briefly into an autoethnographic mode, I (Warwick) reflect that throughout my career as a dance performer, choreographer, and teacher I felt that learning movement was fraught with problems. The origins of this feeling stemmed from my experience as a child when I always had difficulties learning certain movement skills. In ball games or activities such as gymnastics, I was "uncoordinated" and seemed to have a fear of movement. The paradox was that in other areas movement, I felt "natural" (in the sense of being at ease), as I regularly competed successfully at a national and provincial level in athletics and swimming.

In commencing dance classes at the age of eighteen, I found this learning process a struggle made more complex by my notions of what was "right and wrong technique." These notions were based on my perceptions that there existed an ideal, socially sanctioned, dance technique, and my views about how I should look doing it. Attention to physical inner sensation had escaped me. I was preoccupied with achieving the external image of technical perfection no matter what the cost to my body. In the end, I developed chronic back pain, and realize now that my difficulties in learning dance had more to do with my thinking than anything else. I began to transform my attitudes about movement through my growing interest in the Feldenkrais Method of somatic education. Through this way of learning, I began to sense how to make fine discriminations in movement from an inner kinaesthetic perspective. One way I found that somatic education links with dance education was through learning to direct attention to movement on an incrementally fine level. In the field of somatic education, this process of learning movement is termed sensory motor awareness. For this research project, my past experience as a student and my present experience as a somatic and dance educator came together as I observed students experiencing many similar issues that I encountered in my own learning movement processes.

PURPOSE AND ORIENTATION OF THIS STUDY

The purpose of this study was to examine learner perceptions of how somatic education was integrated within contemporary dance technique classes in a pre-professional academic setting. Because of Warwick's commitment to and experience with the practice of the Feldenkrais Method, this particular somatic technique became a central focus. It is one of several methods of somatic education that for over twenty years have been utilized by dancers in pre-professional training institutions in North America, Europe, and Oceania as an adjunct or complementary approach to traditional training methods. As Feldenkrais trainer and kinesiologist Goldfarb expresses it, "The Feldenkrais Method consists of a systemic understanding of the human body's design for motion and a perception orientated pedagogy for changing how people move" (Goldfarb 1990: 1). In other words, through the medium of movement, this method addresses the potential for people to increase their own bodily self-awareness through self-observation of sensory-motor behaviour, which can then act as a catalyst for the improvement of function.

Within the academic and professional milieu of contemporary dance, there are many claims by researchers and teachers, such as Fortin (2003), Fitt (1998), and Cardinal (2000), that somatics has indeed influenced the practices of dance teaching, choreography, performance, and dance medicine in many ways. These influences range from encouraging students to develop self-authority (Green 2001), to assisting in rehabilitation from injury (Cardinal 2000), to the capacity for improving body awareness in dance-technique classes (Lessinger 1996). As a teacher researcher with a background in both contemporary dance and Feldenkrais, I was curious to uncover dancers' perceptions of how the Feldenkrais Method might be integrated within a dance-technique class.

There have been numerous studies on the efficacy of the Feldenkrais Method of somatic education in a number of medical domains (Harris 1996; Ives and Shelley 1998; Stephens 1999), but there are fewer in the field of dance (Fortin, Long, and Lord 2002). Furthermore, from reviewing existing literature in dance and somatics, it appears there is little systematic research examining somatic education and contemporary dance from the perspective of the dancer. Part of this may be due to the fact that somatics as a field of study is relatively new and for the most part research has been focused on an empirical understanding the mechanisms of the different methods and their practical application (Cardinal 2000).

In order to better understand the relationship of somatics and dance from the perspective of the dancer, we address here the following research questions: "How do dancers construct a somatic way of knowing themselves through movement?" and "What were the emerging pedagogical issues around an integrated approach to somatic education and contemporary dance technique?"

METHODOLOGICAL AND EPISTEMOLOGICAL POSITION

The overall paradigm that we used to address the research question was that of qualitative inquiry, shared by both constructivist and ethnographic researchers. The particular advantage of qualitative inquiry in the confines of this study was the value placed on personal experience as the means whereby the researcher can describe, interpret, examine, construct, and understand insiders' world views. As Maykut and Morehouse have expressed it, since qualitative research is "phenomenological in its position," it "examines peoples' words and actions in narrative or descriptive ways more closely representing the situation as experienced by the participants" (1994: 2–3).

Going even further, Peshkin (2001) believes that we are, in fact, never free from viewing the world through a multiplicity of lenses, and delightfully recounts a hiking excursion that narrates a kinaesthetic, aesthetic, olfactory, and visual perception of experiences that not only occur during these leisure activities but also can be accessed on a daily basis in our research endeavours:

> One day on the trail, I decided to attend more seriously to what I was passing by to see if I could enrich the experience of my mountain jaunts. I purposefully identified categories that would focus my attention. The longer I walked, the more focal points or categories I uncovered, all of them quite common, all of them always available, all of them generally ignored. (Peshkin 2001: 239)

As Peshkin developed his metaphor further, he touched on various phenomena existing just outside of our awareness, yet potentially available through selected attention and time spent looking at detail:

The idea, I soon learned, was to select one category at a time as the basis for perceiving and to shut off those others that always are there competing for my attention.... Our wealth of perceptions expands as our awareness of categories expands. (2001: 239)

As a teacher-researcher and somatic practitioner, Warwick found Peshkin's analogy helpful in searching for an entry point to access my research question. Bearing in mind his comments around categories, he realized he could view this study through a variety of lenses, ranging from education to phenomenology, somatics, and the performing arts.

As elaborated above, the epistemological position we chose for this research was constructivism. More specifically, we applied Guba's perspective on constructivism in which inquiry about the nature of knowledge is based in the assumption that if realities exist they do so only in the "form of multiple mental constructions, socially and experientially based, local and specific, dependent for their form and content on the persons who hold them" (1990: 27). Thus, as educational psychologist Thomas Schwandt noted, notions of constructivism have wide usage and yet, of special interest to this research project, are particularly "shaped by the intent of their users" (2000: 119). Schwandt additionally suggests that "human beings do not find or discover knowledge so much as construct or make it. We invent concepts, models and schemes to make sense of experience, and we continually test and modify these constructions in light of the new experience" (2000: 197). In view of the pedagogical backgrounds and specific interest in the pedagogy of somatic education and dance technique of the three of us, we adopted this constructivist orientation because (as is also true from an anthropological perspective) it proposes that knowledge is constructed from personal experience, and that the precise style and patterns of individual actions are developed though a shared social and cultural context encompassing highly personalized ways of communicating and moving.

The somatic approach to contemporary dance technique we adopted in this study fits into the epistemological orientation of constructivism in the sense that it advocates for the individual uniqueness and distinctive sensory experience of each student as a starting point to improve self-knowledge of movement. Knowledge in the context of this study was constructed through investigating the integration of the Feldenkrais Method of somatic education within the contemporary dance-technique classes, and, more precisely, from data collected in the field about the lived experience of four of the dance students and the teacher-researcher as they participated in five classes over a one-week period.

Teacher research is defined by Cochran-Smith and Lytle as a "systematic, intentional inquiry carried out by the teachers themselves" (1993: 7), with the position that "teaching as research is connected to a view of learning as constructive, meaning centered and social" (1993: 101). In this view, teacher research is appropriate within the constructivist position of this study, since it is the teacher and students together who frame the context in which teaching and research takes place. It can also be said that teacher research shares certain characteristics with other interpretive research traditions such as ethnography, but also action research, which supports the idea that raising consciousness leads to social action. Somatic education encourages authorship of personal experience and self-responsibility through advocating increased awareness and consciousness of our daily habits and actions in our environment (Joly 2004; Fortin 2003). We will address the possibility later that emerging outcomes from this study might lead to change, however our present focus is to gain a better understanding of practice in New Zealand by being in the field of the dance studio and interacting with the participants by way of the various ethnographic methods we've described.

SETTING AND PARTICIPANTS

In its entirety, the fieldwork and analysis of this research was conducted between March 2002 and March 2003. As mentioned, the setting was a tertiary education institution in Auckland, New Zealand. There were eleven participants in total, five pre-professional dancers, five professional dancers, and Warwick as teacher-researcher. The pre-professional dance students were enrolled in a bachelor's degree course at the tertiary institution. The professional dancers were part of the independent dance community in Auckland, and taking dance-technique classes through a community partnership with the institution. As the researcher, I initially contacted and consulted the institution's dance program leader who agreed to the institution's involvement in this study.

Ethical approval was obtained from a research ethics committee. The ethical issues in this study concerned the maintenance of anonymity and the safety of participants. All of them signed a consent form and chose pseudonyms, which are used in this chapter.

Due to constraints of length, and in order to reflect the depth of the participants' experience, the synthesis of the teacher-researcher and data from interviews and observations of four students (from the total of the ten students enrolled in the daily classes) are presented in this chapter. Two participants (Amelia and Polly) were pre-professional dance students enrolled in the bachelor's degree course whereas the two other participants (Bevan and John) were professional dancers from the independent dance community, taking classes through the community partnership with the institution. The selection processes employed to choose participants for the study were based on their professional and pre-professional backgrounds, gender, and the depth of articulation of the participant's discourses.

Throughout the five days of classes, participants were asked to

1. Participate in five contemporary dance-technique classes over the course of a week. These classes were videotaped and recorded.
2. Participate in group discussion during or at the conclusion of the class.
3. Participate in in-depth interviews of approximately one hour.
4. Maintain a daily journal.

DATA COLLECTION AND ANALYSIS

During each of the five days, a dance class was offered whose duration was one and a half hours. Each class consisted of four distinct sections: (a) an awareness through movement (ATM) session, usually on floor mats; (b) a transition from movements on the floor to standing and walking; (c) dance-technique exercises; and (d) dance combinations. Both recorded and live music were used as an accompaniment. A warming-down and discussion period followed the conclusion of the dance-combination section. A detailed description of the four sections of the class is presented in Table 1.

The data collection consisted of video recordings of all five classes over the five days; group discussions after each class; the contents of participants' journals; field notes of the teacher-researcher; and audio recordings of four hour-long one-on-one interviews with Amelia, Polly, Bevan, and John. These interviews addressed participants' histories, experiences, and thoughts as they reflected on their participation over the five days of technique classes. Each of these data sources revealed different strengths and possibilities for informing the analysis.

The use of students' journals permitted participants to contribute their thoughts and reflections on their experience in their own time and in their own way. According to Maykut and Morehouse, the goal of a journal is "to let participants speak for themselves as much as possible, to tell their stories without interpretation" (1994: 122). To this end, Warwick asked participants to keep a journal of daily thoughts, reflections, and experiences that they felt related to the classes. He encouraged participants to present this journal in a manner meaningful to them but in a way that was communicable. This was not to preclude graphic or poetic representations of studio

Table 1   Structure and Content of the Class

Section	Time	Description
Awareness Through Movement (ATM)	20 min.	This section was taught primarily through verbal instruction. The focus was to bring students' attention to sensory motor learning, through introducing a series of movement lessons that explored patterns of movement initiation such as flexing, extending, or spiralling. This part of the class was done lying down to reduce the activity in postural muscles through lessening the effects of gravity, and to bring learners' awareness to hidden or parasitic muscular activity.
Transition to standing and walking	10 min.	This section was guided verbally. The aim was to transfer the learning from the ATM lesson to simple functions such as standing and walking, and gradually threading this into the more complex function of dancing.
Dance technique exercises	20–30 min.	This section was similar to a traditional contemporary dance class. It consisted of a series of exercises designed to both sequentially warm up the body for more technically demanding dance phrases and draw attention to alignment and accuracy of movement. The themes and patterns of the ATM lesson were interwoven through both this part of class and the dance combination.
Dance combination	20–30 min.	This section consisted of longer phrases of movement with dynamic movement combinations travelling into the space. The last two sections were taught through verbal instruction, visual demonstration, and modelling from both students and the teacher.

classroom experience. It was important to Warwick that they feel comfortable elaborating upon their experiences in various ways, and to also acknowledge that feelings and sensations of movement cannot always be transposed into the form of language. This open-ended journal process also allowed for the expression of tacit knowledge, that which cannot be spoken yet is known, felt, and perhaps represented in ways other than prose.

At the conclusion of the week of dance classes, my data consisted of eleven participants' journals (including Warwick's). These journals reflected participants' daily experience in class and their related activities and observations emerging through the week. What was missing from the journals, however, was the sense of person, the broader aspects of their experiences in dance and somatics. Warwick found, however, that these broader aspects emerged in the interview process.

After transcribing and reviewing the interviews and studying the participant journals, a data analysis began that was based on a combination of "open coding" (Strauss and Corbin 1990) and the "constant comparative method" (Maykut and Morehouse 1994). Through use these processes, comparison, meanings, and commonalities in the data began to emerge. From this point on, we were able to see more clearly the relationship of fieldwork data to the questions of how dancers constructed a somatic way of knowing, and the emerging pedagogical issues of somatic education and dance technique.

A SOMATIC WAY OF KNOWING

In this section, I (Warwick) slip back into the first person as I synthesize the results of the first question: "How did dancers construct a somatic way of knowing themselves through movement?" The concept of somatic knowing in this study, in the words of Heshusius, is a "knowing evolving from sensitivity toward oneself leading to an awareness that allows more meaningful relationships to the world" (1994: 18). The central tenet of this idea is that of gaining insight into how we come to know ourselves somatically. Questions such as "How do we know we are breathing, moving, standing, balancing and dancing?" invite us to explore somatic ways of knowing ourselves in movement. Four themes emerged from the data, which I have named: refining individual perception, exploring the body's possibilities, questioning through our body, and valuing a plurality of learning experiences. Each theme is outlined below and supported by excerpts from the research participants' observations from the interviews and journal writing.

Amelia—Refining Individual Perception: "You dance for a feeling of pleasure"

Amelia's initial experience with the integration of Feldenkrais and dance technique indicated a certain amount of frustration, but also an openness to explore new ideas from a somatic perspective. As she expressed in the interview:

> At the beginning of the year, you are pushing to your limit. I am finding with these classes, I'm a lot calmer and once I get to doing the phrases, I can feel like I understand what my body is doing and I know where I am, and that actually feels good. I mean to say there's a lot of confusion, but also once I get into doing phrases I can feel where it is in my body that I'm feeling freer and it feels really good. There's always that balance of technique and always judging yourself and trying to be better and then just kind of

free dancing. And then what do you dance for? A feeling of pleasure.... This morning, I found you can create something, create an alignment and create a movement in your body by using other parts of your body. I have to not think about my hip to be able to open up my hips. As soon as I thought about the area it tensed up. If I breathed and I thought about something different, it would work. I found that I knew the movement as well as the feeling I wanted to have while performing it. I didn't have to think so much and yet my body seemed to be accessing the new movement and it felt really easy. (Interview, March 20, 2002)

It was through this kind of language that Amelia described her sense of connection between knowledge of the movement and her feeling of "being in movement." Her aesthetic feeling of movement is embodied somatically. In my analysis of this instance, I felt that Amelia as a dancer did not perceive herself as separate from the dance she was engaged in. In the next quote, it became clear that she was building up what I call "an internal somatic picture" of herself:

When you asked about how I was trying to correct my sacrum [it] was actually through being able to feel what was happening. Because I didn't know really where my sacrum was, and I still don't think I know, but I'm beginning to get an image of that in my brain. And I have to take it from a variety of sources, like I have to see a picture of a skeleton, but maybe for me, seeing a 2-D picture doesn't actually help me. I have to go and see a skeleton. I began to lose weight from my bum last year and suddenly I can feel where my bones are. I've never been aware of that part of my body. It's like I had to learn through a variety of sources where that is inside me before I could kind of begin to change. I had the same thing with my hip joints. I have to learn where they are and what they do inside me because I still have the idea that my hips are wrong, from being told they were wrong. So I have to reconstitute that idea in myself. (Interview, March 20, 2002)

To me, it seemed that Amelia was actively exploring learning different strategies to improve her somatic perception of herself. As she indicated, with new learning there was often confusion, even though her awareness and curiosity continued to lead her to new questions about herself. One theory of somatics advances the notion that integration can occur below the level of our conscious control, and that our soma, through its self-regulatory nature, will gravitate toward the optimum solution to a task if given the right opportunities. The clearer the opportunity in the environment, the easier this will be. However, in the case of a complex or strongly habitual movement, changes may take time. By consciously trying to control all aspects of our movement, as we contemporary dancers are sometimes apt to do, perhaps we may actually inhibit the opportunity for integration or transfer to take place. After a Feldenkrais lesson, I often ask students to notice any new changes or sensations, but not to actively hold on to them. The rationale behind this notion within this pedagogical approach, is that what is important from a specific lesson will make sense and be revealed in the larger context of function such as walking, dancing, or climbing, and not as an isolated sensation. Holding on to specific new sensations, as ends in themselves, can be counterproductive, in that awareness is focused solely on the sensation and less on the integration into function.

Polly—Exploring the Body's Possibilities: "Changing habitual movement"

Polly related to a somatic way of knowing through descriptions of her self-awareness, her ability to create more movement possibilities, and her new-found attention to uncomfortable or restricting movement habits. In her journal on day 1, Polly revealed details of her experience:

> I noticed I was standing with my weight distributed differently over my feet. On the left foot, my weight was all on the outside of the foot whereas on my right foot it was even.... The uneven weight distribution was some-thing I was aware of for the rest of the day, and when walking, I noticed that my right foot rolls outward and then in as I step. (Excerpt from Polly's journal, March 18, 2002)

Often, students commented on their different perceptions of posture after ATM lessons. It was interesting that Polly's awareness remained with her after the lesson. In our interview, we continued to discuss the difference in perception between day 1 and day 2. The rib lesson on day 2 made more sense to her in relation to difficulties she was having with the dance phrase:

> I moved around and did that first phrase and felt more freedom.... I can actually move my ribs without falling over and it gave me that sense that there is the freedom there without losing control. I guess because I've got a lot of ballet training, I tend to, like, hold my torso with a lot of ten-sion and control. When I start to move it more, I kind of think, "Oh, hang on—I'm going to fall over or you know, I'm losing control here." (Interview, March 22, 2002)

Polly spoke further about her emerging awareness of habits and the challenge to maintain awareness and realize when those habits may impede her dancing:

> This week has really allowed me to key into how my body does perform movement, what bad habits I have, where my weaknesses lie and what other areas I can focus on to achieve the same movement. I have felt a greater sense of verticality and this has been achieved through less unnecessary muscle action. I have begun to find new ways to use my legs with greater freedom and stability and felt a sense of freedom and release in my torso. I have noticed a significant change, particularly in ballet where my tendency is to grip muscles. (Interview March 22, 2002)

As did other students, Polly expressed the perception that the contemporary dance classes informed by somatics provided a strong link to ballet classes. It seemed that the strongest relationship between ballet and somatics were the deeply felt sensations that students were able to apply in both contexts. From reading the interview transcripts and journals, ballet seemed to provide a familiar and stable context into which students could bring new somatic awareness and learning. This theme, therefore, suggests that teachers might ask students to notice or identify relationships between the kinds of learning in a somatics class vis-à-vis their learning in other classes they may be entering into during the day.

Bevan—Valuing a Plurality of Learning Experiences: "It's lovely to dance like someone else"

An example that illustrates a plurality of learning and teaching approaches appeared in the journal and interview with Bevan. In a traditional dance class, visual modelling through the teacher's movement is the predominant way of learning. Often, the goal is to replicate the teacher's movement as accurately as possible. In light of this, Bevan raised an interesting observation that equally valued learning through somatic knowledge and learning through visually replicating movement:

> It is the desire to mimic the teacher's style. That's what I was writing in my journal the other day ... that once you came to that point where I had to do it, I was thinking, "How do I move like that anyway?" Like I still wanted to be able to get what you were putting out there. I could see it when you showed the phrase. The main desire, I think, is to be able to try and do that phrase in a way, which fulfills the desire to do something similar. And not

just to do my own version completely. First, the phrase is hard but lovely, so I take a while to figure things out. So for me, what made the biggest impression wasn't what we had done at the start of class (consciously at least) but the way in which you did the phrase, and my desire to move as clearly as you in your movement. (Interview, March 22, 2002)

This is pertinent in light of the relationship between teacher modelling and self-exploration. Bevan said that "as a dancer it's a lovely experience to try and dance like someone else because you actually feel different." He concisely presented a way to re-evaluate the dual benefits of replicating the teacher's movement, and deliberately exploring movement to define one's own personal movement style. As a teacher-researcher, I agreed with Bevan, and responded that I similarly felt a sense of accomplishment when I could interpret someone else's movement. "It's like, 'Oh wow, I've found a new way of doing something.'" This highlighted a paradox for me because I like to encourage autonomy, self-authority, and critical thinking, and yet at the same time think there's a real need for a certain amount of "let's do it exactly like this." The most important realization to come out of this theme was the realization of my own need for balance between fostering self-knowledge and self-authority through (a) encouraging students to engage in their own way of moving while using my movement as a reference, and (b) encouraging students to replicate movement in order to challenge their usual way of moving.

John—Questioning through Our Body: "How aware can I be?"

Technique class, performance, and choreography were the principal mediums through which John constructed his somatic knowledge. Through choreographing and performing his own work, John explored "what it is to have a body" from a somatic base. For John, dance was a vehicle to express different degrees of awareness:

My particular ambition or interest is "How aware can I be?" "How many aspects of my physical reality can I attend to and then articulate, and can that be visible?" Now I feel like I'm getting more interested in a kind of poetic and less Cartesian way of thinking about space. If there was a declarable unified philosophy of "this is what my choreography is about," it seems that part of that is to do with exploration of what it is to have a body, and an avenue to explore what it is to have a body is the somatic frame or the somatic base. I guess for me with Feldenkrais work, it's an avenue for exploration that can lead to movement composition, or a way of creating interesting movement. I have this new information, but I'm not sure how to work with that in standing because I then have to have another lot of learning to do with how to deal with that extra mobility. Sometimes I get quite excited thinking about Feldenkrais and like—oh, it's this great thing, which is like it's going to change the world.... In the studio, if I'm dancing by myself or maybe if I'm improvising, performing ... there can be this kind of engagement with the sublime or the unknown or ... ecstasy.... I just don't know what it is, but it's like I'm chasing this ... divine experience or something. So that's probably influenced by reading what William Forsythe talks about and I think he says something like ... dancing borders on the sublime or it's like at the very edge of what we know or what we can perceive or how we frame the world. (Interview March 20, 2002)

John spoke about a very personal experience of his somatic way of knowing movement and dance, which he found difficult to capture within the constraints of language. For John, but also for Amelia and Polly, dancing seemed to offer the most potent way they could express themselves somatically. As such, words were a secondary tool that could only approximate a part of their somatic knowledge.

From reflecting on the interviews, journals, and the data analysis, I found that integrating a somatics approach with contemporary dance technique, to allow for different learning and teaching styles ranging from student-centred to teacher-centred, was useful in encouraging students to claim a somatic way of knowing and increase awareness of the dance environment they inhabit.

PEDAGOGICAL ISSUES AROUND CONSTRUCTIVISM, SOMATICS, AND DANCE

In the following section, we discuss issues in the literature about constructivism and its relationship to teacher research, pedagogy, somatics, and dance technique. Several authors addressed criticisms concerning the use of somatics in dance teaching and performance, and expressed certain cautions worth noting. The first concerns the apparent difference in context between lying on the floor and sensing minute movements vis-à-vis the technical demands of a strictly prescribed technique such as a classical ballet class (Simpson 1996). The second brings to light how an increase in the value of somatic practices influences dance performance and choreography. In this instance, Schultz (2000) questions whether this trend is leading to a type of dance that is too internalized and self-absorbed, and ultimately detrimental to both technique and performance. Finally, from an aesthetic perspective, Brown suggests that caution may be needed in investing too much in "recent waves of intelligent dancer practice" where the "emphasis within the contemporary dance community upon the 'knowing body,' a body fluent, effortless and released and informed by somatic disciplines, retains an almost modernist formalism and purity" (2001: 23). It has often been a criticism, as well as our own experiences, that somatics sometimes results in a stylized and idealistic way of moving in and of itself, devoid of any functional relationship with ways of being in and interacting with the world. Ironically, this defeats the main purpose of most somatic practices, which are concerned with bringing movement back into function and the consciousness of larger societal issues (Green 2001; Fortin 2003). The dilemma in addressing these criticisms, is not so much the somatic process as the way in which context is created (or not created) by teachers and students to connect somatic ways of learning to the functional demands of dancing, choreographing, and performing.

Beyond the classroom, "context" is created by an institution's curriculum and philosophy. In the cultural environment of New Zealand, as we discussed earlier, differing tertiary institutions have adopted different philosophies, curriculum, and career endpoints that inform the teaching and learning context. The issues raised above have proven true when an institution has "inserted" somatic courses into a degree program without due consideration of the role and nature of the somatic experience. Appropriate contexts for learning and teaching are created when somatics is embedded as a core learning process with a clear rationale and coherent curriculum; not when it is regarded as a "tertiary dance trend" or dualistic opposite to "training."

In contrast to these criticisms, a number of authors have addressed the educational value of somatic practices. These authors have proposed a revision of the traditional way dance classes have been taught in pre-professional training institutions, advocating the value of somatic approaches that direct students' attention to the primacy of process in the experience of learning movement rather than future-orientated, goal-directed process. Sheets-Johnson articulates this in her argument for changing the learning environment, with her observation that traditional methods of dance training are future orientated: "Movement is commonly directed to where I am not yet" (1979: 24). Rather than focusing on the end product of movement, working with the primacy of experience brings focus to the learning experience, and it is only through having that experience that the learner is able to "discriminate and notice change." As Sheets-Johnson states, "the point of noticing and discriminating change is of course learning" (1979: 26). Blank (1987) and Lessinger (1996) also advocate a need for dance training that fine-tunes the kinaesthetic sense in order to facilitate efficient alignment, rather than one that relies on objective visual assessment and mechanical imposition of corrections.

The objective visual assessment of dancers also evokes a teacher-centred approach. Based on empirical data, Green describes the traditional dance studio setting where "the teacher presents specific movements that require rote learning, while students anticipate teacher praise and attention through correction and physical manipulation, the teacher is often viewed as an all knowing expert authority" (1999: 81). And from an anthropologist's view, dance ethnographer Bull (1997) developed a seminal analysis of classical ballet as a dance culture that, as a whole, is rooted in the visual sense. Fortin, Long, and Lord (2002) also maintain that the visual sense has traditionally been the predominant avenue for teaching and learning dance. They add that one problem, for both teacher and student, is how a student can translate what she sees into kinaesthetic sensation. Through their qualitative analysis, Fortin, Long, and Lord demonstrated different ways to encourage exploration of kinaesthetic distinctions and sensory awareness by the use of procedural knowledge as a tool to model and communicate the teacher's perceptions of the movement.

In teaching and learning contemporary dance technique, technical dance steps devoid of sensory awareness might become a sterile representational exercise; on the other hand, overvaluing sensory awareness at the expense of technical schematic function may lead to a type of introspective nebulous movement as criticized by Schultz (2000). According to Howe and Berv (2000), there is reciprocity between our ability to utilize and make sense of both sensory data and conceptual schemes. Sensory data cannot be considered as raw, any more than schemas can be considered as pure, as each has meaning only in the construction of experience (Howe and Berv 2000). One outcome of this research was empirical evidence that students' experiences of new sensation in the Feldenkrais part of the class, and any subsequent interrelationship with dance technique, were interdependent. And this research project has confirmed what I have come to believe: that somatic principles devoid of a relationship with function are spurious, and that creating the context for a meaningful learning environment is one of the most important challenges facing somatic education in dance academia (Fortin 2003).

CONCLUSION

If we take the view that education is primarily about questioning and constructing our values and the way we live in the world, then what does somatic education contribute to understanding our values and ways of moving in contemporary dance-technique classes? If the reality in which we live is subjectively inscribed by social and cultural meanings and values, as anthropologists and cultural critics would have us believe, then our bodies are also a site for the playing out of socially and culturally constructed power relationships (Fortin 2001). The notion of somatic knowledge becomes an important plexus through which relationships of power and socio-cultural inscription take place. Through this study, of a constructivist and ethnographic character, I have been able to observe the power dynamics that occur when a teacher assumes the role of "sole expert," one who possesses knowledge to be distributed to the students. In response, I have observed in the field that when a student feels that he has no participation in the process or its outcome, he tends to dismiss the relevance of the teacher and the relevance of dance in his learning.

According to aesthetics philosopher Shusterman (1999), by way of his proposition for a somaesthetics, the sensing body is central to the guidance of our interactions within the world. I have found, through this study, that rather than assuming the role of docile learners, dancers were able learn, through the practice of somatics, how to take authority in constructing and even transforming their individual bodies within the context of many different (socially constructed) dance styles. This study presents evidence that dancers can learn to balance the notion of constructing their bodies by integrating both internal and external values. Throughout its historical evolution, the teaching of Western theatrical dance technique has primarily been epistemologically based on various theories of dance-based knowledge (Stinson 1998). According to Stinson, dancers have subsumed much of their personal bodily constructions to the demands of choreographic vision or technical style. The findings of this study revealed how dancers' understanding of technique was related to their exploration of relationships that lie between their own awareness in movement and the demands or constraints of technique.

The content of Warwick's class in this study was based on an alternation between a somatic-based knowledge in the Feldenkrais part of the class and a more dance-technique-based knowledge in the other section. The aim of learning, in the Feldenkrais part of the class, was centred more on investigating the self through movement. In this section of class, each person's body became her own sensory reference point for learning and making distinctions through questioning her own perceptions of movement.

A more externally oriented environment typified the dance-technique section, where the internal processes of the Feldenkrais activities were integrated with the external processes of learning through reference to another body (either the teacher or other students). The dance-technique section of the classes addressed the relationship between individual dancers and the content knowledge of the dance technique. This relationship formed a reciprocity, which we see in this study as a dialectic tension and one that required management by both teachers and students over time in the dance classes. In the end, the tension lay between constructing a deeper knowledge of oneself in movement, and integrating that knowledge within the functional demands of dance technique. This present research suggests some future avenues to explore, which include instigating a similar research protocol in the area of classical ballet, investigating the differences between professional and pre-professional dancers, and examining the specific application of somatics in the choreographic process.

Note

We thank the four participants—Amelia, Bevan, John, and Polly—without whom this study would not have been possible. Thanks also to Chris Jannides and Felicity Molloy at UNITEC Institute of Technology, Auckland, for their support and openness. The fieldwork and subsequent thesis emerging from this research were partial requirements for Warwick Long's Master's Degree in Physical Education.

Bibliography

Barbour, Karen. "Journeys in Dance-Making and Research." In Jan Bolwell (ed.), *Tirairaka: Dance in New Zealand*. Wellington, New Zealand: Wellington College of Education, August 2001: 5–11.

Blank, D. "Moving the Dance: Awareness through Movement Classes for Dancers." *Feldenkrais Journal* 3 (1987): 1–8.

Brown, Carol. "Tall Stories." *Dance Theatre Journal* 16, no. 4 (2001): 23.

Bull, Cynthia, and Jean Cohen. "Sense, Meaning and Perception in Three Dance Cultures." In Jane C. Desmond (ed.), *Meaning in Motion: New Cultural Studies of Dance*. Post-Contemporary Interventions Series. Durham, NC: Duke University Press, 1997: 269–88.

Cardinal, M.K. "Trends in Dance Science and Dance Wellness-Related Education, 1990–1997." *Research Quarterly for Exercise and Sport* 71, no. 1 (2000).

Cochran-Smith, M., and S.L. Lytle. *Inside/Outside: Teacher Research and Knowledge*. New York: Teachers College Press, 1993.

Eisner, Eliot. *The Enlightened Eye: Qualitative Inquiry and the Enhancement of Educational Practice*. Upper Saddle River, NJ: Prentice Hall, 1998.

Fitt, Sally. *Dance Kinesiology*. New York: Schirmer, 1998.

Fortin, Sylvie. "Dancing on the Mobius Band." In M. Haregraves (ed.), *New Connectivity: Somatics and Creative Practices in Dance Education.* Papers from Laban Research Conference. London: Laban Centre, 2003: 3–10.

———. "The Self in Dance." In *Proceedings of the Danz Research Forum.* Hamilton: University of Waikato, 2001: 35–41.

———, Warwick Long, and Madeline Lord. "Three Voices Researching How Somatic Education Informs Contemporary Dance Technique Classes." *Research in Dance Education* 3, no. 2 (2002): 155–79.

Green, Jill. "Socially Constructed Bodies in American Dance Classrooms." *Research in Dance Education* 2, no. 2 (2001).

———. "Somatic Authority and the Myth of the Ideal Body in Dance Education." *Dance Research Journal* 31, no. 2 (1999): 81.

Guba, Egon G. *The Paradigm Dialogue.* Beverly Hills, CA: Sage, 1990.

Harris, S. "How Should Treatments Be Critiqued for Scientific Merit?" *Physical Therapy* 76, no. 1 (1996): 175–81.

Heshusius, Lous. "Freeing Ourselves from Objectivity: Managing Subjectivity or Turning towards a Participatory Mode of Consciousness?" *Educational Researcher* 23, no. 3 (1994): 15–22.

Hong, Tina. "Dance Artists and the Curriculum: An Interface." In *Creative New Zealand, Moving to the Future.* Wellington, New Zealand: Creative New Zealand, 2002: 64–70.

Howe, R., and J. Berv. "Constructing Constructivism, Epistemological and Pedagogical." *Constructivism in Education: Opinions and Second Opinions on Controversial Issues* 99, no. 1 (2000): 19–40.

Ives, J., and G. Shelley. "The Feldenkrais Method in Rehabilitation: A Review work." *A Journal of Prevention Assessment and Rehabilitation* 11 (1998): 75–90.

Joly, Yvan, and C. Gillain. "L'éducation somatique: une profession en émergence et un atout dans le domaine de la santé du travail" (2004). http://www.education-somatique.ca (accessed July 1, 2004).

Lake, B. "Moving reflections." *Somatics: Journal of the Bodily Arts and Sciences* 6, no. 3 (1987–88): 37–42.

Lessinger, C. "The Nature of Feldenkrais and its Value to Dancers." In Sally Fitt (ed.), *Dance Kinesiology,* 2nd ed. New York: Schirmer, 1996.

Maykut, P., and R. Morehouse. *Beginning Qualitative Research: A Philosophic and Practical Guide.* London: Falmer Press, 1994.

Peshkin, Alan. "Angles of Vision: Enhancing Perception in Qualitative Research." *Qualitative Inquiry,* 7, no. 16 (2001): 238–53.

Plummer, Caroline, and Ralph Buck. "Negotiating Diversity: Learning About Community Dance." In J. Bolwell (ed.), *Tirairaka: Dance in New Zealand.* Wellington, New Zealand: Wellington College of Education, December 2003: 2–13.

Sansom, Adrienne. "The Meaning of Dance in Early Childhood or, There's More to Dance Than Meets the Eye." In J. Bolwell (ed.), *Tirairaka: Dance in New Zealand.* Wellington, New Zealand: Wellington College of Education (August 2001): 14–23.

Schwandt, Thomas A. "Constructivist Approaches to Human Inquiry." In K. Denzin and Y. Lincoln (eds.), *Handbook of Qualitative Research*. London: Sage, 2000: 119.

Schultz, Marianne. "Looking Ahead: Seeing Dance Trends in New Zealand." *Danz: The Official Magazine of Dance Aotearoa New Zealand* 10, no. 4 (2000): 10–14.

Sheets-Johnstone, Maxine. "The Work of Dr. Moshe Feldenkrais: A New Applied Kinesiology and a Radical Questioning of Training Technique." *Contact Quarterly* (Fall 1979): 24–29.

Shusterman, Richard. Somaesthetics: A Disciplinary Proposal. *The Journal of Aesthetics and Art Criticism* 57, no. 3 (1999): 299–313.

Simpson, M. "Dance Science: A Second Step Approach." *Impulse* 4, no. 1 (1996): 5.

Stephens, J.L. "Awareness through Movement® as a Method of Improving Function and Quality of Life in Individuals with Multiple Sclerosis." Paper presented at the *APTA, Combined Sections Meeting: Physical Therapy Case Reports*, Seattle, WA, 1999.

Stinson, Susan. "A Feminist Pedagogy for Children's Dance." In S. Shapiro (ed.), *Dance, Power, and Difference: Critical and Feminist Perspectives on Dance Education*. Champaign, IL: Human Kinetics, 1998.

Strauss, A., and J. Corbin. *Basics of Qualitative Research*. Newbury Park, CA: Sage, 1990.

CHAPTER FOURTEEN

Dance Education and Emotions

ARTICULATING UNSPOKEN VALUES IN THE EVERDAY LIFE
OF A DANCE SCHOOL

TEIJA LÖYTÖNEN

I became interested in emotion in an institutional context while I was conducting research for my doctoral dissertation. The aim of the study was to explore how dance artists construct their everyday lives in dance institutions by conversing about it. I interviewed fourteen dancers and dance teachers altogether about their work in a contemporary dance theatre and a dance school whose curriculum emphasized classical dance. The format of the interviews was only semi-structured, consisting of open-ended questions, so there was a lot of space to explore any new themes that arose. Emotion in the everyday life of the dance school was one of such theme.

In this chapter, I will explore the commonly held belief about the special link between art and emotion. In addition, I will look into how emotions and morals are entwined. The analysis of one specific emotion, namely loneliness, is an experiment and example of how emotions can open up understanding to the local moral order or the often unspoken values that direct the way of life, in this case, in a dance school.

Because I have worked in the dance world for the whole of my professional career, my position as a researcher in the dance institutions that I was studying was a very subtle one. I was led into this field through enthusiastic training in different modern dance studios in Finland for more than fifteen years. I am neither a professional dancer nor a dance teacher, but in my academic studies in education as well as in aesthetics I focused on dance. After earning a master's degree, my first post was curriculum development within the higher education of dance at the Theatre Academy's Dance Department in Finland. Having worked at the Academy for about six years, my interest moved toward exploring the working cultures in dance institutions. What puzzled me were my experiences in working life, which seemed to include dynamics that were not easily identified. I wanted to understand the often unspoken or tacit dimensions that conduct the way of life within institutions. This led me to training as a process consultant and researcher within dance institutions.

My background in the dance world meant that I knew, in one way or another, all the participants in my study. Some were even very close friends. This led me to explore the researcher's position as a shifting one between the insider and the outsider in my own home field. In order to emphasize the different positions, I used a collaborative research orientation and invited the interviewed dance teachers to take part in joint exploration of the research issues. The idea is that if I permit interpretations to depend only upon me as the researcher, I may be in danger of reinforcing only particular ways of knowing and only particular forms of knowledge. In the words of Patti Lather, the idea of this research orientation can be described as "getting both in and out of the way of participants' stories ... the aim is not so much more adequate representation as a troubling of authority in the telling of other people's stories" (2001).

INTRODUCTION

In everyday thinking, art is very often linked to emotion and, more generally, to a kind of emotional and spontaneous way of relating to the world in contrast to the rational and controlled intellect that science is understood to cultivate. A very common link is also emotion via bodily existence to femininity and the private sphere—i.e., the home (Heinämaa and Reuter 1994: 4; Sihvola 1999: 15). These conceptualizations reveal a tendency toward typically Western dichotomies between art and science, emotion and reason, body and mind, private and public, and woman and man (Domagalski 1999; Sandelands and Boudens 2000).

Furthermore, the working life and one's emotional life have long been seen as separate—that is, emotion does not fit into working life and in this way only emotion-free employees and institutions have been perceived as being efficient. It follows that emotional control, self-restraint, and rationality bolster stability and predictability in working life. Thus, emotions belong somewhere else. Sandelands and Boundens (2000: 48) have even noted that in the Western world there are special quarters for exercise and display of emotion, such as concert halls, movie theatres, sports fields, and therapist's offices. This does not mean, however, that emotions can be eliminated from working life, as many studies on emotion at work have shown (Ashkanasy, Härtel, and Zerbe 2000; Fineman 2000, 2003; Hochchild 1983).

I became interested in emotion in an institutional context while I was conducting research for my doctoral dissertation (Löytönen 2004). The aim of the study was to explore how dance artists construct their everyday lives in dance institutions by conversing about it. I interviewed altogether fourteen dancers and dance teachers about their work in a contemporary dance theatre and a dance school whose curriculum emphasised classical ballet. Both of these institutions are based in Helsinki, Finland. The format of the interviews was only semi-structured consisting of open-ended questions, so there was ample of space to explore any new themes that arose. Emotion in the everyday life of dance institutions was one of such theme.

As noted earlier, this chapter is based on my doctoral dissertation (2004) in which I interviewed dancer teachers from a dance school based in Helsinki, Finland. The semi-structured interviews consisted of open-ended questions giving space to discuss diverse themes around their professional practice. Emotion in the everyday life of dance school was one such theme.

Emotions such as pleasure, satisfaction, and joy, as well as anxiety, fear and sorrow, were commonly expressed in the interviews when the dancers and dance teachers described their diverse everyday lives at the dance institutions. More specifically, emotions came to the fore while the dance teachers openly talked about how they felt about the institutional culture in their work community, where upcoming changes within the dance school (change of the principal and curriculum reformation) had provoked feelings of unhappiness, frustration and uncertainty. However, the most common word used by the dance teachers to describe their everyday life was loneliness. All of the interviewed dance teachers described their work as well as their working community as being lonely.

Here, I will briefly examine emotion and ask, "What actually are emotions?" I will continue by exploring the commonly held belief about the special links between art, artistic expression, and emotion with the help of different art theories. The main emphasis of the chapter is, however, to examine how the interviewed dance teachers described their emotion of loneliness. Their descriptions serve as a bridge to a more general analysis of the meaning of emotion in an institutional context, in which emotion plays a role not only in an individual teacher's experiences but also in the shared culture of dance teachers. In addition to looking at the links between art and emotion, I will formulate a point of view about how emotions and morals are interwoven. The analysis of the "loneliness talk" of the interviewed dance teachers is an example and experiment of how one specific emotion can open up understanding to the local moral order or the often-unspoken values that direct the way of life in a particular dance school. The concept of moral order here does not refer to any stable set of moral norms. Instead, "moral order" refers to a continually constructed and rene-gotiated local understanding of rights and responsibilities, good and bad (Harré 1986; see also Ylijoki 1998: 138; Kurri 2005: 11). Even though the local moral order of a dance school and the entwined emotional culture are often vague, as if an oral tradition largely passed on from one professional generation to the next without much questioning, it is of value to ask to what extent dance teachers in dance schools are capable of recognizing and interpreting emotions collectively and thereby analyzing the moral beliefs that direct the collective activity.

EMOTION

Emotion has been analyzed primarily in the fields of empirical psychology, neurophysiology and cognitive science. Within these disciplines emotion has been understood as biological or genetic in nature. They are consid-ered as unconscious feelings, corresponding tensions or dramas of early family life, which then mould the conduct of everyday life; or as cogni-tive appraisal in which feeling and emotion follow the appraisal process in which meaning is assigned to phenomena (Fineman 2003: 7). Addi-tionally, in the history of Western philosophy emotions have been char-acterised according to various criteria. Emotions have been understood as internal bodily sensations and feelings (pain, pleasure), while another way of understanding emotions views them as non-sensual and "real" (fear, shame, love, sympathy) and, more generally, as frames of mind or moods (joyfulness, sadness). Emotions have also been linked to knowledge and knowing through recognition and familiarity with a thing or a phenom-enon. Sometimes emotions have been understood as mental reactions to outer or inner stimuli (fright, anger), and, in this last conceptualisation, emotions are perceived as reactions that move and possess people, render-ing them in a kind of passive way (passion) (Niiniluoto 1996: 5).

In this chapter I propose an understanding of emotion in a slightly wider sense. In terms of this study, emotions are seen as intentional and thereby always having an object (Harré 1986: 8; Heinämaa and Reuter 1994: 9). All emotions are thus "about" something. For example love, grief, anxiety and fear always have an object in the life-world of the one who is experiencing these emotions. This intentionality does not, however, refer to a straightforward referential relationship because it is not always easy to define what "causes" a feeling. Instead emotions and sensations are attitudes toward the world as well as positions in the world, and their objects are sometimes such that they can be clearly described. On the other hand the objects of emotions can also be unclear or unknown, as Heinämaa and Reuter state (1994: 11). All emotions, sensations and moods have nevertheless meaning for the person experiencing them, providing them with some information about the world.

In this view emotions are thus not simply physiological or mental processes that reside inside a person. Instead they are fundamentally bound to the world, in time and place as well as the social and cultural context of a person. In this way emotions can be understood as social constructions. To say emotion is social is to spotlight the cultural settings in which emotions are both learned and expressed. In the social constructionist view on emotions, language and the use of language are important. As Fineman (2003: 15) states, the key questions are, "What are the emotion vocabularies (emotion words)?" and "Under what conditions are they used (emotion talk)?" It is understood that the ways emotion words are used are bound up with the situations, social context and moral imperatives of the display, feeling and interpretation of emotions (Harré 1986: 2).

Emotions can thus be understood as linked to cultural conventions and community expectations on their members. Emotions have a social function, they are constituted in such a way as to sustain and endorse cultural systems of belief and value. Culturally appropriate emotions serve to restrain undesirable attitudes and behaviour and to sustain and endorse cultural values (Armon-Jones 1986a: 34; Armon-Jones 1986b: 57). Through different kinds of emotions and emotion talk some things are achieved and, on the other hand, some things are rejected. And so, it is easy to see that emotion talk is always socially and politically loaded (Fineman 2003: 16). In understanding emotions it is, indeed, fundamental to see the involvement of the local moral order as Harré (1986: 8) has pointed out. By local moral order he refers to the local systems of rights, obligations, duties and conventions of evaluation.

Before moving on to the empirical part of this chapter, I will explore how the link between art and emotion can theoretically be understood.

ART AND EMOTION

Art has been linked to emotion in lay theories as well as in academic debates and art theories since the time of Plato (Vuorinen 1997: 78). The entwinement of art and emotion is at least twofold: on the one hand it is related to the artist and his or her artistic expression, while on the other hand it has to do with the person viewing or experiencing the art and his or her personal perceptions.

Theories about artistic expression look at the connection between art and emotion in the artist's work, expression and/or the content of the art. Those who have analyzed art from this perspective include Leo Tolstoy (1975/1930), Benedetto Croce (1978), Robin G. Collingwood (1938), Charles Peirce (1958), Ivor A. Richards (Ogden and Richards 1936), and Susanne K. Langer (1953). Even though their theories are quite different, they all view art at least to some extent as an expression of emotion. They variously propose that art expresses emotion and that good art is expressive in character. Art describes human emotions, inner feelings and attitudes; it reveals how a particular individual, namely the artist, perceives the world. Emotional expression has been linked to the content of an art work (what is expressed), as well as the means of expression (how the expression takes place).

Croce's and Collingwood's closely related theories emphasise the artist's role in expressing emotions. In their view, the working process gradually makes the artist more and more aware of his emotional experience, which is crystallized only at the moment when the art work is completed. In this sense, art is a tool through which the artists become aware of themselves and their emotional experiences, and a medium through which the artist expresses his emotions to others. It follows that the viewer can use an art work to become more aware of her own unclear emotions. Langer, on the other hand, sees art as "an image of an emotion": art manifests an idea of emotion in a general sense, beyond that of the artist's personal emotions or the emotions evoked in the recipient. The artist does not express his emotions but his knowledge of an emotion; the artist does not comment on anything or explain things, but creates a symbolic reflection that portrays the emotion (Vuorinen 1997: 27–29; 126–48).

David Novitz (1987: 187) emphasizes the power of the arts in facilitating imagination as well as in understanding moral values. According to him art can serve as a means of acquiring primarily empathetic knowledge. Novitz analyzes art, empathetic understanding and knowledge from the perspective of fictional writing such as the novel, which despite its fictional character, makes claims about the world. Emotional identification with fictional situations and different characters and their emotions can help the reader to understand something that would have otherwise remained unclear or puzzling. In Novitz's view, fictional literature forces the reader to analyze and consider her or his attitudes and values, thereby revealing the complexity and problematic nature of moral questions. In this sense art has an important role as a source of information about values, as well as in understanding and learning about them.

Ronald W. Hepburn (1987: 207) is another writer who sees art as a tool for personal growth, which helps one not only gain more knowledge about the world but also learn more about the emotion. Art can widen one's sphere of emotional experience instead of simply triggering familiar ones. It can free us of emotional clichés, which Hepburn understands to be the stereotypical emotional reactions that are set by the prevailing culture. In this sense art can widen our sphere of emotional freedom.

Although the aforementioned theories mainly use literature or visual arts as examples of emotional experiences, I believe that the dance art is as powerful an art form in providing possibilities for understanding emotions because of its fundamental connection to human existence through the artistic elements of body, time and space. In light of the above theories art can be seen as providing knowledge of diverse emotions and thus makes both personal and even cultural growth possible. With this frame of mind, art can also be understood to serve as a way to learn something about the world and moral values and thus cause us to act in a new way.

The focus of this chapter is not to explore emotions in art, artistic expression, or its reception, so I will now end my overview of the inter-twinement of art and emotion. It is important, however, to bear in mind that art and emotion are interlinked in various ways and that, at least in the theories I've presented here, emotions are seen as an inherent aspect of art and artistic practice. It is important to recognize, however, that art is not all about emotions or emotional expression. Art and artistic prac-tice involve great physical effort, especially in dance, and this is more an apprenticeship to a craft rather than an expression of emotion. Dance art as well as other art forms are also inherently political, a function that mani-fests itself in dance performances through different times and places.

As my emphasis here is to understand how the interviewed dance teachers described their emotion of loneliness, I will not elaborate upon the nature of dance art any further. Instead, I will now continue to explore the culture of the dance school through one specific emotion: loneliness. My intention is to take a closer look at how individuals described the emo-tion of loneliness, and how it was connected to the local moral order of the dance school. What kind of social function was found in the loneliness discourse?

EMOTION IN A DANCE SCHOOL

Dance schools are the main path through which one can become a profes-sional dance artist. Thus, they play a central role in producing dance artists and so in determining who becomes an artist, how one becomes an artist and how one is able to practise dance art (Parviainen 1998: 92, 96). There are altogether nine dance institutions in Finland that provide professional education in dance and only one of them educates professional dancers in classical ballet. It does this in close connection with the Finnish National Ballet. The core of ballet teaching and learning is the coded vocabulary on which the different stylistic features of varying eras of ballet, and slightly discerning national styles, have been based. In the dance school I explored during my research, ballet learning usually starts from about the age of

Figure 1   Entering the dance schools. Photo courtesy Teija Löytönen.

ten, and so ballet students already begin a vocational training as children. It takes a long time to acquire the skills that are needed during the short career, about twenty years, of a professional ballet dancer. After their careers onstage, some dancers start another career in teaching ballet (Salosaari 2001: 15; Wulff 1998: 59). This is the case also with the dance teachers I interviewed for my study.

THE INTERVIEWS AND COLLABORATIVE RESEARCH ORIENTATION

As I have mentioned, the interview extracts are taken from "Discussing the Everyday Life of Dance Institutions," which I completed in 2004. The study's epistemological as well as methodological orientation was based on the tradition of social constructionism, which rejects the idea of any ultimate truth. Instead, knowledge is always bound to certain perspectives and purposes as well as social processes and interactions. In this way, the research project also drew on the traditions of cultural studies as well as institutional ethnography (Burr 1995, 1998; Fornäs 1998; Gergen 1999; Lehtonen 1996; Parker 2002, 1998, 1992; Smith 2001; Wetherell, Taylor and Yates 2001).

The individual interviews, about ninety minutes long, can be described as a collaborative joint effort of the dance teachers and myself, the researcher. In this way, the interviews were meaning-making situations where both parties are necessarily active. This meant attending to the interview process and to the product in ways that are sensitive to the social construction of knowledge (Holstein and Gubrium 1997: 113; Kvale 1996; Lather and Smithies 1997).

One aspect of the construction of knowledge was my role as interviewer and researcher in the dance world. I was not a total outsider, since I have been working in the art world of dance in Finland my entire professional career, first as a curriculum developer within higher dance education at the Theatre Academy Helsinki and later as a process consultant within dance institutions. Process consultation can be understood as way of understanding and facilitating the many different processes and phenomena employees encounter within their daily practices in different institutions and organizations (Schein 1988).

Before my research project on the everyday life of dance institutions, I had been a process consultant in both the dance theatre and the dance school for more than a year, from fall 1995 to spring 1997. Along with the dance teachers, we had discussed their topical issues in thirty meetings, each 90 minutes long. All of these meetings took place in the dance school, which gave me the opportunity to observe their working environment as well as their usual habits when meeting with each other. During the process, I kept a diary about the issues and phenomena we were discussing and experiencing. I did not, however, use these notes as research data because of the confidential nature of the process consultation. I wanted to separate the consultation process from the research process. Only after the process consultation was over, I moved into the research issues and interviewed the dance teachers individually about their everyday life in the dance school. I found that the long process with the dance teachers gave me a unique perspective and background with which to understand their descriptions of their daily life. I felt this also during the interviews when the dance teachers openly and without hesitation described their diverse everyday lives at the dance school.

There are both advantages and disadvantages in working within my own field. First of all, I possess some kind of social capital that structures the idiom in the art world of dance (see also Wulff 1998: 5). Having worked within the field for a long time, I know quite a lot about dance and the working conditions in Finland, and especially in dance schools (this might have won me the trust of the dance teachers). But at the same time, this position creates a problem, which Barbara Czarniawska (1997: 61) calls "home-blindness." It is the taken-for-grantedness of meanings and their modes of construction. What is needed, according to Czarniawska, is an attitude of outsidedness. My attempt to adopt this attitude involves self-reflexivity, the questioning of my position in order to respect the many perspectives and voices of the dance teachers. Such an attitude also entails my allocating equal status to both researchers and participants, as well as of the accounts offered by each. This means that, as the researcher, I must find ways of building opportunities for participants to comment upon their own accounts and those of mine (Burr 1995: 181). I achieved this in my study by using a collaborative research orientation inspired by the works of Patti Lather (Lather and Smithies 1997) and Barbara Czarniawska (1997).

COLLABORATIVE RESEARCH ORIENTATION

The aim of the collaboration was to invite the interviewed dance artists to take part in joint exploration of the research issues. Collaborative inquiry may take many forms, as Gergen states (1999: 98). There are no rules because each form will depend on the aims and hopes of the participants as well as the researcher. In my research, collaboration proceeded in the following way.

I audiotaped and transcribed each interview before it was analyzed. After transcribing the interviews, I sent the transcriptions to the dance teachers for comments and possible completions. Some of them commented on their individual accounts while others did not. At this point, I met three of the six dance teachers to discuss some of their interview themes more deeply. Later, I utilized these discussions when categorizing and analyzing all of the interview data. I categorized the written interview data in the following themes:

Dance Teachers

- Being a dance teacher—the professional dancer's career related to teaching as well as to the general lifespan
- Relationships—within the class, between teachers
- Emotions about being a dance teacher
- Boys—teaching dance for boys, a theme that puzzles one male dance teacher
- Work community—being a part of a community is described as being alone
- Change—experiences of the dance school in a constant state of change

After the dance teachers made comments and we'd held three discussions, I constructed fictive conversations for each of the six themes described above. In the construction of these conversations, my aim was to include descriptions from as many dance teachers as possible. I wanted to emphasize their diverse descriptions of the daily life within the dance school, the polyphony of their workaday life.

When the first drafts of the six fictive conversations were ready, I sent them to each dance teacher to be read. I then met all the dance teachers individually. We discussed the material, during which I wrote down their comments, questions, and suggestions for modifications to the content and form of the fictive conversations. These discussions lasted anywhere from two to five hours.

When editing the "final" fictive conversations, I took their comments into account. It meant expanding the conversations into new themes as well as creating new conversations. One of the issues that the dance teachers commented on was the spoken language I used in the written conversations. It disturbed some of them and made it difficult to read and even to understand the text. The use of spoken language was a conscious choice that I made. With the spoken language, I wanted to emphasize their diverse descriptions of their everyday lives in a detailed manner. When one transforms spoken language into literary language, a great deal of the natural sound of language can be missed: for example, repetitions and pauses. The study was written in Finnish, the native language of the dance teachers and myself—I have translated all the interview extracts from Finnish into English.

Beside the above-mentioned comments, I also paid attention to the dance teachers' intuitive interpretation of the conversations. When working on my own interpretations of the six thematic conversations, I wanted to emphasize their ideas and observations. We also agreed that the dance school would not be identified, nor the dance teachers. That is why they gave themselves pseudonyms, which are also used in this chapter.

I understood the participation of the dance teachers in the research process as a methodological recourse to bring together dualities and recognize the plurality of their realities (Birch and Miller 2002: 94). The collaborative research orientation opened different perspectives for me with which to interpret the interview data. Instead of looking at the interviews just from my perspective, I could discuss the possibilities of the data with the various perspectives of the dance teachers. An active research relationship then involved the exchange of ideas and understanding, and was a shared enterprise. This kind of research orientation can be crystallized in the following words by Patti Lather (2001, see also 1996: 529): "Getting both in and out of the way of participants' stories ... the aim is not so much more adequate representation as a troubling of authority in the telling of other people's stories."

Beside the collaborative discussions with the dance teachers, I used different tools when analyzing the written interview data. The substance (what was told) was analyzed thematically and the way of speaking (how things were told) was analyzed using social constructionist discourse analysis and different narrative approaches (Burr 1995; Parker 1992; Czarniawska 1997, 1998; Riessman 1993; Lieblich, Tuval-Mashiach, Zilber 1998; Saarenheimo 1997, 2001).

In the following section, I interpret the written interview data from two thematic conversations, namely emotions and work community. The perspective is that of entwinement of emotions and morals in the everyday life of the dance school. I use as an example the most common word with which the dance teachers described their work and work community: loneliness.

LONELINESS: A QUEST FOR CONNECTEDNESS

The following extracts describe loneliness through its opposite, namely the quest for connectedness in this particular dance school. In contrast to her present situation, Ritva described how important it would be for her to be able see how other teachers work:

> That we could discuss, thresh out and analyze. Teachers could come to my classes too, make notes and ask questions about things that my teaching calls forth. Opinions. I long to not be so lonely. Anyway, the students are our mutual students, at some point or another. It is very practical co-operation. That is what I long for. I wish we could help one another during the whole year and not only critique each other during assessments. (June 6, 1997)

Ritva ends her comments with student assessments. Students are evaluated at least once a year in order to see what the possibilities are for each student to move forward in ballet training. These assessments are done in special sample classes, which are viewed by the dance teachers of the dance school. Sometimes, students are seen as not being able to continue due to different requirements—for example, those who are not the "ideal" classical dancers might be "assessed out" (Wulff 1998: 66). Jorma contemplates the assessments as well. According to him, the key question is why the objectives of the assessments are not done together:

> If the objectives of the assessments are such that the classes are as good as possible, that the classes are constructed in a way that pleases as many teachers as possible, then why don't we plan them collectively? ... Now the sample class depends only on one teacher and what kind of a class she or he wants to construct. (June 6, 1997)

Both Ritva and Jorma are of the same opinion, wanting more collaboration between the dance teachers of this school. Their explorations of loneliness reveal its central issue, which could be defined as a failure of intersubjectivity, or shared subjectivity. As Wood (1986) points out, there is something very social about loneliness in its essence, as it is at one and the same time the most non-social and the most social of experiences:

It is individual because it refers to the person separated; it is social because what the person is separated from is other people. It is social because it concerns, indeed derives from our capacity for, intersubjectivity; it is individual because it involves experience which is not shared, the failure of intersubjectivity. (191)

The central issue in the failure of intersubjectivity was the lack of sharing and the lack of shared understandings with others. It was the sense of separateness from others, a kind of absence of mutuality that forms the core of loneliness (Wood 1986: 189). This could be found both in Ritva's and Jorma's loneliness discussions: the failure to meet their expectations of sharing teaching experiences and of forming shared understanding—in, for example, sample classes with colleagues—is interpreted as loneliness.

If I follow the social constructionist view that emotions serve a social function in continually constructing and renegotiating cultural values within a community, the following question arises: "What kind of values did loneliness sustain in the dance teachers community?" When analyzing my data, it became obvious that loneliness preserved the values of sharing and connectedness. The content of the loneliness talks was concerned with relationships, mainly—the needs, oughts, and shoulds of interaction with others (Wood 1986: 196). Loneliness can thus be said to have functioned in serving to maintain or recapture closeness within the dance teachers' community. The dance teachers' expressions of loneliness connected them to the collective or the social realm of dance teaching. By talking about loneliness at work, the teachers were in fact talking about their social lives, or lack thereof. There was, however, a paradox within their loneliness and loneliness talk: the ideas and values of sharing and connecting with each other were not carried out in the everyday activities of the dance school. The behaviour of the dance teachers did not seem to change toward the valued shared activities. In order to understand this paradox, it is important to look at other aspects of their loneliness talk.

LONELINESS: A QUEST FOR PRIVACY

The difficulty in realizing the values of sharing and connectedness for the dance teachers interviewed lay in the fact that they all taught classes at the same time. This means that it was actually impossible to observe other dance teachers' classes. And even if this might have been possible, the questions concerning teaching in one dance class were perceived to be so special that they cannot be shared with others let alone be understood by others, as can be seen in Unelma's description:

It is so lonesome and hard work. You know students, they are your own. You can of course discuss with somebody but it is still so much about working within your own class. It is easy for someone else to say what to do, but it does not necessarily work that way. (June 12, 1997)

Even if the collective discussions were valued and hoped for in everyday life, talking about teaching did not seem to interest the dance teachers that much. Orvokki, another dance teacher, describes her view on the dance teachers' discussions:

When we have the possibility to openly talk, when we sit together, why not talk then about these matters? I don't like it when people talk behind each others' back. It is a kind of gnawing, that we are not able to speak out.... This tells me that there is no openness. Openness and being united are very difficult in our dance teachers' community. (June 13, 1997)

The extracts above move the dialogue on loneliness in quite another direction. Instead of the quest for sharing and connectedness, these dance teachers seemed to value dance teaching as a private matter. Loneliness and loneliness talk preserved the value of privacy in the dance teachers' work and working culture.

When analyzing teachers' work in general, Asko Karjalainen argues that there are several myths in teachers' work communities. One of them is the myth of privacy, which he finds powerfully rules the interaction between teachers. Karjalainen (1992: 37) summarizes it in the following normative beliefs:

1. Teachers' work is, like religion and politics, a private matter.
2. Nobody may assess or guide teachers' work.
3. Teachers' problems at work, as well as colleagues' problems, are forbidden topics.

Instead of naming privacy a myth, I understand privacy to be one of the shared values in the dance teachers' work community that I examined. I put forward here that loneliness is appropriate in this context because it appears to sustain and endorse cultural values of respect for the dance teachers' privacy. This can also be understood as the norm of not interfering in one another's teaching. These kinds of values, norms, and rules in the dance teachers' working culture seem to offer relative freedom in ballet teaching. In fact, some of the interviewed dance teachers noted that this kind of relating to one another gives them the possibility of doing what they want "behind closed doors." As nobody comes to observe, no expectations or directions about ballet teaching are expressed. Only once or twice a year in assessment classes will the students be officially evaluated. These evaluations also enable the dance teachers' work to be informally critiqued or praised by their colleagues.

Besides freedom, an interesting view on privacy can also be found in Jorma's account. Jorma was the only male dance teacher taking part in this research and the only one who has an education in ballet teaching. The other dance teachers, all female, earned their knowledge of ballet teaching through their professional career as ballet dancers and/or by way of some short courses in teaching. Jorma, on the other hand, didn't have a career as a performer.

Figure 2 Teaching behind closed doors. Photo courtesy of Teija Löytönen.

Jorma deliberated about the professional practice of ballet teaching in such a way that could be understood as a matter of secrecy: "I don't know, is it that I don't want others to comment on my teaching or is it my professional secrecy, which I don't want to reveal entirely to others?" (June 6, 1997).

This comment led me to think more deeply about the larger cultural context of classical ballet, namely that the ballet world is structured by competition (Wulff 1998: 59, 80). Competition occurs mainly between dancers who are aiming at excellence both in ballet classes, in rehearsals, and also in castings for classical ballet repertoires. Comparisons and evaluations are constant among dancers and, as Helena Wulff (1998: 123) noted in her study on ballet cultures, envy is mixed with admiration and camaraderie.

Competition refers to the success of ballet dancers, the opportunities of moving on with their careers through auditions, débuts, and breakthroughs. Competition refers also to the hierarchical organization of classical ballet companies in which there are invariably only a few dancers on top and a mass of corps de ballet dancers on bottom. Though this has been challenged to change, it is still strongly rooted within the classical ballet world (Wulff 1998: 162). This historical hierarchical ordering might not only direct dancers' everyday life in dance companies but also dance teachers' values, norms, and rules in their educational communities. The professional secrecy that Jorma mentioned might, on the one hand, keep the dance teachers in a hierarchical order in regard to whose ballet students have had the best opportunities or skills to be successful in the competitions of the classical ballet world. On the other hand, by endorsing professional secrecy, Jorma, as the sole male dance teacher, might be sustaining his special "male position" in the social order of dance teachers within the realm of classical ballet, which is very often perceived as "an art of women." As Ann Daly (1999: 112) has noted, dance classicism is an ideology devoted to tradition and to hierarchy of all kinds. One of these hierarchical orderings concerns gender.

THE DISCOURSE OF LONELINESS

By analyzing the loneliness talk of the interviewed dance teachers, my emphasis here has been to articulate some of the unspoken values that lie behind this specific feeling. In my analysis of the data, I found that the dance teachers' discourse of loneliness opened up to two different value systems that produce quite opposite representations of loneliness. On the one hand, loneliness talk represents and sustains the cultural values of sharing and connectedness. On the other hand, loneliness talk represents and preserves the cultural value of privacy, or even the integrity of ballet teaching. By describing their work as being lonesome, the dance teachers had different expectations of their colleagues: closeness and support as well as of non-interference in one another's teaching. Indeed, as this brief analysis and experiment of the connection between the emotion of loneliness and the unspoken values within this dance school shows, the local moral order was not a harmonious whole. Instead, it consisted of values that directed the dance teachers toward quite opposite ways of being and acting within this community. This makes it also understandable why it is so difficult to change one's behaviour. In this case, the values of connectedness (shared intersubjectivity) and privacy (freedom and secrecy) could not be realized at the same time. In citing Zygmunt Bauman (1999: 87), I could say that loneliness is the price one has to pay for privacy.

CONCLUSION

In this study, I found that the local moral order was not necessarily maintained through explicit norms or guidelines. More often, the contrary was true. The most fundamental moral beliefs that directed the dance teachers' lives were those that functioned in a kind of "below-the-surface" way. The self-evident dos and don'ts rooted in the tradition of classical ballet world were the foundation of everyday life at this dance school, along with the evaluation that took place in the form of moral approval and respect or, alternatively, moral contempt and rejection. The local moral order also set out the rights and responsibilities of the dance teachers at this dance school and designated their place in the local social order of the school.

Even when the local moral order, the belief system in a work community affects its activities, it seems that it can be difficult to pin the order down, let alone verbalize it. And so what I propose here is that emotions might serve as a tool for scrutinizing moral values and beliefs within a certain community. The unwritten moral order might also manifest itself more generally in the collective emotional culture of a work community. In Arlie Hochschild's analysis (1996: 29; see also Näre 1999: 263), emotional culture refers to how a work community relates to emotions: what emotions are felt in different contexts and how they are expressed or repressed in different social situations.

Even though the local moral order of a dance school and the entwined emotional culture might often seem vague, I believe it is important to ask to what extent teachers in dance schools are capable of interpreting emotions collectively and thereby the moral beliefs that direct their mutual activity. By careful and in-depth analysis of emotions and emotional culture, a community might become able to change its local moral order.

For me, as a researcher in this dance-education community, the question that has puzzled me during the research process is the gap that is often found between professional practice and research. The descriptions and analysis that are offered here of dance education and emotions do not necessarily have an impact on the dance teachers' daily lives. What I found most important and of value during this research process was the collaborative joint effort with the dance teachers. It is one possibility for bridging the gap between the teachers' and researchers' respective professional cultures.

Bibliography

Armon-Jones, C. "The Thesis of Constructionism." In Rom Harré (ed.), *The Social Construction of Emotions*. Oxford: Blackwell, 1986a: 32–56.

———. "The Social Functions of Emotion." In Rom Harré (ed.), *The Social Construction of Emotions*. Oxford: Blackwell, 1986b: 57–82.

Ashkenasy, N.M., C.E.J. Hartel, and W. Zerbe. *Emotions in the Workplace: Research, Theory and Practice*. Westport, CT: Quorum, 2000.

Bauman, Zygmunt. *Sosiologinen ajattelu*, 2nd ed. Tampere: Vastapaino, 1999. Original work, *Thinking Sociologically*. Blackwell, 1990.

Birch, Maxine, and Tina Miller. "Encouraging Participation: Ethics and Responsibilities." In Melanie Mauthner, Maxine Birch, Julie Jessop, and Tina Miller (eds.), *Ethics in Qualitative Research*. London: Sage, 2002: 91–106.

Burr, Vivien. *An Introduction to Social Constructionism*. London: Routledge, 1995.

———. "Overview: Realism, Relativism, Social Constructionism and Discourse." In Ian Parker (ed.), *Social Constructionism Discourse and Realism*. London: Sage, 1998: 13–25.

Collingwood, Robin G. *The Principles of Art*. London, 1938.

Croce, Benedetto. *Aesthetic. As Science of Expression and General Linguistic*. Translated by Douglas Ainslie. Boston: Nonpareil Books, 1978.

Czarniawska, Barbara. *Narrating the Organization. Dramas of Institutional Identity*. Chicago: University of Chicago Press, 1997.

———. *A Narrative Approach to Organization Studies*. Qualitative Research Methods Series 43. A Sage University Paper. Thousand Oaks, CA: Sage, 1998.

Daly, Ann. "Classical Ballet: A Discourse of Difference." In Jane C. Desmond (ed.), *Meaning in Motion: New Cultural Studies of Dance*, 2nd printing. Durham, NC: Duke University Press, 1999: 111–19.

Domagalski, Theresa. A. "Emotion in Organizations: Main Currents." *Human Relations* 52, no. 6 (1999): 833–52.

Fineman, Stephen. "Emotional Arenas Revisited." In Stephen Fineman (ed.), *Emotion in Organizations*. London: Sage, 2000.

———. *Understanding Emotion at Work*. London: Sage, 2003.

Fornäs, Johan 1998. *Kulttuuriteoria*. Translated by Mikko Lehtonen, Kaarina Hazard, Virpi Blom, and Juha Herkman. Tampere, Finland: Vastapaino. Originally published as *Cultural Theory and Late Modernity*. London: Sage, 1995.

Gergen, Kenneth. J. *An Invitation to Social Construction*. Sage: London, 1999.

Harré, Rom. *The Social Construction of Emotions*. Oxford: Blackwell, 1986.

Hartshorne, Charles, and Paul Weiss (eds.), *Collected Papers of Charles Sanders Peirce*. Vols. 1–6. Cambridge: Belknap Press, 1931–35; vols. 7–8, Cambridge: Belknap Press, 1958.

Heinämaa, Sara, and Reuter, Martina. "Naisten tunneherkkyys: filosofinen keskustelu tunteiden järjellisyydestä" (The Emotional Sensitiveness of Women: a Philosophical Discussion on the Rationality of Emotions). *Naistutkimus* 1 (1994): 4–20.

Hepburn, Ronald. W. "Taide ja tunnekasvatus." In Markus Lammneranta and Arto Haapala (eds.), *Taide ja filosofia*. Helsinki: Gaudeamus, 1987. Original work *The Arts and the Education of Feeling and Emotion*. In R.F. Dearden, P.H. Hirst, and R.S. Peters (eds.), *Education and the Development of Reason*. London: Routledge and Kegan Paul, 1972: 207–25.

Hochschild, Arlie. R. *The Managed Heart: Commercialization of Human Feelings*. Berkeley: University of California Press, 1983.

———. "The Emotional Geography of Work and Family Life." In L. Morris and E.S. Lyon (eds.), *Gender Relations in Public and Private. New Research Perspectives*. London: MacMillan, 1996.

Holstein, James. A., and Jaber F. Gubrium. "Active Interviewing." In David Silverman (ed.), *Qualitative Research. Theory, Method and Practice*. London: Sage, 1997: 113–29.

Ilmonen, Kaj. "Työelämä ja tunteet" (Working Life and Emotions) In Sari Näre (ed.), *Tunteiden sosiologiaa II. Historiaa ja säätelyä* (Sociology of Emotions II. History and Regulation). Helsinki: SKS, Tietolipas 157, 1999: 299–324.

Karjalainen, Asko. *Ammattitaidon myytti opettajayhteisössä* (The Myth of Craftsmanship in Teacher Community). Oulu: Oulun yliopisto. Monistus-ja Kuvakeskus, 1992.

Koivunen, Niina. *Leadership in Symphony Orchestras: Discursive and Aesthetic Practices*. Vammala: Tampere University Press, 2003.

Kurri, Katja. *The Invisible Moral Order. Agency, Accountability and Responsibility in Therapy Talk*. Jyväskylä: Jyväskylä University Printing House, 2005.

Kvale, Steinar. *InterViews: An Introduction to Qualitative Research Interviewing*. Thousand Oaks, CA: Sage, 1996.

Langer, Susanne K. *Feeling and Form. A Theory of Art Developed from Philosophy in a New Key*. London: Routledge and Kegan Paul, 1953.

Lather, Patti. "Postmodernism, Poststructuralism and Post(critical) Ethnography: Of Ruins, Aporias and Angels." In Paul Atkinson, Amanda Coffey, Sara Delamont, John Lofland, and Lyn Lofland (eds.), *Handbook of Ethnography*. London: Sage, 2001: 477–92.

———. "Troubling Clarity: The Politics of Accessible Language." *Harvard Educational Review* 66, no. 3 (1996).

————, and Chris Smithies. *Troubling the Angels: Women Living with HIV/AIDS.* Boulder, CO: Westview Press, 1997.

Lehtonen, Mikko. *Merkitysten maailma. Kulttuurisen tekstintutkimuksen lähtökohtia* (The World of Meanings). Tampere, Finland: Vastapaino, 1996.

Lieblich, Amia, Rivka Tuval-Maschiach, and Zilber Tamar. *Narrative Research: Reading, Analysis and Interpretation.* Applied Social Research Methods Series 47. Thousand Oaks, CA: Sage, 1998.

Löytönen, Teija. "Keskusteluja tanssi-instituutioiden arjesta" (Discussing the Everyday Life of Dance Institutions). *Acta Scenica* 16. Helsinki: Yliopistopaino, 2004.

Niiniluoto, Ilkka. "Tunne-kollokvion avaussanat" (The Opening Words in Emotion conference). In Ilkka Niiniluoto and Juha Räikkä (eds.), *Tunteet* (Feelings). Helsinki: Yliopistopaino, 1996.

Novitz, David. "Fiktio ja tiedon kasvu." In Markus Lammenranta and Arto Haapala (eds.), *Taide ja filosofia.* Helsinki: Gaudeamus, 1987: 187–206. Original work, "Fiction and the Growth of Knowledge." In Joseph Margolis (ed.), *The Worlds of Art and the World.* Amsterdam: Editions Rodopi, 1984.

Näre, Sari. "Sukupuolten tunnekulttuuri ja julkisuuden intimisoituminen" (The Emotional Culture of Sexes and the Intimacy of Publicity). In Sari Näre (ed.), *Tunteiden sosiologiaa I. Elämyksiä ja läheisyyttä* (Sociology of Emotions I. Experiences and Intimacy). Helsinki: SKS, Tietolipas 156, 1999: 263–99.

Ogden, Charles K., and Ivor A. Richards. *The Meaning of Meaning: Study of the Influence of Language upon Thought and of the Science of Symbolism,* 4th ed. London: Kegan Paul, Trench, Trubner and Co., 1936.

Parker, Ian. *Critical Discursive Psychology.* Hampshire, UK: Palgrave Macmillan, 2002.

————. *Social Constructionism Discourse and Realism.* London: Sage, 1998.

————. *Discourse Dynamics: Critical Analysis for Social and Individual Psychology.* London: Routledge, 1992.

Parviainen, Jaana. *Bodies Moving and Moved. A Phenomenological Analysis of the Dancing Subject and the Cognitive and Ethical Values of Dance Art.* Tampere, Finland: Tampere University Press, 1998.

Riessman, Catherine K. *Narrative Analysis. Qualitative Research Methods, Volume 30.* Newbury Park: Sage, 1993.

Saarenheimo, Marja. *Jos etsit kadonnutta aikaa. Vanhuus ja oman elämän muisteleminen* (If You are Looking for the Lost Time. Oldness and Recollection of One's Own Life). Tampere, Finland: Vastapaino, 1997.

————. "Narratiivinen tutkimus ja kertomisen käytännöt asiakastyössä" (Narrative Research and the Practices of Telling in Customer Work). In Merja Korhonen and Birgitta Puustinen (eds.), *Elämä tarinoina* (Life and Counselling in Context)—seminaarin julkaisu. Joensuu: Joensuun yliopisto, 2001.

Salosaari, Paula. *Multiple Enbodiment in Classical Ballet: Educating the Dancer as an Agent of Change in the Cultural Evolution of Ballet. Acta Scenica 8.* Teatterikorkeakoulu. Helsinki: Yliopistopaino, 2001.

Sandelans, L.E., and C.J. Boudens. "Feeling at Work." In Stephen Fineman (ed.), *Emotion in Organizations.* London: Sage, 2000.

Sihvola, Juha. "Antiikin tunneteoriat nykyajattelun lähtökohtana" (The Emotional Theories of Antiquity as the Starting Point of Contemporary Thinking). In Sari Näre (ed.), *Tunteiden sosiologiaa II. Historiaa ja säätelyä* (Sociology of Emotions II. History and Regulation). Helsinki: SKS, Tietolipas 157, 1999: 15–27.

Smith, Dorothy E. "Institutional Ethnography." In T. May (ed.), *Qualitative Research in Action*. London: Routledge, 2001: 17–52.

Tolstoy, Leo. *What Is Art? and Essays on Art*. Translation by Aylmer Maude. London: 1975.

Vuorinen, Jyri. *Taideteos merkkinä. Johdatus semioottiseen taidekäsitykseen* (The Art Work as a Symbol: Introduction to the Semiotic Conception of Art). Helsinki: SKS, Tietolipas 149, 1997.

Wetherell, Margaret, Stephanie Taylor, and Simeon J. Yates. *Discourse Theory and Practice*. London: Sage, 2001.

Wood, L.A. "Loneliness." In Rom Harré (ed.), *The Social Construction of Emotions*. Oxford: Blackwell, 1986: 184–208.

Wulff, Helena. *Ballet across Borders: Career and Culture in the World of Dancers*. Oxford: Berg Press, 1998.

Ylijoki, Oili-Helena. *Akateemiset heimokulttuurit ja noviisien sosialisaatio* (The Academic Tribe Cultures and the Socialization of Novices). Tampere, Finland: Vastapaino, 1998.

CHAPTER FIFTEEN

Black Tights and Dance Belts
CONSTRUCTING A MASCULINE IDENTITY IN A WORLD OF PINK TUTUS IN CORNER BROOK, NEWFOUNDLAND

CANDICE PIKE

INTRODUCTION

The idea for this research was born when the staff at Dance Studio West (DSW) in Corner Brook, Newfoundland, myself included, decided to offer a males-only ballet class, called Boyz Ballet, in hopes of expanding its base of male dancers and to allow male dancers currently taking class to experience training better suited to their needs. Boyz Ballet, like many recreational dance classes, has a teacher who is responsible for planning and facilitating the classes and an assistant who is responsible for demonstrating exercises and so on. As the assistant for Boyz Ballet, I recognized a unique opportunity for sociological investigation as six males came together for a weekly class in the female-centred world of DSW, where, as I found out, they potentially put their masculine status in peril but still managed to find ways of exploring and asserting their unique gender identities.

I came to this study as a native Newfoundlander, young dance teacher, and undergraduate social science student pursuing my research interests in the social construction of gender in the ballet classroom. My research also examined situations in which, from a certain standpoint, I was both an insider and an outsider (for example, being a female studying masculinity or an experienced dancer in a class full of novices). This helped to ensure deep insights and a critical perspective.

The owner and artistic director of DSW, Amy Andrews,[1] began teaching the studio's first all-male ballet class in September 2007, and its participants came from a variety of backgrounds to take part. The weekly classes I observed took place at Corner Brook's[2] only dance studio. Corner Brook is located on the western coast of Canada's most easterly province and is a regional economic hub. It is home to western Newfoundland's only dance school. Through the course of my fieldwork there, I examined what drew these Corner Brook males to ballet, what they perceived the physical goals and aesthetics of ballet to be as compared to those of the hegemonic male ideal propagated by the popular media, how being immersed in the culture of ballet affected their understanding of their own gender identity, and how they subsequently took action to define a masculine status. Unlike other studies of men in dance, which focus on sexuality, my study here focuses on gender identity. It also uniquely focuses on recreational dancers, those who are subjecting themselves to these issues without the prospect of a professional career.

It is my experience (through listing to the commentary of non-dancer friends and jokes in the media) that outsiders often perceive male ballet dancers as effeminate, yet in reality they are involved in a continuous process of asserting and developing their masculine identities in the ballet studio. Prior to this study, the majority of research on males in ballet has concentrated on gender roles that exist in the narratives of ballets or performance issues like costuming and audience reactions pertinent to professional dancers. This study takes a different tack by addressing small-town *recreational* male ballet dancers asking how they fit into a world that is female-centric, where predominant societal roles have switched and they are the *marked* gender. In it, I examine how six dancers experienced masculinity in the ballet studio culture where the aesthetics and training methods are seemingly contrary to typically male-dominated activities.

This study is an investigation of some of the unique issues that this particular group of dancers confronted in the dance classroom. The uniqueness of this study is the particular context within which these men needed to construct their gender identity. Unlike many studies that have focused on how gender construction occurs in male-dominated locations (such as pubs, gyms, and college fraternities; for examples, see Klein 1993 and Tomsen 1997), this one addresses gender construction in a predominantly female domain. Working with the idea that there are as many forms of gender identity as there are individuals, and that males are free to construct their gender identities by exploring multiple masculinities that are unique to the situations they find themselves in, I have found that various forms of "ballet dancer masculinity" exist. The participants in this study illustrate how it is possible to choose ballet as a form of self-expression and subsequently understand how the ballet class functions as a forum through which they can construct a unique gender identity.

METHODOLOGY

In October 2007, I began attending Boyz Ballet class not only in my role as a teaching assistant, but also as an ethnographer. The observations I made over the following six months focused on the way the participants interacted with each other, with the teacher, and with dancers from other classes. I created a set of field notes that recorded important unspoken elements like aesthetics, proxemics,[3] movement types, body shapes, and relationships/friendships that existed in the class. This work was framed in a study of the history of men in dance, current scholarship on masculinities, and current trends in the sociology of dance. The work of sociologist Helen Thomas in particular guided me through this process as I employed her ideas regarding how to study dance and gender through a sociological lens from the standpoint of an ethnographer-dancer and then followed her instructions regarding how to execute a dance ethnography (see Thomas 1993, 2003).

As I conducted interviews with the dancers, I recognized that the information obtained would benefit from observations of the physical aspects of Boyz Ballet and that in my role as a dancer-ethnographer I could help the informants better articulate their ideas about movement and their experiences in the dance studio.[4] I also realized that because of my intimate knowledge and presumptions about the recreational dance world, I would have to be particularly careful to let the interviewees express their own ideas, especially because as class assistant, I was an authority figure.

Because there were so few participants and every individual was a vital part of the class, I felt it was crucial to obtain everyone's perspective. With this in mind, I set up interviews with each of the six participants, who were all Caucasian and ranged in age from sixteen to thirty-one. With the exception of one, who came from England, all were born and raised in Newfoundland—not the typical background of a danseur. With the exception of St. John's, the capital city, very few dance studios exist in the province, and my experiences living in both rural and urban Newfoundland have led me to believe that ballet is not seen as an appropriate career or even recreational activity for males.

At the time of the study, all participants were living in Corner Brook, Newfoundland, or within a twenty-minute commute of the city. With a population of approximately 20,105 people in the city and another 22,000 in neighbouring rural communities (Corner Brook 2005), Corner Brook is not considered a budding metropolis and, although it is technically considered a city, it shares many social dynamics with small-town Canada. There is a small university campus with a theatre and visual arts program, which supports the fifty-year-old city's growing professional arts community. Unlike many Newfoundland communities, Corner Brook's economic base is not rooted in the fishery but in a pulp and paper mill. I perceive that because of this recent working-class cultural heritage, there is not a huge support for the arts and culture community, which is sometimes framed in conversation as frivolous. I propose that it is because of this that artistic people have to work extra hard to carve out a creative niche for themselves. This may be one reason that DSW has the only exclusively male ballet classes on the island, though further research will be necessary to determine what role this mill-town context plays in the dancing experiences of males in Corner Brook.

The interviews I conducted with Boyz Ballet participants included questions regarding identity, dress, perceptions of ballet, perceptions of males in dance, the construction of masculinity, involvement in sports, body issues, the process of learning ballet, friendship, and community. Interviews ranged in length from thirty-five to ninety minutes and were conducted between January 23 and February 6, 2008, either at Dance Studio West or the homes of the participants. Because I saw the participants at least once per week at their ballet class, after the interviews I was able to run ideas past them as a group to ensure that I was interpreting the data accurately from their point of view.

WHO ARE THE DANSEURS?[5]

A brief introduction to the study's participants is beneficial at this point. Each came to ballet at a different period in his life and, although they all joined for similar reasons and share some common characteristics, each of them provided unique insights. Each danseur has been involved, to varying degrees, with both theatre and sports in Corner Brook. None of them were familiar with the history of ballet or the traditional roles of men in ballet and none expressed interest in becoming a professional ballet dancer. Some of the participants had previous dance experience in ballet, other dance forms (like tap and jazz), or both. Each one was also taking at least one additional dance class per week in jazz, tap, hip hop, or modern.

Nick, who at sixteen is the youngest participant, started taking jazz classes the previous year and ballet the year of the study, after being introduced to dance by his older sister. After participating in jazz and tap classes for six years in England with his younger sister, seventeen-year-old Jack had moved to Corner Brook and began taking tap class at DSW the previous year. This was his first full year of ballet training. Ernest, a grade 12 student, started ballet and hip-hop classes the year of this study after participating in a local theatre production. Tom, a university math major, began jazz classes the previous year after developing strong friendships with people in the DSW community and helping them backstage with several productions. This was his first year of ballet. Steve is the husband of studio owner Amy Andrews, though he began taking classes long before their romance started. He is a thirty-one-year-old high school teacher. He began taking dance classes (including ballet) seven years previously as a way to become more involved in the local theatre community. Shannon, a thirty-year-old ski patroller, began his DSW experience when the studio opened nine years ago with a single tap class. He became conscious of a deep love for dancing and had been studying ballet for eight years as of the date I began the study.

FROM SUN KING TO "QUEEN": THE HISTORY OF MEN IN BALLET

Although none of the Boyz Ballet participants were familiar with the history of ballet, to contextualize my interpretation of their interviews it is important to understand certain aspects of its evolution, particularly in terms of male involvement.

In the early days of ballet, when Louis XIV of France created the Royal Academy of Dancing, this form of dance was primarily a courtly pastime throughout Europe, and Louis was himself an accomplished dancer who enjoyed starring in the ballets performed in his court. This was perceived as completely acceptable at the time and, in fact, male dancers were even more respected dancers than female dancers, in part because their costumes were not as restrictive and they could more easily wow the audiences with their "virtuosic" performances (Hanna 1988: 123).

Up until the nineteenth century, there was little stigmatization of or prejudice against male dancers (Burt 1995: 10). However, during the first part of the nineteenth century, the male dancer became an "object of distaste" in Europe, and ballet dancing has not been popularly perceived as an appropriate activity for white males since then (Burt 1995: 1, 24). Burt explains that the change occurred because "since the nineteenth century it has been considered appropriate for men not to appear soft and not to appear emotionally expressive," and also because male dancers impeded the female spectacle that male patrons were paying to see (Burt 1995: 22, 52). Burt points out that, during the same time period, ideas about the body were changing. Critics "seemed to find the male dancer a conflictual figure. He appeared either through association with the degenerate style of the old aristocracy or by his resembling the rude prowess of the working classes. It is these associations which stopped male dancers representing the middle-class male values" (Burt 1995: 50). In a similar vein, Lynn Garafola notes that "as the concept of masculinity aligned itself with productivity, the effeminate sterility of the danseur became unacceptable to ballet's large male public" (2002: 214). What Garafola's historical interpretation proposes is that prejudice against male dancers arose because danseurs did not follow or reproduce social norms of that time and place and, thus, were negatively sanctioned by the men who patronized ballets. This is one reason why I chose not to make sexuality a crucial component of my study even though since that time, male ballet dancing has come to be associated with effeminacy and homosexuality.

It was not until 1909 and the advent of Diaghilev's Ballets Russes in Russia that males began again to experience a little more prestige. Their status increased because new choreography emphasized the spectacular physical feats male dancers could perform, which impressed audiences and gave them a new perspective on danseurs (Garafola 1988: 215; Burt 1995: Chapter 4). The danseurs' standing was raised again in the mid-twentieth century, when dancers from working-class backgrounds such as Edward Villella and Jacques d'Amboise achieved a great deal of professional success, famous dancers like Mikhail Baryshnikov became known as "ladies men" and others, like Rudolph Nureyev, achieved financial success (Fisher 2007: 49–50; Hanna 1988: 143). These prominent danseurs then used their roles as choreographers and spokespeople to further raise the profile of males in ballet.

THE SOCIAL CONSTRUCTION OF GENDER AND MULTIPLE MASCULINITIES

My approach to the study of males in ballet is primarily based on the notion that gender is a social construction. In particular, I use the work of Michael Kimmel, who narrows his focus to look at the construction of masculinity. Kimmel finds that there is not just one ideal type but a variety of "masculinities." Kimmel's colleague, Michael Messner, adds to these ideas by pointing out that males do have some agency in constructing their gender, though they must negotiate social forces in order to do this (2001: 88). This study examines the social forces that must be negotiated for male dancers to construct a masculine identity.

Kimmel and Messner explain that men are the unmarked gender in the sense that that neither society at large nor men themselves "see" their gender (2001: x). This point renders my study more complex by obliging me to contemplate whether or not the participants were "awakened" to their sex when immersed in a female-dominated environment like a ballet school, and to consider the social effects this may have. In this situation, they became the marked gender (that is, they were classified as "male dancers" as opposed to just dancers; there was a class called Boyz Ballet but no "Chick Ballet" class existed).

Another scholar who builds on the theories around the social construction of masculinities is R.W. Connell. Connell writes that during the 1990s a new form of studying masculinities emerged. This new framework was rooted in ethnography and focused on men in specific social locations and the different forms of masculinities that could be found in each unique setting, with many of them taking place in stereotypically male-dominated locations like bars, gyms, and offices (Connell 2001: 56–57). That is precisely the type of ethnography produced by this study—however, in this case, these masculinities are described from the vantage point of a typically female location. Also important to my research is Connell's notion that "masculinities, as patterns of gender practice, are sustained and enacted not only by individuals but also by groups and institutions" (Connell 2001: 57). I am especially interested in how the context of a dance studio can serve as a key influence in the construction of masculinities.

WHY DANCE?

Dance scholars such as Ramsay Burt, Douglas Risner, and Judith Lynn Hanna have speculated as to why men do ballet and, though I have found their insights to be of interest, I needed to explore why the participants of my study began dancing on the basis of the empirical evidence from an actual case study. And, in fact, the reasons articulated by the individuals in my study diverged from much of the scholarly material.

Burt assumes that "often what leads men to start dance training is the discovery of their own unrealised potential; this is frequently brought about by seeing an inspirational performance by another male dancer" (1995: 4). My findings are consistent with the first part of this proposition. For example, Ernest started dancing because Amy told him he had "great turnout" and Tom was also encouraged to begin in part because people told him he had the right body type. However, from the evidence in my study, I would disagree with the second point, an argument also advanced by Risner, that creating "superstar" male dancers has encouraged males to get more involved in both professional and recreational dance in the last twenty years (Risner 2007: 141). Unsurprisingly, only two participants were familiar with the names of any professional danseurs. In contradiction to Burt's and Risner's reasoning, none of the participants stated that a professional had inspired them to take up ballet. There were, in fact, other reasons.

On the other hand, Hanna states that males are drawn to dance because they "seek the pure joy of movement. Narcissism, desire to control audience reactions ... and exhibitionism" all come into play (1988: 120–121). This proved to be a more accurate explanation for why the participants of Boyz Ballet chose to begin dancing. All the dancers I interviewed had been involved with theatre productions (to varying degrees) and enjoyed performing for audiences. They all indicated that they thought dance training could provide them with skills to use in other types of performing or give them an edge in getting acting roles. And so the information from this case study points toward the desire to perform as a prominent reason for taking a ballet class.

The participants also noted other positives of taking part in a ballet class, including physical, artistic, and social benefits. A detailed description of the physical changes the participants discussed can be found in this chapter's section on the body; their examples indicate that there are significant physical benefits (such as increased strength and flexibility) for males who take ballet, even if it is just one class per week.

Both Shannon and Nick also commented on the mental benefits of taking ballet class. By asking them to clarify what this meant, and by drawing on my own experience in ballet, I understood that they saw ballet training not only as a physical challenge but also a mental one. This is because it is necessary to persevere by showing up to every class, pushing yourself, learning new moves and techniques, and understanding that you cannot always do everything on the first try. For them, ballet helps cultivate mental discipline.

One benefit that each of the participants addressed was the social aspect of being involved with DSW and Boyz Ballet in particular. Steve joked that ballet class was a great place to meet girls (he met his wife there) but then commented on how he had also met some of his best male friends in dance class. All class participants felt that they had become part of the DSW community. A conscious effort is made at DSW to cultivate a sense of belonging in all the dancers. Having a pre-existing social community means all dancers, including the males, are drawn to the prospect of friendship and social support from within the institution and benefit from the social stimulation it provides. This is particularly important in Corner Brook, where, at the time of writing, there are relatively few arts-based community groups and even fewer for male youth.

In addition to the community support that exists through involvement in a relatively small dance studio of two hundred dancers, the participants enjoyed Boyz Ballet in particular because of the bond it created based on all members being of the same sex. When asked about the friendships he has in Boyz Ballet class Steve said,

Because it's not even necessarily a friendship, it's a bond. I'm friends with everybody down there, but when you see somebody in a new dance belt it's a different kind of bond. You know something which this person knows which ninety-eight percent of the public has no idea. I didn't know what a dance belt was until I walked into that studio.

Tom also commented on the nature of this special relationship: "There is a weird bond between everyone in the boys ballet class because you are all there struggling with this ridiculous art form." Even as the youngest member of the class, Nick didn't feel isolated or marginalized. He got along well with the other members of the class, was respected by them, and enjoyed the social aspects of the class. This is important to examine because, from personal experience, when I have taught female dance classes, a wide range of ages in the class would normally indicate a certain amount of tension and animosity. However, because of the nature of the class and the specific type of male who is drawn to it, I argue that age differences (a spread from sixteen to thirty-one years old) mean less because the more obvious distinction is between genders.

At the conclusion of his interview, Nick said something that seems to summarize the sentiments of all six males regarding the reasons to take ballet classes:

> Ballet for me—there're a million reasons to not do something but there's only one reason to do it. And the million reasons to not do ballet are … I'm not built for it, I don't have the body shape, I'm not physically capable, people will think I'm girly or feminine or all these different things, or I'll have to compromise my eating habits and there're so many reasons not to. But the reason why I enjoy ballet and I choose to do ballet is not for anybody else but myself. It's a matter of growing to learn who I am, to experience new things, to express myself and that really is why I do ballet.

EXPLORING BALLET; EXPLORING ALTERNATE MASCULINITY

Experiencing ballet for the first time put the participants of my study on a steep learning curve. I examined the unique nature of their experiences by asking about their favourite part of class, the types of competition they find in the class, and how they balance the technical and the artistic requirements of ballet. Exploring these factors also led me to confirm that exploring ballet also means alternate masculinities.

Teaching/Learning Ballet and Gender

The uncommon nature of a male-only recreational ballet class highlights the dance studio's role as a "gendering institution." By signing up for a males-only ballet class, the participants of Boyz Ballet were immediately marked as unique, setting the precedent for others to treat them differently. In looking at the strategies for dealing with teaching ballet to males, Risner notes that "central to most of these strategies is a concerted effort to make gender a conscious variable in all aspects of dance education" (2007: 141). This is certainly true in Boyz Ballet. In the classroom, their gender was constantly commented on by the teacher and each other as they joked about being males who do ballet, learned steps exclusive to danseurs, and found that their bodies all had similar physical limitations that were not experienced by the female teacher. This gender-conscious commentary contributed to their sense of belonging, as they all share these common characteristics.

There is a fairly universal structure for ballet classes, however—each class does, of course, have its own nuances, and Boyz Ballet is no exception (for a more detailed discussion of this "transnational" structure of ballet classes, see Wulff, 1998: 68–70). When asked what makes Boyz Ballet different from other ballet classes at DSW, the participants commented that their class included more push-ups, jumps, work on flexibility, a focus on mastering the basics, and that sometimes non-piano music was used. The most notable difference, in my opinion, though, was that, through the actions and words of the danseurs and their teacher, they were constantly made aware of their gender. This factor contributes to the masculinity they are discovering and constructing because it is based in the most important characteristic of all masculinities: a marked difference from the female.

Boyz Ballet has a female teacher and this, too, contributed to the divide between male and female in the class. I asked the participants to comment on whether they thought having a female teacher and assistant made it difficult to learn given that there are no male models. Everyone said that a woman could understand their bodies and they had not experienced any limitations in consequence either physically or intellectually. Three participants said they would actually have been less comfortable if the teacher had been a male. This was an interesting point that I intend to investigate in future studies and which may provide further insights into gender awareness and socialization in the ballet class.

Favourite Part of Class

Much popular and dance-studies rhetoric suggests that male dancers favour the physically challenging grand allegro portion of class because it is better aligned with traditional male aesthetics of big jumps and the exhibition of strength. Boyz Ballet participants offered another take on this common belief, and their unique perspectives illustrate one way in which they are exploring alternate masculinities. Interestingly, Steve, Tom, and Jack all indicated that the relief they felt at the end of class was their favourite part! Steve viewed it as a time when he could reflect on all that he had learned, a moment to take pride in his achievements, and to let go of the stress he had put his body under. Jack compared the feeling he had at the end of class to the feeling he has had after working out at the gym. Tom said,

> It's a relief because I feel that it's a constant pressure in class, and I'm always like ... when this class ends, because you are under a giant pressure cooker for an hour.... You're trying to do stuff and for the most part your body doesn't want to do it, and when it does do it, it's great, and time passes a little quicker but a lot of times it doesn't or at least you feel like it doesn't or something doesn't look right and you don't feel right and you're tired ... and so it's a relief to leave that behind you. I think it's good to feel that way just so that you can reflect on it.

Nick wasn't able to single out a favourite part of class. He enjoyed the entire physical experience along with the social aspects. Shannon felt the same way. Ernest, however, subverted my expectations when he told me that port de bras was his favourite part of class, noting that he finds it relaxing. Since it occurs after the physically demanding barre portion of class, I interpret his feelings as analogous to those of Steve, Tom, and Jack, who had a similar experience at the end of class. When commenting on each of the different sections of ballet class, Tom surprised me again by not choosing the grand allegro as a preference:

> I like barre. You push yourself ... you have to push your muscles to move in these odd ways. And it's not all about jumping high and moving fast or jumping far or lifting something. It's about you putting your body in the right position and trying to push that position and that's kind of enjoyable—in a masochistic way.

These examples illustrate the unique insights provided by research that concentrates on recreational ballet dancers and non-professionals as well as the need to question generalizations made about male dancers.

Competition as a Masculine Trait

Competition is stereotypically seen as a male characteristic (see, for instance, Kimmel 136 and Hanna 138). But did Boyz Ballet participants exhibit this characteristic in the studio? Five of them said that they competed with others in the class over issues of technical performance and to get compliments from the teacher. Many said they were frustrated if another class member did better. However, the participants also explained that competition helps them learn because it encourages them to listen to and apply corrections. All of the participants also noted that they felt significant internal pressure to do well and that competition with one's self could be overwhelming. This aligns with the male characteristic of competitiveness, but Steve states that this is likely a trait that all dancers share regardless of gender. Given this, it is relevant to question whether ballet's competitive nature attracted these males to class. None of these participants indicated that the desire for competition initially drew them, but their responses show that it is an aspect of the masculinities they were creating. As Christine Williams points out, even men exploring alternate masculinities can "support and identify with hegemonic masculinity" and then incorporate it into the strategies they employ to construct an alternate masculinity (1995: 122).

Perceptions of Traditionalism, Physicality, and Creativity

In their Introduction to *Men's Lives*, Kimmel and Messner advance the notion that in sex-role theory, "masculinity is associated with technical mastery" (2001: xiii). Traditionally, though, masculinity has not always been associated with creativity. Therefore, it is interesting to investigate how males reconcile both technical demands and creativity in a world that employs them both.

Because, as a dance teacher, I see many young students who view ballet as traditional and monotonous, I asked my study's participants if they thought of ballet as innovative or if they perceived it as unchanging. Most responded that there are traditional elements, but that changes can happen when a choreographer uses the classical movements to create something new. Nick acknowledged that because the terminology is old French, and that most people are only exposed to traditional ballets like *The Nutcracker*, there is a common misconception that ballet is always very traditional. He explained it in this way:

> There is a proper way to do things but nobody's ever going to do things the same. No matter how strict the rules are, it depends on whether you put your feet in the right position or move your arms in the right way, but there's so much more to dance than just body movement.

He argued that dancers bring their "entire lives" to their performance, so that even if the steps are done in the same way each time they do not necessarily have the same intention. Others in the class expressed similar sentiments. Shannon said, "Ballet allows me to innovate within a certain determined area. It does have a rigid standard, but contains some flex." Ernest used the example of *Peter Pan*, DSW's most recent production, which used contemporary rock music, combining traditional dance elements with popular music. And Steve also envisioned ballet as innovative and changing, but founded on one "precise technique" that is fixed in stone. However, Tom contradicted this particular assertion when he said that "there's different types of ballet, so I'm sure someone could invent a new type of ballet."

After developing a better understanding of the perceptions Boyz Ballet participants had about the role of creativity in ballet, I asked each of them what, from their point of view, was the most important part of ballet, the technical/physical or the artistic/creative. Because of its association with masculinity and technical mastery, and the focus given to proper technique in their classes, I assumed that they would see the technical and physical aspect as the most important. However, their answers varied, and this variation indicates that, for them, ballet masculinity is different from hegemonic masculinity. The examples below clarify the variations encountered in the course of this study.

Tom articulated that the creative and artistic element of ballet is more important because "you can be as strong and as good at ballet as you want to be but it can still look like shit if it's not artistically put together properly." Steve agreed with him:

> I think you can be totally untechnical. I think it's possible that you can take ten people off the street that have absolutely no dance background and zero technique and make them do something which is totally artistic and innovative, but at the same time it is nice to have that technique because you certainly become limited if you don't have the technique there.

Steve also commented that ballet gives him a personal artistic release and compared dancing to acting, with choreography being interpreted by the dancer, like an actor interprets a script. Jack agreed with Tom and Steve, saying that creativity is more important due to the inherent aesthetic nature of dancing. Shannon commented on the aesthetic nature of ballet as well but saw both elements as equal. He said that "the technical and physical aspects are what makes it ballet. The creativity is what makes ballet beautiful."

Nick's and Ernest's views differed from the others but they provided interesting reasons for their responses. Ernest thought the technical and physical aspects were more important and said "if you can't do it, it's hard to try and do something creative with it." Nick also saw the technical and physical aspects as more important and said,

> You can't really express yourself fully until you have the physical capability to do so. So if you're a singer, for example, if you can't sing, you can't express yourself through song. But if you have the ability to sing well and you can use your breath support and do all the technical things then you're freer to do so.

These examples highlight several views of males who are drawn to ballet. An examination of these views revealed that the type of masculinity developed in ballet class ("ballet masculinity") was not necessarily equivalent to the kind of hegemonic masculinity that encourages competition against other individuals and technical mastery exclusive of creativity. By examining the responses of Boyz Ballet participants, I've come to understand that, although technique was important to these men, mastery was not essential because working toward personal achievements was the key. It was the exploration and cultivation of this attitude that helped construct their ballet masculinity.

TIGHTS AND DANCE BELTS: NEGOTIATING THE DRESS CODE

Everyone who registers to take a class at DSW is provided with a memo that outlines the formal rules, including the dress code. Connell proposes that dress code can be an important factor in expressing masculinity—though his example centres on power suits and not tights (2001: 62). The dress code for danseurs at DSW is a common one for male ballet dancers: a white T-shirt, black male ballet tights (that are thicker, longer, and shaped slightly differently from female tights), a dance belt, and black ballet slippers. Participants are expected to wear this to each class, though, as I discuss in this chapter's section on status, there is some leniency. In this section, I examine how ballet dress code, which is so different from the way Boyz Ballet participants normally dress, affected my participants' perceptions of ballet and masculinity. Because the one thing that most masculinities have in common is their opposition to the feminine (see for instance Kimmel 2006; Kimmel and Messner 2001: xv; Gard 2006: 34; McGuffey et al. 2001: 77), it may be that danseurs appreciate being assigned their own specific dress code to distinguish them from female dancers.

To continue investigating the role of clothing, I asked the participants what they thought of the dress code. Ernest described it as "kind of fruity" but along with the others, was not opposed to wearing the clothes. Nick said that he didn't mind wearing tights because the atmosphere was so relaxed that nobody really cared. Jack said, "It looks like I'm doing the right thing with the proper stuff on," and Tom went further in that sense when he commented that,

> Tights and a dance belt is pretty freeing. I mean, it's constrictive (*laughs*) but when I started … I used track pants and boxers and it's a lot of material.... As soon as I got my dance belt … I could feel a larger range of motion and with tights it's even more and it doesn't feel like there's any material in the way and it's totally practical and necessary now.

Steve also didn't have a problem with the dress code and said that putting on the uniform helps him get in the mood for dancing. He saw it as a requirement and accepted it, stating,

> It was always just one of the norms, I guess, when you go into a different *culture*, for lack of a better word, and ballet is kind of like a culture. I guess you just accept the norms that are already there and just assimilate yourself into that. So I never really questioned it. Wearing a dance belt for the first time was probably a little bit uncomfortable but I don't know if it's as shocking as what we joke about sometimes. I think we kind of overplay the whole dance belt thing sometimes, too, and in the end it's just something that you wear. It's like wearing a jock strap when you're playing hockey.

Shannon said that, even after all the years he has been doing ballet, he has found that the clothes are not "cozy to put on or take off" but he did not mind wearing them once they were on.

These views of recreational dancers are somewhat different than the attitudes of professionals, like NYCB apprentice Giovanni Villalobos, who said, "I tend to wear things that mould to my body.... I don't want to have baggy shirts or pants because I want the teachers to see me and I want to be able to look in the mirror and say my knees are too low, my foot's not pointed right" (quoted in Jarrett 2005: 60). My participants did not share this kind of nuanced, functional aspect of the dress code. However, their responses show that the dress code can create a bond and subsequently allow them to collectively develop one aspect of ballet masculinity. The issue that dressing differently from the girls because they *need* to (i.e., wearing a dance belt) also creates gendered divisions in the ballet classroom, grouping them together as dancers with unique needs and furthering the argument that dance studios are gendering institutions.

MUSCLES, MIRRORS, AND MASCULINITY

Bodies and our perceptions of them are "mediated through society" (Thomas 1993: 70) and ballet pedagogy is all about the body. As previously noted, there are certain training methods, ballet steps, and ways of executing steps that are exclusively for males. This is primarily due to physical differences. Hanna highlights specific aspects of these physical differences: "Women have a higher proportion of body fat distributed differently, less dense bones, wider pelvises, slightly shorter legs relative to the length of trunk and less cardiovascular power.... Men are generally heavier, taller, and more muscular then women, which gives men superior speed and strength" (1988: 157). Thomas insists that it is important for the dance ethnographer to look closely at the body because of the physical nature of dance (2003: 77–78).

Although changing throughout time and within regional variations, ballet has prescribed body types, and professional dancers (particularly female dancers) who do not conform to these types usually have limited success. This ballet-specific body type is a constructed one, as certain muscles are trained in particular by way of highly codified methods through regular ballet classes. However, classes alone are usually not enough to create the ideal aesthetic and many professional dancers also cross-train to build strength and endurance. Paige Edley and Ginger Bihn note that dancers feel pressured to alter their bodies for a number of reasons and state that ballet dancers' bodies are disciplined by both institutions and individual drive (2005: 213, 218).

To begin an investigation of this, I asked the participants what they thought was the ideal body for a male ballet dancer. Though their answers varied slightly, there was a consensus that male dancers should be tall and lean. Each of them pointed out that they came to this conclusion by reflecting on images of professional male dancers, and also by knowing the physical demands of ballet and then conceptualizing what physical characteristics would be conducive to this.

Interestingly, this long and lean male dancer's body imagined by the participants was not analogous to their idea of an ideal body for the hegemonic male. Boyz Ballet participants identified the ideal male body as generally strong and muscular, with toned abdominals, pectoral, and biceps muscles, and of medium height. This is in contrast to the emphasis on lean muscles they described for male dancers, and contributes to the understanding that ballet can also produce a physical masculinity by changing body shapes in addition to the more intangible aspects of identity.

None of the Boyz Ballet participants felt they had the ideal male body. However, not all participants wanted to achieve that kind of body. Inevitably though, all of the participants noted they were striving for physical changes. When I asked them how they would achieve these changes, all informants noted that working out was crucial, while only Jack remarked that dietary changes would be necessary as well. I asked the participants with curiosity if ballet was something that they could use to transform their bodies into some kind of masculine ideal. Steve, Tom, and Shannon said that it could do this, and Nick said doing ballet made him feel fit and flexible. Both Jack and Ernest thought that ballet class was a form of workout and, therefore, was helping them to achieve their physical ideal. Inevitably, all participants commented on the physical/embodied aspects of ballet as contributing to their experience, indicating that they were constructing a physical masculinity through ballet as well as a social one.

To better understand the extent to which the participants relied on ballet to change their bodies, I asked if they had made any lifestyle changes in order to better prepare their bodies for ballet. Shannon, Steve, and Jack all said they had done specific exercises at the gym to prepare themselves for ballet training. Shannon said, "I've changed my whole gym and eating routines to accommodate my ballet"; Jack also noted that he watches what he eats when it comes to sweets and fats and expressed that "taking up ballet had a major role in me starting at the gym." Tom does not go to the gym but has taken up working out in his spare time by skipping, doing push-ups and abdominal exercises, and stretching, as well as practising ballet movements outside of class time. In this way, they are constantly working toward changing their bodies and constructing a new, more masculine, body not only in the ballet class but even outside the class through training methods mediated by their ballet training.

After determining that ballet could construct a physical masculinity, I decided to examine what actual physical changes Boyz Ballet participants have experienced. When probed, Ernest said he had lost some weight; Jack said he was more flexible; Steve said his legs were stronger; and Nick felt he had better balance, more flexibility, and stronger legs. Tom noted that his abdominals were stronger and he has become more flexible; Shannon said he has become stronger, more flexible, and even taller. Because every participant perceived physical results, it became evident that the ballet masculinity they were constructing was flowing over into other parts of their lives and further cementing itself as part of their complete identity—both mentally and, interestingly, physically.

Figure 1 Participants of Boyz Ballet and a new recruit two years after the original fieldwork. They are still dancing, though now in co-ed classes. Their bond and sense of community has developed more and they jokingly refer to themselves as MANCE. From left to right: Tom Cochrane, Shannon Howlett, Ernest Power, Ryan Giles (in his first year of ballet), Steve Perchard, and Nick Fleming. Photo by Tom Cochrane.

GLISSADE-ING UP THE GLASS ESCALATOR

As indicated in popular culture and rhetoric, society often essentializes male ballet dancers. They are often labelled as effeminate or unproductive and men who dance often experience a lower social status than their non-dancing peers. However, this status drop was not replicated for the participants of Boyz Ballet; in fact, the opposite was often true. Participants indicated that dancing gives them a certain "edge" and uniqueness. Because, in society at large, hegemonic masculinity is usually associated with high social status, this edge can be interpreted as one way the participants justified their involvement and became characteristic of the ballet masculinity they were constructing.

In an investigation of males in the ballet hierarchy, Jennifer Fisher notes that male dancers "also enjoy certain privileges in the ballet world, most certainly because of their endangered status" (2007: 52). She also notes that male dancers get more scholarships and opportunities in the ballet world (2007: 52). Similarly Risner says,

Because of the seeming legitimacy men bring to dance, although they comprise a definitive minority, males often receive more attention and cultivation in their classes, training, and scholarship awards. Some research indicates that dance teachers may emphasize the need to make boys and young men in dance "feel more comfortable" ... and by emphasizing the challenge and satisfaction of jumping higher, shifting weight faster, moving bigger and balancing longer. (2007: 141)

My position as a dance teacher at DSW and the assistant for Boyz Ballet allowed me the opportunity to investigate the analogous privileges that male participants in this situation were afforded. I was also able to juxtapose what happened in classes with male participants to what happened in classes with female participants. Also, although I did not ask my study's participants if they believed they were getting any special privileges, many of them commented on it anyway. When discussing the challenges of adapting to a female-dominated environment Steve commented, "It's so easy because you're so accepted. Let's face it, you guys want boys down there and the more the better, and you guys make boys feel pretty special ... because we're such a rare commodity, I guess." Jack noticed that Amy often used a different kind of music in Boyz Ballet (like rock and pop) because the participants didn't enjoy the standard piano music (a sentiment echoed by Ernest in his interview). Jack also mentioned that the most unique thing about Boyz Ballet is that there were no girls. At first, I didn't consider this comment a privilege, but on reflection I realized that there were no classes restricted to female-only registration, so providing this option to the males indicates a special effort being made for them. Additionally, Steve commented that there was not as much pressure for males to have a certain body type, which meant that they had the privilege of being less preoccupied by this requirement.

There were additional privileges for DSW danseurs who liked to perform. Jack recognized that he had been given the lead role in a recent dance production, by and large, because he was a male. Although he is a good dancer, there were several female dancers who were far superior but who received lesser roles. Steve picked up on this idea as well by recognizing that he received more "stage time" than female dancers with better skills. Steve also noted that dancing had helped his theatre career, and that he had been given more roles and more stage time because he studies dance. Tom noticed this, too, and commented that he had received the lead role in a recent community theatre production, to some degree, because of his dance training.

My observations have confirmed that these men were given certain privileges in the ballet classroom as well. For example, the teacher was effectively less strict about the dress code in order to keep the participants happy and motivated to attend. As previously discussed, the required dress was black tights and a white T-shirt; however, many of the participants wore other kinds of T-shirts, like Tom who frequently displayed images and names of music groups on his while Jack's were fluorescent coloured. If a participant forgot their dance belt he was allowed to dance in track pants. This was not allowed in other ballet classes where girls were required to wear solid-coloured bodysuits and those who forgot their tights were expected to dance in bare legs. Also, ballet has traditionally offered males more comfortable attire, particularly as they are not expected to dance on pointe (of course, there are some rare exceptions to that rule, as with the male ballet dancers of Les Ballets Trockaderos). As Kristin Harris points out, "Men are given far greater comfort with their shoes, and don't have to suffer the same physical pain and strain on their bodies in the same way as female ballet dancers" (2003: 6). Because they are not subject to the same uncomfortable footwear, they also are able to enjoy longer careers as dancers (even if it is just in the recreational sense) and this is a privilege they hold over, as well as another notable distinction, the female dancers.

These privileges and status boosters are analogous to what Christine Williams describes as the "glass escalator" effect. Through the course of her research, Williams found that "men and women are still generally confined to predominantly single-sex occupations" (1992: 253), and, although none of the men in Boyz Ballet were intent on pursuing professional careers, their case demonstrates how it is that even recreational ballet tends to be a single-sex activity. Williams further discovered that "in several cases, the more female-dominated the speciality, the greater the apparent preference for men," and that once they have been accepted into a female-specialty field (in this case ballet), they were tracked into higher-status jobs like administrators (1992: 256). This is particularly apparent in the ballet world where male dancers have often held powerful positions like those of choreographer and artistic director, sometimes promoted after relatively short periods in the role of company dancer. When looking at female reactions to this phenomenon, Williams found that "it appears that women are generally eager to see men enter 'their' occupations" and, although they may resent the ease of advancement the men have, they do not take action to bring them down or express this resentment to the men (1992: 260). This was certainly the case in Boyz Ballet. The female dancers of DSW were always excited to hear that more males were getting involved even though they were getting more attention than the best female dancers. As a result, the men felt well accepted by their female colleagues, as Steve has already pointed out.

Williams also stresses that perceptions of status and prestige outside the workplace, or in this case the dance studio, are important as well. She found that because males in female situations are often shunned by the public, they are more readily ushered into "legitimately" masculine jobs. Although the participants of Boyz Ballet were not being pressured into assuming professional positions in the ballet world, they were getting certain privileges, like the leading roles, praise from the teachers, and local media attention, which encouraged Corner Brook residents to perceive their activity as legitimate by affording them a certain power and notoriety. Steve provided an interesting commentary on these dynamics: "I'm not saying it's a bad way that people look at you, because I think I get more respect from people for dancing than a negative vibe or anything." Jack also commented on this when he related that some girls in whom he is interested think the fact that he dances is "pretty cute."

Hanna also notes that heterosexual male dancers have more prestige than gay and female ones (1988: 121), and Williams comments on the dynamics of prestige as well by showing that homosexual male nurses and teachers were not on the same glass escalator as their male counterparts, but were "stuck under the glass ceiling" with the females. Historically, ballet in the West has enjoyed more prestige than other dance forms (Novak 1993: 35). This means that a heterosexual ballet dancer is likely to enjoy a very high status in the dance community. I generally observed that at DSW, the males who have taken ballet are much more popular than the males who take just tap or hip hop. In this case, ballet may be allowing the participants of Boyz Ballet to continue enjoying the high status that is consistent with hegemonic masculinity, particularly because none identify as homosexual.

One issue that arises here is how this phenomenon contradicts the societal goal of equality for everyone. Burt asks, "To what extent can men's achievements in dance be celebrated without at the same time reasserting male dominance and thus reinforcing the imbalance of power between men and women in our society?" (1995: 2). This is not a question addressed within the scope of this study, but it is worth contemplating in a continuing investigation of the status of males in the ballet world.

MASCULINITY AND BALLET

As my capsule history of men in ballet recounts, this dance genre has struggled ever since the beginning of the nineteenth century to be seen as consistent with a masculine identity, and has subsequently become associated with low status and negative stereotyping for males. Risner finds "recent scholarship on male youth in dance education suggests various kinds of prevailing social stigma, including narrow definitions of masculinity, heterosexist justifications for males in dance," and other topics that I explore in this section, where the tension between masculinity and ballet is exposed and questioned (2007: 139).

It is crucial to understand that, while I am approaching this study with the idea that there are as many different masculinities as there are men, men are often compared against a hegemonic standard (Connell 2001: 60). Men who do not fit this ideal type of model may turn to other ways of constructing masculinity—for example, by joining groups with other men (Connell 2001: 60) such as a ballet class.

To disassociate themselves from homosexual stereotypes, Burt observes that male dancers have often tried to overly masculinize their performances (1995: 12). When investigating how male dancers have dealt with effeminate stereotyping, Burt found that

> For most of the twentieth century, the construction of male roles in dance and ballet has generally been overshadowed by the need to counteract this negative image. This has sometimes resulted in a "macho" overcompensation—of trying to prove that ballet is tough really, or that modern dance is not soft like ballet. (1995: 56)

Jennifer Fisher looks in depth at this phenomenon and suggests that to protect male dancers from negative stereotyping and its effects, dance teachers, writers, critics, and dancers have employed the "making it macho strategy" (2007: 45–46). Similarly, Risner noted in 2007 that in the past twenty years, strategies for getting more males involved in dance included comparing it to sports and de-emphasizing the gay population (2007: 141). Fisher argues that this strategy is problematic because ballet is not inherently macho. Instead, she questions whether or not ballet has become too macho and resolves that a "Make it Maverick" solution should be employed (2007: 63). I am also concerned that danseurs may feel pressured to be hegemonically masculine before doing ballet in order to contradict any stereotyping, rather than using ballet to help construct an alternative form of masculinity. While some aspects of the ballet masculinity deviate from hegemonic masculinity, others, like the high status, are consistent with it.

This leads me to wonder if perhaps a balance can be struck. And since ballet masculinity doesn't exist independently from the hegemonic variety, I have needed to consider influences outside of the ballet class in order to understand how it is constructed.

To better understand those influences from outside the ballet studio that constructed the masculine identity of my study's participants, I asked them how they learned to be masculine and who their role models were. Shannon said he learned masculinity from superheroes like Superman, Batman, and Spider-Man, as well as from his grandfather. He said that people know he is a man because he perceives himself as such and this confidence makes others know. Steve, like the majority of participants, said his family contributed to his idea of what a man is by unconsciously forming his view of socially appropriate gender roles. Steve's responses to my questions around the construction of masculinity indicate that he wants to be seen as a man, but understands that he can create his own version of what this means. Steve thinks that to prove masculinity in ballet, you must appear confident and be comfortable with behaving in such a way—traits he sees in all his fellow classmates.

Nick noted that learning to be masculine was "not sudden in the least" but "part of growing up." He commented on how his upbringing illustrated the fluidity of gender:

> I took to my own interests rather than the interests of my gender. I never played with trucks, I never played with dolls. I played outdoors, and I was who I was. And I guess maybe that's why I'm comfortable onstage. I guess things like dance are not really guy things, so if I was brought up in a "guy" way, maybe I wouldn't be doing dance.

When I asked Tom how he learned to be a man, he replied, "I don't think I have yet," indicating that he, too, perceives gender as a learned behaviour. He had to think hard about his models of masculinity:

> I don't know. I guess growing up I looked up to my dad, but the type of guy my dad is, I don't really want to be.... I think now I look up to some friends, like people I've met through the studio and stuff and most of them are a lot older, so I can. It's lame, but I guess you kind of look up to them in a way because they've been through a lot in their own lives and they're real. I guess your own father is old, I perceive him as old and he's not the type of person that I am, or I see myself being at all, but a lot of these people are. We share more similar things and since they are a lot older than I am, I guess I pick up things that I latch onto subconsciously.

Tom went on to discuss how he thinks that his DSW friends provided reliable models of masculinity. Tom's words also bring up an interesting point about the relationships that were developing within Boyz Ballet and how participants helped each other construct a particular identity by influencing and inspiring each other. An analysis of my observations and fragments of dialogue from my field notes confirm that Tom was not the only one experiencing this type of relationship, as he, too, was a role model for some of the younger participants.

Jack noted that he learned about masculinity from his family, friends, and school. He saw his presentation of masculinity as fluid by stating that "[in] some places, you do have to act more manly ... at school, places with girls, you just act like a man." This is different from what Tom perceives because he believed that the members of the class would feel a stronger need to assert their masculinity in the all-male class, because in classes with girls, they are "obviously" male. These examples illustrate that, although participants were taking steps to achieve a collective masculinity in the ballet class, their perspectives on how and when to assert masculinity were different and, as multiple masculinity theories acknowledge, there are as many masculinities as there are males.

In the end, the results of this study support the idea that, although ballet does seem to attract males with a certain (albeit relatively uncommon) world view regarding gender, this is not always the case. There are some men who just do not see taking ballet class as inconsistent with being male.

CONCLUSION

As Kimmel and Messner point out, when scholars study men, they primarily have paid attention to their public roles (2001: ix). This is certainly the case in the ballet world, where the attention has long been focused on danseurs as they perform onstage in terms of the roles they play and the costumes they wear. This study moves beyond public life by exploring the more personal and private location of ballet, the dance studio, and by investigating the unique ways masculinity is constructed there.

Every subsection of this chapter could be elaborated into book-length studies, and further research into each of these expressions of masculine identity in the ballet world will certainly yield fascinating insights. The next stage of research will include follow-up interviews with my informants after their first recital together in order to discover how they felt exposing this part of their identity to the public and what feedback they received. I want to continue exploring the relationship between ballet and masculinity. However, as Thomas notes, "any discussion that focuses on one gender has implications for the other" (1993: 69)—so my incorporating the views of female dancers into this study by conducting a comparative analysis would enrich future research. Hopefully, this glimpse into the world of male dancers by way of the Boyz Ballet class has brought to light some of the vital gender issues facing men in ballet classes and provided a solid case study of how multiple masculinities were constructed. These insights should prove useful not only to dance and gender scholars but also to dance teachers and studio owners as they investigate new strategies in recruiting male students rooted in sociological reasoning.

Notes

1 Amy trained as a dance teacher in St. John's, Newfoundland, and opened DSW in 1997. The thirty-year-old multi-disciplinary dancer has been teaching there as well as choreographing for both professional and amateur theatre on the west coast of the island ever since.

2 All direct quotations and text regarding the Boyz Ballet participants and their opinions have been drawn from my personal interviews with them. Alternatively, remarks derived from field observations are noted as such.

3 The study of proxemics focuses on how individuals create and maintain spatial separation and how these social distances can contribute to the understanding of a culture. My proxemic observations were compared to Kate Bornstein's (2006) method of ascribing gender identities through physical and behavioural clues and the findings were presented in an unpublished version of this paper.

4 Helen Thomas notes that possessing a background in dance is beneficial to the dance ethnographer because it allows her to understand the "difficulties of bringing ideas about the experience of dancing into the domain of the verbal" (Thomas 1993: 76).

5 Though I could have used the Italian term *ballerino* or, the more colloquial, man-a-rina, the participants of my study and the literature seemed to favour this French term. I use it interchangeably with "male ballet dancer" and do not intend it to imply any sort of professional status.

Bibliography

Bornstein, Kate. "Naming All the Parts." In Tracey Ore (ed.), *The Social Construction of Difference and Inequality: Race, Class, Gender, and Sexuality*, 3rd ed. New York: McGraw-Hill, 2006: 187–98.

Burt, Ramsay. *The Male Dancer: Bodies, Spectacle, Sexualities*. London and New York: Routledge, 1995.

Cochrane, Tom. Personal interview, January 25, 2008.

Connell, R.W. "Masculinities and Globalization." In Michael Kimmel and Michael Messner (eds.), *Men's Lives*, 5th ed. Needham Heights, MA: Allyn and Bacon, 2001.

Corner Brook Economic Development Corporation. *Supplement to the Corner Brook Community Profile*. July 2005: 56–70.

Edley, Paige P., and Ginger Bihn. "Corporeality and Discipline of the Performing Body: Representations of International Ballet Companies." In Laura Lengel (ed.), *Intercultural Communication and Creative Practice: Music, Dance, and Women's Cultural Identity*. Westport, CT, and London: Praeger, 2005: 231–38.

Fisher, Jennifer. "Make It Maverick: Rethinking the 'Make It Macho' Strategy for Men in Ballet." *Dance Chronicle* 30, no. 1 (2007): 45–66.

Fleming, Nicholas. Personal interview, January 29, 2008.

Garafola, Lynn. "The Travesty Dancer in Nineteenth-Century Ballet." In Ann Dils and Ann Cooper Albright (eds.), *Moving History/Dancing Cultures: A Dance History Reader*. Middletown, CT: Wesleyan University Press, 2002: 210–17.

Gard, Michael. *Men Who Dance: Aesthetics, Athletics, and the Art of Masculinity*. New York: Peter Lang, 2006.

Hanna, Judith Lynne. *Dance, Sex, and Gender: Signs of Identity, Dominance, Defiance, and Desire*. Chicago: University of Chicago Press, 1988.

Harris, Kristin M. An Examination of the Pointe Shoe as Artifact through Ethnographic and Gender Analysis. *Material History Review* 58 (Fall 2003): 4–12.

Howlett, Shannon. Personal interview, February 6, 2008.

Jarret, Sara. "The Apprentices: Life at the NYCB." *Dance Spirit* (March 2005): 58–63.

Kimmel, Michael S. "Masculinity as Homophobia: Fear, Shame, and Silence in the Construction of Gender Identity." In Tracey Ore (ed.), *The Social Construction of Difference and Inequality: Race, Class, Gender, and Sexuality*, 3rd ed. New York: McGraw-Hill, 2006: 133–50.

Kimmel, Michael, and Michael Messner (eds.). *Men's Lives*, 5th ed. Needham Heights, MA: Allyn and Bacon, 2001.

Klein, Alan M. *Little Big Men: Bodybuilding Subculture and Gender Construction*. Albany: State University of New York Press, 1993.

Lee, Carol. *Ballet in Western Culture: A History of Its Origins and Evolution*. New York and London: Routledge, 2002.

McGuffey, C. Shawn, and B. Lindsay Rich. "Playing in the Gender Transgression Zone: Race, Class, Hegemonic Masculinity in Middle Childhood." In Michael Kimmel and Michael Messner (eds.), *Men's Lives*, 5th ed. Needham Heights, MA: Allyn and Bacon, 2001: 73–87.

McKay, Jim, Janine Mikosza, and Brett Hutchins. "Gentlemen, the Lunchbox Has Landed: Representations of Masculinities" and "Men's Bodies in the Popular Media." In Michael Kimmel, Jeff Hearn, and R.W. Connell (eds.), *Handbook of Studies on Men and Masculinities*. London and New Delhi: Sage, 2005: 270–88.

Messner, Michael A. "Boyhood, Organized Sports, and the Construction of Masculinities." In Michael Kimmel and Michael Messner (eds.), *Men's Lives*, 5th ed. Needham Heights, MA: Allyn and Bacon, 2001: 88–99.

———. "Still a Man's World? Studying Masculinities and Sport." In Michael Kimmel, Jeff Hearn, and R.W. Connell (eds.), *Handbook of Studies on Men and Masculinities*. London and New Delhi: Sage, 2005: 313–25.

Perchard, Stephen. Personal interview, January 23, 2008.

Power, Ernest. Personal interview, January 26, 2008.

Reynolds, Nancy, and Malcolm McCormack. *No Fixed Points: Dance in the Twentieth Century*. New Haven, CT: Yale University Press, 2003.

Risner, Doug. "Rehearsing Masculinity: Challenging the 'Boy Code' in Dance Education." *Research in Dance Education* 8, no. 2 (2007): 139–53.

Sims, Caitlin. "Sascha." *Dance Spirit* (December 2004).

Thomas, Helen. "An Other Voice: Young Women Dancing and Talking." In Helen Thomas (ed.), *Dance, Gender, and Culture*. New York: St. Martin's Press, 1993: 69–93.

———. *The Body, Dance, and Cultural Theory*. New York: Palgrave Macmillan, 2003.

Tomsen, Steven. "A Top Night: Social Protest, Masculinity and the Culture of Drinking Violence." *British Journal of Criminology* 37, no. 1 (1997): 90–103.

Wienke, Chris. "Negotiating the Male Body: Men, Masculinity, and Cultural Ideals." *Journal of Men's Studies* 6, no. 3 (Spring 1998): 255–82.

Wignal, Jack. Personal interview, February 6, 2008.

Williams, Christine. "The Glass Escalator: Hidden Advantages for Men in the Female Professions." *Social Problems* 39, no. 3 (August 1992): 253–67.

Williams, Christine. *Still a Man's World: Men Who Do "Women's" Work*. Berkeley and Los Angeles: University of California Press, 1995.

Wulff, Helena. *Ballet across Borders: Career and Culture in the World of Dancers*. Oxford and New York: Berg Press, 1998.

CHAPTER SIXTEEN

The Construction of the Body in Wilfride Piollet's Classical Dance Classes

NADÈGE TARDIEU AND GEORGIANA GORE[1]

I (Nadège) first met Wilfride Piollet in 1998 when she came to Blaise Pascal University in Clermont Ferrand, France, to give a workshop to students in the master's program, *Anthropologie des pratiques corporelles* (Anthropology of Corporeal Practices).[2] I had completed the program the previous year, during which I had also fortuitously passed the national exam, enabling me to become a physical education high school teacher.[3] By the time I met Piollet, I was undertaking the first of my two *Diplôme d'études approfondies* (DEA) (which at the time was the French degree prerequisite to doctoral studies), and was already beginning to write up a second graduate thesis on the "construction of the body" in dance.[4] In the aforementioned master's program, the body and corporeal practices are examined in a variety of contexts from diverse theoretical perspectives, including those proposed by authors such as Michel Foucault, Gilles Deleuze, and Maurice Merleau-Ponty, among others.[5] Little did I know in 1998 that I would need to spend nearly three years accompanying and observing Piollet in her classes and that these would eventually become multi-sited fields for my PhD. In this chapter, I will present some of the results of this research on the construction of the body in Piollet's classical dance classes, through a narrative which addresses the process of making sense of the realities of field work and the epistemological implications of being a researcher.

A REFLEXIVE APPROACH: THE SUBJECTIVITY OF THE RESEARCHER AND THE CHOICE OF FIELD

My research focuses on the transmission of bodily experience in dance, on how classical dance is taught and learned. I have to state that, until I met Piollet, I had never taken a ballet class; and, although I now teach dance as an extracurricular activity in high school and contribute to organizing a regional dance festival in the city of Castres in southwestern France, I still don't consider myself a "dancer." I discovered dance at university in the mid-1990s through a contemporary dance course in my final under-graduate year. At the time, I played handball and was quite puzzled by the perceptual differences between when I danced and when I played the sport to which my body was accustomed. I felt that my body was constructed totally differently in these two activities, and it was this experience that gave rise to the research topic that I was to pursue for the next ten years. In fact, so profound was this experience that I abandoned all dance or sports activities for a year, only taking up handball again in the context of my teaching, some four years ago.

Throughout my three graduate theses, I struggled to make sense of this experience and to answer my questions concerning the construction of the dancer's body. I decided to apprehend these perceptions from a phenom-enological perspective. From this point of view, the body is considered not as an objective body, a spatial form, or a bundle of functions, but in terms of bodily process—that is, as a present and effective body, as an interlacing of vision and movement (Merleau-Ponty 1964: 16). Through a description of the "lived experience"[6] of space, of time, and of other dimensions of human existence, phenomenology aims to understand the origin of knowl-edge: a primary kind of knowledge. The problem with this approach is that knowledge is considered as constructed from a particular body: an indi-vidual body and not a culturally constructed body.

At that first workshop with Wilfride Piollet in 1998, I was struck by her conception of the body: a body with three levels, three cavities, and rela-tions between these levels (Piollet 1999: 20). (See figure 1.)

It was not, however, until I began my doctoral studies in 2000 that I decided to take Piollet's method and conception of the body as objects of interrogation, and this only after a fruitless search in the contemporary dance community in Paris for a teacher whose method appeared to offer the appropriate context to study bodily construction. Also at this time, I first grasped the importance of education and transmission in the construc-tion of the body. I understood that the body is constructed in a pedagogic relation between students and teacher, in Piollet's case in the context of classical dance lessons.

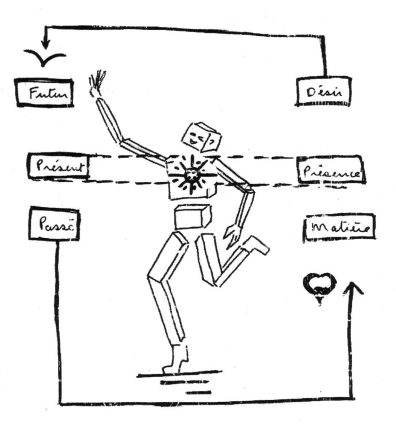

Figure 1 A drawing of her body concept, a body on three levels, by Wilfride Piollet. Excerpted from her pedagogical writing (Piollet 1999: 20).

My doctoral research topic finally became the corporeal knowledge transmitted in the classical dance teaching of Wilfride Piollet, former Paris Opera *étoile* (a title retained even after retiring from performing and the equivalent of prima ballerina), choreographer, and pedagogue. It is an aspect of this research that I share here.

RESEARCHING THE CONTEMPORARY AND THE SINGULAR: ANTHROPOLOGY AT HOME

An Anthropological Approach to Transmission

In this study, I apprehended the corporeal knowledge transmitted not by comparing different methods of teaching but by focusing on a singular and original method, that proposed by Wilfride Piollet, whom I treated as "a typical individuality" (Augé 1992: 31).[7] By this, I suggest that Piollet is a representative of the dance teaching profession, even if her method is not typical of ballet transmission. I questioned the Other, the object of anthropological study (Augé 1992: 28), who is both my alter ego and that which is radically different, in the context of changes characteristic of current contemporaneity: an "anthropology of contemporaneity," as defined by Marc Augé (1992: 55). In this perspective, the researcher must question the ways in which she seeks to understand others similar to herself who are present in the field.

Field in Motion: A Relationship That Is Lived between the Researcher and the Actors of the Observed Field of Study

In the epistemological approach suggested by anthropologist Mondher Kilani, the researcher must explain how the passage from the lived reality to the one constructed intellectually and textually occurs. According to Kilani (1994), it is necessary to specify the relationship between the reality that is experienced and the ways of understanding it.

Because I was working as a physical education teacher in Paris, I was able to observe three years of lessons given by Piollet in two different settings: in the Conservatoire National Supérieur de Musique et Danse de Paris (CNSMDP) and in her studio near Paris. During this time, I became completely absorbed into Piollet's world, and had to negotiate my exit both literally and conceptually in order to write my dissertation.

THE CONSTRUCTION OF THE BODY: A REALITY APPREHENDED FROM THREE EPISTEMOLOGICAL POSTURES

In this research project, I identified three moments corresponding to three epistemological postures, or three perspectives, which contributed to my representations of Piollet's teaching. First, the construction of the body was apprehended from a phenomenological perspective as a phenomenological body, through a process I called "impregnation." Second, my understandings became homologous to those of my informants and I adopted their frame of reference. I named this stage "inclusion." Finally, the process of constructing bodies was materialized and shared in the dance teaching, in the interface between a "bodily reality" postulated by Piollet and the one reinvented in the bodily experience lived by the pupils.

The Schematization of the Body by Wilfride Piollet
At first, using a phenomenological perspective, I tried to explain her conception of the body, a "strange" reality of a body with three levels, and I retained only the notions that resonated with my system of comprehension. I did not initially consider the context of transmission, or the pupils, but only the phrases Piollet used, such as "the intention of the body" or "the body's imagination." I was not "reading"[8] the field, but only interpreting it through my theoretical frame of reference. I later replaced this a priori attitude with another: that of inclusion.

Construction of the Body and Tradition in Classical Dance
In order to put this first attitude aside, I next tried to understand Piollet's teaching method and its specificities. For instance, she refuses to use the barre and the mirror in her classical dance classes. So I undertook research in the texts of ballet masters, from Blasis to Bournonville and Noverre, on the role of these two "traditional" props. I used this historical knowledge to valorize and to justify Piollet's pedagogic choices. And I began to implicate myself in her research, questioning how the traditions of classical dance were appropriated and transformed through Piollet's experience as a dancer and pedagogue.

There are two moments invoked by Piollet to explain the absence of the barre and mirror in her lessons. The first was the experience of rehearsing and dancing a piece choreographed by Merce Cunningham, *Un jour ou deux* (1973). Here, the absence of material props during classes forced her to rely on her own sense of the body in space, and actually made it easier to dance the classical repertory that she was also performing at the time. The second was when she learned to walk on a tightrope. Piollet realized that she had to accept gravity and falling in order to move forward on the rope: that is, falling in order to rise up. The accounts of these moments enabled me to understand that I had to connect experiences that were lived by Piollet to her schematization of the body in the context of transmission of bodily experience.

Transmission and the Construction of the Body: Distancing

It was when I finally managed to gain distance from my own theoretical perspectives that I understood the necessity to connect Piollet's discourses, her conception of the body and her experience lived within the context of teaching. I needed to put aside my own interpretations and, to do so, I began to describe with great precision the classical dance lessons proposed by Piollet.

TO DESCRIBE A REALITY: A CONNECTION BETWEEN OBSERVATION AND INTERPRETATION

Two authors helped in describing the dance lesson from two points of view: the first in relation to the aesthetic of the body favoured by Piollet (Foster 1997), and the second in relation to how this conception of the body is materialized in the dance teaching and shared between the teacher and the pupils (Ness 1996).

Foster conceptualizes the construction of a body as a complex relationship between three bodies, the "perceived," the "aesthetically ideal," and the "demonstrative" (Foster 1997: 237), the latter displaying itself in the body of the teacher who details the parts of the body, the areas of the body, and their relationships in order to present an analysis of the ideal. In this "aesthetic ideal," the teacher uses metaphors and with "repetition, the images used to describe the body and its actions *become* the body. Metaphors that are inapplicable or incomprehensible when first presented take on a concrete reality over time, through their persistent association with a given movement" (Foster 1997: 239).

In the context of classical dance teaching, Piollet favours upward movements in keeping with the classical aesthetic: she points to the heart as the part of the body from which movement is initiated. She deploys the image of a pair of wings to indicate both the iliac wings at the top of the pelvis and the scapulas (shoulder blades). She asks the students to mobilize these parts of the body and to create an oppositional relationship between them through their dynamic interplay.

The second author is Ness, who questions the "learning processes of embodiment" (Ness 1996: 137) from the indications given by the teacher to the student. From her experience of learning a new kind of dance while in the field, Ness asks, concerning the parts of the body mobilized in the movement and the different kinds of movement knowledge, What should be done and how can it be done? She is interested in verbal accounts, contexts of embodiment, tactile corrections, and in the way her teacher's attention was "largely focused on observing how consistently [she] re-incorporated corrections after … instruction" (Ness 1996: 138).

In the lessons proposed by Piollet, the students always experimented with different movements, which they performed in a circle (see figure 4). The relations created by this spatial configuration allowed them to see, on their counterparts, the parts of the body designated by the teacher, and mobilized by the students. Instead of watching themselves in the mirror, the students incorporated corrections through self-observation and observation of others.

The parts of the body designated by Piollet refer to the conceptual schema organizing movement that she has elaborated. In fact, the originality of Piollet's teaching is that she has developed a method based on flexible barres (*barres flexibles*), which dispenses with the mirror and barre of traditional ballet classes. "Their referential functions for bodily construction" are replaced by these flexible barres. This concept was created by the French poet René Char especially for Piollet, by which he means that the movement is explained and constructed from a relationship between defined points in the body. Through visualizing the points during action, the dancer will be able to change his movement and acquire the autonomy and the self-mastery necessary to modify his own movement.

In the lesson proposed by Piollet, she indicates a mobile, unfixed point in the body (such as the heart, which is suspended in the thoracic cavity) and a supporting point in the body from which the movement is organized: by linking these two points, one fixed and one mobile, a flexible barre is constructed, which enables the pupil to organize the body and movement by way of this system of reference.

What follows are a several brief examples of how Piollet explains or constructs these flexible barres during the lesson. The examples are taken from videos that I made of her lessons during my fieldwork.

Piollet explained to the students, "It is the same work as that done at the barre, except that there isn't a barre. It's the same exercise. I could make you work at the barre, but I find it more interesting to know what you are doing, that it's your sternum which goes upwards."[9] She stated, as she touched the student, "It goes forward until you feel that the wing goes up. And it's the heart which makes you do that. Ah, that, [that's] very, very good, the weight-bearing foot all the way to the wing, yes, that's it!"[10]

In figures 2 and 3, Piollet indicates the points in the body that the pupils must visualize in order to make a turn: the heart and the knee. She asks the pupils to put the heart in front of the knee, and to engage in moving from

Figures 2 and 3 Wilfride Piollet with a student in an individual lesson, Studio, Poissy, March 23, 2002. The student sinks by folding the knees and rises using the scarf like a bar. Video still from the author's fieldwork.

the heart in relationship to the knee, which is a gravity point fixed in space. She also indicates that the iliac wing of the supporting leg releases upwards toward the back, while the heart moves forwards.

The bodily reality transmitted to the pupils is not a visible form or a codified system, but rather a dynamic play of forces experienced from points in the body, in relationship and in opposition to three levels within the body. More specifically, the head is directed upwards, the knees and the feet push against the ground and the heart acts as the fictive axis of the body, a mobile point in gravity throughout all three levels.

Then Poillet said, "Next, think about that and put your hands back in place. Think initially about going downwards, then upwards, and then afterwards go back to work, on the weight of all that; leave the lungs which also have weight. Shall we try it?" ... "You are on your toes; you push against the ground, the spine is completely flexible."[11] It is in this kind of visualization of the relationship between the points created by hands and head that the students are made aware of the three body levels.

Figure 4 Wilfride Piollet with first-year students, CNSMDP, Paris, October 1, 2002. Piollet asks the students to place their hands on their head like a crown, and each student must relate this point of contact with the support of the pelvis on the heels, an imaginary axis. Video still from the author's fieldwork.

CONCLUSION

From this anthropological perspective, transmission of dance movement requires that the body be constructed in the interface between the "bodily reality" postulated by Piollet and the one reinvented in the bodily experience lived by the pupils. The flexible barre can be considered as an organizer of the rules of the movement.

Producing an ethnographic description of a dance lesson was not an easy task. How can movements as well as tactile and visual exchanges be put into words? What should be the focus of research: the teacher's actions, those of the students, or what they say? All anthropological approaches force the researcher to question the construction of both the research object and field, to ask what motivates her, how she formulates her questions, how she is transformed through contact with the field. It was only by linking Piollet's ways of putting the body and movement into words, and her ways of acting on her students' bodies in the dance lesson, that I managed progressively to construct my field. In this context, transmission was conceived by myself as the researcher to be a coexistence of opposites—that is, between constraint and freedom, autonomy, and heteronomy. It was also by asking Piollet about her career, the encounters that inspired her, and her own experience as a dancer that I came to understand fully her teaching method: a form of transmission simultaneously inscribed in a tradition, that of French ballet, and in a contemporary practice.

Notes

1 The fieldwork and narrative account are Nadège Tardieu's. Georgiana Gore assisted with the translation and with clarifying the ideas.

2 The then Maîtrise Éducation et Motricité was established in 1996 in the Faculty of Sports and Human Movement Sciences and Physical Education (UFR STAPS) at the same time as the Laboratoire d'Anthropologie des Pratiques Corporelles (LAPRACOR), a research centre devoted to the "anthropology of corporeal practices." The course aimed to provide undergraduate students in the faculty who wished to continue in the human and social sciences with a grounding in cognitive anthropology as applied to the study of techniques of the body. Four years later, in the context of the Europeanization of French university degrees, it became the first year of the following two-year master's programs, the *Master Anthropologie des pratiques corporelles* (Anthropology of Corporeal Practices) and the *Master Anthropologie de la danse* (Anthropology of Dance), the latter being the transformation of the DESS (*Diplôme d'enseignement supérieur spécialisé*) *Anthropologie de la danse*, which opened in 2001. The dance anthropology program has since 2009 become the *Master ethnomusicologie et anthropologie de la danse*, co validated with Paris Ouest University.

3 As there are few doctoral grants in the human and social sciences in France, this exam enabled me to continue my research with a certain financial stability.

Coming from a rural region of central France, the Lozère, and being the first member of my family to go to university, it was important that I specialize in an area which, at the time, ensured me a profession. In 1993, when I went to university, my only intention was to become a physical education teacher. I had no idea that I would eventually undertake research. I very soon became fascinated by my courses in the anthropology of the body and corporeal practices, and decided to specialize in my final undergraduate year. It was also then that I encountered dance as a practice, although I had previously taken theory courses. This was the beginning of a number of intellectual preoccupations that culminated in my doctoral dissertation, "Knowledge Construction in Wilfride Piollet's Classical Dance: An Anthropology of Transmission" (Tardieu 2006), undertaken under the direction of Professor Georgiana Gore at the University Blaise Pascal's LAPRACOR, and as a registered student in UFR STAPS, and in the Arts, Human and Social Sciences Graduate School (École Doctorale Langues, Sciences Humaines et Sociales).

4   While, anatomically, all human bodies may be considered as structurally and functionally the same, when considered from an anthropological perspective as lived bodies in defined cultural milieus, they are conceived as constructed. As Marcel Mauss proposed in 1936 (Mauss 1950) and Bateson and Mead demonstrated in their 1942 photographic analysis of Balinese character, human bodies are fashioned in accordance with the tenets of the society or cultural group in which they are born and raised. This is why it is possible to state in the context of dance teaching that each technique constructs the body in accordance with particular aesthetic norms. This notion of bodily construction is at the heart of my PhD thesis dissertation.

5   These authors analyze bodily practices and experience from three different perspectives: from an anthropological perspective in social and cultural contexts with the concept of "technique of the body" (Mauss 1950); from a philosophico-historical perspective in relation to regimes of power-knowledge, as relayed by the prison and other institutional contexts such as the school (Foucault, 1975); and from a phenomenological perspective with regard to dualistic conceptions of the body–mind relation (Merleau-Ponty, 1945).

6   These words, "lived experience of the time, space and the others," are employed in Merleau-Ponty's phenomenological thought. The aim of phenomenology is to reveal the origin and the process of our perceptive knowledge of things from our manner of acting with others, and in the construction of our spatial and temporal reference points.

7   In the original French, "Toute representation de l'individu est nécessairement une représentation du lien social qui lui est consubstantiel" (Augé 1992: 30).

8   By "reading" the field, I refer to the process of constituting a description based on the interaction of the researcher with the field, rather than on interpretations of observations selected from previously held convictions or theoretical postures.

9   In Piollet's original French, "Ça, c'est le même travail qu'à la barre, sauf qu'il n'y a pas la barre. C'est le même exercice. Je pourrais vous le faire travailler à la barre mais je trouve plus intéressant de savoir ce que vous faites, que c'est votre sternum qui va vers le haut" (CNSMDP, Paris, October 1, 2001).

10 In Piollet's original French, "Ça va vers l'avant jusqu'à ce que tu sentes que l'aile remonte. Et c'est le cœur qui te fait faire ça. Ah, ça très très bien, le pied porteur jusqu'à l'aile, oui, c'est ça!" (Studio, Poissy, March 23, 2002).
11 In Piollet's original French, "Ensuite, vous pensez à ça et vous replacez vos mains. Vous pensez d'abord en bas, puis en haut et vous retravaillez après, le poids de ça, les poumons, il faut les laisser, qui ont du poids. On essaie?" and "On est sur ses doigts de pied, on repousse le sol, la colonne complètement souple" (CNSMDP, Paris, October 1, 2001).

Bibliography

Augé, Marc. *Non-lieux: introduction à une anthropologie de la surmodernité*. Paris: Seuil, 1992.

Bateson, Gregory and Margaret Mead. *Balinese Character: A Photographic Analysis*. New York: Academy of Sciences, 1942.

Foster, Susan Leigh. "Dancing Bodies." In Jane Desmond (ed.), *Meaning in Motion: New Cultural Studies of Dance*. Durham, NC: Duke University Press, 1997.

Foucault, Michel. *Surveiller et punir*. Paris: Gallimard, 1975.

Kilani, Mondher. *L'invention de l'autre. Essai sur le discours anthropologique*. Lausanne: Payot, 1994.

Mauss, Marcel. *Sociologie et anthropologie*. Paris: PUF, 1950.

Merleau-Ponty, Maurice. *Phénoménologie de la perception*. Paris: Gallimard, 1945.

———. *L'oeil et l'esprit*. Paris: PUF, 1964.

Ness, Sally Ann. "Dancing in the Field: Notes from Memory." In Susan Foster (ed.), *Corporealities: Dancing Knowledges, Culture and Power*. London: Routledge, 1996.

Piollet, Wilfride. *Barres flexibles*. Poissy, France: Éditions L'Oiseau de feu, 1999.

Tardieu, Nadège "Savoirs en construction dans la danse classique de Wilfride Piollet: Anthropologie de la transmission." Unpublished PhD dissertation, Blaise Pascal University Clermont 2, 2006.

Revealing Choreographies as Cultural and Spiritual Practices

CHAPTER SEVENTEEN

Vincent Sekwati Mantsoe

TRANCE AS A CULTURAL COMMODITY

BRIDGET E. CAUTHERY

Reflecting on his fieldwork among of the Malagasy speakers of Mayotte in the western Indian Ocean, Canadian anthropologist Michael Lambek questions why the West has such a "blind spot" when it comes to the human activity of trance. Immersed in his subject's trance practices, he questions why such a fundamental aspect of both the Malagasy culture, and many other cultures he has studied around the world, is absent from his own.[1] Lambek provides the jumping-off point for my research into the West's preoccupation with trance in ethnographic research and simultaneous disinclination to attribute or situate trance within its own dance practices. In Lambek's own words, "The question for the West becomes one of understanding why trance has been so rigidly excluded or ignored" (Lambek 1981: 7).

The foundation for this research lies in my interest in the stories dancers tell about their performance experiences: stories about epiphanic, flow, or zone-like physiological experiences that can punctuate a dancer's performance career—stories I myself have told. When I began to look at these experiences in a larger context, beyond their appearance in interviews and in post-performance conversations, I began to see parallels in the extensive body of Western ethnographic literature on trance. Yet unlike ballet dancers and contemporary dancers, the subjects of ethnographic trance research do not reside in the anthropologist's country of origin; they live "in the field"—in lands annexed and occupied by European powers, in smaller, less overtly exploitable areas on the peripheries of the civilized world, or in enclaves of indigenous peoples still recovering from the onslaught of colonization. While trance functions as a part of Western subcultures such as tarantism, Shakerism, Pentecostalism, "new age" dance rituals, and rave, I am seeking to expand its application to include contemporary dance performance and practice. By engaging with an ethnographic methodology—including interviews and participant observation in rehearsals, public discussions, and live performances—I trace how trance is implicated within dance studies and cultural studies, with particular reference to post-colonial theory and, through case studies, examine possible cultural models for trance behaviour.

In 2003, upon learning of my developing interest in trance, a colleague suggested that in addition to my three Canadian case-study respondents, Brian Webb, Zab Maboungou, and Margie Gillis, I might consider South African dancer, choreographer, and healer Vincent Sekwati Mantsoe. After some preliminary research, I learned of Mantsoe's overt relationship with trance and of his connections with a number of Canadian contemporary dance organizations including the National Arts Centre, Fondation Jean-Pierre Perreault, DanceWorks, and the Collective of Black Artists (COBA). I contacted Mantsoe and described my research goals; he readily accepted my invitation to take part in my research.

From the onset, it was clear that, in embarking on this fieldwork, I would need to be cognizant of the elements of difference at play in my relationship with Mantsoe as a respondent. As a white, Canadian, English-speaking woman from southern Ontario, I was aware of the rudiments of difference at many levels—gender, ethnicity, race, skin colour, age, language, country of origin, culture, upbringing, spirituality, colonial legacy, politics, life experience, dance training, and so on. But understanding exactly how our particular difference was constructed was less easy to articulate. The impetus for our meeting was derived from a Eurocentric desire for higher education prefaced on book learning and, in my particular case, on an ethnographic methodology that necessitates identification and analysis of an *Other*. As the black African male subject to the white North American female observer, our interaction could have been predicated on the quintessential, frequently didactic relationship of respondent Other to anthropologist *Self*. Yet, in entering the relationship with an awareness of and appreciation for difference at many levels, a keenly self-reflexive, nuanced perspective was required in order to diffuse the Self–Other dichotomy and to "de-Other" trance as a subject of study.

Additionally, working with Mantsoe provided an interesting angle on the researcher–respondent relationship. With the traditional anthropological model, the researcher typically goes to the home of the subject to observe the person in her native habitat. In my fieldwork example, the opportunity

Figure 1 Vincent Sekwati Mantsoe in *NDAA*, 2003. Photographer: John Hogg.

to meet, interact and observe my subject was occasioned because Mant-soe entered *my* native habitat—all of our interactions occurred in Toronto between 2005 and 2007.

In an article on the transnational elites in global cities, Jonathan Bea-verstock, a professor of economic geography, argues that the "cosmopolitan working, cultural and social practices" of "nomadic, highly mobile and affluent transnational elites in the corporate segments of the service economy are ... highly spatialized and embedded in the network of global cities" (Beaverstock 2002: 527). Though Beaverstock's argument pertains to transnational investment bankers, information technology professionals, business analysts, consultants, and the like, his description could easily be applied to Mantsoe. He is nomadic, highly mobile, and a contributor to the currency of "global culture." Mantsoe's potential to travel the world, create choreography, and bring his work to new stages is limited only by his own endurance and his hosts' capacities to commission him. His work is concentrated in urban centres with existing multicultural communities, ongoing public support for the arts, and a cosmopolitan audience base who patronize his performances. In his own way, he is very much part of a transnational elite that contributes both culturally and intellectually to the proliferation of global cities and to the exchange and adoption of images, sounds, and symbols that cannot be traced to any one culture. It is within this milieu that Mantsoe is active: he, his French wife (who is also a dancer), and their young daughter live and have a studio in Saint Pont, France; he speaks English, French. and several native South African languages; he makes frequent trips home to Soweto; he receives funding from the South African and French governments; his website is hosted in South Africa; and in 2007, he performed in Canada, the United States, Colombia, Sweden, France, the United Kingdom, and Korea. As an active participant in a globalized economy that supports an open market for cultural exports, Mantsoe presents a distinctly postmodern challenge to anthropology. If one accepts that habitus—the universalizing paradigm that supposes an individual's habits, responses, and practices, and that without explicit analysis or meditation, defines what is implicitly "reasonable" and "sensible" for an individual (Bourdieu 1977: 72, 79)—is linked to culture, then it is not unreasonable to suggest that the habitus (and, by extension, one's culture) accompanies a person when he travels through the world, beyond his or her native habitat. If this is the case, then fieldwork conducted away from the respondent's home is no more or less effectively positioned to produce the thick description of traditional ethnography. Mantsoe's "awayness" formed the framework for my fieldwork and was likewise critical to my analysis of the data I collected.

Before considering Mantsoe's particular relationship to trance, I found it necessary to explore trance more broadly as a form of "altered states of consciousness." In 1902, pioneering American psychologist and philosopher William James published *The Varieties of Religious Experience*. On the subject of altered states of consciousness, he writes,

> Our normal waking consciousness, natural consciousness, as we call it, is but one special type of consciousness.... We may go through life without suspecting their existence; but apply the requisite stimulus, and at a touch they are there in all their completeness, definite types of mentality which probably somewhere have their field of application and adaptation. (James [1902] 1985: 16)

A decade earlier, in a *Scribner's Magazine* article entitled "The Hidden Self," James states that the "trance-condition is an immensely complex and fluctuating thing, into the understanding of which we have hardly begun to penetrate, and concerning which any sweeping generalization is sure to be premature" (James 1890: 363). In more than a century, very little has changed. In the 1960s, when American experimental psychologist Charles Tart went looking for a definition of trance for his book *States of Consciousness*, he soon discovered that for every definite characteristic of trance mentioned by an "authority," he found another source that contradicted it (Tart in Inglis 1989: 7). "Even within trancing communities," American ethnomusicologist Judith Becker explains, "the very ambiguity of trance leads to conflicting interpretations" (Becker 2004: 30). This supports the suggestion that tendering any definition of trance is "contentious" (Howard 2000: 363). While transparency is still very much an issue, the wealth of literature on trance—and related subjects of ecstasy, possession, and shamanism—demonstrates a plethora of activity and interest across a number of disciplines.

Reminiscent of James's work, Finnish researcher Anna-Leena Siikala defines trance as a "form of behaviour deviating from what is normal in a wakened state." She continues, describing the "typical features" of trance as including "modifications to the grasp of reality and the self-concept, with the intensity of change varying from slight alteration to complete loss of consciousness" (Siikala 1978: 39). Helmut Wautischer, writing on the philosophy of anthropology, argues that in a state of trance, "perception of reality appears to extend beyond the usual spatial and temporal boundaries that are normally perceived by the sense organs" (Wautischer 1989: 35). Interestingly, he adds that trance is "generally considered *a passage* into another state of consciousness" rather than a state in and of itself (Wautischer 1989: 40). Dennis Wier, the author of two books on trance, believes that trance has "something to do with energy utilization and the potentiation of creativity," where awareness is "focused" and "broad awareness" inhibited (Wier 1996: 23).

Some researchers discuss trance in symbolist, existential terms such as "the space of death" (Taussig 1987: 448) or "symbolic death" (Eliade

1964), or in neo-pagan terms as in the "renewal and awareness of ancient tribal practices" (Partridge 2004: 169). Psycho-spiritual aspects emerge as "ruptures in planes" (Eliade 1964) and/or "a kind of syncope, an absence, a lapse, a cerebral eclipse ... viewed as a manifestation of a divine blessing, or a demonic possession" (Becker 2004: 25). Analyses of trance draw on the field of neuroscience (Lex 1979; D'Aquili 1979; Wright 1989; D'Aquili and Newberg 1999; D'Aquili, Newberg and Rause 2001; Bressan and Crippa 2005; Boso et al. 2006) where the experience is described in terms of "chemical changes" in "the brain's functioning" and the "automatic nervous system" (Howard 2000: 364). Descriptions of trance drawn from the ethnographic literature often appear as catalogues of symptoms including amnesia, depersonalization, derealization, and identity shifts, (Suryani 1993; Card na 1989; Saxena and Prasad 1989; Steinberg 1991); a range of alterations in qualitative functioning including, but not limited to, a disturbed sense of time, changes in body image, change in emotional expression, a sense of the ineffable, feelings of rejuvenation, increased motor skills, hyper-suggestibility, and the deferral of pain (Belo 1960; Ludwig 1966; Laski 1968; Courlander 1972; Kartomi 1973; Bourguignon 1973, 1976; Drewal 1975; Hetherington 1975; Knoll 1979; Newman 1979; Peters and Price-Williams 1980; Lambek 1981; Prince 1982; Foley 1985; Locke and Kelly 1985; Rouget 1985; Heinze 1988; Simpson 1997; Averbuch 1998; Stuart and Hu 1998; Tessler 1998; Coldiron 2004); and, "emotional arousal, loss of sense of self, cessation of inner language, and an extraordinary ability to withstand fatigue" combined with the "loss of sense of time" and "trance amnesia" or the "inability to recall what transpired during trance" (Becker 2004: 29). These symptoms may be "recognized subjectively by the individual himself (or by an objective observer) as representing a sufficient deviation from subject experience or psychological functioning from certain norms" (Ludwig 1969: 9–10).

In 1986, anthropologist Michael Winkelman published his findings on the "psycho-physiological effects of different techniques and procedures" used for "trance induction" and found that trance response was mitigated by auditory stimulation; fasting and nutrition; social isolation and sensory deprivation; meditation; sleep patterns; sexual abstinence or prolonged stimulation; increased motor behaviour; and the ingestion of stimulants such as opiates, hallucinogens, and alcohol (Winkelman 1986: 178–183). The connections between trance and auditory stimulation have been explored through the vehicle of rave culture (Weil and Rosen 1993; Saunders 1996; Collin 1998; Gore 1997; Reynolds 1998; Brewster and Broughton 1999; Fritz 1999; Malbon 1999; Measham et al. 2001; Fatone 2001; Regan 2001; Shapiro 2005), with reference to medicine and healing

(Schadewaldt 1971; McClellan 1991; Gouk 2000; Horden 2000; Howard 2000; Becker 2004; Aldridge and Fachner 2006; Schneck and Berger 2006), alternative spiritualities (Inglis 1989; Partridge 2004; Sylvan 2005), glossolalia and Pentecostalism (Goodman 1972; Kelsey 1981; Holm 1987; Cartledge 2002), and as part of electronic music culture (Prendergast 2000). Collectively, these works effectively demonstrate the presence of trance in Western culture of the twentieth and twenty-first centuries and its manifestation through the combination of music and dancing (as forms of "increased motor behaviour") often, but not exclusively, in concert with recreational drug use. Yet nowhere have these same principles been applied to contemporary *art* dance practice. This would appear to be inappropriate if one considers the following examples:

> Once I get on stage it's like I go into a different place. I don't feel my body, I don't feel my legs, my arms—I don't feel anything. I totally erase my mind; I'm not thinking about anything. I do things that I would never believe that I could do but I do them…. It's just like your heart and your soul is [*sic*] completely open and you're just communicating with the audience somehow and you're talking to them through the dancing. It's like someone from up here [gestures upwards] is using me as a puppet and I don't really have … [trails off] Sometimes I finish the performance and I say [to myself] *what the hell have I done?* (Angel Corella, in Kinberg and Nimerichter 2002)

> There have been certain moments on the stage where I suddenly had a feeling of completeness…. I felt like a total being …it was a feeling of *I am*. At those moments I had the sense of being universal … but not in any specific form. (Erik Bruhn in Gruen 1986: 33)

> When I'm in the studio, when I'm warm, when I'm what people call improvising…. That's when I'm in a certain state where the cerebral powers are turned off, and the body just goes according to directive…. It's at those times that I feel a very special connection to … [trails off] I feel the most *right*. I don't want to become too mystic about this, but things feel as though they're in the best order at that particular moment.
> It's a short period. It lasts, at maximum, an hour. I pay a very great price to be able to maintain that. But—I use the same phrase over and over again—it is that hour that tells me who *I am*. (Twyla Tharp 1993)

In the introduction to his book *Trance: A Natural History of Altered States of Mind*, British journalist and historian Brian Inglis writes,

> Colloquially, trance has a range of meanings, particularly in connection with sport ... commonly used about somebody who is in full possession of his faculties, but in a frame of mind that makes him oblivious to his surroundings.... [Trance has also] been employed to describe a condition when a player feels taken over, almost possessed, by a force which seems to play through him and for him, better than he could hope to play himself. (Inglis 1989: 9)

Understanding dance as a form of high-performance athleticism (Patrick 1978; Arnold 1990; Reed 1998; Dyck 2003; Hargreaves 2007), taken together with some of Winkelman's techniques such as auditory stimulation, fasting and nutrition, social isolation, and increased motor behaviour, one begins to recognize how trance could be an appropriate appellation in respect to contemporary dancers and contemporary dance practice. Yet again, as American medical anthropologist and specialist in transcultural psychiatry, Arthur Kleinman argues, "only the modern, secular, West seems to [in certain circumstances] have blocked individuals' access to these otherwise pan-human dimensions of the self" (Kleinman 1988: 50). It would appear, then, that the West's blind spot is curiously selective. Certainly alongside the statements made by Western-based dancers, Mantsoe's experience of trance states, when he feels "the gods flowing through" him, where he is "elongated," "made whole," at once "infinite" and "finite," "made and unmade," "created," "reborn," "turning" and "being turned," imply that there is a basis from which to not simply draw but to sustain comparison, whether in Johannesburg or Toronto.

Engaging specifically with the work of post-colonial scholars James Clifford—his theories of collecting and identity formation (1988)—and Arjun Appadurai—his theories of commoditization in cultural practice (1986)—I address here the ways in which trance functions as both an artefact and a traded commodity in a globalized economy and how that trade influences embodiment as exemplified by South African shaman and dancer Vincent Sekwati Mantsoe in his performance of his 2003 work *NDAA* (NDAA is a traditional Venda word meaning greetings). Building from descriptions of the differences between artefacts and commodities, I expand on what it means to speak of decolonizing and how this applies to Mantsoe and his work.

Watching Mantsoe dance, I am immediately aware of an intense vitality that is at once contained by his body and radiates outward. Whether he's performing live onstage or on video, the sheer pleasure that he exudes and the precision of his movements make him a captivating performer. Reviews of his work speak of Mantsoe's command, his virtuosity, and his clear and unwavering vision. In speaking with him, one learns that he credits the jubilant life force that audiences attribute to his performances to his ability to enter trance states. Through the vehicle of his living, breathing, dancing body, Mantsoe is able to open himself to the mysteries and healing energy of the spirit world, becoming a vessel for their knowledge and blessings. In his view, it is this rich interior life, based on traditional teachings and the pantheon of his native Zulu culture, mediated by his ability to enter altered states of consciousness, which forms the basis for his gift as a dancer (Mantsoe personal interview 2006).

Mantsoe grew up in the townships of South Africa. As a child and young adult, he participated in youth clubs, practising street dance and imitating the moves of Michael Jackson and other pop artists from American music videos. Throughout his childhood, he woke every day to the sound of his mother playing a drum to greet the ancestors.

In his late teens, Mantsoe began training in earnest with Johannesburg's Moving into Dance Mophatong Company (MIDM). Mantsoe was deeply influenced by MIDM's signature fusion of African ritual, music, and dance with Western contemporary dance forms. With this early training in mind, he continues to describe his work as "Afro-fusion" (Mantsoe 2006).

Though Mantsoe had seen his grandmother, aunt, and mother commune with the spirit world through trance states, for reasons of gender, he was not trained and therefore not permitted to enter them himself. Yet it became apparent to his family that Mantsoe had inherited a propensity for traditional ways—that his "openness" to the spirits and to the *sangoma* or shaman ways was "strong" (Mantsoe personal interview 2006). After consulting the spirits, Mantsoe's aunt and grandmother told him that he was to play a part in the family business: through the vehicle of his dancing, Mantsoe was to bring his family's knowledge and message to the world. The spirits had advised that he was to be a healing "ambassador" and that he was to travel to distant places as a teacher and performer (Mantsoe personal interview 2006). Since the 1990s, Mantsoe has pursued this ordained path, working steadily at the invitation of companies, festivals, and choreographers around the world.

In our encounters, Mantsoe had an unassuming, gracious presence. I was struck by his willingness to be interviewed, to share his knowledge. Our initial meeting, during his residency with COBA in Toronto, initiated a series of conversations and correspondences that took place over coffee, in the studio, via the Internet, backstage, and in the car between engagements. My fieldnotes speak often of his soft-spoken eloquence; his careful turn of phrase; and his enchanting combination of energy, warmth, and humility. He appears to understand that he is an object of fascination but he accepts this as part of his "calling," his "blessing," and does not appear at all perturbed by it. "I am very lucky," he said once. "People respect my work. They are intrigued by what I do onstage, by my relationship with the spirits, but they are always respectful" (Mantsoe, personal conversation 2006). For Mantsoe, my research was another avenue by which he could communicate his message and fulfil his duties to the gods. Conscious of and implicated in the white–black, European–African power imbalance, Mantsoe nonetheless represents himself and his work with equanimity. Far from being disempowered or politically unaware, Mantsoe appears simply to be choosing a means and a message that bridges cultures and understanding, conceived from a unique point of view and cultural experience.

Contextualizing Mantsoe's trade in trance requires understanding trance both as an artefact and as a commodity. According to James, in his seminal work *On Collecting Art and Culture*, an artefact is something prized for its cultural significance and is very much associated with the imperialist anthropological agenda. An artefact comes to signify something that is Other—distanced by time, space, geography, language, and culture, it expands the boundaries of the known world to include that which exists beyond the everyday. It is a reminder of what is achievable and conquerable. Removed from their original context, artefacts form the basis of collections. Simultaneously fixed and indeterminate, they beget identity and signify tenure. One is reminded of Claude Lévi-Strauss's essay "New York in 1941" (Lévi-Strauss 1985), where, according to the author, the city of New York is like a Victorian curio cabinet filled with masterpieces of pre-Columbian, South Asian, Oceanic, Japanese, and Native North American art that is simultaneously prized and forgotten, admired and undervalued.

A commodity, on the other hand, is invested with agency. Wrested from its original context or purpose, a commodity is invested with a value that is jointly created, by buyer and seller, owner and desirer. Even where the value—monetary or otherwise—is artificially inflated by scarcity, demand, or fads, the value to all stakeholders is acknowledged and, though vulnerable to manipulation, respected. Even when two disparate socio-economic systems meet and compete, there is an appreciation and restoration of value through the trade of commodities.

Today, Mantsoe is not an object of ethnographic classification and fascination from whom trance is procured without compensation but an active agent in the transaction. In working with Western dancers, companies and festivals, Mantsoe is participating in a process that subverts and potentially *decolonizes* the traditional flow of contact and information between

Figure 2   Vincent Sekwati Mantsoe in NDAA, 2003. Photographer: John Hogg.

Western and non-Western, wherein trance may be viewed less as an artefact and more as a traded commodity.

Decolonizing entails analyzing and exposing power relationships embedded in the representation of knowledge—who is being studied, by whom and for what purpose—and measuring those responses against imperialist principles that have pervaded academic research. In its most existential form, decolonizing is applied to the notion of subjectivity, bringing into question why one "sees" the way one does. Applied to post-coloniality, decolonizing subjectivity acknowledges that while the dynamics of oppression, trauma, and resistance may manifest in similar ways for all dispossessed peoples, how one experiences the world and one's history is always experienced in a profoundly individual way.

Applied to Mantsoe, decolonizing functions in two ways. First, as the conventional subject of anthropological research, Mantsoe has inverted the traditional flow of knowledge by bringing himself and his use of trance to the attention of the West. Unlike the cultural fairs of the Victorian and Edwardian ages, which saw the importation of indigenous peoples in staged exhibits of the "primitive" and "authentic" for a spectacle-hungry public, Mantsoe positions himself as an active and instigative agent in the exchange within the arena of high culture. Second, Mantsoe is engaged in decolonizing his own subjectivity through his performances of trance—this is particularly clear in *NDAA*. In performing *NDAA*, Mantsoe questions the relationship he has with his multiple audiences—the spirits, spectators, the cosmos, and his own consciousness—challenging both how he sees and is seen. In describing this piece, Mantsoe speaks of an "awakening of the self." From the moment he enters the performance space, he begins the process toward trance. It is there inside him and also hovering on the edge of his kinesphere waiting to be summoned. His awakening begins slowly, tentatively, then his movements gradually expand as the distance between inner and outer is breached. In *NDAA*, as in Mantsoe's habitus, the Self is neither an isolated nor bounded being. It his past, his present and his future, his ancestors, his siblings, his grandchildren not yet born. In performing *NDAA* he asks,

> Is there anyone here, is there something around me that I cannot see or hear? Do I exist between reality and the imaginary? Do you see me? Between us, life passes us without knowing if it ever existed, we breathe the human flesh that we do not see. (Mantsoe 2006)

In *Decolonizing Methodologies* (1999), Linda Tuhiwai Smith looks at the collection of artefacts as an aspect of the colonialist enterprise. "The idea that collectors were actually rescuing artefacts from decay and destruction," Tuhiwai Smith explains, "and from the indigenous peoples themselves, legitimated practices which also included commercial trade and plain and simple theft" (Tuhiwai Smith 1999: 61). Through her writing, it is clear that Tuhiwai Smith wishes to invest the colonized with agency. To view the anthropologists' endeavour as one-sided and limited to their own action, is to deny the colonized their involvement—however coerced—in the colonial enterprise and in its aftermath. Like Homi Bhabha before her, Tuhiwai Smith contributes to the critical discussion of the post-colonial. Where Bhabha liberates the colonized from their "inscription as Europe's shackled Other" and recognizes that the colonized subject can, indeed, speak for him- or herself (Bhabha 1994), Tuhiwai Smith brings the discussion to a much more prosaic level in discussing the act and impact of trade. Here, trade by definition acknowledges the existence and contribution of two sides regardless of the issue of equality or neutrality. The trade of goods—some, as Tuhiwai Smith suggests, were in fact "made to order"—imparts a story of meeting, a declaration of desire, appraisal, debate, resolution, and potential exchange if all prior stages were enacted in a satisfactory manner (Tuhiwai Smith 1999: 61).

For Mantsoe, participating in the trade and acquisition of his cultural and bodily knowledge is part of a moral responsibility he feels is incumbent upon him. He states,

> My purpose is to re-educate, to reintroduce [traditional] practices, to balance traditions with the concerns of modern times. I want to be open, I want to talk about it.... It is important for me to know who I am and where I come from. And to believe that maybe other people can learn something from that. (Mantsoe, in Braun 2006)

While Appadurai's work has focused primarily on issues of modernity and globalization, his theories on the creation and circulation of commodities has particular relevance to this discussion. Building from the premise that commodities, like persons, have "social lives" (Appadurai 1986: 3) Appadurai argues that, through the act of economic exchange, things acquire value where value is something that is attributed to and projected onto the things that are exchanged. By focusing on the things themselves rather than on the form and function that exchange takes allows one to acknowledge that the relationship between exchange and value is determined socially. Understanding why commodities are economically valuable and how they came to be regarded as such presents an opportunity to understand and assess the history of objects, their changes in value, and their trajectories as components or, in fact, foci of social interaction.

Without anthropomorphizing, Appadurai contends that objects have social lives by virtue of the role they play in representing and contesting value both as objects in themselves and in their relation to their owners as properties or assets. If one understands trance as a commodity, as an object of trade, then through Mantsoe's work and his positioning vis-à-vis a globalized economy, one can appreciate how "objects circulate in different regimes of value in space and time," in "specific cultural and historical milieus" and, as a result, acquire social lives (Appadurai 1986: 4).

Watching Mantsoe perform *NDAA*, one is aware through the attunement of his body and focus that he is not alone on stage. As he enters a trance state, he is looking about him, whispering and talking to unseen but present entities. The music for the work features a recording of the everyday chatter and conversation of Gabon's Bibayak Pygmies. In this setting, Mantsoe performs his habitus, thousands of miles from his homeland. *NDAA* is a solo work but Mantsoe performs his place in his community of neighbours, spirits, and ancestors. He is made and defined by them; he is in their presence and they in his—as he says, he inhales the human flesh he cannot see and it becomes part of him. He is not a specimen, he is an individual within a collective of humanity and consciousness, constantly being made and unmade by his relationships with others. His ability to communicate with the spirit world through trance adds another layer to his beingness in the world—a collective beingness that is not defined by an ethnographic lens but is defined by him and his identity in relation to others. Mantsoe's trance states allow him to act as a liaison between a number of different selves. These relationships are produced and reproduced through the trance object that is brought to the attention and into the presence of a consuming audience.

Mantsoe is an active participant in a globalized economy that supports an open market for cultural exports. International co-productions that involve multiple countries and collaborators of various ethnicities and nationalities, working in shared idioms of language and form that defy geographical borders are becoming increasingly common. It is within this milieu that Mantsoe is active. Commodities in this transnational performing arts arena are created out of a desire for the new, the unusual, and the extraordinary and, within this, the authentic. Someone like Mantsoe, who embodies the traditional and the contemporary, is invested with a divine gift yet is equally at ease in the secular, technologized, multinational economy, is keenly positioned to respond to and profit from the current market—this was never as clear to me as when we sat together in an international coffee shop chain in Toronto on an excruciatingly hot day in July with the air conditioning blasting, his iPod hanging around his neck, and Mantsoe telling me that he is descended from a long line of shamans and is himself a shaman (Mantsoe personal interview 2006). "You know, I really am a modern guy," Mantsoe explains to a reviewer in 2005. "I still believe in and am nourished by this modern world" (Braun 2005).

In Mantsoe, trance is an embodied object that he simultaneously brings with him and that moves through him. When one watches Mantsoe dance, there is a sense of a rolling energy building and growing, that follows a transition from intense introspection toward release and revelation. The capacity to enter trance states—like a pilot light that never goes out—resides in his body.

Trance is an intangible action, a mystical concept housed in his body yet in touring around the globe he is circulating and trading in trance. His value as a dancer and trance practitioner is acknowledged equally by his own and his host cultures on either side of the residual West–non-West divide. Even when the West places a monetary value on his skills that cannot truly compensate for their inestimable value, the gods still condescend through their immortal goodness to bring knowledge to the uninitiated through the vehicle of his dancing, trancing body. Mantsoe is the thing in motion, illuminating the human and social dimensions of his existence and his own agency—the globalizing forces of traditional and contemporary, colonial and post-colonial, a human in touch with the divine, a beautiful and exuberant dancer working with the blessings of the gods at the invitation of the patronizing West.

Note

1 This paper is extracted from my PhD dissertation, "Trance as Artefact: De-Othering Transformative States with Reference to Examples from Contemporary Dance in Canada," University of Surrey, 2007.

Bibliography

Aldridge, David, and Jorg Fachner. *Music and Altered States: Consciousness, Transcendence, Therapy, and Addiction.* Philadelphia: Jessica Kingsley, 2006.

Appadurai, Arjun. "Introduction: Commodities and the Politics of Value." In Arjun Appadurai (ed.), *The Social Life of Things: Commodities in Cultural Perspective.* New York: Cambridge University Press, 1986.

Appleman Williams, William. *America in Vietnam: A Documentary History.* Garden City, NJ: Anchor Press, 1985.

Arnold, Peter J. "Sport, Aesthetic and Art: Further Thoughts." *British Journal of Educational Studies* 28, no. 2 (May 1990): 160–79.

Averbuch, Irit. "Shamanic Dance in Japan: The Choreography of Possession in Kagura Performance." *Asian Folklore Studies* 57, no. 2 (1998): 293–329.

Beaverstock, Jonathan V. "Transnational Elites in Global Cities: British Expatriates in Singapore's Financial District." *Geoforum* 33, no. 4 (November 2002): 525–38.

Becker, Judith. *Deep Listening: Music, Emotion, and Trancing.* Bloomington: Indiana University Press, 2004.

Belo, Jane. *Trance in Bali.* New York: Columbia University Press, 1960.

Bhabha, Homi. *The Location of Culture.* London: Routledge, 1994.

Blaut, James M. *The National Question: Decolonizing the Theory of Nationalism.* London: Zed Books, 1987.

Bonn, Moritz J. The *Crumbling of Empire: The Disintegration of World Economy.* London: Allen Press, 1938.

Boso, Marianna, Pierluigi Politi, Francesco Barala, and Enzo Emmanuele. "Neurophysiology and Neurobiology of the Musical Experience." *Functional Neurology* 21, no. 4 (2006): 187–91.

Bourdieu, P. *Outline of a Theory of Practice.* Cambridge: Cambridge University Press, 1977.

Bourguignon, Erika. *Religion, Altered States of Consciousness, and Social Change.* Columbus: Ohio State University Press, 1973.

Braun, Josef. 'Mantsoe Fast.' *Vue Weekly* (2005). www.vueweekly.com/articles/default .aspx?i=2715 (accessed February 12, 2005).

Bressan, Rodrigo A., and José Alexandre Crippa. "The Role of Dopamine in Reward and Pleasure—Review from Preclinical Research." *Acta Psychiatrica Scandinavica* 111, supplement 427 (June 2005): 14–21.

Brewster, Bill, and Frank Broughton. *Last Night a DJ Saved My Life: The History of the Disc Jockey.* London: Headline, 1999.

Caraway, Nancie. *Segregated Sisterhood: Racism and the Politics of American Feminism.* Knoxville: University of Tennessee Press, 1999.

Cardĕna, Etzel. "The Varieties of Possession Experience." *Association for the Anthropological Study of Consciousness Quarterly* 5, vol. 2, no. 3 (1992): 1–17.

Cartledge, Mark J. *Charismatic Glossolalia: An Empirical-Theological Study.* Aldershot: Ashgate, 2002.

Chow, Esther Njan-ling. *Transforming Gender and Development in East Asia.* New York: Routledge Press, 2002.

Clifford, J. "On Collecting Art and Culture." In *The Predicament of Culture: Twentieth Century Ethnography, Literature and Art.* Cambridge, MA: Harvard University Press, 1988.

Coldiron, Margaret. *Trance and Transformation of the Actor in Japanese Noh and Balinese Masked Dance-Drama.* Lewiston: E. Mellen Press, 2004.

Collin, Matthew. *Altered State: The Story of Ecstasy Culture and Acid House.* London: Serpent's Tail, 1998.

Courlander, Harold. "Dance and Dance-Drama in Haiti in Boas." In Franziska Boas (ed.), *The Function of Dance in Human Society.* New York: Dance Horizons, 1972: 41–53.

D'Aquili, Eugene G. *The Spectrum of Ritual: A Biogenetic Structural Analysis*. New York: Columbia University Press, 1979.

———, and Andrew B. Newberg. *The Mystical Mind Probing the Biology of Religious Experience*. New York: Fortress Press, 1999.

Drewal, Margaret Thompson. "Symbols of Possession: A Study of Movement and Regalia in an Anago-Yoruba Ceremony." *Dance Research Journal* 7, no. 2 (Spring/Summer 1975): 15–24.

Dyck, Noel, and Eduardo P. Archetti (eds.). *Sport, Dance, and Embodied Identities*. New York: Berg, 2003.

Eliade, M. *Shamanism: Archaic Techniques of Ecstasy*. Princeton, NJ: Princeton University Press, [1964] 2004.

Esedebe, P. Olisanwuche. *Pan-Africanism: The Idea and the Movement, 1776–1991*. Washington, DC: Howard University Press, 1994.

Fatone, Gina. *We Thank the Technology Goddess for Giving Us the Ability to Rave: Gamelan, Techno-Primitivism, and the San Francisco Rave Scene* (2001). http://www.echo.ucla.edu/Volume3-Issue1/fatone/fatone1.html (accessed April 11, 2007).

Foley, Kathy. "The Dancer and the Danced: Trance Dance and Theatrical Performance in West Java." *Asian Theatre Journal* 2, no. 1 (1985): 28–49.

Fritz, Jimi. *Rave Culture: An Insider's Overview*. Canada: Small Fry Press, 1999.

Geary, Patrick. "Sacred Commodities: The Circulation of Medieval Relics." In Arjun Appadurai (ed.), *The Social Life of Things: Commodities in Cultural Perspective*. New York: Cambridge University Press, 1986.

Goodman, Felicitas, D. *Speaking in Tongues: A Cross-Cultural Study of Glossolalia*. Chicago: University of Chicago Press, 1972.

Gore, Georgianna. "The Beat Goes On: Trance, Dance and Tribalism in Rave Culture." In Helen Thomas (ed.), *Dance in the City*. London: MacMillan Press, 1997: 50–67.

Gouk, Penelope (ed.) *Musical Healing in Cultural Contexts*. London: Ashgate, 2000.

Gruen, John. *The Private World of Ballet*. New York: Viking, 1975.

Hargreaves, Jennifer, and Patricia Vertinsky (eds.). *Physical Culture, Power, and the Body*. New York: Routledge, 2007.

Heinze, Ruth-Inge. *Trance and Healing in Southeast Asia Today*. Bangkok: White Lotus, 1988.

Henry, Annette. *Taking Back Control: African Canadian Women Teachers' Lives and Practice*. Albany: University of New York State Press, 1998.

Hetherington, Ralph. *The Sense of Glory: A Psychological Study of Peak-Experiences*. London: Friends Home Service Committee, 1975.

Holm, Nils G. "Sunden's Role Theory and Glossolalia." *Journal for the Scientific Study of Religion* 26, no. 3 (September 1987): 383–89.

Hordon, Peregrine (ed.). *Music as Medicine: The History of Music Therapy since Antiquity*. Aldershot, UK: Ashgate, 2000.

———. "Connecting on Part I, with a Note on the Origins of Tarantism." In Peregrine Hordon (ed.), *Music as Medicine: The History of Music Therapy since Antiquity*. Aldershot, UK: Ashgate, 2000: 249–54.

Howard, Keith. "Shamanism, Music, and Soul Train." In P. Hordon (ed.), *Music as Medicine: The History of Music Therapy since Antiquity.* Aldershot: Ashgate, 2000: 353–74.

Inglis, Brian. *Trance: A Natural History of Altered States of Mind.* London: Grafton, 1989.

James, W. *The Varieties of Religious Experience: A Study of Human Nature* [1902]. New York: Penguin, 1985.

———. "The Hidden Self." *Scribner's Magazine* 7 (1890): 361–73.

Jameson, F. *Postmodernism, or the Cultural Logic of Late Capitalism.* Durham, NC: Duke University Press, 1990.

Kartomi, Margaret J. "Music and Trance in Central Java." *Ethnomusicology* 17, no. 2 (May 1973): 163–208.

Kelsey, Morton T. *Tongue Speaking: The History and Meaning of Charismatic Experience.* New York: Crossroad, 1981.

Kinberg, Judy, and Jodee Nimerichter. "Born to Be Wild: The Leading Men of American Ballet Theatre." *Dance in America.* DVD. New York: PBS, 2002.

Kleinman, Arthur. *Rethinking Psychiatry: From Cultural Category to Personal Experience.* New York: Free Press and Collier-Macmillan, 1988.

Knoll, Teri. "Dance in Bali: The Reaffirmation of a Sense of Community." *Journal of the Association of Graduate Dance Ethnologists* 3 (Fall/Winter 1979–80): 9–13.

Lambek, Michael. *Human Spirits: A Cultural Account of Trance in Mayotte.* Cambridge: Cambridge University Press, 1981.

Laski, Margharita. *Ecstasy: A Study of Some Secular and Religious Experiences.* New York: Greenwood, 1968.

Lévi-Strauss, Claude. *The View from Afar.* New York: Basic, 1985.

Lex, Barbara. "The Neurobiology of Ritual Trance." In Eugene d'Aquili (ed.), *The Spectrum of Ritual: A Biogenetic Structual Analysis.* New York: Columbia University Press, 1979.

Locke, Ralph G., and Edward F. Kelly. "A Preliminary Model for the Cross-Cultural Analysis of Altered States of Consciousness." *Ethos* 13, no. 1 (1985): 3–55.

Low, Setha. "Protest of the Body." *Medical Anthropology Quarterly Conceptual Development in Medical Anthropology: A Tribute to M. Margaret Clarke,* n.s., 8, 4 (December 1994): 476–78.

Ludwig, Arnold M. "Altered States of Consciousness." *Archives of General Psychiatry* 15 (1966): 225–34.

———. "Altered States of Consciousness." In C. Tart (ed.), *Altered States of Consciousness,* New York: Wiley, 1969: 9–22.

Malbon, Ben. *Clubbing: Dancing, Ecstasy and Vitality.* London: Routledge, 1999.

Mantsoe, Vincent Sekwati. Personal interview. Toronto, June 13, 2006.

———. *Vincent Sekwati Koko Mantsoe: Choreographer / Dancer / Teacher* (2006). http://www.sekwaman.co.za/about.htm (accessed June 17, 2006).

Mbilinyi, Marjorie, and Ruth Meena. "Reports from Four Women's Groups in Africa." *Signs: Journal of Women in Culture and Society* 6, no. 4 (1991): 846–48.

McClellan, Randall. *The Healing Forces of Music.* Rockport: Element, 1991.

Measham, Fiona, Judith Aldridge, and Howard Parker. *Dancing on Drugs: Risk, Health, and Hedonism in the British Club Scene.* London: Free Association Books, 2001.

Newberg, Andrew, Eugene D'Aquili, and Vince Rause. *Why God Won't Go Away: Brain Science and the Biology of Belief.* New York: Ballantine, 2001.

Newman, Anita F. "The Bridge between Physical and Conceptual Reality: The Trance Experience of the !Kung Bushmen." *Journal of the Association of Graduate Dance Ethnologists* 3 (Fall/Winter 1979–80): 1–7.

Ngugi wa Thiong'o. *Decolonising the Mind: The Politics of Language in African Literature.* London: James Currey, 1987.

Partridge, Christopher. *The Re-enchantment of the West: Alternative Spiritualities, Sacralization, Popular Culture and Occulture.* 2 vols. London: T & T Clark International, 2004.

Patrick, Pamela. "Ballet as Sport: Athletes on Pointe." *Frontiers: A Journal of Women's Studies* 3, no. 1 (Spring 1978): 20–21.

Pérez, Emma. *The Decolonial Imaginary: Writing Chicanas into History.* Bloomington: Indiana University Press, 1999.

Peters, Larry G., and Douglass Richard Price-Williams. "Towards an Experiential Analysis of Shamanism." *American Ethnologist* 7, no. 3 (August 1980): 397–418.

Prendergast, Mark. *The Ambient Century: From Mahler to Trance—The Evolution of Sound in the Electronic Age.* London: Bloomsbury, 2000.

Prince, Morton. *The Dissociation of a Personality.* Paris: F. Alcan, 1911.

Reed, Susan A. "The Politics and Poetics of Dance." *Annual Review of Anthropology* 27, no. 2 (1998): 503–32.

Regan, Ciaran. *Intoxicating Minds: How Drugs Work.* New York: Columbia University Press, 2001.

Reynolds, Simon. *Energy Flash: A Journey through Rave Music and Dance Culture.* London: Picador, 1998.

Rogers, Linda, and Beth Blue. "Reframing the 'Field.'" *Anthropology and Education Quarterly* 30, no. 4 (December 1999): 436–40.

Ross, Luana. *Inventing the Savage: The Social Construction of Native American Criminality.* Austin: University of Texas Press, 1998.

Simpson, Faith. "Trance-Dance: An Ethnography of Dervish Whirling." Unpublished MA thesis, University of Surrey, 1997.

Rouget, Gilbert. *Music and Trance: A Theory of the Relations between Music and Possession.* Chicago: University of Chicago Press, 1985.

Saunders, Nicholas. *Ecstasy: Dance, Trance and Transformation.* Oakland: Quick American Archives, 1996.

———. *Ecstasy Reconsidered, with a Bibliography by Alexander Shulgin.* London: Neal's Yard Press, 1997.

Saxena, Shekhar and K.V. Prasad. "K.V.S.K. DSM-III Subclassification of Dissociative Disorders Applied to Psychiatric Outpatients in India." *American Journal of Psychiatry* 146, no. 22 (1989): 261–62.

Schadewaldt, Hans. *Musik und Medizin (Music and Medicine).* Hamburg: Arztliche, 1971.

Schneck, Daniel J., and Dorita S. Berger. *The Music Effect: Music Physiology and Clinical Applications*. Philadelphia: Jessica Kingsley, 2006.

Shapiro, Harry. *Waiting for the Man: The Story of Drugs and Popular Music*. London: Helter Skelter, 2005.

Siikala, Anna-Leena. *The Rite Technique of the Siberian Shaman*. Helsinki: FF Communications, 1978.

Steinberg, Marlene. "The Spectrum of Depersonalization: Assessment and Treatment in Tasman." In Allan and Stephen M. Goldfinger (eds.), *Psychiatric Review*. Washington: American Psychiatric Press, 1991.

Stuart, Kevin, and Jun Hu. "That All May Prosper: The Monguor (Tu) Nadun of the Guanting/Sanchuan Region, Qinghai, China." *Anthropos* 88, no. 1–3 (1993): 15–27.

Suryani, Luh Ketut. *Trance and Possession in Bali: A Window on Western Multiple Personality, Possession Disorder, and Suicide*. New York: Oxford University Press, 1993.

Sylvan, Robin. *Trance Formation: The Spiritual and Religious Dimensions of Global Rave Culture*. New York: Routledge, 2005.

Taussig, M. *Shamanism, Colonialism, and the Wild Man: A Study in Terror and Healing*. Chicago: University of Chicago Press, 1987.

Tessler, Eva Zorilla. "Body and Identity in Afro-Brazilian Candomblé." *Choreography and Dance* 5 (1998): 103–15.

Tharp, Twyla. "Twyla Tharp: Interview, Choreographing the Next Step Forward in Academy of Achievement: A Museum of Living History" (June 25, 1993). http://www.achievement.org/autodoc/page/tha0int-1 (accessed February 28, 2007).

Tuhiwai Smith, Linda. *Decolonizing Methodologies*. New York: Zed Books, 1999.

Wautischer, Helmut. "A Philosophical Inquiry to Include Shamanism in Epistemology." *Journal of Psychoactive Drugs* 21, no. 1 (January–March 1989): 35–46.

Weil, Andrew T., and Winifred Rosen. *From Chocolate to Morphine: Everything You Need to Know about Mind-Altering Drugs*. New York: Houghton Mifflin, 1993.

Wier, Dennis. *Trance: From Magic to Technology*. Ann Arbor, MI: Trans Media, 1996.

Winkelman, Michael. "Trance States: A Theoretical Model and Cross-Cultural Analysis." *Ethos* 14, no. 2 (Summer, 1986): 174–203.

Wright, Peggy Ann. "The Nature of the Shamanic State of Consciousness: A Review." *Journal of Psychoactive Drugs. Special Issue: Shamanism and Altered States of Consciousness* 21, no. 1 (January–March 1989): 25–33.

CHAPTER EIGHTEEN

Anthropophagic Bodies in Flea Market
A STUDY OF SHEILA RIBEIRO'S CHOREOGRAPHY

MÔNICA DANTAS

INTRODUCTION

Approaching the dancing body from the perspective of the dancers who work with Brazilian choreographers is a way of talking about my own trajectory in dance. My training is contemporary dance, and I have also worked as a dancer for Brazilian choreographers. As was true for most dancers in this study, I have always been aware of not merely being an object-body among other object-bodies in the hands of the choreographer because I offer myself to the chosen choreographers, ready to incorporate their universe and to modify myself according to their needs and demands. At the end of this process, I come out feeling transformed and enriched, both artistically and personally.

In a similar way, I have always been interested in understanding the development of theatrical dance in Brazil and for over a decade have been following the work of choreographers who articulate their contemporary dance creation through typical themes, techniques, and procedures of Brazilian culture. I inscribe the issue of contemporary dance with Brazilian characteristics within a broader context, including other fields of cultural production in Brazil, as well as its own theatrical dance history. As I have come to understand it, this history may be seen as the tension between the assimilation and reproduction of consecrated formats and styles—such as classical ballet and different forms of modern dance—as well as a concern with the creation of an indigenous theatrical dance with Brazilian characteristics. The theme of my research stems also from a tradition of thinking about culture and the arts as sources for constructing a national identity.

As Ortiz (1998) points out, this tendency is accentuated in peripheral countries like Brazil, becoming almost a constant thread in Brazilian thinking and producing a "collective intellectual itinerary." I feel that my own intellectual itinerary is a consequence of this theoretical environment, and, in some way, the analysis of work and of the artistic processes of some contemporary Brazilian choreographers allows me a better comprehension of the particularities of Brazil. I would also like to point out that I share these concerns with Eluza Santos, who introduces in this book her own ethnographic study of contemporary dance in Vitória, Brazil (1999).

Hanstein has argued that dance investigation should not move the researcher too far away from the dance experience itself: "We must not forget that at the heart of everything we do in dance is dance and dancing.... Our point of reference must always be rooted in the experience of dancing" (1999: 26). In agreement with her proposition, I decided to follow closely the experiences of two Brazilian choreographers, supporting my investigations by means of an ethnographic approach.[1] In this chapter, I will highlight my research project with choreographer Sheila Ribeiro and the dancers who worked in her company *dona orpheline danse*, focusing on the period when the group was restaging *Flea Market: We Are Used and Cheap*[2] for a tour to three Brazilian cities: São Paulo, Campinas, and Rio de Janeiro. During my fieldwork, I was studying and living in Montreal. And so it was that during the winter of 2001, I followed the preparation for the tour and attended the audition and the rehearsals that followed. The object of these rehearsals was to reassemble the show by way of memory and archival videotapes and/or modification and recreation of the original choreographic sequences. The object was also to adapt the work for a Brazilian audience by translating the spoken text and making certain changes to the songs. But for one, the dancers were the same ones as in the first version: Chris Kauffman, Louis Pelchat, Maryse Richard, and Ribeiro herself. Tara Santini had left the company and was being replaced by Nancy Rivest, who had been chosen during an audition. And so teaching Nancy the choreography, along with the adaptation of her role, was also another objective of the rehearsals.

Between April and June 2001, when the company returned to Brazil, I carried out the interviews: one with each dancer and two with the choreographer. I also collected documents, such as the company's advertising material, the performance program, and press articles, including reviews from arts critics. At the same time, Ribeiro also presented me with a preliminary version of her master's dissertation.[3] It is interesting to note that my entry into the company as a researcher was made easy, largely because I already knew Ribeiro, and so she didn't hesitate in collaborating. In fact, the choreographer and the dancers accepted my presence with no restrictions, facilitating my position in the field as effectively one of *participant* observer. Because of this mutual trust, we all ended up establishing a "small dialogues" dynamic during the rehearsals. Already during my first observation session, Ribeiro intimated her difficulty in sustaining her multiple roles in the company: administrative director, choreographer, the person in charge of rehearsals, and dancer. She then asked me if I would help her to rehearse her solo. Excited by this invitation, I jotted down in my field notes: "I love this idea, very participative observation." Thus, from my role as an observer, I sometimes slipped into that of rehearsal aide for Ribeiro's solo to the point where my name was even placed on the program as an "external advisor" (*oeil extérieur* in the original French).

I have no doubts that, throughout the study, all the stages of the investigation were influenced by the fact that I am a dancer and a Brazilian, which turned me into an insider seeking aspects of my own culture, radically rooted in my experience. Thus, while questioning the presence of certain traces of "brazilness" in Ribeiro's work, I met up with my own experiences and ideas of brazilness. At the same time, the fact that at the time of the study I had been living in Montreal (for a year and a half) deeply affected my experiences and consequently my conceptions about brazilness. Being away from home, living in a society that was not my own, allowed me to better observe from a distance what was going on unnoticed in my society and in my own behaviour (Laplantine 2000). There were many times in Montreal when I felt "more Brazilian" than when in Brazil: for instance, it seemed to me that the way I looked at people, gestured, moved, and even laughed, was quite different from that of native Montrealers. In sum, doing fieldwork with a Brazilian choreographer in Montreal had sharpened my perceptions about Brazil and constantly forced me to reconsider my concepts of brazilness.

The fact that I am a dancer, and that I have lived in several similar situations to the ones I was observing, also influenced my research. During my observations in the field, my experiences as a dancer helped me to better understand things such as the rehearsal settings, the communication difficulties between choreographer and dancers, as well as the creative and reconstructive choreographic processes. At the same time, I wasn't performing the role of dancer. My main task was to observe and take notes, not to dance. Observation of the company's work evoked for me other kinds of emotions. I became enchanted with watching the way in which the dancers worked out the minute details of a gesture, obsessively repeating a movement sequence in trying to find the precise dynamic required. They were so deeply engaged in embodying the choreographic work. I realized that I also felt frustrated because I was not dancing: the appeal of the movement to my body was so powerful that when I finished my fieldwork with the company, I began a solo choreography based on a new reading and deconstruction of the samba.

The field notes, interviews, rehearsal footage, videos from the performances, written documents: they all built up a mosaic of information which I systematically organized and coded, and submitted to further analysis and interpretation. Units of analysis were elaborated from the identification of basic units. At the most advanced stages of the analysis, the notions of ingestion, digestion, and incarnation emerged as categories that corresponded to the *Flea Market* choreographic process, indicating that the dancing bodies' construction in this work followed an assimilation order, leading me to incorporate anthropophagy as one of the main references for this study. I will admit, however, that this interpretation of Ribeiro's work is of my own making and that if the use of anthropophagy in this study appears as consequence of an academic study, it is also the result of my own desires.

DANCING BODIES AS ANTHROPOPHAGIC BODIES

The notion of dancing bodies as "anthropophagic bodies" appears in my study as a consequence of this research. Studying for a doctorate at a moment when concepts like multiculturalism, miscegenation, hybridization, and contamination are constantly evoked by various authors[4] in their dealings with contemporary artistic production has led me to think that it would be important to revisit anthropophagy.

It was the *Anthropophagite Manifesto*, written by Oswald de Andrade in 1928, that introduced and spread the principles of anthropophagy.[5] In it he recaptured the idea of the ritual cannibalism performed by Indians from the Tupinambá tribe in Brazil and proposed an anthropophagical action: to devour the foreign culture, digest it, and selectively assimilate it in order to restore its own cultural patrimony. An anthropophagite is, by definition, a human being who feeds on human flesh. There are many European narratives about cannibalism outside Europe, and these intensified from the sixteenth century on. At the beginning of the twentieth century, anthropophagic artists reclaimed the New World's stereotypes in general and particularly those concerning Brazil—the exoticism, the barbarism, the cannibalism—in order to appropriate them with a large dose of irony and sarcasm. Engaging with those stereotypes is also a way of admitting difference and recognizing distinctiveness. At the same time, anthropophagic artists saw in the ethos of anthropophagy a way to admit the fatality of being colonized and, therefore, of being able to transform it.

> Only anthropophagy unites us. Socially. Economically. Philosophically.
> The world's only law. The masked expression of all individualisms, of all collectivisms.
> Of all religions. Of all peace treaties.
> Tupy, or not tupy that is the question.[6]
> Against all catechisms. And against the mother of the Gracchi.
> The only things that interest me are those that are not mine. Law of man.
> Law of the anthropophagite. (Andrade 1998: 1)[7]

Anthropophagy, however, is not an act of sterile violence, for what it offers is the experience of a transformed violence. More precisely, it is through ingestion and mainly digestion that it is possible to assimilate and incorporate the substance of the devoured object and so bring a new synthesis into being. In other words, anthropophagy is only manifest when it gives form to something new. This product displays the victim's mark, but it is transformed through creative energy.

In order to understand the dancing body as an anthropophagic body, I will illustrate some principles from anthropophagy, such as the ingestion of heteroclite elements (in an analogy to the act of devouring), its digestion (in an analogy to transformation), and its incorporation/incarnation (in an analogy to the assimilation of those elements). It is in this way that the dancing body as anthropophagic body feeds itself on a variety of techniques, practices, and experiences connected to the world of dance. Thus, the learning of different movement techniques and practices, participation in the creation and performance of choreographies, as well as the situations experienced as a dance spectator, can be understood as constituting the elements to be ingested and digested. At the same time, this body feeds itself from other kinds of experiences, apparently not connected to dance. Various artistic practices, sports and leisure activities, meditation, religious experiences, and even love affairs can become nourishment to the anthropophagic body. Those heteroclite practices are digested within this body—decomposed, dissolved and amalgamated—and later assimilated. So, the anthropophagic body can be seen to be constantly reorganizing and transforming itself.

Moreover, the anthropophagic body claims continuity between the everyday body and the dancing body: the dancing body is trained, it masters the movement's techniques, and should be available to creation. This same body that offers itself as material for choreographic creation and that imparts life to the work is the body that sleeps, eats, feels; it is the trained body and also the loving body. There is promiscuity/cross-linking between life and dance, and it is done through the body: the one and same body that lives and enjoys daily life is the body that lives and enjoys dance.

> Sons of the sun, mother of the living. Found and loved ferociously, with all the hypocrisy of nostalgia, by the immigrants, by the slaves and by the touristes. In the country of the big snake.
> A participating consciousness, a religious rhythm.
> The spirit refuses to conceive the spirit without body. Anthropomorphism. The need for an anthropophagical vaccine. For the equilibrium against the religions of the meridian. And foreign inquisitions. (Andrade 1998: 2)

Another characteristic present in anthropophagy that helps in understanding the anthropophagic body is the carnival logic. The *Anthropophagite Manifesto* presents the idea of culture as a party, as carnival. The carnival—the feast of the flesh—is a pagan rite, restored by the Catholic liturgy and celebrated with enthusiasm in Europe during the Middle Ages. Bakhtine (1970) explains that, in opposition to the official celebrations, the carnival represented the temporary loosening of the dominant truth, the temporary abolition of all hierarchic relations, privileges, rules, and taboos. Carnival was introduced in Brazil around 1600 by the Portuguese in keeping with much of the medieval carnival spirit. Even today, Brazilian carnival maintains the characteristics of a social inversion ritual: it is a celebration distinguished by the dissolution of differences, where the moving body exposes and offers itself to the encounter (Matta 1983). Carnival logic is the logic of fusion, of disorder, of pleasure. In this sense, carnival logic can be seen as a component of the anthropophagic body, as one of the elements that allows the dancing body to reconnect to dance through pleasure: the pleasure of movement, and also the pleasure of blending with others. Thus, it is through transgression, delirious and ironic, that the principles of anthropophagy and of the anthropophagic body are stated.

> We were never catechized. What we really did was Carnival. The Indian dressed as a Senator of the Empire. Pretending to be Pitt. Or featuring in Alencar's operas full of good Portuguese feelings.
> We are tired of all the suspicious Catholic husbands put in drama.
> Freud put an end to the woman enigma and to other frights of printed psychology.
> What hindered truth was clothing, the impermeable element between the interior world and the exterior world. The reaction against the dressed man. American movies will inform. (Andrade 1998: 2)

Those traces are also somehow present in Ribeiro's *Flea Market*. It can be said that her work has an anthropophagic character, which is disclosed in its capacity to assimilate multiple influences, among them dancing styles that belong to Eastern traditions such as: ballet and American and German modern dance; Brazilian culture and its popular traditions; mass media information; trends and procedures from contemporary art world practices. Then the work transforms them, incorporates them, and makes a new synthesis come alive, always with a good dose of irony and sarcasm.

ANTHROPOPHAGIC BODIES IN *FLEA MARKET*

Flea Market is structured in three parts: *Haleine, Todo mundo pega trem*, and *Princesse*.[8] Throughout the work short sections follow each other without any apparent connection, resulting in a fragmented mise en scène. The work explores the commercial value of human beings, or as the choreographer said in an interview, "I wanted to put everybody into a showcase and explore their talents" (Ribeiro 2001). This theme serves as a pretext for the choreographic investigation that turns seduction, vulnerability, impossible challenges, mistakes, and the exposition of qualities and weaknesses into some of the leitmotifs of the creation.

As Ribeiro points out, *Flea Market* is not intended as a political manifesto, but its theme—the market value of a human being—does have political and ideological connotations. The choice of this theme was partly nourished by the experiences of a Brazilian woman who, in migrating to Canada, passes through different social roles: a Brazilian artist who comes from a *paulista* middle-class family; a Brazilian university student, and so a Third World "marriagable" woman in Canada; a foreign student earning a master's degree in dance at the University of Quebec in Montreal. She also characterized herself as a person who doesn't identify with foreign clichés about "being a Brazilian," but who actually feels "pretty Brazilian" when living abroad in the sense that she finds empathy for other immigrants of African, Latin, and Algerian origin. The shifting possibilities of all those identities are inscribed in the choreography through the different ways in which she carries her body and behaves on stage. It is in this way that Ribeiro reveals how "the choreography plays with what the human being really is as an animal and with what the human being is as a social being, and it plays with those contradictions and there is lots of ambiguity" (Ribeiro 2001). In a similar vein, the publicity materials for *Flea Market* state: "The four dancers and the actor each have their personal tale, in part representing the animal condition and with allusions to the sex market" (dona orpheline danse 1999: 11). Ribeiro declares that her sources of inspiration are in fact social themes, which she explores from an artistic viewpoint, but without any intention of projecting a specific message: "I have never been interested in denouncing anything, I am interested in sharing with the audience ... a feeling that is it not possible to do anything, or on the contrary, a feeling that, yes, it is possible to do something, it is a feeling of being alive and resisting" (Ribeiro 2001).

The political and social perspectives in Ribeiro's work are neither engaged nor militant, but subjacent to the work's structure; the way form and content are interwoven in *Flea Market* ends up revealing the politic. Irony also plays a fundamental role in this process when, at various moments, the choreography presents a situation in such a paradoxical way that it plays with the audience's perplexity. For instance, at one point a Princess Diana figure glides across the stage on rollerblades, half-naked and wearing a plastic crown on her head.

In the following section I examine how the choreographer and the dancers work with the choreographic substance in order to bring *Flea Market* to life, and how this process contributes to the construction of dancing bodies and in doing so reveals the existence of anthropophagical bodies.

INGESTION AND DIGESTION OF DIFFERENT ARTISTIC PRACTICES

Ribeiro has an eclectic artistic background ranging from contemporary dance to physical theatre, butoh to classic dance, videography to belly dance, and Afro-Brazilian dance. She has staked her ground in the world of artistic dance, as well as identifying with certain artistic movements that have been developed in the big cities of poor countries. She also has an academic background including certification to teach dance through the University of Campinas along with her master's degree in dance from the University of Quebec in Montreal. In *Flea Market* she also participates as a dancer. Like Ribeiro, the *Flea Market* dancers also have diversified backgrounds: Louis Pelchat is a contemporary dancer who also practises and teaches authentic movement;[9] Maryse Richard has training and practice in African dance and yoga, and practises meditation; Nancy Rivest is a contemporary dancer; and Chris Kauffman is an actor, with an emphasis on physical theatre. According to Sheila, the choice of the *Flea Market* cast was not made with the idea of uniformity, since she was not interested in a specific dancer standard. What really interested her were the characteristics of each one and their varied artistic experiences as well as their availability to work on creating and performing the piece. The dancers' reasons for working with Ribeiro varied, but they all shared a desire to explore unusual artistic proposals and become involved in the creation of a contemporary dance work.

Figure 1 *Flea Market*'s touring program—front cover.

How are those references to various dance and artistic forms present in *Flea Market*? How do they inform and transform the dancing bodies? In analyzing the influence of Eastern artistic dance styles, for example, it is possible to verify their use as juxtaposition. As Ribeiro explains in her master's thesis (2003), each section of the performance piece—*Haleine, Todo mundo pega trem*, and *Princesse*—is inspired by specific characteristics of a particular dance style. This way of structuring the piece influenced how the dancing bodies were organized. In *Haleine* the main reference is to the kind of movement fluidity present in certain styles of modern and contemporary dance of North American origin. In the second part, *Todo mundo pega trem*, the source of inspiration is German dance theatre: there is a concern with actually neutralizing references to movement fluidity and to emphasizing a discontinuous gesticulation, going from the dancing movement to gestures and utilitarian behaviours. The third part, *Princesse*, takes butoh as its main point of reference, and so is characterized by slow and centred attitudes in the dancers' gestures.

During one of the rehearsals, Ribeiro explained to Rivest, who had not participated in the creation of *Flea Market*, the differences between the first and the second part. There are differences in the how the sections were conceived and the way in which the body is carried in its relationship to the music. These differences had led to identifying the first part—*Haleine*—with North American modern dance, mainly because of the presence of sequences danced in accordance with the music. The second part—*Todo mundo pega trem*—was more like German dance theatre in the sense that the choreography is structured by "bodily acts" and interruptions in the movement sequences. Ribeiro explains how those choices were intentional and that she wanted "to fool the audience in relation to the choreographic style" (Ribeiro 2001). She also explained differences among the themes from each part: *Haleine* is composed of solos, each with its own quality; in *Todo mundo pega trem* everyone occupies the same space, but do not relate to each other. It is important to Ribeiro that Rivest understand those differences in order for her to find the specific attitudes for each of the sections.

Haleine and *Todo mundo pega trem* are performed by the same three dancers: Maryse Richard, Nancy Rivest, and Ribeiro herself. In *Princesse*, Richard also performs a section directly inspired by aspects of butoh. Ribeiro expects the dancers to corporally maintain the differences and nuances of each section. This might suggest that she demands from the dancers a technical mastery of each of those styles, turning them into truly chameleon dancers, and constituting what Foster calls "hired bodies." Foster explains her concept of the "hired body" as one that is apt to interpret different choreographic propositions without maintaining long-lasting organic and expressive bonds, or incorporating the poetic nuances of the choreography performed, and so transforming themselves into "pragmatic merchants of movement" (1997: 256). But this doesn't seem to be the case for *Flea Market*, since, according to Richard and Rivest, Ribeiro had always been concerned with integrating the dancers fully and deeply into the different moments of creation and re-creation in the piece by giving them the necessary time to understand and assimilate its poetic universe. In a similar way, a more detailed analysis of the work of the dancers in *Flea Market* suggests that instead of simply using the specific skills of the dancers in each style, Ribeiro prefers to incite "corporal states"[10] that refer to these styles, in an interplay between the training and the affinities of each dancer—Richard to Congolese African dance, Rivest to contemporary dance—along with the context and the specific bodily and technical demands of each section. These procedures evoked a feeling of the movement's inadequacy or incompleteness, for the dancers and for the audience, that according to Ribeiro was a desirable and integral part of the work.

The notion of "drive" is central to Ribeiro's process. She defines it as a kind of "primordial energy" that leads to dance, a movement organization principle of the dancing body (Ribeiro 2003). During the rehearsals, drive was one of the words most often used by the choreographer to explain the characteristics of the movements: in Ribeiro's view, this is what determines the intensity and quality of the movements. Further, to perform the movements in the correct drive means to execute them with the precision, impulse, and intent required by the choreography. In this way, the drive is the impulse to perform a movement and also a key to its understanding. It seems to me that the drive acts as the digestive enzyme of the dance techniques in *Flea Market*, since, as a principle of movement organization, it operates across the different dance practices and so allows the dancer a personal means of understanding and assimilating those styles that they do not master to perfection.

Another example of digestion in this study appears within the use of authentic movement, a technique that does not belong to the choreographer's own background but is a main reference for dancer Pelchat. Pelchat's participation in *Flea Market* consists of a solo in which he plays an "almost drag queen." When the scene starts, the dancer is wearing "ordinary" pants and shirt, high-heeled red shoes and a big, colourful wig. He is dubbing a song, according to lip-synching[11] conventions. At a particular moment, Pelchat stops lip-synching and starts to move with his eyes closed and in a way that is fluid and continuous and that can be identified with practices such as authentic movement. Before the song ends, he launches into the lip-synching once again. When the song is over, Pelchat leaves the stage and comes back wearing a short, lime-coloured dress with a long train of little bells that ring as he moves. He is no longer wearing the shoes or wig, and moves once again according to principles of authentic movement. It is striking to observe that authentic movement was not used here in the way it is usually practised. During rehearsals, Ribeiro and Pelchat talked a lot about this process, trying to reconcile those apparently contradictory points of view. For the choreographer, the use of authentic movement allowed for creative exploration of the dancer's intimacy, leading him into a state of vulnerability. Pelchat's concern was with the "aesthetic load" of authentic movement in this context, which isn't usually among its characteristics because it has been considered above all else a pedagogic and therapeutic practice. As Pelchat explains, in this practice the movement is a consequence of feelings that don't necessarily lead to dance. Consequently, his approach to authentic movement in *Flea Market* consisted in being on stage in a "dancing state," without moving away excessively from its principles; in other words, keeping the characteristics of this practice in his body and in his movement. He further explains: "I feel at ease working with authentic movement; I have rules, limits and I understand them ... and I always work with the same material, that is, the feeling" (Pelchat 2001).

INCARNATION AS A METHOD FOR CREATION

Incarnation—*incorporation* in Portuguese—as used by Ribeiro in talking about *Flea Market* is rooted in the "dancer/researcher/interpreter development method" of dance developed by Graziela Rodrigues.[12] Above all else it is about a kind of work with the body and its states of awareness which finds a parallel in the religious rituals of Afro-Brazilian origin in which, through the dance, the body is transformed into a vessel for collective awareness, able to incorporate religious icons. The process of incarnation/incorporation integrates the deity's body with the body of the believer and serves as inspiration for the dynamics of character in creative and interpretative choreographic processes (Rodrigues 1997).

In *Flea Market*, this incorporation implies not only an alteration in the daily body and awareness states, but provokes an alteration in the states of the body generally associated with consecrated styles of Western dance, like ballet and contemporary dance. As Ribeiro explains, it is a matter of leading the dancer into a state of vulnerability that provokes the emergence of the hidden energy within his or her "social body."[13] These procedures make contact possible with very intimate aspects of the dancer's life and personality and aim to lead him or her to transform this energy into material for choreographic creation. In this method the dancers do not incorporate

dona orpheline danse é

uma companhia de dança contemporânea de 9 anos de idade, nascida em São Paulo em 1992 (com o nome de *Asilo*), imigrante em Montréal (Canadá) há 5 anos.

libido+confusão

decadência e delicadeza

a dança da Madame Órfã.

REPERTÓRIO

Flea Market : we are used and cheap (2000 vídeo-dança), *Les querelles de la princesse* (1998), *Haleine* (1997), *I love Maria Lúcia* (1994), *Comida no lixo* (1994 vídeo-dança), *Comida no lixo* (Movimentos de Dança - 1993/Sesc-SP); *Uma nova criação provisoramente intitulada «Banana-Business»* está programada para outubro 2001 e terá trilha sonora de Edgard Scandurra.

« Sua abordagem conceitual me fascina e sua gestualidade me deslumbra. Na minha opinião, Sheila (...) é a coreógrafa mais interessante da nova geração montrealense. » BENOÎT LACHAMBRE

www.donaorpheline.com
donaorpheline@iname.com

Louis Pelchat / Foto: Michaël Slobodian

Figure 2 *Flea Market's* touring program—back cover.

religious deities, but rather images brought from their own daily lives and from the thematic universe pertaining to the choreography. Ribeiro talks of the necessity of scrutinizing—"to snout" is the word she uses—the dancer: "I like to leave the dancers always mentally quite stunned ... and I like to instigate people to get into other mental states, similar to an existential crisis, because those crises will pull the hidden energies to the surface" (Ribeiro 2001). During the creation of *Flea Market*, the dancers had to face frustrating situations.

The dancers who participated in the creation of *Flea Market* recognize the particularities of this process. Richard recalls that in the first rehearsals, Ribeiro invited the dancers to spin until they became a little disoriented and began to shift into an altered state of awareness. Once they were in this state, Ribiero suggested they incorporate certain images. As Richard explains:

> It was very intense, I remember the images of Sebastião Salgado, the Brazilian photographer, I remember that we had worked with the images of this photographer. Then we were supposed to spin around and then incorporate, I mean turn, ourselves into those mine workers ... and there were a series of such experiences. Sheila wanted to work really in depth, forcing us to dive into something; she wanted us to inhabit a certain universe. For a long time, there were things like this and then the choreography started calmly to come out, and Sheila dedicated a long time to work and shape us. (Richard 2001)

This way of working requires an intense personal engagement from the dancers. For Pelchat, it is about the deep work with the dancer's self, his or her desires and limits, and she demands that the dancers devote themselves fully to the work of creation and interpretation. In his words: "To enter in the stage to sing was, in a way, a dream I had always had, but I couldn't find a place for it in my work, and I hadn't managed to make this dream come true" (Pelchat 2001). He continues: "Sheila allowed me to make it come true through a rather ridiculous—a drag queen—and also very intelligent context" (Pelchat 2001). For Pelchat, the relation that Ribeiro establishes with each dancer has a spiritual dimension, which resembles the master/ disciple relation. He explains: "Sheila lets you do what you want, but it is necessary that you also give her what she asks for; and, in some way, that you give it to her in a somewhat blind way, when you don't know exactly where you are going to" (Pelchat 2001). Ribeiro seems to share this point of view because she believes that the choice of art and dance is more than a professional commitment. When I asked her how one can once again recover on stage the states experienced during the processes of creation, she answered that it was by way of courage. For Ribeiro, "it is like a vote the person takes, she must want to do it; she must believe that she is an instrument in service of art.... It is artistic passion, artistic blindness that makes you take the studio choreographic substance onto stage, more than anything; it is a commitment" (Ribeiro 2001).

The idea of incarnation in *Flea Market* is also inspired by butoh. Ribeiro repeatedly refers to the influence of butoh in her work: "There is a butoh in everything I do" (Ribeiro 2001). In a similar way, she explains that her company's training follows butoh ideology, since one of the main characteristics of this dance is "to establish a relationship between the imagination and muscular tonus" (Ribeiro 2001). One of the principles that guides the practice of butoh is the precise materialization of thought and imagination in the body. Thus, it is not about representing something, either emotion or sensation, but it is about becoming something or incarnating this emotion or sensation. The practice of butoh organizes the body by allowing the exploration of particular states which surpass the limits of consciousness and unconsciousness. The butoh dancer becomes what he or she wants to evoke through changes of the body and states of consciousness. For Ribeiro, identification with butoh recognizes that incarnation is as much a principle in practice as are the religious practices that also inspire her creation methods.[14] Moreover, the notions of vulnerability and anonymity—a kind of dilution of the subject—are also present in both practices.

The third part of the work, *Princesse*, is directly inspired by butoh. It is composed of a solo performed by Richard in dim light, with a dense atmosphere created by a slow-moving electronic score. Sheila explains that in this section, the mise en scène is structured through its relationship to time, an intuitive time generated by the dancer. Death is also an important reference, since the princess is Diane, who appears naked on rollerblades. During rehearsals, Sheila asked Richard to improvise on the theme of the dead princess, giving her the following clues: (1) attention to breath, which is heavy since it is a dead body that breathes; (2) the perception/imagination of the digestive tube, bearing in mind the relationship from the base of the anus to the mouth and to the tongue; (3) the fact that it is not actually Richard who is dancing, but that Richard should incarnate the dead body of the princess.

Notions of death, particularly the dead body, constitute one of the core references of butoh. The dead body is not a motionless body, but a body constructed through the idea that it is possible to generate movement beyond the control of "willpower" or the "conscience." This conception of the dead body allows the exploration of different bodily states and highlights the precariousness and frailty of the dancing body. The notion of the dead body can also be seen in the relationship with the idea of the anthropophagical body, since anthropophagy includes the idea of death— through the victim's suffering, the ingestion of their flesh, and the incorporation of their power.

A CONCEPTION OF DANCE AS VITAL ENERGY

In her own words, Ribeiro considers dance, above all, as vital energy, as pulse, as drive. She brings the dancing body closer to the loving one and believes that the vital energy living inside the dance is the same energy present in the sexual act: to dance and to make love demand a similar alternation between the states of awareness, desolation, participation, and vulnerability. Regarding dance, however, it is necessary to refine this energy in a continuous work, which is made mainly through one's training. Training in dance—understood as a systematic practice of one kind of dance, whether self-taught, performed in a community or academic context—allows the dancer to refine the ways of using energy. Thus, Ribeiro considers that in her work, "training in dance is fundamental to do what we do, because it is what is going to give access to the vital energy, to the world of corporal energy" (Ribeiro 2001). And so many types of dance have proved of interest to her: ballet, the various schools of modern and contemporary dance, traditional Brazilian and African dances, belly dance, butoh, and capoeira.[15]

How does this understanding of dance engage with the idea of the anthropophagical body? Ribeiro considers her conception of dance and the dancing body as somewhat closer to the way the body and sexuality are approached in Brazil. She says that living abroad has made her realize that Brazilians have a more playful relation to the body than do North Americans, and that they have a greater ability to yield to and deal with their own body and with those of others, and to deal with emotion and pleasure. Ribeiro's dance shares this bodily desire: "[My dance] has a very strong relationship with the libido, and the libido, not only necessarily as a sexual pleasure, but also as the pleasure of being alive and, at the same time, of being able to resist, a resistant vital drive" (Ribeiro 2001). Moreover, she believes that the construction of the dancing bodies, by which she means the process of becoming a dancer, entails the integration of different "sensitive experiences" that are found both in the dance world and within their daily lives. As she explained:

I am very proud of being a dancer, very, because I think that to be a dancer is to salute life—I know there are many clichés about this, but for me, being a dancer is really to salute life.... When you begin to dance, things are always outside yourself. For example, you make a "*glissade*," the jump is not good and the more you repeat it, the more you understand the jump. Life is also like this: the more you dance, the more you understand what life is about. Because you refine, you bring inside what is outside, you learn how to control this energy, in subtler way, each time subtler and what used to be raw becomes more refined.... It is the practice that allows you to refine the energy and if you look at a dancer—it doesn't matter if he is a ballet or samba dancer—you can see that he is a dancer, because his body manifests this dance energy. (Ribeiro 2001)

This brings me to the notion of continuity between the dancing body—a body that lives and enjoys dance—and the carnival logic that preaches the pleasure in fusion. This being the case, would it not be the anthropophagical body that claims the territory of the promiscuity between dance and life?

In the view of *Flea Market* dancers, the piece finally came to artistic maturity during the performances of the Brazilian tour, for it was contact with the Brazilian reality that allowed them to contextualize the work and to accept the choreographer's propositions more fully. Pelchat talked about his experience in Rio de Janeiro, where he got lost in the night crowd of Lapa, one of the bohemian quarters of the city:

When I saw myself in Lapa, Friday night, under the Arches, and I saw this crowd, I really believed that I was in *Flea Market*; in Lapa, everybody meets everybody: punks, transvestites, heterosexuals, everybody. And, within this exuberance I saw the work and was able to relate this aesthetic to Sheila's, completely exuberant, a fusion of no matter what, everything together and it works.... In Lapa, I was drawn into a nightclub. I, who don't like crowds, who chokes in such places, I found myself in a small night club in Lapa, dancing ... and I danced and danced and everybody around me danced and I couldn't say if they were white, black, Spanish, gringos, men, women. I was there, with a beating heart and I was almost losing myself, losing my own identity. I was in a state of fusion in this sort of crowd; it is very permissive, when you are in a crowd and you dance, you are almost in a trance state; there were bodies touching, and it was not sexual, it was only animal; it is very sensual, but I couldn't tell if there was somebody touching me or if it was me who was touching somebody. (Pelchat 2001)

CONCLUSION

The metaphors of human flesh proposed by anthropophagy are perhaps violent ones, but they may be one of the effective strategies for cultural, artistic, and political statements in countries of peripheral economies. I believe also that anthropophagy differentiates itself from the notions of multiculturalism, impurity, and hybridization because, being less demagogic and consensual, it offers the experience of a transformed violence. If foreign authors who write about Brazilian art and culture have the tendency to interpret most of our production as an inheritance from anthropophagy, it is also true that it has been used to think about art within the context of globalization (Jeudi 1999; Shutz 2000; Laplantine and Nouss 2001).

Just as anthropophagy suggests the assimilation of the devoured object in order to perform new syntheses, the choreographer and dancers of *Flea Market* assimilate the principles (or the substance) of these various bodily practices to configure their dancing bodies. Therefore, the organizing principles of the corporal material specific to each practice are used to the extent that they contribute to poetic needs—that is, they are at the service of the work. In the final product—the choreographic work—these practices are nearly undetectable, for they have been digested and incorporated into the choreography. These digestive practices occur mainly in the dancer's body, generating renewed dancing bodies. Many procedures used in *Flea Market* demand the dancer's complete commitment, for they must look deeply within themselves in order to create and interpret the choreography. At the same time, they needed to accept and absorb the poetic universe and the creative strategies suggested by the choreographer. However, the dancing bodies' reconfiguration in *Flea Market* did not lead to uniformity among the dancers, since the structure of the piece and most of the rehearsals—centred on the solos and trios—had allowed for individualized work from each dancer. Each one was able to appropriate and digest the choreographer's propositions according to his or her own perspectives and desires, allowing them to make their own synthesis and incorporating them into the work. And so it was that those dancing bodies seemed like good examples of anthropophagic bodies, for they ingest, digest, and selectively incorporate a variety of experiences in order to organize and produce new creations while managing to keep their singularities.

Dancing bodies as anthropophagic bodies are not exclusively Brazilian. The *Flea Market* creative and interpretative processes generated anthropophagic bodies through the mixture of different corporal and movement references and by their use of varied creation procedures. In the case of *Flea Market*, those propositions were experienced by Brazilian and North

American dancers alike. There was amalgamation and transformation, but there was also a certain remoteness necessary in order to play with the irony and the sarcasm present in the work. This was most vividly demonstrated by Pelchat, the Canadian dancer who played a drag queen, dubbed Alcione in Portuguese ("I can't feed such a crazy love anymore"), and who suddenly returned to bodily states close to those of authentic movement.

Dancing bodies, like anthropophagic bodies, assert their uniqueness and demonstrate the power of the body. For it is the body that collects and unifies the experiences, whether stemming from dance or from life in general. Dancing bodies are nourished by sexual practices, expressions of affection, dance techniques, artistic creative procedures, "dancing at the party," silent activities like yoga and meditation, and many other activities which then reshape themselves as anthropophagical bodies. In this sense, I consider it important to evoke Rolnik, for whom one of the experiences of the anthropophagic way of life is "the wandering of the desire that makes its connections guided, predominantly, by the body's vibrating point of view and by its willpower" (1998: 136). The vibrating body—the anthropophagic body—reshapes the world by way of knowledge gleaned through vibration and contamination, knowledge which is different from that which is gained through representation and imitation.

Notes

1 This study is part of a broader investigation in which I have aimed to comprehend the way in which participation in the processes of creation, performance, and choreographic reconstruction contributed to the construction of dancing bodies in the context of two Brazilian contemporary choreographers' work. This was the theme for my research, concluded in 2009, within the doctoral program Études et pratiques des arts at the University of Quebec in Montreal. Besides examining the work of Sheila Ribeiro, I also studied the choreography of Brazilian choreographer Lia Rodrigues.

2 The original title in French was *Marché aux puces: nous sommes usagés et pas chers*. In the English version Ribeiro chose to call it *Flea Market: We Are Used and Cheap*. When the choreography was later restaged for a tour in Brazil, Ribeiro translated it into Portuguese as *Liquidação Total: gente usada e barata*. For practical uses in this chapter, I have adopted the English title.

3 The final version of her master's dissertation was called "Marché aux puces, nous sommes usagés et pas chers: la mégalopole et sa chorégraphie contemporaine" (Ribeiro 2003), which earned her a master's of arts in dance at the University of Quebec in Montreal. In her thesis she elaborated a description and analysis of the creative processes of *Flea Market*, with the aim of relating the work of artistic production to the urban context of the megalopolis.

4 From the 1980s on, the production of works with this theme has considerably expanded. In the United States and Canada, the fields of cultural studies and post-colonial studies make the hybridization apology and allow the voices of the colonized to emerge. In Europe, works in favour of syncretisms, such as

L'impureté (Scarpetta 1985), *Le métissage* (La Plantine and Nouss 1997), *La pensée métisse* (Gruzinski 1999) have been published, at the same time as authors such as Filkenkraut (1987) denounced the dissolution of European classic culture.

5   *The Anthropophagite Manifesto*, published for the first time in 1928 in the first is-sue of the magazine *Revista Antropofagia*, and the anthropophagic movement (or simply anthropophagy, according to Andrade in 1928) are benchmarks of mod-ernism in Brazil. In the *Anthropophagite Manifesto*, Oswald de Andrade uses van-guard literary techniques to compose a patchwork of erudite references to the European and Brazilian cultures embedded within the Brazilian popular tradi-tions and within the technological developments of the period. Anthropophagy was compared, on the same level, to other European vanguard movements. It offered the possibility of a renewal of a European culture which was seen as having been suffocated by Christian morality and capitalist utilitarianism. An-thropophagy moved Brazilians beyond the inferiority complex that had long branded their artistic and cultural production.

6   Written in English in the original.

7   In this section, I introduce excerpts from the *Anthropophagite Manifesto* in an English translation by Pedrosa and Cordeiro (see Andrade 1998).

8   Those titles were maintained by Ribeiro in the English translation of the pro-gram. "*Haleine*" means respiration, breath, exhalation. The expression "*Todo mundo pega trem*" means "Everybody gets on a train" and "*Princesse*" means Prin-cess.

9   This is a reference to methods that aim to provide assent to the practitioner to express their inner life through the development of kinaesthetic awareness, while bearing in mind that movement is the personality made visible.

10 In this context, "corporal states" refers to organizing the body in relationship to certain qualities of movement and stage presence.

11 This is an expression used to designate the way drag queens dub a song; lip-synching also includes gestures and even choreography that complements the song.

12 Graziela Rodrigues was Ribeiro's teacher at the Univeristé de Campinas. In her book *Bailarino, pesquisador, intérprete: processo de formação* (1997), Rodrigues elab-orates the principles of her method for teaching dancers and researchers, one which forms the basis for the bachelor's of dance program. Her method begins with a study of certain Brazilian dances, particularly those of Afro-Brazilian re-ligious rituals, from which she developed the principal techniques and symbols with which to structure her approach to the preparation of the body and to the choreographic creative process.

13 In this context, the social body is understood as that which incorporates social structures and rules through the acquisition of behaviours, habits, postures, and gestures of acceptable social comportment.

14 Santos (1999: 187–88) talks about the influence of butoh and Afro-Brazilian reli-gions like Candomblé in the work of the Brazilian dance company Neo-Iaô.

15 Capoeira is an Afro-Brazilian blend of martial arts, game, and dance created by enslaved Africans in Brazil during the sixteenth century. Participants form a *roda* (circle) and take turns playing instruments, singing, and sparring in pairs in the centre of the circle. The game is marked by fluid acrobatic play, feints, and ex-tensive use of groundwork, as well as sweeps, kicks, and headbuts.

Bibliography

Andrade, Oswald. "Anthropophagite Manifesto." XXIV Bienal de São Paulo, 1998. www1.uol.com.br/bienal/24bienal/nuh/i_manifesto.htm (accessed July 7, 2004).

Bakhtine, Mikhaïl. *L'oeuvre de François Rabelais et la culture populaire au moyen âge et sous la renaissance.* Paris: Gallimard, 1970.

dona orpheline danse. Publicity materials from the dance company. Montreal, 1999.

Filkenkraut, Alain. *La défaite de la pensée.* Paris: Gallimard, 1987.

Foster, Susan Leigh. "Dancing Bodies." In J.C. Desmond (ed.), *Meaning in Motion: New Cultural Studies of Dance.* Durham, NC: Duke University Press, 1997: 235–57.

Gruzinski, Serge. *La pensée métisse.* Paris: Fayard, 1999.

Hanstein, Penelope. "From Idea to Research Proposal: Balancing the Systematic and Serendipitous." In Sondra H. Fraleigh and Penelope Hanstein (eds.), *Researching Dance: Evolving Modes of Inqury.* Pittsburgh: University of Pittsburgh Press, 1999: 62–88.

Jeudi, Henri Pierre. *Les usages sociaux de l'art.* Paris: Circé, 1999.

Laplantine, François. *La description ethnographique.* Paris: Nathan Université, 2000.

Laplantine, François and Alexis Nouss. *Métissages, de Arcimboldo à Zombi.* Paris: Pauvert, 2001.

Matta, Roberto. *Carnavals, bandits et héros: ambiguités de la société brésilienne.* Paris: Seuil, 1983.

Ortiz, Renato. *Cultura brasileira e identidade nacional.* São Paulo: Brasiliense, 1998.

Pelchat, Louis. Interview with the author. Montreal, May 22, 2001.

Ribeiro, Sheila. Interview with the author. Montreal, June 27 and July 17, 2001.

Ribeiro, Sheila. "Marché aux puces: nous sommes usagés et pas chers: la mégalopole et sa chorégraphie contemporaine." Mémoire de maîtrise, Université du Québec à Montréal, 2003.

Richard, Maryse. Interview with the author. Montreal, July 15, 2001.

Rodrigues, Graziela. *Bailarino, pesquisador, interpréte: processo de formação.* Rio de Janeiro: Funart, 1997.

Rolnik, Suely. "Anthropophagic Subjectivity." In P. Herkenhoff and A. Pedrosa (eds.), *Arte contemporânea brasileira: um e/entre uutro/s.* São Paulo: Fundação Bienal de São Paulo, 1998. http://caosmose.net/suelyrolnik/textos/Anthropophagic.doc (accessed October 5, 2006).

Santos, Eluza Maria. "The Dancing Voice of Culture: An Ethnography of Contemporary Dance in Vitória, Brazil." Unpublished PhD dissertation, Texas Woman's University, 1999.

Scarpetta, Guy. *L'impureté.* Paris: B. Grasset, 1985.

Schütze, B.A. "Cannibales en ligne." *Le magazine électronique du CIAC* 10 (2000). http://www.cia.ca/magazine/perspective.html (accessed March 15, 2002).

CHAPTER NINETEEN

The Bridge from Past to Present in Lin Hwai-min's Nine Songs (1993)

LITERARY TEXTS AND VISUAL IMAGES

YIN-YING HUANG

INTRODUCTION

In this essay, I will consider Lin Hwai-min's *Nine Songs*, a dance produced by Cloud Gate Dance Theatre in 1993. This dance is inspired by Chinese poet Chu Yuan's poems of the same name. Using Lin's *Nine Songs* as a focus, I hope to shed light on how Chinese poetry has been transformed into a Taiwanese modern dance.

To carry out this research project, I drew upon ethnographic research methods to collect data. In both 1993 and 2000, I observed various rehearsals of *Nine Songs* at the Cloud Gate dance studios and took detailed field notes.[1] To gain a deeper understanding of dance work, I also conducted in-depth interviews with my "informants"—the choreographer and dancers. In this research project, an attempt was also made to analyze the dance work within the sociocultural context of contemporary Taiwan in order to explore how this particular modern dance work, emerging as it does in contemporary Taiwan, might illuminate a contemporary Taiwanese cultural identity. Besides ethnographic research methods, I have also compared dance and literary narratives and used aesthetic analysis to assist my research.

As a Taiwanese dancer-researcher-educator, I strive to present my research from an "insider's perspective." Culturally speaking, I am also Han Chinese and my life is also immersed in Chinese elements. Having been born in Taiwan and lived there much of my life, I also consider myself as a Taiwanese and a member of the contemporary Taiwanese society.[2] This background has assisted me in my identification of various Taiwanese and

Chinese cultural sources in Lin's dance. This also helped me to understand how these aesthetics assist Lin in formulating his dance vocabulary and creating meaning in *Nine Songs*.

Informed by my knowledge of Taiwanese, Chinese, and Asian culture, this chapter seeks to establish a new framework for analyzing contemporary Taiwanese performance. I hope that my findings can help lay the foundations for developing new critical theories of performance for critics in Taiwan, a contemporary Asian society with multiple cultural influences.

HOW A WRITER BECAME A CHOREOGRAPHER

Lin Hwai-min, the choreographer of *Nine Songs*, was born in Chia-yi County, central Taiwan, in 1947. He was a well-known writer in Taiwan before turning to a career in dance. In 1970, Lin won a scholarship to study at The Writer's Workshop at the University of Iowa in the United States. While fulfilling the requirements for his MFA degree in creative writing, he minored in dance and started to compose dances. Upon his return to Taiwan in 1973, he founded the first modern dance company in Taiwan—the Cloud Gate Dance Theatre. Throughout his dance career, he has choreographed many dance works inspired by literature. When Lin transforms a literary work into a dance piece, he often seeks innovative ways to transform the literary text into dance work to articulate a unique interpretation. *Nine Songs* is such a dance.

NINE SONGS: THE CYCLE OF ANCIENT CHINESE POEMS THAT INSPIRED LIN HWAI-MIN'S MODERN DANCE

To begin with, I would like to offer some background information on the literary work *Nine Songs* that inspired Lin's dance. According to Si-yuan Wang, a Chinese literature scholar, *Nine Songs* is one of the oldest literary works of ancient China. It was written by Chinese poet Chu Yuan during the warring states period of China (480–222 BC). As a nobleman of Ch'u, a kingdom occupying the valleys of the central Yangtze River in the southern region of ancient China, Chu Yuan was wrongly accused of treason. He was exiled by his emperor to a barbarian area full of lakes and rivers to the south of his emperor's territories. It was there that Chu wrote *Nine Songs* (Wang 1988: 77), adapting a series of ritual verses used by shamans as sacrificial hymns in ceremonies.

Nine Songs actually consists of eleven poems. According to Wang, "nine" is often used to signify "many" in the Chinese language. In *Nine Songs*, the first nine poems are similar in one respect; in each one, a shaman addresses a local Ch'u deity as if he or she were a lover and invites the deity to earth to be worshipped by the local Ch'u people. In contrast, the tenth poem, "Homage to the Fallen," honours the spirits of Ch'u warriors killed in battle, while the eleventh is a short hymn to conclude the work. Wang points out that these poems are lucid and expressive, as well as layered with levels of meaning. They describe worshippers and a shaman, who, having first purified and perfumed themselves, sing and dance to draw the gods down from the heavens. On the one hand, Chu's poems pay homage to nature and the gods and depict romantic love between humans and the gods. On the other, they seem to express Chu Yuan's criticism of authority, because although there is a recurring focus on expressing love for the gods and goddesses in Chu's *Nine Songs*, there is also an implicit complaint that the gods have either not come, or have come and left too soon. The chiding of the gods implies that Chu believes that his emperor and the gods are alike in that neither pay sincere attention to their loyal people and worshippers (Wang 1988: 77).

Overall, Chu is highly venerated in Chinese society because he is considered both a beautiful poet and an honest, patriotic statesman. Literary scholar Yi-wen Chiou, in her book *Shamanism and Nine Songs*, also stresses the fact that *Nine Songs* are essentially shamans' songs. She attributes *Nine Songs* to the widespread practice of shamanism in the Ch'u region. She also points out that the beauty of the language is key to understanding the *Nine Songs* more fully. The poetry, with its strange mixture of magnificence and melancholy, has had an immediate appeal for many readers throughout Chinese history. According to Chiou, *Nine Songs* has long been considered a great literary accomplishment as well as a mythological representation of ancient China (Chiou 1996: 42).

FROM LITERARY TEXT TO DANCE IMAGES

Lin remarked that he had dreamt of basing a dance on *Nine Songs* for more than ten years before he ever choreographed it. Among his reasons for choosing Chu's *Nine Songs*, the most important, he explained, was its concern with ancient dance ritual. He emphasized, however, that his aim was not to create a "dance reconstruction" of ancient dance rituals. He was interested in "creating a theatrical dance piece from a contemporary perspective, using *Nine Songs* as a springboard for imagination" (Lin Hwai-min, personal interview, July 26, 2000).

To investigate how Lin transformed the literary narrative into dance images, and his choreographic re-imagination of the original literary work,

I will begin by "reading" the dance alongside the literary work scene by scene below. In the following, I will offer a detailed description of the dance work based on findings in my fieldwork, as well as materials I have found through related literature on Chinese literature and aesthetics. In the course of this research project, I witnessed the premiere of the dance in Taipei in 1993, and a performance in New York City in 1995. I also visited the dance company to observe various rehearsals and to collect data in both 1993 and 2000.

Even before the curtain rises, the audience, sitting in the darkness, can see in the orchestra pit along the front of the stage a lotus pond filled with real water and lotus flowers. There is a sound of a quiet rush of water, which gradually increases in volume, suggesting to the audience that they are not far away from a region of lakes, the geographical backdrop to Chu Yuan's *Nine Songs*.

Like Chu Yuan's *Nine Songs*, Lin's dance work takes the form of a dance ritual with the first scene, "Greeting the Gods," echoing the mood depicted in the first half of the first poem of *Nine Songs*, "Monarch of the East":[3]

On a lucky day, good in both its signs,
Let us in reverence give pleasure to the Monarch on high.
I hold my long sword by its jade grasp,
My girdle-gems tinkle with a ch'iu-ch'iang.
From the jewelled mat with its jade weights,
Why not take the perfumed spray?
Meats I offer, flavored with basil, on strewn orchids laid,
I set out the cassia-wine and peppered drink.

As the opening lines of "Monarch of the East," this vivid language describes the preparation for a ritual ceremony that is about to take place. The "I" throughout the cycle of poems is the shaman. She has sprayed perfume on her body and prepared food and drink for the deities.

In Lin's version of this scene, as the curtain slowly rises, a group of celebrants dressed in thin white robes enter the stage from various corners and proceed through a baptism purification ceremony. The celebrants walk toward the lotus pond at their own pace and silently anoint their foreheads with water. They then make a communal circle facing each other in a seated position centre stage. In each celebrant's place are the bamboo sticks, with which they start to beat the floor.

The first dance scene is accompanied by the ritual song of Tsou, which they use in a ceremony to welcome the gods. The Tsou tribe is a group of Taiwanese aborigines in the central mountain area of Taiwan and is one of

nine major aboriginal groups in Taiwan.[4] The use of these mountain dwell-
ers' music adds a solemn atmosphere to the dance creation.

The second scene of the dance "Monarch of the East" corresponds to
the second half of the first poem:

> Now the sticks are raised, the drums are struck,
> To beats distanced and slow the chanters gently sing,
> Then to the ranks of reed-organ and zither make loud reply.
> The spirit moves proudly in her splendid gear,
> Sweetest scents with gusts of fragrance fill the hall.
> The five notes chime in thick array,
> The Lord is pleased and happy, his heart is at rest.

In these lines, the poet tells us that the ritual ceremony has started. The
"spirit," which refers to the shaman, starts to dance. According to Chinese
literature scholar Wang, this shaman plays a central role in Chu's poetry.
In almost every poem of *Nine Songs*, it is the shaman's first-person voice
that addresses each of the deities descending to the human world. The hall
in which the ceremony takes place is now filled with sweet scents and the
sounds of the various instruments. "The Lord," the Monarch of the East,
China's Sun God, has arrived, and is pleased by the worshippers and the
shaman's dance (Wang 1988: 80).

Figure 1 The shaman and group dancers in the dance scene. Photographer: Yu Hui-hung.

In Lin's version of this scene, a red-robed female shaman appears onstage and walks regally into the circle of celebrants. Turning toward the audience, she suddenly begins a frantic and sensual trance-like dance. Her torso bends back and forth in violent, percussive movements. Her long hair flies around her body, while her fingers spread threateningly. She is doing this to summon the gods and goddesses to descend into the human world to bring blessings upon the Ch'u people. As I observed, Lin has made this scene more dramatic than the corresponding scene in the literary text in the sense that the "spirit" represented by the shaman in the dance work is infused with a much sexier and more intense presence.

The first god, the Monarch of the East, appears onstage in response to the female shaman's dance. Chu Yuan describes the god as "pleased and happy, his heart is at rest." This is in stark contrast to Lin's portrayal of a cruel and uncaring Sun God on stage. In the dance, the God arrives on stage standing on the shoulders of two humans. Wearing a fierce, threatening mask, this muscular, aggressive deity jumps to the ground to begin a sexual duet with the female shaman, as the celebrants encircle them. The harshness of this lustful dance is emphasized by its contrast to the spiritual beauty of the lotus pond. Once satisfied, the Sun God deserts the shaman, who is left alone on stage crying. The choreographer referred to this scene as a "rite of fertility" and has compared this female shaman to the "chosen girl" in Nijinsky's *Rite of Spring*. "They were both chosen to dance to call down the deities, to call springtime and life back to the world" (Lin Hwai-min, personal interview, July 26, 2000). In other words, like the chosen girl in Nijinsky's *Rite of Spring*, the female shaman in Lin's *Nine Songs* dances for her people; she sacrifices herself to please the gods for the continuity of their people.

When the Sun God leaves the stage, the third scene of the dance, "Gods of Fate," begins. This scene corresponds to the fifth and sixth poems of *Nine Songs*, "The Big God of Fate" and "The Little God of Fate." Because these two poems are similar in both theme and content, I will include an excerpt of only one part of "The Big God of Fate":

High he flies, peacefully winging,
  On pure air borne aloft he handles Yin and Yang.
He trails his spirit-garment,
  Dangles his girdle-gems.
One Yin for every Yang,
  The crowd does not understand what we are doing.
I pluck the sparse-hemp's lovely flower,
  Meaning to send it to him from whom I am separated.

Age creeps on apace, all will soon be over,
Not to draw nearer is to drift further apart.
He has driven his dragon chariot, loudly rumbling,
High up he gallops into heaven.

Here the Big God of Fate comes down to the human world from heaven. He flies peacefully through the air, balancing yin and yang, the two forces of the universe. The shaman picks a lovely flower for the deity to please him. Soon, however, she is separated from her beloved deity—he has "driven his dragon chariot, loudly rumbling" back to heaven. According to literary scholar Si-yuan Wang, the shaman is sorrowful. This is because the god has arrived, but has stayed for only a brief moment (Wang 1988: 82).

In comparing the literary text and dance scene, I found Lin's translation of these two poems into dance interesting. He did not quite follow the literary text's depiction. The Big God of Fate and the Small God of Fate, who control the fate of human beings, appear on stage at the same time. Upon their arrival, they begin manipulating the worshippers on stage. The bodies of these human beings are twisted and hurled around by the gods. Then the human beings begin to turn on each another, pulling at each other's torsos and trying to hurt one another. In this chaotic scene, the Gods of Fate are clearly depicted as manipulative, destructive, and mean. This scene is accompanied by the Tibetan monks' chanting music.

After a brief intermission, the fourth scene of the dance, "Princess of the Hsiang River," starts. This dance scene corresponds to the third poem of the same title:

The Princess doesn't come, she bides her time.
She is waiting for someone on that big island.
I will check myself in my handsome finery
And set out to find her, riding in my cassia-boat.
May the Yuan and Hsiang raise no waves,
May the waters of the Great River flow quietly!
I look toward the princess, but she doesn't come;
Blowing her pan-pipes there, of whom is she thinking?

Lin's scene echoes these lines, taken from the first half of the poem, in which the River Goddess is waiting for the River God by the Hsiang River. In the dance, the elegant, masked River Goddess enters the stage from the upper right corner. She stands on two bamboo poles, lifted up high in the air by four male attendants, moving across the stage in a processional manner. A "river" of white silk, sprinkled with flowers, flows behind her. Under

367

Figure 2 The princess of Hsiang and a modern traveller are juxtaposed on stage by a real lotus pond. Dancer: Yang Mei-jung. Photographer: Lui Chen-hsiang.

a deep blue sky, several female attendants dance joyously around her, sprinkling flowers over her and the "river." They skip and turn with their fingers held in delicate, curved gestures often seen in classical Chinese dances.

The music accompanying this scene is the high-pitched, soothing voices of Taiwan's Puyumn tribe women, an aboriginal group on Taiwan's east coast. At first, this scene seems to bring us back to a serene world. However, as the scene proceeds, an underlying disharmony starts to appear. The red-robed shaman comes back to the stage and strips off the River Goddess's mask, revealing the sorrow in her face. The River Goddess's movement becomes stiffer and slower. Her attendants have abandoned her and left the stage. She is left alone, feeling lonely and upset. In the end, the River Goddess wraps herself in her own silken "river" and mourns. After a moment, she too leaves the stage, and the stage is left empty.

There is no depiction of a female shaman taking off the River Goddess's mask anywhere in the poem. The choreographer explains that he added this scene to imply that "the gods have their own business to worry about and they have no time to take care of the lives of human beings on earth." He also suggested that "perhaps the gods are in fact masked human beings" (Lin Hwai-min, personal interview, July 26, 2000). It is possible that they look magnificent and pretty in their masks, but their imperfection is revealed after their masks are stripped away.

The God of Clouds enters the stage after the River Goddess leaves. This is the fifth scene of the dance, "God of the Clouds." This scene corresponds to the poem of the same title:

> The spirit in great majesty came down,
> Now he soars up swiftly amid the clouds.
> He looks down on the province of Ch'u and far beyond.
> He travels to the four seas; endless his flight.

This stanza is taken from the second half of the poem, in which the Cloud God is portrayed as majestic and able to "[soar] up swiftly amid the clouds," where he looks down on Ch'u. Lin's transformation of the poetic depiction of the Cloud God into dance is vividly accomplished. Like the entrances of the Sun God and the River Goddess in earlier scenes, the Cloud God enters the stage standing on the shoulders of two human attendants. Remarkably throughout the entire sequence, the Cloud God never sets foot on the ground, showing off a series of flamboyant poses performed on the shoulders and backs of the two human attendants. At some moments, he balances himself on one leg while lifting his other leg high in the air. At other moments, he jumps back and forth between the two attendants, while using his arms to make big, slow, circular patterns around his body. He remains aloof and looks magnificent, while his two human attendants look up at him, painfully struggling in their efforts to support him. In this scene the choreographer seems to be signifying a display of tyrannical power.

Following the God of Clouds, the shy, mournful Mountain Spirit enters the stage, opening the sixth scene of the dance "Mountain Spirit." This scene corresponds to the ninth poem of the same title. The following lines are taken from the first half of "Mountain Spirit":

> It seems there is someone over there, in the fold of the hill,
> Clad in creepers, with a belt of mistletoe.
> He is gazing at me, his lips parted in a smile;
> "Have you taken a fancy to me? Do I please you with my lovely ways?"
> Driving red leopards, followed by stripy civets,
> Chariot of magnolia, banners of cassia,
> Clad in stone-orchid, with belt of asarum,
> I go gathering sweet herbs to give to the one I love.

According to literary scholar Wang, the Mountain Spirit is a deity who lives in the mountains, mingling with the leopards and civets, his chariot decorated with sweet-smelling plants like magnolia, cassia, stone-orchid, and asarum. In the poem, the Mountain Spirit is depicted as shy, but friendly. He may gaze at you, with his lips parted in a smile, and ask you "Have you taken a fancy to me? Do I please you with my lovely ways?" (Wang 1988: 84). In Lin's dance, in contrast, the Mountain Spirit looks terribly afraid. Unlike the other deities appearing in the previous scenes of the dance, the Mountain Spirit is the only deity who does not wear a mask. Indeed, the movements and facial expressions of Lin's Mountain Spirit seem to foreshadow pain. His twisted torso, his tentative prancing around the stage, and his sudden, short movement phrases all make him appear hyper-alert and frightened. This feeling is heightened by the dark, almost-bare stage. His loneliness stands out.

Lin Hwai-min explained that the Mountain Spirit's dance was also based on his impressions of Norwegian artist Edvard Munch's famous painting *The Scream*, in which the subject is depicted with mouth wide open, apparently screaming. Lin even asked Cloud Gate dancer Wen-long Li to view this painting to help him interpret the role. Lin also said that he deliberately portrays the Mountain Spirit as frightened, as if the Spirit foresees something terrible about to happen (Lin Hwai-min, personal interview, July 26, 2000). Indeed, following this scene, a terrible event in Chinese history is represented on the stage.

After circling around the stage and executing several big jumps, the Mountain Spirit exits stage left, concluding the sixth scene. The seventh scene of the dance, "Homage to the Fallen," begins. It corresponds to the tenth poem of the same title in Chu's *Nine Songs* and is dedicated to soldiers who die for their country. The poem reads:

> Grasping our great shields and wearing our hide armour
> Wheel-hub to wheel-hub locked, we battle hand to hand.
> Our banners darken the sky; the enemy teem like clouds:
> Through the hail of arrows the warriors press forward.
> They dash on our lines; they trample our ranks down.
> The left horse has fallen, the right one is wounded.
> Bury the wheels in, tie up the horses!
> Seize the jade drumstick and beat the sounding drum!
> The time is against us: the gods are angry.
> Now all lie dead, left on the field of battle.
> Their long swords at their belts, clasping their elmwood bows.

Head from body sundered: but their hearts could not be vanquished.
Both truly brave, and also truly noble
Strong to the last, they could not be dishonoured.
Their bodies may have died, but their souls are living.
Heroes among the shades their valiant souls will be.

According to Si-yuan Wang (1988), this poem praises those noble soldiers who dare to sacrifice their own lives to protect their country. As it opens, the soldiers grasp their shields, put on their armour, and march into battle. The poet then turns to a cruel description of war—the warriors running among a hail of arrows as the enemy overruns them and kills their horses. Soon all the soldiers lay dead on the battlefield. The last four lines emphasize the bravery of these warriors. The poet believes that although their bodies have died their souls do not, and so they are true heroes of their country and should be forever honoured (Wang 1988: 86).

In transforming this poem into dance, Lin echoes Chu's war theme but does not adhere closely to the details of Chu's poem. In this scene, all the gods and spirits have left the stage, and Lin transports the audience back to the contemporary world. On stage are various scenes recreating historical massacres that have taken place in twentieth-century Chinese history, such as the massacre at Tiananmen Square in mainland China in 1989, and the February 28 event in Taiwan in 1949—a political clash between the local population and the Nationalist Government troops, newly arrived following their withdrawal from China in 1949. During this section, a line of political martyrs from these events slowly enters the stage. All of them have baskets over their heads and hands crossed in front of them, as if tied. For audiences in Taiwan, the baskets are an obvious reference to the way people were led to execution in the February 28 event. As seen in historical photos, those who were sent out to be executed wore baskets over their heads.

Worshippers gradually enter the stage one after another. Together with those political martyrs already on stage, they begin running all over the stage, falling on the floor as if killed in battle. This scene closes with the last young man falling in front of two bright, menacing lights from the back of the stage. According to Lin, this scene refers to the famous photograph of a young man facing tanks before the Tiananmen Square massacre (personal interview, July 26, 2000). On the stage, the young man collapses in a place close to the lotus pond in front of the stage. Suddenly all is quiet, and the stage is set for the final scene.

After the violent drama of Lin's "Homage to the Fallen," the last scene of the dance, "Honouring the Dead," starts by bringing the audience back into harmony with nature, echoing the content of the last poem of *Nine*

Songs, also titled "Honouring the Dead." This five-line poem portrays the final stage of a religious ceremony:

> The rites are accomplished to the beating of the drums,
> The flower-wand is passed on to succeeding dancers,
> Lovely ladies have sung their slow measures.
> In spring, the orchids, in autumn the chrysanthemums,
> So shall it be forever, without break.

As the poet depicts in the last poem, the rites are almost completed. The participants can still hear the drumming, and the flower wand the shaman holds in her hands has been passed down to other dancers—meaning she has completed her task.

In Lin's dance scene, the audience sees all the fallen dancers stand up from the floor as if they were coming back to life again. All the gods and goddesses reappear and take off their masks; they now appear to be human beings. What has just happened on stage seems to have become a part of history. As the solemn ritual song of the aboriginal Tsou people is heard once more, the dancers slowly bring in candles from the two sides of the stage, filling the stage with hundreds of lit candles. They place the candles on the floor to create a stream of flickering light extending from the pond

Figure 3 At the end of the dance, a river of flickering candlelight. Photographer: Lui Chen-hsiang.

to the black backdrop of the stage, suggesting that the river of lit candles extends into the dark, infinite realm of the night sky. The choreographer hoped that "the audience feels a sense of renewal after seeing the dance" (personal interview, July 26, 2000). Indeed, I think that *Nine Songs* serves as a healing ritual for the Taiwanese and Chinese people, who have suffered tremendously because of various political disasters during the past century.

CHINESE VISUAL AND LITERARY AESTHETICS IN LIN'S *NINE SONGS*

I have offered a description of the dance work and given particular emphasis to Lin's imaginative recreation and modification of the characters from the poetry on the dance stage. Below, my emphasis will turn to aspects of the dance that are related to concepts of traditional Chinese visual and literary aesthetics. I will also explain how these concepts assisted Lin in constructing his dance vocabulary.

Lin's *Nine Songs* shares certain concepts of spatial organization with traditional Chinese painting. Based on my analysis of the dance work, three important concepts of Chinese painting—"narrative space," "the insertion of self/author's voice," and "empty space"—are embodied in his choreography.[5] I will explain these concepts and point out where and how they are actualized in the dance. My identification of visual and literary aesthetics in Lin's dance is supported by my cultural knowledge as a Han Chinese growing up in Taiwan, as well as by various scholars' works on Chinese visual art and literary aesthetics.[6]

First, I found that the concept of narrative space from Chinese landscape painting can be recognized in Lin's choreography. The scroll format of a Chinese painting provides enough space and time to develop a narrative. The painting can create more than one scene, and provides a continuous, shifting perspective on a horizontal scroll. This allows the artist to depict an event and not just a single view or an object. The hand scroll allows the viewer to comprehend an event in a succession of images—with no cause-and-effect relationship between the images—while slowly unfolding the scroll.[7]

The eight dance scenes of Lin's *Nine Songs* are put together in a similar fashion and exhibit the concept of narrative space present in Chinese painting. In Lin's dance, each dance scene is capable of being viewed independently as a pure dance piece in itself. When the eight sections are viewed as a unit, a whole dance, they start to form a narrative, like that of a long painted scroll.

The set designer of Lin's *Nine Songs*, Ming-cho Lee, is an internationally recognized Chinese-American artist. Currently teaching at the School of

Drama at Yale University, he was invited by Lin to design the sets for *Nine Songs* in Taiwan. Lee grew up in China and immigrated to the United States as a teenager. According to an article in *Opera News*, Lee studied Chinese landscape painting as a child and considers the aesthetics of Chinese painting to have had a great impact on his stage design (Bowers 1988: 15–18). From my own observations, this seems to be true as well for Lee's design for *Nine Songs*. Lee's design features a real lotus pond with flowers and water in the orchestra pit along the front of the stage. As a result of its position, all eight scenes take place behind the lotus pond like the eight scenes of a horizontal Chinese scroll painting.

The insertion of self/author's voice is the second concept I have examined in Lin's dance.[8] Past and present are juxtaposed at several junctures in *Nine Songs*. A particularly salient example of this is a "traveller" dressed in a modern black suit who appears from time to time, suitcase in hand, walking slowly across the stage.[9] The traveller is Lin's invention; there is no such role in Chu Yuan's literary text. The traveller can be seen as representing the choreographer himself, a modern Taiwanese person who travels back to the world depicted in ancient Chinese literature to participate in the ancient dance ritual described by Chu Yuan in *Nine Songs*.[10] The insertion of this traveller echoes the idea of inserting the painter's voice in a traditional Chinese painting—the technique of "insertion of self."

According to Chinese aesthetics scholar Hsiun Chiang, traditionally the painter's goal in Chinese paintings was to capture the essence of nature with a distinct personal voice, rather than just record its physical likeness (Chiang 1993). To reconnect to our traveller by placing himself in the dance work, Lin can reflect upon his process of making meaning. History indeed comes alive in this traveller who journeys back and forth between the present and past to create meaning.

Another important concept in Chinese painting is empty space, also clearly demonstrated in Lin's choreography (Chiang 1993: 112). In a Chinese painting, completion of a work of art does not lie in a self-contained act of creation that covers an entire canvas, but in the harmony and proportion between the painted and empty spaces. This represents a balance like that between yin and yang in Chinese Taoist philosophy. Empty space is not equivalent to empty space in the Western sense—nothingness does, in fact, suggest something more. The use of empty space allows the viewer to use his or her imagination, suggesting both the notion of infinity and the idea that "less is more" (Chiang 1993: 112).

When Lin choreographs, he leaves a great deal of empty room on stage. Even the original set design was more complicated than the final one. Lin and the set designer, Ming-cho Lee, decided to remove some of the set pieces, reasoning that the audience would then be afforded room for contemplation and imagination.[11]

There is yet another use of empty space that I observed in *Nine Songs*. As mentioned above, the cycle of poems from which Lin's work derives was written and set in the fog- and cloud-filled lake region of southern China. Maximizing the amount of empty space on stage helps capture that atmosphere in the dance piece. As is typical in Chinese painting, water, river, fog, clouds, and sky are often represented by empty space (Chiang 1993: 122).

Lin's choreography also displays traits of Chinese literary aesthetics, which may be due to its inspiration from a literary text. A fondness for symbols in Chinese literary tradition is also reflected on Lin's choreography. According to the standards of Chinese art it is in bad taste to express ideas in too straightforward a manner. According to Chinese aesthetician Tse-ho Li (1996: 151), Chinese artists are fond of using symbols because they allow for indirect and poetic expression.

Lin has remarked that an important theme he tries to convey in his work is "death and rebirth." In *Nine Songs*, he adopts the lotus flower, a classical Chinese symbol for nature and the cycle of death and rebirth. Lin finds the lotus flower an especially potent symbol for communicating this message. As he explained, "Lotus flowers bud in spring, blossom in summer, wither in autumn, rot in winter—and return again in the spring." He even asked his set designer to try to include the lotus flower as the major motif in this piece. As a result, a lotus flower is painted on the backdrop and a profusion of real lotus flowers float in the pond at the front of the stage (personal interview, July 26, 2000).

Water is another powerful symbol in Lin's dance, appearing in *Nine Songs* in various shapes and forms. As I observed, the sound of water flowing in the opening sequence tells the audience that the dance is taking place in the lake region. Then there is the lotus pond where the celebrants engage in ritual cleansing before their ceremony. In "Homage to the Fallen," as the shamans wash the wound of the young boy killed for his country, water becomes a sign of purification. In addition to serving as a symbol, water itself is depicted in various scenes—for instance, when the long white scarf of the River Goddess is used to represent a spring stream.

In summary, Lin uses various traditional Chinese aesthetic concepts in *Nine Songs* in innovative ways. These aesthetic concepts not only assist him in restoring a distinctively Asian sensibility to his modern dance, but also provide a vehicle for him to bridge the past and the present as he articulates his contemporary interpretations of Chu's ancient poetry.

A DANCE MADE IN TAIWAN

As an island off mainland China, Taiwan has always been a part of, and at the same time apart from, mainstream Chinese society. Although the majority of Taiwanese people are Han Chinese and identify with their Chinese cultural roots, contemporary Taiwanese people also feel that they are not exactly the same as people in contemporary China. They cherish their own distinct cultural identity. As a Taiwanese woman, I ask myself why Lin Hwai-min, a Taiwanese choreographer, turned to Chinese literature and visual aesthetics to seek inspiration for his dance. Were his attitudes toward his "Chinese heritage" and his identity as a Taiwanese choreographer revealed in his dance creation? I will attempt here to read the dance work within the sociocultural context of contemporary Taiwan. One premise of my study is that a dance is a cultural product of the society from which it comes, and that the aesthetic analysis of a dance would be incomplete if it were taken out of its sociocultural context.

Besides drawing upon Chinese aesthetics and literary materials in *Nine Songs*, Lin has also juxtaposed various kinds of "non-Chinese" elements, as demonstrated in his choice of musical accompaniment. According to Lin, although Chu's *Nine Songs* was meant to be a ritual performance that could be sung, the original music for *Nine Songs*, like the dance, has long been lost. Reflecting on his process of choosing music for *Nine Songs*, Lin stated that the ritual music of the Taiwanese aboriginal people was his first choice. He believes that this has to do with his rich exposure to and fascination with Taiwanese aboriginal music in Taiwan. In fact, he intentionally refrained from using traditional Han Chinese music in this piece to avoid giving the audience the impression that his dance was a faithful reconstruction of an ancient Chinese ritual dance (personal interview, July 26, 2000).

Lin uses three pieces of Taiwanese aboriginal music in his *Nine Songs*. He chose the ritual music of the Taiwanese aboriginal Tsou tribe for the first scene of the dance, "Greeting the Gods," and the last, "Honouring the Dead," while using a women's festival chant of the Puyumn tribe for the dance scene "Princess of Hsiang River." Currently, there are nine major Taiwanese aboriginal tribes in Taiwan, and as the earliest inhabitants of Taiwan, they are often considered to be the most representative of authentic culture originating in Taiwan. The use of aboriginal music to reinterpret *Nine Songs*—a piece of classical Chinese literature—can be seen as Lin's strategy to claim that *Nine Songs* is the Taiwanese version of the literary piece. It was, after all, choreographed by a Taiwanese choreographer, performed by a Taiwanese dance company, and accompanied by indigenous Taiwanese music.

Lin also uses music from other Asian sources. For example, he chose Japanese court music for the "God of Clouds" scene, a Tibetan chant for the "Gods of Fates" scene, and Indian flute music for the "Mountain Spirit." It seems clear that Lin's music choice points to the truly complicated cultural history and identity of the Taiwanese people and the undeniable influence of increased globalization. From my perspective as a Taiwanese researcher, Lin's employment of diverse cultural sources can also be seen as a strategy to shake up stereotypes held by the uninitiated Westerner, who assumes that Taiwan, as an Asian society with deep roots in Chinese cultural heritage, is impervious to global modernization and too mired in Chinese tradition to change. In fact, contemporary Taiwanese culture has already taken its own course of development as a result of historical and geographical factors. It has grown into a culture with its own identity that is reducible neither to that of historical China nor to that of contemporary China. The importance of Chinese cultural heritage can be seen in Lin's choice to use Chu's poetry, *Nine Songs*, as a device to reconnect to his Chinese cultural heritage. However, to gain full understanding of contemporary Taiwanese culture, one also needs to consider the various other cultures that have greatly influenced Taiwan, such as indigenous Taiwanese cultures, other Asian cultures, and even Western cultures.

When *Nine Songs* was presented at the Brooklyn Academy of Music in New York in October 1995, the choreographer revealed in a performance review (Dekle 1995) that "[his] travels to Bali and India gave [him] the feeling of how [he] would present this piece." Clearly, Lin did not limit himself to Chinese cultural influences in representing Chu Yuan's *Nine Songs* on a contemporary stage. Rather, he acknowledged the multiple cultural influences acting on him as a Taiwanese choreographer and enriching his dance work.

As post-colonial cultural theorist Homi K. Bhabha (1994) has articulated, cultural identity is a question everyone encounters in the contemporary world. According to him, the concept of cultural identity is related to how we define our culture and how we differentiate our culture from other cultures. Bhabha assumes that biology is not the only factor that determines one's identity; rather, one's sociocultural history and experiences also shape identity. Indeed, by observing Lin's *Nine Songs*, one can clearly see that, although Lin is a descendant of Han Chinese, his living experience in Taiwan and the United States has familiarized him with Taiwanese aboriginal music, various other Asian traditions, and American modern dance. By integrating various cultural elements into his dance work, the choreographer and Cloud Gate Dance Theatre contribute to the illumination of a contemporary Taiwanese cultural identity that has deep roots in ancient Chinese culture but also departs from it, having been influenced by a wealth of other non-Chinese cultures.

CONCLUSION

Lin's dance generates a life of its own. By drawing upon ethnographic research methods to collect data, and analyzing the dance from an insider's perspective, I have found that Lin does not just slavishly translate Chu Yuan's poetry into dance images. Through the information I gathered at rehearsals of the dance company, at interviews with the choreographer, and my attempts to read this dance within the broader cultural context of present-day Taiwan, I have discovered that the choreographer has added layers of contemporary meanings into the dance. This study also provides insights into how a Taiwanese choreographer today comes to terms with his Chinese cultural past, his current experience in Taiwan, as well as cultural influences from other parts of the world. Indeed, in this landmark modern dance piece, Lin Hwai-min bridges the past and the present and, in so doing, rejuvenates the classical literary work and makes it relevant to our time once again through dancers' moving bodies.

Notes

1 *Nine Songs* was produced by Cloud Gate Dance Theatre and premiered at the National Theatre of Taipei on October 22, 1993. The company was also later invited to perform this choreography at various international arts festivals, such as the Next Wave Festival of the Brooklyn Academy of Arts in 1995, and the Olympic Arts Festival in Australia in 2000. From 1993 to 2007, *Nine Songs* was performed ninety-seven times in Taiwan, Hong Kong, Australia, Germany, United States, Colombia, Australia, and New Zealand.

2 Taiwan used to be a deserted island in the Pacific Ocean off mainland China. It was occupied by the Dutch and the Spanish during the eighteenth century, and the Japanese between 1889 and 1945. Taiwan's significance in Chinese history emerged in the past several centuries. Before many Chinese people had moved to Taiwan, the island was primarily occupied by Taiwanese aborigines. Due to the lack of arable land in southern China, a large number of Chinese people began to immigrate to Taiwan in search of a better life during the Ching dynasty (1616–1912 AD). They gradually became the majority of the population in Taiwan. In 1949, when the Communists took over China and the original Nationalist government, led by President Chiang Kai-shek, withdrew to Taiwan to establish a government. Following the Nationalist government, a second wave of Chinese immigrants came to Taiwan. From then on, Taiwan and Mainland China were under a situation of separation, and for four decades people on the two sides of the Taiwan Strait were not permitted to visit each other.

3 For the English translation, I primarily used Arthur Waley's translation of Chu Yuan's *Nine Songs* (1955).

4 See Yenzen (1993: 95). There are nine major aboriginal tribes in Taiwan living primarily along the eastern coast and in the central mountainous area of Taiwan. The nine aboriginal tribes are Atayal, Saisiyat, Bunun, Tsou, Paiwan, Rukai, Puyuma, Ami, and Yami. Each of these tribes has its own language and cultural characteristics. They are the earliest habitants of Taiwan. Today, although they have been more or less influenced by the descendants of Han Chinese people in Taiwan, they still keep a comparatively traditional lifestyle, and dance and music still constitute an important part of their festivals and ceremonies.

5 In his book *A Contemplation on Chinese Art* (1993: 96–114), Hsiun Chiang, an important Taiwanese scholar of Chinese aesthetics, proposes these three important concepts of Chinese aesthetics based on his study of traditional Chinese painting and arts.

6 To identify the Chinese aesthetics in Lin's dance, I have also consulted Yeah (1996) and Li (1996).

7 For a more extensive discussion of the concept of narrative space in Chinese art, see "Time and Space in Chinese Art" in Chiang (1993: 83–88).

8 A more extensive discussion of the concept of insertion of self/author's voice in Chinese art is also found in "Time and Space in Chinese Art" in Chiang (1993: 83–88).

9 This mysterious traveller appears from time to time in Lin's *Nine Songs*. The "traveller" is listed as a specific role in the dance program of *Nine Songs* (1993).

10 Lin also agrees that the traveller can be interpreted as himself. He adds, however, that he purposely kept the traveller's identity a mystery, preferring to leave the question open to the viewer's interpretation (personal interview, July 26, 2000).

11 This story is recounted in a book by journalist Kei-chen Hsu. See Lin, Hsu, and Ji (1993: 157).

Bibliography

Bhabha, Homi. *The Location of Culture*. New York: Routledge, 1994.

Bowers, Faubion. "Dean of Design." *Opera News* (March 1988): 15–18.

Chiang, Hsiun. *A Contemplation on Chinese Art*. Taipei: Hsiung-shih Art, 1993.

Chiou, Yi-wen. *Shamanism and Nine Songs*. Taipei: Wen-wei, 1996.

Chu, Yuan. *Nine Songs*. Taipei: Chiu-po, 1998.

Cloud Gate Dance Theatre. *Nine Songs*. Printed program. National Theatre, Taipei, August 10, 1993.

Cloud Gate Foundation. *Cloud Gate at Twenty*. Taipei: Cloud Gate Foundation, 1993.

Dekle, Nicole. "Stirring Still Waters: Nature and Ritual Meet Politics in Chinese Dance." *Village Voice*, October 24, 1995.

Li, Tse-ho. *Chinese Aesthetics*. Taipei: Shan-Min, 1996.

Lin, Hwai-min. *Source and Transformation*. Taipei: Cloud Gate Foundation, 1995.

———. Personal interview. July 26, 2000.

Lin, Hwai-min, Kei-chen Hsu, and Huei-ling Ji. *Lin Hwai-min's Nine Songs*. Taipei: Ming-shen, 1993.

Nine Songs. Choreographed by Lin Hwai-min and performed by Cloud Gate Dance
    Theatre. Video. Taipei: Joy Communication, 1993.
Waley, Arthur. *The Nine Songs*. London: George Allen and Unwin, 1955.
Wang, Si-yuan, ed. *Ch'u Tz'u*. Taipei: Jin-fun, 1988.
Yeah, Lang. *A History of Chinese Aesthetics*. Taipei: Wen-Jin, 1996.
Yenzen, Kunpen. *Taiwanese Aborigines*. Taipei: Chen-chin, 1993.

CHAPTER TWENTY

Revealed by Fire

LATA PADA'S NARRATIVE OF TRANSFORMATION

SUSAN MCNAUGHTON

Revealed by Fire was produced and performed by Canadian choreographer Lata Pada in March 2001 at Premiere Dance Theatre in Toronto. It was a work that called on multiple forms of media to embody not only the memory of the events that inspired it, but Pada's journey of self-discovery in the process of its making and performance. In what follows, I explore the ways in which the dance project *Revealed by Fire* "danced against" the idea of delivering an unproblematic world of sense to the audience and instead located itself in the "productive conflict of different ways of knowing" (Marks 2000: 239). My ethnography examines the creation of *Revealed by Fire*[1] as a microcosmic event and follows its trajectory in connection to the larger sociocultural issues of which it forms a part.

I conducted multi-site ethnographic research in Toronto and Chennai in partial fulfillment of my MA in dance at York University from 2000 to 2001. My fieldwork in Chennai, India, was conducted among bharatanatyam performers, choreographers, dance scholars, and critics for the purpose of comparative study. I was able to view performances at Kalakshetra,[2] research written accounts, and collect oral histories of Indian dancers and choreographers. In a confluence of serendipitous events, I was invited to perform in a contemporary dance festival, The Other Festival, in Chennai in 2000, where I was able to participate in, as well as observe, the multi-faceted interface between contemporary dance and classical dance tradition. While I was in Chennai, India, the opportunity arose to participate in the annual Natya Kala Conference, a venue where dance critics, classical and contemporary dancers, and scholars had the opportunity for debate and discussion on what such an interface implied for bharatanatyam.

Formal and informal interviews with Pada and her collaborators were conducted between July and December 2001, during the conception and performance of *Revealed*. These form the foundation of my study. I recorded and transcribed only formal interviews as the more informal interviews were often conversations wedged between rehearsals, or the collaborators' other rehearsals and engagements. Recording devices seemed intrusive and disruptive. I took extensive field notes in the working rehearsals Pada held with her dance company in studio as well as tech/dress rehearsals that took place in Pada's home studio, the performance dress rehearsal, and all performances at Premiere Dance Theatre.

My exploration of bharatanatyam and its practitioners had two sources. One source was my close relationship, an apprenticeship actually, in the informal but daily study of Sankhya philosophy and Sanskrit under the insightful guidance of Mantri Lal, a former lawyer from Lahore, Pakistan. What struck me most besides his seemingly voluminous knowledge of Indian shastras were his wit and shrewdness in dealing with the racism and cultural stereotyping he often had to face in Toronto. We would sometimes walk or take public transit through Toronto and he took every opportunity to introduce himself to complete strangers as "Peter the Paki handyman" and to "shoot the breeze" with anyone who would talk to him. It seemed to me he did this in order to break the spell of being treated as if he were from another time instead of a geographically distinct place. Even in these exchanges, his intensity and his interest in others were heightened by his unassuming manner. His ability to shift between the roles of a casual labourer and that of a mentor in Vedic lore, traditional religious practices, shastras, and jyotish brought me closer to understanding his own journey through the muddy waters of the global diaspora.

The second source was the study of anthropology. Although dance is no longer my main focus, the story of bharatanatyam had led to my pursuit of a doctoral degree in social anthropology [awarded posthumously in December 2010—ed.]. At the time of this research I was struck by the ability of bharatanatyam practitioners to act as a powerful tool for social change during the period of British colonization. The question that took me over the threshold of the anthropology department was: So what was it about the bharatanatyam dancer, now, that seemed to inhabit and influence the everyday spaces of the global/local?

In the analysis and writing-up process, I moved in and out of ethnography, valuing immediate experience but also questioning some of the assumptions that underpin ethnographic practice in relation to Indian dance. Geertz warns that "ethnographic contextualizations are as problematic as aesthetic ones, as susceptible to purified ahistorical treatment" (Chow 1993: 39). At the same time, bharatanatyam's colonial genealogy, while important, is not the whole story in the context of contemporary dance. As I write this I am confronted once again with the conundrum of writing about bharatanatyam as a Western woman brought up in a primarily Judeo-Christian environment who remembers being unabashedly dazzled by my first viewing of the bejewelled bharatanatyam dancer in her red and gold sari. Her opulence pointed to historical origins and cultural contents I could only guess at. How was I to write without confining the bharatanatyam dancer's body or body of work to exclusionary terms? Talking about bharatanatyam as a culturally specific practice opened a Pandora's box to questions of identity/otherness, ethnicity/race, and class/caste. This dilemma was ever-present throughout the ethnographic process as Pada herself struggled against the reifying image of the temple dancer and sought to tell her own story.

At the time of this project I was active as a contemporary dancer, choreographer, and teacher. Pada and I met as students in the MA program in dance at York University; it was there that I learned about her work as well as her story. A large part of the appeal of this research was Pada's courage in putting such a personal and life-changing moment on stage; more important was her willingness to avoid dwelling in psychological depths in telling her story and her decision to de-emphasize the virtuosic bharatanatyam body so highly valued among performers. I admired her journey along her circuitous route of memory, being willing to represent it as a layering of fragmented experience that defied closure or an evolutionary progression toward an inevitable conclusion.

DANCING THE GLOBAL/LOCAL

In 2001, the fusion of hip hop, Bollywood-style dance, and bharatanatyam was beginning to be popular among young second- and third-generation South Asians dancers in Toronto. Dance fusion of this kind was creating a lot of excitement at this time in part because it blurred the lines between Indian classical and popular dance genres, creating a style of popular dance that appealed across cultures and generations. Because the style was eclectic it could be performed in diverse theatrical venues—from nightclub dance spots like Verve on Toronto's Queen Street West to proscenium arch stages. I attended a unique performance of what has come to be known as "Bollywood style" dancing in the spring of 2000. It was held in the auditorium of the Federal Labour Organization (FLO) in Toronto, where, attended by two hundred and fifty older, primarily first-generation South Asians, a big celebration of the FLO's anniversary was under way.

The large assembly hall buzzed with news that professional bharatanatyam dancers accompanied by the Bombay Rhythm Orchestra were arriving from India for the occasion. Instead of the advertised "classical" Indian dance performance, the dancers performed a fusion of classical Indian dance gesture and Bollywood- style dance to an eclectic musical mix of hip hop/bhangra and rock. I expected mild shock from the audience, but I saw instead that many were humming and clapping along with the music and recognized the movement style from Indian cinema. A few brave audience members jumped to their feet and started dancing together after the dancers left the performance area, signalling the rest to do the same. The audience was clearly enthusiastic. The woman next to me exclaimed, "This is just like Indian cinema!" A very different experience from the classical bharatanatyam programs I had seen, this one seemed to not only elicit enthusiastic audience response but also invite audience participation.

Bharatanatyam has historically been a site of hybrid approaches and practices, and yet the relatively recent changes that have taken place in the approach to and performance of this style are often viewed suspiciously by more traditional practitioners. Classical training is notoriously rigorous and elaborate and often requires a special relationship with a teacher. Conventional training follows the guru-shishya *parampar* tradition,[3] including the meticulous study of music and rhythm especially in the performance of *alarippu*.[4] The dancers I met in Chennai felt it more important to honour their teacher's repertoire than explore, invent, or innovate on their own. A student's commitment to upholding their teacher's approach to tradition is an unspoken, but often critically important, part of their relationship.

But what of *arangetram*[5] programs and the careful practice of *abhinaya*[6] in a globalized consumer culture where students no longer want to devote a decade of their lives to one teacher? It seemed the once-reliable map of heritage and history was no longer able to describe the territory in which contemporary bharatanatyam dancers found themselves, but had become the territory. Almost anyone could emulate it.

Due to the increased sophistication in simulation technologies a new "real" had slipped with little warning into the place of acceptable bharatanatyam practice, resulting in a bricolage of traditional and popular dance forms that blurred the boundaries of both. The "traditional" appeared to be effaced or superseded by the signs of its existence etched into the speed and transparency of mass communications. Not only the Bollywood film industry but music videos featuring henna-painted and sari-clad stars like Madonna, singing *Shanti Ashtangi* and dancing in homage to the Indian deity Vishnu, had managed to capture the image of a "virtual" bharatanatyam dancer. Contemporary bharatanatyam in particular was clearly informed by contentious influences.

Bharatanatyam thus made an impact far beyond the performative expression registered in the dancer's own body. Its intersection with contemporary dance and music styles was shaped by, but also shaped, the social, cultural, and economic conditions that underpinned its transformations. Modern power, in the form of the globalized movement of people, goods, communication technologies, and culture had created conditions in which new kinds of desire and new kinds of possibility emerged. For better or worse, a market for a transnational aesthetic had been created.

But what were the means of interpreting, legitimating, and resisting categorical identities in contemporary contexts among contemporary bharatanatyam practitioners? What was fusion and what was appropriation? Concerns among dance practitioners collided over the seemingly inevitable cultural homogenization that followed in the wake of culture industries in spite of the claims on their attention for adherence to traditional values. Bharatanatyam dancers participated in both traditional and hybridized events, yet found praise on one side for upholding traditional values and criticism on the other for polluting or corrupting the form with choreographic innovation. At the same time, important values of the home culture were constantly being reformulated to include dancers' own present cultural environment and values.

In conversations with Toronto-based bharatanatyam dance artists and choreographers it became clear to me that changes to the contemporary Indian dance scene were part of a larger discourse, one complicated by issues of identity and social personhood. The current trend of performative practices, some argued, merely evoked nostalgia for India's imagined past and provided, at best, a means of self-expression for an educated global consumer. The production of South Asian-ness as easily digestible and marketable within a corporate transnational marketplace was revealing of the contemporary processes of identity formation and the ways in which place, race, and nation came to bear on these representations. In the gaps between a politics of representation and identity the dance artists' stories, lives, and experiments were enacted. Their individual voices register less as individualistic self-expression and express instead dissent, re-emphasizing heterogeneity over homogeneity.

The interface of Indian classical dance, film, and video, at times by accident and at times by design, facilitated a multidisciplinary perspective that cut across boundaries of historical, temporal, and geographical specificities.

On one hand South Asian dance artists were in a unique position to "speak between" audience and performer in ways that did not merely reconstruct or re-evoke the narrative of a monolithic past. But on the other hand, the crossing of boundaries between popular interpretations and the lineage of classical dance tradition was, in part, the effect of a tactic of strategic essentialism that enabled continued survival as artists. Dancers learned to "perform" cultural identity to counter the contradictory demands often imposed upon them to simultaneously produce their culture as a commodity for the changing "tastes" of the market and also as a fixed essence capable of display. Such a dance vernacular invokes a two-way trajectory: the first moves back into the quasi-mystical past and the other shoots forward to its present as a commodified sign, with an auratic quality that seems to vanish as quickly as it is recuperated.

In another conversation with a dancer, born in the United States to South Asian parents, I was told the story of her performing experience at a promotional event for Air India and the Indian Board of Tourism. Because she "looked Indian" and the dance she performed fulfilled the organizer's expectations of what they considered "authentic," she found herself performing short set pieces before an audience as they munched canapés and sipped white wine. The audience, wanting to be seduced into visiting India, was most impressed, to her chagrin, with the costume, jewellery, and her flower-decorated hair. After the performance, a German art historian who worked in India as a guide, approached her saying, "Your technique is as good as dancers in India but you have to work on your presence. It is too self-confident. Women in India are not like that!"[7]

Lata Pada, based in Toronto, is internationally known for a performing career that spans twenty-five years. She is acknowledged particularly by Toronto audiences as a choreographer, founder, and artistic director of Sampradaya Dance Creations.[8] Her goal is to create work that takes risks, "to be vulnerable and most critically to learn from the process."[9] *Revealed by Fire* was unlike any of her previous dance work in that it told her personal tale of loss and tragedy, and also challenged her to confront the paradox of her lived experience that compelled her, without always allowing her, to identify as a Canadian artist.

Pada had already made complex adjustments as a contemporary bharatanatyam dancer and choreographer working outside of India. She spoke to me of the tension she felt being encouraged to develop and maintain South Asian traditional forms while simultaneously feeling under pressure to create new and more challenging artworks. Her experience testified to the cracks between "official" national/ cultural histories and her lived history, revealing the fuzziness between culture, history, identity, and tradition. As she embarked upon this project she could not but be implicated in the power relations upon which the work reflected. In the creation of *Revealed by Fire* Pada was confronted by a double remoteness in relation to Toronto's dance community at large and to an imagined Indian source of origin. As Marks observes in the context of intercultural film, cultural diaspora can involve both productive as well as destructive processes:

> When experience takes place in the conjunction of two or more cultural regimes of knowledge ... [artists] must find ways to express this experience that cannot be in terms of either: experimental form helps to express the emergent knowledge conditions of intercultural experience. (Marks 2000: 10)

In a post-production conversation Pada explained: "It was December 1999 when I realized that this work was about me, but I was still playing it safe. Not until August 2000 did I actually decide to be specific in telling my own story.... This was hugely liberating" (Pada 2000).

"BETWEEN BOMBAY, INDIA, AND THOMPSON, MANITOBA, THERE ARE SEVEN STEPS. WHERE AM I? / WHERE AM I GOING?"[10]

Revealed was a multidisciplinary work that juxtaposed text, sound score, and film footage with bharatanatyam and improvised dance. It brought together artists from diverse backgrounds pushing the disciplinary boundaries between videography, film, music, dance, and dramaturgy. It was an ambitious work that attempted to come to terms with the past, both Pada's own as well as the historical narratives that haunt bharatanatyam. Though she attempted to take deliberate steps in *Revealed*'s creation, inevitable irruptions occurred as the process evolved as she and her collaborators shared the creative navigation of an explosive terrain necessary to its own creation.

The inspiration for *Revealed by Fire* was the tragic loss of Pada's family in the Air India bombing of 1985. On the morning of June 23, 1985, Flight 182, en route from Toronto to Bombay, India, disappeared from all radar screens and subsequently was lost to a mid-air explosion over the Atlantic Ocean, one hundred miles from the southwest coast of Ireland. It was declared the largest aviation disaster in Canada's history. Of the 329 passengers aboard the flight, 156 were Canadian, three of whom were Pada's husband and two daughters.

In thinking about how to craft this piece, Pada decided at first to represent her experience allegorically, mediated by Indian mythology and framed in terms of an aesthetically pleasing performance. Instead it became necessary to explore and expose a moment in her life that, like the aftermath of a bombing, was potentially desolate and discouraging, even alien. The death of her husband and children, her cultural isolation in Canada, as well as the gender and class exclusions she faced as a widow in India, resulted in a form of socialized *sati* and the sublimation of female identity that is expected of widows. Creating and performing *Revealed* soon became a precarious undertaking.

At the same time, as work began on the choreography there had been a lot of press coverage of the Air India tragedy.[11] Prior to opening night, sixteen years after the event, the Royal Canadian Mounted Police arrested two suspects, catapulting *Revealed by Fire* and Lata Pada to front-page news in many national daily newspapers, provoking a flood of media interviews. One effect of this media attention could be seen in the busy box office at Harbourfront and a guaranteed sold-out run. At the same time, coincident with the rehearsal and performing period, the local Sikh community held fundraisers to support the legal costs of the newly arrested suspects (Rudakoff 2002). Pada and her collaborators were all too aware they had a fine line to walk between producing a theatrical event that would portray the reality of the event but also not allowing it to become sensationalized by press coverage. A large portion of her audience was South Asian, and there was no way of knowing whether they would embrace or shun *Revealed*.

The opening of the dance begins with Pada, alone in a simple white sari, rehearsing in a dance studio in Bombay, awaiting the arrival of her family. She is jolted out of her concentration by the sound of an abnormally loud phone ringing, a sound that will ultimately change the course of her life. We hear her voice in a pre-recorded text as "Lata": "It was an ordinary day. I was rehearsing. The phone rang." As she is told the terrible news of the crash, Pada comes out of the shock which had frozen her to the spot and reaches up to tear down the panels of red and gold saris streaming from the cyclorama. The stage appears engulfed in a mass of flames. Fire, a central metaphor of the work, represents both the explosive moment of the plane crash that took her family but also the burning ground of memory; fire both onscreen and onstage, evoked destruction as well as emergence:

> Fire ... is a symbol of both the creative and destructive elements in my life. It is also a metaphor for the transformative process that I have had to undergo and the catharsis that can occur when one is plunged into the depths of sorrow or tragedy. (Pada 2001)

The image widens out across the back of the stage, giving the impression that Pada herself is engulfed in flames: the flames of sati, the flames of half a life that has disappeared forever. Within the fire we see the photos of her husband Vishnu and her two daughters, Brinda and Arti, drift across the screen as if caught in a fire draught, their smiling faces curling and dissolving in the heat of the flames. This is followed rapidly by single images of each of them smiling, in a happier time and place. A scrapbook of her life is disappearing into ash and smoke. These images become embers, then ash disappearing in a gust of wind. Pada sinks to her knees, reaching up to the screen as if to try and recapture their faces for one more moment. The screen goes black.

This powerful opening forms a keyhole through which Pada leads us into a world which we come to see, as the dance continues, is actually two worlds. Pada describes how, in creating this work, she became aware of an intersection between the physical state of reliving the shock and the psychological state of recalling the tragedy. By working through it again in the form of a danced self-narrative, she allows these two states to meet and mirror each other. She distinguishes the irrevocable rift between the life

Figure 1 From the section "Obstructions" of *Revealed by Fire*. Lata faces the challenges of society in rediscovering her voice and identity. Dancers: Lata Pada (centre) and (left to right) Lakshmi Venkataraman, Suba Navaratnasingam, Aneela Maharaj, Rajkumari Chatterjee, Anandhi Narayanan. Photographer: Andrew Oxenham.

she knew prior to the plane crash and the life following it. Her past is represented as a dream-like memory in which her individuality is defined as a member of a family and that family as a member of a larger community.

The creation of this dance work took over two years and underwent considerable transformation. Pada originally wanted to approach the themes of loss, transformation, and her journey of fire allegorically—as Sita experiencing *agni pareksha*.[12] The unabashed expression of her personal experience stood in direct opposition to the proscribed value of distancing oneself from personal experience by framing it in the context of Indian mythology. She balked at an autobiographical performance. Having to excavate the painful past was only one challenge; communicating it to three collaborators with strong opinions of their own in the creation of the project was another. The artistic intuition that accompanies beginnings had yet to come ... how to begin? How could she turn a personal landscape which had effectively been scarred and burned by loss into theatre?

> About two years ago there was a documentary on my life aired on Vision TV. A couple of days later, I had a phone call from a woman. Here was this woman who was absolutely grief-stricken, almost incoherent. She didn't tell me her story, all she could say was that this documentary had an incredible impact on her life and she was able to put her own grief into context. I didn't ask any questions but I understood what she meant. I think that gave me the strength and the motivation to tell this story. (Pada 2001)

The dance consists of seven sections. Beginning with the news of the plane crash as Pada is rehearsing in her guru's studio in Bombay, *Revealed* is told in flashbacks to her childhood, then forward to her marriage and immigration to Canada. Describing the sections as frames, Pada viewed the work cinematically and created an intricate storyboard which articulated the multiple time periods the story covered, as well as the psychological dimensions she wanted it to reflect. Film footage depicting an array of images—images of India, a winter parka, the first gift from her husband upon arriving in Manitoba, images of nature—shifted and dissolved continuously in the background, providing powerful metaphors for the geographical and cultural boundaries Pada had crossed. Liminal symbols of passage from one state to another also flashed across the screen—vignettes of her childhood, her marriage in India, motherhood in Manitoba—expressing the corporeal transformation that represented her submersion in and re-emergence from the past.

Pada, along with her collaborators—musician Tim Sullivan and visual artist Cylla von Tiedemann (whose photo of Pada is found on the cover of

REVEALED BY FIRE :: SUSAN MCNAUGHTON

this book)—created a storyboard that set out the multiple real-life time periods as well as the "memory" time periods the story covered. Von Tiedemann's videography gave the memory sections a dream-like quality that changed spatial location and also created the illusion of an interior and exterior stage space. This effect was emphasized by the visual impact of the embodied images shifting from a weighty horizontal to a lighter filmic verticality. At times the performing area appeared as if extended both in a downstage direction toward the audience and upstage toward the film images on the cyclorama. The effect gave the scenes of the air crash and Pada's solo a sense of being caught in a threshold and an appearance of the story shifting from past to present. Pada was able to move between the interstices of the particular, the personal and psychological dimensions important to the realization of the work, and she also found the detachment and self-control necessary to produce and coordinate the performance. She wanted her story to connect with those of her audience, many of whom had also lost loved ones in the plane crash. She wanted her audience to move and learn with her that there are new ways of looking at things.

Viewing the work cinematically gave Pada the opportunity to explore other movement possibilities in the transitions between scenes and the spaces in which narrative fragments occurred. This exploration closed the gap between the poles of representation / subjectivity and nostalgia / familiarity. Encouraged by her collaborators, Pada gradually came to recognize a way of structuring the dance by committing to, rather than avoiding, the potentially cathartic nature of the work. The "self" she became in the course of the dance shifted her conception of "self" to whom these tragic events happened. It became evident in the process of creation that, while reframing the events of the past for theatrical presentation, she was effectively rewriting her autobiography—putting the pictures in the scrapbook according to her own chronology.

In *Revealed by Fire* dance performed a number of important functions: a constant companion, a restorative place, a creative force, and a means of self-remembering. The dance onstage formed the point of connectivity around which events past and present took place; her body was not a passive object inscribed with meaning but a source of meaning and sensuously informed knowledge. Throughout these seven sections memory is actualized in bodily sensations. The opening scenes introduce the primary metaphors that help blend the story with solo bharatanatyam, group choreography, and the multimedia theatricality of the dance work.

"IN A TINY BLACK BOX, THE FINAL MOMENT RECORDED. HOW DO I UNLOCK THE BOX? WHAT'S THE COMBINATION? I SLEEPLESSLY TURN LEFT, TURN RIGHT, TURN LEFT."

The creation of *Revealed* meant all participants—collaborators and dancers—had to move through uncharted waters. Because of the highly personal nature of the work, sensitivity and trust had to be built slowly to dispel apprehension on everyone's part and to allow the intensity of the material, Pada's memories, to come forward. Though there was an unavoidably strong psychological and therapeutic component underpinning the creation process, this was an artistic endeavour, not a therapeutic one. *Revealed* became, however, a form of autoethnography conveyed through dance and text that in the absence of other records became a vehicle of Pada's memory and future dreams for her family.

Autoethnography was a transformative tool for Pada in discovering her place in the "new" world of awakened memory by linking forms of storytelling and connecting the autobiographical and personal to the cultural, social, and political. Through the combination of text, dance, and film, Pada was able to explore, keeping interpretive possibilities open while also circumventing artificial closure:

> This work is part of a long ... emotional and spiritual journey for me that started about 15 years ago.... I felt that I had a story that could be told through dance but I wasn't quite sure if I had the courage to tell it. It was a story inside me that found voice only about two years ago. (Pada 2001)

Themes of disruption and difference, boundary crossing both literal and metaphorical, and citizenship and belonging were all a part of her narrative. Pada's arrival as an immigrant from India many years ago, the beginning of her new career in Canada, a country informed by different metaphors, marked a turning point in her work as a solo bharatanatyam artist and her uncovering of another dance "voice," which departed in important ways from the iconography of her traditional bharatanatyam work. The multidisciplinary nature of this theatre work brought to light the ways in which dance is a social act, embodying social relations, and is therefore also an expression of place and voice within a social field of various and at times competing discourses.

At a time of profound shock time stands still; a similar movement arrested the process of this work. Little by little, going back to the minute animations and tactility of her daily life after the crash began to recapture her attention. Certain primary experiences surfaced, creating a plot line that Pada, her collaborators and her audience could inhabit. The difficulty of memory excavation grew less arduous, and along with it her trust in the collaborative creative process enabled her to move between her past into the present toward the future. As audience members we could also savour the immediacy of memory images: the feel and smell of a sari on her skin, her wedding jewellery, her widow's shroud, the feel of wet stones beneath her feet. One scene depicting Pada's widowhood after the crash showed the dancers circling around Lata, stripping her of her wedding jewellery and clothing, then pressing their blood-stained hands against white cloth reminiscent of widows' sati. An image juxtaposed with huge red banners floated, wave-like, across the cyclorama. Such metaphors gave her memory-body substance, showing the "slippage between the symbolic and the 'real' and [the fact] that the 'real' in dance, the body, holds in its hands our well-being, our mortality" (Hamera 2002: 32).

Figure 2 From the section "Resistance" of *Revealed by Fire*. Dancers (left to right): Suba Navaratnasingam, Lakshmi Venkataraman, Rajkumari Chatterjee, Anandhi Narayanan. "These images of blood-stained hands on a white cloth are a potent metaphor for the total sublimation of women's identities. The women of Rajasthan imprint walls with their hands before they gave themselves to the funeral fire of their husbands in the ritual of sati, rather than suffer the fate of negation of personal identity" (Rudakoff 2002). Photographer: Andrew Oxenham.

"THE EXPERIENCE OF BEING EMBODIED IS NEVER A PRIVATE AFFAIR"[13]

The dance work was conceived in multiple locations as Pada and videographer von Tiedemann travelled in order to film an Indian imaginary evocative of Pada's remembered past. Though their relationship was strained almost to the breaking point on a trip through India, Pada said that it later helped her "to confront the reality of my culture, of my history, of my past." In a conversation among ourselves, Pada and von Tiedemann described the circuitous beginnings of the project and von Tiedemann's arguments for the work to become personal:

> **Pada:** I thought that Cylla [von Tiedemann], with her photographic artistry and her love of India, and I could trace the nexus between dance and sculpture found in the [Indian] temples, and how those [*devadasi* dance] compositions evolved out of the temple and why they were so deeply devotional and philosophical in content.... But underlying it was always [my] story that wanted to be told. Maybe at first I didn't feel comfortable about it being the right kind of story because in India people are very, very private. We will do everything on the stage but we will not talk about a personal issue on the stage. It's just not done. [...]

> **McNaughton:** It seems very courageous to put such a life experience on stage [...]

> **Von Tiedemann:** You can't believe how many barriers there were—emotional barriers. That was a very deep wound that Lata had healed with many, many patches. But I think it never heals, it cannot heal. So I always knew you (Lata) had it in you [to do this piece] but it was so deeply buried. It was like unpatching, like taking everything off until you got to the bare wound again. There was a lot of resistance on your part.

> **Pada:** There was. You're always afraid to take the scab off an old wound because you don't know what is going to happen.... But I guess you just get to a point where you say, it's worth making that leap—both ways, both artistically and emotionally. And they just seemed to come together. [...]

> **Von Tiedemann:** When we actually got to putting down the storyline in Shridhari we began to imagine how it could look and how we'd deal with it. It was a really good exchange. I thought it was the first step in a true artistic collaboration. That's where we had the idea of the storyboard. It was in India. [...] (Pada, Sullivan, and von Tiedemann 2001)

A central challenge for Pada in the creation of *Revealed* was deciding how much of her personal experience could and should be revealed. Her decision to dramatize her own story rather than create a generic narrative was pivotal to the creative tension inherent in the piece between therapeutic techniques of self and expression of aesthetic values. While such a decision to "lay bare the dream" seemed straightforward to me, having worked in particular theatrical conventions that value the exploration and expression of emotions, it was a decision Pada struggled with.

In contrast to the South Asian tendency to reticence, her primary collaborator von Tiedemann urged her to explore the dimension of psychological realism and theatrical audacity, and remarked, "Here in North America, we do exactly the opposite. [Performers] strip themselves naked on stage to talk about their emotions and share everything. It's an incredible cultural difference" (von Tiedemann 2001). It was an approach that took both of them some time to adjust to. For Pada it not only meant relinquishing her identification with the institutions and social practices from which bharatanatyam had originated and recapitulating the loss of her family in the Air India tragedy, but it also meant a new and unprogrammatic approach to choreography.

Classical Indian dance is comfortable with the "storying body," which, as Foster puts it, are "no bodies," or in the case of the colonial enterprise, the quintessential Indian body (Foster 1996: 332). Aware of the critical view that traditional bharatanatyam practitioners have regarding choreographic innovation, which they perceive as narcissistic experimentation, Pada said:

> There are very specific ways of showing emotion in Indian dance, but it's very stylized.... If you want honesty and real emotions to come through then you have to put aside stylization because it has to be lived in the body. I had to then strip away all my training, put it aside.... How did I react as a human being, not a dancer? How did I react and what would my body have said? (Pada 2001)

At the same time, grappling with the creative space between tradition and innovation became more complex when her guru questioned her motive: "Why would you tell your story onstage? It is the lives of the gods and goddesses who must be celebrated." Pada said, "He thought I was bringing the work to a mundane level by telling my own story, and somehow cheapening the art form as a result. I knew I would be breaking with cultural conditioning with this work: my own and my audience's" (Pada 2001).

Transplanted traditional social and cultural orders were also mediated by the dancers' own bodies. Colonial and post-colonial reconstructions of bharatanatyam deployed in the reification of images of Indian culture and notions of idealized feminine embodiment continue to inform the contemporary practice of bharatanatyam (Meduri 1996). Yet what interested Pada the deeper she got into this project was not tradition but the highly charged, overlapping synaesthesia of all the senses that are involved in rhythm, language, visual art, and movement (Ram 2000). The intersection between notions of heritage and contemporary bharatanatyam practice were also revealed:

> My exploration had to do with an internal cultural examination of my own identity in my growing years and then ... [moving] to northern Manitoba, while remaining an Indian dance teacher, being a mother, being a wife ... then suddenly, being stripped of all those identities and having to forge a new identity. Those were the underlying things that I felt I needed to resolve. (Pada 2001)

The shape of the piece came into focus in fits and starts. Though sections of dance and music had been completed, the ambient music, spoken text, and video and film images had yet to be finalized. It wasn't until December 2001 that the final narrative storyboard was up and finalized, leaving only two months until the premiere.

"IN THE BOXES I FOUND A TAPE OF THE GIRLS' VOICES ... THIS IS THE INTIMACY THAT DEATH FORCES UPON US"

Pada's uncovering of personal identity was a participatory process for all her collaborators. The pre-recorded text allowed Pada to structure her role theatrically and give textual form to her ideas. It served as a kind of Ariadne's thread through the central metaphors and memories of the past. Her voice narrates the series of events that she, and her inventive company of five dancers, describe as her journey of self-transformation. The role of Lata as narrator erased the need to give her every action a precise value associated with specific images and intentions and inspired another layer of recovering and uncovering personal identity. Dramaturge Judith Rudakoff said:

> We talked in real theatrical terms about the character of "Lata" as opposed to Lata the person, and what the character of Lata's role within the theatrical narrative of *Revealed by Fire* was in communicating these things to an audience.... What we had to do was strike a balance between the universal story that Lata wanted to communicate, a story of female empowerment

and reconnecting with personal identity and place in the world, and her personal story. (Rudakoff 2001)

Pada's decision to integrate particularly vivid audio records of the past dispelled any anxiety Rudakoff and Sullivan had about approaching sensitive material. Rudakoff's suggestion of incorporating the sound of the phone call itself at the opening of the piece rather than beginning with Lata's reaction to the news of the crash evoked a more visceral level of intensity, evocative of the transformative journey she would describe. The self she became in the course of the dance shifted from the self to whom these tragic events happened.

Pada and Tim Sullivan, musician and creator of the sound score, spoke about the importance of retracing the grieving process:

> **Pada:** To collaborate with someone who can get into the skin of your work is very important because collaboration can be very superficial or incredibly confrontational. [In the latter case] you start building walls around yourself and you want to keep that territory to yourself because you don't want to become vulnerable again. It requires an enormous amount of strength on both sides to be able to get that [understanding].... Timothy pushed me to understand or actually reflect and contemplate and open up those wounds—to talk about it, because it was important to him to also figure out what textures and emotions and what moods he needed to bring to the sound score. (Pada 2001)

> **Sullivan:** One of the things we did was see some process of this piece as one of grieving following Kübler-Ross's[14] model. The second section is an immediate movement into Lata's past ... a state of shock. And then there's the remembering, of her marriage, her life in India before finally getting to the air crash, which is the point where the past meets the future. We graphed what happens when you're riding these waves between reality ... between the present and the memories. You move away from the memories back to the present and then drift back to the memories, back to the present, back to the memories and the two finally converge. (Sullivan 2001)

A riveting moment of convergence took place at the sound of the tape-recorded voices of her daughters. Pada had saved the taped phone recording of her daughters' last phone message before they boarded the plane. The unforgettable memory of their voices was retrieved in the process of making the sound score. She once said, "I used to go to bed at night wondering what the girls wore on the plane, if they had eaten, if Vishnu [her husband] had been tired." Pada's decision to use it in the sound score of the dance had an electrifying impact on the audience.

She had never listened to it until the making of *Revealed*. The collaborators themselves were unprepared for the intensity of the experience. The sound of weeping could be heard throughout much of the performance. Many of the spectators had suffered personal losses in the Air India tragedy, but others were experiencing Pada's trial by fires mediated by their own experience. But at the sound of her children's voices there wasn't a dry eye in the theatre. The trace of their voices gestured to a past and more importantly to a past which had never been present.

"ALL MY MOTHERS, A LINE THROUGH ME, A SOUNDING OF VOICES, WHO AM I? ALL MY MOTHERS ARE LIVING THROUGH ME. WHO AM I? I AM THE JOURNEY. THE ONLY WAY OUT IS THROUGH"

A thought that kept coming back to me throughout the creative process, as the collaborators were working to retrieve memory images, sounds, tastes, was the idea that the trauma of losing her family seemed to mean a loss of parts of her own corporeality. As Grosz (1994) observes, studies of the phantom limb phenomenon show that disturbance in body image affects not only the way an individual perceives and experiences her own body, but also the individual's ability to relate her present position to wished-for goals of action. In a related manner, objects "external" to the body are often incorporated by the body image; objects or implements and, I would add, people with whom the subject continually interacts become unconsciously invested parts of one's body image and, in turn, sense of self. By Grosz's account, the extent to which body image operates as a kind of body-knowledge is essential to one's ability to move forward, to act, making clear the inextricable link between corporeality and agency. As the work on *Revealed* progressed, it began to develop a tactile and contagious quality, something the audience could brush up against as though it were another body. Thus the "psychical mapping" Pada invested through recuperating memory but also sensation was an important factor in the expression of the character of Lata with which the work concerned itself (Grosz 1994: 36).

THE SOLO: "ALL MY MOTHERS, A LINE THROUGH ME. BEGINNING WITH THE ENDING. END OF ALL BEGINNINGS. WHO AM I? I AM THE JOURNEY. I HAVE ALWAYS BEEN HERE."

The cross-fertilization between artistic genres expanded the possibilities for Pada's dance work. The multimedia nature of this work multiplied the metaphors as well as their contexts. This was most apparent in her solo (see photographic image on book cover), which was improvised each perfor-mance and was the only unchoreographed moment in the whole program. It formed the climax of the piece.

Lata's movement seemed weighed down, as if she struggled against great pressure, barely able to pull herself off the ground. At the same time her arms and upper body were in a frenzy of activity and rage; abandoned, homeless, and adrift, she knew she couldn't go back and was unsure of the future. As the stage was lit by shards of diagonal light, Lata attempted, tentatively, to walk as if looking for some path, stubbornly attempting to navigate her fate. Spoken text over the movement and wild film images resonated as a kind of talking-back to fate. She was not looking for resolu-tion but was possessed by frenzy like someone needing to surface through deep water for air. The solo was a kind of voluntary disorientation, a loss of control even over the meaning of the solo, a moment of contradiction in which she has not yet discovered the new being which it affirms.

It was in the solo that the narrative reached an apex, a beginning and an end of mourning, a search for loved ones who cannot be recalled, except partially. These lost loved ones were not only family but places and even ways of inhabiting the world. It was in the creation of personal symbols that Pada was able to overcome the terrors of the past: privation, guilt, and loss. Such healing of the past is a necessity that can occur within both cul-tural and personal life (Epp 1998: 69). One of the last images in the dance was Lata walking along a rocky shore. She appears to want to leap into the ocean, whose engulfing presence urges her to swim or die, to become a convergent point through which the ocean's divergent forces flow ... it is a starting over.

CONCLUSION

Intercultural dance artists are now in a position to question the historical archive, both Western and traditional, in order to read their own histories in its silences or to force a gap in the archive so that they have a space in which to speak (Marks 2000). But to undertake this kind of work often requires the sometimes traumatic interrogation of personal and family memories, only to create an empty space where no history is certain, and can be a psychically draining experience. These lost loved ones were not only family but places and even ways of inhabiting the world.

Revealed by Fire gave Pada a way to question her relationship not only to her family and her past but to a way of living. The multimedia collaboration destabilized a narrative she had cultivated about what forms of knowledge could be embodied by classical dance while mobilizing other forms of expressiveness. The reconceptualizing of social space allowed for the creation of a distinctive cultural space that may be defined and redefined not by fixed, unchanging categorical relations of class, ethnicity, or gender, but by a constantly shifting array of culturally defined relations (Jeyasingh 1998). Individual voices have a double claim: to personal self-expression as well as dissent, asserting the freedom to articulate alternative visions over pressures to represent an entire culture. *Revealed by Fire* marked a means for Pada of challenging hierarchical religious and cultural paradigms.

Revealed by Fire went beyond the dramatization of one woman's world, demonstrating that mythological containers are also the repositories of individual experience. Her grief may be individual or widely shared but in *Revealed by Fire* it became a collective experience in which the dancer, her company, her collaborators, and her audience could all share. *Revealed by Fire* was the result of a tentative process of creation that began in a time of grieving: in effect, the scent that arises from funeral garlands. This work described a process that moved from deconstructing dominant social and cultural histories to creating new conditions for stories—the holding of artefacts of culture in order to coax from them memories, and from memories, stories.

Notes

1 *Revealed by Fire* is a dance work that incorporates spoken text co-written by Lata Pada and dramaturge Judith Rudakoff. Film and film design by dance photographer Cylla von Tiedemann; Carnatic music score by R.A. Ramamani; and sound engineering and composition by musician and composer Timothy Sullivan.
2 Well-known school and theatre founded by Rukmini Devi in her effort to revitalize bharatanatyam in the late 1930s.
3 In the *paramparâ* system, knowledge is passed down through successive generations of teacher-disciple, literally "an uninterrupted series or succession." Often, the student remains with his guru as a family member.
4 Refers to the first full dance piece that most bharatanatyam dancers learn and symbolizes the awakening of the dancer's body.
5 The first public recital given by a dancer.
6 A mode of expressiveness that may require mimetic ability on the part of the dancer or other forms of theatrical finesse.

7 Chatterjee and Moorty (2001).
8 At the time of performance company members included Rajkumari Chatterjee, Aneela Maharaj, Anandhi Narayanan, Shubha Navaratnasingam, and Lakshmi Venkataraman.
9 Excerpt from the mission statement of Sampradaya Dance Creations.
10 Textual headings are quotations from the play text written and developed for *Revealed by Fire* by Pada and Rudakoff unless otherwise indicated.
11 It took until June 21, 2006, for a full government inquiry to be held into the Air India bombing. However due to miscommunication and political hostilities between the investigating governmental agencies, CSIS and the RCMP, key pieces of evidence were destroyed. To date, though Inderjit Singh Reyat has been convicted of supplying materials for bombs, many of those who lost family members hold little hope that explanations will be forthcoming on how such a catastrophe could occur and why it took over twenty years to mount an inquiry will ever be forthcoming. [The final report of this Canadian *Commission of Inquiry into the Investigation of the Bombing of Air India Flight 182* was released on June 17, 2010. It concluded that "there were structural failures and operational failures; policy failures, communications failures and human errors. Each contributed to, but none was the sole cause for, Sikh terrorists being able to place a bomb in the checked baggage loaded aboard Flight 182 without being detected." Report website is http://epe.lac-bac.gc.ca/100/206/301/pco-bcp/commissions/air_india/2010-07-23/www.majorcomm.ca, accessed June 30, 2011.—ed.]
12 Allusion to the Indian epic *Ramayana*, in which the famous wife of the god-king Rama, Sita, undergoes voluntary self-immolation to prove her fidelity and so putting to rest any doubt about her character.
13 Tamisari (2000: 274).
14 A five-stage model (denial, anger, bargaining, depression, and acceptance) of the process by which people deal with death and terminal illness was introduced by Elizabeth Kübler-Ross in *On Death and Dying* (1969).

Bibliography

Chatterjee, Sandra, and Shyamala Moorty. "BiDentities, Not Binaries: Using Choreography and Writing to Investigate Bi-Cultural Experiences." Paper presented at the annual international American Popular Culture Conference, Toronto, 2001.

Chow, Rey. *Writing Diaspora: Tactics of Intervention in Contemporary Cultural Studies.* Bloomington: Indiana University Press, 1993.

Epp, Linda Joy. "Violating the Sacred? The Social Reform of Devadasis among Dalits in Karnataka, India." Unpublished PhD diss., York University, Toronto, 1998.

Foster, Susan. *Corporealities: Dancing Knowledge, Culture and Power.* London: Routledge, 1996.

Grosz, Elizabeth. *Volatile Bodies: Toward a Corporeal Feminism.* Bloomington: Indiana University Press, 1994.

Hamera, Judith. "I Dance to You: Reflections of Irigaray's *I Love to You* in Pilates and Virtuosity." *Cultural Studies* 15, no. 2 (2001): 229–40.

Jain, Kajiri. *Gods in the Bazaar: The Economies of Indian Calendar Art.* Durham: Duke University Press, 2007.

Jeyasingh, Shobana. "Imaginary Homelands: Creating a New Dance Language." In Alexandra Carter (ed.), *Routledge Studies Dance Reader*. London: Routledge, 1998: 46–52.

Kübler-Ross, Elizabeth. *On Death and Dying* [1969]. London: Tavistock, 1973.

Marks, Laura. *The Skin of the Film: Intercultural Cinema, Embodiment and the Senses*. Durham: Duke University Press, 2000.

Meduri, Avanthi. "Nation, Woman, Representation: The Sutured History of the Devadasi and Her Dance." Unpublished PhD diss., New York University, 1996.

Ram, Kalpana. "Listening to the Call of Dance: Rethinking Authenticity and Essentialism." *The Australian Journal of Anthropology* 11, no. 3 (2000): 261–74.

Pada, Lata. Interview with author. May 22, 2000, Toronto.

———, and Judith Rudakoff. Pre-performance conversaton. January 26, 2001, Janak Khendry's Studio, Toronto.

———, Timothy Sullivan, and Cylla von Tiedemann. Group interview with author. February 4, 2001, Toronto.

Ratnam, Anita. Administrator of The Other Festival. Interview with author. December 22, 2000, Chennai, India.

Rudakoff, Judith. "Shifting Boundaries and Crossing Borders: Dramaturging Lata Pada's *Revealed by Fire*." *Theatre Forum* 20 (2002): 13–20.

———. Interview with author. August 10, 2001, Toronto.

Srinivasan, Amrit. "Reform and Revival: The Devadasi and Her Dance." *Economic and Political Weekly* 20, no. 44 (1985): 1869–76.

Sullivan, Timothy. Interview with author. July 4, 2001, Toronto.

Tamisari, Franca. "The Meaning of the Steps Is in Between: Dancing and the Curse of Compliments." *The Australian Journal of Anthropology* 11, no. 3 (2000): 277.

von Tiedemann, Cylla. Interview with author. September 10, 2001, Toronto.

CHAPTER TWENTY-ONE

Spectres of the Dark

THE DANCE-MAKING MANIFESTO OF LATINA/CHICANA CHOREOGRAPHIES

JUANITA SUAREZ

Women, let's not let the danger of the journey and the vastness of the territory scare us—let's look forward and open paths in these woods.
—Anzaldúa and Moraga 1983: v

MAPPING THE TERRAIN

The Mexican-American modern dance experience is an emerging artistic development in the world of dance. Due to the currency of its inception as well as other social-political factors, published research on this new dance-making phenomenon is non-existent. Consequently, we know little about Mexican-American modern dance choreographers in terms of artistic vision or process.

Hence, this chapter is about listening and reflecting on the cultural, political voices of Mexican/Mexican-American women dance-makers who create modern concert dance works. For clarification, a Chicana is both Mexican/Mexican-American and a Latina, but a Latina is not necessarily a Chicana because the term "Chicana" has feminist overtones, which many Latinas do not identify with.[1] Second, although the identifier "Latina" applies to females who come from other Latin countries such as Mexico, Puerto Rico, Brazil, and Cuba, for the purpose of this writing and to avoid literary awkwardness, the term "Latina" will serve as a referent for a Mexican or Mexican-American female.

During my literary excavations into the world of the Latina/Chicana art world, I came to realize how, after thirty years of dance-making, I could not speak about other Mexican-American choreographers, a community of contemporary concert dance-makers whose roots are anchored within the Mexican-American experience. I did not know if there were other dance-makers who made dances by drawing from the Mexican-American experience. If there were others like myself—I assumed there were or would be—how do they speak through dance and how do their dances voice a cultural aesthetic particular to the Mexican-American experience? For if "dancing like speaking, is a social act, produced by and within given discourses" (Goellner and Murphy 1995: 22), then what discourses were taking place within the works of other Mexican-American contemporary dance-makers? And so I felt a need to make visible the invisible by asking, "What would it take to locate these voices?"

In order to hear the voices of this particular population of Latin modern dance-makers, I networked with dancers and arts administrators in the field who knew the whereabouts of the voices I sought. I connected with a dance professional, the program director for the American Dance Festival, who forwarded a lengthy list of Latino dance artists and organizations that he knew of. Participants I identified as relevant to this study had to be Mexican-American, female, and currently involved within the discipline of contemporary dance. They could be included if they were Mexican and lived in the United States for a long period of time.

One Los Angeles dance company, Danzantes, had a female director by the name of Licia Perea. After an introductory telephone call, I connected with Licia, gleaning information about her work, which fortunately met the parameters of my study. Licia had graduated from the University of New Mexico in 1993 with an MA in choreography.

Some of the questions I initially asked were, "How long have you been dancing and making dances?" "What kind of dance style or styles do you work with?" "What kind of world are you creating through dance-making?" "How would you describe your aesthetic?" "How has your work changed over time?" "Do you know other Latina dance-makers in your area who are creating modern dance works?" At the culmination of our initial telephone conversation we made arrangements to meet at Licia's home in Los Angeles for our first interviews and she became the first research participant for this study.

The pathway leading to Eva Tessler's door was not as direct. During my stay at a fellow graduate's home in Tucson, Arizona, I heard about Eva Tessler (her maiden name is Eva Concepción Zorilla Saldaña), a Mexican modern dance-maker who graduated from the University of Arizona, Tucson, dance program in 1991 with an MFA in Theatre Arts. My hostess suggested Eva as a possible participant for my research since she was a Latina

SPECTRES OF THE DARK :: JUANITA SUAREZ

modern dance-maker living in the area, but there was a serious drawback. Eva's husband, Daniel Nugent, a professor of cultural anthropology at the University of Arizona in Tucson, and managing editor of the Journal of Historical Sociology, had suddenly passed away two weeks earlier (October 12, 1997), which meant Eva was in mourning. My concern that Eva would turn down my research request gave me reason to pause. I asked my hostess for Eva's telephone number so I could contact her later. Six months passed before I decided to call Eva.

During our initial telephone conversation, I offered a personal introduction and posed the same questions I asked of Licia. Eva's dance-making development met the criteria established for the study and so I invited Eva and she consented to join us. We concluded our telephone conversation by making arrangements to meet in Tucson the following summer. Through the help of friends and by word of mouth, a net was cast that allowed me to connect to the women of this study. The blueprint for this study is one utilized by many qualitative researchers seeking to understand "a reality that is of 'whole cloth.' That is, all aspects of reality are interrelated" (Erlandson, Harris, Skipper, and Allen 1993: 11).

Creating a dance universe involves a unique form of artistic/cultural negotiation that vibrates between the world of ideas and the material universe, giving form to those ideas. To listen to the voice that guided the process of creating such a cosmos, it was imperative I observe each dance-maker's repertoire with the choreographer close by. This entailed residing for one week in Los Angeles with Licia Perea (May 19–25, 1998), and five days in Tucson with Eva Tessler (July 18–22, 1998).[2]

I walked through individual dances with each choreographer and worked to reconstitute as much of "the worlds" of choreographing, rehearsing, and performing as possible. By presenting questions and listening to the artistic voice of each choreographer, I was able to derive materials that would not have been possible had I just observed the works. In essence, I was trying to qualitatively experience, reflect upon, and interpret their creative worlds.

When entering the research as a dance-maker, I was confronted by my own enthusiastic relationship to the dance-making process and had to hold in abeyance self-reflexive tendencies to interpret for the choreographer. I wanted to choreograph our encounters, embracing with enthusiasm similarities between their narratives and mine. I soon learned how I would increase the risk of making erroneous assumptions and ultimately had to settle into an understanding: whatever needed to be found would make itself apparent. Moving back and forth in "a spiral between generalizations and specific observations, abstractions and immediacies, looking from the 'outside' and trying to understand the vantage points 'from the inside'" (Geertz 1973: 482), I danced the dynamics of the hermeneutic circle.[3]

Initially, the data collected from each dance-maker created a realm of ambiguity, which only revealed the hefty challenge of connecting threads, recognizing patterns, and crystallizing relationships among disparate parts in creation of a "whole cloth." I found the weavings of choreographic voice to be multi-faceted. And so theory evolved out of this process and surfaced slowly over time.

Open-ended interviews were conducted in the natural setting of each choreographer's home, with each interview lasting three to four hours. In order to acknowledge the authority of personal voice coming from within each work, active participation on behalf of the interviewee became essential. Interviews focused on how expressive voice issued forth, echoing the practice of a cultural, yet critical, oral tradition. From this urge to get "inside" the dance narrative, it was important that a pattern of interviewing, dance viewing, and post/secondary viewing, concurrent with a running dialogue, was established with each choreographer, while all dances were encountered through captured video images. We proceeded chronologically through each choreographer's obra or work, beginning with early dance studies and culminating with established signature works.

By having each choreographer describe her work prior to viewing, I could "listen" then look for comparative variations between verbal and movement narratives. After the initial viewing with the choreographer, each dance was viewed again. The second viewing—accompanied by ongoing commentary by each choreographer—"thickened the description"[4] of each movement narrative (Geertz 1973: 6–7). The conceptual basis for each dance was central to our conversations. Discussions included those interactive layers of development and contextual realities that directly impacted the development of each choreographic statement. I came to call these contextual realities lived text because these danced/lived narratives enlivened the choreographic mixture between the "world created" and the "world lived." Supplementary comments pertinent to the material production of the dance were also addressed in our discussions. Audio recordings of each interview were created and transcribed (Erlandson et al.: 1993), while journals chronicled my impressions of each choreographer's living/ studio space. Interviews with co-collaborators enhanced the dimensions of the research process by providing additional insight especially as it pertained to the lived text. By drawing from the insights of fellow creative participants, I was able to triangulate and give weight to my own observations. The data I collected and analyzed was based on discussions with each choreographer, as well as the dancers each dance-maker worked with over time, and my observations of the creative and performance process that spanned eight years. When interview transcriptions were completed, a copy was forwarded to each dance-maker and co-collaborator for review and approval (Rubin and Rubin 1995). Participant feedback or member checking validated the content/results of the interview process.

Artefacts that reflected the afterglow of each choreographer's creative life were made available. By delving into a feast of colours, textures, symbols, and stories that enhanced a "narration of meaning," I was able to piece together a fascinating tapestry of material relationships. Journals by both choreographers contained significant notes that were descriptive and comprehensive. In addition, Eva's thesis from the University of Arizona enabled me to view in detail an intricate and revelatory progression of ideas leading to her thesis production.

From the resumés of these two women I was able to discern a chronology of growth, survey artistic influences, identify education backgrounds, understand migratory patterns resulting from new locations/geographies, affirm discipline roles chosen by each choreographer, and ensure correct spelling of Spanish names and titles. Individual biographies provided additional information as to heritage and creative interests.

Photographs captured a theatrical and psychological presence for study and reflection. Ultimately, each portrait served as a source for descriptive phenomenological renderings. By creatively exploring identities projected in a photograph, I came closer to establishing an empathic connection with the subject at hand. Fraleigh elucidates further stating, "the process of identification ... relates directly to the subjective/affective source of aesthetic experience as founded in sense perception and emotional responsiveness" (1999: 193).

In order to help me retrace my steps, each choreographer supplied me with selective memorabilia that would carry me back to those significant moments of our encounter. In the form of papered announcements, musical tracks, and captured video images, I could continue to hear the tenor of the choreographer's voice from a distance.

On my return home, I looked for various narratives that could possibly surface within each work. As I looked at the dancing female body as a meta-narrative of current and past influences, my attention was drawn to how personal and cultural inscriptions or "bodily writings" surfaced simultaneously. For example, a complex of individual narratives created ongoing discourses and included the following conceptions of the body: (1) the historical body; (2) the body symbolic of "otherness"; (3) the representational body that through motions/emotions symbolizes death, joy, anger, and vulnerability; (4) the kinaesthetic body as a source for physical

Figure 1   Licia Perea's character portrayal of Frida Kahlo. Photographer: Dorit Thies.

and emotional engagement; (5) the phenomenological body, which aims at "insightful description of that which presents itself to consciousness" (Fraleigh 1987: 11); (6) the spiritually lucid body that conveys a "meaningful semantic universe by the process of symbolic mediation" (Nicholson 1987: 93); (7) the body as a place of located knowledge, where the intersection of race, class, gender, and ability are made manifest; and (8) the autobiographical as translated through the body, "where one's life experience is embodied in the narrative text of a dance" (Albright 1997: 119).

Another research strategy was accomplished through a phenomenological rendering of the dance narratives. And so it is, through self-study, "I nevertheless accept that I am there in my attention to phenomena ... to arrive at what is most basic" (Fraleigh 1987: 7). Furthermore, in learning their dance, by physically immersing myself as a dancer, I inhabited momentarily a "projection from the interior." I discovered, as did Deirdre Sklar, that "qualitative movement analysis ... is neither vague nor mysterious but a matter of developing our inherent capacity to navigate between sensory modalities.... It is the kinetic qualities of movement that provide clues to the experiential meaning of people's movement knowledge (2001: 3). The kinetic/kinaesthetic experience of dancing a phrase enabled me to chart the distance between what appears and what exists. I came to learn how each dance-maker's physical facility, composition, and personality determined and shaped the physical renderings of tales told. For "there must be some appreciation of how getting oneself physically through a choreographic moment can affect a human being, and how it can affect one's own cultural understanding" (Ness 1992: 3).

Relevant because of my Latina heritage, I was always/already the subject-for-study, as well as the one who studies. And so I entered the woods of my own making by studying *La Llorona* or *The Weeping Woman* (1980), a work that looks at how stories within stories (my stories) can point to a deeper subtext and, hence, cultural meaning. As a cultural narrative, *La Llorona* is a gender-specific tale that models and conveys the lives of two women, one mythical and the other real. Through memory recall and video viewing, I attended to the creative consciousness I was engaged with at the time of its creation. The dance, as metaphoric narrative, addresses Chicana-specific images and symbols I find compelling. *La Llorona* evolved since its inception in 1975 and in particular has responded to changes I moved through as a Chicana dance artist.

Another strategy involved visiting the dance through reconstruction. *La Llorona* was restaged in order to listen to the choreographic voice that entered the narrative years ago. In order to establish a visceral relationship with the work, the dance was reproduced with the help of two dancers from SUNY College at Brockport, New York, and performed for Scholar's Day.[5] During the following semester, *La Llorona* was presented again for El Corazón de Mexico,[6] a dance ensemble composed of Mexican migrant farm workers from the Brockport, New York, area. I included *La Llorona* within the presentation because her character is relevant and familiar to the cultural/political ideology of Mexican migrants who work the local area. Also, members of El Corazón come from these migrant families. The farm workers' response was immediate. They spoke of historical continuities and provided me with family variations of an old story. Strong connections to the Mexican oral tradition rest within the ancient character of *La Llorona*, whose voice echoes through the centuries. Chicana scholar Irene I. Blea recognizes *La Llorona* as the one who straddles the historical period of the Spanish Conquest as well as Indian history to be "the oldest living female influence in the Americas" (Blea 1992: 27).

THE BRIDGE THAT CALLS ME BACK[7]

Mexican-American modern choreography is a nascent voice in the field of dance, and thus little dance literature exists to theoretically illuminate these spirited narratives. Yet many tangential connections between literary/art themes and choreographic narratives exist as various forms of symbolic mediation permeate the tales of each medium. Based on this reality and for contextual purposes, an excursion into the work of Chicana artmakers serves to move our journey onward since these artmakers actively seek to reclaim culture through their work. By braiding various threads of a cultural legacy through the imaging of Latina artistry, I hope to present a womanly cultural mosaic of an emergent collective voice. I will take this opportunity to identify the various social/cultural/political elements that inform us of an evolving artistic Chicana identity. But the course of our journey is complicated. Chicanas draw from elements inherent to Mexican-American legacies—isolation/disconnection/connection—to remember through artmaking how we as a people are evolving.

If we listen to our literary sisters we can discern "a growing corpus of critical thought and praxis [that] evinces an evolving infrastructure of a Chicana feminist theory" (Rebolledo 1995: 2). Through theoretical reflection Chicanas have discovered that "for the minority artist and writer ... self-definition is fraught with multiple views, with angles that reflect both universal and individual images of self" (Rebolledo and Rivero 1993: 75). The Chicana, as educated woman, can also mean we are thinking subjects from working-class origins (Anzaldúa 2000). In translation, "it means being concerned with the ways knowledges are invented ... challenging institutionalized discourses ... being suspicious of the dominant culture's interpretation of 'our' experience, of the way they 'read' us" (Anzaldúa 2000: xxv).

The personal voice of the Chicana artist continues to reveal a sense of identity encumbered with dialectical complexities. Issues such as isolation, invisibility, silence, assimilation, the realities of a bicultural world, and the intersection of gender, class, race as well as heritage (Rebolledo

1995) continue to plague her. The task is not simple. By paying attention to select voices from the field, we recognize complexity as characteristic of Chicana thought and voice.

Chicana artistic traditions foreshadow cultural/aesthetic renderings found within Latina choreography. Theories derived from the critical cultural-analytic traditions of Chicana writers and artists were coupled with observations from the field to create a platform for discussing specifically the work of Latina dance-makers. We begin by trekking through the creative world of Chicana culture.

SISTERS OF THE SNOW

Chicana artists are in the process of establishing a culture-specific artistic language. As translators of foreign mail (Cervantes 1981)—that is to say, as scribes of an alien/public language and as interpreters of individual/universal realities—we discovered that our search for personal voice founded our need for "a language with which to communicate with ourselves, a secret language" (Anzaldúa 1987: 55). This need to connect through language is thematically prevalent among Chicana creative forms, and for good reason. Culture-based forms of isolation and exclusion founded on language and distance created an absence of collective voice. We discovered that "if we do not speak for ourselves—about what we do, what it means, and why it is important—others will speak for us. Or no one will speak at all about those issues we hold most dear, as though we do not even exist" (Stinson 1994: 6).

Identifying the Chicana voice as a self-in-relation[8] is not new. Chicana oral traditions come from singing over old bones. By listening to our mothers' and grandmothers' stories, the "powerful sister of our dream language" (Estés 1992: 471), Chicanas have developed a cultural record passed down from generation to generation. Sharing stories about women who lived lives of courage and fire, cantadora storytellers also impressed the listening ear with stories of isolation and exclusion. These soulful biographies paint a lonely path for heroines caught in the crossfire of time and culture.

Chicanas have explored dusty historical manuscripts and out-of-print books. And although Mexican-American oral traditions can be traced to the Bancroft Narratives (1870), "the silenced voice, the voice of the subaltern" (Rebolledo and Rivero 1993: 279), the roots of our written tradition, can be found as far back as the late seventeenth century. The first female intellectual of Mexico, a woman considered a troublemaker by church officials, Sor Juana Inés de la Cruz (1648–95), defied socially constructed gender patterns by committing herself to a life of seclusion and reading, turning to her books for salvation (Hahner 1976: 25). Her intellectual and literary life challenged the social, cultural, and religious mores that kept women physically and mentally confined (Arenal and Powell 1994: vii). Sor Juana chose the scholarly isolation of the convent over the compulsory isolation of marriage expected of women during her time.

Pat Mora, Chicana writer, poet, and educator, identifies with the image of seclusion that Sor Juana evoked but transposes her experience through the modern-day lens of a motel room:

> Motels are my convents.
> I come alone
> Give workshops, readings.
> I lock my door twice,
> smell solitude, taste quiet
> away from fast music, telephones,
> Children tugging, "Mom, Mom." (Mora 1993)

In light of our modern sensibility, isolation can be precious for a woman writer for a writer's voice surfaces best under quiet, secluded conditions. But, at times, listening to one's own voice must compete with the reality of family constraints. For many Chicanas this means addressing tasks/schedules that challenge limited energies. Yet, through the act of writing, Mora shows her commitment to community, to having the Latina voice heard and valued in this country. Sandra Cisneros believes it is important to be "one of many voices and not the voice, for we know the grand variety in our community, and we want others to recognize this human wealth" (Mora 1993: 45). Hence, the need to survey and assess our community of voices, to actively make tracks away from isolation, becomes evident. Mora's poetic modern vernacular text establishes connections between heroic women of the past and everyday events.

Another pioneering spirit in literature is Jovita Gonzalez, a writer/academician of the 1920s and 1930s. Recognized as one of the first Mexican-Americans to write in English about the Chicano culture, Gonzalez created a bridge that spanned from one culture to another. A lonely voice in the academic wilderness, Gonzalez was courageous for bringing forward existent conditions and relationships between Anglos and Chicanos, as can be seen in her highly political work *With the Coming of the Barbed Wire Came Hunger* (Cotera 1977).

When listening to the voice of the Chicana artist, I hear a refrain of isolation as a pervasive, multi-faceted presence. Many Chicanas find themselves in the middle of a borderland, struggling to cross barriers imposed by human social constructs of gender. In her crossing she awakens to the sound of her own potential, her many selves that quietly wait for her arrival. For actresses Socorro Valdez and Diana Rodriguez of El Teatro Campesino,[9] an "awakening" took place when they resisted stereotypical gender-role casting. In terms of creative autonomy, they claimed:

> We both ended up in the role of fighters because that's what was needed to get the men's heads to a place where they would be able to discuss something with you. We would have open meetings where the shit would fly across the room. (Cordova et al. 1990: 167)

According to Rodriguez, El Teatro had a very limited view of women and had no intention of changing their "cardboard" perspective (Cordova et al. 1990). Socorro's creative response and strategy involved playing a male role, which "provided a new adventure in role-playing: as a male she was now in an active position" (Cordova et al. 1990: 175).

Chicana playwrights also find themselves waging a gender war. Some Chicana playwrights who contribute to the contemporary New York theatre scene are Denise Chavez, Josefina Lopez, and Cherríe Moraga. Although "Latinas have always been present in the theater, for various reasons, patriarchal reasons, ethnic reasons, racist reasons, they haven't always been recognized" (Durnell 1994: 9). And this lack of recognition has spanned three decades: "Ever since the first Chicana writer, Estela Portillo Trambley published her first play *The Day of the Swallow* in 1971, it has been clear that sexism was to be an important theme among Chicana writers" (Tierney 1990: 55).

It is important to understand how a feminist voice can be heard through the various characters within a Chicana play, but it is a distinctly different voice, one that stays close to community: "instead of looking back at the previous generations of women and pushing them away, the Latina writer and feminist seeks strength from the past and from women like their mothers, aunts, and grandmothers" (Durnell 1994: 10). Chicanas choose to keep good company, as can be seen in Denise Chavez's Novena Narratives. The narrator/character Isabel states, "When I feel alone, I remember behind me stand my grandmother, my mother, all the women who have come before me" (Herrera-Sobek and Viramontes 1988: 88).

Another form of connection came when Chicanas took their art to the people. Visual artists Graciella Carillo de Lopez, Consuelo Mendez Castillo, Irene Perez, and Patricia Rodriguez studied at the San Francisco Art Institute and came to be known as Las Mujeres Muralistas (The Women Muralists). As a collective, they painted eleven large outdoor murals between

1973 and 1976, principally in the Mission district of San Francisco (Rubin-stein 1982: 431). To promote ethnic pride and self-determination for Latin people, they avoided harsh, political images sometimes used by their male colleagues in order to reach out to the community.

The murals depict a number of pre-Columbian symbols, motifs, deities, figures, corn, birds, and dancers (Barrio 1975). The history of our struggle, an integral theme of these murals, allows Chicano viewers a chance to engage with the past and the present with a coruscating eye for the future. The visual script of past glories keeps cultural amnesia at bay and our connections to the past open.

Judith Francisca Baca has risen from her role as premiere muralist of the streets of Los Angeles to that of international chronicler of Chicano culture. Baca's stature in the art world escalated with her project, called the *Great Wall of Los Angeles*, the largest outdoor mural project in the world, 2,435 feet long by 13 feet high (Cockroft and Barnet-Sánchez 1990: 80). It is clear how the "mural rewrites, in a strong and direct visual language, aspects of the history of California that have been blurred, hidden and/ or forgotten in the official narratives and popular mentalities" (Zamudio-Taylor, as cited in Sullivan 1996: 327).

By bringing together urban youth from diverse cultural backgrounds, Baca has been able to realize several hundred murals. Her project *World Wall: A Vision of the Future without Fear* is a "participatory mural that explores the material and spiritual transformation of a society toward peace! For each country that exhibits the portable mural, a native artist will add a panel" (Zamudio-Taylor 1996: 327). Baca's commitment surfaces: "I struggle not to distance myself from my culture, because ... my work is informed by the connection" (quoted in National Women's History Project 1991: 37). Amalia Mesa-Bains tells us how: "The community participatory process Baca developed, which involves input from historians, cultural informants, storytellers, community residents and young artists, has become an important model for collective murals. The collective process was based on the need to create murals by Chicanos for Chicanos" (Cockcroft and Barnet-Sánchez 1993: 81).

Literary shaman sisters have had much to say about the Chicana experience through either prose or poetry. They have conducted a "quiet revolution" (Rebolledo 1995) by listening with great attention to the winds of a private discontent. By putting pen to paper these visionaries wrestle with shadowy figures of their own and a collective identity that, at times, can be quite elusive. Chicana identities struggle, and thrive, at the confluence of two bicultural rivers where currents stream through the brown consciousness of the Chicana scribe. These rivers or testimonios have led many of us out of the wilderness.

Lorna Dee Cervantes eloquently rides the winds of poetic furor in her classic work, "Poem for the Young White Man Who Asked Me How I, an Intelligent, Well-Read Person, Could Believe in the War between Races" (1981). In this excerpt, she glares at the reality that stands before her.

> I am a poet
> who yearns to dance on rooftops,
> to whisper delicate lines about joy
> and the blessings of human understanding.
> I try. I go to my land, my tower of words and
> bolt the door, but the typewriter doesn't fade out
> the sounds of blasting and muffled outrage.
> My own days bring me slaps on the face.
> Every day I am deluged with reminders
> that this is not
> My land
> And this is my land. (Rebolledo and Rivero 1993: 287)

As the title suggests, cultural realities are not always in sync with each other. The hyphenated experience of the Mexican-American reflects a life lived on the margins, as Pat Mora's poem "Legal Alien" openly admits:

> American but hyphenated,
> viewed by Anglos as perhaps exotic,
> perhaps inferior, definitely different,
> viewed by Mexicans as alien,
> (their eyes say, "You may speak
> Spanish but you're not like me"). (Rebolledo and Rivero 1993: 95)

Chicana language has evolved out of a collective dialogue and a need to formulate connections with others. Through writing, speaking, possibly dancing, Chicanas connect and create a larger, historical sense of personal/ cultural self. In dichotomous fashion, the emergent voices of Chicana writers turn to language as a tool, a weapon to question the precariousness of their relationship with language. Because of the "English/Spanish language question that subsumes Chicano culture, no matter what language they speak, Chicana writers always feel a void, an exile from language (Rebolledo 1995: 157). By way of personal example I remember this: My first day in kindergarten ended with my American teacher attaching a note to my sweater. The note stated I could no longer speak Spanish in school. Not allowed. Since I spoke fluent Spanish, it was clear to my family I would have to shift linguistic gears to comply with her (the school's demands). This infuriated my father, a migrant farm worker, who refused to speak the language of those who paid so little. Consequently, our relationship dissipated. He lived in a world of Spanish and I moved into a world of English. Now I understand why, on the day of his funeral, I wanted to be at a school picnic instead of by his side.

THE BRIDGES WE CROSS

When looking at our work through a theoretical lens, we can see how the creative and political entanglements we Latina dance-makers engage in through dance-making are similar to those artistic/political entanglements Chicana artists, writers, and actors connect to when they draw from personal, cultural sources. The concepts identified within both art forms reveal a beneficial dynamic of opposites, disconnection, fragmentation, pluralistic paradigms of engagement, as well as isolation as a cultural artefact. To facilitate this discussion, I will use the term "Chicana artist" inclusively to embrace visual artists, writers, and actors discussed so far and, at times, Latina dance-makers.

For the Latina dance-maker, stories of "otherness" are narratives about physical and psychological migrations, a spiritual searching for self-worth, a restless "transitoriness'—of character, space, and time—in which the Latina voice is actively engaged with a personal dispossession that is ignited when cultural narratives warrant attention to past and/or current infractions of character.

Migrant voices feed into and are fed by the creative process; a Latina who makes dances by drawing from a cosmology of "otherness" listens to all the voices in escort as they guide her to places where the sound of a familiar voice resonates with her own experiences as a woman of colour. The work and the world of "otherness" created by the Latina dance-maker simulate the dramatic and creative movements inherent within the work of Chicana artists—the spiritual searching for one's own voice, the elusive self among the many voices encountered.

Within the created subaltern world of the Latina dance-maker and Chicana artist, dramatic tensions arise when the protagonist (the heroine within our narratives) finds herself without "voice" and, hence, without agency. Yet, it is at this place where created intersections, which require a crossing for both the protagonist and the Latina dance-maker, begin to differ from those prescribed by history to become something else. Chicanas who speak to female minority experiences through artmaking develop creative and cultural skills for shaping the dimensions of their crossings through the blank page, the canvas, or the stage. Like their creative sisters who live a life in the borderlands, Latina dance-makers also possess the creative, cultural knowledge needed to begin to transcend and, hence, subvert the nature of the borders they, as women of colour, experience.

Out of a return to origins, to cultural sources through artmaking, the Chicana artist not only creates a world, but puts into motion a vehicle for change when the artwork as vessel connects to and is empowered by all her creative cultural voices. By empowering the protagonist, the Chicana artist/Latina dance-maker empowers her own womanhood and, in a communal way, the womanhood of other women like herself, as each new interpretation of a woman's life contributes not only to the momentum of personal change taking place within her but also the community of women she represents and/or connects to.

A BENEFICIAL DYNAMIC OF OPPOSITES

When reflecting on the dances women create and perform that mirror an under-represented kind of cultural experience, it is possible to notice the emergence of a symbiotic dynamic. The dancer's corporeality on stage contrasts with that of the culture under discussion to create an *oppositional yet mutually beneficial dynamic between cultures.*

Dances based on the racial or cultural historicized text of a woman's life draw from the silences that surround her, for hers is a life that has either been spoken for or has been interpreted, unwittingly, on her behalf. In essence, she is invisible in that she lacks a voice and a body that locates her. In similar fashion, Chicana artists make known the unknown; they make visible the invisible, and audible the silence women have experienced; they "bring flesh and blood, color and form" (Suarez 2006) to women's lives through the voice of their work, making the Chicana artist and Latina dance-maker agents of change for herself and for others like herself. In a new and significant way, by "breaking her silences," the Chicana artist and Latina dance-maker who does not represent mainstream culture is in a position to contest the unattended void between the past/present when she intertwines her life/voice with her culture.

When a new interpretation of a woman's life connects to and is compatible with another interpretation and then another, a network of understandings among women begins to develop, a communal comprehension as well as an agency, a "faculty of action" (O'Neill, cited in Jaggar and Bordo 1989: 68). In other words, Chicana artists and Latina dance-makers

Figure 2 *Grandmother Turns 100*, choreography and performance by Eva Tessler. Photographer: Steve Clarke.

are poised to make the most of these gender- and culture-imposed silences. By drawing from this vocal stillness to orchestrate the sound of a new reflective and reflexive inner quiet, which comes to audiences/readers/ viewers when they become aware of the catastrophic implications of cultural silences within and between cultures, the Chicana artist/Latina dance-maker, who represents the underrepresented, exposes the murky, obscure territories that separate and divide us into political unknowns.

Another symbiotic dynamic between opposites can be found in the concept of disconnection. When the Chicana artist/Latina dance-maker researches the concept of "otherness" she comes to understand in a profound way what it means to be viewed as the "other." Growing up in the United States for the woman of colour can be liberating, an experience full of opportunities, and/or it can be viewed as a racial, gender-based borderland, an entrapment determined by her sense of "otherness." Chicana artists/Latina dance-makers fruitfully draw from this felt sense of "disconnectedness."

A beneficial dynamic of opposites within the realm of creativity requires a world of solitude, a self-imposed isolation. Dance-making finds us "churning bits and pieces of the everyday with the worlds of our own creation" (Suarez 2006); this kind of activity requires a self-imposed solitude and the silence that a creative space demands. A life of isolation that comes from being a Chicana artist/Latina dance-maker, as well as a contemporary, educated professional, seamlessly interconnects to create a world where isolation becomes a cultural artefact, a synergistic counterpoint that reverberates between and within the real world and the world created.

By remembering the stories of those who came before, by studying the lives and meaningful intentions of those who vicariously may have shaped her, Chicana artists and Latina dance-makers lessen the cultural gap between the past and the present and by so doing stave off the likelihood of cultural amnesia.

Another beneficial dynamic of opposites is expressed through the poetics of literary, visual, embodied narration in which the Chicana artist and Latina dance-maker, wittingly or unwittingly, uses fragmentation as a strategy for creative action, in that she creates to recreate the whole of a woman's life, not by telling in chronological detail significant events that identify her but by "filling in the pieces" that fall by the historic wayside. According to Maria Lugones, fragmentation enters the work through the guise of "other world" subjectivities, in which the main characters either reflect on or expose to us the gypsy voice of the nomadic "other," the life of the "world traveler" (Garry and Pearsall 1989). The psychological movements that take place when one must survive, of relocation from one self to another, tells us a story as only that side of a subjective self can tell it. By locating and shifting the voices of her heroines within the terra firma of her colour-based experiences, the Chicana artist and Latina dance-maker present perceptions particular to and representative of "other" respective cosmologies, which can only evolve through the lived experiences of growing up female and brown. The culturally based nomadic self within the voicing of the creative work takes leave when the character of one's culture is attributed stories that are untenable—that is, the story's message points to a prescribed series of events or relationships that, in precedential fashion, eradicate culture.

From one migrant to another, the voices within *la familia*, the Chicana artist/Latina dance-maker and her protagonists/characters, speak when spoken to *and* speak to each other. The array of voices function not only as a syncretic space that cannot be heard unless you are of "this place," for there is that element in their work, but also as a collage of voices in which multiple messages are being communicated and negotiated concurrently and through counterpoint in order to determine, for the culture and the artist, new directions in which to move and create. The concurrent narratives within this kind of work, reminiscent of "the stereo sisters" (a vernacular term that means the narratives speak at once), "play off" of, buoy each other to recreate for the artist/viewer/listener a world rich in narrative detail. Such narratives replicate the perceptual, cultural, and linguistic "worlds within worlds" of its maker.

A PLURALISTIC PARADIGM OF ENGAGEMENT

Creative blood drawn from the lived experiences of the Chicana artist/Latina dance-maker creates a fusion of forms, imagistic and linguistic. The weave of their movements in life and on the page/stage, reflect a dialectical multiplicity of forms, *pluralistic paradigms of engagement*, one in which the Chicana artist/Latina dance-maker draws from several cultural sources: lived experience (private/public), multicultural experiences (various linguistic terrains), and female legacies (past and present). Creating a world that means to "say something" of their experiences as women of colour insinuates their involvement as negotiators of multiple narrative forms, as they struggle to embody, through the created work, their myriad stories. For Quintana "the entire Chicana literary text is analogous to a musical fugue; both employ polyphony, with separate voices maintaining comparative integrity, throughout a composition" (1996: 36). In translation, the Chicana artist/Latina dance-maker participates in "cultural kinds of double speak" when she moves back and forth between linguistic and/or cultural territories that are, at times, conflictive and/or contradictory.

The strategy of developing a space for herself and the many voices that reflect the various communities she inhabits can be found in the work of the Chicana artist. As Quintana points out, "synthesizing ancestral and modern perceptions, [Denise] Chávez shows how Chicanas today fashion a cultural identity by combining traditional cultural attitudes with ... postmodernist perceptions" (1996: 98–99) to reflect yet another pluralistic paradigm of engagement.

The Chicana artist/Latina dance-maker who draws from "other" sources is always already in a position to draw from the sources of the "One," since she has access to public voice. The Chicana artist/Latina dance-maker embodies the protagonist with the voices of a multicultural people, always in transition, moving between the panoply of voices she possesses, shedding skins when necessary, defining her movements by the restless hemispheres she inhabits.

In order to contextualize the pathways of the Chicana artist/Latina dance-maker, it is important to note how personal and creative empowerment through artmaking is not completely innocent. A relationship between disparate parts surfaces when the narrative voices of the artmaker and protagonist intertwine to create a braiding of sorts in which the vocal strands of the One (the Chicana artist) stands in relief against the strands of the "other" (the protagonist) to create a configuration of "difference." As a creator of worlds, Chicana artists/Latina dance-makers control the terms of the stories they choose to tell by manipulating the way they tell it, deciding which perspectives to draw from in the telling, and determining how to conclude her protagonist's (her culture's) story.

CONCLUSION

Mexican/American/Latina/Chicana artmaking is shaped by a border consciousness. But borders serve a function. They are set up "to define the places that are safe and unsafe, to distinguish us from them. A borderland is a vague and undetermined place created by the emotional residue of an unnatural boundary. The prohibited and forbidden are its inhabitants" (Anzaldúa 1987: 3). For Chicana writers who see themselves as cultural workers and translators of foreign mail, the border can arise whenever the traditional (Old World) collides with the transitional (New World). In translation, this means our horizon is in a chronic state of flux.

Still, Chicana artists/Latina dance-makers are positioned for creative autonomy. In questioning those borders and crossroads where race, class, and gender meet, we derive a sense of agency as can be seen when Cisneros experienced an artistic/cultural epiphany:

> It was not until this moment when I separated myself, when I considered myself truly distinct that my writing acquired a voice. I knew I was a Mexican woman, but I didn't think it had anything to do with why I felt so much imbalance in my life, whereas it had everything to do with it! My race, my gender, my class! That's when I decided I would write about something my classmates couldn't write about. (Telgen and Kamp 1996: 85)

421

In studying the work of Latina dance-makers through the lens of Chicana art, I came to understand not only the parallels that exist between us but also the way in which we mobilize a multitude of creative strategies to serve our needs to make possible through a critical connection to language and artistic, cultural literacy a creative world of consequent empowerment.

Figure 3 Promotional photo for the Latina Dance Project's *Coyolxauhqui ReMembers*, 2006. Dancers in photo, clockwise from left: Eva Tessler (in Zoot Suit), Eluza Santos, Licia Perez, and Juanita Suarez. Photographer: Dorit Thies.

Notes

1 A Chicana is a Mexican-American woman who is proud of her heritage and who actively seeks a connection to her indigenous roots. Chicana, as a term, is politically charged due to the fact that it evolved out of the Chicano movement, which took place concurrently with the civil rights and women's movement of the 1960s. A humorous definition is offered by Dan Guerrero, son of the Father of Chicano music, Lalo Guerrero, who stated in his show *Gaytino!* (January 12, 2006) that "the term Chicano stands for a Mexican who means it."

2 Eventually, Eva Tessler, Licia Perea, Eluza Santos, and I co-founded the Latina Dance Project (2000), which allowed me to observe, perform, and co-create a dance concert *Embodying Borders* and *Coyolxauhqui ReMembers*. This series of activities spanned an eight-year period. The Latina Dance Project evolved out of a telephone conversation Eluza Santos and I had in 2001. During the course of this conversation, I pointed out to Eluza, "I am a Latina, you are a Latina, and I am working with two Latinas who are subjects in my dissertation. Maybe they would be interested in joining us and we could perform as a group. You can contact them through email. What do you think?" Eluza was excited by the idea. As a result, the Latina Dance Project came into existence. Eluza invented the name for the group, since we were not interested in becoming a company but instead strove to invest in a process, and so Eluza produced our first concert at the University of North Carolina at Greensboro. The results have been rewarding. I was able to study, up close, the work of each woman choreographer and to continue dialoguing about the dances with each dance-maker. I was also introduced to new works as they evolved. Sometimes pertinent information about the dances or choreographer's life appeared "out of the mist," revealing a side to our work I would not have encountered had we not created the project.

3 Denzin and Lincoln (2000: 286). The hermeneutic circle is "a process of analysis in which interpreters seek the historical and social dynamics that shape textual interpretation." In translation, "critical researchers engage in the back and forth of studying parts in relation to the whole and the whole in relation to parts."

4 Geertz (1973). Geertz acknowledged that he borrowed this term coined by Gilbert Ryle.

5 Performed by Kristine Willis and Elizabeth Lefrois, the dance and paper were presented concurrently in a session titled "Dance as Autobiography: The Reclamation of Embodied Culture for Scholar's Day," which took place March 30, 1999, at SUNY College at Brockport, New York. The term "embodied culture" is ironic since it would have made choreographic/cultural sense to work with Latina dancers but the dance program at SUNY Brockport did not have any Latina dancers I could work with. As stated in the first chapter of this study, it is and has been difficult to find dancers from these ethnicities to work with.

6 *La Llorona* was presented for El Corazón de Mexico (The Mexican Heart) on October 2, 1999. El Corazón de Mexico is a local dance company composed of undocumented farm workers who farm the fields of western New York. As artistic director I worked collaboratively with Macrina Alarcon, then director of the ministry.

7 Moraga and Anzaldúa (1983). The section titled "The Bridge That Calls Me Back" is a play on words of this book title.

423

8 Jordan et al. (1991). According to Janet L. Surrey, "Our conception of the self-in-relation involves the recognition that, for women, the primary experience of self is relational, that is, the self is organized and developed in the context of important relationships."

9 El Teatro Campesino, under the direction of Luis Valdez, is a migrant theatre company that addresses the plight of the Mexican migrant farmer as well as that of the Mexican-American living in the United States.

Bibliography

Albright, Ann Cooper. *Choreographing Difference: The Body and Identity in Contemporary Dance*. Hanover, NH: Wesleyan University Press, 1997.

Anzaldúa, Gloria. *Making Face, Making Soul/Haciendo Caras: Creative and Critical Perspectives by Women of Color*. San Francisco: Aunt Lute, 2000.

———. *Borderlands/La Frontera: The New Mestiza*. San Francisco: Aunt Lute Books, 1987.

Anzaldúa, Gloria, and Cherríe Moraga (eds.). *This Bridge Called My Back: Writings by Radical Women of Color*. Watertown, MA: Persephone Press. Reprinted, New York: Kitchen Table Women of Color of Press, 1983.

Arenal, Electa, and Amanda Powell (eds.). *Sor Juana Inés de la Cruz/The Answer/La respuesta: Including a Selection of Poems*. City University of New York: Feminist Press, 1994.

Arrizón, Alicia. *Latina Performance: Traversing the Stage*. Bloomington: Indiana University Press, 1999.

Barrio, Raymond. *Mexico's Art and Chicano Artists*. Greenville: Ventury Press, 1975.

Blea, Irene. *La Chicana and the Intersection of Race, Class and Gender*. Westport, CT: Praeger, 1992.

Cervantes, Lorna Dee. *Emplumada*. Pittsburgh: University of Pittsburgh Press, 1981.

Cockroft, Eva S., and Holly Barnet-Sánchez (eds.). *Signs from the Heart: California Chicano Murals*. Venice, CA: Social and Public Art Resource; Albuquerque: University of New Mexico Press, 1993.

Cordova, Theresa, Norma E. Cantu, Gilberto Cardenas, Juan Garcia, and Christine Sierra. *Chicana Voices: Intersections of Class, Race, and Gender*. Albuquerque, NM: NACS, 1990.

Cotera, Martha. P. *The Chicana Feminist*. Austin, TX: Information Systems Development, 1977.

Creswell, John W. *Qualitative Inquiry and Research Design: Choosing among Five Traditions*. Thousand Oaks, CA: Sage Press, 1998.

Denzin, Norman K., and Yvonna S. Lincoln. *Handbook of Qualitative Research*, 2nd ed. Thousand Oaks, CA: Sage Press, 2000.

Durnell, L.E. "This Time of Truth and Talent: Latina Playwrights Conquer Center Stage." *The Creative Woman* 14, no. 3 (1994): 9.

Erlandson, David.A., Edward L. Harris, Barbara L. Skipper, and Steve D. Allen. *Doing Naturalistic Inquiry: A Guide to Methods*. Newbury Park, CA: Sage Press, 1993.

Estés, Clarissa P. *Women Who Run with the Wolves: Myths and Stories of the Wild Woman Archetype*. New York: Ballantine, 1992.

Fraleigh, Sondra. *Researching Dance: Evolving Modes of Inquiry*. Pittsburgh, PA: University of Pittsburgh Press, 1999.

———. *Dance and the Lived Body: A Descriptive Aesthetics*. Pittsburgh, PA: University of Pittsburgh Press, 1987.

Garry, Ann, and Marilyn Pearsall (eds.). "Playfulness 'World' Traveling, and Loving Perception." *Women, Knowledge and Reality: Explorations in Feminist Philosophy*. Boston: Unwin Hyman, 1989.

Geertz, Clifford. *The Interpretation of Cultures*. New York: Basic, 1973.

Goellner, Ellen W., and Jacqueline Shea Murphy (eds.). *Bodies of the Text: Dance as Theory, Literature as Dance*. New Brunswick, NJ: Rutgers University Press, 1995.

Hahner, June E. (ed.). *Women in Latin American History: Their Lives and Views*. Los Angeles: Regents of the University of California, 1976.

Herrera-Sobek, María.H., and Helena MaríaViramontes (eds.). *Chicana Creativity and Criticism: Charting New Frontiers in American Literature*. Houston, TX: Arte Publico Press, 1988.

Jaggar, Allison M., and Susan R. Bordo (eds.). *Gender/Body/Knowledge: Feminist Reconstructions of Being and Knowing*. New Brunswick, NJ: Rutgers University Press, 1989.

Jordan, Judith V., Alexandra G. Kaplan, Jean Baker Miller, Irene P. Stiver, and Janet L. Surrey. *Women's Growth in Connection: Writings from the Stone Center*. New York: Guilford Press, 1991.

Mora, Pat. *Nepantla: Essays from the Land in the Middle*. Albuquerque: University of New Mexico Press, 1993.

Moraga, Cherríe, and Gloria Anzaldúa (eds.). *This Bridge Called My Back: Writings by Radical Women of Color*. Watertown, MA: Persephone Press. Reprinted, New York: Kitchen Table Women of Color of Press, 1983.

Ness, Sally Ann. *Body, Movement and Culture: Kinesthetic and Visual Symbolism in a Philippine Community*. Philadelphia: University of Pennsylvania Press, 1992.

Nicholson, Shirley. *Shamanism*. Madras, India: Theosophical Publishing House, 1987.

Quintana, Alvina E. *Home Girls: Chicana Literary Voices*. Philadelphia, PA: Temple University Press, 1996.

Rebolledo, Tey Diana. *Women Singing in the Snow: A Critical Cultural Analysis of Chicana Literature*. Tucson: University of Arizona Press, 1995.

Rebolledo, Tey Diana, and Maria Theresa Márquez. *Women's Tales from the New Mexico WPA: La diabla a pie*. Houston, TX: Arte Público Press, 2000.

Rebolledo, Tey Diana, and Eliana S. Rivero (eds.). *Infinite Divisions: An Anthology of Chicana Literature*. Tucson: University of Arizona Press, 1993.

Rubin, Herbert J., and Irene S. Rubin. *Qualitative Interviewing: The Art of Hearing Data*. Thousand Oaks, CA: Sage Press, 1995.

Rubinstein, Charlotte S. *American Women Artists*. Boston: Avon, 1982.

Sklar, Dierdre. *Dancing with the Virgin: Body and Faith in the Fiesta of Tortugas, New Mexico*. Berkeley: University of California Press, 2001.

Stinson, Sue. *Research as Choreography*. Reston, VA: National Dance Association, 1994.

Suarez, Juanita. "A Migrant's Tale." *Introduction to Dance Workbook*. Dubuque, IA: Kendall Hunt Publishing, 2006.

Telgen, Diane, and Jim Kamp (eds). *Notable Hispanic American Women*. Detroit: Gale Research, 1993.

Tierney, Helen (ed.). "Literature, Arts and Learning." *Women's Studies Encyclopedia*. New York: Greenwood Press, 1990: 9–14.

Zamudio-Taylor, Victor. "Chicano Art." In E. Sullivan (ed.), *Latin American Art in the Twentieth Century*. London: Phaidon, 1996: 315–29.

CHAPTER TWENTY-TWO

Not of Themselves

CONTEMPORARY PRACTICES IN AMERICAN PROTESTANT DANCE

EMILY WRIGHT

And as the ark of the LORD came into the city of David, Michal, Saul's daughter looked through a window and saw King David leaping and dancing before the LORD and she despised him in her heart.
— 2 Samuel 6:20

INTRODUCTION

As a child, I attended weekly dance lessons in Martha Graham–based modern technique, a half-hearted attempt to fulfill a middle-class expectation for extra-curricular activities. It was not until I discovered Christian dance, as a member of a church dance ministry, that I discovered my passion for dance. This group, which included the pastor's wife, was composed of women in their thirties and forties with little formal dance training and led by a local high school drama teacher. The movements were usually literal interpretations of Christian song lyrics performed in unison or quasi-mimetic narrative set to instrumental music. The emphasis in performance was purity of spiritual intention: seeking to worship God with our hearts through our best attempt to dance with our bodies. Our leader encouraged us to focus on God while we were dancing and not on the congregation watching us. Our goal was to enhance the worship experience for the congregation by adding a layer of physical and visual meaning to the words of praise songs or a sermon. Mistakes were opportunities to be reminded of our human imperfections before God. Any praise we received was to be redirected toward God, who alone was worthy to receive all the glory.

So compelling were my experiences with this group, and much to my parents' amazement, considering I had shown very little passion for dance as a child, I decided to pursue a bachelor's degree in dance at a Christian college. There I encountered a very different experience of Christian dance. We still prayed together before each technique class, asking that God would be glorified by our hard work, that our efforts would be for His glory and not our own, that we would have the wisdom to make good decisions when taking care of our bodies, our instruments for God's service. For ninety minutes, five days a week, we wore black leotards (with a one-inch strap for modesty) and pink tights, hair in buns, no jewellery. Auditions for roles in performances were competitive. This led to frustration, disappointment, and disillusionment for dancers who had a strong desire to worship God through dance but lacked the technical excellence required.

I learned a tremendous amount, technically and personally, but I chafed at the inconsistencies between Christian doctrines of love and community and certain practices in the dance department.

One of the central debates of my experience among Christian dancers is the importance of the attitude of the heart and purity of intention versus the technical excellence of the dancer. In this chapter, I will discuss my ongoing research into the complex practices of American Protestant dancers. By making Christian dance the focus of my research, I hope to initiate dialogues among academic and Christian dance communities at an intersection of faith and practice.

Figure 1 *Not Yet* choreography by Emily Wright and dancers. Dancers (from left to right): Jessica Mumford, KristinTovson, Julia Vessey, Janie Ross, Holly Wooldridge, Avery Yanez, and Sara Malan-McDonald. Photography: Tim Trumble Photography, Inc.

When one hears the phrase "American Protestant dance," many things may come to mind. Or, perhaps, nothing at all. Yet throughout Christian history, dance has been present in some form, whether in the group circle dances and catacomb processions of the early Church, the spontaneous dances of the priests on medieval feast day celebrations, or the distinct shaking movements of the nineteenth-century Shakers. On the other hand, many people are also aware of the historic tensions between dance and the Christian Church. In the United States in the twentieth and twenty-first centuries, Christian religious dance has been experiencing a rebirth and revitalization. This period in the history of Christian dance follows on the heels of an "anti-dance" period, a time stretching from the Reformation to the end of the nineteenth century, in which mostly Protestant churches denounced dancing as something antithetical to the Christian way of life. What is contemporary Christian dance? And why should it be of interest to the dance academy?

Although there are several helpful texts by contemporary practitioners within the Christian dance community, relatively few studies are available by dance scholars addressing Christian dance; similarly, few religious-studies volumes examine aspects of dance within the Christian tradition.[1] As Kent De Spain noted in his paper, "Invisible Communities or Blind Scholars: Critical Issues in American Liturgical Dance" (presented in Florida at the 2005 Congress on Research in Dance Conference), the lack of scholarship examining Christian dance is surprising "considering the historical relationship most organized churches in America have toward the dancing body" (De Spain 2005).

My purpose here is to demonstrate the application of religious-studies scholarship to a field study of a professional, "Christian faith–based" dance company. My goal in pursuing this thread of scholarship is to further the nascent academic conversation concerning the phenomenon of contemporary Christian dance in the North American context by engaging a qualitative paradigm: to make the world of Christian dance "strange" to myself for the purpose of greater objectivity and discovery in critical analysis and to make Christian dance more "familiar" to the academic dance community. I achieve this by developing a choreographic strategy that frames Christian ideas of worship and religious experience in more recognizable movement forms. With the ever-increasing visibility of Christian dance, the academic dance community will be better able to process interactions from a more informed perspective. This study presents a dual challenge to myself as a researcher because not only am I an insider to the Christian faith, but I am also an insider to the practice of Christian dance. Conversely, my position as an insider to Christianity and Christian dance has provided me with insight into the sometimes unarticulated aesthetic ideals and choreographic intentions of this little known and vaguely formed group.

The field of religious studies provides helpful models for examining Christian dance, as it has quickly become apparent that the focus of my inquiry is also where the dancers often place it: on the religious experiences as embodied by dance, rather than on the movements themselves. The integration of religious studies scholarship involves the historical grounding of the treatment of dance within the tradition of Protestant Christianity through the examination of primary source material, such as the "anti-dance" literature, the secondary scholarship of religion and dance historians, and the application of a phenomenological methodology for engaging the religious experience of others to the process of creating choreography for concert performance. The eventual outcome of this project will be a choreographic reflection of my experiences as a researcher and a performer of "imaginative empathy" in which I demonstrate the potential of dance as a mediator for religious experience between the Christian and secular dance communities. The hard data of my research findings will undergo two translations: that of my own personal responses to the material based on my "particular body" of history, ideas, and ways of moving and the "particular bodies" of the dancers who will then learn the choreography from me. This process of "embodied experience" serves as an experiment in experiencing the experience of others. My choreographic method for this mediation is derived from Kimerer LaMothe's analysis of Dutch phenomenologist Gerardus van der Leeuw's braided methodology of imaginative empathy, suspended judgment, and willingness to move between chaos and form, which I will describe in detail at the end of this chapter.

By applying religious-studies scholarship to the investigation of Christian dance, I hope to further the dialogue in dance scholarship concerning how Christian ideas of the body and religious experience in America influence the practice of dance in the twenty-first century. Works such as Ann Wagner's text, *Adversaries of Dance: From the Puritans to the Present*, and Elizabeth Aldrich's essay, "Plunge Not into the Mire of Worldly Folly: Objections to Social Dance in Nineteenth-Century America," provide an overview of the historical Christian polemic against dance, which illuminates the legacy of ideas about the body and dance in Western, and particularly American, contexts. Aldrich's essay relies heavily on Wagner's delineation of arguments against the "essential nature of dance" as disorderly, trivial, anti-intellectual, and artificial, and the "incidental characteristics of dance" as leading to sexual immorality, the squandering of time and resources, unnecessary health risks, and participation in "worldly" pleasures to the peril of the immortal soul (Wagner 1997: 363–78).

However, Aldrich's specific focus on "anti-dance" literature, a collection of essays, sermons, and other publications written primarily by Protestant pastors from the Reformation to the early twentieth century, demonstrates the dramatic increase in negative attitudes toward dance post-Reformation (Aldrich 2006). Wagner concludes, "The vast majority of American anti-dance arguments [are] derived from incidental characteristics surrounding the act of dancing" (Wagner 1997: 378). While these texts focus primarily on American social dance in a broad milieu, their narratives stem directly from a religion-based dialogue within American Protestantism that continues to influence dance practices in secular and religious frameworks. In this chapter, I will explore the impact of these ideas on contemporary dancing practices in American Protestant contexts.

BACKGROUND

Robert Orsi, in *Between Heaven and Earth: The Religious Worlds People Make and the Scholars Who Study Them* (2005), encourages religious fieldworkers to rethink the us–them boundary by acknowledging one's own context for the subject being studied while simultaneously enacting "the necessary disciplines of fieldwork, scrupulous attention to the practices encountered in their social field, the necessary historical framing, (and) the resolute difference of our sources and their autonomy." In recognition of this scholarly tradition, I have provided this glimpse at the context in which I am conducting this study based on secondary scholarship, data provided by my informants, and my own experiences as a practitioner of Christian dance. The term "Christian dance" specifically refers to predominantly white, American Protestant Christian dance in the twentieth and twenty-first centuries. There are two main delineations of dance in this context: spontaneous dance, occurring almost exclusively within the context of corporate worship services, and choreographed dance, which also takes place in corporate worship but can be performed in "secular" contexts, such as a concert venues or public festivals.[2] I will be referring exclusively to choreographed Christian dance here. Christian dance is sometimes also called liturgical dance, sacred dance, or interpretive movement, but each term carries with it an implied context. *Liturgical* can indicate a "high church" sensibility, often of the Catholic or Anglican traditions. Therefore, Protestant evangelical dancers sometimes resist this term. *Sacred dance* is also employed by dancers in religious traditions other than Christianity and is, thus, viewed as too broad. *Interpretive movement* is favoured by some "low church" denominations, particularly those whose members tend to resist the idea of dance in church altogether; interpretive is seen as a less threatening form of movement that is not quite dance. Consequently, Christian professional dancers tend to resist this label as conveying a more simplified, mimetic movement often executed by less trained or untrained dancers.

Simply defined, Christian dancers are first Christians. They believe, like other Christians, in the God of the Bible and in Jesus Christ as Saviour. Secondly, they are dancers. The form that this Christian belief takes in a dance context is widely varied, from teachers who construct technique classes that incorporate Christian prayer and scripture readings, to choreographers who organize movement around Christian music or thematic content, to performers who orient their attention to God in worship. Others choose *not* to operate within a specifically Christian context, but they employ Christian beliefs when making choices about training, choreography, and performance. These choices may not reflect specifically Christian sentiment, but they adhere to a normative principle when participating in dance; in other words, they do not participate in practices that are expressly prohibited by the Bible, but there may be individual variations in practice based on personal convictions on "grey areas" of scripture where an activity is not mentioned as permissible or not permissible.[3] Christian dance can occur in a variety of contexts, from church sanctuaries and fellowship halls, to schools and studios, to concert venues, to private homes, to parks and public squares. There is not necessarily something inherent in the movement that makes the dance Christian, although several gestures have developed that are often utilized by Christian dancers, such as "prayer hands" and "praise arms." Instead, they believe it is the attitude of the heart of the dancer as a Christian that "sanctifies" the movement. A more basic understanding is that a Christian dancer is a dancer who is Christian, or a Christian who dances.

Historically, the relationship between the Church and the dancing body can be traced in the following manner. Scholars note that neo-platonic thought in the intellectual community surrounding the early Church and interpretations of specific scriptures in the New Testament merged to create a mind–body dualism that has remained in Christian religious practices to varying degrees since its inception.[4] The early Church in Rome was surrounded by pagan religions, many of which made use of dance as part of their religious practices. Additionally, the intellectual community of the day, the Neo-Platonists, looked down on pagan religious practices, including their dances. In his text, *Dancing: The Pleasure, Power and Art of Movement*, Gerald Jonas writes that "the early church fathers, believing that the body was inferior to the spirit, were drawn to the Neo-Platonic concept of the ideal body free of unseemly lusts. This was the kind of body that, properly purified and controlled, could perform sacred dances to the greater glory of God" (Jonas 1998: 42). The early Church aligned itself with the intellectual community against the pagan practices of the day in order to establish itself as distinct from other religions and as a worthy member of the intellectual community.

During the period following the Reformation and into the early twentieth century, texts known as "anti-dance" literature reveal the increasing antipathy of Christianity to the dancing body. Written primarily by Protestant pastors, the anti-dance literature is a collection of essays, sermons, and other publications that denounced contemporary social dancing as evil and sinful. These claims were based on a variety of arguments, such as the interpretation of certain Bible passages as forbidding dance, health concerns that dancing weakened the body, that dance was an improper use of leisure time, and the idea of the dancing woman as victim or temptress (Aldrich 2006: 5–11). Concurrently, religious scholarship traces the reification of the definition of Protestant religious experience as private, intellectual, and internal through the writings of prominent Protestant theologians, such as Jonathan Edwards, who were attempting to situate Protestant Christianity between what they viewed as the two cultural extremes of the Enlightenment (no religion) and 'enthusiasm' (too much religion) (Taves 1999: 34–35). I would suggest that the significance of the surge in anti-dance literature correlates to the developing notion among Protestants of true or good religious experience as that which denies bodily participation in favour of internal, private, and intellectualized expression. The role that contemporary choreographed Christian dance has played in the Church simultaneously reifies and subverts this notion. By integrating the use of the body in corporate worship settings, Christian dancers subvert the notion of religious experience as private and internal. However, for those who situate themselves in the choreographed dance camp, as opposed to the use of spontaneous dance or untrained dancers, religious experience is reified as internal and private as the dancers resist individual response that might deviate from choreographed movements during performance in favour of communicating the choreographer's interpretation of a praise chorus or sermon point. This tension is exemplified by the commonly held belief within Christian dance that the role of the dancer in the congregational setting is "not for themselves," which will be explored further as the dual purpose for the dancer in the congregational worship setting.[5]

From its foundations, Protestantism has been concerned with the incorporation of the visual into Christian worship practices. In contrast to the pervasive use of visual art within Catholicism—from stained-glass windows depicting Biblical scenes to statues of the Virgin Mary, Baby Jesus, and many Saints, to the very architecture of the cathedral—traditional Protestant churches usually consist of some variation of simple wooden pews or chairs facing an elevated platform on which the pulpit stands, orienting the Protestant worshipper to the primacy of God's Word. Sometimes, the Lord's Table or a baptismal font or a choir loft is also a permanent fixture, but the basic simplicity of Protestant sanctuaries remains a constant. What has changed within the culture of American Protestantism that accounts for the current popularity of a kinetic art form such as dance? The sanctuary certainly does not provide an inviting location for large body movement. The elevated platforms are too small for much dancing; sometimes, the pulpit is permanently attached, presenting a large visual obstacle for congregational viewing. The empty space at floor level between the platform and the congregational seating is usually narrow, necessitating an uncomfortable proximity between viewers and dancers. Some more recently built Protestant churches have actually attempted to remedy the shortage of performance space for worship bands, dramatic skits, and dance by replacing the small platform with larger, concert-style stages. By making the concert stage a permanent fixture of the sanctuary, these churches are sending a strong message about the shift in priorities from exclusion to inclusion of the performative. The rhetoric associated with this shift often emphasizes God as the Creator-God, the first and greatest Artist, and that Christians, as part of being made in the image of God, are to participate in creative activities "to the glory of God." Others see the visual arts as a tool to help Christianity remain relevant to the increasingly visual nature of contemporary American culture. Whatever the reasons, the practice of visual arts are increasing within American Protestant worship practices and choreographed dance demonstrably so.

FIELDWORK

The subject group for this qualitative ethnographic study is the AZ Dance Group, a contemporary Christian faith–based ballet company under the artistic direction of Kenda Newbury in Anthem, Arizona. Although my fieldwork is ongoing, a definition of the dual purpose of the dancer in the Christian worship service has emerged which corresponds to my personal experiences in this area. The Christian dancer in the context of a congregational worship setting, views herself as a worshipper of God and a communicator of truth to the audience.[6] Sometimes referring to themselves as a "movement ministry," Christian dancers see their dance as first an act of worship.[7] One company member strongly links the music accompanying the dance in describing her experience as "representing the music to people and showing praise with my body."[8] For her, the performance is less about displaying what the body can do in terms of technical virtuosity, but rather displaying what the body can do in terms of illustrating feelings of worship and adoration to God. To that end, this company member, in her own choreography, often specifically chooses less complicated movement so that her mind is less focused on the difficulties of the performance and the image of her movement to the congregation and is more able to focus on the feelings of worship stimulated by the words or music to which she is dancing. The Christian dancer's second purpose in the context of corporate worship is communication. Much like the contested Christian practice of speaking in tongues, these dancers believe that the dancer should not offer a dance to be viewed by the congregation unless the "interpretation" of that dance is easily discernable to the congregation. Otherwise, the dancer will appear to be dancing for herself, which, in the context of corporate worship, is unacceptable. The underlying message seems to be that in the context of corporate worship, only that which is beneficial and edifying for the entire congregation is appropriate. This belief illuminates the aesthetic choices of Christian dancers: the movement choices are often simplistic and performed in unison (although unison is also employed to convey a sense of the unity of the Body of Christ); the movement also relies heavily upon song lyrics as a shaping force for the choreography.

I observed first-hand the implementation of these beliefs in the performance of the AZ Dance Group's "Prayer." Set to a lyrical duet sung by a man and a woman, the dancers were sometimes divided into two groups, each performing movements while one voice was singing and stopping when the other voice and the other group of dancers began. When the two voices sang at the same time, all of the dancers performed together as well. Interspersed throughout the generally balletic vocabulary were accents of "prayer hands," referring to the prayer about which the vocalists were singing. For a more sophisticated audience, this dance might seem too literal, but to congregational audiences who generally have little reference for watching dance, the dance can be powerfully demonstrative of the potential of the human body to add to the communication of truth or a message within Christianity.

This aspect of the role of the Christian dancer as communicator leads to a debate within the Christian dance community about the use of trained versus untrained dancers in the corporate worship setting. The Sacred Dance Guild, as early as 1958, has documented this debate in its organizational newsletters. On the one hand were those who felt, due to the responsibility of Christian dancers to communicate a message, that trained dancers were the most equipped to carry out this responsibility. Thus, those who aspire to be Christian dancers should seek to increase their training experiences. On the other hand were those who felt that the attitude of the heart in worship to God was primary and, thus, Christian dancers should seek continued depth of devotional practice and experiences to draw them closer to God.[9] The director of the AZ Dance Group specifically situates herself and her company in the former camp. To that end, her company holds formal ballet auditions and makes selections based on the technical merit of the performer. In articulating the Christian aspect of her company, she emphasizes that it is "Christian faith–based," but "all faiths are welcome." She permits any qualified dancer to join the company as long as he realizes that some choreographic and musical content will be explicitly Christian and he can willingly invest in that as a performer.[10] As a Christian, I question the appropriateness of a dancer who is not a Christian potentially being asked to "perform" the emotions and actions of worship toward God without the actual heart attitude or heart relationship to God that Christians believe establishes their authority to approach God in this way. In response to my questions, the company's director emphasized the "comfort zone" and willingness of the performer to engage with religious ideas in which he does not believe, rather than addressing the conflict between performing and worshipping. During our conversation, she stated, "I believe I've been given this gift and I can share this gift. It is emotional; it is connecting to others in the audience ... so it's not your movement, it's God's movement."[11] I interpret her position to be that regardless of the performer's belief system, if he is sincerely emotional, God is still the inspiration and the recipient of that movement.

CHOREOGRAPHIC METHOD

As I thought about the shape of my choreographic responses to my interaction as researcher with this Christian dance company, I realized that, although my tendency as an insider is to determine whether their expressions of faith are similar or different to what I know to be "true" of Christianity and, thus, authentic or legitimate, as a scholar that would be inappropriate and as a choreographic responder, ineffective. An embodied experience method, developed by Dutch phenomenologist, Gerardus van der Leeuw, and delineated by Kimerer LaMothe, requires that I resist this tendency by engaging in a braided approach to the study of religious experience, weaving together strands of fact through historical and social scientific examination, meaning through a phenomenological lens, and truth through theology in the sense of a "dynamic, incomplete and ongoing reflection on the forms of God" (LaMothe 2004). To that end, van der Leeuw developed three responsibilities for the religious scholar when engaging with the religious experiences of others based on his simultaneous definitions of religion and dance as experiences/expressions of power. For van der Leeuw, the phenomenological researcher-scholar seeks to understand the meaning that a phenomenon has for a practitioner as a function of the meaning that it has for the researcher-scholar. He acknowledges that not all instances of power are religious. Religion appears as an experience or expression of power at the intersection of the "horizontal plane," the field of human agency, and the "vertical plane," or the appearance of a power that interrupts human agency. By this definition, van der Leeuw enacts a sense of religion as having to do with the ultimate, or as he puts it, "the last word." Similarly, dance, or "beautiful movement" appear as "moments in history when someone experiences human motion as a conduit for an experience of beauty. Such a moment is also religion if it is experienced as conducting an experience of power." As a form that contests verbal translation, dance also operates as a "last word," an expression of the ultimate through human movement (LaMothe 2004: 159–78). Obviously, the definitions of religion and dance are many and varied. I have found the fields of religious studies and dance strikingly similar in their struggle to define essential terms. However, for my purposes, these definitions clarify the connections between religious experience and dance experience in terms of my choreographic project.

Van der Leeuw's first responsibility, "imaginative empathy," asks the researcher to "transpose" or surrender her own experience to draw closer to the *shape* of another's and "interpolate" or mobilize the reaches of her own experience to match the perception of the movement of another's experience. Van der Leeuw is careful to explain that imaginative empathy does not ask that the researcher give up her sense of who she is, what her experiences have been, and so on. Rather, the scholar acknowledges that "reality is always my reality" in the sense that we can only fully know our own experiences and attempt imaginatively to understand the experiences of others through what we recognize as having meaning from our own experiences of meaning (LaMothe 2004: 143–47). As I develop my choreographic responses to this study, I have specifically geared my interview questions to generate descriptive responses from my participants about their religious experiences through movement. Then I have identified, through comparative analysis, outstanding points of similarity or difference in our experiences as American Protestant Christian dancers. When I begin working with my cast, whom I choose to work with me will be based on their willingness to explore ideas of religious experience through movement, rather than adherence to a particular religious affiliation. We will engage in van der Leeuw's imaginative empathy by (re)membering bodily experiences that will draw us close to the shape of what members of my participant group have described as their bodily experience of religion. Drawing from Carl Bagley and Mary Beth Cancienne's *Dancing the Data* (2004), we will work with text from interviews and video images from rehearsals and performances to develop personal vocabularies of imaginatively empathizing movements as a foundation for choreographic construction.

Van der Leeuw's second responsibility, the suspension of judgment, speaks directly to this choreographic process (LaMothe 2004: 147–49). Before I began this study, I had hoped to dissect the aesthetically unappealing elements of Christian dance and develop a new movement vocabulary that was less limiting than what I had observed in Christian dance presentations. This vocabulary could be used by other Christian choreographers more effectively. As I have mentioned, I quickly realized that to engage critically with the material would be at cross-purposes with my imaginative empathy in achieving the choreographic result of making the "strange" world of Christian dance more familiar to an academic audience. Van der Leeuw encourages the religious scholar to resist the desire to question the truth of a religious experience, to see another's experience as a challenge to your own. In this, he reveals his own Protestant context, in that Protestant Christians are encouraged individually to "test the spirits to see if any of them is from God" rather than rely on a designated authority to make those pronouncements. A prominent element of my religious experience as a Christian has been to "test the spirits" by critically evaluating the words and actions of others who call themselves Christians, particularly teachers, or those who present themselves as participants in truth, to determine if they match my experience of truth. Embracing suspended judgment has necessarily changed the focus of my project and my thinking about engaging the religious experience of others. In data analysis, I have focused my attention on interview responses rather than descriptions of the actual movement of dancers. Whether or not I enjoy the aesthetic of my participants' dances has become much less important when compared to the potential for imaginative empathy found in their descriptions of their religious experiences through movement. I realize that in focusing on the interview responses rather than movement observation I am continuing the Christian reification of religious experience through words, but I also recognize that Christians still primarily articulate their religious experiences through words and that it is in their words that I find the richest and most complex material for choreographic response.

Van der Leeuw's final responsibility, willingness to move between chaos and form, is still emerging in my project. Van der Leeuw describes this responsibility as a spiral of exposing oneself to a broad range of experiences while continually revisiting and (re)membering past personal experiences. This spiral takes place in a linear progression in which exposure to the experiences of others influences and changes you so that your awareness of your own experiences is also changed. This in turn influences further engagement with the experiences of others and so forth. For van der Leeuw, this spiralling movement also guarantees accountability and the constant assessment of your own conclusions (LaMothe 2004: 149–58). For me, this book is part of the accountability process, as is my inclusion of dancers of varying religious backgrounds in my choreographic project. In the context of my insider relationship to the world of Christian dance, I recognize the similarities and differences in my experience through comparative analysis of my participant group. As a dancer, researcher, and choreographer in the academic context, I expose my experiences and the experiences of my participant group to a much wider base of experiences through the interpretations of my dancers and, ultimately, my audience. I anticipate that this will result in some very fluid aspects of the choreographic presentation based on the fluid nature of moving between chaos and form.

CONCLUSION

Viewing Christian dance can be uncomfortable for the academic dance audience. It can seem ineffective, inappropriate, trite, clichéd, even embarrassing or offensive. I would suggest that this is partly because many Christian dancers are trying to utilize a standardized form of movement (ballet) because it is recognizable and accessible to their audiences without the necessary training in that discipline to accomplish their choreographic goals effectively, but that is a topic for another discussion. Christian dance can also be powerful and innovative, especially in light of the historical treatment of the body within the context of Christian practice. Western dancers in general are uniquely equipped to empathize with the religious experiences of Christian dancers, not only because we come from a generally Western dance background, but also because we can identify with the Christian dancer's dual roles as worshipper and communicator. Although we dance for many different reasons, the communication of a thought, idea, or emotion is often prominent in our motivations. In choreography, we ask ourselves, "What is my intent?" "Is my intent clearly discernable to my audience?" If not, then the dance is deemed "unsuccessful." Although most Western dancers would not couch their experience of dance as an act of worship, the concept of dance as an experience of power, whether it be a self-actualizing power from within or a separate power from without, provides a bridge to understanding the religious experience of Christian dancers. In this way, dance can be a mediator for the understanding of Christian religious experience between Christian and non-Christian dancers.

But why is mediation even needed? Christian dance is still most often performed in Christian religious ceremonies, where those who have no interest in Christianity will probably not be present. Is this study of value only to people like me who happen to be members of both Christian and secular dance communities? Christian dance is a growing movement. Again, as Kent De Spain (2005) has noted, Christian dance websites indicate Christian dance groups are increasing in many parts of the United States. This is a stimulating and significant time within Protestant Christianity, as the incorporation of bodily practices, such as dance, encourages a richer, more dynamic religious experience in the long-neglected sphere of the physical body. However, this movement remains largely disconnected from the larger professional and academic communities. I have alluded to several problematic areas in Christian dance, including the debate over the use of trained versus untrained dancers and the choice of balletic movement vocabulary, which I see as counterproductive to their aims to reincorporate the body into Christian worship practices. I have not yet mentioned other debates within Christian dance over thematic content; movement; accompaniment and costume choices; the appropriateness of incorporating dance into certain physical sites within the church building; and the portrayal of the dancing body, particularly the female dancing body, in worship. Christian dance could be well served by the critical-subjective eye of dance scholars. And as Christian dance continues to filter through into secular performing venues, dance scholars would be better equipped to process these interactions and cope with the "strangeness" of Christian dance from a more informed perspective.

Acknowledgements

I wish to thank Kenda Newbury and the members of the AZ Dance Group for inviting me into their creative, spiritual and personal spaces. I also thank Lindsey Bauer, Dena Davida, Naomi Jackson, Beverly Lucas, Nicole Manus, Beau Seegmiller, Konden Smith, Jennifer Tsukayama, and Tisa Wenger for their encouragement and editorial advice. Finally, I thank the cast of my MFA thesis concert for their willingness to take this journey with me.

Notes

1 For examples of texts by contemporary practitioners, see *The Spirit Moves: A Handbook of Dance and Prayer* by Carla De Sola; *Imagine: A Vision for Christians in the Arts* by Steve Turner; and *Liturgical Dance: An Historical, Theological and Practical Handbook* by J.G. Davies. For examples of Christian dance studies by dance scholars, see *Dance as Religious Studies*, edited by Doug Adams and Diane Apostolos-Cappadona; and Kent De Spain's paper, "Invisible Communities or Blind Scholars: Critical Issues in American Liturgical Dance," from the CORD 2005 conference proceedings.

2 Here, the term "corporate" indicates a public, group setting, as opposed to private, individual worship and is derived from the Christian belief that the Church is the *body* of Christ (Rom. 12:5; 1 Cor. 12:12).

3 The normative principle of worship within the context of Christianity teaches that that which is not expressly prohibited by scripture is permissible in the worship service. By contrast, the regulative principle of worship teaches that only that which is explicitly commanded in scripture is permissible in the worship service. Different traditions within Christianity embrace either normative or regulative, and while those who operate under the normative principle are more likely to include dance, those who utilize the regulative principle are not necessarily opposed to dance, just dance within the context of the congregational worship setting.

4 Specific Biblical references include, "I discipline my body and make it my slave" (1 Cor. 9:27) and "If there is a natural body, there is also a spiritual body" (1 Cor. 15:44).

5 Kenda Newbury, personal communication to author, September 30, 2006.

6 Although Christian dancers are sometimes males, they tend, as in secular Western dance communities, to be in the minority. The AZ Dance Group is entirely composed of females; therefore, references to Christian dancers in this paper are in the feminine.

7 Kenda Newbury, personal communication to author, September 30, 2006.

8 Nicole Rennell, personal communication to author, October 13, 2006.

9 Carlynn Reed, *And We Have Danced: The History of the Sacred Dance Guild, 1958–1978* (Sharing Company, 1978).

10 Kenda Newbury, personal communication to author, September 30, 2006.

11 Kenda Newbury, personal communication to author, October 28, 2006.

Bibliography

Adams, Doug, and Diane Apostolos-Cappadona, eds. *Dance as Religious Studies*. New York: Crossroad Publishing Company, 1990.

Adams, Doug, and Diane Apostolos-Cappadona. "Changing Biblical Imagery and Artistic Identity in Twentieth-Century Dance." In Doug Adams and Diane Apostolos-Cappadona (eds.), *Dance as Religious Studies*. New York: Crossroad Publishing Company, 1990: 3–14.

Aldrich, Elizabeth. "Plunge Not into the Mire of Worldly Folly: Objections to Social Dance in Nineteenth-Century America." Unpublished article, 2006.

Bagley, Carl, and Mary Beth Cancienne. "Educational Research and Intertextual Forms of (Re)Presentation: The Case for Dancing the Data." In Carl Bagley and

Mary Beth Cancienne (eds.), *Dancing the Data*. New York: Peter Lang Publishing, 2002: 3–19.

Bauer, Susan. *A Choreographed Lecture Demonstration of Sacred Dance in the Christian Tradition*. Master's thesis, Arizona State University, 1976.

———. "Dance as Performance Fine Art in Liturgy." In Doug Adams and Diane Apostolos-Cappadona (eds.), *Dance as Religious Studies*. New York: Crossroad Publishing Company, 1990: 167–83.

Brooks, Lynn Matluck. "Christianity and Dance: Medieval Views." In *International Encyclopedia of Dance*. New York: Oxford University Press, 1998: 164–66.

Buckland, Theresa J. (ed.). *Dance in the Field: Theory, Methods and Issues in Dance Ethnography*. New York: St. Martin's Press, 1999.

Bogden, Robert C., and Sari Knopp Biklen. *Qualitative Research for Education: An Introduction to Theories and Methods*. Boston: Pearson Education Group, 2003.

Davies, J.G. "Christianity and Dance: Early Christian Views." In *International Encyclopedia of Dance*. New York: Oxford University Press, 1998: 162–64.

———. *Liturgical Dance: An Historical, Theological and Practical Handbook*. London: SCM Press, 1984.

De Spain, Kent. "Invisible Communities or Blind Scholars: Critical Issues in American Liturgical Dance." Unpublished conference presentation, Florida, 2005.

De Sola, Carla. *The Spirit Moves: A Handbook of Dance and Prayer*. Washington DC: Liturgical Conference, 1977.

———. "And the Word Became Dance: A Theory and Practice of Liturgical Dance." In Doug Adams and Diane Apostolos-Cappadona (eds.), *Dance as Religious Studies*. New York: Crossroad Publishing Company, 1990: 153–66.

Eisner, Elliot W. "The Promise and Perils of Alternative Forms of Data Representation." *Educational Researcher* (August-September), 1997.

Gruber, Gerald L. "Dance in the Bible." In *International Encyclopedia of Dance*. New York: Oxford University Press, 1998: 448–49.

Gundlach, Helga Barbara. "New Approaches to the Study of Religious Dance." In Peter Antes, Armin W. Geertz, and Randi R. Warne (eds.), *New Approaches to the Study of Religion Volume 2: Textual, Comparative, Sociological, and Cognitive Approaches*. Berlin and New York: Walter de Gruyter, 2004: 139–63.

Jackson, Anthony (ed.). *Anthropology at Home*. London and New York: Tavistock Publications, 1987.

Jonas, Gerald. *Dancing: The Pleasure, Power and Art of Movement*. New York: Harry N. Abrams, 1998.

Kaeppler, Adrienne. "The Mystique of Fieldwork." In Theresa J. Buckland (ed.), *Dance in the Field: Theory, Methods and Issues in Dance Ethnography*. New York: St. Martin's Press, 1999: 13–25.

Kealiinohomoku, Joann. "Field Guides." In *New Dimensions in Dance Research: Anthropology and Dance—the American Indian*. New York City: the Congress on Research in Dance, 1974: 245–60.

Koutsouba, Maria. "'Outsider' in an 'Inside' World, or Dance Ethnography at Home." In Theresa J. Buckland (ed.), *Dance in the Field: Theory, Methods and Issues in Dance Ethnography*. New York: St. Martin's Press, 1999: 186–95.

LaMothe, Kimerer L. *Between Dancing and Writing: The Practice of Religious Studies.* New York: Fordham University Press, 2004.

Mascarenhas-Keyes, Stella. "The Native Anthropologist: Constraints and Strategies in Research." In Anthony Jackson (ed.), *Anthropology at Home.* London and New York: Tavistock Publications, 1987: 180–95.

Noll, Mark A. "Contemporary Uncertainties." In *Between Faith and Criticism: Evangelicals, Scholarship and the Bible in America.* San Francisco: Harper & Row, Publishers, 1986: 162–85.

Orsi, Robert A. *Between Heaven and Earth: The Religious Worlds People Make and the Scholars Who Study Them.* Princeton and Oxford: Princeton University Press, 2005.

Reed, Carlynn. *And We Have Danced: The History of the Sacred Dance Guild, 1958–1978.* Sharing Co., 1978.

Repp, Dianna Louise. "Christian Religious Dance in Evangelical and Charismatic Churches in Tucson, Arizona." Master's thesis, Arizona State University, 1998.

Sklar, Deidre. "Movement Observation Guidelines." Unpublished paper, 2006.

———. "Performance Observation Guidelines, Parts I & II." Unpublished paper, 2006.

Styers, Randall. *Making Magic: Religion, Magic, and Science in the Modern World.* Oxford: University Press, 2004.

Taussig, Hal. "Dancing the Scriptures." In Doug Adams and Diane Apostolos-Cappadona (eds.), *Dance as Religious Studies.* New York: Crossroad Publishing Company, 1990: 67–79.

Taves, Ann. *Fits, Trances, and Visions: Experiencing Religion and Explaining Experience from Wesley to James.* Princeton: Princeton University Press, 1999.

Taylor, Margaret. "A History of Symbolic Movement in Worship." In Doug Adams and Diane Apostolos-Cappadona (eds.), *Dance as Religious Studies.* New York: Crossroad Publishing Company, 1990: 15–32.

Turner, Steve. *Imagine: A Vision for Christians in the Arts.* Downers Grove: InterVarsity Press, 2001.

Wagner, Ann. *Adversaries of Dance: From the Puritans to the Present.* Urbana and Chicago: University of Illinois Press, 1997.

———. "Christianity and Dance: Modern Views." In *International Encyclopedia of Dance.* New York: Oxford University Press, 1998: 166–69.

Wenger, Tisa A. "The Practice of Dance for the Future of Christianity: 'Eurythmic Worship' in New York's Roaring Twenties." In Laurie F. Maffly-Kipp, Leigh E. Schmidt, and Mark Valeri (eds.), *Practicing Protestants: Histories of Christian Life in America 1630–1965.* Baltimore: Johns Hopkins University Press, 2006.

Wolcott, Harry F. *The Art of Fieldwork.* Walnut Creek: Alta Mira Press, 2001.

Theory That Acts like Dancing

THE AUTOETHNOGRAPHIC STRUT

LISA DOOLITTLE AND ANNE FLYNN

Directions for use:
Stand up and hold book in left hand. Imagine you are strutting down the streets of any big city wearing two-inch heels and tight-fitting polyester clothes, sternum lifted, head rotating from side to side, feet slightly outward rotated and striking the ground with solid weight and steady rhythm. It is hot and noisy. In your head, you are singing to yourself this Bee Gees pop hit from 1978, "Stayin' Alive":

Well, you can tell by the way I use my walk,
I'm a woman's man, no time to talk.
Music loud and women warm, I've been kicked around
Since I was born.
And now it's all right, it's okay,
And you may look the other way.
We can try to understand
The New York times effect on man.

Whether you're a brother or whether you're a mother,
You're stayin' alive, stayin' alive.
Feel the city breakin' and everybody shakin',
And were stayin' alive, stayin' alive.
Ah, ha, ha, ha, stayin' alive, stayin' alive
Ah, ha, ha, ha, stayin' alive.

Pause, but remain standing.

Anne: This is not how I was dancing in 1978. It was all around me in popular media, but this was not my dance. This was a parallel but separate reality that I observed (and well the rhythm of it did get under my skin and stimulated the neural networks of all the social dancing I did as a kid), but this is not how I expressed my dancing then. Instead, I was sitting in my office in the physical education building at the University of Calgary, flipping through the Yellow Pages looking for listings under "Dance." I had recently accepted a nine-month contract as a sessional instructor and was trying to get a sense of the dance scene in Calgary. Under "Dance," I saw a listing for something called "Co-Motion." I can't remember now if the listing was just a name or if there were other descriptors as well, but I decided to dial the number. The phone rang and a woman answered saying, "Co-Motion." This woman was Lisa Doolittle. She was founder of an experimental dance collective in a funky loft in downtown Calgary, and I had just left an improvisational ensemble in New York to teach in the University of Calgary's physical education faculty. (I literally ran from the dance studio, after changing clothes in the bathroom, out to the tennis courts to get the ball machines set up in time to teach Tennis I.) Lisa and I talked for a long time that day and I can still remember exactly where my desk was in relation to the window and the outside view. I can remember the elation I felt finding someone who knew all about the New York modern and experimental dance scene. Geography shrunk and suddenly Calgary was not so far away from New York.

Continue imaginary strut and singing:

Well now, I get low and I get high,
And if I can't get either, I really try.
Got the wings of heaven on my shoes,
I'm a dancin' man and I just can't lose.
You know it's all right, it's okay
I'll live to see another day.
We can try to understand
The New York times effect on man.

Lisa: I was an independent choreographer working in a dance collective making serious, complicated contemporary dances for very small serious audiences. But I couldn't make a living doing this in Calgary, Alberta, in 1978, so how would I stay alive? In a refurbished elementary school called the Wildflower Arts Centre, my dance colleague Norma Wood and I reinvented ourselves as disco dance instructors and I found myself instructing the hustle, which, just in case you can't remember it, was a group disco line dance (step–cross–step–touch; step–cross–step–touch, other side) to eager young couples and mums and dads in the suburbs. Maybe it was not "the real thing," but we watched *Saturday Night Fever*, we read the instructions in a disco dance teaching manual, we had a lot of fun and made some cash. At night, I could go with my girlfriends to the gay clubs in town and dance my face off to the same music, using none of those same steps. I reinvented myself as the urbane nightclubber—something to match my life as a downtown dancer with a funky loft—with a new dance colleague from the big city. Geography shrunk and suddenly New York was not so far away from Calgary.

> Life goin' nowhere. Somebody help me. Somebody help me, yeah.
> Stayin' alive.

End of epilogue preamble. You may remain standing, move around, or sit comfortably as you continue reading.

Sometimes, moving around (as in dancing, exercising, or playing sport) changes our sense of the world, our consciousness. And, sometimes, words do. The words in *Fields in Motion* have provided all kinds of moments for slipping into imagined realities by offering the reader vivid descriptions of the movement and choreography, in addition to the perspectives, of the choreographers, dancers, ethnographers, and others. From single voices scattered across numerous disciplines we have here a concentration of voices in a single volume devoted to dance, to the field of dance studies. Paying respect to pioneering dance scholars such as Kealiinohomoku, Fraleigh, Foster, and Novack, who insisted that dance was important to humanities scholarship, this collection of writers have brought us carefully documented and considered studies. And *Fields in Motion* effectively demonstrates that, within dance scholarship, concert dance forms such as contemporary dance and ballet are no longer privileged as high art forms that exist outside the "ethnic" realm. With this shift in consciousness, other actions and ideas can move ahead.

Standing here, at the end of this volume, what can we write about what happens next—the futures this research has put into motion? An epilogue, definitions tell us, is a speech or piece of text that is added to the end of a play or book, often giving a short statement about what happens to the characters/people after the play or book finishes, deriving from the Greek *epi-* ("upon, in addition") and *logos-* ("a speaking"). The ideas and actions stirred up by the authors' investigations, all those "characters" developed in these pages, are now poised to leap—to where, and to accomplish what?

Arjun Appadurai has coined the term *ethnoscapes* (Ashcroft, Griffiths, and Tiffin 1995: 469) to refer to "the landscape of persons who constitute the shifting world in which we live"—our situation as dynamic participants in the global drama of rapidly evolving cultural encounters. As Appadurai claims, the ethnographic perspective is not just interesting in these times, it is necessary. Necessary, because when forms and ideas circulate so quickly, we may neglect careful translation from context to context in their global movements. Contemporary concert dance forms, teaching and choreographic strategies all reflect the realities of transnational movements of people and things. Dance participates in global economies where new cultural commodities and unanchored cultural ideas circulate at a fantastic rate of exchange. It is necessary not to forget that the use of words or movements by artists and teachers, audiences and students, and scholars and readers "may be subject to very different sets of contextual conventions that mediate their translation into public representations" (Ashcroft, Griffiths, and Tiffin 1995: 471). Hyphenated transnational identities demand a hyphenated transdisciplinary scholarship. Local subjects appropriate, transform, and consume global phenomena. Trance, for transcontinental South African choreographer Vincent Mantsoe, and classical southern Indian dance, for Indian-Canadian émigré Lata Pada, come to have numerous meanings in different spaces. The perspectives taken in this volume bring minute detail into focus—for example, the gesture of a hand—then nudge us to notice where that small gesture is located in relation to a much bigger set of actions. What if the repeated Christmastime performance of the "ethnic" dances in the *Nutcracker* ballet all across North America (combined with the self-reflective practice instigated by the take-home interview technique Fisher employed to analyze the phenomenon) could illuminate North Americans' perceptions and actions relating to exotic others? What if an improvised dance solo that embodies the ongoing response of an Indian-Canadian woman to the loss of her family in a plane-hijacking incident (in concert with McNaughton's exploration of innovation in Indian classical dance) could mobilize the power of grief to face international terrorism, or to empathize with a diasporic newcomer? What if the analysis of power relations between choreographer and interpreter/dancer in a Montreal workshop (in lockstep with Newell and Fortin puzzling through the dynamics at play between researchers and subjects) could deepen understanding of political choreographies in other groups—including participatory democracy?

The *What if?* question drives these essays in the same way it drives new experimental dances. Common theoretical influences such as ethnography, phenomenology, and critical analysis, as outlined, are getting a creative workout by a new generation of dance writers who slip through and bounce over the boundaries within dance's subcultures. Ethnographic and phenomenological method anchors the exploration and creates an intersection for diverse areas of dance study, such as creative process, technique and training, dance studies, and methodology. The autoethnographic method seems here to have unleashed new abilities. Twisting, darting, flailing, and shimmying, the authors have gotten past the pitfalls of talking about movement as representation, as if movement was somehow static.

The autoethnographic approach, for all its interpretive power, has some troubling aspects that require us as researchers to be attentive and continuously questioning the purpose of our work. Using oneself, one's own artistic or pedagogical practice, in the research picture is a tricky business, and unlike fiction writers, who have enormous artistic licence and write for a broad audience, academic researchers are governed by narrower conventions and speak to a more limited readership. When you are situated as subject, it is acknowledged that subjective context will structure perspective and, thus, all knowledge. Emily Wright, in the final chapter of this volume, explores subjectivity, explaining phenomenologist Gerardus Van der Lieuw's concept of imaginative empathy: "The scholar acknowledges that 'reality is always my reality' in the sense that we can only fully know our own experiences and attempt imaginatively to understand the experiences of others through that which we recognize as having meaning from our own experiences of meaning." Readers can, presumably, see through the perspective of the writer into the material, and judge for themselves the value of the writing. This is a sincerely practised post-colonial strategy for those of us on top to acknowledge/apologize for our *topness*, to acknowledge the constructedness of all selves including ourselves, and thus to leave space for other kinds of selves and knowledges. But, at times, the method allows readers to find out more about the writer than the material itself, and the result is more autobiography than ethnology. Again, in this more experimental style of academic discourse, the researcher has more challenges in integrating multiple voices and perspectives, but the results can be subtle, complex, and revelatory. They can be more like dancing, more like life.

Animated by the vibrant presence of movement through the autoethnographic approach, *Fields in Motion* illustrates not just *that* contemporary concert dance has an ethnicity but *what*, in fact, the new knowledge of this ethnicity can accomplish. Research can and will influence and enrich the practice of dance, dance teaching, and dance creation. These new dance stories, never known before, will now begin to circulate and enter into other stories. They will create more conversations and more conversations and more conversations. In the dance milieu, the work will inspire dance students to go on to graduate school and become dance researchers. It will educate non-dancers about the importance of movement/dance in cultural studies. It will honour the work of dance artists whose body of choreography receives so little consideration by artistic analysts. It will help dance teachers to think about the best way to develop highly skilled performers. It will guide producers and presenters of contemporary dance as they address issues of diversity in dance and its global packaging.

The essays in this collection deepen a dialogue, through corporeality, with other disciplines. Investigating choreography with ethnography helps choreographers, in their notoriously and too often needlessly obscure creative process, understand what they are doing and why. Investigating the dance studio with ethnography brings new perspective to the too-little-examined habits and what theorist de Certeau would call the *habitus* of dance training. Conversely, dance perspectives push at the boundaries of academic theory and method. The dance teachers' ways of putting bodily experience into words are here mobilized to contribute to phenomenological, ethnographic, and pedagogical theory. As Fisher suggests, "If ethnography as it is rooted in cultural anthropology is to survive its colonialist roots, more methods that move toward collaboration need to emerge. Who better," she adds, "to develop them than scholars who know that the elite form of ballet evolved from folk dance; and who better to call on for collaboration than people who do and watch ballet, because they are the folk who are involved now?" Tardieu's dance research (chapter 16 with Gore), in allying itself with ethnographic methodologies, identifies a limitation in phenomenological theory, finding that "the problem with this approach is that knowledge is considered as constructed from a particular body, an individual body and not a culturally constructed body," and that including her own subjective experience of learning became an essential methodology unlocking new analyses of transmission of bodily knowledges. Theoretical perspectives from non-dance disciplines are rechoreographed; choreography, performance, and pedagogy are retheorized.

Nodding to the autoethnographic methods so exhaustively elaborated here, from our vantage point as "characters" in the field, we acknowledge that our own work has been immeasurably enriched by interdisciplinary research methods applied in dance studies. Our current research on folk dancing would not in the past have been considered worthy of the serious artistic or critical analysis accorded to high-art dance. Nor would dancing, of any kind, formerly be given serious consideration in discussions of nationalism, globalization, ethnicity, and human rights. Thanks to our mentors, who have worked to break down unproductive segregation of scholarly categories, we have been allowed to view dancing in a much wider landscape of human ideas. Layered into this scholarly guidance we can trace the widening of our scope to our own lived experiences. Our earliest dancing selves inhabited the small sphere of experimental modern dance. Often compelled by circumstance more than conscious personal choice, we found ourselves teaching disco to suburbanites; or international folk dance to kinesiology students; or adapting contemporary dance training to the needs of actors; or writing about movement for yoga magazines; or creating dance performances for seniors, or children, danced by themselves, for themselves. Continually stepping outside that earliest sphere led us toward a more inclusive ethnographic perspective, enabled us to see other ways that people are fully engaged in and satisfied by their dancing. Our ideas are still in motion.

Dances like the cells in our bodies exist only in movement—never in stillness. The writers in this volume contend with an object of study that is always in flux; the researcher has to be able to dance with the object of study. The varied approaches and subjects found in *Fields in Motion* suggest a fluidity of thinking in the study of dance ethnography. The classroom, the book, and the stage are just diverse settings connected by the action of dancing. We readers see the connections, not the final answers. The researchers' eyes are soft and wide, the nervous systems open and explorative, the breath is easy and full. Thinking and writing like a mover moves.

And now it's all right, it's okay
And you may look the other way.
We can try to understand ...

Bibliography

Ashcroft, Bill, Gareth Williams, and Helen Tiffin (eds.). *The Post-Colonial Studies Reader*, 2nd ed. Routledge: London and New York, 1995.
"Stayin' Alive." Music and lyrics by The Bee Gees from the soundtrack *Saturday Night Fever*. RSO, Reprise, 1977.

List of Contributors

Karen Barbour is a senior lecturer in dance in the School of Education at the University of Waikato, New Zealand. Returning to academic study after dance training presented rich spaces for negotiation and tension between traditional and dancerly forms of knowledge and inspired her doctoral thesis on women's solo contemporary dance. Karen's work as a dance lecturer encompasses choreography, contemporary dance, improvisation, and performance. Barbour has just published *Dancing across the Page: Narrative and Embodied Ways of Knowing* (2011), choreographs professionally, creates digital dance works, and publishes articles in a range of academic journals.

Ralph Buck is associate professor and head of Dance Studies, University of Auckland. He holds a PhD from the University of Otago. His research interests are in dance education, curriculum, pedagogy, and community dance. Ralph has presented his research in networks such as Congress on Research in Dance, World Dance Alliance (WDA), Dance and the Child International. He has given keynote addresses at national and international conferences. He is chair, Education and Training Network, WDA: Asia-Pacific; chairperson, Executive Council, World Alliance for Arts Education; and is an honorary life member of the Australian Dance Council.

Bridget Cauthery is a lecturer, journalist, and arts consultant based in Toronto, Canada. She received her doctorate in dance studies from the University of Surrey, UK, in 2007, where her research focused on the applicability of trance to Western concert dance forms. She lectures in the dance department at York University and in the theatre department at Ryerson University and is currently working with ten international choreographers on a book project provisionally titled *Choreographing the North*, funded by the Canada Council for the Arts.

Anne Cazemajou completed an MA in philosophy, two DEA in the performing arts, and, in 2010, a PhD in dance anthropology at Université Blaise Pascal, Clermont Université. Her doctoral research examines the body's experience of transmission in a case study of a contemporary dance class for dance-interested adults in which the teacher, Toni D'Amelio, had integrated a yoga technique. Since 2007, she has taught the Université Blaise Pascal, Clermont Université, Université Paris 13 and Université Paris 8. Cazemajou practises Iyengar yoga and is a founding member of the Atelier des Doctorants at the Centre National de la Danse in Paris.

Mônica Dantas earned her PhD in the program "Études et pratiques des arts" at the Université de Québec à Montréal. She has a master's in human movement sciences, and since 1995 has been a professor at the Federal University of Rio Grande do Sul in Porto Alegre, Brazil, teaching in the physical education department and the master's program of performing arts. She has published articles in scientific journals on the subject of contemporary dance, and in 1999 authored the monograph *Dança, o enigma do movimento (Dance, the enigma of movement)*. Dantas is also a practising contemporary dancer and choreographer.

Dena Davida, an American living in Montreal since 1977, earned her MA in movement studies from Wesleyan University (1995), and later her PhD in the Études et pratiques des arts program at the Université du Québec à Montréal (2006), where she taught improvisation, composition and theory classes for twenty-five years. She co-founded the Festival international de nouvelle danse in 1978 and, in 1981, Tangente, Quebec's first dance performance space, for which she remains co-artistic director. She is also a veteran contact improviser, contemporary dancer, and dance curator who has published numerous essays in dance journals and magazines on issues of contemporary dance, ethnography, and culture.

Lisa Doolittle is professor in theatre arts at the University of Lethbridge. She holds an MA in Movement Studies from Wesleyan University, and has worked as a dancer, choreographer, journalist and lecturer in the USA, Canada, UK, Italy, and Japan. With Anne Flynn, her SSHRC-supported

research examines indigenous and "folk" dance in Canada, national identities, and Canadian multicultural policy. International presentations and
publications include studies of Canadian dance in the twentieth century,
concepts of folk dance and social dance, and the roles of performance in
social change. Her community-based performance projects have focused
on immigrant issues and health promotion in Lethbridge, London (UK),
and Malawi.

Jennifer Fisher, PhD, is the author of *Nutcracker Nation: How an Old World
Ballet Became a Christmas Tradition in the New World* (Yale University Press,
2003), which won the de la Torre Bueno special citation. Co-editor, with
Anthony Shay, of *When Men Dance: Choreographing Masculinities across Borders* (Oxford University Press, 2009), she is an associate professor in the
dance department of the University of California, Irvine, where she created
Dance Major Journal, a publication for undergraduate writing. She has written about dance for *The Globe and Mail* (Toronto), the *Los Angeles Times*,
and *The New York Times*, as well as for scholarly journals.

Anne Flynn has long been involved in the Calgary dance community as a
performer, artistic director, teacher, writer, administrator, and dance education advocate. She earned her MA in movement studies from Wesleyan University. Professor in the Department of Dance at the University of Calgary,
Faculties of Arts and Kinesiology, her dance research on Canadian women,
multiculturalism and identity, health promotion, and education has been
presented and published internationally. In collaboration with Lisa Doolittle, she co-founded *Dance Connection* magazine (1987–1995), edited *Dancing Bodies, Moving Histories* (2000) and has essays forthcoming in a themed
issue of *Discourses in Dance* on "folk."

Sylvie Fortin earned her PhD in dance from Ohio State University and is
currently a professor in the dance department of the Université du Québec
à Montréal, where she has taught since 1986. Her research interests focus
on somatic education, research methodology, dance medicine, and feminist studies. A certified teacher of the Feldenkrais Method, she also has a
wide experience in other somatic education methods. She has published
numerous articles in scientific journals and has presented her work at conferences in Canada, England, United States, Australia, Germany, Portugal,
Brazil, New Zealand, and France. In 2008, she edited the anthology *Danse et
Santé*, based on her four-year research project on dancers' health.

Janet Goodridge has a background in dance training and academic study. She holds a BA in drama/music (Bristol University), postgraduate diploma in Social Anthropology (London School of Economics), and PhD in Anthropology (University College London). She initiated and contributed to several UK university/college courses, and taught as visiting artist at various US universities. In 1993 she took early retirement from teaching to develop independent work in research, writing, music (percussion) and performance projects—teaching occasional courses in Laban studies, theatre movement and Tai Ji. Publications include *Drama in the Primary School* (1970), *Rhythm and Timing of Movement in Performance: Drama, Dance and Ceremony* (1999), and journal articles.

Georgiana Gore completed undergraduate and postgraduate training at the University of Keele, UK, where she was artistic director of *Kontradance Theatre*. Until 2008 she directed the *Laboratoire d'Anthropologie des Pratiques Corporelles* at *Université Blaise Pascal*, where in 2001 she created France's first master's program in dance anthropology and currently co-directs the Masters in Ethnomusicology and Anthropology of Dance. Her research interests include the anthropology of the body and dance, the politics of performance and dances of the Nigerian Edo. She has lectured in numerous countries, and contributed to many seminal publications including the anthology *Anthropologie de la danse: Genèse et construction d'une discipline* (2005–2006), co-edited with Andrée Grau.

Yin-ying Huang holds an MA in performance studies from New York University and a PhD in Dance from Temple University. Native to Taiwan, she is currently assistant professor of English and Performance at Chang Gung University and has also taught at Taiwan University and Taipei National University of Arts. Her research interests include dance theatre/ethnography, intercultural performance, feminist theatre. She has served as editor of *Performing Arts Review* and presented her research at conferences in the US, England, France, Portugal, and Germany. She has published articles in *Dance Research Journal*, *Arts Review*, *International Journal of Humanities*, and *Hong Kong Theatre Journal*.

Naomi Jackson is a dance scholar who has published and presented papers extensively in Europe, Canada, Russia, and the United States. She received her BA in philosophy and art history from McGill University, her MA from the University of Surrey, and PhD from New York University. Dr. Jackson has taught at the Juilliard School and is currently an associate professor in the School of Dance at Arizona State University. Her books include

Converging Movements: Modern Dance and Jewish Culture at the 92nd Street Y, Right to Dance; Dancing for Rights (editor), and *Dance, Human Rights and Social Justice* (co-edited with Toni Shapiro-Phim).

Inka Juslin is a post-doctoral dance researcher undertaking research since 2007 in performance studies at New York University and also at the Dance in Nordic Space Project, University of Tampere in Finland. Her research interests include world theatre, and dance in conjunction to video and new media. She is also a Finnish dancer and choreographer currently based in New York City, collaborating with Melinda Ring Special Projects while continuing dance and media projects with artists Susan Kozel and Svitlana Matviyenko. Juslin has choreographed dance and video works in Finland, in Asia, North America, and Europe.

Warwick Long holds a master's degree in physical education, University of Otago New Zealand and is a Certified Feldenkrais Practitioner. He currently teaches in the dance departments of the Université du Québec à Montréal and Concordia University. Long has danced professionally in Australia, Canada, and New Zealand and taught in the Dance Studies program at the University of Otago and UNITEC Institute of Technology in New Zealand. He published texts in *Danse et Santé : Du corps intime au corps social* (2008), *Feldenkrais Journal* (2004), and *Research in Dance Education* (2002), and presented at the Congress on Research in Dance (2005). He is finishing studies in osteopathy in Montreal.

Teija Löytönen holds a master's degree in education (University of Helsinki) and earned her doctorate in dance with a study of discourses in dance institutions (Theatre Academy in Finland). Currently she is a senior researcher at Aalto University School of Art and Design. Her particular research interests include higher arts education, teaching cultures in arts education as well as collegial collaboration in relation to professional development and knowledge creation. She has published in several refereed journals and presented her research in various conferences. She is affiliated with CORD (Congress on Research in Dance) and NOFOD (Nordic Forum for Dance Research).

Susan McNaughton earned her MA in fine arts–dance, an MA in social anthropology, and was awarded a posthumous PhD, also in social anthropology, at York University. Susan danced with the *Toronto Dance Theater*, the *London Contemporary Dance Theater* (England), and independent Canadian and American artists. She managed and taught at Pavlychenko Studio, an early Toronto training ground and performance space. Her choreography has been performed in Europe, the US, and Chennai, India. McNaughton's doctoral research explores how the socio-cultural and political affiliations within the Sri Lanka Tamil diaspora in Toronto shape, and are shaped by, faith-based commitments. She passed away in December 2010.

Michèle Moss is a choreographer, dancer, and educator. She completed her MA in interpretive studies in education and is currently a tenured assistant professor in the Department of Dance, at the University of Calgary in Canada. She co-founded *Decidedly Jazz Danceworks*, a professional dance company whose mission it is to preserve and promote jazz. She presents her research both textually and embodied in concert, and has been performing and choreographing since the mid-1980s. She also teaches and conducts ethnographic research in Cuba and Guinée, West Africa.

Pamela Newell received her master's degree from the Université du Québec à Montréal (UQAM) and has been a member of Concordia University's Contemporary Dance faculty since 1998. Her research on the choreographer–dancer relationship in the creative process won awards from the Society for Canadian Dance Studies and UQAM. She is a regular contributor to *The Dance Current* magazine. Pamela has created a dozen choreographic works, including *Being Susan Sontag* (2006) and *Ultreya!* (2004). She is rehearsal director for *Compagnie Marie Chouinard* and danced with that company from 1992 to 1998. Pamela is pursuing certification in Bartenieff Fundamentals/Laban Movement Analysis.

Candice Pike is a graduate of York University's MA in dance. Her chapter in this volume is the culmination of her work in a BA in social cultural studies from Memorial University's Grenfell Campus. Her primary research interests include the construction of gender and status and community in ballet pedagogy, dance and popular culture, and research in the recreational dance world. Pike teaches recreational dance to dancers of all ages and levels. She is currently working on research and practical projects related to dance, masculinity, and community in Corner Brook, Newfoundland, Canada.

Eluza Santos, a native of Brazil, holds a PhD in dance from Texas Woman's University. Her dissertation, *The Dancing Voice of Culture: An Ethnography of Contemporary Dance in Vitória, Brazil*, analyzes the cultural origins of Brazilian concert dance. She has presented scholarship, choreographed, and performed in Brazil, the US, and other countries. Santos was an associate professor of dance at the University of North Carolina, Greensboro, now lives in Brazil, and continues her professional activities as artist, scholar, and educator. She is a co-founding member of Latina Dance Theater Project (in the US) and founder of EluzArtes (in Brazil).

Juanita Suarez holds a PhD in Dance from Texas Woman's University, and is associate professor of Dance, serving a joint position in the Department of Dance and Arts for Children Program at the College at Brockport SUNY. A co-founding member of the Latina Dance Theater Project, an international, interdisciplinary, performance ensemble, Suarez has also taught/ performed creative dance in China (2000–2009) and Brazil (2010). In 2001, she received a Rockefeller Grant U.S.-Map Fund for Culture to study Mexico's history through dance and music, culminating her research with a theater/dance production titled *Visible Line/Invisible People* featuring Mexico City's Luz y Fuerza.

Nadège Tardieu holds a PhD from the Laboratoire d'Anthropologie des Pratiques Corporelles at the Université Blaise Pascal de Clermont-Ferrand, France. She is a dance researcher and a physical education instructor from France. From extensive fieldwork with innovative ballet teacher Wilfride Piollet and her students in various settings, her research examines questions of how she apprehended the realities and implications of being a researcher in her "own field" and how dance is transmitted and bodies were constructed in the particular cultural context of Piollet's pedagogy.

Priya Thomas is a dancer, musician, and yoga educator with a background in South Asian art, comparative religion, and Sanskrit. Trained for twenty years in the classical South Indian dance form Bharatanatyam, her teacher was the primary pupil of Balasaraswati. She holds a BA from McGill University in comparative religion and a MA from York University in dance. Currently a doctoral candidate in dance studies at York University, she is working on a dissertation on modern yoga scholarship. She founded and edits the digital journal *Shivers Up the Spine: The Yoga Examiner*. She is also a musician with a catalogue of critically acclaimed solo releases.

Joëlle Vellet is a maître de conférences at the Université de Nice Sophia Antipolis in France and holds a doctorate in aesthetics from the Université de Paris 8. She directs the dance section in the arts department of the UFR LASH (UNS) and is a member of the Centre de recherche RITM (EA 3158) at the Université de Nice. She taught for many years at the Université Blaise Pascal de Clermont-Ferrand, where also co-directed the master's program.

Her research is situated at the crossroads between aesthetics and dance anthropology (*anthropologie poïétique*). Her experiences as a dancer, choreographer, and teacher are important to the direction of her work.

Emily Wright, MFA, is a specialty instructor for dance at Belhaven University in Jackson, Mississippi. She received her BFA in dance from Belhaven University in 2002 and her MFA in dance, with an emphasis in performance and choreography, from Arizona State University in 2007. Ms. Wright has presented her research on contemporary trends in American Protestant dance from both insider and outsider perspectives in the context of current and historic tensions at numerous national and international conferences. She employs an autoethnographic approach to choreography as well as in her collaborations with Front Porch Dance, a Jackson-based contemporary dance company.

COPYRIGHT ACKNOWLEDGEMENTS

Chapter 5 was published in an earlier version as Kristin M. Harris, "An Examination of the Pointe Shoe as Artifact through Ethnographic and Gender Analysis," in *Material History Review/Revue d'histoire de la culture matérielle* (now called *Material Culture Review/Revue de la culture matérielle*) no. 58 (Fall 2003): 4–12.

Chapter 11 was previously published in French in Sylvie Fortin, ed., *Danse et Santé : Du corps intime au corps social*, as "Dynamiques relationnelles entre chorégraphes et danseurs contemporains" (Montréal: Presses de l'Université du Québec, 2008), 87–111.

Chapter 14 was published in an earlier version as Teija Loyötonen, "Emotions in the Everyday Life of a Dance School: Articulating Unspoken Values," in *The Dance Research Journal* 40, no. 1 (Summer 2008): 17–30, published by the Congress on Research in Dance.

Chapter 20 was published in an earlier version as Susan McNaughton, "Revealed by Fire: One woman's narrative of transformation," in the e-journal *In*Tensions, no. 4.0 (Fall 2010), published by Fine Arts Cultural Studies, York University.

Epilogue. "Stayin' Alive" words and music by Barry Gibb, Maurice Gibb, and Robin Gibb. Copyright © 1977 (Renewed) Crompton Songs LLC and Gibb Brothers Music. All rights for Crompton Songs LLC administered by Warner-Tamerlane Publishing Corp. All rights reserved. Used by permission of Alfred Music Publishing Co., Inc.

"Stayin' Alive" from the motion picture *Saturday Night Fever*. Words and music by Barry Gibb, Robin Gibb, and Maurice Gibb. Copyright © 1977 by Universal Music Publishing International MGB Ltd., Warner-Tamerlane Publishing Corp., and Crompton Songs LLC. Copyright renewed. All rights for Universal Music Publishing International MGB Ltd. in the U.S. and Canada administered by Universal Music – Careers. International copyright secured. All rights reserved. Reprinted by permission of Hal Leonard Corporation.

Index

abhinaya practice, 384
Abu-Lughod, Lila, 49
acculturation, 22, 27n7
Advinha quem vem para dançar? 148, 152
aesthetics: of ballet, 90, 278; Chinese visual and literary, 362, 364, 373–76, 379n5n6; crossing between aesthetics and anthropology, 223; gestural description and, 221; indigenous performance, 127; of Lavendar, 41; of *Luna* choreography, 41; traditional male dance, 287; of Merleau-Ponty, 108, 177, 212, 306, 314n5n6; models, 6; movement, 154; multimodal performance, 184; Shustermann and somaesthetics, 6, 251; unspoken element in field notes, 279; video, 177; Western schemes of, 171
African dance: African drumming, 124; Vincent Sekwati Mantsoe (South African dancer), 319–38; West African, 70, 76
agency, 282, 328, 331, 416, 421, 437
Air India tragedy, 388, 395, 397–98, 401n11
alarippu, 384, 400n5
Albright, Ann Cooper, 105–10
Aldrich, Elizabeth, 430–31

Alter, Judy, 2
amateur: ballet dancers, 51, 57, 87; dancers and dance companies, 50; insider , 87
American Protestant Christian Dance and dancers, 427–34
Andrews, Amy, 277, 281
Angelwindow (Juslin), 173–87
anonymity: in butoh, 353; of participants, 199, 240
anthropology, xiii, xiv, 3, 7, 10, 14, 119, 123, 126, 138, 382; cognitive, 54; of contemporaneity, 308; of corporeal practices, 305, 313n2; crossing of aesthetics and, 223; cultural, 60, 119, 450; dance, 29, 31, 119, 127; epistemological approach, 308; of performing arts, 11; philosophy of, 323; Popcock's "personal," 19; social, 126, 382; theatre arts and, 130
anthropopagy: anthropophagic body, 344, 354; *Anthropophagite Manifesto* and movement, 358n5; Oswald de Andrade and, 342; assimilation of human flesh, 354, 356; principles, 342–43
Appadurai, Arjun, 448
arangetram programs, 384
Armstrong, Robert Plant, 94

Wilfride Piollet's class (France), 305–
18; replication of teacher's movements, 194, 213; somatic education
(*see* somatics); structure for men's
ballet class, 286
dance presenting, 41–42
dancer-researchers, 103, 450; credibility, as insider, 149–51; critical dance researchers, 423n3; as
dancer-researcher, 2, 31, 49, 145, 160,
166–67, 199, 361; double subjectiv-
ity/multiple positioning, 3; embodied, 113; in equal status with/politi-
cal balance with participants, 34,
228, 263–64, 448; as exploitive, 151;
minority researchers, 149; multiple
positioning, 49; as protagonist in
study, 2, 145; researcher's posture/
position, 3, 19–24, 28, 255–56; self-
research, 68, 183, 409; self-transformation through research, 5, 41–42,
183, 243, 396; as tourist, 79
dancers' issues: autonomy, subjectivity,
identity, 195; creative authenticity, 212; dancer appropriation, 194,
197; dancer identity, 221; dancer as
"movement ministry," 434; dancer
roles in creative process, 194–96;
dancer self-authority and awareness, 237; experience of power, 199;
gender identity, 278, 298; health,
192–93; performing cultural identity,
386; personal discernment process,
200, 208–12; replaceability, 212;
rights and ownership, 193; safety,
193; status, recognition, working conditions, 192; unionization
192–93; use of trained vs. untrained
Christian dancers, 432–35, 440
dance studies, xii, 14, 49, 64n6, 287,
320; Christian dance studies, 441n1
Dance Studio West (Corner Brook, Newfoundland), 277, 280
dance teachers/educators: Amy
Andrews, 277, 281; Leslie Burrowes,
132–33; Toni D'Amelio, 19–22,
25;Warwick Long, 233–43, 251
dance theory, dance-based, 2

dance training institutions: Dance
Centre Studio (London, UK), 133;
Dance Studio West (Corner Brook,
Newfoundland), 277, 280; Loudoun School of Ballet (Canada), 56;
National Ballet School (Toronto), 57
dance writing, 8, 112, 172; Juslin's "corporeal language dialect," 182
data: collection and analysis, 31, 49,
70, 73, 148, 153, 197–98, 200, 223,
227–28, 236, 240–41, 243, 250, 271,
322, 361, 430; "dancing the data,"
438; sensory data, 250
de Andrade, Oswald, 342–44, 358n5
death, 18, 20; in anthropophagy, 354;
dead body, 323; Kübler-Ross's five-
stage model, 401n14; rebirth cycle,
375; trance as symbolic, 323
de la Cruz, Sor Juana, 411
Deleuze, Gilles, 27n10, 305
de Spain, Kent, 429, 440
Devi, Rukimini, 400n2
Diaghilev and Ballets Russes, 282
Diaz, Gene, 75
diversity: awareness of, 235; in ballet
world, 58; cultural, 127; in dance,
450
dona orpheline danse, 340
Duboc, Odile, 222–32
Duncan, Isadora, 96
Dunlop, Rishma, 172
Duo Cia. De Dança, 148, 152–54

East, Alison, 110
écriture du mouvement/chorégraphique
(corporeal languages), 221, 231n2
El Corazón de Mexico dance company,
423
emic and etic, 26n1; emic perspective in data collection, 236; gaining
distance, 19–28, 225; negotiation of
emic/etic position, 19, 224, 230
emotion, 258–59: arousal in trance,
324; art and, 260–61; Brazilian
emotionally charged body, 155;
importance of expression in dance,
154; link to morals; 255; loneliness of dance teachers, 255, 257,
261, 266–72; opposed to intellect,